PLEASE BE A

FOURTH EDITION

ANA
Leading the Marketing Community

THE LEGAL REFERENCE GUIDE
FOR THE ADVERTISING EXECUTIVE

DOUGLAS J. WOOD

PLEASE BE AD-VISED
Table of Contents

Part I—Please Be Ad-Vised
The Creative Side of Advertising

Part II—Please Be Ad-Vised
The Business Side of Advertising

Appendix

About the Author

Douglas J. Wood practices law in New York City and is General Counsel of the Association of National Advertisers. He has over 25 years' experience representing national and multinational companies in advertising and unfair competition, intellectual property, and Internet matters and serves as legal adviser to several worldwide advertising industry trade organizations. Mr. Wood is the founder, Chairman, and U.S. member of the Global Advertising Lawyers Alliance (GALA), an alliance of independent lawyers located throughout the world with expertise in advertising, marketing, and promotion law. In addition to *Please Be Ad-Vised*, Mr. Wood's authorship credits include co-author of *Legal Problems in Advertising*, published by Matthew Bender & Co. He also co-wrote *The Internet and Advertising Law*, a chapter in *Advertising Law in Europe and North America*, published by Kluwer Law International. He is a regular columnist for *The Advertiser* and is Editor of the  on-line newsletter, *Adlaw By Request*. Mr. Wood is a frequent guest speaker, writer and media commentator on a variety of subjects involving advertising and marketing related legal topics for the Association of National Advertisers, the World Federation of Advertising, the International Advertising Association, the Advertising Festival, the American Marketing Association, and advertising agency networks and ad clubs throughout the United States.

Mr. Wood is admitted to practice law in New York, New Jersey, and Bucharest, Romania. He holds a Juris Doctor degree from the Franklin Pierce Law Center, where he is Chairman of the Board of Trustees. He received a Masters in Law degree in Trade Regulation from New York University School of Law and a Bachelor of Arts degree in Political Science from the University of Rhode Island. Mr. Wood is a member of the Board of Directors and past President of the Touchdown Club of America, a non-profit organization dedicated to awarding college scholarships to deserving high school scholar athletes.

Mr. Wood lives in Wyckoff, New Jersey, with his wife, Carol Ann, and children, Joshua, Meghan, and Andrea and can be contacted via email at douglasjwood@hotmail.com.

About the ANA

The Association of National Advertisers leads the marketing community by providing its members insights, collaboration and advocacy. ANA's membership includes 370 companies with 8,000 brands that collectively spend over $100 billion in marketing communications and advertising. The ANA strives to communicate marketing best practices, lead industry initiatives, influence industry practices, manage industry affairs and advance, promote and protect all advertisers and marketers. For more information visit: www.ana.net.

ANA Mission Statement

ANA provides indispensable leadership that drives marketing excellence and champions, promotes and defends the interests of the marketing community. We will accomplish our mission through:

- **Insights**

  ANA advances marketing decision-making by acquiring, developing and disseminating unique and proprietary insights to ANA members. Our intellectual capital covers all aspects of the communications process, including brand building, integrated marketing communications, marketing accountability and the marketing organization.

- **Collaboration**

  ANA consistently brings members together with industry thought leaders to promote fresh thinking, develop new ideas, provide professional training and facilitate industry-wide networking. The ANA convenes constituents across the entire marketing spectrum including peer marketers, agencies, the media, associations, consultants, vendors, production companies and academicians.

- **Advocacy**

  ANA is the voice of the marketing community. ANA leverages its leadership to advance the industry's agenda – engineering progress and transformation while defending core marketing interests and freedoms. On behalf of the industry, we address legislative and regulatory issues, promote industry policies and practices, strengthen the marketing supply chain and align the marketing community towards solutions for societal concerns.

Please Be Ad-Vised

Acknowledgment

I owe thanks to many people who helped make the substantially revised 4th edition of *Please Be Ad-Vised* a reality.

First, this book came together largely through the dedication of Nancy Schulein, my right arm and administrative assistant, and Geri Clark, my firm's marketing director, together with her assistant, Andrea Mouzakis. Over the years this book took shape and was revised, they stayed involved through it all, making sure I met deadlines and finished the many re-writes relatively on schedule. They tolerated all of my last minute changes and unreasonable requests. And I knew Geri was only kidding when she said she was ready to throw something at me. At least I think she was! Thanks also go to Kate Catenacci and Marisol Cancel for their help in putting the manuscript in proper form, a task that is far more difficult than I ever imagined. This edition also could not have come about without the assistance of Heather Fenby who lent her hand to provide professional editing. Heather's contributions were invaluable in making this edition a quantum leap forward from the past iterations. I'm thankful to a host of professional colleagues for their collaborative efforts, particularly Richard B. Rodman (Mergers and Acquisitions), Steven Goldberg and Charles Wern (Sales Tax), Lawrence M. Hertz (Multimedia Contracts), Char Pagar, John Hendrickson, Bill Heberer, and Alan H. Feldstein (Home Shopping, Infomercials and Telemarketing), Jennifer Koester and Lindsay Schoen (Advertising to Children), Jeff Edelstein and Marilyn Colaninno (Self-Regulation and Network Clearance), Michael Barkow, Peter O'Reilly, and Shalom Stevens (Sweepstakes and Contests), Elky Stone (Celebrity Contracts and Talent Unions), Felix Kent (Agency/Client Agreements), Stephanie Shulman and Marc Roth (Sales Promotion), Darren Cohen, Fawn Horvath, Susan Rosenfeld, and Cathy Shore-Sirotin (Copyrights and Trademarks), Cynthia Rosenberg (assistance with research materials), and Tami Morachnick (a little bit of everything).

Most importantly, however, this book would have never existed were it not for the encouragement and vision of the Association of National Advertisers, Inc. I am especially grateful to Robin Webster and Barbara Bacci-Mirque for their support, enthusiasm, and helpful suggestions. And to the rest of the folks at the ANA, including Ada Agrait, Michelle Hunter and Rick Knecht — all consummate professionals — for managing the behind-the-scenes efforts.

Finally, to my wife, Carol Ann, and my children, Joshua, Meghan, and Andrea, who patiently tolerated my spending upwards of four hours a day working on this book while on vacations. We missed a lot of time together on the beach. This edition is again dedicated to them.

Please Be Ad-Vised

Preface

Most advertising and marketing executives cannot claim a mastery of advertising and marketing law; yet, it is an area we deal in almost every day. Are we aware of the repercussions some of our decisions can have? Probably not. Douglas Wood explains why we should be. In *Please Be Ad-Vised*, Mr. Wood gives us the knowledge and know-how we need — and points out countless legal landmines along the way.

Who should read this book? Certainly CEOs, creative directors, and CFOs will find it an important reference tool in managing their company's advertising and business activities. In addition, this book provides hands-on guidance to the brand manager, account executive, media planner, copywriter, producer, human resource manager, and business affairs manager. Those who teach or study advertising and marketing will find it a valuable resource, as it is packed with examples of common problems and their practical solutions. In short, it should be read by anyone involved in the day-to-day business of advertising.

Mr. Wood has written an easy-to-read, practical reference guide on advertising law. Part I covers the Creative Side of Advertising, while Part II is an in-depth text on the Business Side of Advertising. There are over 20 sample contracts for everything from Agency/Advertiser contracts to Web site development agreements to television production contracts.

In addition to the many forms, Mr. Wood has included strategies, guidelines, and checklists that will be helpful. Many of the forms are written from an agency point of view, since advertising agencies most commonly use such forms. In the case where the advertising function has been brought "in-house," the forms will require modification. A word of caution about using the sample forms. Laws vary in each state or foreign jurisdiction. As such, readers may want to check with local counsel to determine whether any unusual state law provisions require the forms to be modified. Don't be surprised if your lawyer changes the forms — particularly if he/she does not have industry experience.

The Association of National Advertisers, Inc. is pleased to again publish this invaluable work. The narrative sections are quick lessons on the issues, while the "Why It Matters" and "Warning" sections are essential cautions and real world examples of problems that can or have occurred.

As so many of Mr. Wood's examples warn us, often the addition of a single fact — or the absence of one — seemingly of no significance to a non-lawyer, can change the outcome of a case 180 degrees. But for the marketing or advertising executive, or even for a lawyer of other specialties, Mr. Wood calls attention to areas for caution and further examination that might otherwise, by default, have disastrous results.

The Creative Side of Advertising

Please Be Ad-Vised

CHAPTER 1
Ownership and Protection of Creative

1. Ownership of Creative Materials

a. What Does the Advertiser Own?

The ownership of creative materials is one of the most hotly contested issues in negotiating agreements between advertisers and advertising agencies. Usually, however, the debate is largely academic, as advertising agencies increasingly agree to very broad ownership provisions that favor the advertiser. Today, it is not uncommon to see an agency agree to the following concessions:

1. The advertiser owns even mere ideas presented by the agency.

2. The advertiser owns everything the agency presents, even if the advertiser has not used the concepts.

3. The advertiser owns the creative materials presented by the agency even if it has not paid for them, thereby subverting any connection between ownership and payment.

It is not a matter of what is fair. After all, it really does not make sense that an advertising agency should forgo any claim to use mere ideas it has generated and presented, materials that the advertiser has rejected, or materials for which the advertiser has not paid. The inequity in favor of the advertiser has more to do with competitive pressures in the marketplace and the ebbs and flows of the economy.

Why It Matters

Unless a contract provides otherwise, ideas are as free as the wind and anyone can use them. On the other hand, if a contract provides that an idea is owned by one of the parties, then the other party is no longer free to use it.

For example, if an agreement between an advertising agency and an advertiser provides that ideas are owned by the advertiser, then no matter what idea the agency comes up with—even if the client rejects it—the advertiser owns it, and the agency cannot use it for any other client. In other words, that idea is now in the bank of ideas owned by the original advertiser client.

The result is rather absurd. Any other advertiser or advertising agency, not a party to the contract, could use the idea. While an argument can be made that the idea is in the public domain once used by another, such an argument may fail if refuted by a contractual provision to the contrary.

Thus, when drafting a provision dealing with ownership, focus on the tangible expression of ideas–e.g., campaign strategies, proposed advertisements or commercials, storyboards and scripts, logo designs, and so forth–rather than on mere ideas, which should, ideally, not be owned exclusively by either party. The agreement should be silent in that respect thereby leaving use of ideas free to either party.

---

b. What Does the Outside Supplier Own?

Outside suppliers, particularly photographers, are very astute in copyright ownership. Their form contracts typically provide that copyright ownership is retained by the supplier, and that the advertiser or advertising agency receives only a license to use the materials for a limited period of time. Unless the advertising agency secures signed agreements from outside suppliers agreeing to a transfer of ownership, no transfer occurs; ownership is retained by the supplier, regardless of what may have been the oral understanding. This becomes important if the advertising agency's agreement with its client requires that the agency secure full ownership of any materials it incorporates in the advertising it produces. But since few suppliers of outside creative will grant outright ownership, it is unrealistic for an Agency/Client agreement to require such full ownership.

In reality, most outside suppliers of creative materials provide the advertiser and advertising agency with a license to use the materials in specific media and geographic areas for a specified period of time. This is a perfectly acceptable form of doing business, provided the agreement clearly specifies the rights obtained, the term of use, the area of use, and the compensation to be paid. Such agreements must be in writing and signed by the supplier.

Why It Matters

In the absence of a signed agreement, the supplier retains ownership, regardless of what an unsigned advertising agency or advertiser form may provide or what may have been either the oral understanding or an understanding recited in call reports or similar internal memoranda.

Consider the following case: A sculptor was commissioned by a nonprofit organization to create a work of art representing a nonviolent message supported by the organization. He was paid a fee, and the organization reviewed the sculptor's progress, making suggestions along the way. Nothing was in writing between the parties.

After displaying the completed work in Washington, D.C., the organization decided to take it "on the road" and display it in cities throughout the United States. The sculptor sued to enjoin such use, fearing it would damage the sculpture and claiming that, since there was no written document between the parties transferring ownership, ownership was retained by him and moving the art work required his approval.

In a 1988 decision that sent shock waves throughout the advertising industry, the United States Supreme Court agreed with the sculptor. The Court held that strict compliance with the provisions of the Copyright Act must be followed to transfer ownership. Under the Copyright Act, a transfer of ownership can only occur if the transfer is memorialized in a written agreement signed by the party who created the work. Absent a signed agreement, no transfer occurs, and the party who created the work retains ownership.

In an aside, the Supreme Court specifically noted that it was aware of the impact its ruling would have on the advertising industry. The Court felt it was compelled, however, to rule as it did under the law as adopted by Congress, particularly since the law was a result of hard-fought legislative compromises. There has been no change in the law in this regard, and the ruling stands.

Therefore, in the absence of a written agreement signed by the supplier, the law is clear that no transfer of ownership occurs. Any advertising agency or advertiser that does not monitor its suppliers and obtain written agreements risks justified criticism concerning its business practices.

c. Who Owns Masters and Related Materials?

Contrary to the opinion of many production houses, absent a written agreement indicating otherwise, production houses do not own masters, and the advertising agency or advertiser has a legal right to have masters delivered to them or to an editing house. Even if an advertising agency or advertiser fails to use the proper form or secure a written, signed agreement with a production house, ownership should remain with the agency/advertiser, since mere film stock is not itself subject to copyright protection. If it were, advertising agencies and advertisers would need written agreements with Kodak transferring ownership every time they used Kodak film! While the images that appear on the film are subject to copyright protection, the actual creation of such images is generally done by the advertising agency and usually pursuant to a production contract that vests copyright ownership in the advertising agency on behalf of its advertiser client.

Some production houses will nonetheless argue that they own the master and that the advertising agency or advertiser is entitled only to prints from the master. Such an argument defies logic. A production house no more retains ownership of the master than a print shop retains ownership of a mechanical. Furthermore, what is the point of its owning the master—except to hold it for ransom in a fee dispute—given that the production house has no right to use the commercial independently of the advertising agency or advertiser? Unless the advertising agency or advertiser foolishly signs a form from the production house providing otherwise, masters are owned by the advertiser.

Nor is there any such thing as a "printer's lien" on materials in the possession of printers that otherwise belong to an agency or advertiser. Such a notion presumably came from the various liens that are automatically applied by state law to certain transactions, e.g., construction contracts. Such is not the case, however, with respect to printers (or commercial producers, for that matter). Thus, while a printer may withhold materials as leverage to gain payment, doing so is technically an illegal conversion of the materials and exposes the printer to liability for their full cost or value. By improperly asserting a printer's lien, the printer has, in effect, purchased the goods from the agency and owes the agency the cost or value of the materials withheld, which is often far more than the agency will ever owe the printer.

Why It Matters

Production houses will hold masters until they are paid in full for services rendered. This can be problematic if there is a dispute as to what is owed. That is why it is important to spell out the audit rights in the agreement with the production house and to clearly state that withholding the masters is not a right of the production house.

---

d. Who Owns Creative Materials Presented at a Speculative Pitch for a New Account?

It is common for an advertising agency to present speculative creative work to a prospective advertiser during pitches for its business. In some cases, hundreds of thousands of dollars are spent on speculative creative work by the advertising agency that comes in "second place," only to see its creative work used by the advertising agency that wins the account.

The law in this area is somewhat unsettled, but generally, in the absence of a written agreement between the advertising agency and the advertiser in which the advertising agency agrees that the advertiser will own the speculative creative presented, ownership remains with the advertising agency. If the advertising agency was paid for its presentation, the advertiser can argue that there was an implied transfer of ownership or usage rights. Absent a written agreement, the U.S. Supreme Court holds that a transfer of ownership cannot occur. However, a court might hold that an implied license has been entered into between the parties, allowing use by the advertiser.

Advertisers today are becoming increasingly aware of the risks regarding ownership of speculative creative. As a result, it is not unusual for an advertiser to require that an advertising agency participating in a "pitch" sign over ownership of creative and other materials presented. While some nominal consideration usually is paid, it rarely covers the advertising agency's costs.

In the event that an advertiser allows presentation of speculative creative without an agreement as to ownership, it is recommended that the advertising agency include its own copyright notice on any materials presented. In some instances, an advertising agency may even want to register such materials with the U.S. Copyright Office, e.g., if the creative is considered particularly original and likely to be used even if the advertising agency loses the pitch. Such registration does, however, mean that the creative becomes part of the public record; the advertising agency may prefer to keep the creative confidential. In either event, the materials should bear the advertising agency's copyright notice.

It should be noted that even if the advertising agency fails to include a copyright notice, copyright ownership still vests in the agency. The absence of a copyright notice does not transfer ownership or place the work in the public domain. The best business practice, however, is to include the notice and, where appropriate, register the materials.

Ideally, the advertising agency should openly address the issue of ownership with the advertiser before the pitch is made, and put the understanding in writing.

2. Copyrights

a. Notice

Generally speaking, copyright notice should appear on all materials produced by an advertising agency for its advertiser client. Proper notice is as follows:

1. For print advertising, notice should include an encircled "c" or the word "copyright" or "copr.," the year the material was first published, and the advertiser's name (or advertising agency's name if ownership is retained by the agency); e.g., © 1999 XYZ, Inc. The notice may be located anywhere in the advertisement and be in a small font size so long as it is legible to the reader.

2. For television commercials, notice should include an encircled "c" or the word "copyright" or "copr.", the year the commercial was first broadcast, and the advertiser's name (or advertising agency's name if ownership is retained by the agency); e.g., © 1999 XYZ, Inc. If the length of the commercial is 60 seconds or less, notice may be placed on the leader or slate of the commercial. For longer commercials, notice should be placed as a video super at either the beginning or end of the commercial.

3. For radio commercials, notice should include an encircled "c" or the word "copyright" or "copr.", and also a "p" in a circle (the "p" claims protection for the actual sound recording; the "c" claims protection for the copy and sound track in the commercial itself), the year the commercial was first aired, and the advertiser's name (or advertising agency's name if ownership is retained by the agency); e.g., © (P) 1999 XYZ, Inc. The notice should appear on the label of the cassette, cartridge, or reel-to-reel tape. There is no need to audibly state the copyright notice during broadcast.

It is important to remember that the first year of publication or broadcast is the year that should always be used in the notice, regardless of the actual year in which it is published or broadcast. Thus, an advertisement or commercial first published or broadcast in 1997 should bear "1997" in its copyright notice in any year it is published or broadcast thereafter. If new material is added to the advertisement or commercial, the copyright notice can be updated by including both the first year of copyright and the year the new material was added, e.g., © 1997, 1999 XYZ, Inc.

Why It Matters

The lack of copyright notice will not dedicate a work to the public domain, free for anyone to copy. However, lack of notice gives an infringer a legal defense of "innocent infringement" that might leave the copyright owner with a weakened case. Some form of copyright notice should be mandatory on all advertising. Since the law forgives the absence of notice, abbreviated notice may be an acceptable form of warning against would-be innocent infringers. Thus, if including the year date is problematic, it can arguably be eliminated, leaving the notice reading: e.g., © XYZ, Inc. Even without the year date, an infringer would be hard-pressed to assert innocent infringement in an action. The law on this point, however, is not yet settled, and unless there is a very strong creative reason not to include the date, the full form of notice should appear.

b. Copyright Registration

Except under certain circumstances not relevant to this discussion, there is no legal requirement to register advertising with the U.S. Copyright Office. While such a registration is not expensive and may help secure higher monetary damages in case of litigation, it is generally done only for campaigns that contain original, highly valuable music or artwork, or when there is a particular concern that the materials may be copied by third parties without authorization. Given the low cost involved and the fact that registration forms can be completed and filed without the assistance of legal counsel, some advertisers insist that all advertising prepared by their advertising agencies be registered. They may also require it in their contracts with advertising agencies. The forms for registering commercials and print advertising are included in Appendix 1.

3. Trademarks

a. Trademark Clearance

Before a new name, tag line, slogan, logo, symbol, Internet domain name, or e-mail address is adopted by an advertiser, a detailed trademark search—comprising a federal registration, state registration, common law (marks in use for which registration may never have been sought), and domain name search compiled by a professional trademark search company—should be conducted to research and review what other uses have been made in the marketplace of the same or similar trademarks. These searches are simple, take about seven business days (or fewer in the event of urgency) to complete, and are relatively inexpensive, with prices ranging from about $1,000 to $2,500 per trademark searched. Before undertaking a full search, it is advisable to conduct a trademark "scan," comprising a "knock-out" online search (i.e., a search that disqualifies a trademark) of the records of the U.S. Trademark Office and the trademark registers of the individual 50 states, to see if there are any applied-for marks which would present an immediate problem and thus dictate that a different proposed mark be chosen. Such preliminary searches can be conducted in-house by trademark counsel, usually with a quick turnaround and for a fraction of the cost of a full search. A full search, however, should always follow any preliminary clearance efforts.

The searches, whether preliminary or full, should be reviewed by legal counsel expert in trademark law. An advertiser should not rely upon the opinion of its advertising agency unless it is backed by the written legal opinion of qualified counsel.

Why It Matters

Failure to conduct a trademark search can be very costly if the trademark later turns out to be preempted by someone else's prior use or registration. A revision in advertising copy and in labeling can be very expensive, irrespective of any damages to the other party.

An advertising agency may run such searches as a matter of courtesy, but the agency can be liable to its advertiser client if the search is negligently performed.

The written search opinion is discoverable in a legal action should one arise, and evidence of conducting proper legal clearance through competent trademark counsel can deflect a claim of bad-faith adoption.

WARNING

Even the most complete trademark search cannot uncover every use in the marketplace of identical or similar trademarks. Therefore, advertising agencies and advertisers should understand that there is always some risk, although it can be minimized through proper procedures.

Many advertisers and agencies have adopted the practice of clearing potential marks by searching the website of the United States Trademark Office. Under no circumstances should this type of search be relied upon, as the results are usually incomplete and give no indication of the true risk involved in adopting a particular mark.

b. Trademark Notice

Wherever possible, proper trademark notice should be used in advertising produced by an advertising agency or advertiser. Such notice is ™ for an unregistered trademark, ˢᴹ for an unregistered service mark (see discussion of service marks), and ® for federally registered trademarks and service marks. The notice should appear at the upper or lower right-hand side of the trademark. While this notice need not appear every time the trademark is used in advertising, it should at least appear at the first, most prominent, instance of the trademark. In addition, a footnote (e.g., "Coca-Cola® is a registered trademark of The Coca-Cola Company") is recommended.

Some advertisers take a very conservative approach and require that notice appear in advertising whenever the trademark is used. This is particularly true of advertisers that own trademarks weakened because they are commonly used by consumers in everyday speech when referring to a generic product, e.g., "Please give me a kleenex" (improper use), as opposed to "please give me a Kleenex tissue" (proper use). Proper trademark notice should be liberally used in similar cases where consumers have begun using a brand name to refer to a generic product (e.g., "Sanka," "Sweet'N Low," and "Band-Aid"), and great care should be taken to use the trademarks themselves correctly (e.g., "Sanka® brand decaffeinated coffee," "Sweet 'N Low® brand sugar substitute," and "Band-Aid® brand adhesive bandages"). In other words, the proper use of a trademark is as an adjective modifying the generic name of the product or service, never as a noun.

Some trademarks, however, are so strong and distinctive that the likelihood of loss through occasional improper use is rare. In this category, commonly referred to as "coined" marks, are trademarks that have no commonly known meaning independent from their form. Examples include "Exxon" for gasoline, "Kodak" for film, and "Polaroid" for cameras. While these companies may, nonetheless, be very conservative regarding use of their marks, some creative freedom in advertising can be allowed for trademarks with such strength and uniqueness. For example, the Ford Motor Company for many years used the tag line "Have You Driven a Ford Lately?" Such use of its trademark, "Ford," is technically improper because "Ford" is used as a noun rather than as an adjective. Nonetheless, no one would realistically believe that another automobile manufacturer would seize upon this improper use and start calling its automobiles "Ford's." Other examples of "safe" uses that are technically improper include "I want my Maypo!" (as opposed to "I want my Maypo cereal!") and "Leggo my Eggo!" (as opposed to "Leggo my Eggo waffle!").

This concept should be kept in mind when developing a trademark: The more distinct and less descriptive the trademark is of the product to which it will be applied, the stronger the trademark. Unfortunately, a truly strong mark may then take years to build if it is truly distinct and totally nondescriptive of the product. It is unlikely that anyone knew what "Kodak" or "Polaroid" meant when the companies first introduced their products. Today, such trademarks are among the strongest in the marketplace.

Why It Matters

Many trademarks have been lost because of improper use in advertising that contributed to consumers using such trademarks as generic designations for the products sold rather than as a brand name from a particular source. For example, "Aspirin," "Dry Ice," "Nylon," "Yo-Yo," and "Escalator" were once trademarks that were lost when they became generic descriptions of the products marketed under their names, largely on account of improper use in advertising.

The Thermos Company, manufacturers of hot and cold beverage containers, lost its trademark, "Thermos," when it challenged Aladdin, a competitor that used the trademark in its advertising to describe Aladdin containers. The court held that "Thermos" had become a generic reference for such containers and that Aladdin was free to use it.

Thus advertising agency creative directors or art directors who complain about conservative rules of advertisers regarding use of their trademarks should be reminded of the tales of aspirin, dry ice, nylon, escalator, and thermos.

---

c. Guidelines for Use of Trademarks in Advertising

1. Always use a trademark as an adjective. Use a trademark or service mark as you would any other adjective. Never:

   + pluralize a trademark or service mark;
   + use a trademark or service mark in the possessive form;
   + use a trademark or service mark as a verb; or
   + fail to follow a trademark or service mark with a generic noun.

2. Do not deviate from the form of the trademark as registered. Never:

   - abbreviate a trademark or service mark;
   - hyphenate, coin new words from, or change the spelling of a trademark or service mark; or
   - use colors for graphic trademarks and service marks inconsistent with those claimed in the registration.

3. Always use proper trademark notice. If a trademark registration has been granted by the U.S. Patent and Trademark Office, use the symbol ® or an asterisk with a footnote reading, "Reg. U.S. Pat. & Tm. Off." or words to similar effect. If a trademark is not federally registered or an application for federal registration has not yet been granted, use the symbol ™ for a trademark or SM for a service mark, together with a footnote reading "Trademark/Service Mark of (Company Name)" or words to similar effect.

4. If using the trademarks of others in advertising, give the other trademarks the respect they are due. Always:

   - use all trademarks and service marks in their correct form, i.e., the form as registered by the owner or as used by the owner on its own packaging or in its own advertising;
   - use proper notice of the other company's trademark or service mark; and
   - consult with legal counsel to determine if permission is required to use the other trademark.

d. Service Marks

Some confusion exists in the marketplace as to the difference between a trademark and a service mark.

On the one hand, a trademark is used to indicate the source of tangible goods. Coca-Cola® is a registered trademark for a carbonated cola beverage; Pepsi-Cola® is a registered trademark for a competitor's carbonated cola beverage.

A service mark, on the other hand, is used to indicate the source of a service rather than of tangible goods. AAdvantage® is a registered service mark for American Airlines' frequent flyer program; "Fly the Friendly Skies" is a registered service mark for United Airlines' passenger air-travel services.

In most ways, the distinction is not important in advertising so long as the marks themselves are properly used.

Proper notice, however, is one area where concerns can arise.

A service mark is really just another form of a trademark. The symbol ™ can be used for either an unregistered trademark or unregistered service mark. On the other hand, the notation SM should only be used for service marks, never for trademarks. Thus, when in doubt, use the ™ symbol.

If a trademark or service mark is registered, of course, the ® should always be the symbol used in the notice.

e. The Federal Trademark Registration Process

1. Intent-to-Use Trademark Applications

   It is possible to protect a potential name, design, tag line, logo, or slogan prior to actually using it in the marketplace by filing an intent-to-use application with the U.S. Patent and Trademark Office (PTO). The filing is valid, however, only if there is a true and "bona fide" intent to use the mark in commerce within the foreseeable future. While the mere filing of an intent-to-use application does not confer any trademark rights (trademark rights are created upon use), it can serve as notice to the public that trademark rights will be claimed. Most important, the date of filing an intent-to-use application will ultimately serve as the "priority" date against third parties once a mark becomes registered. To obtain a registration, use must be demonstrated; the PTO will allow an applicant three years from the date the application is issued a "Notice of Allowance" to evidence use. Even if use by the registrant is not commenced for a significant length of time after filing, a trademark owner, once registration has been obtained, can assert that earlier filing date as its constructive date of first use against infringing parties, even those whose use pre-dates that of the registrant. Intent-to-use applications can be validly filed even if use has already commenced.

The option of filing an intent-to-use application is particularly significant when a tag line or logo is an important element of an advertising campaign or product introduction that will take months or more to prepare and launch. In such instances, intent-to-use-applications should be filed to be certain that rights to the trademark or service mark are not lost because another company uses it before the campaign or product hits the market.

Unless proof of use is filed prior to approval of the intent to use application, an intent-to-use application will take longer to process than a use-based application, simply because it entails a second examination period (based on the evidence of use) after approval of the application. The extra length of time it takes to obtain a registration will depend on how long it takes the trademark owner to commence use. As a general rule, it should take four to six months after filing for the PTO to examine an application and send its first report, known as an "Office Action," to an applicant. The Office Action sets forth objections or corrections to an application. If multiple Office Actions occur, the entire registration process can take roughly one and a half to two and a half years, and even longer if there are any third party objections.

The assistance of legal counsel is recommended to prepare, file, and process both intent-to-use and use-based applications.

2. Use-Based Trademark Applications

A use-based trademark application requires an applicant to certify, under penalty of perjury, that it believes it has the right to receive federal protection. The application is accompanied by samples of the use of the trademark or service mark. For an intent-to-use application, the samples are submitted any time after use of the mark begins. To be valid, use must be interstate, territorial, or international. A PTO Trademark Examiner is assigned to the application. He or she reviews the filing and compares it to previous filings to determine if there are any conflicts. He or she will also determine if the trademark is entitled to registration or if it should be denied protection for a variety of proscriptions under federal trademark law, including descriptiveness (i.e., the trademark literally describes either what the product is or a key element of the product). Typically, if a proper search was conducted before the application was filed and advice on availability of the trademark was obtained from expert legal counsel, this process should go smoothly and should cost, including legal fees, from $2,500 to $3,500. The costs will be higher, however, if the examiner challenges the right to registration and the applicant is forced to appeal the denial to the Trademark Trial and Appeal Board (TTAB). Third-party objections will add to this cost as well, and are also heard by the TTAB. At that point, the costs can become considerable, as is the case with any litigated matter.

The process is inexpensive when compared to the investment made in purchasing media time and production costs for most advertising campaigns. It is therefore a mystery why so many advertising agencies and advertisers often fail to take advantage of the protection a registration offers.

f. The State Trademark Registration System

Virtually every state has its own trademark registration system. State registrations are sometimes desirable where a trademark owner will only use its mark within a limited geographic scope or cannot validly assert nationwide trademark rights due to rights of a prior user in a separate geographic region. While state registration does not provide the same scope of remedies as a federal registration, obtaining a state registration is faster. It is therefore often advisable to file for state registration simultaneously with filing for federal registration. By doing so, a public record of the claim to trademark ownership is made as quickly as possible. Thus, the original claimant's rights are better protected in that a trademark search of the various databases in the marketplace will discover that a claim has been made to the trademark, dissuading potential users from adopting the trademark. As yet, states do not have intent-to-use applications.

Chapter One Forms

Form I.1.1 Advertising Agency Ownership of Speculative Creative

Agreement made this_____day of_____, 20___, by and between [Advertiser and address] (the "Advertiser") and [Agency and address] (the "Agency").

Whereas the Agency has [been invited by the Advertiser/requested the Advertiser for the opportunity to (choose one)] present creative materials (the "Materials") for consideration by the Advertiser and the Advertiser desires to consider the Materials for use in its advertising and marketing plans; and

Whereas the Advertiser and the Agency desire to set forth the rights of ownership and rights to use the Materials presented.

Therefore, the parties agree as follows:

1. The Advertiser agrees that all rights of ownership and rights of use of the Materials are the sole and exclusive property of the Agency until such time as the Advertiser and the Agency agree otherwise in writing. The Advertiser agrees that it will not make any use whatsoever of the Materials without the written consent of the Agency.

2. Notwithstanding the foregoing, any part of the Materials that are in the public domain, were known or developed by the Advertiser prior to presentation by the Agency, or were presented to the Advertiser by a third party not affiliated with or obligated to the Agency, shall not be subject to the restrictions contained in paragraph 1 hereof. The Advertiser agrees to promptly notify the Agency if it believes that, pursuant to this paragraph 2, any of the Materials presented by the Agency are subject to use by the Advertiser without permission of the Agency.

3. The Agency shall be responsible for all costs and expenses related to the presentation, and the Advertiser will not be obligated to reimburse the Agency for any such costs or expenses.

IN WITNESS WHEREOF the parties have set their respective signatures on the day and date that first appears above.

[Advertiser]   [Agency]

By: _____   By: _____

Form I.1.2 Advertiser Ownership of Speculative Creative

Agreement made this _____ day of _____, 20___, by and between [Advertiser and address] (the "Advertiser") and [Agency and address] (the "Agency").

Whereas the Agency has [been invited by the Advertiser/requested the Advertiser for the opportunity to (choose one)] present creative materials (the "Materials") for consideration by the Advertiser and the Advertiser desires to consider the Materials for use in its advertising and marketing plans; and

Whereas the Advertiser and the Agency desire to set forth the rights of ownership and rights to use the Materials presented.

Therefore, the parties agree as follows:

1. The Agency agrees that all rights of ownership and rights of use of the Materials will be the sole and exclusive property of the Advertiser upon presentation, and the Advertiser will be free to use the Materials without the further consent of or compensation to the Agency. The Agency agrees that it will not make any further use whatsoever of the Materials without the written consent of the Advertiser. The Agency agrees to execute such further documents as the Advertiser may require in order to transfer any rights of ownership in the Materials to the Advertiser.

2. Notwithstanding the foregoing, any part of the Materials that are in the public domain shall not be subject to the restrictions contained in paragraph 1 hereof.

3. The Advertiser agrees to pay the Agency the following:

   a. Reimburse the Agency for all its costs and expenses related to the presentation; and
   b. A creative fee of $_____.

   Payments pursuant to this paragraph 3 will be payable within ten (10) days following the presentation of the Materials by the Agency to the Advertiser.

4. The Agency warrants and represents that the Materials are free and clear of any claims by third parties and that it has full right and authority to transfer ownership of the Materials to the Advertiser. If there are any restrictions on the Advertiser's use or ownership of the Materials, the Agency will notify the Advertiser at the time of presentation. Any such limitations so noticed will not be subject to this warranty or representation.

5. In the event the Agency breaches any warranty or representation made by the Agency contained in this Agreement, the Agency agrees to indemnify and hold the Advertiser harmless from and against any costs, expenses, attorneys' fees, or other damages that may be incurred by the Advertiser on account of such breach.

IN WITNESS WHEREOF the parties have set their respective signatures on the day and date that first appears above.

[Advertiser]   [Agency]

By: _____   By: _____

CHAPTER II
Copyright and Trademark Infringement

1. The Distinction Between Copyright and Trademark

Copyright protects the manner in which an idea is expressed; it does not protect the basic idea itself. For example, there is no copyright protection for the idea or format of a hidden-camera testimonial or a side-by-side taste test. What can be protected, however, is the actual dialogue, copy, layout, photography, music, or other expression used in the material created from the idea. Put another way, it is not the creative approach that is protected but rather what is actually said, performed, or photographed.

Importantly, copyright protects only original expressions of ideas. If someone simply copies work that was produced by someone else, that person can claim no copyright interest in it. It is no more the copier's than it is any other party who might copy it. The original creator, if anyone, holds the copyright. Nor does copyright protect materials that are in the public domain. Anyone may copy materials in the public domain. While determining if a work is in the public domain is somewhat complicated, in general, if a work is more than 100 years old, it is safe to assume it is in the public domain; if less than 100 years old, research is advised.

Finally, copyright does not protect individual words or short expressions, slogans, or advertising lines. Such things are protected, if at all, as trademarks.

Often confused with copyright, a trademark, unlike a copyright, is a word, name, slogan, logo, or symbol that distinguishes one product or service from another, e.g., Coca-Cola® versus Pepsi-Cola®. By definition, a trademark (or service mark, as some forms of trademarks are called) must be used in such a way as to conjure up in the consumer's mind the actual product or service and the company that sells the product or offers the service. As discussed in more detail below, the more original the word, name, slogan, or symbol, the greater the protection available under the trademark laws; e.g., wholly coined words such as "Kodak" are very protected, whereas trademarks using common English words are considered "weak" marks.

Note that a trademark need not be just the name of the product. A phrase or slogan commonly associated with it can also be a trademark. "Budweiser" is a trademark, as is "The King of Beers." In both instances, the trademarks describe the product: beer brewed by Anheuser-Busch. Indeed, a trademark can also be a musical "tag" or series of notes, e.g., the melody to Roto-Rooter's jingle, "Call Roto-Rooter, that's the name, and away go troubles down the drain." More recently, Harley Davidson motorcycles registered the distinctive idling sound of its motorcycles as a trademark.

Why It Matters

The distinction between copyright and trademark is important.

First, a copyright will eventually fall into the public domain, making the material it protected free for anyone to copy. On the other hand, a trademark can be protected in perpetuity as long as it continues to be used properly.

Second, copyright protects against copying by anyone, regardless of the respective fields of competition. On the other hand, trademark protection is generally available only within a particular field of competition. Thus, while Anheuser-Busch could undoubtedly stop another brewer from using the tag line "This Bud's for You," it was unable to stop a florist from using the same line to sell its flowers. Some trademarks are so strong, however, that they are given protection even against noncompetitive uses. Among the trademarks which have been enforced against noncompeting products are "Rolls Royce," "Tiffany," "Dunhill," "Beefeater," "Dior," "Bacardi," "Playboy," "Esquire," and "Kodak."

2. Copyright Infringement

a. Generally

The unauthorized taking of a substantial portion of a copyrighted work constitutes copyright infringement. While the concept is easily stated, in practice it is both vague and complex.

As a first step, an analysis must be made as to the originality of the work upon which the claim of infringement is made, seeking answers to the following questions:

1. When was it created? If created more than 100 years earlier, the work is probably in the public domain, and free to be copied.

2. When was the work first published? If before 1978, inquiry should be made if it was ever published without proper copyright notice prior to 1978. If so, the copyright to the work may have been lost to the public domain.

3. Who is claiming ownership to the work? Make sure the claimant has adequate documentation of its ownership and check the records of the U.S. Copyright Office.

4. What is alleged to have been copied? Usually a side-by-side analysis is made, comparing the original work with the sections that are claimed to have been copied.

5. Are all of the parts of the first work claimed to have been infringed original in and of themselves? Quite often, the portion of a work copied is not original even though the first work in its entirety is sufficiently original to be copyrightable. The actual expression taken must be original in its own right.

6. Is the expression in the allegedly infringing work truly similar to the expression in the original work? Remember that originality is the key to copyright protection.

7. What was the nature of the copying? If it was for reporting or educational purposes or to respond to or criticize the original work, it may be fair use to copy portions of the first work. Likewise, some copying may be protected under the First Amendment, e.g., comparative advertising or protected parody, defenses discussed in more detail below.

In the area of advertising, some courts have also adopted the so-called "look and feel" test. After comparing the respective works, if the expression of the second work has the same "look and feel" of the original expression contained in the first work, infringement has occurred. This test has sometimes been expressed as a "but for" test, i.e., in looking at the second work, it is clear that but for the first work, the second work would have never been expressed in the fashion in which it was published.

Why It Matters

Cases make it clear that copyright protection is broad in the context of advertising. Courts have not shown great sympathy for the advertiser or its advertising agency when copyrighted materials have been "borrowed." Some examples follow:

1. In an early case, California creative Chuck Blore wrote and produced a television commercial for a California radio station that utilized an attractive actress as the sole on-camera talent, using close-up photography, short scenes, quick cuts, and numerous costume changes. 20/20 Advertising, Inc., a Midwest advertising agency, saw Blore's commercial and produced a commercial for an eyeglass retailer, using the same actress and incorporating short scenes, quick cuts, and costume changes. At trial, 20/20 argued that the copied elements were commonly used in the advertising industry and in the public domain. The court rejected the defense and found that the defendant's similar juxtaposition of otherwise common techniques captured the "total concept and feel" of Blore's work and constituted copyright infringement.

2. In 2002, athletic-shoe maker Nike sued computer game company Sega Corporation, alleging that Sega's commercial for its "NBA 2K2" basketball video game infringed a 1996 Nike commercial titled "Frozen Moment." This case is interesting because Nike seeks to apply the look-and-feel standard to commercials, relying on the approach in the 20/20 case. Nike claims that the Sega commercial copies the sequence, theme, tone, acting characters, mood, pace, music, and setting of "Frozen Moment."

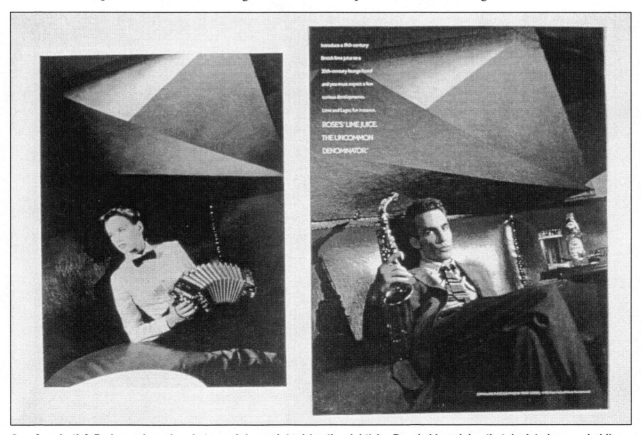

2.a Ammirati & Puris used a color photograph in a print ad (on the right) for Rose's Lime Juice that depicted a man holding a saxophone at the same table with the same background similar to the photograph on the left.

3. Ammirati & Puris was sued by a well-known photographer who had taken a black-and-white photograph of a woman holding an accordion while sitting at a table in a New York nightclub. An art deco painting was hanging on the wall behind the woman and the camera angle was pointed up at her. Ammirati & Puris used a color photograph in a print ad for Rose's Lime Juice that depicted a man holding a saxophone at the same table with the same background. (See picture 2.a.) The point of view of the photo was also up at an angle. The advertising agency pointed out that neither the nightclub nor the wall hanging was owned by the plaintiff and that the photographic techniques used were commonplace. The court held that there were enough similarities between the arrangement of the elements in the two photos to allow the issue of copyright infringement to go to a jury. The case was reportedly settled for $300,000.

4. General Dynamics and Wyse Advertising were sued by a stock photographer over the use of a photograph of a wheelchair on a porch. The photo was arguably similar to the stock photographer's photo of former President Franklin D. Roosevelt's wheelchair. (See picture 2.b.) The agency initially used the stock photographer's image in a proposed layout for a General Dynamics print advertisement. When the photographer wanted too much money to license the shot for use in the actual ad, Wyse commissioned another photographer to shoot a wheelchair on a porch. A different wheelchair and a different porch were used. Nonetheless, the court felt that the same "look and feel" existed between the original photograph and the one used in the print advertisement. It cited the similar use of an old wheelchair, the porch setting, and the camera angle. The photographer was awarded $60,108 in compensatory damages and $80,000 in legal fees—a lot more than the license

2.b General Dynamics and Wyse Advertising were sued by a stock photographer over the use of a photograph of a wheelchair on a porch.

fee originally quoted to Wyse. There is another important lesson in this case. The use of stock photography or other copyrighted material by agencies in presentations to advertisers without permission from the copyright owner is very risky. Nor does it help that the industry commonly refers to such use as "rip-o-matics" or "steal-o-matics." If what is ultimately published resembles the original work in any substantial manner, there is a serious risk of copyright infringement.

b. Public Domain

Works in the public domain may be freely copied without permission of the original author or owner of the copyright. While the statement seems simple enough, it can be quite complicated to determine which works are in the public domain.

If a work was published before January 1, 1978, it is in the public domain if it was first published on or before December 31, 1903. Some works first published between January 1, 1904, and December 31, 1977, may also be in the public domain depending upon when they were first registered for copyright and whether they were renewed. In those instances, research is needed to determine the status of the copyright.

While not immediately pertinent to the present marketplace, any work published after January 1, 1978, will enter the public domain as follows:

1. If created by an individual author, it will become public domain 70 years following the author's death.

2. If owned by a corporation or entity, it will become public domain 95 years after the date of publication or 120 years following the date of creation, whichever comes first.

While it may at first seem simple to determine the age of a work or the date of death of an author, it is often easier said than done. In addition, many works are authored by more than one individual. In such cases, the date of death of the last surviving author is determinative. Copyright research firms can be a useful resource in these matters, but it is a good idea to consult with legal counsel regarding the potential risk of infringement.

As a general rule of thumb, however, if a work was first published prior to 1903, it is in the public domain.

Since it will be many years before works created after January 1, 1978 go into the public domain, there is little point to discussing the post-1977 period. Once pre-1978 works, however, are determined to be in the public domain, it is important to be certain that what is copied is, in fact, part of the work as originally published and that what is created does not inadvertently infringe upon subsequent versions of the work, which may be subject to copyright protection.

Why It Matters

The following examples illustrate the distinction between an original work, which is in the public domain, and subsequent versions, which are not.

1. The characters, Frankenstein and Dracula, are in the public domain. They originated in stories first published prior to 1903. However, the portrayal of the characters in the movies by Boris Karloff and Bela Lugosi are not in the public domain and are protected by copyright law. If an advertiser used the image of Karloff as Frankenstein or Lugosi as Dracula, it would constitute copyright infringement. If one depicts the characters as originally described in the originating novels, consumers might not immediately identify them unless the copy specifically identifies them by name.

The original Frankenstein did not have the high forehead or the spikes in the side of the neck; Dracula was gaunt, decidedly unattractive, and had extremely long fingernails.

2. The early Sherlock Holmes novels by Sir Arthur Conan Doyle are in the public domain. Thus, the characters Sherlock Holmes and Dr. Watson are as well. However, later novels are not, since they were first published after 1903. An advertiser would be well advised to carefully consider any use of the Sherlock Holmes character, because an incorrect analysis could result in copyright infringement.

3. The novel *The Wizard of Oz* is in the public domain. The costuming and visual depictions of Dorothy, the Tin Man, the Lion, and the Scarecrow, portrayed by Judy Garland, Jack Haley, Bert Lahr, and Ray Bolger, respectively, are not. They are the property of Turner Entertainment, which owns the motion picture. Thus, in using any of the characters in a commercial, care must be taken to avoid copying them as portrayed in the motion picture.

Strategies

1. Never assume something is in the public domain. Keep in mind that an adaptation of a public-domain work may be subject to copyright protection. This is particularly true of musical compositions. While an underlying composition may be in the public domain, a musical arrangement or other version may still be under copyright.

2. Require evidence of copyright ownership from the party granting rights to a work. Request a copy of the copyright registration certificate and any existing copyright assignments or licenses that have been granted or registered. If another author or owner is indicated, be wary until it is clear who has the rights to convey the license. Make sure the license has an indemnity regarding ownership so that if a third party makes a claim, the licensor is responsible to defend against it.

3. Don't play the game of: How close can I get to the original work and not infringe it? The proper answer to the question is: Not close enough to satisfy what you want to accomplish. Either license a copyrighted work, or avoid it altogether and create an original. After all, isn't creating original works in large part what an advertiser pays its advertising agency to do?

4. Be careful when instructing a music production house concerning the "feel" of the music desired. Avoid using comparisons to actual compositions. Use the generic genre of the style, e.g., jazz, rock, blues, etc. Too often, an advertising agency will instruct a producer to compose music to sound like a popular composition. In many such instances, the composer crosses the line and infringes the original work.

5. When in doubt, conduct a copyright search to determine the status of copyright and its ownership. Such searches should be obtained through legal counsel to preserve the results as privileged information in the event of litigation. A search typically costs from $750 to $1,250.

6. Retaining an expert may be advisable in borderline cases or where the advertiser or its advertising agency wants to be certain of its rights. In the area of print materials, legal counsel is usually qualified to render formal opinions, provided he or she is expert in copyright law. In the area of music, a musicologist is the best expert to compare the work created for the advertiser with other copyrighted works. In other areas, film or television historians may be the best bet for expert advice. When using musicologists or other non-lawyer experts, it is most often advisable to have a law firm commission the work in order to best preserve its confidentiality in the event of litigation.

7. If an owner of a copyrighted work denies permission to use the work when asked, avoid using anything even remotely similar to the work requested. While the test for infringement should not differ legally even if one asked for permission and was rejected, the reality is that courts look with a jaundiced eye upon defendants who asked for permission, were denied it, and then created something arguably similar. If the answer is "no," it's best to move on to another creative approach.

3. Trademark Infringement

a. Generally

If a name, symbol, slogan, or logo is used in such a fashion that it causes potential confusion among consumers with another, preexisting trademark, whereby consumers are likely to mistakenly believe that the goods and/or services sold or rendered under the respective marks originate from the same company or legal entity, trademark infringement has occurred.

Like copyright infringement, the concept is easily stated but difficult to apply.

First, when a claim of infringement is made, it should be determined whether the party making the claim actually owns the trademark and how strong its claim of rights to that trademark is. This is generally accomplished by conducting the same type of trademark search as when developing a new trademark, which will not only verify the claimant's assertions but also give a clear view of the field and whether there are coexisting similar marks that would restrict the claimant's enforcement rights. In addition, ordering the "file wrapper" of a registration or application from the U.S. Patent and Trademark Office (PTO) may be worthwhile. The file wrapper shows the entire record of the application process before the PTO, and indicates precisely what protections were challenged, denied, and granted. It is not unusual, for example, to find that in the process of obtaining a trademark, an applicant disclaimed the exclusive right to certain words or designs included in the trademark, usually because such elements (e.g., a descriptive word or geographic location) cannot be protected apart from the mark as a whole. Inspecting the file wrapper can also reveal the nature of the claimant's use of a particular mark by way of the samples of use filed (if not the subject of a pending intent-to-use application), or reveal omissions or errors in the application by the Trademark Office that would render the underlying application or registration vulnerable to attack.

Second, the potential for consumer confusion should be viewed in the context of the entire presentation of the challenged trademark. If there are adequate indications of ownership or if disclaimers are used to dissuade any consumer from being confused, a claim of trademark infringement may not be viable. On the other hand, if a trademark is particularly strong, e.g., Kodak, it is unlikely that any disclaimer would defeat a claim of trademark infringement. In some instances, it may be necessary to conduct consumer research to determine if confusion exists. Such research, however, can become expensive if a product is distributed nationally.

Third, the respective markets—both geographic and customer—should be examined. In order for potential confusion to exist, there must be some overlap in the customer base. Without that, any claim of trademark infringement is doubtful unless, once again, the original trademark is particularly strong. If there is no federal registration and the owner's use of the mark is limited, for example, to a few West Coast states, a company using a similar trademark in New England will face an uphill battle to claim infringement, because it will only have "common law" rights. Under common law, a prior user of a mark has superior rights over subsequent users only in the specific geographical region in which the prior user has used the mark or has a substantial reputation. (However, a prior user, even without a federal trademark registration, may be able to successfully challenge another user's federal application by demonstrating prior use of that mark anywhere in the United States.) Thus, both the market and the natural zone of expansion of the market should be explored.

Finally, consider asking for a trademark license if trademark infringement occurred either because a mistake was made or a search report failed to disclose a prior user. Many trademark owners are satisfied with an acknowledgment of ownership and a license agreement at some agreed-upon compensation level. Some owners may also be amenable to selling their marks through assignment or some other coexistence arrangement.

b. Use of Another Company's Trademark

When using a competitor's trademark in a non-trademark fashion, i.e., in comparative advertisements, try to use it exactly as the competitor does, including the manner of trademark notice. While this rule is not etched in stone, misuse in this area can result in charges of dilution of the competitor's mark, especially if that mark is particularly well known or famous (see the discussion on trademark dilution). Comparative advertising is risky enough. There's no need to add a potential trademark infringement action when defending a comparative advertising case. In addition, avoid using the other company's trademark in a confusing manner to describe one's own goods. For example, it would be risky to describe a Hyundai automobile as "Honda-like."

c. Implied Endorsements

Care must be taken that the use of someone else's trademark does not imply an endorsement. While disclaimers can sometimes help in such instances, they are not necessarily the answer. Even when used, they must be very clearly stated.

Why It Matters

1. It is common practice to use well-known products in advertising to make a point, e.g., a Porsche to illustrate the speed of a computer program. An argument can be made that such use is improper without the permission of Porsche Cars. Porsche Cars could argue that such use is trading on their good will and potentially diluting the value of their trademark in the marketplace.

2. A Louisiana federal court held that famous New Orleans chef Paul Prudhomme stated a valid cause of action in a lawsuit against Procter & Gamble for trademark infringement in a commercial for Folgers coffee. Prudhomme alleged that the use of a look-alike was an implied endorsement. The case was settled.

3. *Consumer Reports* publishes the results of independent tests comparing competing products with ratings from best to worst. Those manufacturers who "win" in such tests like nothing more than to use the results in advertising. Consumers Union, publisher of *Consumer Reports*, has a strict policy against use of the magazine in advertising. For example, Consumers Union sued The New Regina Corporation, manufacturers of Regina vacuum cleaners, to prevent Regina from naming the magazine in an ad and referring to its published test results. Pending trial, the court refused to preliminarily enjoin the advertisement, in part finding that the disclaimer, "*Consumer Reports* is not affiliated with Regina and does not endorse Regina products or any other products," was adequate to eliminate confusion among consumers. Consumers Union also claimed that Regina's publishing of the results was copyright infringement. In a later motion by Regina to dismiss the

case, Consumers Union presented survey evidence that showed 19% to 23% of consumers surveyed believed that *Consumer Reports* was "affiliated" with Regina. On the basis of the survey, the court held that the issues of confusion and copyright infringement should be determined at trial and not by motion.

WARNING

Some states have laws prohibiting the use of the name of a nonprofit organization in advertising without written permission. While the results from *Consumer Reports* can be used in advertising, the name of the publication should not be used. Nor should a reprint be used. Instead, a reference such as "a leading consumer magazine" should be used, and the results should be stated in the advertiser's own words. In addition, any advertiser using the results in advertising must be very careful to report the results accurately, otherwise Consumers Union may have a cause of action against the advertiser for falsely reporting the results of the tests.

4. Trademark Dilution

The primary focus of the Federal Trademark Dilution Act is the protection of famous trademarks, including slogans and service marks, from dilution by others. In pertinent part, the law provides:

> *The owner of a famous mark shall be entitled, subject to the principles of equity and upon such terms as the court deems reasonable, to an injunction against another person's commercial use in commerce of a mark or trade name, if such use begins after the mark has become famous and causes dilution of the distinctive quality of the mark.*

> *The term "dilution" means the lessening of the capacity of a famous mark to identify and distinguish goods or services, regardless of the presence or absence of:*
> > *1. competition between the owner of the famous mark and other parties, or*
> > *2. likelihood of confusion, mistake, or deception.*

Thus, under the Act, dilution can occur when a famous trademark is misused by another person or company, or where a famous mark is used by another person or company in a manner that may dilute the distinctive value of that trademark. For example, "Kodak" teddy bears would dilute the long-established goodwill and unique identity of the Kodak trademark held by Eastman Kodak Co.

Generally, the factors considered in determining whether a mark is "famous" are:

1. the degree of inherent or acquired distinctiveness of the mark;
2. the duration and extent of use of the mark;
3. the duration and extent of advertising and publicity;
4. the geographical extent of the trading area in which the mark is used;
5. the channels of trade;
6. the degree of recognition of the mark in the trading areas and channels of trade used by both the mark's owner and the party against whom the injunction is sought;
7. the nature and extent of use of the same or similar marks by third parties; and
8. whether the owner of the mark has a valid federal registration. It is important to note that federal registration is not required to assert a valid claim of trademark dilution, but is merely one factor weighed in the determination of fame.

Trademarks that clearly fall within the category of "famous trademarks" are company names (and their products or services bearing the same name) like "H&R Block," "Coca-Cola," "Reebok," and "Rolls-Royce"; product names like "Tide" detergent, "Cheerios" cereal, and "Jeep" vehicles; slogans like "It's the Real Thing" and "Always Coca-Cola"; and service marks like American Airlines' "Something Special in the Air" and Allstate Insurance Company's "You're in Good Hands with Allstate."

Dilution has been found when an unauthorized use causes "blurring" or "tarnishment" of the famous mark in the public mind. "Blurring" has been described as the "whittling away" of the distinctive nature of a famous mark when the mark is used in connection with an unrelated or noncompeting product or service. "Tarnishment," on the other hand, can occur when the unauthorized use is derogatory or otherwise casts the famous mark in a negative light.

Courts have generally held that the owner of a famous mark need not prove competition or likelihood of public confusion. However, a 2003 United States Supreme Court ruling sheds some light on how difficult it may nonetheless be for a plaintiff to establish the burden of proof required to succeed under a claim of trademark dilution.

In 2003, the Supreme Court, in a case where Victoria's Secret tried to stop a local retailer from using the name "Victor's Secret," ruled that the Federal Trademark Dilution Act requires proof of *actual harm*, as opposed to a mere showing that consumers would likely associate the claimant with the challenged trademark. The Supreme Court strongly questioned the impact "Victor's Secret" would have on a well-established business like Victoria's Secret. Victor's Secret argued that many widely known businesses shared their names, with no apparent ill effects, and argued that objective evidence—such as a survey—was necessary to determine if dilution of the famous mark had occurred.

The Court ruled that Victoria's Secret had failed to meet its burden of proof that its famous mark had actually been diluted or otherwise weakened, and the mere fact that the use of "Victor's Secret" created a mental association by the public with Victoria's Secret did not automatically result in dilution. The case was remanded to the lower court to determine whether actual harm has been inflicted on the Victoria's Secret mark, which may result in a clearer definition of dilution and the burden of proof needed to be met to bring a successful action.

Prior to the Victoria's Secret case, rulings of the lower courts have been mixed, which was clearly an impetus for the Supreme Court to hear the case. For example, Hasbro, owner of the trademark CANDY LAND, was successful in its attempt to enjoin a company from using the name "Candyland" to identify a sexually explicit Internet site. The court found that Hasbro demonstrated a probability of proving that defendants had been diluting the value of Hasbro's mark and were causing irreparable injury to Hasbro by such use of the mark. But compare the Hasbro result to a case where The Ringling Bros. and Barnum & Bailey circus sued a bar owner, alleging violation of its rights to the phrase "The Greatest Show On Earth." The court held that the circus failed to show a likelihood that "The Greatest Bar on Earth" diluted its well-known mark. Indeed, the outcome of the Hasbro case may have been quite different had it been decided today, in light of the recent Supreme Court ruling.

While the general provisions of the Dilution Act impact advertising (particularly in establishing when a mark is famous), the one sentence section of the Act dealing with comparative advertising is of particular interest. It provides that "Fair use of a famous mark by another person in comparative commercial advertising or promotion to identify the competing goods or services of the owner of the famous mark" is not actionable.

At first blush the exception seems quite broad. The key to any analysis, however, is whether the use is "fair," a term not defined in the Dilution Act. Thus, in the case of comparative advertising, the pivotal issue is whether a defendant's use of a plaintiff's famous mark was "unfair" and caused dilution within the statutory scheme. The legislative history is virtually silent on the issue, but at least one case referenced in that history is instructive of the intent and scope of the legislation.

The case involved a comparative advertisement for MTD's lawn tractor, Yardman, targeted against its primary rival, Deere & Company. The Yardman commercial converted the static image of the deer in John Deere's logo to an animated version of a deer smaller than a vicious little dog depicted in the commercial chasing the animated deer. The District Court characterized the commercial, in pertinent part, as follows:

> *The advertisement … displays an animated version of Deere's logo, a two-dimensional leaping male deer, in order to demonstrate the MTD tractors are of comparable quality but less expensive than those made by Deere. The animation makes the deer appear small, weak, and frightened … "poking fun" at a directly competitive product also risks "diluting the selling power of the mark that is made fun of." Moreover, the scope of protection under the statute "must take into account the degree to which the mark is altered." Alterations of the kind made by MTD, in which the Deere logo is diminished in grace and power and made to look fearful, crossed the line.*

It can be assumed that MTD's use of the John Deere logo was "unfair" in the context of this statute. As such, it illustrates the kind of creative that would be actionable under the statute. Key to the analysis is the uncomplimentary animation of the John Deere logo. Manipulating a logo or trademark in a fashion that ridicules the trademark may constitute trademark dilution.

In addition to the federal dilution law, more than half the states have trademark dilution statutes. Similar to the federal law, these state laws allow courts to enjoin the use of a trademark owned by another company even in the absence of actual or likely consumer confusion. They prohibit the use of a trademark where such use may dilute the distinctiveness of a trademark by "whittling away" at its uniqueness.

The lesson here is a simple one: If an advertiser intends to use the logo of another company in comparative advertising, the logo should not be altered in any manner. It should be used it as the competitor uses it.

Why It Matters

1. In 2003, fashion designer Tommy Hilfiger failed to stop novelty gift merchant Nature Labs LLC from selling a pet perfume called "Timmy Holedigger" and branding it with trade dress similar to Hilfiger's. Its display featured the slogan "Strong enough for a man, but made for a Chihuahua." Hilfiger alleged trademark infringement and dilution. The court found Nature Labs was entitled to some degree of First Amendment defense for its parody of Hilfiger's brand and that consumers would most likely recognize the target of the joke.

2. Anheuser-Busch was successful in preventing a company that made a floor wax impregnated with an insecticide from using the slogan "Where there's life … there's bugs," claiming, in part, that it diluted and tarnished the value of its slogan "Where there's life … there's Bud." Note the difference in result between the case with the floor wax company and Anheuser-Busch's loss when it tried to enjoin the florist from using the slogan "This Bud's for You" for its flowers. In the case of the florist, a dilution argument failed since the use did not tarnish Anheuser-Busch or its products.

3. Jeans manufacturer Jordache was unsuccessful in preventing an Arizona company from using the trademark "Lardashe" for its line of jeans for heavyset women. The court in that case found that the use, while disparaging in the purest sense, was not likely to cause confusion as to the source of the jeans (i.e., consumers would not think Jordache was marketing the "Lardashe" jeans), and that the use was a humorous and satirical comment on the marketing by Jordache of its jeans. The use of humor and satire, commonly known as parody, is discussed in greater detail in section 5 of this chapter.

4. Athletic shoe manufacturer Nike convinced Volkswagen to pull a print campaign for its Corrado model car that used the headline "Air Jörgen" as an obvious play on Nike's trademark "Air Jordan." VW also agreed to drop plans to use the ad as an in-dealer poster. (See picture 2.c.)

Note, however, that it has long been the position of the Federal Trade Commission that otherwise truthful advertising, no matter how disparaging it may be, is wholly permissible, provided the net impression of the advertising is not deceptive. In 1979, the Federal Trade Commission released its "Statement of Policy in Regard to Comparative Advertising," which provides, in part, as follows with respect to the issue of disparagement:

> *Some industry codes which prohibit practices such as "disparagement," "disparagement of competitors," "improper disparagement," "unfair attacking," "discrediting," [and] may operate as a restriction on comparative advertising. The Commission has previously held that disparaging advertising is permissible so long*

2. c Athletic shoe manufacturer Nike convinced Volkswagen to pull a print campaign for its Corrado model car that used the headline "Air Jorgen."

as it is truthful and not deceptive. Comparison may have the effect of disparaging the competing product, but we know of no rule or law which prevents a seller from honestly informing the public of the advantages of its products as opposed to those of competing products.

Thus, while a charge of trademark dilution is a possible risk in comparative advertising, it is a difficult case to win, provided the advertising is truthful and the use does not create confusion among consumers.

5. Fair Use

Not all copying is illegal. Under the concept of "fair use" some copying is permissible, depending upon the circumstances surrounding the use.

a. Copyrights

The U.S. Copyright Act provides a four-factor test to determine whether an unauthorized use of a copyrighted work will constitute permissible "fair use":

1. The purpose and character of the use, including whether the use is of a commercial nature or is for nonprofit educational purposes;

2. The nature of the copyrighted work;

3. The amount and substantiality of the portion used in relation to the copyrighted work as a whole; and

4. The effect of the use upon the potential market for or value of the copyrighted work.

WARNING

Advertisers should be aware of a case involving the incidental use of a work of art in the background set of a television show. The court found infringement and rejected the defendant television producers' argument that the use constituted de minimis infringement or fair use, as the artwork had appeared for a short period of time and was out of focus, and as no visually significant aspect of the work was discernible. In another case, a court refused to dismiss a copyright infringement case against retailer the Gap when it inadvertently used the copyrighted sunglasses of the plaintiff on a model in a print ad. The plaintiff argued that the use infringed his copyright and was not fair use, particularly since the Gap sold other sunglasses and not those made by the plaintiff. While these decisions appear to be very fact-specific, one should be aware of them when considering use of copyrighted material as background or props in advertising materials.

---

b. Trademarks

While the trademark laws do not specifically contain the same fair-use language or factors, the analysis is quite similar to the approach under copyright law insofar as advertising is concerned.

In the context of advertising, the defense of fair use usually falls into one of two areas, parody or comparative advertising, discussed in more detail below.

c. Parody

The term "parody" is often misapplied when describing the use of copyrighted materials or trademarks in advertising. Many people believe that anything humorous is parody. Humor is not, however, the pivotal test in determining defensible parody. To be defensible, parody must satirize the original work. Some courts have described parody as requiring that the offending work must actually ridicule the original copyrighted material. The parody defense is rare in trademark infringement cases. The Jordache case discussed in the previous section is one of a few such cases. However, there have been decisions that trademark parodies have constituted infringement, especially when the courts considered the parodies offensive. For example, a court held that Mutual of Omaha's trademark was infringed by a company's use of "Mutant of Omaha" on T-shirts and other items. Another court granted The Coca-Cola Company a preliminary injunction against the producer of a poster proclaiming "Enjoy Cocaine."

The issue of parody as a defense is more defined in the context of copyright infringement.

The general rule is that a parody is permissible as a fair use as long as it does not take more from the original than necessary to (1) conjure up the original and (2) make the satirical comment, i.e., the point of the parody. The courts have recognized that a parody "frequently needs to be more than a fleeting evocation of an original in order to make its humorous point." One federal court has stated: "A parody is entitled at least to conjure up the original. Even more extensive use would still be fair use, provided that the parody builds upon the original, using the original as a known element of modern culture and contributing something new for humorous effect or commentary."

Why It Matters

The results of copyright infringement cases involving a parody defense have been mixed. The cases tend to be very fact-specific.

1. A court found that a Coors beer commercial using the actor Leslie Nielsen wearing a bunny suit and parodying the famous Eveready "Energizer Bunny" campaign constituted a fair use. The court ruled that "The Coors spot did not borrow an impermissible amount of the Eveready commercials for the purposes of the fair use/parody analysis.... Rather, Coors' ad merely incorporates certain elements of those commercials necessary to conjure an image of the Eveready spots for humorous effect."

2. In a New York case, the rap group Fat Boys sued Miller Brewing Company over a television commercial in which actor Joe Piscopo of Saturday Night Live fame, portrayed the lead singer of an obese rap group extolling the virtues of Miller Beer. A court held that a commercial for Miller Beer using a parody of the Fat Boys rap group did not constitute fair use. The court stated its view that "appropriation of copyrighted material solely for personal profit, unrelieved by any creative purpose, cannot constitute parody as a matter of law." The court also stated that the parody of the Fat Boys did not qualify as a fair use because the commercial "in no manner builds upon the original, nor does it contain elements contributing something new for humorous effect or commentary."

3. The scope of the parody defense in advertising became the focus of attention by the U.S. Supreme Court in March 1994, when it decided the controversial 2 Live Crew/Oh, Pretty Woman case. The Supreme Court upheld as parody ribald lyrics sung by rap group 2 Live Crew to the tune of Roy Orbison's classic song "Oh, Pretty Woman."

The Supreme Court held that the parody defense must be evaluated on a case-by-case basis and that a profit motive, however egregious it may be, is not a deathblow to a parody defense. Quoting from 18th-century politician and historian Samuel Johnson, Supreme Court Justice David Souter, who wrote the court's opinion, noted that "No man but a blockhead ever wrote except for money." Thus, the fact that all advertising has a profit motive should not undermine a parody defense.

Justice Souter, however, in an effort to distinguish between legitimate commercial use of parody (2 Live Crew's song) and less-favored commercial use of parody, wrote: "The use, for example, of a copyrighted work to advertise a product, even in a parody, will be entitled to less indulgence under the ... fair use inquiry, than the sale of a parody for its own sake...." This comment, totally unnecessary to the court's argument, shows the lack of sympathy the Supreme Court has for advertising's use of the parody defense, when sued by writers of materials that are mainstream entertainment. Advertisers should take note that advertising will not necessarily be given the full range of the parody defense, thereby dictating that caution be the rule.

4. In 2001, a U.S. Court of Appeals overturned a Georgia court order that prohibited publisher Houghton Mifflin from publishing the novel *The Wind Done Gone*, an alleged parody of the classic *Gone with the Wind*. The book extensively used characters, plot points, and settings from Margaret Mitchell's novel. Mitchell's heirs claim that the novel infringed on the copyright of the original work. The Court accepted Houghton Mifflin's arguments and chided the trial judge for overstepping his authority by granting the injunction. The decision in this case lends credence to the argument that parodies of stories that remain under copyright protection are protected by the "fair use" exception in copyright law.

d. Comparative Advertising

In the context of comparative advertising, the First Amendment affords further protection from copyright infringement.

If a manufacturer publishes advertising that compares the relative merits of its products with those of a competitor, it may reproduce materials created by the competitor to illustrate the comparison. Thus, the advertiser is free to use the competitor's trademarks, although care should be taken to include proper trademark notice when doing so. Similarly, the advertiser may use copyrighted materials of the competitor as well. For example, the publisher of a guide for television programming competitive to the leading magazine in the category, *TV Guide*, was allowed to reproduce the entire cover of *TV Guide* in a print advertisement comparing the listings in the two magazines. The court in that case held that free speech protection under the First Amendment is a defense to a claim of copyright infringement, opining that truthful comparative advertising must be allowed considerable freedom in using the materials of competitors to make comparisons.

CHAPTER III
Rights of Privacy and Publicity

As a general rule, the name, photograph, or likeness of a living person may not be used in advertising without his or her written consent. Unauthorized use violates the individual's right of privacy, a right recognized in every state. The law covers celebrities and politicians, as well as foreign nationals. The only exception rests upon First Amendment grounds, for advertising by certain kinds of media, e.g., magazines, regarding the content of their publications or programming. Thus, a commercial for a news program can mention the names of people who will be the subject of a report in an upcoming show. Similarly, in advertising promoting the purchase of a magazine, the magazine may mention the names of people featured in their editorial content.

WARNING

The use by media, e.g., magazines, of photographs of individuals without permission is a narrow exemption. Technically, the photos must be used legitimately in an editorial context. Any use in advertising must be in connection with marketing such editorial and must include only those photographs that actually appeared in the editorial content of the publication. While there is some practical leeway to this technical approach, the case law itself is very narrow.

The use of the name, photograph, or likeness of a deceased celebrity is an area of legal uncertainty, with laws differing from state to state. As such, it is becoming increasingly risky. Under umbrella of the so-called "right of publicity," a number of states have enacted laws that give certain heirs of a deceased celebrity the right to control the use of the celebrity's name and likeness for commercial purposes for a stated period of time following death, usually from 50 to 100 years. Whether or not a celebrity is protected by such right may depend on a number of circumstances, although the trend in legislatures and the courts is increasingly in favor of the recognition of the right.

On the other hand, New York has specifically rejected the survivability of such a right, although there is almost always legislation pending in New York to bring New York's position in line with the majority of those states that have ruled on the issue. The prudent advertiser and advertising agency should operate under the assumption that the right exists for at least 50 years following the celebrity's death, and research each use on a case-by-case basis to determine if permission from an heir is necessary before using the celebrity in advertising.

The use of look-alikes and sound-alikes of celebrities is also risky. If the public is deceived and believes that it is seeing or hearing the actual celebrity but is, in fact, seeing or listening to an impersonator, that celebrity may have a cause of action against the advertiser and advertising agency. Where the impersonator appears in a television commercial, the impersonation may be apparent to the viewer, and the risk is minimized. However, in some states, e.g., California and Indiana, even use of an impersonator in which it is obvious the real celebrity is not performing can be risky.

These rights continue to expand. In the early 1990s, the Estate of singer Bobby Darin sued McDonald's for use of the "performing style" of Mr. Darin in a commercial. The ad portrayed a fictitious character, whose head was shaped like a crescent moon, sitting at a piano as it floats through the sky and singing parody lyrics to "Mack the

Knife." While McDonald's had rights to use the music, it did not have any permission to mimic Darin's performance. McDonald's settled the case rather than defend it, presumably in light of the expense involved and the possibility that a California court might agree with the Estate. Courts in California, where the case was brought, generally favor celebrities.

Why It Matters

Considerable damages have been recovered by celebrities. The trend is certainly detrimental to the advertising industry.

1. In 2003, mass retailer Best Buy was sued by "Sopranos" star James Gandolfini on account of its use of his photograph from "The Sopranos" in a print advertisement offering a DirecTV satellite system with three months of free HBO, the network that airs "The Sopranos." The advertisement included the headline "Call the Boys" and copy that read, "They got all the shows a guy wants, plus "The Sopranos." What, you got a problem with that?" The ad also included a visual from the program that included Gandolfini and other cast members. Despite the fact that Best Buy had a right to refer to HBO programming in its DirecTV offer, it is not clear whether it also had the right to show photographs of celebrities who appear in the programming.

3.a A court enjoined Christian Dior from using a Jackie Onassis look-alike in an ad.

2. A New York court enjoined Christian Dior from using a Jackie Onassis look-alike in an ad. The court held that use of a look-alike was equivalent to the use of Jackie O's actual likeness and required written permission. (See picture 3.a.)

3. Another New York court accepted Woody Allen's argument that his "persona" was a trademark, and enjoined a use of a look-alike, finding the use was an implied

3.b A court accepted Woody Allen's argument that his "persona" was a trademark and enjoined the defendant's use of a look-alike, finding the use was an implied endorsement in violation of federal law.

endorsement in violation of federal law. The case reportedly settled for $300,000. (See picture 3.b.)

4. A California court awarded singer Bette Midler $400,000 in damages against Young & Rubicam for use of a singer who sounded like Midler's singing "Do You Want to Dance" in a television campaign for Lincoln-Mercury. Interestingly, Lincoln-Mercury was dismissed from the case, successfully claiming that it relied upon Y&R for the creative approach and was not to blame for the infringement of Ms. Midler's right of publicity.

5. Another California court affirmed a $2.4-million damage award against Frito-Lay and its advertising agency, Tracy-Locke, for using a sound-alike of singer Tom Waits in a radio commercial for Doritos brand corn chips. The award included punitive damages of $1.5 million against Tracy-Locke and $500,000 against Frito-Lay.

6. Actor Bert Lahr sued the makers of Lestoil liquid cleaner over a commercial that used an animated duck with a voice that sounded like Lahr's. While the court rejected the privacy claim based on similar voice, it upheld a possible defamation claim that the commercial suggested Lahr "stoops so low as to do anonymous voice-over." It also upheld a claim for unfair competition because the advertiser obtained an "enhanced value" or benefit from Lahr's apparent participation in the commercial.

7. In a Texas case, singer and guitarist Carlos Santana of the rock group Santana brought suit against Miller Brewing Company for its use of the composition "Black Magic Woman" in a commercial for Miller Beer. While Miller had secured permission from the music publisher to use the song, Santana claimed that he was so closely associated with the composition that its use was tantamount to the use of his identity. The case was reportedly settled for more than $100,000.

3.c Former Governor Michael Dukakis of Massachusetts successfully forced a software company to stop using his photograph in a print advertisement.

8. In another aspect of the Fat Boys vs. Miller case discussed above, the Fat Boys claimed the commercial was a violation of their rights and misappropriated their performance. A judge declined to dismiss the case and held that the facts were sufficient to proceed to a jury trial. The case subsequently settled for an undisclosed amount.

9. Even politicians get into the act. Former Governor Michael Dukakis of Massachusetts successfully forced a software company to stop using his photograph in a print advertisement for its presentation software under the headline "There are some people even we couldn't make more persuasive." (See picture 3.c.)

10. In a reported case that can only be described as extreme, Iraqi officials objected to the use of Saddam Hussein's photograph in an advertisement for Prophesy, a price reporting system for the treasury investment market published in the United States and Japan. The headline read: "History has shown what happens when one source controls all the information," and the copy referred to "dictators." According to published reports, the advertiser offered to substitute Stalin when Iraqi diplomats stationed in Japan objected on behalf of Hussein. (See picture 3.d.)

3.d Dictator Saddam Hussein objected to the use of his photograph in an advertisement for Prophesy.

Nonetheless, commercials have been produced that use politicians without permission and without incident.

1. In 2003, the U.S. Court of Appeals in California upheld the dismissal of a case brought by the Diana, Princess of Wales Memorial Fund against the Franklin Mint. The Fund accused the Franklin Mint of unlawfully using Diana's likeness on dolls, jewelry, plates, sculptures, and its advertisements for its products. The court held that the law of Great Britain, not California, applied. Great Britain does not recognize the right of publicity. The court also upheld the trial court's dismissal of the Fund's allegation of false endorsement, holding that there must be evidence of customer confusion as to an actual endorsement. In this case, the court found that there was no likelihood of confusion as to the origin of Franklin Mint's Diana-related products.

2. In 1989, Hal Riney & Partners, the advertising agency for The Stroh Brewery Co., produced and aired a number of commercials in a campaign that featured footage of actual foreign politicians,

including Fidel Castro and Daniel Ortega. Their words were replaced by dubbed voiceovers praising Stroh's beer. While any one of the politicians used in the campaign could have asserted their right of privacy in the United States, it was presumably a safe bet that none of them would. The bet apparently paid off, and the commercials ran without any material claims against them.

3.   It is not unusual to see look-alikes or sound-alikes of current or former presidents of the United States used in advertising. While such use is technically illegal, usually they do not object. Advertisers should be cautioned, however, that former President Clinton has objected to the use of his voice or likeness, and successfully convinced Molson Breweries to discontinue use of a print advertisement that used his image to promote Molson beer in England. Even though Great Britain does not recognize the right of privacy as it is recognized in the United States, Molson, nonetheless, agreed to discontinue publication of the advertisement. (See picture 3.e.)

Therefore, the proposed use of politicians in advertising needs to be evaluated on a case-by-case basis. Use of celebrities, however, is far riskier.

Unfortunately, the trend in cases and legislation is hardly supportive of the advertising industry.

For example, Indiana protects not only the name, voice, likeness, and photograph of celebrities, it also protects mannerisms and expressions. Such a right is also protected after the death of the celebrity upon the claim of any heir having more than a 50% interest in an estate. Thus, the expression "Go ahead, make my day" presumably could not be used in advertising without the written consent of Clint Eastwood. While the con-

3.e President Clinton objected to the use of his voice or likeness and successfully convinced Molson Breweries to discontinue use of a print advertisement that used his image to promote Molson beer in England.

stitutionality of the Indiana statute is questionable, its scope nonetheless illustrates the legislative trend toward broadening celebrity rights.

A case involving game-show hostess and sometime actress Vanna White illustrates how far celebrity rights are being applied.

In 1994, Vanna White won a verdict of $400,000 against electronics giant Samsung over a print ad that used a blond female robot dressed in an evening gown standing in front of a letter board similar to that used on the TV game show "Wheel of Fortune." (See picture 3.f.)

The court found that Samsung violated White's right of publicity because the advertisement misappropriated her "identity." In rendering its decision, the court effectively acknowledged that no one in his or her right mind could have believed that the robot was Vanna White. Nor was there any evidence that the advertiser attempted to deceive the public into believing that White was in any way involved with the advertisement. The mere fact that her image inspired the advertisement, and that "but for" her, the visual would probably never have been produced, gave her a right under California law.

Taken to its extreme, the White decision means that any time the public might be reminded of a celebrity in an ad or promotion, the advertiser must first obtain consent from that celebrity, or run the risk that it will be sued for invasion of the celebrity's right of publicity.

3.f Vanna White won a verdict of $400,000 against electronics giant Samsung over a print ad that used a blond female robot dressed in an evening gown standing in front of a letter board like the one used on the TV game show "Wheel of Fortune."

To make matters worse, the American Law Institute(ALI) adopts the White approach in its highly influential *Restatement of Law*, a publication often relied upon by lawyers and judges in considering legal rights and remedies where specific state statutes do not exist.

The *Restatement of Law* now defines the right of publicity as follows: "One who appropriates the commercial value of a person's identity by using without consent the person's name, likeness, or other indicia of identity for the purposes of trade is subject to liability...." This restatement supports White's victory and creates a cause of action in virtually any situation where some element of an advertisement reminds the public of a celebrity.

To illustrate the potential impact of the definition, here are a few creative advertising concepts, suggested by some of the leading creative directors in the country, that could, under the *Restatement*, give rise to a lawsuit. The name of the potential celebrity "plaintiff" follows each example.

- A fat woman screeching the national anthem—Roseanne

- An old comedian with a bad toupee and a large cigar—George Burns

- A shapely blond woman wearing a pointed brassiere—Madonna

- A white glove on a piano bench—Michael Jackson

Despite strongly warning of the consequences of right-of-publicity infringement, the Vanna White decision and the *Restatement* provide virtually no guidance in determining how much, if any, of a celebrity's identity may be used without permission. In addition, the decision and the *Restatement* completely ignore the likelihood that claims may be made by lesser-known persons alleging a violation of their right of publicity based on something contained in an ad that reminds them of themselves. Moreover, there is no discussion in either the decision or the *Restatement* of the treatment of parodies, which have traditionally been afforded broad protection under the First Amendment.

The only sensible voice heard from the judicial bench during the White debate came from Judge Alex Kozinski, a highly respected federal judge. He wrote, "Something very dangerous is going on here.... [I]t's now a tort for advertisers to remind the public of a celebrity.... [T]he panel's opinion is a classic case of overprotection.... [I]t's bad law.... In the name of avoiding the 'evisceration' of a celebrity's rights to her image, the majority diminishes the rights of copyright holders and the public at large. In the name of fostering creativity, the majority suppresses it. Vanna White and those like her have been given something they never had before, and they've been given it at our expense. I cannot agree."

The Vanna White case was followed by the truly bizarre case of Wendt v. Host International, Inc. Actor George Wendt and his co-plaintiff, John Ratzenberger, played the barfly characters Norm and Cliff in the television series "Cheers." Paramount Pictures, the owner of the series, granted Host a license to set up bars in airports modeled after the set from "Cheers" and to use the trademark "Cheers." Host also set up "animatronic robotic figures" named Bob and Hank that were based on the Norm and Cliff characters from the television series, although neither had the facial features of Wendt or Ratzenberger. (See picture 3.g.)

The actors sued under the California Right of Privacy statute and under the Lanham Act, a federal trademark protection act, claiming that the robots, though bearing different names and faces, were nonetheless sufficiently based upon their likenesses to constitute a cause of action. At first consideration, the District Court granted summary judgment to the defendant, finding that the robots did not look like the plaintiffs and that, as Paramount owned the copyright to the characters used in the program and was free to license them, the actors portraying those characters did not attain rights to them.

On appeal, the Court of Appeals reversed, holding that the District Court's comparison of photographs of Wendt and Ratzenberger with photographs of the animatronic figures was not sufficient to resolve their claims.

After remand, the District Court reconsidered the matter and again granted summary judgment to Host. Again, the court found that there was no similarity between the plaintiffs and the robots, except that one robot was heavy and the other was slight.

On appeal, the Court of Appeals again reversed. The judges disregarded the District Court's finding that there was no resemblance and held for the plaintiffs on all counts.

The Court of Appeals, as in the Vanna White case, gave a very broad interpretation of "likeness" for statutory purposes, saying that it may include an "impressionistic resemblance." In effect, the court held that even though there was no true similarity between the actors and the robots, and despite the fact that Paramount owned the underlying characters, the public nonetheless remembered the actors as having played those roles in the TV series. According to the Court of Appeals, that was enough to give rise to a cause of action.

As if that were not enough, the court held that the plaintiffs had a valid claim for "unfair competition" under Section 43(a) of the Lanham Act. Because one robot was heavy and the other slight, as were the actors who played Norm and Cliff, the court found that these physical similarities gave rise to a claim for false endorsement, holding that there was a likelihood of confusion that the plaintiffs were endorsing the defendant's "Cheers" bars.

After years of litigation, the case was eventually settled.

Do the White and Wendt cases and the ALI Restatement represent aberrations that other courts will disregard?

Actor William McFarland, known primarily for his performance as the character "Spanky" in the original "Our Gang" series, brought suit against a restaurant named "Spanky's," in Ocean City, New Jersey. McFarland claimed that use of the name Spanky violated his rights of privacy and publicity under New Jersey law, even though he had signed away any personal claim to the name when he contracted to perform the character many years earlier. The New Jersey court agreed with McFarland, finding that he had become so associated with the character that he and the character were effectively indistinguishable, making them one and the same. Use of the name Spanky, therefore, violated his rights, despite his having signed away any interests in the character. In arriving at its decision, the court cited the White case as support for its holding.

On the other hand, a Michigan court threw out a case brought by William Levine, popularly known as "Mitch Ryder" of the rock group Mitch Ryder and the Detroit Wheels, against Molson Breweries and its advertising agency, Lintas: New York. Levine claimed a commercial produced by Lintas for Molson used a sound-alike in the song "Devil with a Blue Dress On," one of the few hits Mitch Ryder and the Detroit Wheels enjoyed. The court rejected the argument, specifically finding that the California decision in favor of Bette Midler against Lincoln-Mercury was not accepted as precedent in Michigan. Levine did not appeal.

3.g The actor George Wendt (top), from the television series Cheers, and the robotic figure "Bob" (bottom), based on his television character, were the basis of the suit Wendt vs. Host International Inc. in which plaintiffs claim that the robots, though bearing different names and faces, were none-the- less thier likeness.

CHAPTER IV
Comparative Advertising

One of the most controversial areas in advertising today is comparative advertising; i.e., advertising that compares the relative merits of competitive products or services. Any advertising agency or advertiser embarking on a comparative advertising campaign must exercise the greatest degree of caution. While the area is replete with risks, the rewards for a successful, truthful campaign are considered by many to be worth those risks.

Real-estate brokers claim there are three important things to consider when buying a house—location, location, location. When it comes to producing comparative advertising, there are, similarly, three important things to remember—substantiation, substantiation, substantiation.

While all advertising needs to be supported by adequate substantiation for claims made in the copy, the need triples in the case of comparative advertising. The risks are simply too high to take the need for substantiation lightly. At least one company went bankrupt over a false comparative newspaper campaign, which was distributed in the Southwest only! In other instances, advertising agencies have lost very valuable clients on account of sloppy procedures or cutting corners with respect to the substantiation needed to support comparative advertising. In virtually every case, the problem could have been solved had the advertiser or its advertising agency taken simple precautions in producing the advertising in the first instance. In some cases, simple word changes in the copy, e.g., "our prices are the lowest" to "nobody has lower prices," were all that would have been required to avoid the problem. The former is a superiority claim, requiring extensive market studies to substantiate; the latter is a parity claim, requiring a lesser degree of substantiation and a policy to meet any lower price in the marketplace.

1. Producing Comparative Advertising

a. Proper Claim Substantiation

In comparative advertising, the net impression of the advertising, i.e., the consumer take-away, is critical. It is rare for a comparative advertisement to deliberately make a false statement. More often, everything said is literally true, but the net impression is false or misleading. As a result, great care must be taken to determine the consumer's net impression and to be certain that the net impression is clearly supported by the substantiation.

Therefore, consumer surveys or independent data available from marketplace researchers, e.g., IRI, Nielsen, FIND/SVP, Polk, Consumers Union, etc., must be carefully reviewed to be certain they support the claim made in the advertising within the context of the net impression of the advertisement taken as a whole.

Why It Matters

Hyde Athletics, the manufacturer of Saucony walking shoes, claimed in a print campaign that it ranked "Number 1" in a survey of women's walking shoes conducted by Consumers Union and reported in its publication, *Consumer Reports*. In truth, however, Avia's women's walking shoes were on the top of the survey list. Hyde argued that since the Saucony shoes had, in the aggregate, more favorable ratings among the listed criteria in the survey than Avia, it was, in fact, the winner. Consumers Union confirmed, however, that its criteria were weighted and that the order of ranking as listed in the survey reflected the actual order of superiority. Avia filed suit under a federal statute that prohibits false or deceptive comparative advertising. Within weeks, Hyde settled and agreed to stop publishing the claim.

Generally, the issue of adequate claim substantiation centers upon an evaluation of whether the advertiser and its advertising agency have a reasonable basis upon which to base the claims made. A "reasonable basis" is hard to define and will depend upon a number of factors. However, the reasonable basis needed to support a claim in comparative advertising may be even heavier than that needed to support the truth of a claim in a challenge brought by the Federal Trade Commission.

To illustrate the high level of substantiation required to show a reasonable basis for a claim in comparative advertising, it is instructive to compare what the Federal Trade Commission requires in challenges brought against advertisers and advertising agencies for false and deceptive advertising. In reviewing advertising for compliance with the Federal Trade Commission Act, the FTC has identified that the following factors determine the truth of claims made in advertising.

1. The type of product advertised—In advertising for drugs, foods, or other potentially hazardous consumer products, the level of substantiation is higher than for goods that pose no immediate danger if properly used, e.g., clothing. In cases involving health and safety issues, the FTC generally requires a relatively high level of substantiation; i.e., scientific tests. The same level of substantiation is required in comparative advertising.

2. The type of claim made—If an advertisement makes health, medical, dietary, safety, or other similar claims that refer to specific facts or figures, rather than making generalized statements regarding product performance, a high level of substantiation is required, e.g., scientific tests. A high level of substantiation is also required for claims whose truth or falsity is difficult or impossible for consumers to evaluate by themselves. The same holds true for comparative advertising.

3. The benefits of a truthful claim—The FTC has stated that it is concerned about ensuring that the level of substantiation which it requires is not likely to prevent consumers from receiving potentially valuable information about product performance. Thus, if a product is particularly beneficial to consumers, e.g., a very low interest rate on a mortgage, the Commission will tolerate a lower level of substantiation. In a comparative advertisement, however, it is not clear that the courts will agree with the FTC approach. Where a comparative claim is made, regardless of the product's benefit to consumers, the advertiser and its advertising agency must be certain to substantiate claims made against competitors.

4. The ease of developing substantiation for the claim—How costly and difficult is it to obtain substantiation for the claim? The FTC considers this factor in conjunction with the third factor, above, and may be lenient in some cases. Such a defense would never prevail in a comparative advertising case as an excuse for not conducting thorough research to support a comparative claim.

5. The consequences of a false claim—If personal injury, property damage, or extensive monetary loss may result as a result of reliance on a claim, the FTC requires a high level of substantiation. This factor ties in closely with the first factor. In comparative advertising, however, it is unlikely that even a slight risk of injury or loss would require substantiation any less supportive of a claim than a more severe risk.

6. The amount of substantiation that experts in the field agree is reasonable—For drugs, the FTC considers the substantiation standard generally applied by the scientific and medical community and by the Food and Drug Administration. The standard is probably the same for comparative advertising.

A full copy of the FTC's Policy Statement Regarding Advertising Substantiation is included in Appendix 2.

Why It Matters

There have been any number of comparative advertising cases, costing many thousands and sometimes millions of dollars, involving product categories as diverse as shampoos, toilet bowl cleaners, beverages, drugs, motor oils, pet foods, computers, razor blades, and cigarettes. For example:

1. U-Haul, a company that rents trucks and trailers used by consumers when moving, was awarded $40 million in damages against competitor Jartran for statements in a newspaper campaign that falsely claimed newer trucks, gas savings features not on U-Haul trucks, better fuel efficiency, and easier handling. Jartran went bankrupt as a result of the award. (See picture 4.a.)

2. BMW obtained a restraining order against the now-defunct maker of the Sterling automobile for use of a commercial depicting a luxury car—a BMW—being vandalized. The judge found that the commercial, produced by Hal Riney & Partners, falsely implied that BMW did not provide a standard security system, as did Sterling. The judge issued a temporary restraining order on one day's notice. Sterling agreed to permanently pull the ad eight days after the temporary restraining order was issued.

3. Razor blade manufacturer Wilkinson Sword was held liable for $953,000 in damages to Gillette for false claims regarding superior smoothness for Wilkinson's blades when compared to Gillette's blades.

4. ALPO Pet Products obtained a $12.1 million judgment against Ralston-Purina for false claims in a Ralston dog food campaign. The award was based on $3.6 million in ALPO advertising needed to counter the Ralston campaign and $4 million for the delayed introduction of ALPO's puppy food due to Ralston's campaign. The court then increased the damages by 50% under a special provision in the federal law that can be applied to comparative advertising.

4.a U-Haul was awarded $40 million in damages against competitor Jartran for statements in a newspaper campaign with false claims.

b. Measuring Deception in Comparative Advertising

It is not necessary that a majority, or even near a majority, of consumers be potentially misled by the challenged claims. In challenging or defending advertising in a lawsuit, both sides typically rely upon consumer surveys to support their case.

Survey results tend to be given considerable weight by the courts to ascertain the net impression conveyed to consumers. Survey reliability, however, depends on whether: (1) the sample tested is representative of the consuming public; (2) the sample included enough consumers; (3) the questions were properly phrased to avoid bias; (4) the manner in which the study was conducted was developed by experts; (5) the interviewers were unaware of any litigation; and (6) the survey was supported at trial by expert testimony.

The adequacy of the sample, in numerical and geographical terms, is a significant factor. Courts have not established any absolute number of consumers necessary to form a sufficient sample, but they have provided guidance. Based upon generally accepted principles of survey research, the television networks, for example, have established that consumer testing should be conducted in at least four regions of the country, with at least 50 consumers in each region.

In evaluating the significance of survey results in cases involving the issue of likelihood of confusion, courts have determined that an "appreciable" number of consumers potentially deceived is not a majority. Courts have found that 15-20% confusion rates are enough to find confusion.

Why It Matters

1. The Coca-Cola Company challenged Tropicana Products, Inc. over a commercial that featured Olympic Gold medalist Bruce Jenner, who, after squeezing an orange and pouring it into a Tropicana orange juice container, stated, "It's pure, pasteurized juice as it comes from the orange." Coca-Cola, the manufacturer of Minute Maid orange juice, charged that the advertisement was false because it represented that the orange juice is unprocessed and fresh-squeezed when, in fact, it is pasteurized and sometimes frozen prior to packaging. The court granted an injunction based on consumer perception tests that showed only 15% of the

4.b The Coca-Cola Company successfully challenged Tropicana Products, Inc. over a commercial that featured Olympic Gold Medalist Bruce Jenner.

consumers tested were misled. The injunction was affirmed on appeal, where the court pointed out that since the claim was false on its face, no consumer perception studies were needed for the lower court to enter an injunction. This was a pivotal ruling in comparative advertising. If a plaintiff can show that claims made by the defendant are false, regardless of evidence of actual consumer confusion or market impact, a court may grant an injunction. (See picture 4.b.)

2. The Upjohn Company claimed that advertising for Advil, American Home Products' over-the-counter ibuprofen analgesic, caused consumer confusion as to the source of Advil and the substitutability of Advil for Motrin, Upjohn's brand of the prescription form of ibuprofen. Questions were asked of 214 subjects, half men and half women, in five geographically dispersed shopping malls. Thirty-three percent of the respondents stated that Advil was the name of the prescription drug, and 76% selected the Motrin tablet when asked which of the two tablets was pictured in the

ad. The court considered these responses to show that a "not insubstantial number" of consumers were deceived. American Home Products revised the commercial by including a visual clarification of the color of Advil, adding supers, and revising the language.

It is important to note that, as in Upjohn, courts frequently will pay far more attention to responses to unaided questions in a survey, e.g. What does the advertisement tell you?, than to the responses to directed questions, often skillfully devised to elicit a desired response.

2. Naming the Competitor in Comparative Advertising

It is not a defense to a comparative advertising lawsuit that the competitor was not specifically named. As long as the target of the comparative claim was the competition, any competitor that might be potentially affected has standing to bring a lawsuit. Thus, neither the advertiser nor its advertising agency should take any solace in thinking that avoiding direct references to the competitor diminishes its risk. Note that in many of the cases discussed in this chapter, the competitor was never specifically named.

Indeed, failing to specifically name the competitor against whom the claim is made may increase liability, since any competitor affected can bring a lawsuit. Thus, if the advertiser has failed to prepare substantiation against the "other" competitor who brings suit, it may find itself having no defense in a lawsuit. Therefore, it is often better to name the competitor and focus the risk assessment on known entities.

3. Comparative Advertising Litigation Time Frames

It is possible to stop false or deceptive comparative advertising in a matter of days. While such a result is unusual, it is becoming increasingly common as advertisers become more familiar with the application of comparative advertising laws and the courts become more educated in the importance of swift justice in advertising disputes, where a shift of as little as a fraction of a market share can mean millions of dollars in lost sales. Such was the case when BMW was granted a temporary restraining order against the maker of the Sterling automobile after a one-day hearing.

4. Advertising Agency Liability for Deceptive Advertising

Advertising agencies generally have not been found independently liable for false or deceptive comparative advertising in lawsuits brought by a client's competitor, although it is common practice to name the advertising agency as a codefendant. The lack of decisions holding agencies independently liable is due more to the fact that most cases settle than to there being no legal foundation for liability. Indeed, advertising agencies clearly have independent liability for actions brought by the Federal Trade Commission for false or deceptive advertising. The same logic applies in finding liability for false or deceptive comparative advertising; i.e., if the agency actively participated in the production of the advertising and was or should have been aware of the falsity of the claims made, it is independently liable.

5. The Fine Line between Advertising and Public Relations

In 2003, the United States Supreme Court agreed to hear an appeal from athletic-shoe giant Nike. Nike appealed a 2002 decision of the California Supreme Court that Nike must stand trial for false advertising under California law for statements it made in corporate advertising and public relations releases. The statements defended against accusations by public interest groups that Nike supported child labor and poor working conditions in Asian plants where its goods are manufactured. The California court found that because Nike's comments on the issue affect consumer purchase decisions, the ads and public relations statements—even though they did not directly sell any Nike products—were entitled only to the limited protection afforded "commercial speech" and not the higher level of First Amendment protection afforded noncommercial speech. Nike argues that it critics should not be permitted to take full advantage of an uninhibited and wide-open debate under the First Amendment unless Nike is permitted to address those charges with the same freedom.

If the U.S. Supreme Court allows the California decision to stand, the Nike case points out a very significant limit to corporate free speech and the distinction between commercial and noncommercial speech under the First Amendment. Historically, public relations and issue advertising was not burdened with the same substantiation requirements as more traditional offers for products or services. As far as California is concerned, every statement in a public relations release, annual report, or public statement by a CEO or other corporate officer can be attacked if believed to be unsubstantiated. Such a burden has a very chilling effect on open corporate communications to shareholders and consumers on important public issues.

6. Media Liability for Deceptive Advertising

Generally, the media is not liable for false or deceptive advertising that appears in its pages or is broadcast over its facilities. If it can be shown, however, that the media recklessly disregarded what it should have known was false or deceptive, liability may, in fact, exist. In the most extreme example, *Soldier of Fortune* magazine was held liable in 1992 for $4.3 million in damages to the sons of a victim of a contract murder. The case involved an Atlanta businessman whose killers were hired through a classified advertisement placed with the publication. The ad began "Gun for hire" and ended with "all jobs considered."

7. The Costs and Alternatives to Litigation

Litigating a comparative advertising case is a very expensive proposition. Initiating or defending what may seem like even the simplest case can cost hundreds of thousands of dollars.

Because of the expense involved in litigating a comparative advertising lawsuit, the first consideration should be the practicality of bringing or defending such a lawsuit. This may depend on the strength of the case, the "litigation attitude" of the respective advertisers, the skill and funding of legal counsel for each side, and the attitude and schedule of the judge assigned to the matter.

Most comparative advertising lawsuits are settled, not tried. Where the deception is obvious and the judge is available and sympathetic, or where the plaintiff has an overwhelming economic advantage over the defendant, a settlement can come quite quickly after the instigation of a lawsuit. Indeed, a quick settlement is the scenario most hoped for when bringing a comparative advertising case. Thus, from the outset, it is important for both sides to focus on the essential ingredients of any potential settlement.

It can be assumed that any settlement would include a cessation of further broadcast or publication of the offending advertising. The faster the advertising is pulled, however, the greater the cancellation and associated costs, not to mention the possibility that an entire campaign may be aborted because the advertiser has no backup advertising.

There are alternatives to litigation. They include challenges to the television networks (ABC, CBS, and NBC—Fox and others do not have a formal procedure), and challenges before the National Advertising Division of the Council of Better Business Bureaus (NAD). The NAD and each of the networks have detailed challenge procedures that can be far less expensive and complicated than litigation. The procedures of the NAD are reproduced in Appendix 3.

If an advertiser has decided that it has no alternative other than to commence a lawsuit for false comparative advertising under the Lanham Act, the first thing to do is prepare the materials the lawyers will need to bring the case. Similarly, if an advertiser finds itself on the receiving end of a lawsuit, it must also prepare key materials for its attorneys before the case can be defended. A checklist appears at the end of this chapter. If the tasks and the materials in the checklist are undertaken and collected before the lawyer is called, considerable legal expenses can be avoided.

Chapter Four Forms

Form I.4.1 Checklist in Considering a Comparative Advertising Lawsuit

A. For all comparative advertising cases:

☐ 1. Full corporate name of the advertiser, state of incorporation, and principal officers.

☐ 2. All subsidiaries, divisions, or affiliates of the advertiser.

☐ 3. Name and address of the advertiser's advertising and promotion agencies and, with regard to any agency involved in any advertising being questioned, the name, title, and phone number of the principle contact at the agency and a copy of the advertiser's contract(s) with the agency(ies) involved.

☐ 4. Copies of all advertising, promotion, and collateral materials then presently being published, broadcast, displayed, or distributed by the advertiser; copies of then-inactive advertising published within six months prior to the date of the challenge; and copies of advertising planned to be published in the future.

☐ 5. Copies of all correspondence, memoranda, layouts, storyboards, scripts, photoboards, copy tests, call reports, focus groups, meeting notes, and the like pertaining to the advertising in question, including relevant records then in possession of the advertiser's agency(ies).

☐ 6. Written summaries of all oral communications between the advertiser and the opposing advertiser relating to (i) the questioned advertising or (ii) prior advertising published by either advertiser.

☐ 7. Details of pending or prior lawsuits, regulatory actions, or other formal challenges relating to the advertiser's advertising or marketing practices, particularly any lawsuits or challenges between the advertiser and the opposing advertiser.

B. For comparative advertising cases where the advertiser is the plaintiff:

☐ 1. Copies of the offending advertising and evidence as to where it has been published.

☐ 2. A memorandum from the plaintiff detailing what the plaintiff considers false or misleading in the offending advertising and the plaintiff's reasoning in support of its position.

☐ 3. Measures, if any, taken or planned to be taken by the plaintiff to counteract or otherwise respond to the offending advertising.

☐ 4. Copies of all research, testing, focus groups, perception studies, reports, anecdotes, or other evidence relating to (i) consumer reaction to, or net impression of, the offending advertising and (ii) what effect the advertising had on the perception of the plaintiff's and the defendant's products or services advertised therein.

☐ 5. Details and evidence of the immediate and long-term impact on the manufacture, inventory, distribution, and sale of the advertiser's goods or services if the challenged advertising were to continue to be published.

C. For comparative advertising cases where the advertiser is the defendant:

☐ 1. Copies of the challenged advertising, together with the location of where it has been, or is planned to be, published.

☐ 2. The names and addresses of all companies and persons involved in the creation, production, or publication of the challenged advertising.

☐ 3.   The cost of production of the challenged advertising.

☐ 4.   A media schedule (including the costs) for the challenged advertising, showing both past and planned publications.

☐ 5.   Copies of all reports, tests, research, or other material supporting the truth of the claims challenged in the advertising or the quality, safety, and efficacy of the advertiser's products and services, together with the sources and principal contacts of those who prepared the substantiation.

☐ 6.   Copies of any network clearance reports if the challenged advertising was submitted for broadcast clearance.

D.   For cases where the advertiser is claiming a defendant has diluted its trademarks in comparative advertising:

☐ 1.   Copies of the advertiser's federal, state, and foreign trademark or service mark registrations, together with any trademark searches, abandoned filings, refusals to register, oppositions, or cancellations relating to the advertiser's marks.

☐ 2.   Copies of all research relating to (i) consumer reaction to, or net impression of, the offending advertising and (ii) the defendant's products or services advertised therein.

☐ 3.   A memorandum from the plaintiff detailing why the advertiser feels the defendant's use or depiction of the mark(s) dilutes the value and prestige of the mark(s) in the marketplace, together with any reports, tests, research, or other materials in support of the advertiser's beliefs.

☐ 4.   Details and evidence of the immediate and long-term impact on the manufacture, inventory, distribution, and sale of the advertiser's goods or services if the offending advertising were to continue to be published.

Chapter V
Sales Promotion

1. Sweepstakes, Contests, and Sales Incentives

a. General Rules and Distinctions

There are many federal, state, and local laws and regulations governing sweepstakes and contests, two very popular promotional techniques.

As a general rule, a sweepstakes or contest becomes a "lottery" and, thus, illegal under federal and state laws, if all of the following three elements are present: Prize promotions, consideration, and chance.

1. Prize is always present in such promotions.

2. Consideration, in the majority of states, generally means that the entrant has to make a purchase or payment (e.g., buy the product) while in others, the entrant must do something substantial (e.g., go to the store to get or deposit the entry form). Most states follow the "standard lottery rule"—defining consideration as a purchase or payment. A handful of states include substantial expenditure of effort within the definition. Store visits may be problematic in certain states. Simple tasks like watching a television show, completing a questionnaire, or reading a brochure are generally permissible. A requirement that return postage be included is generally not deemed to be consideration (except in Vermont) when the consumer requests game material by mail (i.e., a game card, entry forms or rules).

It is perhaps the store visit requirement that has caused the most controversy in recent years. Two states, Ohio and Michigan, have specifically held that requiring a consumer to visit a retail outlet in order to enter a sweepstakes may constitute consideration rendering such a promotion an illegal lottery. However, the Ohio Attorney General effectively repealed an Attorney General Opinion that held store visits to be consideration. For many years, Ohio prohibited store visits. Upon review of the rule, however, the Attorney General held that so long as a consumer may have gone to the retail location for some reason other than to enter into the sweepstakes, consideration was not present. In Michigan, the Attorney General has informally indicated that the store visit rule would be invoked only if multiple visits were required.

Why It Matters

Montgomery Ward was cited by the State of California for what seemed an innocent promotion. The promotion was a garden-variety random draw sweepstakes designed to increase store traffic. The promotion was supported by broadcast and print media together with point-of-sale materials, all of which informed consumers that they could enter the drawing by depositing entry blanks at the store or by mailing in their entries.

Under an obscure California statute that was intended to apply to promotions designed to induce a consumer to visit a location and attend a sales presentation, detailed disclosures are required in advertising materials. The statute was designed to apply to time-share promotions and similar sweepstakes in which consumers are notified that they have won a prize, but must visit the time-share location or sit through a sales presentation in order to claim it. Despite the legislative history of the statute, the California Attorney General took the position that the statute applied to the Montgomery Ward promotion on the theory that nothing more was necessary to bring a promotion within the ambit of the statute than that persons were induced to visit a location. Since the Montgomery Ward promotion did not include all the disclosures required by the statute, the law was violated. Despite the fact that the position had never before been taken and that it rendered virtually every fast-food promotion subject to the disclosure requirements, the Attorney General stood firm. The case was reportedly settled for an amount in the six figures. Other promotions in California involving store visits have not been challenged since, and the Montgomery Ward case may likely be an isolated aberration.

3. Chance means that the winner is selected at random (e.g., a drawing, a preselected number, a rub-off card randomly distributed, etc.).

The distinction between a sweepstakes and a contest is that in a sweepstakes, the element of consideration must be eliminated because the winner is selected by chance. In a sweepstakes, the entrant cannot be required to pay or do anything substantial to enter. In a contest, the element of chance is eliminated and the winner is selected solely on the basis of skill. In a contest, it is generally permissible to require a purchase in order to enter, except in certain states. With respect to sweepstakes, the laws and interpretations among the different states as to what constitutes consideration are highly uncertain and frequently changed. With respect to contests, similar controversy exists as to what constitutes "skill."

All sweepstakes and contests should be accompanied by official rules that are clear and unambiguous. Disclosures required in advertising a sweepstakes or contest will vary depending on the nature of the promotion and the state in which it is running. Special care should be taken that advertising of the promotion is consistent with the rules.

It should also be noted that the states of Florida and New York require that certain sweepstakes (those with a combined prize package valued in excess of $5000) be registered and that a deposit be made or surety bond posted to cover the value of the prizes. Florida requires registration with the Department of Agriculture and Consumer Services, and New York requires registration with the Secretary of State. Rhode Island requires registration of sweepstakes in which local retail stores are involved and the total prize package exceeds $500. No bond is required. Arizona requires registration of certain types of skill contests. All games of chance that use a 900-number pay-per-call alternative are illegal in California.

Sales incentive programs are often a hybrid of the sweepstakes and contest. In a typical incentive program, a salesperson is given the opportunity to receive something of value, like a prize, if he or she reaches a certain sales goal. Presumably, a certain level of sales skill is required to succeed. In such programs, however, every salesperson who reaches the set goals must be awarded the prize. If the goal is set too low, the sponsor may be awarding more prizes than it wants to. On the other hand, if the goal is set too high, there may be no incentive for most of the sales force to participate. As a result, many companies opt to use the sweepstakes format in their incentive programs. Rather than setting specific goals, a salesperson gets an entry into a sweepstakes for each sale he or she makes or each time he or she performs some other task requested by the sponsor, e.g., sells a customer an extended warranty.

The controversy concerning sales incentives that use the sweepstakes format is whether they constitute lotteries, since one could argue that all three requisite elements are present. Certainly, prize and chance are present. It could be argued that consideration is also present on one of two grounds. First, the salesperson is expending effort to the advantage of the sponsor. Is that effort consideration? The conventional wisdom is that it is not, since the salesperson's efforts in making the sale are really nothing more than what he or she was hired to do in the first place. Thus, since the effort was a condition of employment, it cannot be deemed consideration in a sweepstakes. Second, the sponsor is receiving revenues directly related to the purpose of employment, i.e., the sale of the product or service it offers. In this instance, however, the consideration is paid by the consumer, not by the salesperson. Since the consumer is not receiving a chance for a prize, the promotion is not a lottery insofar as the consumer is concerned. Conversely, since the salesperson is not paying any consideration, it is not a lottery as to the salesperson either. While neither of these arguments has been tested in court, most experts in the field agree that either one should prevail. (See Form I.5.1.)

b. Frequently Asked Questions

There are certain questions commonly asked regarding sweepstakes, contests, and sales incentive programs. A compendium of frequently asked questions appears at the end of this chapter.

c. Enforcement and Special State Laws

Enforcement of state lottery laws is handled principally by the state Attorney General. In some states, like California, the laws can also be enforced by local law-enforcement officials. Enforcement activity has increased with the increased visibility and power of the National Association of Attorneys General (NAAG). Recent legislation in several states evidences a definite trend toward more restrictive requirements, particularly in the area of disclosure. Penalties include fines and imprisonment, but most disputes are resolved by consent decrees. On the civil side, there has been a noticeable increase in civil class actions.

The following is a discussion of some of the issues involved in particular techniques used in sweepstakes and contest promotions. It is not all-inclusive, but will give the reader an idea of some of the concerns that must be resolved in developing sweepstakes promotions. In addition, if any of the formats discussed is proposed for a campaign, expert legal counsel should be consulted because the laws in this area change constantly.

1. In-Pack Promotions

    The free method of entry must be disclosed on the outside of the package to avoid lottery considerations. Some states have special rules. Alabama and Hawaii have special rules applicable to bottle-cap and on-pack promotions, i.e., free bottle caps must be made available at retail outlets. In Minnesota and Wisconsin, participation must be made available without purchase by mail, toll-free telephone, or from the retailer; the outside of the package and all advertising must state the free method of entry and the termination date; upon the request of the retailer, the sponsor must provide game pieces sufficient to permit free participation by the retailer's customers; and, upon request of the state, the promoter must provide a list of major prizewinners. In Kansas, winning game pieces or tokens may only be redeemed for the sponsor's product or one product authorized by the sponsor from another manufacturer.

2. Retail Promotions

    Promotions run by or through retailers are subject to restriction in certain states. For example, Connecticut prohibits sweepstakes by retail grocers. The definition of "retail grocer," however, is very narrow. If any nonfood items are sold, the retailer is not a retail grocer. In Florida, rules must be posted in all retail outlets if the promotion is subject to bonding and registration. Moreover, all print advertising pieces for such promotions must contain the full (not abbreviated) official rules. In Michigan, a description of the number of prizes and geographic area must be disclosed in all retail outlets. In New York and Rhode Island, the minimum number and value of prizes, geographic area, and rules must be posted in all retail outlets.

3. Direct Mail Promotions

Both federal and state statutes regulate direct mail promotions. These statutes include many onerous disclosure requirements, and compliance can be very difficult. The federal statute requires that all sweepstakes delivered through direct mail include an address or 800 number for persons to be removed from the list for future sweepstakes mailings, and that full rules accompany all communications that include entry materials. Colorado and Texas also have comprehensive statutes. Colorado requires, among numerous provisions, that complete official rules accompany all sweepstakes announcements and that these rules include a section entitled "Consumer Disclosures," which must contain very specific provisions. The Texas law affects only those promotions communicated through direct mail with a single prize valued at $50,000 or more.

4. "Everybody Wins" Sweepstakes

Indiana law imposes stringent disclosure requirements. Many other states have so-called "special selection" statutes making it problematic to use the phrases "you have won" or "you have been selected to receive," or words to similar effect. In addition, many recent settlements between states and direct-mail marketers prohibit use of "everybody wins" promotions. In approaching this type of promotion, it is best to first consult legal counsel as the laws are ever changing.

5. "Giftstakes" Promotions

Promotions in which a consumer is notified that he or she has won a prize but must make a purchase or payment in order to claim or redeem the prize, require special scrutiny. Several states prohibit such promotions while many others impose special disclosure requirements or, among other mandates, set specific limitations on how much a consumer can be required to spend.

6. Other State Rules

Some states have special disclosure requirements that may affect what must be included in the rules and where the rules must be distributed. Maryland requires disclosure of the exact number and retail value of prizes, odds, whether all prizes will be awarded, where and when a winner's list can be obtained, and when winners will be determined. These disclosures are required on the first page of the solicitation. Massachusetts requires disclosure in all advertising, including broadcast advertising, of all prizes, verifiable retail value of all prizes, quantity of prizes, odds, the geographic area covered by the promotion, start and end dates for the promotion, and any conditions or limitation on receipt of the prize. It also requires additional disclosures on entry forms and disclosure at retail outlets of how to obtain a winners list. In Michigan, the rules must disclose at retail outlets or on entry forms a description and number of prizes, and geographic area covered. In New Mexico, promotions in which consideration is required must disclose prize descriptions, odds, amount of consideration required, geographic area, opening and closing dates, name and address of the sponsor, method of selection of winner, and start and end dates. Rhode Island requires rules to be posted in all retail outlets. Broadcast advertising should disclose where rules are available. Finally, Texas requires disclosure at retail outlet or on game card of the geographic area, and minimum number and value of prizes.

d. Official Rules

Official Rules serve as the contract between the sponsor and the consumer, and are easily the most critical element of the promotion. Great care must be taken to avoid ambiguities in the rules, as they may create administrative nightmares. (See Form I.5.4.) It is also critical that all statements made in advertising for the promotion be consistent with the official rules. Two checklists—one for sweepstakes and one for contests—appear at the end of this chapter.

e. Interactive Promotional Games

As promotion marketing vehicles, sweepstakes and skill contests are more popular than ever; marketers eagerly use them to attract consumers to their websites. But beware—these types of promotions have always been subject to intense legal and regulatory scrutiny, and now marketers must grapple with a host of new issues unique to online media. Chapter 6, Marketing on the Internet, includes a discussion of the legal issues unique to interactive promotional games.

2. Avoiding Promotional Pitfalls

a. Choice of Suppliers

It is sometimes amazing how cavalier an industry that spends so many millions of dollars can be when choosing outside suppliers. Time and time again we read of disasters in the marketplace because of poor suppliers, or promotions poorly designed by suppliers.

Why It Matters

1. Kraft Foods nearly gave out hundreds of cars on account of a printing error in a promotion tied in with a major auto manufacturer. In the Kraft promotion, consumers could win a car if they matched two halves of a game card, comparing the half they received at home with one on a store display. As a result of a printing error, virtually every consumer who compared his or her half with the store display had a winner. Kraft eventually settled a class-action suit and an Illinois Attorney General inquiry, which reportedly cost the company a small fortune.

2. Hunt-Wesson settled a case for millions on account of a promotion tied in with the Superbowl. In the Hunt-Wesson promotion, consumers scratched off hidden boxes on a game card to determine if they had a winning card. Every card was a possible winner, depending upon which boxes the consumer chose to scratch off. One consumer, however, was able to determine the pattern on the cards and submitted hundreds of winning cards totaling millions of dollars.

3. Anheuser-Busch faced its own printing disaster in a promotion for its flagship brand, Budweiser. As a result of a printing and production error on game pieces, hundreds of thousands of consumers received winning game cards. The rules of the game provided, however, that in the event of a print-

ing or production error, Anheuser-Busch would award the prizes originally offered in a random drawing from all verified winning-prize claims. Enforcing the rule as written would have alienated tens of thousands of presumably loyal Budweiser buyers who thought they were holding winning tickets. Instead of relying upon the literal wording of the rules, Anheuser-Busch decided to award the prizes originally offered to all verified winners (discernible based upon special markings on the game cards that were the actual winners), and to award an identical number of prizes in a separate, random drawing from among all consumers who made a claim for a prize regardless of whether their game card was verified as a winner. Anheuser-Busch took out full-page newspaper advertisements announcing the resolution.

4. In perhaps the most bizarre case, an announcer misread the winning number in a sweepstakes sponsored by the Pepsi-Cola Company in the Philippines, making countless consumers winners of a $100 shopping spree. When the error was announced, riots ensued and Pepsi headquarters in Manila was reportedly firebombed.

It is therefore vital to carefully evaluate suppliers, particularly in light of the development of new technology—both hardware and software. Some things to consider in evaluating a supplier include:

1. How long has the supplier been in business?

2. What does a LexisNexis or other database search reveal? Database information can be quite revealing and is useful in many areas; researching outside suppliers is one of them.

3. Has it had any regulatory problems?

4. What insurance does it carry? Printers can obtain insurance against losses resulting from printers' errors. But check the coverage. Some printers take shortcuts with high deductibles and limited coverage for damages sustained by the advertiser or its advertising agency; e.g., coverage only for costs of printing, and not claims of consumers.

5. Who else has it represented or performed services for? Contact its former and current clients for an opinion of its performance.

6. How tested is its technology?

While there is no absolute protection against a printing error, such errors are undoubtedly the source of the largest liability risks in the promotion business. The lesson is clear: be extremely careful in choosing a printer, and go only with those printers that have a proven track record.

b. Additional Preventive Measures

Here are some other steps to follow.

1. Do not assume that the same legal counsel that clears general advertising has the expertise to clear sweepstakes and contests. Verify their experience. Make them sign off in writing. While a formal legal opinion letter may be expensive, it is money well spent in the event a problem should arise.

2. Retain an experienced judging and promotion company to draft the rules of the promotion, judge the promotion, monitor its progress in the marketplace, and resolve any conflicts. By retaining an independent judging organization, the sponsor goes a long way in insulating itself from some of the problems that can be encountered from consumers and regulators.

3. Cross-check all elements of the promotion—the game pieces, advertising, and collateral must all be consistent with one another and with the official rules.

4. If a regulatory problem should arise, visit with the regulator personally, together with the fulfillment company and expert legal counsel. Most of the problems that arise can be resolved informally if quick action is taken. The sponsor that decides to "wait it out" only creates more problems for itself.

5. Respond to consumer inquiries as fast as possible, giving consumers a refund if they are dissatisfied with the promotion—no questions asked. The cost of the refund will be far less than the legal fees incurred in answering a regulatory inquiry.

3. Promotional Tie-ins and Co-Promotions

Tie-ins with another company to co-sponsor a promotion are a growing marketing technique. The reasons are obvious. It costs less, and the brand identification by consumers increases participation in a promotion. Outlined below are some special considerations to bear in mind with respect to a co-promotion. (See Forms I.5.5 and I.5.6.)

a. Identify the Participants and their Respective Roles and Goals

A co-promotion or co-branding opportunity can serve a variety of goals. Perhaps its goal is nothing more than to raise brand or product awareness. More likely, its goal is to introduce a new product, test a new campaign, target very specific demographic markets, develop a customer list, or even to create a whole new ancillary market for a product.

b. Ownership of Jointly Produced Materials

Who owns the materials jointly produced? Generally, ownership in each element contributed by either of the partners is retained by the partner contributing the element. But what about material original to the promotion, e.g., music, special artwork, or even a premium item offered in the promotion? Care should be taken in defining ownership of such materials.

c. Clearance of Creative Material

Perhaps the single greatest source of failure in a co-promotion is deviating from the agreed-upon standards or, even worse, contradicting the offer intended to be made to the consumer. Is a free ticket on an airline subject to restrictions? Is the discount on a future purchase of the partner's product subject to limitations? Creative material should be cleared by all participants in the promotion or by a qualified coordinator to be certain that all conditions are properly disclosed in the materials given to consumers. While allowing time for the clearance process can certainly slow down a promotion, the danger of failing to coordinate this effort can be exorbitant.

d. Exclusivity

It is unlikely that a partner would be pleased to see its co-partner running the same promotion with a competitor during a promotion or, at times, even after a promotion ends. The best protection is to forbid a similar promotion for a period of time, such as six months, or to require a right of first refusal to run the promotion again as partners before either party can go to a competitor.

e. Fulfillment Obligations

Fulfillment obligations are not to be taken lightly. The Federal Trade Commission and the U.S. Postal Service have caused some promoters to be sent to jail (through intervention e.g., by the U.S. Attorney) for failing to fulfill consumer offers in accordance with the offer made, or otherwise violating federal law. Make sure the fulfillment obligations are clearly set forth in the contract and that any fulfillment company that may be contracted to provide service is qualified and capable of satisfying the anticipated demand.

f. Adding Additional Participants

All too often, adding additional participants to an offer, particularly a multiple-coupon offer, is left to the discretion of one party. That's fine for the party that has the discretion. Strong consideration, however, should be given to a requirement that additional participants be approved by all present participants. For example, one can only wonder how The Coca-Cola Company might react if Taco Bell, owned by PepsiCo, Inc., suddenly became a co-participant in a multi-advertiser promotion.

g. Customer Lists

Databases are an integral part of the new wave of direct marketing. As a result, one of the most valuable products of a co-promotion can be the customer list that it generates. This brings up important considerations. Who owns the customer list generated by the co-promotion? Is it owned jointly? If so, are there any limits on use of the list? Is there a limit on time? Is there a limit on how the user can tie itself with another brand? The value of the customer list should not be underestimated, and its exploitation should be contractually covered in any co-promotion that may generate one.

Chapter Five Forms

Form I.5.1 Sweepstakes and Contests FAQ

Sweepstakes

Q. Can the sponsor of a sweepstakes extend the end date of a promotion?

A. Generally, no. Sweepstakes rules are the contract that a sponsor offers to the consumer. Just as the consumer is bound to comply with the rules, so is the sponsor. Above all else, the sponsor must be sure not to do anything that lessens the odds of winning for those consumers who entered the promotion by the deadline date in the rules. Extending the deadline after a promotion has begun allows more people to enter and thereby lowers the odds of winning from what they would have been had the promotion ended as originally provided. Consumers who entered before the original deadline date are thus harmed by lesser odds. While the promotion's rules could theoretically allow for an extension, such a provision in the promotion's rules is risky and could run afoul of some state laws requiring an end date.

Q. Can a sponsor require that a consumer visit a store in order to enter?

A. Generally, yes. Most states allow a requirement that a consumer must visit a retail store to enter a promotion. Though Ohio and Michigan have both challenged promotions that required a store visit as a condition of participation, more than 10 years have passed since the last case. Generally, conventional thinking concludes that neither state will challenge a promotion so long as it required only one store visit. If multiple store visits are required in Michigan, or if the consumer must interact with a salesperson, or if retail outlets are few and the consumer must travel considerable distances to enter, the smartest thing to do is allow a mail-in entry as well.

Q. Can a sponsor require an entrant to be present at a drawing in order to win a prize?

A. In most states, yes. There are some states, however, that prohibit requiring an entrant to be present to win.

Q. With so many state statutes, how can a sponsor effectively structure a national promotion?

A. In truth, it's not that difficult if one has experience. After all, every major package goods company conducts them, and rarely runs into problems. The smart sponsor, however, does not try to do it alone. An experienced sweepstakes fulfillment house is a must, as is careful legal review of the rules, disclaimers, and advertising. A good printer is also an important partner. The laws change constantly and their interpretations vary state to state (and sometimes even county to county or city to city), so it's important to retain professionals experienced in the field. While it will add to the cost of a promotion, foregoing preventive measures at the outset can result in devastating cost for later mistakes.

Q. Can a promotion require purchase of another product of the sponsor to win a prize, e.g., a free soda with the purchase of a hamburger?

A. This type of prize is suspect and should not be referred to as a prize but considered an offer, even if it is a lower-level prize. In the 1970s, in response to zealous time-share promoters, a number of states passed legislation making it illegal to require any purchase to receive a prize or gift. In recent years, other states have passed similar statutes, generally targeted at telemarketing. The language in most of these statutes, however, is broad and technically could cover any sweepstakes promotion. While states have not generally targeted traditional sweepstakes under these various statutes, any sponsor that includes a purchase requirement is well advised to consult legal counsel to assess the risk on a case-by-case basis. As recently as 2003, in a case that was settled for a substantial sum, California cited a retailer that advertised a discount as a prize.

Q. If a winner doesn't want the prize, can a sponsor give it to the winner's relative, e.g., the parent or child, or even to a friend?

A. The conservative answer is that the prize can be given to a relative or other person only if the rules specifically allow it. If the rules are silent and the prize is given to someone other than the winner originally selected, those consumers who entered and lost could argue that the sponsor awarded the prize to an ineligible consumer who never entered the promotion in the first place. If that is the case, a sponsor could be forced to draw another winner and award the prize in accordance with the rules, leaving the sponsor with a choice between awarding two prizes or facing negative public relations when it refuses to give the prize to a relative or friend of the first drawn winner.

Q. Is a cash alternative for a prize required?

A. No. While it is often done for high-end prizes, it is not legally required. Nor does a cash alternative have to be equal to the retail value of a prize.

Q. When is a 1099 tax form required, and what happens if the winner challenges the value reported on the 1099?

A. The value of a prize is income to the winner and must be reported as such on the winner's income tax return. In order to help the IRS keep track of higher-value prizes, a sponsor is required to file with the IRS and issue a 1099 tax form to a winner of any prize worth $600 or more. The reported value of the prize must be its retail value on the date it was awarded to the consumer. For prizes that are paid out to the winner over time, there are special IRS rules on reporting the income for 1099 purposes.

Q. Do unclaimed prizes have to be awarded in a second-chance drawing?

A. Generally, no. Though some state statutes do require that all prizes offered be awarded, the FTC and other regulators have held that unclaimed prizes need not be awarded, provided the official rules of the sweepstakes specifically state that they will not be awarded. Many sponsors, however, do award unclaimed major prizes to a charity or to consumers in a second-chance drawing to avoid adverse publicity that they never awarded what they offered.

Q. Can a sponsor cancel a promotion that is not drawing the store traffic or sales a sponsor projected?

A. Generally, no. Once the offer is made, the sponsor must complete the offer in accordance with the official rules. While the rules could provide for the possibility of cancellation if certain events fail to occur, keying such cancellations to sales or store traffic is ill advised as it could run afoul of some state laws prohibiting the funding of a promotion's prizes from sales revenues.

Q. Are affidavits of eligibility required from winners?

A. Affidavits of eligibility are not legally required. They are advisable, however, for any major prizes. By requiring them, a sponsor shields itself from criticism if it mistakenly awards a prize to an entrant who was ineligible.

Contests

Q. Can a sponsor require a purchase to enter a contest?

A. Generally, yes. Several states, however, have laws that may prohibit certain entry fees, out-of-pocket expenses, or purchase requirements, or that require onerous disclosures when requiring a purchase to participate. A sponsor should consult with counsel if any of those states is involved in a contest. Sponsors should also take care that the skill required in the promotion is a truly verifiable skill.

Q. Can the judges in a contest be employees of the sponsor?

A. Yes. Except in rare instances, there is no legal requirement that judges must be totally independent, although it is generally a better policy. By using independent judges, a sponsor shields itself from criticism that there were irregularities in the judging process because of improper motives of the sponsor. Even unfounded allegations can cause investigations that can destroy an otherwise successful promotion.

Q. If there is a tie, can the winner of a contest be determined by a random drawing from among those entrants who tied?

A. If there was any consideration incurred by the entrants, most states would regard it as illegal to resolve ties by a random drawing. If entry into the contest is free and the effort by the entrant minimal in entering, a random tiebreaker may be proper, but it is always risky. A legitimate contest should choose winners based upon objective standards, not chance.

Q. Does a list of the criteria that will be used to determine the winner in a contest promotion need to be included in the rules?

A. Generally, yes. It is always better to list them so that the entrant has an idea of what criteria will be used and that allegations that winners were chosen on an arbitrary, chance basis can be prevented. The basic integrity of a contest is its objectivity in choosing winners. Stated criteria insure that objectivity is maintained.

Q. Do contests have to be registered and bonded like sweepstakes?

A. Certain contests need to be registered in Arizona. They do not need to be bonded or registered in New York, Florida, or Rhode Island as do sweepstakes.

Q. Who owns the material submitted by an entrant in a contest?

A. Unless the rules specify that the material is owned by the sponsor, it is not clear if ownership passes to the sponsor upon entry by a consumer. Even if the rules state that ownership transfers, there are some types of works, particularly essays or photography, whose ownership cannot be transferred unless the creator, i.e., the entrant, signs the entry form transferring ownership. Therefore, if a sponsor desires to use entries for marketing or advertising purposes, it is well advised to require entrants to sign written transfers with entry.

Q. Must a sponsor take into account the relative ability of different consumers to win in planning a contest, e.g., age brackets?

A. While there is no rule that entrants must all have equal ability in a contest, it is generally advisable to consider the relative abilities of entrants in designing a contest. For example, if a sponsor conducts an essay contest, it makes little sense to judge entries of 10-year-olds with those of college students. Therefore, the astute sponsor balances the ability to win by restricting eligibility, e.g., 18 years of age or older to compete, or by specifying tiers of entry ages, e.g., 10–12 years of age, 13–17 years of age, 18–21 years of age, etc.

Sales Incentive and Business-to-Business Promotions

Q. Can a sponsor exclude employees of competitors in a business-to-business sweepstakes or contest promotion?

A. Yes. Official rules can exclude employees of competitors.

Q. Does a sponsor have to tell an employer that it is offering the employer's employees an incentive for sales of the sponsor's products?

A. Yes. It is illegal to give incentives, including prizes in contests or sweepstakes, to employees of third parties who sell a sponsor's product unless the employer of the entrant is aware of the incentive.

Q. Does a trade sweepstakes have to be bonded and registered in Florida and New York?

A. No. While the literal wording of the statutes could be read to apply to trade sweepstakes, neither state requires the registration of trade programs.

Q. How does a sponsor handle a policy that prohibits employees of its customers from accepting prizes?

A. The best way to handle this problem is to provide in the rules of the promotion that if such a policy exists, the entrant is disqualified and another winner will be selected.

Q. Can a sponsor give a salesperson a chance in a sweepstakes for each sale of the sponsor's product made by the salesperson?

A. This is a controversial issue. In the automotive industry, so-called "pull boards" are used, where for each car a salesperson sells he or she gets to pull a token from a play board to see if he or she has won a prize. If the dealer sells only one make of car, a pull board may be defensible, arguing that the effort of the salesperson is nothing other than what is required of the employee. If the dealership sells more than one brand, however, the incentive and effort given to one of the car brands could be seen as special consideration, making the promotion a lottery. While there has been little, if any, enforcement in this area, it is unclear if such incentives are legal or illegal.

Form I.5.2 Checklist for Preparing Official Rules for Sweepstakes

- ☐ 1. Entry instructions
- ☐ 2. Limit on entries
- ☐ 3. Specify per person, per household, per e-mail address
- ☐ 4. Odds of winning
- ☐ 5. Seeded games, probability games, and preselected numbers games must give numerical odds
- ☐ 6. Calculate cumulative odds of receiving all game pieces in "Collect and Win" games
- ☐ 7. Prohibition on facsimile entries (if desired)
- ☐ 8. Prize description, number available, and approximate retail value
- ☐ 9. Eligibility
  - ☐ a. Age
  - ☐ b. Residence
  - ☐ c. Occupation
  - ☐ d. Exclusion of sponsor-related parties
  - ☐ e. Employees
  - ☐ f. Agents
  - ☐ g. Suppliers
  - ☐ h. Family members (immediate or all)
  - ☐ i. Members of household
- ☐ 10. Duration
  - ☐ a. Commencement date
  - ☐ b. Termination date
  - ☐ c. Winner selection date
- ☐ 11. Limitation on sponsor's liability
- ☐ 12. Disclaimer of liability for lost, late, misdirected mail
- ☐ 13. Voiding clause
- ☐ 14. Taxes on prizes
- ☐ 15. Affidavit of eligibility
- ☐ 16. Winners list
- ☐ 17. Reservation of publicity rights
- ☐ 18. Entries property of sponsor
- ☐ 19. Judges' decisions final
- ☐ 20. Minors clause

☐ 21. Releases (publicity, liability, travel)

☐ 22. Sponsor name and address

☐ 23. For Online Games, add the following Internet liability limitations:

    ☐ a. Fraud clause (virus or other system malfunction)
    ☐ b. Faulty transmission
    ☐ c. Entry deemed made by holder of e-mail account
    ☐ d. Time zones
    ☐ e. Right to amend, modify, or terminate promotion
    ☐ f. Link to sponsor's privacy policy

☐ 24. For Instant Win/In-Pack Games, add the following:

    ☐ a. Duration: For requests for free game pieces
    ☐ b. All properly claimed prizes will be awarded
    ☐ c. "Kraft" clause: Printing, typographical, and other errors.

Form I.5.3 Checklist for Preparing Official Rules for Contests

In addition to everything listed in Form I.5.2, add the following:

☐ 1. Detailed description of judging criteria and qualification of judges

☐ 2. Non-return of entries

☐ 3. Notification that entries become property of promoter

☐ 4. Limitation of number of times one may enter

☐ 5. Warranty as to originality or ownership of entry

Form I.5.4. Sweepstakes and Contest Fulfillment Contract (Long Form)

<Fulfillment Company Letterhead>

<Date>

<Sponsor Name>

<Street Address>

<City, State, Zip>

<Salutation>:

This agreement sets forth the final and complete understanding of the parties. It is understood and agreed that there are no other representations with respect to this agreement and this agreement supersedes all prior discussions, agreements, and undertakings relating to the subject matter hereof. It is further agreed that the rights, interests, understandings, agreements, and obligations of the respective parties pertaining to the subject matter of this agreement may not be amended, modified, or supplemented in any respect except by a subsequent written instrument evidencing the express written consent of each of the parties, duly executed by the parties. Any terms inconsistent with or additional to the terms set forth in this agreement, which may be included with a purchase order, acknowledgment, invoice, and so forth of either party, shall not be binding on the other party hereto unless previously communicated in writing and approved by both parties.

SERVICE AND FEES

RANDOM DRAW SWEEPSTAKES

ADMINISTRATIVE SERVICES AND FEES

The administrative services we will provide to you in connection with random draw sweepstakes promotions are as follows:

1. Render our advice and counsel on all elements of the sweepstakes that could contribute to maximum effectiveness. This includes our advice on sweepstakes duration, preparation of entry forms, and rules and related materials.

2. A helpful advisory service to provide you and your counsel with our practical knowledge of postal, federal, state, and local laws and regulations which could significantly affect the sweepstakes.

3. Review all copy pertinent to the sweepstakes prior to production of same.

4. Submit our draft of rules that will govern the sweepstakes.

5. Assign suitable post office boxes for use during the campaign.

6. Count all entries received by accurate weight measurements.

7. Submit bimonthly written reports in a form that has been approved by you on the volume of entries received, etc.

8. Conduct random drawings in accordance with our standardized procedures with our personnel in the presence of your representative for all major prize drawings to award all prizes from among all eligible entries received in accordance with the printed rules governing the sweepstakes.

9. Arrange for clearance of major prizewinner(s) before formal announcement. Clearance will be accomplished via mail correspondence only, and receipt of the potential winner's required documentation including an Affidavit of Eligibility and/or Release of Liability within specific time parameters.

10. Submit a certified list of winners to you after all clearances have been concluded.

11. The official major winners list will include all prizewinners' names and full addresses. We will provide separately to you all major prizewinner's social security numbers, for any tax liabilities.

12. Guarantee that names of contestants and other pertinent information relating to your program are secure against unauthorized use. We will not utilize the names in any manner other than as you direct or authorize.

13. We further guarantee the absolute non-collusion of our employees with your agents, parents, affiliates, and employees. We indemnify and hold harmless you and your agents, parents, affiliates, subsidiaries, and employees from any and all loss, cost, or expense which they might incur by reason of any claim or action arising out of our performance in executing our services on your behalf. Nothing herein contained, however, shall be deemed to constitute any representation or indemnity with respect to the legality of the promotions under federal, state, or local lottery or related statutes, including the Federal Trade Commission Act, except where such legality may depend upon the proper performance of the duties assumed by us hereunder including, but not limited to, the objectivity of the selection of winners.

We indemnify and hold harmless you and your agents, parents, affiliates, subsidiaries, and employees against any claims or actions relating to any name, title, or slogan created and owned by us that is used by you with our authorization. In the event that a particular name, title, or slogan affixed to the sweepstakes is not owned or created by us, any and all claims or actions relating to the use of the name, title, or slogan will be your responsibility and you will indemnify and hold us harmless with respect to the cost of the defense of any such claim or action, including reasonable attorneys' fees. In any such event, the indemnified party will promptly inform the indemnitor of any claim or action which has been received or commenced. The indemnitor will promptly assume the defense thereof on behalf of the indemnified parties. In the event any indemnified party wishes to participate in the defense of any such claim or action through its own counsel, it may do so at its own expense.

Our fee for the administrative services outlined above is $_____.

Additional costs and fees that may be expected in connection with sweepstakes promotions are as follows:

1. Filing Surety Bonds, if necessary, and filing the details of the promotion with the Secretaries of

State of Florida, New York, and Rhode Island—$ _____ per state plus out-of-pocket filing fees.

2. Providing post office boxes for receipt of entries and receipt of winners list requests, at our cost per box per six-month period or part thereof.

3. If we are charged with the responsibility for procuring merchandise prizes, the cost of such prize procurement will be true delivered cost as documented by supplier's actual invoice(s) to us plus _____%.

4. For sweepstakes promotions in which more than _____ prizes are offered, our fee for the selection of additional prizewinners will be $_____ per name (or $_____ per name if duplication elimination is not mandatory).

5. A personal investigation of major prizewinner(s), if requested by you, can be accomplished at true cost plus _____ %; alternatively, affidavit clearances are priced at $_____ each. Affidavit clearances will be obtained via mail only, and consist of a notarized document verifying the potential winner's name, address, social security number, and that they have complied with all the rules and regulations of the specific program.

6. Notifying major prizewinners in writing of the prize won. If winners may select among multiple prizes, ascertain if the selected prize is available. This service is billable relative to the number of notifications required but would not exceed the sliding scale provided below, plus materials (billable at true cost plus _____ %) and postage (as incurred). The number of prizes and costs are:

    1–5 major prizes—$ _____ each;
    6–10 prizes— $ _____ each;
    11–25 prizes— $ _____ each;
    26–50 prizes— $ _____ each;
    51–100 prizes— $ _____ each;
    101+ prizes— $ _____ each.

    Below a certain prize value level (to be determined by you and us), a separate notification letter is not warranted, but a congratulatory note may be included with the prize award. The cost of this type of notification with prize award is $ _____ per thousand ("M").

7. Printing and fulfilling winners list requests. Printing is chargeable at true cost plus _____%; fulfillment is chargeable at $ _____/M.

8. Fulfillment of additional entry forms or game pieces, if applicable, is billable at $ _____/M.

9. Prize fulfillment, as required, including receiving and handling of prizes, would be billable at a predetermined cost per thousand after agreement upon prize parameters including who is procuring the actual prizes, and their sizes and quantities.

10. Prize storage after _____ days and insurance for prizes, if we are not procuring prizes, would be billable at $ _____ /sq. ft./month and $ _____/$100 value/month, respectively.

11. Miscellaneous services requested in writing by you, and not identified above as part of the administrative services—$ _____ per hour, or at a cost per response agreed upon by you and us, dependent upon the service requested.

12. Preparation and issuance of 1099 forms to all prizewinners receiving awards of $600 or more will be charged at $ _____ each. If this service is not requested by you, we will prepare all information necessary for you to issue at the close of each promotion program.

13. Any amounts paid by you hereunder shall be deemed to include all applicable taxes, duties, and charges. We are responsible for all tax filings required by any authority with regard to a sweepstakes, except filing 1099s for the winners.

CONTESTS

ADMINISTRATIVE SERVICES AND FEES

The administrative services which we provide to you in connection with contests of skill are as follows:

1. Render our advice and counsel on all elements of the contest that could contribute to maximum effectiveness. This includes, without limitation, our advice on contest duration, preparation of entry forms, rules, and related material.

2. A helpful advisory service to provide you and your counsel with our practical knowledge of postal, state, and local laws and regulations which could significantly affect the contest.

3. Review all copy pertinent to the contest prior to production of same.

4. Submit our draft of rules that will govern the contest.

5. Assign suitable post office boxes for use during the contest.

6. Receive, open, and extract all entries.

7. Submit formal bimonthly written reports in a form that has been approved by you on the volume of entries received, including a hand-counted tally of all entries opened and extracted.

8. Judge and determine winners in accordance with the contest rules. If outside "expert" judges are to be obtained, you reserve the right to approve all third-party judges.

9. Arrange for clearance of major prizewinner(s) before formal announcement. Clearance will be accomplished via mail correspondence only, and receipt of the potential winner's required documentation including an Affidavit of Eligibility and/or Release of Liability within specific time parameters.

10. Submit a certified list of winners to you after all clearances have been concluded.

11. The official major winners list will include all prizewinners' names and full addresses. We will provide separately to you all major prizewinners' social security numbers, for any tax liabilities.

12. Guarantee that names of contestants and other pertinent information relating to your program are secure against unauthorized use. We will not utilize the names in any manner other than as you direct or authorize. Our fee for the administrative services outlined above is $ _____ ... for consumer programs and $ _____ for trade programs per contest, plus judging. The judging fees will vary depending upon the time and complexity involved in the actual judging process, but would normally fall between $ _____ and $ _____ per thousand. This variable cost would be agreed upon in advance and in writing, but deals with parameters including, but not limited to, expertise of judges, time involved in preliminary screening of entries, and required facilities, if necessary.

13. We further guarantee the absolute non-collusion of our employees with your agents, parents, affiliates, and employees. We indemnify and hold harmless you and your agents, parents, affiliates, subsidiaries, and employees from any and all loss, cost, or expense which they might incur by reason of any claim or action arising out of our performance in executing our services on your behalf. Nothing herein contained, however, shall be deemed to constitute any representation or indemnity with respect to the legality of the promotions under federal, state, or local lottery or related statutes, including the Federal Trade Commission Act, except where such legality may depend upon the proper performance of the duties assumed by us hereunder including, but not limited to, the objectivity of the selection of winners.

We indemnify and hold harmless you and your agents, parents, affiliates, subsidiaries, and employees against any claims or actions relating to any name, title, or slogan created and owned by us that is used by you with our authorization. In the event that a particular name, title, or slogan affixed to the sweepstakes is not owned or created by us, any and all claims or actions relating to the use of the name, title, or slogan will be your responsibility and you will indemnify and hold us harmless with respect to the cost of the defense of any such claim or action, including reasonable attorneys' fees. In any such event, the indemnified party will promptly inform the indemnitor of any claim or action which has been received or commenced. The indemnitor will promptly assume the defense thereof on behalf of the indemnified parties. In the event any indemnified party wishes to participate in the defense of any such claim or action through its own counsel, it may do so at its own expense.

Additional costs and fees which may be expected in connection with contest promotions are as follows:

1. Filings with Arizona—$ _____ plus out-of-pocket filing fees.

2. Providing post office boxes for receipt of entries and receipt of winners list requests—at our cost per box per six-month period or part thereof.

3. If we are charged with the responsibility for procuring merchandise prizes, the cost of such prize procurement will be true delivered cost as documented by supplier's actual invoice(s) to us plus _____ %.

4. For sweepstakes promotions in which more than _____ prizes are offered, our fee for the selection of additional prizewinners will be $_____per name (or $ _____ per name if duplication elimination is not mandatory).

5. A personal investigation of major prizewinner(s), if requested by you, can be accomplished at true cost plus _____ %; alternatively, affidavit clearances are priced at $ _____ each. Affidavit clearances will be obtained via mail only and consist of a notarized document verifying the potential winner's name, address, social security number, and that they have complied with all the rules and regulations of the specific program.

6. Notifying major prizewinners in writing of the prize won. If winners may select among multiple prizes, ascertain if the selected prize is available. This service is billable relative to the number of notifications required but would not exceed the sliding scale provided below, plus materials (billable at true cost plus _____%) and postage (as incurred). The number of prizes and costs are:

    1–5 major prizes—$_____ each;
    6–10 prizes— $_____ each;

11–25 prizes— $ _____ each;
26–50 prizes— $ _____ each;
51–100 prizes— $ _____ each;
101+ prizes— $ _____ each.

Below a certain prize value level (to be determined by you and us), a separate notification letter is not warranted, but a congratulatory note may be included with the prize award. The cost of this type of notification with prize award is $ _____ /M.

7. Printing and fulfilling winners list requests. Printing is chargeable at true cost plus _____%; fulfillment is chargeable at $ _____ /M.

8. Fulfillment of additional entry forms or game pieces, if applicable, is billable at $ _____ /M.

9. Prize fulfillment, as required, including receiving and handling of prizes, would be billable at a predetermined cost per thousand after agreement upon prize parameters including who is procuring the actual prizes, and their sizes and quantities.

10. Prize storage after _____ days and insurance for prizes, if we are not procuring prizes, would be billable at $ _____ /sq. ft./month and $ _____ /$100 value/month, respectively.

11. Miscellaneous services requested in writing by you, and not identified above as part of the administrative services—$ _____ per hour, or at a cost per response agreed upon by you and us, dependent upon the service requested.

12. Preparation and issuance of 1099 forms to all prizewinners receiving awards of $600 or more will be charged at $ _____ each. If this service is not requested by you, we will prepare all information necessary for you to issue at the close of each promotion program.

13. Any amounts paid by you hereunder shall be deemed to include all applicable taxes, duties, and charges. We are responsible for all tax filings required by any authority with regard to a sweepstakes, except filing 1099s for the winners.

PRESELECTED WINNER SWEEPSTAKES (MATCHING TYPE)

ADMINISTRATIVE SERVICES AND FEES

Preselected Winner Sweepstakes is a technique utilized in direct-mail sweepstakes programs in which mailings are made to a preselected sample population. Based on a computer selected "random selection" process, a winner has already been selected, but it is the responsibility of the consumer to mail back or activate their entry.

The administrative services which we provide to you in connection with preselected winner sweepstakes (matching type) are as follows:

1. Render our advice and counsel on all elements of the sweepstakes that could contribute to maximum effectiveness. This includes our advice on sweepstakes duration, preparation of entry forms, rules, and related materials.

2. A helpful advisory service to provide you and your counsel with our practical knowledge of postal, federal, state, and local laws and regulations which could significantly affect the sweepstakes.

3. Review all copy pertinent to the sweepstakes prior to production of same.

4. Submit our draft of rules that will govern the sweepstakes.

5. Assign suitable post office boxes for use during the campaign.

6. Count all entries received by accurate weight measurements.

7. Submit bimonthly written reports in a form that has been approved by you on the volume of entries received, etc.

8. Conduct random drawings in accordance with our standardized procedures with our personnel in the presence of your representative for all major prize drawings to award all prizes from among all eligible entries received in accordance with the printed rules governing the sweepstakes.

9. Arrange for clearance of major prizewinner(s) before formal announcement. Clearance will be accomplished via mail correspondence only and receipt of the potential winner's required documentation including an Affidavit of Eligibility and/or Release of Liability within specific time parameters.

10. Submit a certified list of winners to you after all clearances have been concluded.

11. The official major winners list will include all prizewinners' names and full addresses. We will provide separately to you all major prizewinners' social security numbers, for any tax liabilities.

12. Guarantee that names of contestants and other pertinent information relating to your program are secure against unauthorized use. We will not utilize the names in any manner other than as you direct or authorize.

13. We further guarantee the absolute non-collusion of our employees with your agents, parents, affiliates, and employees. We indemnify and hold harmless you and your agents, parents, affiliates, subsidiaries, and employees from any and all loss, cost, or expense which they might incur by reason of any claim or action arising out of our performance in executing our services on your behalf. Nothing herein contained, however, shall be deemed to constitute any representation or indemnity with respect to the legality of the promotions under federal, state, or local lottery or related statutes, including the Federal Trade Commission Act, except where such legality may depend upon the proper performance of the duties assumed by us hereunder including, but not limited to, the objectivity of the selection of winners.

Our fee for the administrative services outlined above is $ _____.

Additional costs and fees which may be expected in connection with "matching type" preselected winner sweepstakes promotions and instant win promotions using on-shelf seeding are as follows:

1. Filing Surety Bonds, if necessary, and filing the details of the promotion with the Secretaries of State of Florida, New York, and Rhode Island—$ _____ per state plus out-of-pocket filing fees.

2. Seeding. Our fee for personally inserting each major prizewinning symbol at random throughout the full print or circulation universe will be $ _____ per day on premise of seeding location plus out-of-pocket expenses (coach airfare, travel, hotel, etc.).

3. Fulfillment of additional entry forms or game pieces, if applicable is billable at $ _____ /M.

4. Receiving and verifying instant winner prize claims is chargeable at $ _____ /M.

5. Providing post office boxes for receipt of entries and receipt of winners list requests—at our cost per box per six-month period or part thereof.

6. If we are charged with the responsibility for procuring merchandise prizes, the cost of such prize procurement will be true delivered cost as documented by supplier's actual invoice(s) to us plus _____ %.

7. For sweepstakes promotions in which more than _____ prizes are offered, our fee for the selection of additional prizewinners will be $ _____ per name (or $ _____ per name if duplication elimination is not mandatory).

8. A personal investigation of major prizewinner(s), if requested by you, can be accomplished at true cost plus _____ %; alternatively, affidavit clearances are priced at $ _____... each. Affidavit clearances will be obtained via mail only and consist of a notarized document verifying the potential winner's name, address, social security number, and that they have complied with all the rules and regulations of the specific program.

9. Notifying major prizewinners in writing of the prize won. If winners may select among multiple prizes, ascertain if the selected prize is available. This service is billable relative to the number of notifications required but would not exceed the sliding scale provided below, plus materials (billable at true cost plus _____ %) and postage (as incurred). The number of prizes and costs are:

    1–5 major prizes—$ _____ each;
    6–10 prizes— $ _____ each;
    11–25 prizes— $ _____ each;
    26–50 prizes— $ _____ each;
    51–100 prizes— $ _____ each;
    101+ prizes— $ _____ each.

    Below a certain prize value level (to be determined by you and us), a separate notification letter is not warranted, but a congratulatory note may be included with the prize award. The cost of this type of notification with prize award is $ _____ /M.

10. Printing and fulfilling winners list requests. Printing is chargeable at true cost plus _____%; fulfillment is chargeable at $ _____ /M.

11. Fulfillment of additional entry forms or game pieces, if applicable, is billable at $ _____ /M.

12. Prize fulfillment, as required, including receiving and handling of prizes, would be billable at a predetermined cost per thousand after agreement upon prize parameters including who is procuring the actual prizes, and their sizes and quantities.

13. Prize storage after _____ days and insurance for prizes, if we are not procuring prizes, would be billable at $ _____ /sq. ft./month and $ _____ /$100 value/month, respectively.

14. Miscellaneous services requested in writing by you, and not identified above as part of the administrative services—$ _____ per hour, or at a cost per response agreed upon by you and us, dependent upon the service requested.

15. Preparation and issuance of 1099 forms to all prizewinners receiving awards of $600 or more will be charged at $ _____ each. If this service is not requested by you, we will prepare all information necessary for you to issue at the close of each promotion program.

16. Any amounts paid by you hereunder shall be deemed to include all applicable taxes, duties, and charges. We are responsible for all tax filings required by any authority with regard to a sweepstakes, except filing 1099s for the winners.

INVOLVEMENT GAMES

ADMINISTRATIVE SERVICES AND FEES

The administrative services which we are prepared to provide to you in connection with involvement games are as follows:

1. Produce and secretly identify with anti-counterfeiting devices all winning versions of the sweepstakes symbol in the presence of your representative. This procedure is undertaken by us to safeguard the integrity of the official prizewinning entries and to invalidate any counterfeit or altered claims.

2. Personally "seed" winning versions of all major prize symbols at magazine or newspaper printing plants or at packaging plants, in compliance with our official procedures for seeding. Your representative may be on site to witness or verify seeding of all major prizes. In the case of minor prize symbols, arrange with the management of the appropriate media for management "seeding" under the terms of the prize distribution program. Affidavits for seeding procedures will be executed in writing and will be in a form approved by you.

3. Receive and verify prize claims. The following will confirm the procedures to be employed with regard to receiving and verifying prize claims:

Registered or Certified Claims:

a. All claims sent certified or registered mail are signed for at the post office by our employee indicating date received.

b. Claims sent to us are given to our production supervisor.

c. All envelopes are stamped with a sequential number and are logged in a journal to indicate: the sequential number, registered or certified number, whether a return receipt was required, name and address of claimant, and the date received. This procedure is accomplished by supervisory personnel.

d. The envelope (containing sequential number) and contents of the envelope are photocopied.

e. Any empty envelopes received are immediately brought to the Vice President of Production who enters on the envelope the words "no contents" and signs the envelope, as does the supervisor. The envelope containing the sequential number, the notation that nothing was included, and both signatures is photocopied. The claim is logged in the register.

f. A list is typed or computer list generated of all verified claims received. Prize fulfillment is accomplished based on the list indicating claimant's name and address and prize claimed.

g. All originals and photocopies are stored in two separate secure locations. Should any claim be questioned, the log is utilized to determine the date the original claim was received and the photocopy of the claim can be retrieved immediately. Non-winning entries will be retained for at least 60 days after all prizes have been awarded. A letter will then be sent to you requesting permission to destroy, or designating shipping instructions. Winning entries will be retained for seven years.

h. Photocopied claims are stored by sequential number; original claims are stored by date.

Non-Registered or Non-Certified Claims:

a. All non-registered or "non-certified" claims are picked up at the post office by our personnel and transferred to our production facility.

b. All responses are opened, extracted, and verified as to their contents.

c. If a major prize claim is included with these responses, the claim and the envelope is brought to the supervisor and the response is handled as it would be if it were sent registered or certified.

4. Determine winners in accordance with the promotion rules.

Our fee for the administrative services outlined above is $ _____ per promotion.

Additional costs and fees which may be expected in connection with "instant winner games" preselected winner sweepstakes promotions are as follows:

1. If requested, creative presentation of layouts, and production of final art for game pieces including preparation of the mechanical, overlays, and photostats are chargeable at true cost plus _____ %.

2. If requested, game piece production and supervision is chargeable at true cost plus _____ %.

3. Seeding. Our fee for personally inserting each major prizewinning symbol at random throughout the full print circulation would be billable for out-of-pocket expenses (coach airfare, travel, hotel, etc.) only when we are given the assignment of producing game pieces; otherwise, a seeding fee of $ _____ per day we are required to be on the premises of seeding location, plus out-of-pocket expenses.

4. Fulfillment of additional entry forms or game pieces, if applicable, is billable at $ _____ /M.

The above outline of services and fees is intended to cover the development and execution of all conventional prize promotions and services that you may reasonably be expected to execute during the term of this agreement. Should we be assigned the development or execution of any prize promotion or service not covered by the above, we will provide a separate outline of services and fees to you.

With regard to any questionable or noncompliant submissions, we will communicate with your consumer service department for dispensation and handling.

All forms for written notifications to potential winners, including, but not limited to, congratulatory letters, Affidavits of Eligibility, Releases of Liability, etc., will be sent to you for approval prior to submission to potential winners.

While the term "major prize" has been utilized throughout this agreement, the specific "major prize" level will be determined on a promotion-by-promotion basis, and will be stated in writing on each individual promotion document.

ADDITIONAL TERMS AND CONDITIONS

1. Billing Procedures. Upon receiving invoices for providing the services described above (the "Services"), you will pay us the agreed amounts on or before the due date specified thereon, but in no event shall payment be required earlier than _____ days after receipt of an invoice or earlier than _____ days after we have completed the Services with respect to which the billing relates. All invoices shall include such supporting information and documentation as you may reasonably request.

2. Retention and Inspection of Records. We will maintain records of all contracts, papers, correspondence, proof of payment, affidavits of performance, ledgers, books, accounts, and other information relating to the payments made by you for the Services hereunder. You may inspect, examine, and review such records (and make copies thereof) at any time during normal business hours. These records will be retained for a maximum of three years.

3. We represent, warrant, and covenant that:

a. We are a corporation duly organized and validly existing under the laws of the State of _____.

b. We are not insolvent, are not in a bankruptcy proceeding or receivership, nor engaged in any litigation, arbitration, or other legal or administrative proceeding or investigation of any kind which would have an adverse affect on our ability to perform our obligations under this agreement. We will promptly notify you of any materially adverse change in our financial condition and any litigation, arbitration, or other legal proceeding which would have an adverse affect on our ability to perform our obligations under this agreement.

c. All of the Services hereunder will be performed in keeping with the highest professional business standards and will be subject to review and approval by you.

d. We will make prompt payment of all bills submitted by third parties relating to the Services in order to obtain all available discounts, rebates, and credits.

e. During the agreement term, we will not become involved in any situation or occurrence which brings us into public disrepute, contempt, scandal, or ridicule or which tends to shock, insult, or offend the community or which reflects unfavorably upon the reputation of your products.

f. We will comply with all applicable federal, state, and local laws, executive regulations, and orders in carrying out our obligations under this agreement.

4. Term. This agreement shall be effective as of _____ and shall remain in full force and effect until _____. You shall have the option, but no obligation, to renew this agreement for another one-year term on the same terms and conditions, provided you give us written notice of your intent to renew at least thirty (30) days before the end of the initial term. In the event you exercise your option to renew this agreement, the renewal term shall be on the same terms and conditions

as provided herein, except for the agreement fees, which shall be subject to negotiation in good faith and agreement by the parties for the renewal term.

5. Termination. You may terminate this agreement immediately at your sole discretion by giving us written notice upon the occurrence of any of the following events:

a. Where lawful, if we make a general assignment for the benefit of creditors, shall have been adjudicated bankrupt, shall have filed a voluntary petition for bankruptcy or for reorganization, or effectuated a plan or similar arrangement with creditors, shall have filed an answer to a creditor's petition or a petition is filed against us for an adjudication in a bankruptcy or reorganization, or if we shall have applied for or permitted the employment of a receiver or a trustee or a custodian for any of our property or assets.

b. If there is a default by us under any provision of this agreement and we have failed to cure the default within thirty (30) days after being given written notice by you.

c. If you are prohibited by law, regulation, or order from engaging in or utilizing any of the activities described in this agreement.

In the event of such a termination, without prejudice to any other remedies that you may have, you shall be entitled to withhold further payments to us. In addition, you may elect to have us complete any previously agreed-to Services even though the work may not be completed until after termination, or you may elect to stop all work on all Services.

6. Insurance. We will, at our expense, secure and maintain in full force and effect during the term of this agreement at least the following insurance coverage:

a. A comprehensive general liability policy in an amount not less than $ _____ to cover liability for personal injury, death, property damage, and other related harm suffered by those who may be adversely affected by this agreement;

b. A policy of insurance for fire, extended coverage, vandalism, and burglary covering any materials stored by us, whether on our premises or on any other premises, for you, in an amount not less than the reproduction costs of such materials. In the event that any materials (premiums) which are your property are stolen, lost, misplaced, or destroyed while in our possession, we will, via our insurance coverage, reimburse you for the loss incurred; and

c. Workers' Compensation and Unemployment Insurance coverage as required by applicable state law. We will provide you with certificates of insurance naming you as an additional co-insured evidencing the existence of these insurance policies within ten (10) days after execution of this agreement.

7. Independent Contractor. We and our employees and all others with whom we contract to perform services hereunder shall be and remain independent contractors and shall not be deemed your employees. We will be solely responsible for compensating our employees and all others supplied by us to perform Services hereunder. We are not authorized to act for, financially commit, speak for, or represent you in any dealings with third parties unless expressly authorized by you in writing.

8. Governing Law. This agreement shall be governed by and construed and interpreted in accordance with the internal laws of the State of _____.

9. Notices. Any notices required to be given pursuant to the provisions of this agreement shall be in writing and given either in person or by certified mail postage prepaid and mailed to us at [insert address] or to you at [insert address] or to such other addresses as the parties may specify in writing in accordance with the terms of this paragraph.

10. Non-assignability; Subcontracting. The rights and obligations of this agreement may not be assigned or subcontracted by us without your prior written consent.

11. Confidentiality. Any non-public information, data, or plans learned by us from you or your agents in connection with this Agreement, and all such information created for you by us shall be considered by us to be strictly confidential, provided that such confidentiality shall not be required with respect to information disclosed publicly or become generally known under circumstances not involving a breach of this Agreement by us, or which is received by us from third parties lawfully entitled to disclose such information. Unless you have given your express prior written consent, we will not at any time disclose such information, data, or plans to anyone, and we will endeavor in good faith to prevent our agents, employees, or representatives from disclosing same.

If you agree with the foregoing terms and conditions, kindly sign two copies of this letter and return one signed copy to us at your earliest convenience.

Very truly yours,

<Fulfillment Company>

By: _____

ACCEPTED AND AGREED:

<Sponsor>

By: _____

Form I.5.5 Sweepstakes and Contest Fulfillment Contract (Short Form)

<Promotion Sponsor Letterhead>

<Date>

<Fulfillment Company>

<Street Address>

<City, State, Zip>

<Salutation>:

This letter, when signed by you and by us where indicated below will constitute the agreement between you and us concerning your involvement in the <insert name of promotion> promotion (the "Promotion") more fully described below.

1. Description of the Promotion

    <Insert description of promotion>

2. The Promotion Plan

    <Describe media plan>

3. Fulfillment Company Obligations

    <Describe specific fulfillment company commitment. This includes the specifics of their various obligations, e.g., securing of prizes, premiums, and merchandise (the "Merchandise"), mail-fulfillment obligations, returns, defective-goods handling, subcontracting, deadlines, handling of consumer and regulatory inquires, etc.>

4. Terms of Payment

    <Insert payment terms>

5. Term

    The term ("Term") of this Agreement shall commence on <insert start date> and end on <insert end date>. We shall have the right to terminate this agreement on not less than <insert number of days> notice, effective at the end of such <insert number of days> day period.

6. Ownership of Trademarks and Copyrights

a. You hereby acknowledge, recognize, and accept all of our rights and interests in and to any of our trademarks, service marks, or trade names (collectively the "Trademarks"). No right, title, or interest in such Trademarks is granted to you hereunder. You agree not to claim any right, title, or interest in or to the Trademarks or to at any time challenge or attack our rights in or to the Trademarks for any reason whatsoever, without limitation.

b. You hereby acknowledge, recognize, and accept all of our rights and interests in and to any of our copyrights (collectively the "Copyrights"). No right, title, or interest in such Copyrights is granted to you hereunder. You agree not to claim any right, title, or interest in or to the Copyrights or to at any time challenge or attack our rights in or to the Copyrights for any reason whatsoever, without limitation.

c. In the event that any of the services supplied by you hereunder or the product thereof is copyrightable subject matter, you hereby agree that for the purposes of this agreement all such materials shall be considered work-made-for-hire and our property. In the event that any material which is the subject of this agreement is not copyrightable subject matter, or for any reason cannot legally be a work-made-for-hire, then and in such event you hereby assign all right, title, and interest to such material to us and agree to execute such documents as may be necessary to evidence such assignment(s).

7. Miscellaneous Provisions

a. Indemnification and Insurance

You guarantee the absolute non-collusion of your employees with our agents, parents, affiliates, and employees. You indemnify and hold harmless us and our agents, parents, affiliates, subsidiaries, and employees from any and all loss, cost, or expense which we or they might incur by reason of any claim or action arising out of your performance in executing your services on our behalf. Nothing herein contained, however, shall be deemed to constitute any representation or indemnity with respect to the legality of the promotions under federal, state, or local lottery or related statutes, including the Federal Trade Commission Act, except where such legality may depend upon the proper performance of the duties assumed by you hereunder including, but not limited to, the objectivity of the selection of winners.

You indemnify and hold harmless us and our agents, parents, affiliates, subsidiaries, and employees against any claims or actions relating to any name, title, or slogan created and owned by you and used by us with your authorization. In the event that a particular name, title, or slogan affixed to the sweepstakes is not owned or created by you, any and all claims or actions relating to the use of the name, title, or slogan will be our responsibility and we will indemnify and hold you harmless with respect to the cost of the defense of any such claim or action, including reasonable attorneys' fees. In any such event, the indemnified party will promptly inform the indemnitor of any claim or action which has been received or commenced. The indemnitor will promptly assume the defense thereof on behalf of the indemnified parties. In the event any indemnified party wishes to participate in the defense of any such claim or action through its own counsel, it may do so at its own expense.

b. Breach

If you or we breach any terms of this agreement, the breaching party shall have the right to remedy the breach within thirty (30) days following written notice of such breach.

c. Notices

Service of all notice under this agreement will be sufficient if given personally, mailed, telefaxed, or telegraphed to the addresses hereinabove provided or to such other address as either party hereto may notify the other in writing. Any notice mailed, telefaxed, or telegraphed pursuant hereto shall be deemed to have been given on the day it is mailed, telefaxed, or telegraphed or, if delivered in person by hand, on the day it is delivered.

d. Relationship Between Parties

This agreement shall not create or be deemed to create any agency, partnership, or joint venture between you and us. Each party hereto is acting as an independent contractor.

e. Assignment and Sublicense

This agreement may not be assigned or sublicensed by you or us without the prior written approval of the other party. Any assignment or sublicense shall not relieve you or us of our respective obligations hereunder to one another.

f. Entire Agreement

This agreement is intended by you and us as a final and complete expression of our mutual agreement, and supersedes any and all prior and contemporaneous agreements and understandings relating to it.

g. Modifications and Waiver

This agreement may not be modified and none of its terms may be waived, except in writing signed by both you and us. The failure of either you or us to enforce or the delay by either you or us in enforcing any of our respective rights shall not be deemed a continuing waiver or a modification of this agreement.

h. Severability

If any part of this agreement shall be declared invalid or unenforceable by a court of competent jurisdiction, it shall not affect the validity of the balance of this agreement.

i. Governing Laws

This agreement shall be governed by and interpreted in accordance with the laws of the State of <insert jurisdiction> applicable to agreements entered into and to be performed wholly in <insert jurisdiction>.

j. Force Majeure

If for any reason, such as strikes, boycotts, war, acts of God, labor troubles, riots, delays of commercial carriers, restraints of public authority, or for any other reason, similar or dissimilar, beyond their control, any party hereto is unable to perform its respective obligations in connection with the Promotion, such non-performance shall not be considered a breach of this agreement.

k. Full Power

Each party hereto represents and warrants that it has full power and authority to enter into this agreement and to assume the obligations hereunder, and that the execution, delivery, and performance of this agreement will not infringe upon the rights of any third party or violate the provisions of any other agreement to which such party is bound.

l. Confidentiality

You covenant and agree that you will not disseminate, reveal, or otherwise make available to others, or use for its own purposes, any information of a proprietary or confidential nature owned by us and learned by you in the course of fulfilling your obligations hereunder, regarding, but not limited to, trade secrets and confidential information, advertising materials, ideas, plans, techniques, and products.

m. Audit Rights

We shall have the right to audit your financial records which pertain to the rendition of your services hereunder, during ordinary business hours on not less than two (2) days' prior notice.

n. Default

You shall be in default of this agreement if you:
(1) file a petition in bankruptcy, are adjudicated bankrupt, or if a petition in bankruptcy is filed against you;
(2) become insolvent, make an assignment for the benefit of your creditors, make an arrangement pursuant to any bankruptcy law; or
(3) discontinue your business, or if a receiver is appointed for you or your business.

If the above meets with your approval, kindly sign where indicated below and return a signed copy of this letter to us.

Very truly yours,

<Sponsor>

By: _____

ACCEPTED AND AGREED:

<Fulfillment Company>

By: _____

Form I.5.6 Co-Promotion Contract

<**Primary Sponsor Letterhead**>

<**Date**>

<Co-Sponsor Name>

<Street Address>

<City, State, Zip>

<Salutation>:

This letter, when signed by you and by us where indicated below, will constitute the agreement between you and us concerning your involvement in the <insert name of promotion> promotion more fully described below.

1   The Promotion

<Insert description of promotion>

The Promotion is being administered by <insert name of judging organization, if any>, an independent judging organization. The judging organization will, among other duties, prepare a set of Official Rules, judge all winning claims, and properly register and bond the Promotion on behalf of <insert name of primary sponsor>. <Insert names of co-sponsors> (the "Co-Sponsors") will participate in the Promotion as more fully described below. Among the prizes and premiums offered in the Promotion will be the following:

<List prizes>

2.   The Media Plan

To advertise the Promotion, the following media plan is intended:

<Describe media plan>

3.   Co-Sponsor Commitment

<Describe specific co-sponsor commitment. This is usually done by a separate contract for each co-sponsor. One does not generally let co-sponsors see the full commitment of each other co-sponsor, unless deemed important as a deal point.>

4.   Co-Sponsor Media Exposure

<Insert media exposure expected for individual co-sponsor>

<If estimates of media exposure are indicated, e.g., minimum GRPs etc., insert the following: All media values are estimates and all parties understand that such media values can not be exactly

measured. It is the intent of all parties, however, that best efforts will be used to achieve the above results. Proposed layouts, storyboards, or scripts will be submitted to each co-sponsor affected or its authorized agent for approval. Once approved, any assured media exposure (other than GRPs, etc.) shall be deemed achieved, provided no material changes are made from layout, storyboard, or script to production.>

5.   Ownership of Materials

You acknowledge that you have no right, title, or interest, and agree that you will not claim any, in or to the materials produced hereunder (other than those, if any, produced by you), or in or to any of <insert name of primary sponsor>'s or the other Co-Sponsor's trademarks, service marks, trade names, or copyrights.

6.   Miscellaneous Provisions

a.   Exclusivity

During the Promotion Period, you agree not to enter into any promotion or advertising campaign as a Co-Sponsor or participant with any other company or organization in competition with the Co-Sponsors of the Promotion.

b.   Warranty and Indemnification

You hereby indemnify and undertake to defend <insert name of primary sponsor> and the other Co-Sponsors and our respective agents and licensees against all claims, suits, loss, attorneys' fees, or damage resulting from your breach of this agreement; provided that prompt notice is given to you of any such claim or suit and provided, further, that you shall undertake and conduct the defense of any suit so brought.

Similarly, <insert name of primary sponsor> hereby agrees to indemnify you and undertake to defend you against, and hold you harmless from all claims, suits, loss, attorneys' fees, or damage arising out of any breach by <insert name of primary sponsor> or any of the other Co-Sponsors of any terms or conditions of this Agreement; provided that prompt notice is given to us of any such claim or suit and provided, further, that we shall undertake and conduct the defense of any suit so brought.

- OR -

<Insert name of primary sponsor> agrees to indemnify, defend, and hold harmless <insert name of co-sponsor> from and against any regulatory or legal actions arising from the <insert name of promotion>. It is understood that <insert name of primary sponsor> assumes responsibility for the content of advertising, and any other promotional materials prepared by, paid for, and sponsored by <insert name of primary sponsor> for use in the <insert name of promotion>.

<Insert name of co-sponsor> agrees to indemnify, defend, and hold harmless <insert name of primary sponsor> with respect to any regulatory or legal actions arising from the use by <insert name of primary sponsor> of material or products furnished by <insert name of co-sponsor> for use in the <insert name of promotion>. It is understood that <insert name of co-sponsor> assumes responsibility for the fulfillment and performance of its obligations in connection with its participation in the <insert name of promotion>.

c. Breach

If you or we breach any terms of this agreement, the breaching party shall have the right to remedy the breach within thirty (30) days following written notice of such breach.

d. Notices

Service of all notice under this agreement will be sufficient if given personally, mailed, telefaxed, or telegraphed to the addresses hereinabove provided or to such other address as either party hereto may notify the other in writing. Any notice mailed, telefaxed, or telegraphed pursuant hereto shall be deemed to have been given on the day it is mailed, telefaxed, or telegraphed or, if delivered in person by hand, on the day it is delivered.

e. Relationship Between Parties

This agreement shall not create or be deemed to create any agency, partnership, or joint venture between you and us or between or among any other Co-Sponsor. Each party hereto is acting as an independent contractor.

f. Assignment and Sublicense

This agreement may not be assigned or sublicensed by you or us without the prior written approval of the other party. Any assignment or sublicense shall not relieve you or us of our respective obligations hereunder to one another.

g. Entire Agreement

This agreement is intended by you and us as a final and complete expression of our mutual agreement, and supersedes any and all prior and contemporaneous agreements and understandings relating to it.

h. Modifications and Waiver

This agreement may not be modified and none of its terms may be waived, except in writing signed by both you and us. The failure of either you or us to enforce or the delay by either you or us in enforcing any of our respective rights shall not be deemed a continuing waiver or a modification of this agreement.

i. Severability

If any part of this agreement shall be declared invalid or unenforceable by a court of competent jurisdiction, it shall not affect the validity of the balance of this agreement.

j. Governing Laws

This agreement shall be governed by and interpreted in accordance with the laws of the State of <insert jurisdiction> applicable to agreements entered into and to be performed wholly in <insert jurisdiction>.

k. Force Majeure

If for any reason, such as strikes, boycotts, war, acts of God, labor troubles, riots, delays of commercial carriers, restraints of public authority, or for any other reason, similar or dissimilar, beyond their control, any party hereto or another Co-Sponsor is unable to perform its respective obligations in connection with the Promotion, such non-performance shall not be considered a breach of this agreement.

l.   Full Power

Each party hereto represents and warrants that it has full power and authority to enter into this agreement and to assume the obligations hereunder, and that the execution, delivery, and performance of this agreement will not infringe upon the rights of any third party or violate the provisions of any other agreement to which such party is bound.

If the above meets with your approval, kindly sign where indicated below and return a signed copy of this letter to us.

Very truly yours,

<Primary Sponsor>

By: _____

ACCEPTED AND AGREED

<Co-Sponsor>

By: _____

CHAPTER VI
Marketing on the Internet

The Internet has matured into a legitimate media, and continues to rapidly grow. In general, the law cannot keep pace with this rapid growth. Thus, gaps between existing laws and the demands of online media remain complex and confused. However, while regulation of the Internet is in constant flux, there are a number of areas where the law has become somewhat settled or at least where the issues have become relatively clear.

Many of the novel issues identified in the early years of the Internet are largely resolved, including (1) the dichotomy between traditional trademark laws and the domain-name system; (2) the liability of website owners for defamatory or infringing materials posted on their sites; (3) the collection and use of personally identifiable information as it relates to children; (4) the complex issues raised by conducting online sweepstakes, games, and contests; and (5) the future of the domain-name system itself.

This chapter is intended to assist advertising and marketing executives to identify key issues and deal with legal developments and proposed legislation affecting online advertising, marketing, and promotional activities. Because the area is evolving, however, the reader is encouraged to visit www.adlaw.com for updated information.

1. Internet Domain Names

a. Clearance

Internet domain names (the shorthand reference for the url address used to access a website) should be cleared and protected like any other trademark.

Before adopting a domain name, a trademark search and domain-name search should be conducted. A domain-name search begins by conducting a "WHO IS" query on the Internet Network Information Center (InterNIC) website found at http://www.internic.net/whois.html. A WHO IS search can quickly knock out a desired domain by revealing that it has been already registered and is not available. Even if a WHO IS search shows the domain name is available, a would-be registrant is advised to conduct a full trademark search on the domain name before investing in the establishment of a website or other use of the domain.

b. Registration Process

There are many organizations that will register domain names, all of which are available online. Registrations, however, are made on a first-come, first-served basis, something critics have characterized as "first come, only served" policy. Regardless, the process favors those who are quick to register.

c. Protecting a Domain Name

1. Register as Trademarks

    Website owners should register their names not only with the registrar through which the domain name is initially registered, but also with the U.S. Patent and Trademark Office (www.uspto.gov) and foreign trademark registries when advisable. The United States Patent and Trademark Office has issued guidelines on registering domain names as trademarks at http://www.uspto.gov/web/offices/tac/tmep/1200.htm#_Toc2666059.

Not all domain names will be protected as trademarks or service marks. For example, generic or descriptive words (e.g., books.com), domain names for billboard sites, and domain names used only as e-mail addresses may not qualify for protection.

2. Monitor Use

Marketers should periodically "surf" and monitor the Internet to be certain that others are not improperly using their trademarks, trade names, and logos. Commercial Internet watch services are available to monitor and "surf" the Internet to keep marketers apprised of unauthorized use of brand names and trademarks in domain names, website content, and on bulletin boards.

d. Domain Name Disputes—Cybersquatters and Typosquatters

The domain-name system illustrates a fundamental dichotomy between trademark law and Internet commerce. While traditional trademark law permits more than one owner of the same mark, so long as consumer confusion is avoided, on the Internet only one company can own a specific domain name. For example, while the mark DELTA can be used and registered as a trademark for an airline and for faucets, only one company can own delta.com (Delta Airlines).

It may be advisable for parties with equal rights in a trademark to couple a generic word with their non-unique trademark in order to avoid consumer confusion and costly turf battles. Using the example above, one owner could register deltaairlines.com and the other could register deltafaucets.com. Another proposed solution is the creation of directories—much like the Yellow Pages telephone books—which would direct consumers to various websites listed under the applicable heading. An example of a voluntary directory open to businesses is available at http://www.io.io.

Cybersquatters: Much of the litigation surrounding domain names has been between legitimate trademark owners and cybersquatters—individuals who register domain names that represent well-established trademarks of other companies or individuals. Because Internet policy allows registration of domain names on a first-come, first-serve basis, cybersquatting was quite common in the early years of the Internet.

The courts and self-regulatory polices of Internet registrars, however, have substantially limited cybersquatting, generally finding that registration of a famous trademark as a domain name by someone other then the trademark holder constitutes trademark dilution. A trademark dilution claim requires proof that the mark being infringed is a "famous mark" and that the defendant has made a "commercial use" of the mark. In domain disputes, courts have been quite liberal in applying these threshold requirements.

Foreign Cybersquatting. International cybersquatters also found fertile ground to register infringing and/or diluting domain names in the country code Top Level Domains (ccTLDs) such as ".to" for the Republic of Tonga and ".tm" for Turkmenistan. All of the countries recognized by the United Nations have been allotted a ccTLD. Each country has sovereignty to decide what restrictions, if any, it will impose on entities seeking to register domain names in its ccTLD. As a result, most of the more than 180 ccTLDs require that a registrant have a "local presence" in the country (such as a corporation or an agent). This local presence requirement has successfully deterred many cybersquatters who cannot afford to comply with the requirement. However, approximately 70 of the ccTLDs do not impose any restrictions on domain name registration. Some countries which currently do not require a local presence include: Denmark (.dk), Ecuador (.ec), Hungary (.hu), Israel (.il), Luxembourg (.lu), New Zealand (.nz), Puerto Rico (.pr), South Africa (.za), Switzerland (.ch), and Tuvalu (.tv). Generally, it is too expensive and time-consuming for trademark owners to attempt to register their trademarks in each ccTLD. While foreign cybersquatters were a major concern in the early days of the Internet, they do not appear to create much controversy today.

Why It Matters

1. Hasbro, Inc., the owner of the trademark CANDY LAND for children's games, successfully sought a preliminary injunction against the defendants for using the domain name "candyland.com" in connection with a sexually explicit website. The court ruled that the plaintiff had demonstrated a likelihood of prevailing on its claims that such use tarnished and thereby diluted the famous CANDY LAND trademark.

2. Intermatic, a manufacturer of electronic products and services, brought an action against Dennis Toeppen, who was using the domain name "intermatic.com" with a home page showing a map of Champaign-Urbana, Illinois. The court felt that while there was no cause of action for trademark infringement because the marks were being used on different goods, the plaintiff could prevail on a trademark dilution theory.

3. Panavision International, the owner of federal registrations for the trademarks PANAVISION and PANAFLEX also sued Mr. Toeppen, over his registrations of "panavision.com" and "panaflex.com." The court ruled in favor of Panavision, noting that Toeppen's registration of these domain names with the intent to sell them, followed by subsequent offers to sell them, constituted a violation of Panavision's rights and a dilution of its trademarks.

Typosquatters: Typosquatters—persons who register domain names consisting of likely typographical errors for heavily trafficked sites, e.g., amazon.com instead of amazon.com—are variations of cybersquatters. While the courts and self-regulatory bodies that govern the Internet are not as sophisticated against typosquatters as they are against cybersquatters, the Internet has developed to a point where even typosquatters are not finding much of a market for such activities.

WARNING

In a conflict situation, the current dispute-resolution procedure may still favor the party who can provide a valid U.S. or foreign trademark registration. This is a disadvantage to companies that may have relied upon state registrations or common-law usages or that use a design element with their trademarks. Thus, companies with established marks or brand names that have heretofore relied upon state registrations or common-law usages would be advised to obtain a federal registration for their domain names, before a dispute develops. Otherwise, a challenge to a federal or foreign registration may be sufficient to at least tie up the domain name. The dispute-resolution procedure may also encourage unscrupulous companies to obtain quick foreign registrations abroad.

Trademark owners should employ watch services to police potentially infringing domain-name registrations in the ccTLDs. If the cybersquatters are residents of the U.S., then the typical causes of action for infringement and dilution can be brought against the cybersquatter in the U.S., and the courts can wield their power to punish for contempt if the registration abroad is not withdrawn. If, however, neither the cybersquatter nor the ccTLD registrar is in the U.S., the trademark owner's sole remedy may only be found in a foreign court with jurisdiction over the cybersquatter.

2. Domain Name Governance—United States Government View

Prior to 1998, day-to-day operations of the Internet were controlled by a number of nonprofit and profit organizations, each with its own responsibility. The Internet Assigned Numbers Authority (IANA) was responsible for dolling out strings of numbers that allow for unique identifiers for each Internet address (URL). The Internet Engineering Task Force (IETF) had the responsibility for the design and technology that operates as the backbone of the Internet itself. Both IANA and the IETF were nonprofit organizations that operated largely by consensus and were managed by only a handful of individuals. Throughout the world, there were just over a dozen nonprofit organizations, from educational institutions to quasi-governmental bodies, that operated key computer systems (root servers) that acted as various portals to direct the traffic on the Internet. Network Solutions, Inc., a for-profit company based in Virginia, was responsible for assigning individual applicants their particular Internet domain address, e.g., apple.com for Apple Computers. Virtually all of the financing for these activities and the Internet itself came from the U.S. Treasury. In 1998, however, the U.S. Department of Commerce announced that the United States would not renew a private contract with Network Solutions, Inc., and invited the nonprofit private sector to submit proposals to operate the domain-name system, the Internet's root server system (the network of key computers that act as the backbone of the Internet), and Internet security as a nonprofit entity. IANA, the IETF, and the various root-server operators remained intact, but under the coordination of the new entity.

In late 1998, the Department of Commerce selected the Internet Corporation for Assigned Names and Numbers ("ICANN") as the nonprofit successor to govern the Internet domain-name system.

Since its establishment, ICANN has been a controversial organization. While it has made significant progress in Internet governance with the addition of new top-level domains to compete with .com and .org, i.e., .info, .biz, etc., those domains have not had the popularity many predicted, in large part because it took ICANN nearly four years to introduce them. In addition, ICANN, working with the World Intellectual Property Organization (WIPO), has developed a detailed procedure to resolve disputes among domain-name owners and trademark owners concerned with a particular domain name. And while the WIPO procedures have been widely used, the results have been inconsistent and criticized by both brand owners and organizations fearful of large trademark owners gaining too much control over domain names. ICANN is also challenged by the many organizations that own or control the country code domain name authorities (ccTLDs). Each country has a two-letter domain suffix assigned to it. The United States is ".us," Great Britain is ".uk," etc. The organizations that control each of the ccTLDs are either government agencies and private groups. While these two-letter domain suffixes are not as popular as the three-letter domain suffixes, e.g., .com, .org, etc., there are nonetheless many disputes regarding trademarks in the ccTLD system. ICANN has struggled in creating cooperative agreements with the various ccTLD administrators. Finally, ICANN has received considerable criticism from both private and public organizations and agencies. Suffice it to say that ICANN, despite its efforts to be diligent, has far to go before trademark owners can feel their rights are adequately protected on the Internet. Trademark owners should remain informed about developments in Internet domain-name governance through popular or trade press, the ICANN website (www.icann.org), and the Department of Commerce website (www.ntia.doc.gov/ntiahome/domainname). Brand owners should also voice their concerns individually or through their trade associations, and participate in new developments.

3. Website Content

a. Traditional Advertising Regulations Apply

Laws applicable to traditional advertising apply equally to advertising on the Internet. Various federal and state regulatory agencies routinely enforce traditional advertising regulations on the Internet.

1. Federal Enforcement and Regulation

    The Federal Trade Commission (FTC) (http://www.ftc.gov) is aggressive in enforcing regulations prohibiting false and deceptive advertising on the Internet. Most of the cases have been brought against deceptive programs involving scams such as credit-repair schemes, work-at-home businesses, self-improvement products, and easy get-rich-quick pyramid schemes, and against websites that have violated the privacy rights of consumers.

2. Private Enforcement

    The National Advertising Division of the Council of Better Business Bureaus (NAD) (http://www.bbb.org/advertising) also investigates activities on the Internet. Many challenges brought before the NAD concern advertising claims made on the Internet.

b. Foreign Exposure

As a practical matter, it may be virtually impossible to check the legality of any advertising campaign on a worldwide basis. The following are some practical steps a marketer may consider to substantially reduce the risk.

1. Avoid "regulated" industries or products.

2. Obtain opinion of foreign counsel in key jurisdictions (e.g. those in which the marketer has a presence or assets). Assistance in this regard is available from the Global Advertising Lawyers Alliance (www.gala-marketlaw.com).

3. Consider additional insurance coverage.

4. Keep in mind that certain product categories and types of marketing programs are subject to differing international laws. Examples include alcohol, tobacco, health-related products, children's advertising, comparative advertising, and sweepstakes, contests, and games.

c. The Rights of Third-Party Suppliers

The rights of third-party suppliers such as photographers, freelancers, stock photo houses, and others who have licensed materials for use online must be carefully checked to insure that the appropriate rights have been obtained.

Releases and licenses should provide for use in electronic media. Releases limited to use in broadcast or print may not be sufficient to cover online usage.

Internet use equates to worldwide publication. Therefore, releases and licenses must provide for worldwide usage. Failure to properly check third-party releases could result in violations of the underlying contracts as well as infringement of the supplier's copyright. Future contracts should be drafted with Internet usage in mind.

Special rules apply to using music online. The use of music on the Internet requires appropriate synchronization licenses and may require performance licenses from the publisher (the representative of the writer of the underlying composition) and owner of the master recording (the recording company that owns the actual master, assuming prerecorded music is used).

d. Rights of Privacy and Publicity

Websites sponsored by marketers of products and services are likely to be viewed as advertising, rather than entertainment, irrespective of content. All living individuals, from employees of advertising agencies to celebrities and politicians, enjoy a right of privacy, i.e., the right not to have their names, photographs, or likenesses used in advertising without their written consent.

Particular attention should be paid to the rights of celebrities. In addition to the right of privacy, celebrities enjoy a right of publicity, that is, the right to control the commercial exploitation of their names, photos, or likenesses. The right of publicity accorded to celebrities has been expanding, with some jurisdictions extending the right beyond name, photograph, and likeness to include expressions and mannerisms.

If existing advertising materials are to be uploaded, contracts with any underlying talent must be reviewed to ensure that the contracts permit such electronic usage, and more importantly are not limited in geographic scope. It is quite rare for agreements with established talent to provide for worldwide usage. (See Chapter 3 for a detailed discussion of the rights of privacy and publicity, all of which is applicable to the Internet.)

e. Hyperlinking

Linking to another owner's website without permission, while commonly done, may give rise to a legal challenge, particularly if the link takes viewers deep into the other owner's site, bypassing its home page.

In Scotland, the *Shetland Times* sued the *Shetland News*, objecting to the *Shetland News'* linking newspaper headlines on its site to articles on the *Shetland Times* website. The Scotland Court of Sessions entered an interim edict, the equivalent of a U.S. injunction, prohibiting such linking. Later, the case was settled and the *Shetland News* agreed not to continue its linking activities.

In another hyperlinking case, Ticketmaster sued Microsoft over Microsoft's use of unauthorized hyperlinks that connected users from Microsoft's Seattle Sidewalk website to the ticket-sales portion of Ticketmaster's website, bypassing the advertising appearing on Ticketmaster's home page. Ticketmaster alleged unfair competition, deceptive trade practices, and trademark dilution. Microsoft's position was that because links are an inherent part of the Web, any entity operating on the Web has granted or implied license for others to link to any page on its site. The case was settled, and Microsoft agreed that its link would go to Ticketmaster's home page.

While not necessarily clearly required legally, the best practice is to seek permission to hyperlink to another site.

f. Framing

Framing is a practice whereby a website owner superimposes its own "frame" around another linked website in order not to lose the visitor. Without the frame, the visitor would go directly to the linked site without any continuing reference to the original website. The practice of framing has been challenged under theories of copyright and trademark infringement, and unfair competition.

In 1997, the *Washington Post* and several other media publishers challenged the practice of framing by Total News, a website that displayed advertising messages surrounding the Total News site. When a user clicked on a link to another site, the content of the second site was shown on the space inside the static Total News frame. The user continued to see Total News' advertisements. Although the case was settled (Total News agreeing not to display the content of other sites within its own frame), the case remains instructive and dictates caution if framing is being considered.

g. Special Rules for Online Marketing to Children

Websites directed at children are subject to the special rules and guidelines of the Children's Advertising Review Unit (CARU) of the Better Business Bureau (http://www.caru.org). Important guidelines are provided below.

1. Advertising sites should be clearly designated as such.

2. Site owners should avoid linking to sites containing material inappropriate for children.

3. Children should be encouraged to use nicknames or screen names.

4. Bulletin boards and chat rooms should be monitored and parental consent required.

5. Parental consent should be required before processing any orders.

6. Children's sites must have a clearly and prominently posted privacy policy conforming to FTC Guidelines (see Privacy Section below).

h. Electronic Bulletin Boards

The use of electronic bulletin boards may expose a website owner to several types of liabilities for content posted to the site by third parties:

1. Defamation

    Electronic bulletin board operators may be held liable for defamation by system users if they know or had reason to know of the existence of the defamatory statements. There are, however, certain limitations.

    Under the Communications Decency Act of 1996 (the CDA), "[n]o provider or user of an interactive computer service shall be treated as the publisher or speaker of any information provided by another information content provider." This provision (known as the "Good Samaritan" provision) was intended to remove the disincentives to self-regulation by forbidding the imposition of liability on service providers who sweep their sites.

    Two 1998 legal decisions against America Online (AOL) construed the Good Samaritan provision broadly and immunized online access providers from liability. One case immunized AOL from liability for defamatory statements posted through its services, even though AOL allegedly had notice that the statements were posted. The court found that even assuming that AOL satisfied the "knowledge" standard of liability, it was entitled to the immunity. In the second case, the court held that AOL could not be held liable for defamatory statements contained in a gossip column that it carried, even though AOL paid the columnist a royalty each month for his column and had the right to remove content that violated AOL's then-standard terms of service.

2. Copyright Infringement

Decisions clearly establish that website operators may be held liable for copyright infringement if users post infringing material to bulletin boards.

In two 1996 California cases, game maker Sega Enterprises successfully obtained relief against operators of commercial bulletin boards and their system operators. In the first case, Sega challenged an operator who encouraged users to upload Sega's computer game software so that others using software sold by the defendants could download it. Notably, the court also analyzed the operator's liability under a theory of contributory infringement and applied the following test: "One who, with knowledge of the infringing activity, induces, causes, or materially contributes to the infringing conduct of another." In the second case, a California court held that a bulletin-board operator was liable for contributory infringement when subscribers uploaded a number of Sega video games to its bulletin board. Although the operator claimed to have no actual knowledge of the illegal uploads, the court found that there was "reason to know" of the infringement where the board contained a directory listing the names of approximately 20 Sega video games as well as the trademark "SEGA."

Playboy Enterprises, Inc., publisher of *Playboy* magazine, has similarly been successful in three cases against bulletin-board operators and their service providers. In an early 1993 Florida case, the court held that the operator of an "adult" electronic bulletin-board service infringed Playboy's copyright to 170 photographs when subscribers uploaded the pictures to his bulletin board. Although the defendant claimed that he did not know that the photographs had been posted, the court dismissed the defense, stating that intent or knowledge is not an element of infringement and thus even an innocent infringer is liable. In a 1997 Ohio case, the court held that the operators of an electronic bulletin-board system that distributed and displayed copies of Playboy's adult photographs in violation of Playboy's copyrights were directly liable for copyright infringement. The court noted that the defendants were more than just passive providers of space. The facts showed that the defendants encouraged subscribers to upload files, and screened all uploaded files before moving them into the general files available to all subscribers. Such actions made the defendants active participants in the infringement process. The defendants were also liable for contributory infringement by encouraging subscribers to engage in infringing activity by uploading plaintiff's copyrighted photographs. And in a 1997 Texas case, a court held that individuals who have supervisory control over infringing activities might be vicariously liable for infringement. In that case, the court found that a website operator that stored Playboy's photographs on its computers and provided subscribers with access to those photographs for a monthly fee was directly liable to Playboy for copyright infringement. In addition, the individuals who controlled and supervised the website were found to be vicariously liable for copyright infringement.

i. The Digital Millennium Copyright Act

The Digital Millennium Copyright Act (DMCA) establishes limitations on the liability of Internet and online service providers for copyright violations by their subscribers, provided that certain conditions are satisfied. The DMCA immunizes an Internet or online service provider from claims for monetary relief by reason of its storage of infringing materials on its system at the direction of the user of those materials. Providers are also shielded from claims based on their referring or linking users to a site containing infringing materials.

WARNING

The foregoing limitations on liability do not apply, however, if the Internet or online service provider knew or had reason to know that the materials concerned were infringing, derived a financial benefit from the infringing activity, or failed to remove the infringing materials expeditiously upon notice, as provided in the DMCA.

---

4. E-Commerce Sites

Sites through which actual sales transactions are consummated raise special issues. Sellers should take the following steps to reduce their risk of liability:

a. Periodically check e-mail system to be sure it is functioning properly, including the conduct of periodic e-mail tests.

b. Check any hypertext links embedded in the site to be sure they are functioning properly.

c. If the site features limited inventory, prices, or other time-sensitive information subject to change, indicate when the pages were last refreshed.

d. Remind visitors to direct their browsers to refresh images of the pages.

e. Be sure to securely save and back up customer records.

f. Prominently disclose important disclaimers such as warranties, limitations of liability, or material restrictions or conditions of sale.

g. Consider the use of "click wrap" agreements. These are arrangements whereby the user must indicate their agreement to terms on a given page by clicking on a designated area of the page. Unless the user affirmatively clicks, he or she cannot navigate through the website or submit an order.

5. Protecting Online Content

Theft of copyrights and trademarks on the Internet is rampant, as words, graphics, images, and brand names are freely stolen and used without permission of the owner. The following steps can help guard against this:

a. Include a proper copyright notice on the site; e.g., © 2003 Newco, Inc.

b. Consider registering the site with the U.S. Copyright Office (http://cweb.loc.gov/copyright). The copyright office will accept either printouts of each page of the site or a disk containing the entire site plus five representative pages in print. The website owner may also wish to submit the HTML code.

c. Include identifying marks such as serial numbers or digital watermarks.

d. Include warnings about unauthorized use of copyright materials in a website Legal Page.

e. Periodically surf the Internet to look for infringements and the use of meta tags—invisible code embedded in the hypertext language used to create websites. Although invisible to the users, the meta tags are picked up by search engines. Companies can effectively bury the trademarks of well-known competitors within these meta tags so that a user searching for the well-known competitor will pick up the lesser-known competitor's site as well.

6. Website Legal Pages

The use of a legal page on a website represents a cost-efficient way of responding to the increased risk of liability. While the legal impact of the legal page remains untested, the legal page can be used to address various areas of liability by including the following:

  a.   A well-defined privacy policy

  b.   Copyright and trademark notices for protected materials

  c.   Restrictions on permissible uses of website materials

  d.   A disclaimer of liability for materials posted by others on the site

  e.   A disclaimer of liability for advertising materials posted on the site and for the content of linked sites

  f.   Choice of law and venue provisions

  g.   Limitations on liability for damages

  h.   A "click-wrap" agreement, if a visitor's express agreement to certain terms and conditions is necessary

Examples of legal pages appear at the end of this chapter.

7. Online Privacy and Unsolicited E-mail ("SPAM")

Personal information about website visitors is being used by website owners in a variety of ways. At the most elementary level, aggregate website traffic information is necessary to induce advertisers to pay fees to advertise at the website. On a more sophisticated level, the personal information of individual site visitors is collected in databases and used to target direct mailings. In many cases it is also being provided to other direct mailers for a fee.

Personal information is collected through the use of online registrations and surveys that frequently accompany sweepstakes and contests. It is also collected in a more subtle way through the use of Internet cookies stored on the hard drive of website visitors. Internet cookies enable website owners to create a record of the visitor's interests and preferences based upon his or her activities at the website.

Each time a visitor accesses a website, each time a consumer makes a purchase, every time they use the telephone, every time they order a pay-per-view movie, the information is collected in a database. The list of how data is collected from consumers goes on and on. Even at supermarkets, the traditional check-cashing card has been exchanged for a card with its own scannable "signature," recording every product purchased by that consumer, providing invaluable information to manufacturers and sellers. All this information on what consumers do each day in their lives can be used to bring them discounts on what they really want and need, save them the time of finding where a particular product might be, and afford them the ability to "do other things" —or so the story goes. Yet that same information may be of the most private nature.

There are three factors regarding privacy that have attracted the attention of various regulatory authorities and industry groups. First, the need to adopt mechanisms to minimize the impact of unsolicited and unwanted marketing e-mail. Second, the need to develop responsible practices to market and advertise to children (see discussion below). And third, the desirability of notifying visitors to a website of the nature and use of the personal information gathered at the website, the extent of the disclosure of such information to third parties, and the right to elect to suppress any retransmission of such information.

a. Overview of Regulatory/Legislative/Industry Privacy Initiatives

With the exception of the Children's Online Privacy Protection Act of 1998 and legislation targeting specific industries, e.g., insurance and banking, there is no law explicitly barring or otherwise regulating the collection of personal information on Internet users or the reuse or sale of such information. At any given time, however, there are seemingly countless bills pending in Congress. Such bills have failed to be reported out of their committees or have languished on the floor of the House and Senate. It is generally considered unlikely that Congress will enact a comprehensive national privacy policy.

Various trade associations, however, are very active in establishing best practices with regard to consumer privacy. Internet marketers should review the suggestions of these various organizations in adopting a comprehensive privacy policy, including the following: The Council of Better Business Bureaus (www.bbbonline.org/understandingprivacy) and The Direct Marketing Association (http://www.the-dma.org/privacy).

There is no "form" for a privacy policy. Each website operates differently, and using a form approach may cause a website owner to be too conservative. The better approach is to design the website for whatever legitimate purposes the owner elects, and then address the privacy policy issue. A questionnaire that can assist the reader in developing an appropriate privacy policy appears at the end of this chapter.

b. European Union Directive

The European Parliament has passed many Directives regarding advertising practices in an effort to harmonize the divergent laws in Europe. Among these is the European Union Directive on Data Protection. It mandates certain minimum standards for, among other things, the collection, disclosure, and transmission of personal data. This Directive, through implementing legislation in each member state of the European Union, will not only restrict the flow of personal data within the European Union, but also from member states to countries outside the European Union where the European Commission determines such countries do not provide adequate levels of protection for personal data.

Legislation on privacy protection in the United States does not meet the standards required by the Directive. Although the United States has enacted national legislation restricting the disclosure of certain limited types of information (e.g., credit, medical history), the United States generally favors voluntary industry self-regulation. This, of course, may change should any of the proposed privacy bills be enacted.

To avoid a conflict with the European Union, U.S. Department of Commerce and the European Commission negotiated a "safe harbor" framework whereby U.S. companies that comply with the requirements of the agreement avoid violations of the Directive.

Becoming an adherent to the safe harbors is self-effectuated and requires the participant to register via the Department of Commerce website dedicated to the program at http://www.export.gov/safeharbor.

To enjoy protection under the safe-harbor provisions, website owners must comply with the following minimum standards:

1. Notice. A variety of notices must be provided to consumers who visit a website, including (i) the purposes for which the website collects and uses information about visitors, (ii) how visitors can contact the website owner with inquiries or complaints, (iii) the types of third parties to whom information will be disclosed, and (iv) the choices and means the website offers visitors to limit the website owner's use and disclosure of personal information derived from the visitor.

2. Choice. The website owner must give visitors the opportunity and means to choose not to have their personal information disclosed to third parties. This option is known as the "opt-out" option. If the information derived from the visitor is "sensitive information," the website owner must give the visitor the choice to opt in, without which the website may not disclose such information. This is the most controversial part of the safe-harbor provisions and still diametrically opposite virtually all rules in the U.S.

3. Transfers to Third Parties. If a website owner does disclose information to a third party, it may do so if it determines that the third party also subscribes to the safe-harbor provisions or is subject to the actual Directive (either literally or because of its own self-regulated policies). To be safe, the website owner can satisfy this requirement by entering into a written agreement with the third party whereby the third party agrees that it will comply.

4. Access. The website owner must establish a procedure whereby the visitor has access to their personal information in the website owners' database. They must also be given a mechanism to correct, amend, or delete information that is inaccurate.

5. Security. A website owner must take "reasonable precautions" to protect personal information from loss, misuse, unauthorized access or disclosure, alteration, and destruction. It is unclear what constitutes "reasonable precautions."

6. Data Integrity. Whatever personal information is derived from visitors, it must be relevant for the purposes for which it is to be used. Thus, a website owner must take "reasonable steps" to ensure that data is relevant for its intended use, and accurate, complete, and current. Again, it is not clear what constitutes "reasonable steps."

7. Enforcement. In the self-regulatory mold, the website owner must adopt procedures that ensure it will abide by the rules. This can include establishing "readily available and affordable independent recourse mechanisms" to resolve complaints, specific procedures to periodically monitor compliance, and remedies, including self-imposed sanctions, to address failures to comply. How such measures are given any teeth is anyone's guess.

As of March 2003, over 300 companies have registered as participating in the safe-harbor protections. It is interesting to note, however, that a 2002 memorandum from the European Commission reported that over half of the companies registered with the Department of Commerce are not complying with the safe-harbor provisions, most particularly with respect to providing the access and ability to correct information. It is therefore unclear if the safe-harbor provisions actually work for U.S. companies.

c. Special Children's Issues

While online privacy is certainly an important issue among regulators, consumer groups, and website operators, the collection and use of such information gathered from children presents the greatest concern. The FTC indicated in a 1998 Report to Congress that 89% of the 212 child-oriented websites it visited collected personally identifiable information directly from children, and only half of them disclosed their information-collection practices. Fewer than 10% of those sites provided for some form of parental control over the collection of information from their children. Those observations gave rise to the FTC's recommendation that Congress enact legislation to provide greater protection for information collected from children.

Congress swiftly responded by enacting the Children's Online Privacy Protection Act of 1998 (COPPA). Specifically, COPPA requires any operator of a website or online service directed or targeted to children under 13 or any operator of a website that knowingly collects personal information (name, physical and e-mail address, telephone number, social security number) from children under 13, to provide notice on the website of what information is collected, how the operator uses such information, and the operator's disclosure practices for such information. COPPA also requires operators to obtain verifiable parental consent before collecting information from children under 13.

COPPA defines "verifiable parental consent" as any reasonable effort (taking into consideration available technology) to ensure that a parent receives notice of the operator's collection, use, and disclosure practices, and authorizes such collection, use, and disclosure of the personal information. The COPPA Rule enacted by the Federal Trade Commission lists the following acceptable methods of obtaining verifiable parental consent: (i) a signed consent form from the parent returned via mail or facsimile; (ii) a toll-free number which parents can call to give their consent to trained personnel; (iii) requiring a parent to use a credit-card number in connection with a transaction; (iv) a digital certificate that uses public key technology; or (v) the provision of an e-mail message with a PIN or password obtained by one of the aforementioned methods. The required method of consent will be based upon how the operator is using the child's information that it has collected. For instance, if the information is being disclosed to third parties, a more reliable method of obtaining verifiable parental consent, such as the use of a credit card, is required.

COPPA provides several exemptions from this prior consent requirement. Prior consent is not required where an operator collects only a child's e-mail address and such e-mail address is used only once to respond to a one-time request from the child and then deleted after the one-time use. For example, if when a child registers for an online sweepstakes by providing only his or her e-mail address, the e-mail address is only used to notify the child if he or she was a winner and the e-mail address is deleted after completion of the sweepstakes, the operator would not need to obtain prior parental consent. Prior consent is also not required where a child's e-mail address is collected to respond more than once to a specific request of that child and is not used beyond the scope of that request, provided that after the initial response to the child, the operator uses reasonable efforts to provide notice to the child's parent of the information collected and the purpose(s) for which it is to be used, and an opportunity for the parent to request that the operator no longer use or maintain the information.

The Act also requires an operator to provide to a parent whose child has provided personal information, upon proper identification of that parent, a description of the specific types of personal information collected from the child and a reasonable (and lawful) means for the parent to obtain such information. An operator is required to allow a parent the opportunity at any time to refuse to permit the operator's further use or maintenance, or future online collection, of the collected information. This last provision is referred to as an "opt-out" requirement.

Operators are also required to establish and maintain reasonable procedures to protect the confidentiality, security, and integrity or personal information collected from children. The Act also prohibits conditioning a child's participation in a game, the offering of a prize, or another activity on the child disclosing more personal information than is reasonably necessary to participate in such activity.

The Act requires the FTC to provide incentives for self-regulation efforts that track the regulations described above. The Act provides a "safe harbor" for operators that adopt guidelines issued by marketing or online industry associations or self-regulatory bodies approved by the FTC. The FTC must either approve or deny a submitted safe-harbor guideline within 180 days. The Children's Advertising Review Unit, Entertainment Software Rating Board, and TRUSTe have been granted safe-harbor program status.

Operators of websites directed at children under 13 should adopt policies and procedures to ensure that parents are provided with adequate notice of and control over the information their children submit to the site.

Private-sector resources are readily available on the Internet to assist marketers to children and compliance with COPPA. They include:

1. The Children's Advertising Review Unit of the Council of Better Business Bureaus (www.caru.org).

2. The Center for Media Education (CME), a nonprofit children's advocacy organization based in Washington, D.C. (http://www.cme.org), and the Consumer Federation of America (CFA) have jointly proposed a set of guidelines for protecting children's privacy on the Internet, which generally mirror the provisions of the Children's Online Privacy Protection Act. The "Guidelines for the Collection and Tracking of Information from Children on the Global Information Infrastructure and in Interactive Media" :

    a. Collection limitation. Data collectors may not collect personal information from children, unless it is relevant, necessary, and socially acceptable;

    b. Disclosure. Each data collector must prominently display a privacy statement which discloses what information is being collected or tracked, how it is collected, how it will be used, who is collecting it, and who will use it;

    c. Parental consent. The child must understand that he/she must get parental permission before visiting areas where personal information is collected. The burden is on the collector/tracker to obtain valid parental consent;

    d. Use specification/use limitation. Personal data should not be disclosed, made available, or otherwise used for purposes other than those specified in the disclosure statement;

    e. Data quality and security. Personal data should be protected against loss, unauthorized access, destruction, use, modification, or disclosure;

    f. Parental participation: access, correction, and prevention of future use. The data collector must provide access to the information it has collected about the child. It must also allow the parent the ability to correct erroneous data, have data deleted, and/or prevent further use.

d. Unsolicited Electronic Mail ("Junk" e-mail/Spam)

Spamming, the practice of sending multiple copies of unsolicited or "junk" e-mail for commercial purposes over the Internet, is a hot topic on the Internet and on federal and state lawmakers' minds. Those who engage in the practice do so because e-mail provides an opportunity to reach a wide audience quickly and at virtually no cost to the sender.

Numerous objections have been raised to this practice, including:

1. The enormous volume of mass mailings processed by commercial online service providers such as CompuServe and America Online places a tremendous burden on their computer resources;

2. The use of false return addresses on junk e-mail results in an enormous volume of misaddressed e-mail being returned to the network supervisor of the server that has responsibility for the false return address. The practice by junk e-mailers of using false return addresses arose in part as a strategy to increase the likelihood that a message would be opened rather than deleted by the recipient and in part to bypass filters designed to filter out junk e-mail;

3. Recipients of junk e-mail usually respond by sending angry return messages to the authors of the junk e-mail, and this only increases the number of messages that get routed ultimately to the network supervisor of the server that has responsibility for the false return address; and

4. Subscribers are forced to incur incremental time charges to access, read, and delete unwanted e-mail messages.

There have been several cases trying to block spamming practice.

In 1996, a Pennsylvania Federal court held that Cyber Promotions did not have a First Amendment right to send unsolicited e-mail through America Online. The court also held that America Online was within its rights to use blocking software to prevent junk e-mail from being delivered to its members. The court rejected the First Amendment argument based on the fact that America Online is a private company.

However, in 1997, another Pennsylvania court held that an Internet service provider (not AOL) could not unilaterally terminate Cyber Promotions' access to the Internet without honoring its contractual obligation to provide a 30-day notice of termination. The court granted Cyber Promotions a preliminary injunction, forcing the ISP to reactivate Cyber Promotions' Internet access service to enable it to avoid the harm likely to occur if it was denied access while attempting to secure a new Internet service provider.

The battle between spammers and ISPs is ongoing and not expected to change at any time in the near future, despite legislation at the state level.

On the federal legislative front, a number of bills have been promulgated in an attempt to curb the practice. None of these proposals, however, have ever been brought to a vote, and Congress has yet to pass federal legislation directed at spam. Nor do observers believe it will any time soon.

To date, legislation has been enacted in twenty-six states: Arkansas, California, Colorado, Connecticut, Delaware, Idaho, Illinois, Iowa, Kansas, Louisiana, Maryland, Minnesota, Missouri, Nevada, North Carolina, Ohio, Oklahoma, Pennsylvania, Rhode Island, South Dakota, Tennessee, Utah, Virginia, Washington, West Virginia, and Wisconsin. A list of the highlights of the state statutory scheme appears at the end of this chapter. Suffice to say that enforcement of the state statutes is limited when compared to the volume of spam and its seemingly geometric growth. In general, however, the state statutes address minimum disclosure requirements and specific penalties.

The majority of statutory penalties are limited to monetary damages and injunctive relief. Monetary damages include actual damages suffered by the recipient or ISP that initiated the lawsuit as well as statutory damages ranging from $10 per e-mail to $25,000 per day. A judge can also award reasonable attorney's fees and court costs. Nine states, however, do provide for criminal penalties: Arkansas, Connecticut, Delaware,

Nevada, Pennsylvania, South Dakota, Utah, Virginia, and Wisconsin. These criminal penalties include fines up to $10,000 and/or imprisonment ranging from one month to eight years.

Some states broaden the application of their statutes to parties who "assist the transmission" of unsolicited e-mail. Such assistance is most broadly defined as providing "substantial assistance or support which enables any person to formulate, compose, send, originate, initiate, or transmit a commercial electronic-mail message if the person providing the assistance knows or consciously avoids knowing that the initiator of the commercial electronic message is engaged, or intends to engage, in any practice which violates" this or other consumer-protection laws.

Assuming an Internet marketer were to elect spam as a viable method of reaching consumers, compliance with the following will limit exposure under state law:

1. Unsolicited e-mail should be sent from a valid e-mail address.

2. The header, routing, and transmission should not be forged or falsified.

3. No third party domain name or e-mail address should be used without permission.

4. The subject line should begin with "ADV" or "ADV-ADLT," as appropriate.

5. A valid e-mail address should be provided for recipients to unsubscribe from receiving future e-mail.

6. A statement describing how recipients can unsubscribe should be included.

7. Unsubscribe requests should be promptly honored.

Although sending unsolicited e-mail advertisements is not a crime, the FTC will challenge spam if it contains representations that may be unsubstantiated or deceptive or may violate any of the rules or guides the FTC is empowered to enforce.

The FTC has also published a list of the top 12 most common types of spam scams, in this order:

- Business Opportunity Scams

- Making Money by Sending Bulk E-Mailings

- Chain Letters ("You are about to make $50,000 in less than 90 days!")

- Work-at-Home Schemes (envelope stuffing and craft assembly)

- Health and Diet Scams ("scientific breakthroughs," "miraculous cures," "exclusive products," "secret formulas," and "ancient ingredients")

- Easy Money ("Learn how to make $4,000 in one day," "Make unlimited profits exchanging money on world currency markets")

- Get Something Free (high-tech pyramid schemes)

- Investment Opportunities

- Cable Descrambler Kits (Kits usually don't work and stealing cable service is illegal.)

- Guaranteed Loans or Credit, On Easy Terms (Loans turn out to be lists of lending institutions, and the credit cards never arrive.)

- Repair Scams (No one can erase a bad credit record if it's accurate, and using an Employer Identification Number to set up a new credit identity is against the law)

◆ Vacation Prize Promotions (Consumer has been selected to receive a "luxury" vacation at a bargain-basement price. But the accommodations aren't deluxe and upgrades are expensive.)

Any marketer engaged directly or indirectly with such marketing activities should proceed with caution.

8. Sweepstakes and Contests

Conducting promotional games such as sweepstakes or contests on the Internet raises unique lottery issues. Lotteries, except those that are state operated, are illegal under federal law and the laws of all 50 states. A lottery is generally defined as a promotion in which all three of the following elements are present: prize, chance, and consideration. Accordingly, one of these three elements must be removed before a promotion can lawfully proceed. A chance promotion always contains the elements of prize and chance. Therefore, the element of consideration must be eliminated to render the promotion lawful. (See Chapter 5 for more details on sweepstakes and contests in general.)

a. Sweepstakes and Consideration Issues

1. Internet Access Fees. Access to the Internet invariably involves the payment of some fee by the user, which, for lottery purposes, may be deemed to constitute consideration. It is important to know how a game entrant is billed for access to an electronic service on which the promotional game is conducted. This factor may determine whether a free, alternative method of entry is required. Clearly, if the service is a premium service, for which a direct payment is required to access, an alternate method of entry is required. Do not, however, assume that just because the service is a free rather than a paid subscription service, no alternative method of entry is required. Even if the website on which a promotion presented is a free site, a fee must nonetheless be paid to some service provider to gain access. While the argument may be made that a promotion conducted on a free website is no different from a promotion conducted via television, the fact remains that a payment of some sort must be made to a service provider to access that website. As the Internet becomes more accessible through various free means, the rule of thumb has become that if a non-ISP, such as a package-goods company, is running an Internet-only promotion, the consideration does not flow directly to the sponsor, but to a third party. Thus, the fee is not prohibited consideration. This argument does not work in instances where an ISP such as AOL is sponsoring a promotion and requires a subscription to their services as a condition of entry. The "consideration," however, does not flow to the sponsor, but to the ISP. Accordingly, no regulator has challenged the now-common online-only game. The conservative approach would suggest including an alternative, free method of entry or limiting entry to those persons with Internet access as of a certain date prior to the start date of the promotion, although few sponsors now follow this approach, even where games are advertised off-line. It should be noted, however, that no state has brought an action alleging that the fee charged by an ISP is consideration in connection with a promotion run on an independent website. Florida has specifically eliminated the requirement that there be a free off-line method of entry for Internet promotions. As a result, fewer and fewer Internet promotions are offering alternate methods of entry.

In certain types of sweepstakes, an off-line method of entry may not be practical. In such cases, the following factors should be considered in assessing the risk:

a. How is the website accessed? Is it freely accessible on the Web or accessible only through a commercial online service?

b. Where is the promotion being advertised? Is the promotion being advertised in other media?

c. How much online time is required? How many visits to the site are required?

d. What is the duration of the promotion? How large are the prizes?

2. Equal Opportunity to Win. If an alternate, free method of entry is to be incorporated into the promotion, it must have equal dignity with the electronic method of entry. Any disparity in opportunity to win between the electronic method of entry and alternate method of entry may render the alternate method invalid. Achieving parity with an alternate method of entry may be particularly challenging with certain interactive promotions. Beware of interactive promotions in which speed of response is an element determinative of winner selection.

3. Degree of Effort. While consideration is generally deemed to constitute a purchase of the sponsor's product or payment of a fee, consideration may also be found to exist in a promotion where the entrant is required to expend a substantial degree of effort in order to participate. Promotions requiring the entrant to spend considerable time navigating a website may be subject to challenge on that basis. Federal law and the various states follow the "standard lottery rule," under which consideration may be found to exist by virtue of certain non-monetary requirements if a "substantial effort" is required of the consumer. Lottery challenges based on non-monetary consideration, however, are rare.

4. Consumer Data. Many promotions on the Internet require or request entrants to answer various survey questions. Some of these surveys seek highly personal, sensitive data. To the extent that entrants are required to provide sensitive or proprietary financial or other personal data, consideration may be deemed to be present in the promotion. If the survey questions are extensive, thought should be given to making the answers to those questions optional.

5. Consent to Receipt of Future E-mails. In an effort to build e-mail databases, many sponsors of promotions require consumers to agree to accept future spam as a condition of entry. As passing anti-spam legislation becomes a priority for state and federal legislatures, this practice may become risky. In such promotions, it is best to allow the consumer to opt-in to receipt of future e-mails from the sponsor and third parties.

6. Use of Sponsor's Software. A sweepstakes or game requiring use of certain software packages or a specified browser may inject the element of consideration into the sweepstakes.

b. Skill Contests

Properly structuring a free method of entry is generally a key issue in formulating a sweepstakes. An alternative to providing a free method of entry is to structure the promotion as a bona-fide game of skill. If the game is a pure skill contest, then the element of consideration can generally be present, since the element of chance has been eliminated. Marketers should be aware, however, that structuring a bona-fide skill game is highly complex. Care must be taken to ensure that the element of chance is not present in any form. If the element of chance enters into the skill promotion in any manner, it taints the entire promotion. In addition, even if the game is structured as a bona-fide skill game, a number of states still prohibit any fee or payment as a condition of entry.

The language of state statutes must be carefully reviewed to determine which ones apply to online games. Some statutes refer expressly to a payment to the sponsor; other statutes are triggered only when certain representations are made and appear to be targeted by direct mail. Some of the states restricting consideration in skill contests permit consideration if certain disclosures are made. The Federal Direct Mail statute also has specific provisions directed towards contests of skill. Accommodating these provisions may be easier in an online context.

If consideration is going to remain present in the promotion, the sponsor must be certain that the promotion will pass muster as a bona-fide skill contest.

1. The skill needed to win must be bona fide.

2. Contestants must be judged based on objective criteria.

3. Skill must determine and control the final result.

4. In determining whether a game is one of skill or chance, most states follow a "dominant element theory." So long as skill is the dominant factor in determining the winner, the promotion is a game of skill.

5. Ties must be broken on the basis of skill.

WARNING

Beware of speed as an element of skill in an online promotion, and carefully review game specifications to determine if the game is compatible with all platforms and software.

---

c. Games for Games' Sake

The Internet has become fertile ground for the conduct of games conducted purely for entertainment value or profit to the sponsor. To the extent that such games do not involve the promotion of an underlying product or service and permit entry for a fee (even if not required), certain states have suggested that such games may run afoul of the gambling statutes, e.g., Ohio, South Carolina, and Texas.

d. Worldwide Legal Exposure

Given that Internet promotions create worldwide legal exposure, the prudent approach is to limit eligibility to residents of the United States unless the promotion will be cleared legally in other key markets, i.e., those in which the sponsor has contacts or assets. The limitation of eligibility to United States residents should be prominently disclosed not only in the official rules, but also directly at the point of entry. Many countries have extremely strict data-protection laws that make running online games in those countries cost-prohibitive. Other countries outlaw games of chance entirely. The risk of worldwide exposure can also be reduced by choice of law and venue provisions specifying that the laws of the United States apply and that any claims must be resolved in the United States.

e. Privacy

Since completion of an entry form necessarily requires disclosure of personally identifiable information, a privacy policy should be disclosed at the point of entry. If an entrant's name and personal information are being solicited for marketing purposes, the prudent approach is to disclose this in the official game rules and include a link from the game rules to the Sponsor's privacy policy. For online games directed towards children or on websites directed towards children, special care should be taken to follow all of the guidelines of CARU and especially the COPPA guidelines for collecting personal information from children online.

f. Other Special Official Rules Provisions

There are a number of other unique situations posed by online promotions that should be handled by special provisions in the official game rules.

1. The deadline for online entries must specify not only the date of the deadline, but also the time of the deadline and the time zone for the deadline, e.g., 11:59 p.m. EST. Also, remember that the deadline for online entries must be parallel with the postmark date for mail entries.

2. Technical personnel must work closely with those drafting the "How to Play" instructions to be sure that any special technical requirements are adequately set forth in the rules. For example, if a grid must be completed in a certain way, or if an entrant must use exactly the same name each time he or she plays to be sure a score is properly aggregated, this must be set forth in the rules.

3. A provision should be added indicating that in the event of a dispute regarding who submitted an online entry, the entry will be deemed submitted by the holder of the e-mail account.

4. Given the complexities inherent in an online promotion, unpredictable and uncontrollable problems can arise from bugs or failure in the server, hardware, or software. In addition, a promotion may be plagued with unforeseen failure of data to transmit failure; or lost, delayed, or corrupted data transmitted by participants. Sponsors should disclaim liability for all such problems.

5. A disclaimer of liability should also be added for any damage to a user's system occasioned by participating in the promotion or downloading any information necessary to participate in the promotion.

6. In some instances, particularly where the game is fairly complex, it may be advisable to require entrants to indicate their acceptance of the official rules, such as by clicking on an "I Accept" button.

Chapter Six Forms

Form I.6.1 Website Legal Page / Disclaimer Form (Informal)

Wow, you actually came to this page. Our lawyers made us include it and made us use a precious button on our home page to get you here. At first, we thought the lawyers were a real pain. But then we read the page. What a Netwakening! It's really important stuff. We took the legalese the lawyers wrote and translated it into readable English. So be a smart nethead and read the stuff on this page. It could prevent you from hearing from our lawyers, or worse yet, from really nasty people, like prosecutors.

Here's the deal:

We run this website so that people like you (and people you like) can use it for personal entertainment, information, education, communication, and cybergratification. So go ahead and browse around all you like. You can even download stuff from the website, but only for noncommercial, personal use. If you do, though, don't fool around with the copyright and other notices all over the stuff. They're there for a really good reason. And don't even think about distributing, modifying, transmitting, reusing, reposting, or anything else uncool with any of the stuff, including the text, images, audio, and video, for public or commercial purposes unless we give you written permission. And it's not likely we will.

If you visit our website, you're also legally obligated to (read: stuck with) the terms and conditions listed below and any other law or regulation that applies to the website, the Internet or, the World Wide Web. You shouldn't access or browse the website if you have a problem with that, because once you start, there's no turning back—you are bound by (read: stuck with) the terms and conditions.

So here's the scoop on the Top Ten Rules for Cybersurfers who hang out on our website:

1. For everyone's sake, just assume that everything on the site is copyrighted unless we say it's not. So you can't use the stuff, except how we say you can, on this page or anywhere else on the website, without our written permission. And like we said before, it's not likely we'll give you permission anyway. In fact, even if we wanted to, the lawyers are likely to veto any deal anyway. So it's better you don't even ask.

2. While we try to include accurate stuff on the website, we're not promising you it's accurate. In fact, we're not promising you anything except fun and entertainment. So if you use stuff on the website, you're using it at your own risk. Don't call us if there's a problem because we assume no liability or responsibility for errors or omissions on the website.

3. We, and anybody else who helped us create, produce, or deliver the website, are not liable for any damages you suffer when you use it. In particular, the lawyers want you to know that our disclaimer includes "direct, incidental, consequential, indirect, or punitive damages arising out of your access to, or use of, the website. Without limiting the foregoing, everything on the website is provided to you 'AS IS' WITHOUT WARRANTY OF ANY KIND, EITHER EXPRESSED OR IMPLIED, INCLUDING, BUT NOT LIMITED TO, THE IMPLIED WARRANTIES OR MERCHANTABILITY, FITNESS FOR A PARTICULAR PURPOSE, OR NON-INFRINGEMENT. Please note that some jurisdictions may not allow the exclusion of implied warranties, so some of the above exclusions may not apply to you. Check your local laws for any restrictions or limitations regarding the exclusion of implied warranties." Ugh! What a mouthful

from the mouthpieces. We put all of that in quotes because we couldn't figure out any other way to say it that the lawyers would accept. But here's the bottom line—we're not responsible if you're browsing around and the website damages you or your computer or infects it with any nasty viruses. We sure hope that doesn't happen, but if it does, don't call us.

4. If you don't want the world to know something, don't post it on the website, in any bulletin board or anyplace else. That's because anything you disclose to us is ours. That's right—ours. So we can do anything we want with the stuff you post. We can reproduce it, disclose it, transmit it, publish it, broadcast it, and post it someplace else. We can even send it to your mother (as soon as we find her address). Not only that, we can even use any ideas, concepts, know-how, or techniques you post any way we want to, including developing, manufacturing, and marketing products or other stuff using the information you post.

5. Pictures of people or places shown on the website are either our property or someone else's property we're using with their permission. No matter what, it's definitely not your property. You or any of your net-friends can't use it unless we said you could on this page or somewhere else on the website. And guess what—we won't say yes. So be careful, Bunky, because unauthorized use may violate all sorts of nasty laws. Be smart; keep the stuff you download to yourself.

6. There are also a lot of trademarks, logos, and service marks on the website, including ones like [insert names of trademarks] that either we own or we're using with someone else's permission. So don't think you have any kind of license or right to use them, because you don't and we're not about to give you one. If you don't leave them alone, and you mess with the trademarks, logos, and service marks on our site, we'll probably go ballistic—so will the companies that own the other trademarks, logos, and service marks. That means that we're likely to sue you or to ask a prosecutor to come after you for messing around with our property or the property of others.

7. You'll probably notice we've linked our website to lots of others. While that's cool, it doesn't mean we've looked at all those sites, much less checked them out periodically to see what's going on. So don't blame us if some site you visit is bad or has stuff on it that offends you or your pets. Go ahead and click on it, but remember, you're doing it at your own risk.

8. That brings us to what you do on our website. While we occasionally listen in on chat groups or look at the posts in our discussion groups or on our bulletin boards, we take no responsibility and assume no liability for the content of those locations or for any mistakes, defamation, libel, slander, omissions, falsehoods, obscenity, pornography, or profanity you might encounter when you visit such places on our website. And please don't post or transmit any unlawful, threatening, libelous, defamatory, obscene, scandalous, inflammatory, pornographic, nasty, mean, or profane material, or any material that law enforcement types may consider a criminal offense, that could get someone in court on a civil lawsuit, or that violates any law—anywhere, anytime. While we certainly respect your privacy, we have no choice but to fully cooperate with any law enforcement authorities or court that might ask us who might have posted nasty stuff on our site.

9. Software that you can use on this site is protected by all sorts of patriotic U.S. laws. Because of that, you can't download or send the software to anyone in the vacation travel spots of Cuba, Iraq, Libya, North Korea, Iran, Syria or any other country where the United States has embargoed goods; or (get this) to anyone on the United States Treasury Department's list of Specially Designated

Nationals, the U.S. Commerce Department's Table of Deny Orders, or the FBI's Most Wanted Internet Creeps List (just kidding on the last one). As if that were not enough, if you live in or are a national of any of those lovely places, you're not even supposed to be reading this page, so beat it!

10. We're also allowed to change this page and anything else on the site anytime we want to. That's because it's ours and we have the programmers to do it. If we do change the page, then you're bound by (read: stuck with) those changes, too, whenever you visit our site. If this all sounds kind of mean and undiplomatic, you should have seen what the lawyers gave to us in the first place. We had to remind them that human torture and sacrifice was outlawed in the United States. Boy, did they look disappointed!

Form I.6.2 Website Legal Page (Formal)

[Site Owner] maintains this site (the "Site") for your personal entertainment, information, education, and communication. Please feel free to browse the Site. You may download material displayed on the Site for non-commercial, personal use only provided you also retain all copyright and other proprietary notices contained on the materials. You may not, however, distribute, modify, transmit, reuse, re-post, or use the content of the Site for public or commercial purposes, including the text, images, audio, and video, without [Site Owner]'s written permission.

Your access to and use of the Site is also subject to the following terms and conditions ("Terms and Conditions") and all applicable laws. By accessing and browsing the Site, you accept, without limitation or qualification, the Terms and Conditions and acknowledge that any other agreements between you and [Site Owner] are superseded and of no force or effect.

Terms and Conditions

1. You should assume that everything you see or read on the Site is copyrighted unless otherwise noted and may not be used except as provided in these Terms and Conditions or in the text on the Site without the written permission of [Site Owner]. [Site Owner] neither warrants nor represents that your use of materials displayed on the Site will not infringe rights of third parties not owned by or affiliated with [Site Owner].

2. While [Site Owner] uses reasonable efforts to include accurate and up-to-date information in the Site, [Site Owner] makes no warranties or representations as to its accuracy. [Site Owner] assumes no liability or responsibility for any errors or omissions in the content of the Site.

3. Your use of and browsing in the Site are at your risk. Neither [Site Owner] nor any other party involved in creating, producing, or delivering the Site is liable for any direct, incidental, consequential, indirect, or punitive damages arising out of your access to, or use of, the Site. Without limiting the foregoing, everything on the Site is provided to you "AS IS" WITHOUT WARRANTY OF ANY KIND, EITHER EXPRESSED OR IMPLIED, INCLUDING, BUT NOT LIMITED TO, THE IMPLIED WARRANTIES OF MERCHANTABILITY, FITNESS FOR A PARTICULAR PURPOSE, OR NON-INFRINGEMENT. Please note that some jurisdictions may not allow the exclusion of implied warranties, so some of the above exclusions may not apply to you. Check your local laws for any restrictions or limitations regarding the exclusion of implied warranties. [Site Owner] also assumes no responsibility for, and shall not be liable for, any damages to, or viruses that may infect, your computer equipment or other property on account of your access to, use of, or browsing in the Site or your downloading of any materials, data, text, images, video, or audio from the Site.

4. Any communication or material you transmit to the Site by electronic mail or otherwise, including any data, questions, comments, suggestions, or the like, is, and will be treated as, non-confidential and non-proprietary. Anything you transmit or post may be used by [Site Owner] or its affiliates for any purpose, including, but not limited to, reproduction, disclosure, transmission, publication, broadcast, and posting. Furthermore, [Site Owner] is free to use any ideas, concepts, know-how, or techniques contained in any communication you send to the Site for any purpose whatsoever including, but not limited to, developing, manufacturing, and marketing products using such information.

5. Images of people or places displayed on the Site are either the property of, or used with permission by, [Site Owner]. The use of these images by you, or anyone else authorized by you, is prohibited unless specifically permitted by these Terms and Conditions or specific permission provided elsewhere on the Site. Any unauthorized use of the images may violate copyright laws, trademark laws, the laws of privacy and publicity, and communications regulations and statutes.

6. The trademarks, logos, and service marks (collectively the "Trademarks") displayed on the Site, including [insert names of trademarks], are registered and unregistered Trademarks of [Site Owner] and others. Nothing contained on the Site should be construed as granting, by implication, estoppel, or otherwise, any license or right to use any Trademark displayed on the Site without the written permission of [Site Owner] or such third party that may own the Trademarks displayed on the Site. Your misuse of the Trademarks displayed on the Site, or any other content on the Site, except as provided in these Terms and Conditions, is strictly prohibited. You are also advised that [Site Owner] will aggressively enforce its intellectual property rights to the fullest extent of the law, including the seeking of criminal prosecution.

7. [Site Owner] has not reviewed all of the sites linked to the Site and is not responsible for the content of any off-site pages or any other sites linked to the Site. Your clicking on hyperlinks and visiting any other off-site pages or other sites is at your own risk.

8. Although [Site Owner] may from time to time monitor or review discussions, chats, postings, transmissions, bulletin boards, and the like on the Site, [Site Owner] is under no obligation to do so and assumes no responsibility or liability arising from the content of any such locations nor for any error, defamation, libel, slander, omission, falsehood, obscenity, pornography, profanity, danger, or inaccuracy contained in any information within such locations on the Site. You are prohibited from posting or transmitting any unlawful, threatening, libelous, defamatory, obscene, scandalous, inflammatory, pornographic, or profane material or any material that could constitute or encourage conduct that would be considered a criminal offense, give rise to civil liability, or otherwise violate any law. [Site Owner] will fully cooperate with any law enforcement authorities or court order requesting or directing [Site Owner] to disclose the identity of anyone posting any such information or materials.

9. Software from this Site is further subject to United States Export Controls. No software from this Site may be downloaded or exported (i) into (or to a national or resident of) Cuba, Iraq, Libya, North Korea, Iran, Syria, or any other country to which the United States has embargoed goods; or (ii) anyone on the United States Treasury Department's list of Specially Designated Nationals or the U.S. Commerce Department's Table of Deny Orders. By downloading or using the software, you represent and warrant that you are not located in, under the control of, or a national or resident of any such country or on any such list.

10. [Site Owner] may at any time revise these Terms and Conditions by updating this posting. You are bound by any such revisions and should therefore periodically visit this page to review the then-current Terms and Conditions to which you are bound.

Form I.6.3 Internet Privacy Policy Questionnaire

If a site owner cannot answer all of these questions in the affirmative, the owner is advised to consult with legal counsel and review the privacy policy posted on the site.

1. Is the name, address, and telephone number of the entity operating the site clearly stated in the privacy policy?

2. Does this privacy policy accurately reflect the online practices of the company?

3. Is it clear how users contact the site with questions regarding the site's privacy practices?

4. Does the policy state what both personally identifiable information (i.e., name, address, e-mail address, telephone number, age) and non-identifiable information (e.g., site usage patterns) is collected on the site?

5. Does the policy state how the identifiable and non-identifiable information is used by the site?

6. Does the policy state if the personally identifiable information is shared with third parties? If so, does it state what types of third parties can gain access to the information (e.g., affiliates and subsidiaries, branding partners)?

7. Does the policy state if and how personal information may be used for any other purpose other than the purpose for which it was provided to the site (e.g., to send the user e-mails)?

8. Is the policy clear whether information collected on the site is combined with other sources of information?

9. If used, does the policy disclose that the site uses cookie technology, Web bugs, or other information collection methods?

10. If permitted, does the policy state that third parties on the site may use any such collection methods?

11. Does the site collect IP addresses? If so, does the policy state how this information is used?

12. Is any financial information collected on the site? If so, does the policy state how it is used and whether it is shared with third parties?

13. Does the site collect demographic information? If so, does the policy state how it is used and whether it is shared with third parties?

14. Is the site directed towards children under the age of 13 or does it knowingly collect personal information from children under the age of 13? If so, has the site owner reviewed and complied with the requirements of the Children's Online Privacy Protection Act (COPPA)?

15. Can the user access and correct and/or delete any personal information collected on the site? If so, is the process by which they can do so stated in the policy?

16. Does the site have links to third-party sites? If so, is there a disclaimer regarding liability with respect to activities once the visitor links to the third-party site?

17. Does the site use third parties to help administer the site? If so, are those third parties identified on the privacy page?

18. Are there bulletin boards or other public areas of communication on the site? If so, does the privacy policy adequately address content of such communications, and issues concerning libel or other unacceptable content?

19. Are there security measures in place to protect against misuse of personal information posted by visitors?

20. Does the policy state how a visitor whose information has been collected can opt out of any further collection practices, e-mail communications from the site, or sharing of such information with third parties?

21. Is information collected from European visitors and shared with third parties? If so, has the site owner reviewed and complied with the European Directive on Data Protection or its safe-harbor provisions?

Form I.6.4 Overview of State Anti-Spam Laws (as of January 2003)

The state statutory requirements regarding unsolicited e-mail can be broken down into broad categories: advance permission; labeling; mandatory unsubscribe option; accurate e-mail address; accurate header and routing information; accurate subject line; and prohibition against sexually explicit materials.

1. Advance Permission

   Delaware: Prohibits sending unsolicited e-mail for advertising, promoting, marketing or soliciting interest in goods, services or other enterprises without the recipient's prior authorization.

2. Labeling

   California, South Dakota, Tennessee, Utah: The subject line of unsolicited e-mail must begin with the letters "ADV:". If the unsolicited e-mail contain materials which can only be accepted if the recipient is over 18 years of age, the subject line of unsolicited e-mail must begin with the letters "ADV:ADLT".

   Colorado: The subject line of unsolicited e-mail must begin with the letters "ADV:".

   Kansas: The subject line of unsolicited e-mail must begin with the letters "ADV:" unless there is an established existing relationship between the parties or the recipient expressly consents to receive the unsolicited e-mail, other than adult e-mail, which is sent to less than 500 recipients per month. The subject line of sexually explicit or adult e-mail must begin with the letters "ADV:ADLT".

   Minnesota: The subject line of unsolicited e-mail must begin with the letters "ADV:" or "ADV:ADLT" if the unsolicited e-mail contain materials which can only be accepted if the recipient is over 18 years of age, unless the recipient has expressly requested the unsolicited e-mail or the sender has a business or personal relationship with the recipient.

   Nevada: Unsolicited e-mail must be readily identified as an advertisement or contain a statement that it is an advertisement.

   Pennsylvania: The subject line of unsolicited e-mail which contain sexually explicit material must begin with the letters "ADV-ADULT".

   Wisconsin: The subject line of unsolicited e-mail which contain sexually explicit or obscene material must contain the words "ADULT ADVERTISEMENT".

3. Mandatory Unsubscribe Option (a/k/a Opt-Out)

   California, Minnesota, Missouri, Rhode Island, Tennessee, Utah: Sender must include valid toll-free telephone number or e-mail address to unsubscribe, and must honor such requests.

   Idaho, Iowa: Sender must include valid e-mail address to unsubscribe, and must honor such requests.

   Colorado, Delaware, Kansas, Nevada: Sender must advise recipient how to unsubscribe, and must honor such requests.

4. E-mail Address

   Arkansas, Illinois, Kansas, Minnesota, Nevada, Rhode Island, South Dakota, Utah, Washington, West Virginia: Sender may not use third party domain name without permission.

Colorado, Idaho, Iowa, Maryland: Sender may not use third party domain name and/or e-mail address without permission.

Colorado: Sender must disclose its actual e-mail address.

Kansas, Utah, Nevada: Sender must include valid sender return e-mail address, legal name of sender, and physical address or toll-free telephone number.

West Virginia: Sender must include date and time message is sent, sender's name, and sender's return e-mail address.

5. Header/Routing/Transmission Information

    Arkansas, Colorado, Delaware, Idaho, Illinois, Iowa, Kansas, Louisiana, Maryland, Minnesota, Nevada, North Carolina, Oklahoma, Rhode Island, South Dakota, Utah, Virginia, Washington, West Virginia: Sender may not falsify, forge or misrepresent routing, header and/or transmission information.

6. Subject Line

    Arkansas, Illinois, Kansas, Maryland, Minnesota, Nevada, South Dakota, Washington, West Virginia: Sender may not falsify, forge or misrepresent information in subject line.

7. Sexually Explicit Material

    West Virginia: Sender may not send unsolicited e-mail that contains sexually explicit material.

CHAPTER VII
CD-ROM and Interactive Multimedia

1. Overview

Many advertisers use multimedia platforms, usually CD-ROM, DVD products, or other computer-accessed technology. Before embarking on any interactive multimedia project, however, the following issues should be resolved.

a. Ownership rights for works created specifically for an interactive product generally fall under one of four categories—works of employees, works-made-for-hire, assignments, or licenses. Occasionally, the ownership to a work will be held jointly, but such joint ownership is rare.

  1. Employees. The rights to original works created by an employee of the advertiser are automatically owned by the advertiser and may generally be used for any purpose without further payment.

  2. Works-Made-for-Hire. An advertiser has similar rights if original works are created by an independent contractor, e.g., its advertising agency or other freelancers, for one of nine purposes set forth in the United States Copyright Act, provided there is a contemporaneously executed written contract that specifically designates such materials as a "work-for-hire." Where the material is a work-made-for-hire, the advertiser owns the materials and may deal with the rights as it sees fit.

  3. Assignments. Rights to materials that do not qualify as a "work-for-hire" may be obtained through an appropriate assignment. In such instances, the advertiser again owns all rights transferred and may generally exploit them without limitation, although in some instances there may be conditions on an assignment, e.g., royalties, territories, etc.

  4. Licenses. For most purposes, any one of the first three methods of obtaining ownership (i.e., works of employees, works-made-for-hire, or assignments) is more preferable to the advertiser than a license. Where such ownership is not available, however, the advertiser may have to rely upon a license. Under a license, ownership is not transferred and the advertiser obtains limited rights from the copyright owner to use the work for a limited period of time.

  It is not unusual to see a combination of all forms of ownership in a single project. Therefore, monitoring proper handling of ownership rights is critical to a project.

b. Printed media such as a book or magazine are comprised of text, illustrations, and photographs. These elements may be incorporated into an interactive product without a license if the work is in the "public domain" (i.e., a work for which the copyright term has expired worldwide). If the work is still subject to copyright protection, electronic media rights to each of these elements must be obtained from the publisher of the book or magazine. In some cases, the publisher may not have obtained the electronic media rights; the original author may have retained them. In other cases, the document by which the publisher acquired its rights may be silent or ambiguous on the subject (common in contracts drafted prior to the advent of electronic media), or contain specific limitations on the use of the work (such as prohibitions against unauthorized editing), or simply not permit further sublicensing. In all of these cases, the advertiser must negotiate with the copyright holder for a license to use the work in the multimedia product.

   c.   Motion Pictures. Use of a film clip presents similar problems. The owner of the copyright for the film may not have the right to license clips for use in a multimedia product because of rights retained by a screenwriter or the author of the original novel upon which the screenplay is based. Similarly, the composer and arranger of the score may have retained rights to the film score. Additionally, the use of clips containing the image or voice of union talent will usually necessitate payments of royalties and residuals to such talent, and pension fund payments to the appropriate union or guild.

   d.   Many states, including New York and California, provide statutory or common-law protection against the commercial exploitation of a person's name, image, or likeness without the consent of the person or his or her estate if such person is deceased. Some states even provide protection against the unauthorized use of another's voice. Indiana even protects expressions and mannerisms for 100 years following the death of a celebrity. Such consent and the associated license and fee arrangements are a necessary consideration, whether the work to be used in an interactive product involves public or private figures, and even where the copyright term for the work has expired.

   e.   The concept of *droit morale* originated in Europe and describes the right of a creative artist to protect the moral integrity of the original work. Moral rights are widely recognized abroad and appropriate caution must be exercised in situations where the laws of a foreign jurisdiction may be relevant. Such rights are occasionally being acknowledged in the United States. The debate over colorization is an example of the area, although colorization is only part of the issue, and a minor one at that. Federal law presently protects the integrity of famous fine art and sculptures but does not extend to other works.

At least two states (New York and California) have adopted statutes granting creative artists limited rights to approve alterations to works that fall within certain defined categories. Similar rights to approve alterations to a work are frequently granted by contract. Clauses precluding alteration of the original work may be found in the contract for the production of the work, the director's contract, or any applicable union contract.

Interactive multimedia projects may likely face similar challenges since the original work, once digitized for incorporation into a product, can be easily manipulated by either the producer or the end user. For this reason, waivers should be obtained from the holders of any contractual rights and from those who may assert any statutorily protected moral rights. In the absence of effective waivers (e.g., in a jurisdiction where statutorily protected rights may not be waived), indemnification should be obtained from the licensor as part of the license agreement.

   f.   A common misconception is that the party financing the development of a software program automatically owns the program. This is not always true. Ownership of programs and databases produced domestically are subject to U.S. copyright law. Whoever holds the copyright has exclusive rights to exploit the product, to grant others rights to exploit (i.e., duplicate, display, adapt, distribute, or otherwise use) the product, or to prevent others from exploiting the product. The copyright holder is the only one who can grant rights to develop the program for alternative operating systems (e.g., Macintosh or Windows), or specific platforms (e.g., CD-ROM). Under the work-for-hire doctrine discussed above, an advertiser automatically owns the copyright for works prepared by an employee within the scope of his or her employment. However, the work-for-hire doctrine also provides that the copyright for specially ordered or commissioned works prepared by persons other than true employees will be owned by the commissioning party only if the work falls within one of nine categories set forth in the Copyright Act (programs and databases generally fall within up to four of these categories) and there is a contemporaneous writing designating the work as one made for hire. This means that if there is no agreement, if the agreement is silent on the issue, or if the agreement is executed after the development is completed, the advertiser does not hold the copyright.

In many situations, the software developers and advertisers negotiate ownership over the program's screen displays or "end-user interfaces." If the program uses only visual design elements that create a "look and feel" unique to the advertiser's multimedia presentation, the advertiser has a strong interest in owning the copyright to the end-user interfaces. For programs that incorporate some elements standard to the developer's products, perpetual, irrevocable, royalty-free license to use, modify, and sublicense must be arranged. (Caution: the case law addressing the copyrightability of individual elements of the end-user interface is in a state of flux, and discussion is beyond the scope of this book.)

    g. A development agreement should include: (1) specifications and specific deliverables (e.g., source code need not be delivered unless provided by agreement); (2) a payment schedule triggered by delivery of the various software modules, the successful completion of beta testing, and the end of the warranty period; (3) a warranty that the program will perform in accordance with the functional specifications for a specified warranty period; (4) an indemnification for third-party claims against the sponsor that the program breaches their intellectual property rights; and (5) a delineation of marketing rights.

If the developer retains control of the source code, the advertiser will be entirely dependent on it for maintenance and enhancements to the interactive product. In such circumstances, a product-support agreement should be negotiated at the same time as the development agreement, and should include provisions that specify the extent to which the developer is obligated to attempt to correct any errors or limitations in the program and to provide telephonic or on-site services after the expiration of the warranty period.

Another problem inherent in development agreements is an arrangement that allows the developer to retain control of the source code. Without the source code, an advertiser is unable to correct defects in or enhance the program without the cooperation of the developer. In this situation the advertiser risks a potential loss in value of the multimedia product if the developer provides inadequate maintenance or goes out of business. A source-code escrow agreement typically provides for the release of the source code to the advertiser upon the developer's bankruptcy or failure to provide maintenance. In some situations, additional triggering events for the release of the source code may be negotiated, such as the breach of specific terms of the maintenance agreement.

2. Negotiating Contracts with Multimedia Producers

Multimedia producers, unlike advertising agencies, often ask for profit participation as part of their fee. This takes several forms, including a percentage of the sales price of a CD-ROM or of any products sold through an Internet site.

One consequence of growing specialization in this area is that it is incorrect to assume that a single producer can fulfill all roles in a production. A good deal of subcontracting can occur. For example, in the development of a home page on the Internet, one entity may be responsible for designing the initial site, another assigned the task of writing the software, and yet others given the responsibility for updating that site, converting text into a format that is compatible to operating software (e.g., HTML), providing a server, and/or paying for telephone lines (e.g., T-1s, between the server and the Internet, etc.). Whether such responsibilities lie with the original producer, the advertiser, the advertiser's agency, or another party should be clearly delineated.

Another problem is the ever-changing technology and the increasing desire to have better quality in images and higher speed in downloading or operating. For example, high volumes of information cannot be quickly transmitted over present telephone lines. Some designers have begun creating products that require both a CD-ROM disk and an online connection to improve speed.

Other general areas of concern include the following:

a. Interactive Product Description and Concept. Quite often, the parties are not clear what the product will look like or how it will work. It is important to remember that, unlike traditional advertising, multimedia products evolve during development as technological problems are overcome or avoided.

b. Production Schedules. Production schedules should be kept loose to anticipate technological problems and changes in the product. Don't expect to be able to produce a viable multimedia product or home page in a short time frame. Even allowing as much as six months may not be long enough.

c. Budgets. Expect budgets to change as the project progresses. Overages are common, and the advertiser must be certain to monitor costs closely throughout a project and to require that the contractor obtain the advertiser's written approval for every overage.

d. Creative Materials. Extant creative materials such as scripts, storyboards, photoboards, layouts, film, videotape, or packaging may require many changes in the process of creating digitized images. Some may be entirely unusable. Therefore, don't assume that producing a multimedia product will be less expensive because there are extant creative materials.

e. Source Code. The key to the operation of a software program is its "source code," essential software instructions buried deep in the program and often protected from independent alteration. Without it, a program cannot be modified or fixed if a bug should occur. It is therefore critical that the source code be available to the advertiser, either outright within the purchase price, or subject to disclosure if the producer fails to fulfill its obligations. Source-code escrow agreements are commonly used to ensure that the key information is available should the producer fail in its performance.

f. Hacker Protection. The development of any multimedia product should be sensitive to actions by potential hackers, who might invade the software and install a virus, sometimes also called a "time bomb," "Trojan horse," "worm," or "drop dead" device. The issue should be a matter of serious attention between the advertiser and developer until the advertiser is satisfied that its multimedia product is protected.

g. Audits. Audit rights are important in multimedia contracts, given the typical variations from budgets that can be expected as a project develops. In addition, if the producer is to receive any profit participation or royalty, the audit rights will be reciprocal; i.e., each party may audit the other.

CHAPTER VIII
Infomercials

1. Overview

Cable television and deregulation of the airwaves have created many changes in broadcasting. While the additional channels and new policies have opened up opportunities for networks, local programming, syndicators, cable operators, and home shopping, they have brought consumers controversial forms of marketing as well. These include infomercials, advertisements for products or services that, some critics say, deceptively take on the appearance of programming, but are, in fact, long-form commercials doing nothing more than selling a product. Indeed, early pioneers in the infomercial industry faced many state and federal regulatory actions, which alleged deception and misrepresentation. Despite the critics, however, infomercials are clearly legal. The industry has matured, and infomercials have become standard fare for viewers.

The major issues cited by regulators fall into three categories: (1) false or unsubstantiated product claims; (2) false or misleading endorsements or paid endorsements without adequate disclosure; and (3) misrepresentations as to the format of the infomercial, i.e., is it programming or a commercial?

In regard to (2), the FTC guidelines concerning the use of testimonials and endorsements outline how a consumer, expert or celebrity endorser, or spokesperson may be used in advertising. Although the guidelines do not have the force of law, they express how the FTC views these representations and should therefore be followed.

The most comprehensive guidance in this area, however, is gleaned from consent decrees entered into by the FTC and infomercial producers alleged to have engaged in deceptive practices in violation of Section 5 of the Federal Trade Commission Act. They typically contain the language and levels of substantiation the FTC requires of infomercial producers, which, in most cases, mirror general advertising law principles. For example, early infomercial consent decrees require that testimony offered by consumer endorsers be the "typical" experience that a user of the advertised product can expect. In addition, most infomercial consent decrees prohibit producers from claiming that any endorsement or testimonial represents the typical experience of those who have used the product unless the claim is substantiated or is accompanied by a prominent disclaimer.

FTC consent orders have included a wide range of penalties: e.g., (1) banning the offending infomercial from further broadcast; (2) barring a producer from making false or deceptive claims concerning a product; (3) prohibiting a producer from making efficacy claims concerning drug products unless supported by scientific or medical substantiation; (4) requiring disclosure that an infomercial is a paid commercial (usually noted by the phrase "The program you are watching is a paid advertisement for [the product or service]"); (5) providing funds for consumer refunds; (6) paying fines; and (7) mandating that all principals keep the FTC apprised of their business activities.

The penalties are heavy if mistakes are made. While the laws are technically no different for infomercials than they are for any other advertising activity, the penalties for violations seem more extreme, perhaps because the industry began with a few too many operators that skirted the rules.

Why It Matters

1. In January 2003, the FTC appealed the dismissal of an action against former baseball star Steve Garvey. Garvey was a codefendant in a case against infomercial producer Enforma. The FTC charged that claims for Enforma's products, "Fat Trapper" and "Exercise in a Bottle," were unsubstantiated and false. Enforma settled. Garvey, the star in Enforma's infomercials, however, refused to settle, arguing that he was nothing more than a celebrity spokesperson and could not be personally liable for the efficacy of the products. While a federal district court agreed with Garvey and dismissed the case, the Commission, by a 5-0 vote, authorized an appeal. While the outcome of the appeal will certainly be of interest to Garvey, the FTC position is more important as a indication of the Commission's intent to hold endorsers liable if circumstances, in the FTC's opinion, indicate that the celebrity was more than just a scripted shill. In Garvey's case, the FTC claimed Garvey was very active in the creation and production of the infomercial. Infomercial producers and celebrity performers are on notice that their relationship may create greater liability than has been the case in the past.

2. The FTC's enforcement activity in this area has not been limited only to televised infomercials. In January 1998, the FTC settled charges with eight marketers of self-help and health-related products promoted in radio as well as television infomercials. The FTC alleged that Kevin Trudeau and several other individuals who developed infomercials for various products under the name "A Closer Look" formatted the infomercials to appear to be radio and television entertainment programs or talk shows. The defendants paid a total of $1.1 million to settle the charges, and Trudeau was required to establish a $500,000 escrow account, which was to be used to repay consumers should he commit similar law violations in the future.

3. In December 1996, Natural Innovations, its president, Dr. William S. Gandee, and World Media TV, Inc., agreed to settle FTC charges stemming from the advertising and sale of the "Stimulator," a purported pain-relief device widely advertised in an infomercial titled "Saying No To Pain." The FTC alleged that the defendants did not have adequate substantiation for claims that the Stimulator could relieve virtually all types of pain and provide immediate, long-term pain relief superior to other forms of pain relief. The settlements require that the defendants have competent and reliable scientific evidence, including, in most cases, well-controlled clinical testing, to support pain relief and pain elimination claims in the future.

4. One of the most publicized settlements in the infomercial area involved a 1996 case against the manufacturer of NordicTrack exercise equipment. The FTC alleged that NordicTrack, Inc. had made false and unsubstantiated weight-loss and weight-maintenance claims in advertising for its cross-country-ski exercise machine. Specifically, the FTC charged NordicTrack for relying on flawed research to support its claims. The FTC asserted that the research relied upon by NordicTrack reflected only the experiences of a select population of purchasers who were able to integrate the product into their regular, weekly exercise regimen. Moreover, the FTC felt the studies did not take into consideration the participants' dietary habits and were based on consumers' own reports of changes in their weight. The settlement prohibits NordicTrack from misrepresenting future weight-loss study results and requires it to have competent and reliable evidence to substantiate weight loss, weight maintenance, and related claims for any exercise equipment it sells.

The industry has not been silent in the face of these government actions. To thwart further intrusion by the regulators, the industry adopted much-needed standards of conduct. The guidelines include or disclose the following:

a. A "paid advertisement" disclosure at the beginning of the infomercial and at each ordering opportunity

b. Disclosure of the name of the sponsor

c. No misrepresentations as to format, and no false claims, deception through omission, or indecent or offensive materials within the infomercial

d. Sufficient quantity of product to meet anticipated demand

e. A "reasonable basis" for all claims

f. All testimonials must be voluntary and honest and generally representative of average experience or otherwise disclosed

g. If offered, a copy of any warranty must be available prior to sale

2. The Talent Union's Role in the Production of Infomercials

The talent unions have promulgated a proposed code for talent appearing in infomercials. For an infomercial producer, becoming a signatory to such a code can have significant ramifications. Unquestionably, the most significant impact is that signatories must pay all talent, whether they are a union members or not, at least the minimum compensation established by the union plus a percentage of the union member's compensation to the pension and health funds of the unions. A signatory producer also becomes bound by a host of other rules governing production and editing.

While the union's present minimum fees are not excessive, they will in time grow and become as significant a factor in the production of infomercials as they are in commercials. The conclusion is inescapable—become a signatory to the unions' code at the last possible moment. Hold on to nonunion status as long as possible.

Many infomercials employ celebrity talent. In many instances, celebrities are paid a portion of the profits as well as minimum guarantees. A form celebrity contract for infomercials, with commentary, appears at the end of this chapter.

Chapter Eight Forms

Form I.8.1 Celebrity Contract for Infomercials (with commentary)

Introduction

Direct-response marketing includes any form of advertisement that solicits a product order or inquiry from the consumer. The order or inquiry may be placed by telephone or in writing. The half-hour television infomercial and short-form direct response commercial (:30, :60, and two minutes) are two of the better-known forms of direct response. Direct response, however, also includes home-shopping programming, the Internet, catalog, credit-card syndication, and direct-mail advertising. Ultimately, the "back end" of many direct response campaigns is retail distribution, both domestic and international, and many direct response campaigns are designed from the outset to drive retail sales.

Most direct-response celebrity-spokesperson agreements provide for a royalty to be paid to the celebrity based on the direct response marketing company's gross sales of the subject product. Although "net" deals are sometimes used, they are more often than not the exception. The royalty rate will depend upon the status of the particular celebrity and, generally speaking, may range from one percent to five percent of gross sales generated through television direct response, and possibly increased rates for nonbroadcast sales. It is also customary to provide the celebrity with either an annual guaranty (against which the royalties will be applied as a credit), or an annual minimum (which must be paid as a condition of renewing or extending the term of the agreement, but which need not be paid if the infomercial company elects to end the marketing after the initial term).

The following agreement sets forth standard provisions for engagement of a celebrity as an on-camera spokesperson for an infomercial product. Based upon the level of celebrity, it may be modified as suggested in the accompanying comments.

THIS AGREEMENT is made and entered into, and shall be effective as of, this [date], by and between [Infomercial Company] ("Company") and [Loan-Out Corporation] ("LOC"), relative to LOC furnishing the services of Artist ("Artist") as described herein below. In consideration of the mutual covenants and conditions as set forth herein below, the parties agree as follows:

1. Infomercial Production and Test:

A. Infomercial: Company hereby engages Artist and LOC agrees to provide the services of Artist as an on-camera spokesperson in one (1) thirty-minute infomercial and still photographs promoting a [description of product] (hereinafter referred to as the "Product Line").

Comment:

In some instances, the description of the product line may be lengthy. In such cases, either a separate paragraph may be inserted in the body of the agreement defining the product line, or an exhibit attached to the document listing the components thereof.

B. The rendition of Artist's services will be at such times and locations as the parties shall reasonably agree, subject to reasonable prior notice to Artist and Artist's prior professional commitments.

Comment:

Artist will request an outside date for the infomercial shoot, so that he/she will not be committed under the Agreement for an indefinite time period.

C. All services to be rendered by Artist will be in accordance with Company's reasonable instructions and under Company's control. LOC and Artist shall have approval over all product representations to be made by Artist in the infomercial and commercials, as well over all photographs and likenesses of Artist. In connection with the foregoing, LOC and Artist consent to the use of Artist's name, image, likeness, photograph, voice, and signature for such purpose. The parties agree that Artist's services are unique in character and, therefore, may not be delegated for any purposes under this Agreement.

Comment:

The approvals granted to the Artist will vary significantly from agreement to agreement, depending in part upon the status of the Artist, the Artist's role (if any) in developing the product line, and the extent to which the parties anticipate that the Artist will become closely associated in the public eye with the Product Line. Paragraph 16 of the Agreement provides that all rights of approval must be exercised in a reasonable manner. In some instances (e.g., where approvals will be extensive), it may be appropriate to set forth all approval rights in a separate paragraph. Celebrity talent will often ask for broad approval rights, including approval over the script, format, product extensions and improvements, selection of cohosts, and all uses of their name, image, likeness, photograph, voice, and signature. The reason for the breadth of requested approval rights has its genesis not just in the high failure rate of the infomercial and the desire to improve the odds, but also in the fact that, over the course of the twenty-eight-minute infomercial, there is plenty of room for errors and misstatements regarding product attributes, as well as for good, aggressive product promotion. In negotiating the approvals paragraph in the celebrity talent agreement, there always room for give and take, but there is usually one clear line which the talent will not be able to cross—and that is the line which separates the creative process, on the one hand, from strategic marketing decisions, on the other. Although there are exceptions, the general rule is that marketing decisions remain the bastion of the infomercial company, in large part because it is its money at risk.

D. Compensation: Company shall pay LOC, in consideration for the services of Artist as set forth hereinabove and the use of the results thereof, the sum of $_____ (the "Session Fee"), said sum to be credited against all union minimum payments due under this Agreement and to be paid upon completion of the shoot. Such payment shall be nonrefundable but recoupable against Royalties due LOC pursuant to Paragraph "2E," below. Company shall make or cause to be made payment of all sums required to be paid to the applicable pension, health, and welfare funds arising out of Artist's services referenced hereinabove. LOC agrees to pay any required income, employment, or other taxes relating to the compensation paid to LOC by Company hereunder and shall indemnify and hold Company harmless against the paying of any such taxes.

Comment:

Under the AFTRA infomercial agreement with producers, an on-camera performer or host is entitled to a minimum Session Fee for the first day of work (currently $957.45) and for a reduced fee for each additional day (currently $478.70). Payment of the Session Fee entitles the producer/ infomercial Company to air the infomercial on basic cable or broadcast television for a period of ninety (90) days. The producer may air the material for subsequent ninety (90)-day periods, provided that it pays to the performer a sum not less than the minimum Session Fee for each such subsequent period and for each media (cable or broadcast) in which the material airs. Notwithstanding the union minimums, it is not unusual for the Artist to receive a Session Fee which exceeds, and is credited against, the union minimum. The amount will depend upon the status of the Artist, as well as the other compensation provisions of the Agreement (Artist may, for example, forego a larger Session Fee in order to obtain a greater Royalty or Guarantee). Session Fees for major talent range from $25,000.00 to $100,000.00. In addition to the Session Fee, the producer must pay a sum to the appropriate union health and retirement fund equal to a percentage of the gross compensation paid to the Artist (e.g., 12.1% under the AFTRA agreement). Such contribution is payable only with respect to compensation paid for services covered by the applicable union agreement; no health and welfare contribution is payable with respect to royalties paid to the Artist. Because of the high failure rate and the necessity of a test phase in most infomercial projects, the majority of infomercial companies will not pay any guaranteed compensation to the talent (other than a session fee for the infomercial shoot) until completion of the infomercial test. As the test cannot be performed until after the infomercial has been produced, the result is that months may pass between the signing of the celebrity agreement and the completion of the test. On top of this, most celebrity agreements provide for some degree of exclusivity for the celebrity's services during the term of the agreement within a given product category and sometimes within defined media. If no guaranteed money is payable during this period, the argument is sometimes made that the infomercial company is getting the equivalent of a free option to utilize the celebrity (although this is not really the case, since the infomercial company is usually investing substantial monies in product acquisition as well as in the infomercial production and test). In order to address these concerns of the celebrity, infomercial companies usually agree to reasonable time constraints relative to their production of the infomercial, completion of their testing, and their election whether or not to proceed with a roll-out. In addition, they typically will agree to pay a nonrefundable advance upon roll-out, usually recoupable against the royalties otherwise payable to the celebrity. Once a roll-out has commenced, the financial concerns mentioned above are no longer a problem because of the guaranteed compensation and/or royalties which then go into effect.

E. Test: The infomercial will test, at the discretion of Company, on cable stations, network affiliates, and independent stations over a period not to exceed ninety (90) consecutive days in total.

Comment:

The failure rate of new infomercials and direct-response commercials is high, in large part because of the ever-increasing cost of media and the impact of such costs on profitability. Although statistics vary, media buyers will verify that the success rate for new infomercials is somewhere between 1 out of 10 and 1 out of 20; others will say the that true figure is closer to 1 out of 30. Whatever the figures, the risks are high.

Therefore, most infomercial companies will "test" a new infomercial on air prior to a full-scale roll-out of an infomercial campaign. The "test phase" will usually last for a period from thirty to ninety days (although many tests are completed in just one or two weekends of strategically placed advertising). The stakes are high because, by the time of the test, the infomercial company may have expended from $100,000 up to $500,000 for the infomercial production, and additional monies in product acquisition and development, with no assurance that the infomercial will pay out any additional compensation once aired. The foregoing risk and cost factors hold implications for the typical celebrity-talent deal. Some celebrities are reluctant to be involved at all with a high-risk venture such as infomercials. In the direct-response industry, there is usually a point at which an infomercial is determined to have tested successfully (so that a roll-out is merited), or to have tested poorly, in which case the project will be dropped, and the news—good or bad—gets published in the trades and otherwise discussed among industry insiders and outsiders. Further, the celebrity's concern with failure may be compounded by a concern of being associated with the infomercial industry and a perceived lack of credibility and integrity in the industry as a whole. Although the industry is a far cry from what it was at its inception, it still has a long way to go. Its attempts at self-regulation have been of moderate success, and the Federal Trade Commission has found fertile ground for its regulatory practices. Fortunately for the industry, a number of major celebrities have made appearances in infomercials, and, as a result, the "stigma" has diminished, but it is not altogether gone. In light of the foregoing, celebrity talent will sometimes request time and geographic restrictions in the testing of their infomercials. Certain markets—New York, Chicago, and Los Angeles— are sometimes excluded from the territory of permitted test airings, and testing during prime time may also be prohibited. Although additional restrictions may also be requested, they are usually not granted because of their potential impact on the reliability of the test results. Most infomercial companies consider their test protocol to be tantamount to a trade secret and, thus, they are reluctant to permit any third parties to dictate how the test should be conducted.

2. Marketing:

A. Option: Company will have the option, exercisable in writing following completion of the Test Phase, to elect to proceed with the marketing of the Product Line utilizing the infomercial, commercials, and/or still photography produced as referenced hereinabove, with Roll-Out to occur not later than _____. The phrase "Roll-Out" shall be defined as the first exhibition of the infomercial and/or commercials following completion of the Test Phase. It is specifically understood and agreed by and between the parties hereto that Company has the right not to proceed with such option, for any reason whatsoever or for no reason, and that neither party shall have any liability whatsoever to the other arising solely out of Company's election not to proceed.

Comment:

Company will want to have sole discretion over the decision whether to proceed with a roll-out of the infomercial, and talent is virtually never given any approval right over this decision. The decision to roll out is usually based on an analysis of the "cost per order" (CPO) generated during the infomercial test. The CPO is defined as the media dollars expended to generate one product order. In general (but subject to many exceptions based on the specific economic factors of each deal), if the cost per order exceeds 50 percent of the sales price of the product (e.g.: less than a 2-to-1 ratio of price to cost), the test results will be deemed unsuccessful and a roll-out will not occur without further testing and revision of the infomercial.

B. Term: The term of this Agreement shall commence upon execution hereof and shall, thereafter, run for a period of one year (the "Initial One Year Term") beginning on the date of a Roll-Out, if any, subject to renewal pursuant to Paragraph "___," below. The Agreement will terminate immediately at such time as Company elects not to proceed with a Roll-Out, and in such event there shall be no further use of the materials in any manner.

Comment:

The term is significant in that it defines the time period during which (i) the infomercial company is permitted to use the celebrity's endorsement, and (ii) the celebrity's services may be exclusive (if so negotiated). Infomercial company will want the right to terminate the agreement in the event that the test is unsuccessful.

C. Area of Use: The area of use for the advertising materials shall be the universe.

Comment:

The majority of agreements provide for a grant of worldwide rights. However, in some cases, the parties may agree to limit the area of use to domestic usage only (e.g.: the U.S. only, or the United States and Canada).

D. Consents and Responsibilities in the Event of a Roll-Out:

(1) In the event that Company exercises its option to proceed with a Roll-Out as referenced hereinabove, LOC and Artist consent to the use of Artist's name, image, likeness, photograph, voice, and signature in connection therewith for the duration of the Initial One Year Term and all Renewal Terms thereof. Such consent shall extend to all uses incident to Company's marketing of the Product Line, inclusive of infomercials, commercials, print advertisements (e.g.: advertisements in newspapers, magazines, catalogs and other periodicals; credit card inserts; and direct mail), product packaging and inserts, and sales literature, through any and all manner, media, and channels of distribution throughout the universe, including direct-response and retail distribution, and electronic/interactive media of all kinds, including the Internet. With respect to the foregoing uses, LOC and Artist shall have the same rights of approval as are set forth in Paragraph "1A," above.

(2) At the option and upon the request of Company, LOC will provide the services of Artist during the Initial One Year Term (and any Renewal Terms thereof), at specific dates, times, and places to be mutually agreed upon in good faith by the parties, taking into consideration Artist's other professional obligations, for the purpose of shooting additional footage to update the infomercial and/or commercials, including still photography, or for shooting footage for a new infomercial and/or commercials, including still photography (which new infomercial and/or commercials may be tested on air either prior to expiration of the then-current contract term or following renewal thereof). With respect to the foregoing services, LOC and Artist shall have the same rights of approval as are set forth in Paragraph "1A," above. In consideration for such services, Company will pay LOC the minimum session fee due in accordance with the applicable collective bargaining agreement.

Comment:

Typically, the infomercial company will request that the Artist render his or her services for several days during each one-year term in order to provide for updating of the infomercial footage or for shooting a new infomercial and for the testing of same prior to expiration of the current term (in order to decide whether to renew). Such services will entitle the Artist to payment of an additional session fee (either the union minimum or a negotiated overscale fee). The session fees typically remain level from year to year, the rationale being that the celebrity's upside will come from his or her royalty on sales.

E. Compensation:

(1) Royalty Payable to LOC: In the event of a Roll-Out, Company shall pay to LOC, for the Initial One Year Term of the Agreement and any Renewal Terms thereof, a royalty (the "Royalty") equal to _____ percent (__%) of the Gross Sales of the Product Line by Company (or by any Company Affiliate, successor, or assign). "Gross Sales" shall be defined as the total dollars paid from all sources to, and received by, Company (or by any Company Affiliate, successor, or assign) for the sale of the Product Line, less refunds or rebates to customers, shipping and handling charges, and sales and use taxes. "Affiliate" shall be defined as an entity that controls or is controlled by, is under common control with, or is related by at least majority common ownership with, a specified entity.

Comment:

Royalty rates are fully negotiable and depend upon the status of the Artist, the number of other celebrity endorsers involved, and the economics of the project. Most agreements now provide for a royalty calculated as a percentage of gross income, although net percentages were formerly used. Common royalty rates are between 2% and 2½% of gross sales. Where a product is marketed under the celebrity's name (e.g., Mr. A's Miracle Cream), the royalty may be as high as 5%.

---

(2) Payment Schedule: The foregoing royalty shall be due and payable on a quarterly basis within forty-five (45) days following the close of each calendar year quarter. Each payment shall be accompanied by a complete, detailed, and accurate statement of accounting, describing the quantity and description of products sold, gross receipts, and applicable deductions (subject to audit by LOC pursuant to Paragraph "5," below).

(3) Guarantee: In the event of a Roll-Out, Company hereby guarantees to LOC that the total amount paid to or on behalf of LOC for the Initial One Year Term (including any royalties earned in connection with the Test Phase) shall not be less than $_____. In addition, in the event of renewal(s) pursuant to Paragraph "3," below, Company guarantees that the total amount paid to or on behalf of LOC for each Renewal Term shall not be less than $_____. In the event that total payments made to LOC in connection with any Term or Renewal Term do not equal $_____, the balance of the Guarantee shall be paid within forty-five (45) days following the close of the calendar year quarter in which such Term or Renewal Term expires.

Comment:

In part because of the Artist's exclusivity to the infomercial company (as set forth in Paragraph "8" of the Agreement), he or she will insist on some form of guarantee. As with the other compensation provisions, the amount of the guarantee depends, in part, on the stature of the Artist and the economics of the project. In addition, the amount may depend upon the level of exclusivity agreed to by the parties.

(4) Crediting of Payments: All compensation as referenced above shall be credited against any and all union minimum payments due under this Agreement (excluding pension, health, and welfare fund contributions). LOC agrees to pay any required income, employment, or other taxes relating to the compensation paid to LOC by Company hereunder, and shall indemnify and hold Company harmless against the paying of any such sums.

3. Renewal:

COMPANY shall have the sole right to renew this Agreement for three (3) successive one-year terms upon the same terms and conditions, exercisable in writing not less than thirty (30) days prior to the expiration of the then-current contract term.

Comment:

The infomercial company will want the right to renew or extend the term of the agreement for a substantial period of time. An initial one-year term and the right to extend for three additional one-year terms is not unusual. The artist, on the other hand, may not want to grant consent to the use of his or her endorsement for an extended period, and may not want to be bound to the exclusivity provision of the agreement for an extended period. As media costs rise and it becomes increasingly necessary to look to back-end marketing for profitability, infomercial companies will insist on liberal renewal rights.

4. Indemnity/Insurance:

A. LOC and Artist warrant and represent that they have the right to enter into this Agreement and to grant the rights as set forth hereinabove; that there are no contractual obligations preventing the fulfillment of this Agreement, or materially impairing or diminishing the value of the rights granted hereunder; that they will not make any agreements, commitments, or arrangements whatsoever with any person or entity that may, in any manner or to any extent, affect the rights of Company under this Agreement; and that they have not, and will not, either themselves or by granting authority to any other person or entity, exercise any right or take any action which directly derogates, impairs, or competes with the rights granted to Company hereunder, or directly derogates the names or reputations of Company, the Product Line, or any of the officers, directors, or shareholders of Company.

Comment:

Counsel will want to make sure that Artist's other contractual obligations or commitments do not interfere with his or her ability to render services under the Agreement. Failure to do so could result in the infomercial company having to defend against an application for temporary restraining order seeking to bar airing of the infomercial (after having invested hundreds of thousands of dollars in product development and production of the infomercial).

B. LOC and Artist agree to defend, indemnify, and hold Company harmless from and against any and all losses, costs, damages, charges, claims, legal fees, recoveries, judgments, penalties, and/or reasonable expenses which may be obtained against, imposed upon, or suffered by Company by reason of any breach of any representation, warranty, or agreements made by LOC and/or Artist under this Agreement.

Comment:

Also, the infomercial company may have valid concerns that the celebrity may make comments at a later date (e.g., in interviews on television or in the print media) which reflect negatively on the product, the infomercial, the infomercial company, or the industry as a whole. Therefore, it may be wise to include restrictions on such conduct in the Agreement

C. Company warrants and represents that it has the right to enter into this Agreement and to grant the rights as set forth hereinabove. Company warrants and represents that it is an AFTRA and SAG signatory. Company will defend, indemnify, and hold LOC and Artist harmless from and against any and all losses, costs, damages, charges, claims, legal fees, recoveries, judgments, penalties, and/or reasonable expenses which may be obtained against, imposed upon, or suffered by LOC or Artist by reason of the use or content of the advertising materials produced hereunder or the Product Line advertised therein. During the term of this Agreement and each Renewal Term thereof, Company shall include LOC and Artist as additional named insureds under Company's product and general liability insurance policies and shall provide LOC and Artist, upon request, with certificates of insurance evidencing such coverage.

Comment:

The Artist will want the infomercial company to assume the burden of maintaining adequate insurance coverage relative to the advertisements and the product line.

5. Right to Audit:

Company shall maintain complete and accurate books of account and records relating to all Gross Sales of the Product Line. LOC and Artist shall have the right, upon reasonable written notice during the Term, to inspect, or have their designated representatives inspect and make copies of, all such records relating to such sales and payments. Such inspections shall take place during Company's normal working hours at the offices of Company. Such inspections shall be performed at the expense of LOC and Artist; provided, however, that should any inspection disclose monies owed by Company to LOC and Artist in an amount equal to three percent (3%) or more of the proper contract rate of compensation, the reasonable accounting fees incurred in such inspection shall be paid by Company.

Comment:

As most celebrity compensation is based on gross revenues and not net income, the issues which arise in audits are fewer in number and usually easier to resolve than in agreements that depend upon net profit distributions. As a result, the infomercial company will desire to restrict access for audit purposes to documentation relating to the components of Gross Sales as defined in the Agreement (as opposed to documents disclosing project costs and profitability), and the Artist will usually agree with this approach.

6. Successors and Assigns:

    Subject to the restrictions on delegation of duties contained elsewhere in this Agreement, this Agreement shall be binding upon and inure to the benefit of the parties hereto and their respective executors, administrators, heirs, successors, and assigns, as the case may be.

7. Exclusivity:

    For the duration of this Agreement and any renewal(s) thereof, neither LOC nor Artist shall develop, manufacture, endorse, or market, or appear in any infomercial, commercial, or print advertisement for the purpose of endorsing or marketing, any other _____. In addition, commencing upon execution of this Agreement and continuing thereafter for a period of one year following a Roll-Out under Paragraph "2A," neither LOC nor Artist shall in any way participate or appear in any other infomercial, regardless of the product or service being advertised therein. This provision shall not preclude Artist from appearing in the entertainment, news, or information portion of any radio, television, motion picture, or other entertainment program, including live performances, regardless of sponsorship.

Comment:

Exclusivity is typically one of the most negotiated provisions of the Agreement. From the Artist's perspective, he or she does not want to be unfairly prohibited from accepting other work. From the infomercial company's perspective, acceptance of other work competitive with the product endorsement may dilute its effectiveness. Further, the appearance of the Artist in other (even noncompetitive) infomercials may diminish the effectiveness of the endorsement. Typically, the Artist agrees at a minimum not to endorse any other product in the same product category (in all forms of advertising) for the duration of the Term. If the guaranteed compensation to the Artist is substantial, complete exclusivity for all direct-response advertising may be negotiated.

8. Attorneys' Fees:

    In the event that any legal action is commenced to enforce any term of this Agreement or to seek recovery for any breach thereof, the prevailing party in such action shall be entitled to recovery of its reasonable attorneys' fees and actual costs incurred in such action.

9. Controlling Law:

    This Agreement shall be governed by and construed in accordance with the laws of the State of _____. The parties agree and consent that jurisdiction and venue of all matters relating to this Agreement will be vested exclusively in the federal, state, and local courts within the State of _____ unless otherwise superseded by the arbitration provisions contained in any applicable collective bargaining agreement to which the parties are signatories. The prevailing party in any action arising out of this Agreement shall be entitled to an award of its reasonable attorneys' fees and actual costs incurred therein.

Comment:

With respect to guild productions, the AFTRA and SAG infomercial agreements each provide for mandatory arbitration of disputes between producer and talent.

10. Entire Agreement:

This Agreement contains the entire agreement of the parties and supersedes any prior agreements, understandings, and memoranda relating thereto. This Agreement may not be changed, altered, or modified in any way except in writing signed by the parties hereto.

11. Severability:

If any clause or provision of this Agreement shall be adjudged to be invalid or unenforceable by the arbitrator(s) selected or appointed to hear any controversy arising hereunder, or by operation of any applicable law, such adjudication shall not affect the validity of any other clause or provision, which shall remain in full force and effect.

12. Consent in the Event of Death:

The parties agree that, in the event of Artist's death during the contract term or any renewal(s) thereof, Company shall have the option to continue marketing the Product Line utilizing Artist's name, image, likeness, photograph, voice, and signature in connection therewith, for the duration of the contract term and any renewal(s) thereof, under the same terms and conditions as set forth in this Agreement. In the event that Company shall instead elect to terminate such marketing, Company shall pay to LOC the royalty as provided in Paragraph "2E(1)," above, through date of termination (including post-termination sales that are generated by use of the materials), and the Guarantee provided in Paragraph "2E(3)" shall be prorated to date of termination.

Comment:

Although an infrequent occurrence, the death of a spokesperson raises the issue of whether his or her endorsement can continue to be used. This can usually be resolved by the granting of such consent in the Agreement, so as to avoid the uncertainty (and delays) of requesting consent from the heirs or other authorized persons following date of death. Even when the parties anticipate no airing of the infomercial in the event of death, there may still be inventory of the product, which needs to be disposed of, as well as spots for the infomercial already purchased. Absent advance consent, the infomercial company may have no right to continue utilizing the endorsement in any capacity. With regard to proration of the Guarantee in the event of death, this seems to be a common method for handling the issue fairly.

13. Ownership of Product Line and Advertising Materials:

The Product Line and all advertising materials produced hereunder will be and remain the absolute property of Company forever, including, but not limited to, all intellectual property interests therein. LOC and Artist acknowledge that they have no right, title, or interest in or to same, and hereby assign all rights to the Product Line and advertising materials to Company. Notwithstanding the foregoing, it is agreed that, except as otherwise permitted herein, Company may not use Artist's name, image, likeness, photograph, voice, signature, or reputation after the termination or expiration of this Agreement.

Comment:

Infomercial Company may want to request a sell-off period after expiration of the term in order to dispose of inventory containing the endorsement of Artist.

14. Independent Contractor:

It is understood and agreed that LOC's relationship to Company is that of an independent contractor, and nothing contained in this Agreement shall be construed to create any partnership, joint venture, principal/agent relationship, or any other fiduciary relationship between the parties hereto. The parties expressly disclaim the existence of any third-party beneficiaries to this Agreement.

15. Approvals:

All rights of approval and/or consent provided under the terms of this Agreement shall be exercised in a fair and reasonable manner, with no such approval or consent being unreasonably withheld. In all instances where the right of consent or approval is provided, same shall be deemed to have been given in the absence of written disapproval of the subject material within five (5) business days following LOC's receipt of a written request for approval.

16. Confidentiality:

The parties acknowledge that the terms and provisions of this Agreement, and any disputes arising thereunder, are confidential in nature and, therefore, agree not to disclose the content or substance thereof to any third parties (not affiliated by common ownership, employment, or other form of agency relationship), other than the parties' respective attorneys and accountants or as may be reasonably required in order to comply with (i) any obligations imposed by the Agreement, or (ii) any statute, ordinance, rule, regulation, other law, or court order.

17. Notices:

A. Service of all notices under this Agreement will be sufficient if given personally, mailed, or telefaxed to the following addresses: [fill in]

B. Any notice shall be deemed to have been given on the day it is mailed or telefaxed or, if delivered in person by hand, on the day it is delivered.

18. Applicable Union Agreements:

This Agreement is subject to all of the terms and conditions of the representative contracts of the union(s) having jurisdiction over the services covered by this Agreement, except as same may be, and are hereby, superseded, amended, or supplemented.

Comment:

AFTRA has jurisdiction over services provided in connection with infomercials recorded on videotape or by any other means except recordation by motion picture film photography.

IN WITNESS WHEREOF, the parties have set their respective signatures hereto on the day and date as first above appears.

[Infomercial Company]   [Loan-Out Corporation]

By: _____   By: _____

CHAPTER IX
Home Shopping

1. Overview

Home shopping is an area that deserves particular attention as it continues to expand. With home shopping, there is no sales agent in a home. There is no product to pick up and touch. There is no competitive product to compare. One might say that this is really no different than mail order, but in truth the difference is like night and day. Consumers can be motivated and manipulated by a television program with far greater ease and impact than by any mail-order catalog. In addition, the audience is far more susceptible, with a diverse composition of children, the elderly, and the housebound. It's like the worst of the door-to-door salesmen, only this time they don't even knock. How is the quality of products sold on home shopping channels controlled? What protection should the consumer have to return goods? Should return policies be freely dictated by the home shopping network, as they are presently by retailers at shopping malls? Is the pricing on a home shopping network really better, as is often claimed? What must the network do to substantiate a price claim? After all, its market is the entire United States. How can it possibly know if its price superiority is true everywhere? What is the manufacturer's liability? And what about guarantees and warranties? In the past, the consumer could get a copy of a guarantee or warranty at retail before purchase, or read it in a catalog. Now what?

2. Agreements with Home Shopping Broadcasters

Understanding the important elements in an agreement with a home shopping broadcaster may mean the difference in failure or success in bringing a product to the attention of the viewer.

In dealing with a home shopping network, consider the following issues and how they impact on any offer.

    a.   Type of show: e.g., a show with multiple products by the same advertiser or a show where products by multiple advertisers are featured. If the former, involvement with the channel and how the product or service is sold will be far greater than if the advertiser's product is one of many offered in a segment.

    b.   How is price determined and who is responsible for purchase processing, delivery of the goods, and returns, if any? If goods are on consignment, the advertiser has a greater risk, since it will only receive revenues from products actually sold. On the other hand, if the channel is responsible for a minimum inventory, it will have the right to control pricing and other key elements of the marketing of the product on the channel.

    c.   What exclusivity is available, i.e., what other competitive products will the channel sell and in what time slots? If exclusivity is granted, how long does it run after the last segment offering the advertiser's product is broadcast? It may make a big difference if a competitor comes on in a half hour as opposed to the next day.

    d.   While all major channels currently handle fulfillment, be certain that tight controls are in place to comply with FTC and other laws and regulations relating to purchases by mail.

e. Who owns the customer databases and lists that will be generated? This is often one of the most valuable products of an offer. While the advertiser naturally has a right to know the names of its customers, can the channel do anything independently with the list? What about other data learned about the customer?

f. For longer programs, the advertiser may be asked to contribute to advertising the channel or the program in which its product is featured. If so, what will the advertiser receive in return? Are other vendors being asked for similar support? What assurances does the advertiser have that the money will be spent on advertising? What will be the content of the advertising?

g. The choice of time slot can be critical. Targeted markets and demographics should dictate the slot. This is particularly important since channels measure success by dollars-per-hour sales.

h. Will the channel's host offer the product, or will the advertiser use a celebrity spokesperson? If a celebrity is involved, a separate agreement needs to be negotiated. While such agreements are similar to endorsement contracts used in more traditional forms of advertising, e.g., television commercials, some provisions are unique. For example, it is not unusual for the celebrity to receive a percentage of sales.

Any final agreement with a channel or a celebrity requires consideration of many more provisions, e.g., territory, term, renewals, back-end residuals, etc. Given the fast-evolving nature of distribution via home shopping networks, standard forms are to be avoided. Each deal should be reviewed on its own merits.

CHAPTER X
Telemarketing

Disclaimer:

After this edition went to press, the Federal Trade Commission's Do Not Call Registry was activated. Before engaging in any telemarketing, it is important to review the FTC rules regarding the Registry and its operations. See http://www.ftc.gov and htpp://www.donotcal.gov for more details.

---

1. Federal Laws

a. The Telephone Consumer Protection Act

The Telephone Consumer Protection Act of 1991 (TCPA) and rules issued by the Federal Communications Commission under TCPA regulate marketing activities where the promoter initiates the call to the consumer.

In general, the TCPA divides telemarketers into two categories—those who use "automatic telephone dialing systems" or artificial or prerecorded voices, and telemarketers who use live operators for their calls. An automatic telephone dialing system is defined by the FCC as equipment that "has the capacity to store or produce telephone numbers to be called using a random or sequential number generator and to dial such number."

Under the TCPA it is unlawful to make any call with an automatic telephone dialing system to (1) an emergency telephone line, (2) the room of a hospital, elderly home, or similar institution, or (3) a paging, cellular, or similar telephone system where the recipient is charged for the call. The law also prohibits such a call to a residential telephone line unless the call is initiated for "emergency purposes" or is exempt by FCC rules.

Under FCC rules, a telephonic solicitation to a residential subscriber, regardless of how it is initiated, is subject to the following disclosure requirements and limitations:

1. At the beginning of the call, the telemarketer must state his or her name, the name of the entity on whose behalf the call is being made, and the telephone number or address of the telemarketer.

2. Calls are not allowed prior to 8 a.m. or after 9 p.m. (local time of called party). Some states have stricter limitations.

3. The caller must maintain a list of consumers who do not wish to receive calls from the telemarketer. The telemarketer must (1) adopt a written policy on how "don't call" requests are handled by its employees, (2) train its employees on the existence and use of the no-call list, (3) add "do-not-call" requests to its no-call list as appropriate, and (4) desist from calling any consumers on its no-call list in future solicitations. "Do-not-call" requests apply only to the entity or person making the call (or on whose behalf the call is being made) and not to any of its affiliates, unless the consumer "reasonably would expect them to be included given the identification of the caller and the product being advertised."

FCC rules allow the following non-emergency calls to residential telephone lines using an automatic telephone dialing system (providing that at the beginning of such an AutoDial call, the message must state the identity of the entity initiating the call and the telephone number or address of such entity):

4.   Calls made with the express prior consent of the party called

5.   Calls not made for a commercial purpose

6.   Calls made for a commercial purpose, but that do not include the transmission of an "unsolicited advertisement" (defined as "any material advertising the commercial availability or quality of any property, goods, or services which is transmitted to any person without that person's prior express invitation or permission")

7.   Calls made for a commercial purpose to a person with whom the caller has an established business relationship at the time the call is made

8.   Calls made for a commercial purpose by a tax-exempt nonprofit organization

The TCPA also prohibits using telephone facsimile machines to send unsolicited advertisements to either residences or businesses.

b. Telemarketing and Consumer Fraud and Abuse Prevention Act

Under the Telemarketing and Consumer Fraud and Abuse Prevention Act, the Federal Trade Commission has issued the Telemarketing Sales Rule, a comprehensive set of rules designed to regulate abusive and deceptive telemarketing practices. The Telemarketing Sales Rule was amended by the FTC in early 2003, and the revised Rule went into effect on March 31, 2003.

The primary forms of direct-response activity subject to the rule are outbound calls and "upsells"—sales solicitations that take place in an inbound or outbound telephone call after the initial transaction with the consumer. Some of the major highlights of the amended rule are:

1.   Mandatory Disclosures. Telemarketers have to disclose promptly the identity of the seller, the purpose of the call, and the nature of the goods or services being offered. They must also clearly and conspicuously disclose, prior to obtaining the consumer's billing information: the total costs of goods or services; all material restrictions or conditions on the purchase or use of the products and services; the terms and conditions of any refund, exchange, or cancellation policy mentioned in the offer; and the fact that the sale is final, if such the case.

2.   Prize Promotions. If any prize promotion is involved, the telemarketer must disclose the fact that no purchase is necessary to enter, and give instructions on how to enter for free or an address or local toll-free telephone number to which customers may write or call to find out how to participate for free. The odds of winning must be told. These disclosures apply to both inbound and outbound calls and can be made either in writing prior to the call or during the course of the call. Under the timing requirement imposed by the rule, these disclosures must be made before a customer pays for the goods or services offered.

3.   "Negative Option" Offers. For telephone offers which include a "negative option" feature—i.e., where the consumer's silence or failure to take an affirmative action to reject goods or services or to cancel the agreement is interpreted by the seller as an acceptance of the offer—the telemarketer, prior to obtaining the

consumer's consent to be charged, must disclose the fact that the consumer's account will be charged unless he or she takes some affirmative action to avoid the charge(s), as well as disclose the date(s) the charge(s) will be submitted for payment and the specific steps the customer must take to avoid the charges. Typical negative-option offers include continuity programs, and free-to-pay conversion, automatic renewal, and continuous service offers.

4. Prohibited Misrepresentations. The rule contains broad prohibitions against misrepresentations regarding any of the information that is required to be disclosed under the rule or regarding any aspect of the performance, nature, or characteristics of the goods and services.

5. Consumer Consent to the Transaction. A consumer's express informed consent to be charged is required for all telemarketing transactions, and a seller may not cause billing information to be submitted for payment unless the consumer has been provided with all of the disclosures required under the rule and has affirmatively and unambiguously given his or her consent to be charged. If the transaction involves the use of "preacquired account information"—i.e., the account number or other billing information to be used is not obtained directly from the consumer during the call and in connection with the particular telemarketing offer—the telemarketer must identify the account to be charged with sufficient specificity for the customer to understand what account will be charged, and obtain from the customer his or her express agreement to be charged and to be charged using the identified account number. If the transaction involves both the use of preacquired account information and a "free-to-pay conversion" offer—one in which the customer receives a good or service for free for an initial period and will incur an obligation to pay for the good or service if he or she does not take an affirmative action to cancel before the end of the free trial period—the telemarketer must obtain the last 4 digits of the account number to be charged from the customer, obtain the customer's express agreement to be charged and to be charged using this account number; and make and maintain an audio recording of the entire telemarketing transaction.

6. Novel Payment Methods. The customer's express verifiable authorization is required for all telemarketing transactions in which payment is made by a method other than a credit or debit card. This can be satisfied either in writing, or orally during the call if the call is taped and during the call disclosure is made of the number and amount of payments or charges, the date(s) these charges will be submitted for payment, a telephone number for customer inquiries, the vendor's name and billing information, and the date of the oral authorization. A written confirmation of the transaction, which contains all of these same disclosures and a statement of the procedures by which the customer can obtain a refund, may also be used to satisfy this express verifiable authorization requirement for all transactions except those involving preacquired account information and a free-to-pay conversion offer.

7. Aiding and Abetting. Under the rule, a person can be held liable for having provided substantial assistance to a telemarketer found to be in violation of the rule if the person knows or consciously avoids knowing that the seller or telemarketer is engaged in any act or practice that violated the rule. To the extent that infomercial production companies, fulfillment agencies, credit card processors, and the like are providing support services to telemarketers, this provision is of key importance.

8. Calling Restrictions. The rule prohibits placing calls before 8 a.m. or after 9 p.m. or placing calls to anyone who has indicated they do not want to be called.

9. National Do-Not-Call Registry. A national do-not-call list containing the telephone numbers of con-

sumers who do not wish to receive outbound telemarketing calls will be maintained and administered by the FTC. Beginning in October 2003, telemarketers will be required to obtain a copy of the national do-not-call list and to refrain from placing telemarketing calls to any telephone numbers appearing on the list. There are exceptions, however, for calls from sellers that the consumer has authorized in writing to place telemarketing calls, as well as for calls from sellers with which the consumer has an established business relationship. In addition, there is a "safe harbor" for inadvertent calls to a number on the national do-not-call registry. A seller will not be liable for violating the do-not-call provision of the new TSR, provided that the company has established and implemented written procedures to comply with the do-not-call requirements, has trained its personnel to comply with these procedures and monitors and enforces compliance, uses a process to prevent calls to names on the national do-not-call list using a version of the list less than three months old and maintains records documenting this process, and that any subsequent call made to a consumer appearing on the do-not-call list is the result of error.

10. Caller ID. Beginning January 30, 2004, telemarketers will be required to transmit their telephone number and, where made available by the telephone carrier, name to any caller ID service in use by the consumer being called.

11. Abandoned Calls. Telemarketers are prohibited from abandoning any outbound call—which is defined as failing to connect the call to an operator within two seconds of the consumer's completed greeting when answering the call. There is a safe harbor, however, which provides that the telemarketer will not be liable for the placement of an abandoned call—provided it uses predictive dialer technology that ensures no more than a three-percent abandonment rate on a per-day, per-campaign basis, allows the phone to ring at least 15 seconds or 4 rings before hanging up, and retains records establishing its compliance with these requirements. Beginning in October 2003, the telemarketer will also be required to play a recorded message that states the seller's name and telephone number whenever an operator is not available to speak to the person answering the call within 2 seconds after the person's completed greeting.

12. Transfer of Unencrypted Account Information. Sellers and telemarketers may not disclose or receive, for payment or other consideration, a consumer's unencrypted (i.e., complete) account information for use in telemarketing, other than to process a payment for goods or services in connection with the particular telemarketing transaction at issue.

13. Recordkeeping. Telemarketers must maintain various records for a period of two years, including customer names and addresses, records of goods and services purchased, and the names of employees involved in telephone sales.

14. Enforcement Authority. The rule is enforceable not only by the FTC but also by the 50 state Attorneys General. Violations of the rule may result in civil penalties of up to $10,000 per violation.

There are, however, exemptions to the Telemarketing Sales Rule. The Rule contains a blanket exemption for television and other mass-media forms of advertising, unless the advertising is for an investment opportunity or credit repair service. Accordingly, infomercials are generally exempt from the rule entirely. Marketers should also note that calls initiated in response to receipt of a catalog are exempt as long as the seller does not attempt during the course of a call to resolicit the customer to purchase an item not contained in the catalog. Calls made in response to direct mail solicitations are exempt to the extent that the material terms and conditions of the offer are disclosed in the direct mail piece. The rule also exempts calls in which the transaction is completed only after a face-to-face meeting, and business-to-business calls (except those involving the sale of office or cleaning supplies).

Why It Matters

The FTC has been extremely vigilant in its enforcement of the Telemarketing Sales Rule.

1. In April 1997, the FTC announced the results of "Operation False Alarm," which addressed "badge-related" fundraising telemarketing fraud. The initiative, which involved the FTC, 50 state attorneys general, secretaries of state, and other state charities regulators, targeted the deceptive activities of for-profit fundraisers who misrepresented ties with police departments, firefighters, and other community organizations. One defendant, Southwest Marketing Concepts, Inc., d/b/a *The Journal— The Voice of Law Enforcement*, and its principal, Stephen Inmon, agreed to settle the FTC's charges that they misrepresented, to businesses solicited by phone and mail in almost every state, their affiliation with law enforcement, and that advertising in *The Journal* was a meaningful way for businesses to support important causes such as fighting crime or preventing drug abuse. The settlement prohibits the defendants from making similar representations in the future, and required payment of a $40,000 monetary judgment.

2. The Telemarketing Sales Rule also prohibits a telemarketer who guarantees consumers a loan or other form of credit, or who claims he or she can arrange such credit for a consumer, from asking consumers to pay any money before they receive the loan or credit. In January 1998, the FTC, the state attorneys general of Illinois and Missouri, and the Idaho Department of Finance announced a coordinated action against 37 telemarketing firms and individuals who allegedly engaged in these activities, commonly referred to as "advance-fee loan scams." The initiative also involved Canadian law enforcement authorities. According to the complaints filed in these actions, the targets of these scams included U.S. military personnel and senior citizens.

c. **Mail and Telephone Order Rule**

Telemarketers are also subject to the Federal Trade Commission's Mail and Telephone Order Rule. When originally adopted in 1975, the rule applied only to mail order and was largely in response to growing complaints regarding delays in shipment by direct-mail marketers. Similar complaints against telemarketers prompted the FTC's decision to expand the scope of the rule to include telephonic sales.

The critical issue is time needed to ship the merchandise ordered. Here, telemarketers should be very conservative, allowing extra time in delivery to cover the many unpredictable events that can occur in the marketplace. If a telemarketer fails to provide itself enough time, it will find compliance with the rule costly. Worse yet, if the telemarketer fails to specify a time of delivery, it must ship the goods within thirty days.

If a shipping date longer than thirty days is desired by the telemarketer, the longer period must be disclosed to the consumer in a "clear and conspicuous" manner. In other words, it must be prominent and cannot be buried in disclaimers. In addition, the telemarketer must have a reasonable basis for believing that shipment will be made within the time period stated.

Depending upon the method of payment, the "clock" on the time period before shipment must be made varies. If payment is by check, cash, or money order, the clock begins to run from the date payment is received by the telemarketer. If the payment is by credit card, the clock begins to run from the date the credit information is given to the seller, irrespective of when the buyer's account is actually debited.

If there is any delay in the promised shipment date, the telemarketer must provide notice of the delay to the consumer and give a new shipment date. If the original shipment was promised in less than thirty days, the telemarketer can require that the consumer notify the telemarketer if he or she wants to cancel and not accept a new delivery date. Otherwise, it is presumed that the new date is acceptable. On the other hand, if the original shipment date was more than thirty days (as is usually the case), the telemarketer must presume that the consumer does not accept and must cancel the order unless the telemarketer receives an affirmation of the consumer's consent to the new date. If an order is canceled, a refund must be issued within seven (7) days, including shipping and handling charges.

Why It Matters

1. Telebrands Corporation and its principal, Ajit Khubani, were charged in 1996 with failing to comply with the Mail Order Rule by not notifying consumers that there would be a delay in shipping their orders and by failing to deem an order canceled and make a prompt refund where the company failed to ship the order. The FTC noted that this was the second time Khubani had violated the Mail Order Rule, the first time as the owner of a Virginia mail-order company called Direct Marketing of Virginia. Telebrands and Khubani agreed to pay a $95,000 civil penalty.

2. In December 1996, Mattel, Inc. agreed to settle FTC charges that it failed to make timely deliveries or prompt refunds in connection with the sale of its Barbie collectible dolls. The FTC alleged that, beginning in 1994, after having received orders for the dolls by mail or by telephone, Mattel failed to ship the dolls to buyers within the Rule's applicable time. Mattel agreed to refrain from violating, directly or through any corporation or fulfillment house, any provision of the Rule in the future, and to pay a civil penalty of $146,186.

3. In May 1998, Dell Computer Corporation paid $800,000 for its alleged violations of the Rule. The FTC alleged that Dell violated the Rule when it advertised and sold computer systems bundled with a suite of third-party software that was not ready to be shipped. Instead of offering buyers the option to cancel their order until the suite was ready and loaded on the machines, Dell shipped the computers with a coupon redeemable for the suite when it became available. The FTC charged that Dell failed to notify buyers that the computers were not ready to be shipped as advertised, and failed to offer to cancel their orders if they did not want their computer without the suite.

d. Telemarketing and the Federal Trade Commission's "Dandelion" Theory

One of the most powerful tools that the Federal Trade Commission has in actions regarding telemarketing is the "dandelion theory." The name reflects the FTC's authority to go after not only the fraudulent operators but also companies and individuals that provide services that aid and abet the fraudulent operation. In 1994, Christian S. White, then acting director of the FTC's Bureau of Consumer Protection, described why the FTC favors the theory. White testified before a Congressional Committee that by using the approach, the FTC "has [not only] been able to reach those entities that distance themselves from the deceptive consumer transaction but [those persons] whose behind-the-scene participation is essential to its success." While the FTC can use the theory in any case, in recent years it has most often been used against fraudulent telemarketing activities.

Why It Matters

1. In a case against Pioneer Enterprises, a telemarketer for itself and others, the FTC alleged that Pioneer ran fraudulent schemes promoting the sale of a variety of products and fraudulent schemes for other telemarketers. In settling with the FTC, Pioneer agreed to cease certain activities and to disclose information to consumers in all its future telemarketing activities. It also agreed to pay $1.5 million in consumer redress. Those aspects of the case, however, are only half the story.

   Pioneer must also monitor its employees' compliance with disclosure requirements contained in the settlement and must fire any employees who violates the provisions three times within any 18-month period. As to other telemarketers for whom Pioneer provides services, Pioneer is required to (a) investigate the nature of products offered by the other telemarketer, (b) verify the accuracy of any claims made for the products, (c) obtain written agreement from the telemarketer to comply with Pioneer's consent decree, and (d) monitor the telemarketers' compliance. In order to assist the FTC in monitoring Pioneer's compliance, Pioneer is required to seed its customer lists, including those sold or rented to others, with names provided by the FTC.

2. The FTC used the dandelion theory against CitiCorp Financial Services. In the Citicorp case, the FTC charged that CitiCorp aided and abetted Credit Card Travel Services Inc., in a deceptive telemarketing scheme for Credit Card Travel's Bankcard Travel Club. The FTC alleged that CitiCorp continued to process credit card sales for a period of four years despite excessive consumer requests that authorized charges not be paid to Credit Card Travel (known as "chargebacks"). In so doing, the FTC charged that CitiCorp knew or should have known that the telemarketer's program was fraudulent. Credit Card Travel Services Inc. paid $2 million to settle the charges brought by the FTC. In its settlement with the FTC, CitiCorp agreed to investigate merchants with high chargeback rates and to terminate relationships with those CitiCorp merchants found to be engaged in fraudulent or deceptive schemes.

3. In 1994, the FTC attacked telefunding in a series of three cases. In its case against National Clearing House Inc., the FTC charged that NCH, among other things, misled consumers regarding their chance to receive a prize in exchange for a contribution to a charity named Operation Life. In a case against a Las Vegas food bank, the FTC charged that the telefunder deceived consumers regarding prizes donors could receive if they made a donation and the manner in which the funds would be used. Finally, in its case against United Holdings Group, Inc., the FTC charged that United Holdings misled consumers about chances of winning a prize in a sweepstakes promotion when it sought donations to a charity named the Express Line Foundation. In each case, the FTC also challenged the legitimacy of the charities themselves.

Importantly, however, the FTC also named a number of the telefunders' suppliers, including those who provided donor leads, customer service support, and prizes.

The message from the FTC is clear. Suppliers, including advertising agencies, should conduct their own investigations before undertaking the performance of services for telemarketers. Failing to do so may result in burdens imposed by the FTC that could affect a supplier's entire operation, not just the services provided to the telemarketer engaged in fraudulent activities.

2. State Laws

Generally, federal telemarketing law does not preempt state laws, and states can adopt stricter limitations. Some state law provisions that impact telemarketers include the following:

a. State autodial laws may bar activities permitted under the TCPA. For example, some states have time-of-day restrictions for the use of autodials that are more restrictive than the TCPA, and others prohibit calls on state holidays and Sundays. Some states, such as Arizona and Connecticut, prohibit their use outright, with no exemptions, if used to solicit goods or services.

b. Some states, including Colorado, Florida, Idaho, Kansas, Maryland, and Texas, require a "cooling-off period" during which a consumer may cancel a purchase made over the telephone. In most cases, such statutes also require that a written agreement be obtained from the consumer in order to have an enforceable deal. Some transactions, however, are generally exempt from these requirements including those involving (1) a preexisting relationship with the person called; (2) the availability of a refund within seven days of receipt of the goods, provided the refund is processed within thirty days; or (3) a sale made after the consumer has had the opportunity to examine a brochure or advertisement that contains the name of the seller, a description of the goods, and any material limitations or restrictions on the offer.

c. Many states require that specific information be disclosed if a prize, premium, or gift is offered by a telemarketer as an incentive to purchase a product or service. Some states (Hawaii and Texas) even prohibit offering such items.

d. Some states, including Illinois, Kansas, Kentucky, Oregon, South Carolina, and South Dakota, require telemarketers who solicit the sale of goods or services to ask the called party whether they may continue with the solicitation after identifying themselves and stating the purpose of the call. Other states, such as Arkansas, Illinois, Kansas, Kentucky, Mississippi, Oregon, Pennsylvania, South Carolina, South Dakota, Utah, and Washington, prohibit a telemarketer from continuing a sales call if at any time during the call the called party gives a negative response to a question concerning the goods or services offered. Jurisdictions with these requirements are considered "no rebuttal" states.

e. Some states require that telemarketers be registered and licensed by the state, regardless of whether they operate within that particular state or call into it from another state (Alabama, Alaska, Arizona, Arkansas, California, Colorado, Florida, Hawaii, Idaho, Indiana, Kentucky, Louisiana, Maine, Mississippi, Nebraska, Nevada, North Carolina, Ohio, Oklahoma, Oregon, Pennsylvania, Rhode Island, South Dakota, Texas, Utah, and Washington). Other states require licenses for both the sellers and the individual salespersons who make the actual calls. However, many of these statutes provide exemption for the following classes of calls:

    1. Calls to consumers with whom the caller has a preexisting business relationship
    2. Calls concerning the sale of magazines or periodicals of general circulation
    3. Calls on behalf of public companies
    4. Calls concerning the sale of goods subject to rules enforced by the Federal Trade Commission.

CHAPTER XI
Music in Advertising

1. Acquiring Original Music

Mistakes in the acquisition of original music for commercials can be very costly. For example, if the supplier is careless, the music they produce might infringe the copyright of another composer or publisher. It should also be made clear who owns what rights with regard to the particular piece of music. (See Forms I.11.1 and I.11.2.)

Another controversial area is the collection of royalties for so-called "performance rights" in a composition. Performance rights royalties are paid by television and radio stations for the right to broadcast compositions controlled by one of a number of performing rights societies, of which the two best known are the American Society of Composers, Authors, and Publishers (ASCAP) and Broadcast Music, Inc. (BMI).

ASCAP and BMI collect the royalties from the stations, and through a complicated formula, distribute the money to composers and publishers who have assigned the performance rights administration to ASCAP and BMI.

Until the 1980s, music that was performed in commercials was not included in calculating royalties and jingle writers did not receive any payments from ASCAP or BMI. When this policy changed, composers sought to keep the performance rights to make claims for the royalties from ASCAP and BMI. In turn, however, some advertising agencies and advertisers decided to set up their own publishing companies, register them with ASCAP and BMI, and collect their share of performance rights royalties. If an advertiser ran a considerable amount of network advertising, the economics of setting up a publishing company made some sense.

As a result, the right to collect performance royalties as a publisher became a matter of considerable negotiation between composers and advertisers. After the dust settled, however, few advertisers or advertising agencies set up or retained publishing companies. Except in rare instances, the battle is no longer at issue. Most advertisers and advertising agencies freely leave the performance rights to the composer.

The forms for this chapter include a contract that is typical of what is used today, leaving the performance rights to the composer, but otherwise acquiring all rights for the advertiser. It should be noted that there is some controversy regarding the grant-back to the advertiser, which gives the advertiser the right to use the composition royalty-free for broadcast purposes. ASCAP has objected to this provision and has stated that any member of ASCAP who agrees with the provision forgoes all royalties for that composition from ASCAP. As a practical matter, if the clause were eliminated from the form, it would not be a material problem today. Virtually all radio and television stations carry the necessary licenses from ASCAP and BMI. Nonetheless, conservative practice dictates at least attempting to cover the possibility that things could change.

2. Licensing Existing Music

Acquiring rights to existing music is entirely different than commissioning new music. It is rarely, if ever, purchased outright. It is generally only licensed for a limited period of time within a specified geographic area.

The keys to negotiating a music license agreement include:

a. Do not limit the number of commercials in which the music can be used. Doing so may run into problems, particularly if a number of versions of a commercial are produced, e.g., a 30- and 60-second version, dealer versions, etc.

b. Provide for options for future use beyond the current term. Remember—an option should cost nothing until it is exercised. The same holds true for expanded geographic coverage.

c. Include use of lyrics in print if intended as part of the campaign. All too often, an advertiser or advertising agency overlooks this point and improperly uses the lyrics to a licensed composition in print advertising. Most standard music license agreements allow only for broadcast use. Print use must be negotiated separately. Provided it is negotiated in the beginning, it should be inexpensive.

d. Pay close attention to exclusivity and warranties. Exclusivity should be as broad as possible, preferably complete exclusivity if the budget can afford it. The warranty should not be limited to the license fee paid.

e. Note that many forms disclaim any right to use a sound-alike of the performer who originally recorded the composition. This is understandable given the ever-widening protection given to performers. Take it as a warning, and be careful when recording the composition for the commercial soundtrack. (See Form I.11.3.)

3. Licensing Master Recordings

The original recording of a performance of a musical composition as recorded by the musicians and vocalists is the master recording. As of 1972, master recordings are protected by copyright. Recording companies responsible for the distribution of the recordings are usually the copyright owners of the master recordings but do not necessarily own copyright of the compositions performed on them. Thus, in the rare instance where the advertiser or its advertising agency desires to use the master recording in a commercial, separate negotiations are necessary with the record company that owns the master. What is important to remember is that a separate license is also required from the publisher of the composition and possibly from the recording artist as well.

Chapter Eleven Forms

Form I.11.1 Acquisition of Music Rights (Limited Rights)

[Licensee Letterhead]

[Date]

[Music Supplier]

[Address]

Dear _____:

The following constitutes the agreement between you and us on behalf of our client, _____("Client").

1. You have created and written a certain "work" which is the ( ) music ( ) lyrics ( ) arrangement (check which is applicable) of a musical jingle, a copy of which is annexed hereto, for the purpose of advertising the products or services of our client.

2. You hereby agree that the work is a work-made-for-hire and the sole property of Client. In the event that the work is for any reason deemed not to be a work-made-for-hire, then and in such event, you hereby assign all your right, title, and interest in the work to Client. Without limiting the foregoing, it is specifically understood that we have the right to alter, expand, adapt, and make any arrangements of said work, and we shall have the sole right to decide whether and in what manner the work will be published, advertised, publicized, performed, or exploited by us, our successors, or assigns. We have the further right to secure a statutory copyright therein anywhere in the world in the name(s) of such person, firms, or corporations as we may elect, and we or our designees have the right to secure extensions and renewals of such copyright registrations. All score sheets, lead sheets, folios, master tapes, duplicate tapes, or other elements of the production of the work, if any, shall be our exclusive property and provided to us upon request.

3. We agree to pay to you, and you agree to accept in full consideration for all services rendered by you and for all rights herein the sum of $_____, to be paid by us within thirty (30) days following completion of your services and submission by you of appropriate invoice.

4. You represent and warrant to us that

    (a) The work created by you is original;
    (b) It does not and will not infringe upon or violate the copyrights or any other rights whatsoever of any person or entity;
    (c) No adverse claim exists with respect to it;
    (d) It has not heretofore been published or exploited in any form anywhere in the world;
    (e) You own and control said work and all rights in it throughout the world;

(f) You have the full and exclusive right and authority to enter into this agreement and to make the grant herein contained; and

(g) Any and all materials that are incorporated in the work are works-made-for-hire and free from any reversionary rights therein.

5. You agree to hold us, our Client, and their assigns and licensees harmless from and against any loss, damage, or expense, including court costs and reasonable attorneys' fees, that we, our Client, and their assigns and licensees may suffer or incur as a result of any breach or alleged breach of the foregoing warranties.

6. We hereby grant back to you the performance rights to the work, subject, however, to the following conditions:

(a) You warrant and represent that you are a member of ASCAP or BMI;

(b) The performance rights to the work will not be licensed on behalf of any other advertiser;

(c) ASCAP or BMI, as the case may be, will license the work on radio and TV stations and networks throughout the U.S.A., without any special compensation therefore by stations, networks, or us, such rights to be granted under the license agreements with stations and networks;

(d) In the event we shall desire to use the composition on stations or networks which have not entered into a license agreement with ASCAP or BMI, this agreement shall be deemed to constitute a license for such use, without any limitation or further compensation; and

(e) Neither you nor anyone deriving any rights from you shall at any time interfere with or hold up the performance of the work in any manner whatsoever or for whatever reason.

Please evidence your acceptance hereof and agreement hereto by signing in the place indicated.

Very truly yours,

[Agency/Advertiser]

By: _____

ACCEPTED AND AGREED:

[Music Supplier]

By: _____

Form I.11.2 Acquisition of Music Rights (All Rights)

[Licensee Letterhead]

[Date]

[Music Supplier]

[Address]

Dear _____ :

The following constitutes the agreement between you and us on behalf of our client, _____("Client").

1. You have created and written a certain"work" which is the ( ) music ( ) lyrics ( ) arrangement (check which is applicable) of a musical jingle, a copy of which is annexed hereto, for the purpose of advertising the products or services of our client.

2. You hereby agree that the work is a work-made-for-hire and the sole property of Client. In the event that the work is for any reason deemed not to be a work-made-for-hire, then and in such event, you hereby assign all your right, title, and interest in the work to Client. Without limiting the foregoing, it is specifically understood that we have the right to alter, expand, adapt, and make any arrangements of said work, and we shall have the sole right to decide whether and in what manner the work will be published, advertised, publicized, performed, or exploited by us, our successors, or assigns. We have the further right to secure a statutory copyright therein anywhere in the world in the name(s) of such person, firms, or corporations as we may elect, and we or our designees have the right to secure extensions and renewals of such copyright registrations. All score sheets, lead sheets, folios, master tapes, duplicate tapes, or other elements of the production of the work, if any, shall be our exclusive property and provided to us upon request.

3. We agree to pay to you, and you agree to accept in full consideration for all services rendered by you and for all rights herein the sum of $_____, to be paid by us within thirty (30) days following completion of your services and submission by you of appropriate invoice.

4. You represent and warrant to us that

   (a) The work created by you is original;
   (b) It does not and will not infringe upon or violate the copyrights or any other rights whatsoever of any person or entity;
   (c) No adverse claim exists with respect to it;
   (d) It has not heretofore been published or exploited in any form anywhere in the world;
   (e) You own and control said work and all rights in it throughout the world;

   (f) You have the full and exclusive right and authority to enter into this agreement and to make the grant herein contained; and

   (g) Any and all materials that are incorporated in the work are works-made-for-hire and free from any reversionary rights therein.

  5. You agree to hold us, our Client, and their assigns and licensees harmless from and against any loss, damage, or expense, including court costs and reasonable attorneys' fees, that we, our Client, and their assigns and licensees may suffer or incur as a result of any breach or alleged breach of the foregoing warranties.

Please evidence your acceptance hereof and agreement hereto by signing in the place indicated.

Very truly yours,

[Agency/Advertiser]

By: _____

ACCEPTED AND AGREED:

[Music Supplier]

By: _____

Form I.11.3 License for Existing Music

AGREEMENT made this _____ day of _____ year of _____ by and between _____ ("Publisher") located at _____ and _____ ("Licensee") located at _____ as agent for _____ ("Client").

1. During the "Term" hereof, Licensee shall have the non-exclusive, irrevocable right and license to use and record the copyrighted musical composition entitled _____ (the "Composition") by _____ in synchronism with television and radio commercials for the purpose of advertising Client's products or services. Licensee may also use the lyrics to the Composition in print advertising.

2. Notwithstanding the above, Publisher hereby acknowledges that it will not grant any license to use the Composition in the advertising, marketing, or promotion of any products competitive with Client's products or services in any media throughout the Territory from the date hereof and continuing thereafter for the duration of the Term and any extensions hereof.

3. In consideration of the license granted herein, Licensee shall pay the sum of $_____ to Publisher, such payment to be made within ten (10) days of execution of this agreement.

4. Publisher warrants and represents that it is a member of ASCAP and BMI.

5. (a) ASCAP or BMI, as the case may be, will license the Composition on radio and television stations and networks throughout the United States without any special compensation therefor by stations or Licensee, such rights to be granted under the license agreements with stations and networks; and (b) In the event Licensee shall desire to use the Composition on stations or networks which have not entered into a license agreement with ASCAP or BMI, this agreement shall be deemed to constitute a license for such uses, without any limitation or further compensation.

6. This license is granted for the "Territory" comprising _____.

7. The "Term" of this license shall be for one year, from _____ to _____. Licensee shall thereafter have an option to renew the Term hereof for an additional period of one year upon the same terms and conditions upon notice of no less than thirty (30) days preceding the end of the "Term" and upon the payment to Publisher of the sum of $_____ not later than _____ (   ) days succeeding the end of the "Term" hereof.

8. Licensee shall have the right to alter, expand, adapt, and make any arrangements of the Composition, and Licensee shall have the sole right to decide whether and in what manner the work will be published, advertised, publicized, performed, or exploited by us, our successor, or assigns. Licensee shall have the further right to secure a statutory copyright therein anywhere in the world in the name(s) of such person, firms, or corporations it may elect, and it or its designees shall have the right to secure extensions and renewals of such copyright registrations.

9. Publisher hereby represents and warrants to Licensee that:

   (a) The Composition is original;

   (b) The Composition does not and will not infringe upon or violate the copyrights or any other rights whatsoever of any person or entity;

(c) No adverse claim exists with respect to it;

(d) Publisher owns and controls the Composition and all rights in it throughout the world; and

(e) Publisher has the full and exclusive right and authority to enter into this agreement and to make the grant herein contained.

10. Publisher agrees to hold Licensee and its Client and their respective assigns and licensees harmless from and against any loss, damage, or expense, including court costs and reasonable attorneys' fees, that they and their assigns and licensees may suffer or incur as a result of any breach or alleged breach of the foregoing warranties.

11. This agreement shall be construed in accordance with the laws of the State of _____.

IN WITNESS WHEREOF, the parties have set their signatures hereto on the day and date as first appears above.

PUBLISHER: LICENSEE:

By: ` _____   By: _____

CHAPTER XII
Government Regulation

1. The Regulatory Environment

The Federal Trade Commission is the primary regulator of advertising. Its regulatory tools are many, including fines, restitution, and corrective advertising. Corrective advertising requires an advertiser found to have violated the Federal Trade Commission Act to openly admit it in its future advertising.

Why It Matters

In a 1994 case, Eggland's Best, Inc. claimed clinical tests prove that eating a dozen of Eggland's Best eggs a week as part of a low-fat diet will not increase serum cholesterol. The claim was challenged, and pursuant to a consent agreement, Eggland's Best agreed to place clearly and prominently on its egg products packaging the statement "There are no studies showing that these eggs are different from other eggs in their effect on serum cholesterol."

Other Federal agencies, such as the Food and Drug Administration, the U.S. Postal Service, the Bureau of Alcohol, Tobacco and Firearms, and the Securities and Exchange Commission, also have regulatory authority over advertising practices.

At the state level, The National Association of Attorneys General, popularly known by its acronym, NAAG, is increasingly active, particularly in the environmental area. Over the past ten years, task forces have investigated a wide range of industries, including automobiles, diet plans, insurance, long-distance telephone services, funeral homes, and investment services, among others. Their most celebrated efforts culminated with the 1997 Tobacco Settlement.

Coping with a multiple-state investigation can be an eye-opening experience and is to be avoided at virtually all costs.

2. Preventive Measures to Control the Risk of a Regulatory Challenge

While it is not always feasible to have all advertising copy reviewed by legal counsel, television copy and new campaigns, especially, warrant such review. Often, an advertising agency can pass the legal costs on to the advertiser.

Neither agency nor advertiser should rely solely on the advertiser's legal counsel to review advertising unless they are expert in the area.

Independent review by an agency's legal counsel is also important because an agency can be held liable independent from its client.

It is the position of the FTC that an advertising agency will have an affirmative defense in an action against its client only if the agency can show that it identified for its client, in writing, all the performance claims which it reasonably believed were contained in the advertising, and exercised due care to assure itself that the client possessed and relied upon a reasonable basis for those claims.

The FTC cases make it clear that, before preparing and placing advertising, an advertising agency is under the following obligations:

a. To examine and relate to the client all possible representations or claims made in advertising prepared by it; and

b. To exercise due care to assure itself that the advertiser possessed support which constitutes a reasonable basis for the claims.

Why It Matters

An advertising agency has liability for false and deceptive advertising separate and apart from its advertiser client. An advertising agency cannot hide behind the advertiser, and the order against the advertising agency can often be worse than the penalty against the advertiser. A Federal Trade Commission case involving advertising for Lewis Galoob Toys, Inc. produced by Towne, Silverstein & Rotter illustrates the problem. In the Galoob case, the FTC challenged certain video depictions in a commercial as misleading to children because they were exaggerated and could not be reasonably reproduced by children in a play environment. In settling the case, Galoob agreed to cease using such depictions. The advertising agency agreed to cease using such depictions not only for Galoob but for all its other advertiser clients as well.

3. Routinely Request and Review Claim Substantiation

When an objective, provable claim is made, the advertiser must have adequate substantiation for the claim, before the advertisement is published or the commercial is broadcast. It is illegal to publish or broadcast a claim that is only later substantiated. The law takes the position that consumer interest mandates that the advertiser have the proof in hand before it makes the claim. (See Form I.12.1.)

Substantiation requires that the advertiser have a "reasonable basis" for the claim. Obviously, what constitutes "due care" and a "reasonable basis" will vary, depending upon the scope of the claims made and the nature of the product or service advertised. For example, claims about a dishwasher detergent will require a much lower level of substantiation than claims about a drug product, given comparative health and safety considerations. The FTC has, however, defined a "reasonable basis" as follows:

> A "reasonable basis" shall consist of a competent and reliable scientific test or tests, or other competent and reliable evidence including competent and reliable opinions of scientific, engineering, or other experts who are qualified by professional training and experience to render competent judgments in such matters.

Often, counsel and the marketing group will differ on what constitutes a "reasonable basis" for a given product claim. There are no hard and fast rules, and lengthy discussions are more the norm than the exception. In most instances, the advertising copy can be revised to comply with substantiation rules to everyone's satisfaction.

4. Educate Employees on Legal Risks

Proactive advertising managers will want to ensure that their employees understand the laws and regulations they need to follow and the consequences of failing to uphold them. Periodic legal seminars are perhaps the best way to insure an ongoing program to minimize risks. Seminars can be conducted in-house, or personnel can attend any number that are available in the marketplace.

5. The Concept of "Unfair" and "Deceptive" Advertising

Unfairness is a very broad standard, one that the FTC rarely applies due to controversy surrounding its use.

Under federal law, an "unfair" act or practice is defined as one that "causes or is likely to cause substantial injury to consumers which is not reasonably avoidable by consumers themselves and not outweighed by countervailing benefits to consumers or to competition." The definition requires a three-prong analysis. First, the challenged act must be shown to cause or be likely to cause substantial consumer injury. Second, the act must be such that a consumer could not have reasonably avoided the injury. Third, any injury sustained must be weighed against the countervailing benefits to consumers and competition in general. Thus, not all injuries are actionable, even if substantial and unavoidable by consumers.

Deception, on the other hand, is a very real and active standard by which the FTC and courts judge advertising. While clearly false or misleading claims are always considered deceptive, a decision as to whether a borderline advertisement is "deceptive" will most often be based upon the "net impression" of the entire advertisement. Even if every statement made is literally true, an advertisement will nonetheless be considered deceptive if the overall net impression left with the consumer is misleading. Anything ambiguous will be construed against the advertiser. Perhaps the most important principle in advertising regulation is that the net impression is controlling, regardless of whether every individual claim made is true. For example, if you claim that four out of five doctors surveyed recommend your product, but fail to disclose that only a small sample of doctors was surveyed, the literal truth of the claim is irrelevant; consumers will believe that a significant number of doctors were involved, thereby leaving a misleading net impression and exposing the advertising agency and the advertiser to a charge of deceptive advertising.

Put simply, if an individual claim in an advertisement or the net impression of the advertisement is false or misleading, the advertisement will be considered deceptive and subject to FTC or other regulatory action, unless the injury to consumers is insignificant or the consumer was not acting reasonably, i.e., could easily have realized the claim was merely puffery and not based on established fact.

The FTC may, in lieu of attacking a particular advertiser, adopt a broad, industry-wide Trade Regulation Rule respecting unfair or deceptive acts or practices, provided it first finds that such acts or practices are prevalent in the industry. The FTC can make a determination that the acts or practices are prevalent only if it has issued cease-and-desist orders regarding the acts or practices, or "any other information available to the Commission indicates a widespread pattern of unfair or deceptive acts or practices."

Importantly, the law requires the FTC to examine how its resources are allocated and to identify areas that are most appropriately enforced by the states. Presumably, this alleviates some of the problems associated with multiple actions by both the FTC and interested states.

Recently, FTC commissioners have warned that we can expect to see significant activity in deceptive advertising investigations, particularly in the areas of consumer health and safety, dietary-supplements, high-octane gasolines, computers, toys, environmental marketing, product demonstrations, and use of survey data, and where "fat," "cholesterol" and/or "calories" are used in food ads. And, certainly, the FTC has added the Internet as a major area of focus.

Since the potential impact on advertisers and advertising agencies is significant, depending on how aggressively the FTC uses its powers, advertisers and advertising agencies should carefully evaluate FTC Commissioner appointments for signals of how aggressively the FTC may enforce its powers.

6. Puffery

An advertiser seeks to show its product or service in the best light possible. This is as true for food products as for any other products. As a result, superlative claims like "delicious," "tasty," "zesty," and "mouth-watering" are common. Also common, and more troublesome, are comparative claims such as "X tastes better than Y," objective claims dealing with product attributes, and similar claims which cross the line from puffery to claims that require substantiation. The key to analyzing such claims under principles of advertising law is the distinction between hyperbole, or puffery, and actual or implied product claims.

Puffery has been said to be as difficult to define as pornography, although judges appear to share the ability to know it when they see it. However, the word is usually used to describe a claim, typically a statement of opinion, that is so vague or so hyperbolic that no reasonable person would suppose that the statement was intended to be taken seriously. As one court put it, "Puffery is the advertiser's right to lie his head off because no consumer will believe him anyway."

Terms such as "great-tasting" and "fabulous flavor" would normally be considered puffery. In contrast, if a statement appears to be a statement of fact or an assertion that can be proven or not proven, such as "best-" or "better-tasting," it will not be considered puffery and will be considered a product claim that must be adequately substantiated.

Why It Matters

1. Milk has been recognized by some nutritionists as the most nearly perfect food, and though yogurt does preserve all of milk's nutrients, the advertisement of yogurt as nature's "most perfect food" was held by the FTC to be more than puffery.

2. A cigarette company conducted a taste test between its brand of cigarettes and various competitors' cigarette brands. Based on the test, the advertising announced that the advertiser's brand was the "National Smoker Study Winner." The test methodology consisted of participants smoking the two cigarettes, after which they were told the tar content of the cigarettes (the advertiser's was lower) and then asked which cigarette they preferred. The court ruled that the Smoker Study results were deceptive because of the disclosure of tar content to the test participants just before they were asked which cigarette they would prefer to smoke.

3. The Advertising Standards and Guidelines of the broadcast network, ABC, Inc., state that taste claims which give the impression of being objective rather than simply being personal opinion must be supported by competent taste testing data. ABC, Inc. defines objective claims as those "that generally deal with performance, efficacy, preference, taste, and other tangible attributes which are measurable and verifiable." On the other hand, another ABC, Inc. guideline provides: "Subjective or puffery claims cannot be verified. Since they deal with subjective preferences or hyperbole, they cannot be proved or disproved. They are generally acceptable without support as long as the clear net impression that they are likely to make upon the viewing public is subjective personal preference or puffery."

---

7. Product Demonstrations

The use of a demonstration can be a powerful vehicle to illustrate or convey a product's attributes or capabilities, because it invites consumers to make purchasing decisions based on what they see.

Accordingly, product demonstrations must be completely accurate and may not use mock-ups of any kind without disclosure. It is no defense that a video mock-up depicts an appearance that is identical to the natural or unembellished product or that the mock-up was necessary due to the nature of photography or video reproduction, or to difficulty in producing a natural-looking image other than by artificial means.

The production of any television demonstration or print ad depicting a demonstration should be carefully monitored, and accurate records of all details of the production should be kept. It is a wise precaution to obtain an affirmation from the producer, photographer, or person responsible for the advertising providing all details of the demonstration, and attesting to its authenticity.

Why It Matters

Volvo and its advertising agency produced a commercial showing a "Big Foot" truck driving over the roofs of a line of cars. The collection of cars involved one Volvo. All the cars, except the Volvo (proving its renown as a strong and safe car), crushed under the weight of the truck. Part of the copy read, "Can you spot the Volvo?" (See picture 12.a.)

While a single take in filming probably would have shown the results depicted in the commercial, in production there were reportedly concerns over the damage that might be done on repeated takes. To solve this concern, the Volvo was structurally reinforced. The car manufacturer and its advertising agency did crush, however, under the weight of the Texas Attorney General and the FTC, to whom they paid over $600,000 in fines for a mocked-up demonstration. The advertising agency also lost the $40 million account and many people lost their jobs.

12.a Volvo and its advertising agency produced an advertisement showing a "Big Foot" truck driving over the roofs of a line of cars. The collection of cars involved one Volvo. Proving its renown as a strong and safe car, all the cars, except the Volvo, crushed under the weight of the truck. Unfortunately, the demonstration was rigged.

8. Common Claims and Practices

a. Guarantees

According to the FTC Guides for the advertising of warranties and guarantees, any advertisement that mentions a warranty or guarantee must contain certain required statements or explanations.

Advertisements for consumer products priced above $15 must contain a statement "with the clarity and prominence as will be noticed and understood by prospective purchasers" that the consumer can review a written copy of the guarantee or warranty prior to purchase, and where such copy can be obtained.

The FTC Guides do not specify any type size or locations for the required statements in print advertisements. In television commercials, the statement should be given simultaneously with or immediately after the mention of the warranty. It can be either in the audio portion of the commercial or in a super of at least five seconds' duration.

Advertisements that mention a guarantee must also specify whether the guarantee is full or limited. A "full" guarantee is one with no restrictions. Most guarantees, however, are "limited" ones, although common usage of the only term "guarantee" seems to apply to limited guarantees not full guarantees. It is recommended that any material limitation or condition placed on the guarantee be clearly disclosed in order to avoid problems with federal and state regulators.

There are additional requirements relating to guaranteed satisfaction and lifetime guarantees and similar types of representations. Any advertisement featuring a guarantee should be carefully reviewed by qualified counsel.

b. Testimonials

The consumer's own words are sometimes the best advertising for a product. Thus, testimonials are very popular. As in other areas of advertising, however, the FTC has adopted very specific guidelines on the use of testimonials. Included in these guidelines are the following:

1. The testimonial must actually reflect the experience of the endorser, i.e., it must be truthful; also, he or she must have had sufficient experience with the product to make the statements attributed to him or her. For example, it would be improper for someone to say his watch was the best he ever owned if he had only owned the watch for a month.

2. The testimonial must reflect what other consumers can expect to experience. It would be illegal to have a consumer say his car battery lasted five years if most consumers typically had to replace it after three years, unless the advertisement clearly disclosed that his was not a typical experience.

3. The testimonial must be obtained in a manner that does not bias the opinion. If the advertiser tells the endorser his statements will be used in advertising before the testimonial is obtained, the testimonial is misleading unless clear disclosure of the procedure used to secure the testimonials is made in the advertising.

4. All statements involving product claims made by the consumer must be subject to direct substantiation. It is no defense to simply say the endorser was only giving his or her individual opinion.

Special rules apply to celebrity and expert endorsements. Special rules also apply to certain product categories such as alcoholic beverages and drugs. In addition, each of the networks has its own requirements for testimonials. Properly executed testimonial releases must be secured from anyone whose testimonial is used in advertising. While a powerful advertising tool, the use of testimonials must be carefully monitored and reviewed. In some instances, you may have to disclose that a payment was made in exchange for a testimonial.

It should be noted that the FTC announced in 2003 that it would review the Testimonial Guidelines. Given the FTC's concerns regarding testimonials in infomercials and in advertising to the elderly, and for sensitive products and product categories such as weight loss, nutrition, and drugs, marketers are well advised to stay aware of changes should they occur.

c. "New"

There are two rules relating to the use of the word "new" in advertising, both resulting from FTC Advisory Opinions.

First, for a product to be described as "new," it must be legitimately new or reformulated in a material respect related to product performance. A mere cosmetic change is not sufficient to justify use of the word "new."

Second, the term "new" may only be used to describe the product for a period of six months from initial distribution of the product to which the term is applied. An exception is permitted where the product is first tested in markets not exceeding 15% of the U.S. population. In such cases, six months in test market may precede the general six-month period, thus allowing a maximum theoretical period of one year during which the word "new" may be used.

As a practical matter, many advertisers find it difficult to adhere to those time limitations when a product is being introduced into the market on a roll-out basis. The networks have generally been more diligent in enforcing this rule than has the FTC.

d. Deceptive Pricing and "Free" or "Cents Off"

The FTC has adopted specific guidelines for use of the words "free," "cents off," or words of similar effect. State and local regulatory bodies that have adopted similar guidelines are more active in enforcement than is the FTC in this area.

In summary, a "free" or savings claim may be used only when:

1. The amount of saving claimed or the cost of the merchandise described as "free" is truly borne by the advertiser, and not recouped from the consumer. A free product has to be legitimately free.

2. All conditions of the offer are clearly stated. For example, if a consumer must buy a product to take advantage of the free offer, that condition must be conspicuously stated in the advertising.

3. The offer is discontinued after a reasonable period of time. For example, if a "buy one, get one free" offer is used for two years, the true cost of the "free" merchandise may, in fact, have been absorbed into the basic cost of the product.

Other, more detailed, federal and state rules apply to coupons and other similar offers. Such "savings" promotions should be carefully reviewed by qualified counsel to ensure conformity to applicable guidelines.

Why It Matters

1. Colorado sued the May Department Store chain for violating state law by use of artificially inflated "regular" or "original" prices for the purpose of advertising later reductions. The chain was ordered to cease and desist from similar practices in the future, make restitution to certain consumers, and pay the state's costs and attorneys' fees.

2. The Connecticut Supreme Court upheld as constitutional a Connecticut consumer protection regulation requiring that the net price, after rebates, of an item offered for sale must be shown in all advertising offering the rebate. Simply listing the original price and the amount of a rebate is not sufficient under the Connecticut regulation; the net price is also required.

3. Sears, Roebuck and Co. was found liable for deceptive advertising when it advertised a saw at a reduced price during a holiday sale where some of the Sears stores failed to have sufficient inventory of the saw to meet consumer demand. The New York court held that "[R]easonable demand must be calculated from the commencement of the sale rather than defendant's delivery cycle … especially when the advertisement is directed at last-minute holiday shoppers. Demand cannot be subject to the vagaries of the inventory control practices of each separate store."

e. Use of Flags, Money, and Stamps

It is generally unlawful to use domestic (federal and state) and foreign flags in advertising. However, the incidental use of a flag, such as when it appears in front of a building being photographed, is permissible.

The use of photographic reproductions of paper currency in print is permitted if it meets the following specifications:

1. It must be more than 150% or less than 75% of the actual size of the currency.

2. The photographic plates must be destroyed after use.

3. Color illustrations are permitted if the illustrations are one-sided.

These restrictions do not apply to the use of currency on videotape or film. Photographic reproduction of coins is permitted.

Uncanceled postage stamps (U.S. and foreign) may be reproduced in color if the reproduction is less than 75% or more than 150% of the size of the original, or in exact size if in black and white. United States canceled stamps may be reproduced in exact size and in color. Foreign canceled stamps may be reproduced in exact size but only in black and white.

f. "Made in the USA"

The Federal Trade Commission has a specific policy statement regarding claims that a product was made in the USA, a claim that is often considered advantageous to sales. The Enforcement Policy Statement on U.S. Origin Claims is reproduced in Appendix 4 of this volume. In essence, however, an unqualified U.S.-origin claim must mean that all or virtually all of the product was made in the United States. Thus, if a marketer makes an unqualified claim that a product is "Made in USA," it should, at the time the representation is made, possess a reasonable basis that the product is in fact all or virtually all made in the United States.

9. The Robinson-Patman Act and Promotional Allowances

The Federal Trade Commission staff has issued Guides on Advertising Allowances—commonly known as the Fred Meyer Guides—under the Robinson-Patman Act, a very confusing and often ignored piece of federal legislation presumably enacted to protect small retailers from the clout of larger ones.

At the end of this chapter is a compilation of frequently asked questions relating to promotional allowances. Suffice it to say that any company offering promotional allowances to any of its wholesalers, distributors, or retailers must review such plans carefully under the Robinson-Patman requirements.

10. Licensing of Stock Photography

Claims against advertisers and advertising agencies from models and other individuals whose pictures were used for advertising purposes without written permission is particularly common in cases where an advertising agency has licensed stock photography. Time and again, advertising agencies license photographs from so-called stock photo houses without obtaining written assurance that the stock photo house has obtained rights from the people whose pictures appear in the stock photos. As a general rule, stock photo houses only guarantee that they have rights from the photographer. On rare occasions will they warrant that they have rights from the individuals depicted in the photography. In fact, the terms and conditions on the back of the typical stock photo house contract specifically provides that the stock photo house makes no such warranty and that the advertising agency or advertiser has the responsibility to obtain permission.

Best practices dictate that the advertising agency carefully review forms from the stock photo house and inquire regarding the necessity of permission from individuals in the photos. Where such rights are not clearly established, an advertiser's use of the photography is unwise.

When dealing with stock photography houses, advertising agencies are well advised to take note of the penalty for the loss of any transparencies that may be given to the advertising agency for consideration. It is quite common for a stock photography house to deliver dozens of transparencies. All too often, these are misplaced and cannot be found. The terms and conditions in stock photography house forms generally provide that the stock photography house is entitled to thousands of dollars for each lost transparency. This can amount to significant damages that are not generally covered by insurance. The best practice is to review any such forms and to object to any such damage clause prior to accepting delivery. Alternatively, objection to any such clause should be clearly stated in the initial order.

11. File Retention of Advertising-Related Materials

There is no perfect record-retention policy with respect to advertising-related materials. Even a policy that calls for retaining all documents and discarding none is not perfect. First, it requires considerable cost. Second, there may be some documents that are better left discarded in certain situations involving litigation. At times, the absence of a document can be better than its presence.

As a general rule, however, documents should be retained as provided in the form at the end of this chapter, except where such documents are the subject of an audit or litigation, in which case such documents should be retained for the period stated following the conclusion of the audit or litigation (the notation "P" means the document should be kept permanently). The policy should be reviewed with counsel, however, before discarding any documents presently in possession.

Chapter Twelve Forms

Form I.12.1 Demonstration Commercial Producer's Affirmation to Support a Claim

[Advertising Agency]

[Advertiser]

[Commercial Title]

[Commercial #]

[Production Company]

[Producer]

1. Location of shooting:

2. Day and time of shooting:

3. All persons present, participating in, or observing demonstration:

4. Product(s) demonstrated:

5. Competitive products demonstrated:

6. Where products were obtained:

7. Who obtained products?

8. Exact description of demonstration, including the functions of the different participating personnel. (Use extra sheet of paper, if necessary):

9. What was done with products following the demonstration?

10. If demonstration included any kind of mock-up, give complete description thereof:

11. How often was the demonstration performed on the set or location prior to shooting, and did the demonstration work each time? If not, why not?

I certify that no undisclosed procedures were employed in the production of this commercial (these commercials) and that the filming or taping was done in a truthful and accurate manner.

Producer _____

Form I.12.2 Frequently Asked Questions Regarding Promotional Allowances

The following is a question-and-answer discussion of ten common issues that arise when dealing with the Robinson-Patman Act and pricing policies. Caution must be exercised, however, because every case will depend on its own facts. The following discussion must therefore be viewed as a general one, and specific legal advice should be sought for individual programs.

1. What are the restrictions applicable to co-op advertising?

    Because co-op advertising is one of the many types of promotional allowances subject to the Robinson-Patman Act, this question provides a good framework to review some basic principles.

    The Act prohibits a seller from granting allowances or furnishing services to promote the resale of its products unless the allowances or services are made available to all competing customers on proportionally equal terms. In other words, a seller cannot single out a particular customer to receive an "irresistible offer." The Act applies to all types of payments or promotional services that are designed to stimulate the resale of the seller's products.

    Discrimination related to granting promotional allowances or other merchandising services are per se violations. An adverse effect on competition does not need to be proven. The only defense is if the discriminatory payment or allowance is made to "meet the actions of a competitor." Remember that the provisions of the Robinson-Patman Act apply only to payments or allowances made in connection with the sale of goods of like grade and quality. Services are not covered.

    Four essential requirements must be met when offering a co-op advertising program or any similar promotional allowance:

    (a) The allowance must be offered to all competing customers;
    (b) All competing customers must be notified that the allowance is being offered;
    (c) The allowance must be reasonably available. This means it must be usable in a practical sense by all competing customers. If the basic allowance is not usable in a practical sense by all competing customers, alternatives must be offered; and
    (d) The allowance must be available to all competing customers on proportionally equal terms.

2. Who are competing customers?

    The following three basic elements are involved in determining competing customers:

    (a) The respective customers must be at the same functional level. A retailer will not be considered a competing customer of a wholesaler unless the wholesaler is also in the retail business. On the other hand, where a manufacturer sells directly to wholesalers and retailers, the retailers who buy from the wholesalers will be considered competitors of the retailers who buy directly from the manufacturer.
    (b) The customers must compete in the resale of products of like grade and quality. Thus, if a company that makes televisions and computers offers a co-op advertising allowance to retailers selling its televisions, it need not offer the same promotional allowance to retailers selling its computers. What about products which are more similar in nature? As a general rule, if there are real physical differences between the products and the differences affect the use or performance of the products, the products will not be considered of like grade and quality. One question

that frequently comes up in this area is whether identical products sold under different brand names will be considered of like grade and quality. Unfortunately, there is no clear answer to this issue. The facts of each individual case must be analyzed.

(c) The customers must compete in the same geographic area. Thus, a small grocery store in Chicago would be considered a competitor of an A&P in Chicago, but would not be considered a competitor of a grocery store in New York. Care must be taken, however, not to arbitrarily draw geographical boundaries when structuring a regional promotion. Some products compete across geographic lines. For example, a consumer might travel to New Jersey or Connecticut for things like a fur coat or furniture, but certainly would not travel that far for a container of milk.

3. What type of notification to customers is required?

The FTC Guides set forth a number of methods by which notification can be given, such as direct contact, releases in trade publications, and notices on shipping containers.

In a case against The Gillette Company several years ago, Gillette was charged with failing to make its advertising allowances available to its smaller retailers. The FTC required that Gillette provide all of its retailers, on a recurring basis, with a written statement describing its advertising allowance program, including all available alternatives. In addition, the FTC required that Gillette state its advertising allowance policy on all shipping containers and in all promotional literature sent to wholesalers.

Liability for failing to provide notice has generally been found only where the seller made no effort or only a token effort to inform its customers. As a general rule, if a manufacturer makes a good-faith effort to notify customers by any of the methods mentioned in the Guides, there should be no problem.

It is rarely a problem for a manufacturer to provide notice to customers that buy directly from the manufacturer. A more difficult problem exists for companies that distribute to both wholesalers and retailers and must therefore also provide notice to the customers of its wholesalers. In most cases, a company does not know the identity of its wholesaler's customers. While it is acceptable in such circumstances for a manufacturer to ask its wholesaler or some other intermediary to provide notice to the retail customers, the ultimate responsibility rests with the manufacturer. If it is relying on wholesalers or other intermediaries to notify customers of promotional allowances, the manufacturer should have a written agreement with the wholesaler or intermediary that specifies the details of the program and how the retailers will be notified. The current FTC Guides also recommend that the manufacturer conduct spot checks at 90-day intervals; however, this requirement has been eliminated in the proposed Guides.

4. How do you insure that the allowance is reasonably available?

Reasonable availability means that the allowance or service must be usable in a practical sense by all competing customers. For example, a co-op advertising plan that provides reimbursement only for television and radio advertising would not be functionally available to small retailers who do not advertise through these media. Alternatives such as reimbursement for advertising in local newspapers or through handbills or circulars would have to be offered. A proposal for a coupon program that requires the use of scanning devices would also need to offer alternative allowances for smaller retailers who do not typically have this equipment.

Some court decisions, however, reject the notion that the seller must offer a plan that is usable by even the smallest retailer. In one case, a car dealer challenged a co-op advertising program offered by Suzuki that required dealers to make a minimum purchase in order to qualify for the advertising allowance. The dealer claimed that the minimum purchase requirement was too large. The court said that as long as the minimum purchase requirement was low enough for the average dealer to meet, which in Suzuki's case it was, the program satisfied Robinson-Patman requirements.

5. What is proportional equality?

Trying to achieve proportional equality is a little like maintaining the speed limit on an interstate highway. Neither you nor anyone around you complies; each driver simply tries to stay within a reasonable range. Even the FTC has stated that no single way to proportionalize is prescribed by law. The goal is to be fair to customers. It is important to remember that the goal is not to treat all customers equally, but to treat them proportionally. The FTC has suggested two methods of proportionalizing the allowance: on the dollar volume or on the quantity of units purchased by the customer during a specified period of time. Thus, for example, a program would comply that offered each customer $1.00 per unit or dollar volume purchased for advertising in newspapers and for advertising in some alternative way, such as handbills, if newspapers were not available.

On the other hand, a plan that has graduated rates based on the amount of goods purchased—for example, allowance of 1% of the first 1,000 cases purchased, 2% of the second 1,000 cases purchased, and 3% for all purchases over 2,000 cases—is not proportional, because only the larger-buying customers are earning the higher rate.

The FTC has also suggested that the payments can be proportional to the customer's cost of providing the service. An example of this approach would be a plan under which the seller agrees to pay 50% of its customer's cost of advertising in newspapers and of advertising in some alternative way, such as handbills or circulars, if newspapers are not available.

One of the main criticisms of the FTC's approach to proportionalizing, which is commonly referred to as the "cost approach," is that it fails to take into account the value to the seller of the promotional services being provided by the customer. Critics of the cost approach believe that the seller should be able to vary the rates at which it will pay for various promotional services in proportion to the value that the seller will be receiving from the promotional service. Under this theory, commonly referred to as the "value theory," if one customer advertises on television and another customer advertises in local newspapers, and the television advertising is likely to be twice as effective in selling the product as the local newspaper advertising, the customer who advertises on television should be able to receive twice as much of an allowance per dollar or unit volume purchased than the customer who advertises in local papers. There has been some judicial support for this approach. In what is commonly referred to as the Soap Cases, a co-op advertising plan was approved that granted higher allowances per case of soap for newspaper advertising than for advertising through handbills and radio. The court in that case stated that "the law does not require a seller to pay at the same rate per unit of product sold for types of services which are of unequal cost or value."

6. Can the retailer or wholesaler be liable?

One of the ironies of the Robinson-Patman Act is that although it was passed in an attempt to curb the power that large chain stores were wielding, the Act itself contains no specific provision for buyer liability when the buyer unknowingly accepts a discriminatory allowance. It is well established, however, that a buyer who knowingly induces a disproportional advertising allowance may be prosecuted under Section 2(f) of the Robinson-Patman Act or Section 5 of the Federal Trade Commission Act. One of the interesting developments in this area is that a number of courts have been reluctant to find liability for violations of the spirit of the Robinson-Patman Act unless there is a showing of competitive injury.

Competitive injury need not be proven to hold a seller liable for violating Robinson-Patman.

7.   Is it legal to withhold co-op allowances from discount retailers?

The FTC Guides specifically state that a manufacturer should not refuse to contribute to the cost of ads that feature prices other than the manufacturer's suggested retail prices. The Commission's position had been that this would constitute a per se violation of the Sherman Act prohibition against price fixing. In May of 1987, however, the Commission announced that it would look at such denials under a rule of reason , i.e., on the facts of each case, and not as per se illegal. Some recent decisions have also adopted a rule of reason. Several years ago, for example, a Nissan co-op advertising plan that limited reimbursement to ads that contained Nissan's suggested retail prices was challenged. The court rejected the notion that the program was a per se violation of the Sherman Act. The court said that there was no price fixing or restraint of trade, because the dealers were free to sell cars at whatever price they chose and could advertise whatever prices they chose in ads they paid for. They simply waived the right to participate in Nissan's co-op plan. The proposed revisions to the Guides would eliminate the statement that such a resale price restriction on co-op advertising allowances is per se illegal. As long as retailers have the flexibility to set their own prices, the Guides would allow manufacturers to refuse to contribute to advertising that lists prices below those recommended by the manufacturer.

8.   How does the Push Money Rule impact trade promotions?

The FTC's Push Money Rule provides that it is unlawful for manufacturers to give anything of value to a salesperson employed by the manufacturer's customer in order to induce the employee to push the sale of the manufacturer's product, without the knowledge and consent of the salesperson's employer. Thus, any special incentive programs directed to dealers or other sales personnel must be disclosed to the employers of the dealers or salespersons. As long as the program is fully disclosed to the employer, there should not be a problem. A word of caution, however, is in order. Many employers have policies prohibiting employees from receiving incentives from suppliers.

You should also remember that push money payments or benefits are promotional allowances under the Robinson-Patman Act. Therefore, to the extent that push money payments are available only to the employees of selected companies, there may be a Robinson-Patman problem.

9.   Can you offer discount coupons that result in a sale below cost?

As a general rule, sales below cost are not *per se* illegal. Whether a particular sale below cost violates the law will depend on the facts of the particular sale.

Sales below cost are prohibited when the sales are made for the purpose or intent of destroying a competitor. Sales below cost for the purposes of advertising or stimulating business are acceptable. Thus, the use of loss leaders is an acceptable business practice.

Whether or not a sale below cost will be deemed for the purpose or intent of destroying competition may depend on a number of factors. Obviously, if there is any written correspondence or communication indicating an intent to destroy competition, then the predatory intent will be shown. Similarly, if the sales below cost occur in a geographic area where there are only one or two competitors, or where there has been a recent new entry into the market, predatory intent may be inferred. In addition, a continuous and sustained practice of selling below cost can be viewed as predatory intent. A program of limited duration is less likely to be viewed as having the requisite predatory intent.

Many states also have specific statutes that prohibit sales below cost when done with the purpose or effect of injuring competition. In certain states, sales below cost of certain items, such as dairy products and gasoline, are strictly prohibited.

In short, before commencing any sales-below-cost program, you have to look at the particular geographic area in which the program is to be conducted, the structure of the market, and the products involved.

10. Is Robinson-Patman likely to be a priority of the FTC in the future?

The Robinson-Patman Act had its heyday in the 1950s and 1960s, but is hardly a top priority for the FTC today. That doesn't mean that the Act is ignored. The potential exists for a private litigant to bring an action for treble damages—a significant private remedy that exists under the Act. Generally speaking, however, as long as a company makes a good-faith effort to comply with the law and the Guides, the likelihood of a serious challenge is minimized.

Form I.12.3 Records Retention Policy Checklist

Category	Retention Period (In Years)
Animatics, etc. (following production of campaign)	1
Audit Reports	P*
Authorizations & Appropriations for Expenditures	7
Bank Records	7
Budget Work Sheets	2
Call Reports	3
Cash Receipts and Disbursements Records	7
Claim Substantiation (following completion of campaign)	3
Client Papers or Other Property	P
Confidentiality Agreements	P
Contracts, Government	P
Contracts, Other (following termination)	7
Copyright Certificates	P
Cost Accounting Records	7
Employee Records	P
Expense Reports, Employees	7
Invoices (other than Property, Plant, and Equipment)	6
Licenses	P
Masters	P
Payroll Records	7
Plates & Mechanicals (following completion of campaign)	7
Procedures for Compliance with ADA, FMLA, etc.	P
Storyboards (following completion of campaign or rejection)	3
Talent Payment Records (following last use of materials)	7
Tear Sheets (following completion of campaign)	7
Tissues of Potential Campaigns (following completion of campaign or rejection)	2
Trademark Certificates	P
Transparencies	7

*P = permanent

Chapter XIII
Private Regulation of Advertising

1. The NAD and NARB

The early 1970s gave birth to the National Advertising Division (NAD) and the National Advertising Review Board (NARB) as the advertising industry's self-regulatory bodies. In rough comparison to the traditional judicial system, the NAD is the equivalent of a trial court and the NARB, similar in nature to appellate courts, resolves appeals from the NAD. Unlike the judicial system, however, compliance with NAD and NARB rulings is voluntary, although responsible advertisers and agencies generally comply with such rulings. Created by four major associations of the advertising industry (the Council of Better Business Bureaus, the American Association of Advertising Agencies, the American Advertising Federation, and the Association of National Advertisers), the NAD and NARB have gained widespread acceptance in the advertising industry. Indeed, one court has noted that "Voluntary compliance with NAD's decisions has been universal." Nevertheless, a decision of the NAD or NARB is not binding on the participants and, of course, is not binding upon a court of law, even when the court reviews the exact same issues argued before the NAD or NARB.

The NAD monitors advertising and its compliance with accepted standards of claims substantiation. It is staffed with attorneys who are highly experienced in reviewing advertising. The NAD can institute proceedings against an advertiser on its own or as a result of a complaint filed by a competitor, trade association, consumer, or consumer group. Established procedures, while far more informal than court actions, provide for meetings and the submission of papers by all sides of a controversy.

If a party subject to an adverse ruling of the NAD takes exception to the NAD's findings, it may appeal the ruling to the NARB. The NARB will convene a panel of five executives from the advertising community who will sit at a hearing, consider arguments presented by the NAD, the challenged advertiser, and the challenger, and render an opinion either affirming, reversing, or modifying the NAD ruling. There is no further appeal.

Findings of the NAD and NARB are published and often reported in trade publications like *Advertising Age* and *Adweek*. On occasion, mainstream press will also pick up a decision. For the most part, however, NAD and NARB proceedings are resolved quietly.

WARNING

If an advertiser objects to an NARB ruling, it is faced with a dilemma. While not legally bound to follow the ruling, advertisers who fail to do so run the risk of having the NARB refer the matter to the Federal Trade Commission. When egg marketer Eggland's Best, Inc. chose to ignore an NARB ruling, the NARB referred the case to the FTC. By the time the FTC was finished with Eggland's Best, the company had agreed to corrective advertising, admitting it had made false claims in prior advertising. It would have been far better off complying with the NARB ruling.

---

2. Network Clearance

One of the great misconceptions among some in the advertising community is that network clearance is tantamount to legal clearance. The fact is that most advertising that is challenged by the FTC or is the subject of a lawsuit was cleared by the networks. Equally important is the networks' right to refuse advertising based solely on policy grounds, regardless of its truth. An advertiser not familiar with network guidelines on advertising can find itself in a very embarrassing situation with regard to perfectly legal commercials that are nonetheless refused by the networks.

While network clearance does involve some review of substantiation and other legal issues, it is also concerned with policy issues unique to each network. For example, NBC, ABC, and Fox will not allow the on-camera consumption of beer or wine in a commercial. CBS, on the other hand, will permit it, provided specific guidelines are followed. CBS allows moderate consumption of beer and wine.

Why It Matters

1. Prince Manufacturing, Inc., the maker of Prince tennis equipment, found itself with a "split" approval on a commercial it aired during the 1994 U.S. Open tennis tournament. The CBS Network was the live broadcaster of the event and USA Network had the cable rights. While USA agreed to air a commercial showing an actor portraying God losing a shot to an opponent who was using a Prince racquet, CBS refused on the grounds of poor taste.

2. In 1991, athletic footwear manufacturer L. A. Gear, Inc. found itself with approval only from NBC and ABC in a campaign that used the tag line, "Everything else is just hot air." CBS refused to air the spot, claiming that the tag line was an unsupported superiority claim against competitors Nike and Reebok.

3. Print Media

Some print media, e.g., *Good Housekeeping*, have sophisticated review procedures for the advertising they print. Most, however, do not. Because their liability is so limited, even for false or deceptive advertising, most print media do not consider advertising clearance of great importance. Print media do not, for example, have to periodically renew their licenses to be in business, as do broadcasting stations. Thus, the networks consider the clearance process far more important than do print media.

4. Regulated Industries

Some regulated industries have their own requirements regarding advertising. Perhaps the best known is the code of advertising of the Distilled Spirits Council of the United States (DISCUS). Under the DISCUS Code, for example, distillers are discouraged from broadcasting commercials for hard liquor. However, since the DISCUS Code was updated to permit responsible television and radio advertising of distilled spirits in commercials not targeted at individuals below the legal purchase age, in 1996, a few distillers have disregarded the voluntary ban by broadcasting hard liquor commercials. Under the revision, advertising on electronic media, including television, is permitted by the DISCUS Code.

5. Advertising Directed at Children

Advertising directed at children deserves specific mention. It is an area of considerable concern to the advertising community, the media, and legislators. While there are a few specific laws that relate to the content of advertising directed at children, they tend to be in areas of little controversy, for example, advertising for 900 pay-per-call services directed at children.

At the federal level, the Federal Trade Commission has brought a number of actions against advertisers and their advertising agencies on the basis of problems unique to children's advertising. Thus, the FTC challenged a commercial for an instant rice where a child was shown too close to a boiling pot on the stove without adult supervision. Similarly, the FTC has stopped advertising of children's toys where video techniques used in commercials portrayed a toy's performance that could not be replicated by children. It is important to note that in virtually every case involving children's advertising challenged by the FTC, the order against the advertising agency was broader than that entered against the advertiser. In most cases, the order against the advertising agency applied to all the clients of the agency, not just the advertiser client challenged by the FTC.

At the legislative level, the attacks have sharpened. In May 1997, the FTC issued a complaint against R.J. Reynolds Tobacco Company alleging that the use of Reynolds'"Joe Camel" cartoon figure in

SURGEON GENERAL'S WARNING: Quitting Smoking Now Greatly Reduces Serious Risks to Your Health.

13.a The FDA's attack on R.J. Reynolds' Joe Camel campaign presents serious First Amendment issues.

a Camel cigarette advertising campaign constituted an unfair act or practice in violation of the FTC Act. Underlying the complaint were concerns that the advertising campaign was targeted at children and would lead more children to smoke or to smoke more. These issues were similar to those considered by the FTC in its 1993–94 inquiry into the same advertising campaign in which the Commission voted to end its investigation, citing insufficient evidence that the advertising campaign would lead more children to smoke. (See picture 13.a.)

Then, in June 1997, the major tobacco companies reached a historic settlement with 40 state attorneys general who had sued to recover Medicaid money that their states had spent for the treatment of smoking-related illness. In addition to the payment of substantial amounts of money, the settlement would have banned billboard advertising, people in ads (i.e., the Marlboro Man), cartoon characters like Joe Camel, brand sponsorship of sports, and photos or color in print ads that children see. That settlement died, however, in Congress. Finally, in 1998, the 40 states entered into a settlement agreement with the major tobacco companies accomplishing, something Congress could not.

Within the context of the self-regulatory area, however, the advertising community has attempted to address major concerns before advertisers and advertising agencies become subject to legislative action. Under the auspices of the Council of Better Business Bureaus, the advertising community funds the Children's Advertising Review Unit (CARU). CARU routinely monitors children's advertising for compliance with a set of guidelines it established. While these guidelines are sometimes controversial in their admittedly subjective nature, the astute advertising executive embarking on a children's advertising campaign is well advised to be fully familiar with CARU's Guidelines and Procedures, which are available online at http://www.caru.org/guidelines/index.asp.

CHAPTER XIV
Handling Unsolicited Ideas

1. Rejection/Acceptance Policy for Unsolicited Ideas

The most effective way to deal with unsolicited ideas is to adopt a strict and unvarying practice of refusing to consider unsolicited ideas unless submitted in the regular course of business by professionals in the field. There are at least two good reasons to refuse to consider unsolicited ideas:

(a) It is extremely unlikely that any idea submitted by a member of the general public will not already be known to the advertiser or its advertising agency or, if it is not generally known, will have any merit; accordingly, refusing to consider unsolicited ideas will constitute no hardship.

(b) By refusing to consider all unsolicited ideas, the chances of having to defend a lawsuit are minimized.

The procedure commonly used by companies that follow the rule of refusing to consider any unsolicited ideas is to immediately send any unsolicited idea that is received to a specified non-creative person (an administrative or financial officer). That person promptly returns the entire package to the submitter with a form letter that explains the company's position and states that the idea will not be considered by the company. Before returning the package, a copy of its contents should be made in order to avoid any future controversy as to what was submitted. The copy should be retained under the control of a person who has no connection with the creative or advertising process.

A second approach, which is followed by some national advertisers, is similar to the first approach in its initial steps. The unsolicited idea is immediately forwarded to a non-creative person. He or she, in this approach, then notifies the submitter that the company's policy is to refuse to consider any unsolicited idea unless the submitter signs the company's standard form of contract governing the submission. In essence, the contract provides that even if the idea is used, in no event will it be deemed to have a value in excess of a modest sum that is set forth in the contract. If agreed to, the contract will permit the company to consider the idea while, it is hoped, limiting the company's financial exposure to the stipulated contract sum. (See Form I.14.1.)

2. Risks in Accepting Unsolicited Ideas

Accepting unsolicited ideas is not without risks. The smart thing to do is avoid them whenever possible. Otherwise, get a signed agreement stating agency policy. Failing to take protective measures to instruct all personnel on how to handle unsolicited ideas can cost many thousands of dollars in damages and legal fees.

Why It Matters

1. A creative consultant produced a commercial for Eastern Airlines that started with nine separate five-second, silent, black-and-white frames. The ad also included video supers "selling" various services offered by Eastern. The final frame showed a sunset, in color, and included a voice-over tag. Eastern decided to use the commercial only in Canada. The consultant (who had retained the rights

to the commercial) then wrote the president of United Airlines suggesting that United hire him to produce a silent commercial for its U.S. market. United never hired the consultant, but did air a silent commercial on U.S. television. United's commercial contained nine five-second frames, the first eight of which were black and white, with supers fading in and out, from frame to frame. The last frame was in color and showed an airplane taking off. The word "Roarrr" was superimposed over the final frame, but there was no sound. The consultant sued, and the court held that the case should be tried to determine whether United copied Eastern's commercial by similar juxtaposition of video depictions of airplanes with silent video "supers" showing the destinations and prices.

2. Burger King Corporation was sued for allegedly misappropriating an advertising theme entitled "Burger King Town." The plaintiff's previous submission to Burger King was a campaign using the theme "Everywhere you go in America there is a Burger King Town." The trial court's dismissal of the case was reversed, and the trial court was ordered to allow the plaintiff to show that his idea was novel and disclosed in confidence to Burger King.

Chapter Fourteen Forms

Form I.14.1 Idea Submission Agreement (for use when ideas will be considered)

Name:_____

Address: _____

Telephone: _____

The above (the "Submitter") desires to submit certain materials (the "Material") to [insert name of company] (the "Company") to evaluate and review. The parties understand and acknowledge as follows:

1. The Company is continuously engaged in active research and development programs that may have ideas, functions, features, or other aspects that are similar or identical to the ideas, functions, features, or other aspects of the Material.

2. Other persons, including the Company's own employees, may have submitted to the Company or to others, or may in the future originate and submit, material which is similar or identical to the Material. It is agreed that no compensation will be paid to the Submitter for use of the Material because of the Company's use of such other similar or identical material not created by the Submitter.

3. Submitter agrees that the Company assumes no obligation to (i) return the Material submitted, (ii) compensate the Submitter in any way for the use of the Material in accordance with the evaluation specified herein, (iii) proceed with negotiations of any kind respecting the Material, or (iv) furnish Submitter with any information respecting the results of the Company's evaluation or its reasons for not proceeding further.

4. Inasmuch as the disclosure to the Company of information that is considered by Submitter or a third party to be confidential could have an adverse impact on the Company's rights in products or ideas arising out of the Company's research and development program, the Company is not interested in gaining access to information that is considered by Submitter or a third party to be confidential. In order to ensure that there is no future misunderstanding of the respective rights of the Company and Submitter, the Company has developed a policy under which it will not undertake to review or evaluate information that is claimed to be confidential by any person or entity outside the Company.

5. The Company agrees that it will not use the Material for any purpose other than evaluation hereunder without entering into a formal written agreement with Submitter giving permission to the Company to do so. The foregoing does not apply to any material which is similar to or identical to the Material, but which was independently developed (without the use of the Material) by the Company or a third party.

6. Submitter has retained at least one copy of the Material, and releases the Company from any and all liability for loss of or damage to the copy or copies of the Material submitted to the Company hereunder.

7. Submitter represents that the material is original with Submitter, that Submitter is the owner of the Material, that Submitter has the exclusive right to submit the Material to the Company, and that Submitter has the power and authority to grant the Company any and all rights in the Material.

8. Submitter agrees that Submitter will not use the potential interest of the Company with respect to any material submitted to the Company in any promotional activity nor disclose to any other person that the Company is evaluating the Material.

9. Submitter hereby acknowledges and agrees that there are no prior or contemporaneous oral or written agreements in effect between Submitter and the Company pertaining to the Material submitted hereunder or any other material (including, but not limited to, agreements pertaining to the submission by Submitter of any ideas, formats, plots, characters, or the like). Submitter further agrees that no other obligations exist or shall exist or shall be deemed to exist unless and until a formal written agreement has been prepared and executed by both Submitter and the Company, and then Submitter's rights and obligations, and the Company's rights and obligations, shall be only such as are expressly set forth in such formal written agreement.

10. Nothing contained in this Agreement shall be construed as creating any obligation or an expectation on the part of either party to enter into a business relationship with the other party, or an obligation to refrain from entering into a business relationship with any third party. Nothing contained in this Agreement shall be construed as creating a joint venture, partnership, or employment relationship between the Company and Submitter, it being understood that the Company and Submitter are independent contractors vis-à-vis one another. Except as specified herein, no party shall have the right, power, or implied authority to create any obligation or duty, express or implied, on behalf of any other party hereto.

11. Submitter agrees that the terms of this document shall control the rights and obligations of the Company and Submitter respecting the Material, however disclosed or provided to the Company, including verbal disclosure thereof, and notwithstanding any legends, markings, or other restrictions embodied in, attached to, or accompanying such Material. The terms of this document may not be amended or superseded except by written amendment that refers to this document and is signed by both parties.

12. Submitter agrees that no oral representations of any kind have been made to Submitter.

13. This Agreement sets forth the entire understanding and agreement of the parties with respect to the subject matter hereof and supersedes all other oral or written representations and understandings. The formation, interpretation, and performance of this Agreement shall be governed by the laws of the State of [insert State], excluding its conflict of law rules, and any action relating to this Agreement or its enforcement shall only be brought in a state or federal court in [insert City and State]. In the event that any provision hereof is found invalid or unenforceable, the remainder of this Agreement shall remain valid and enforceable according to its terms.

14. Submitter certifies that Submitter has read this Agreement and that Submitter understands it. SUBMITTER UNDERSTANDS THAT THE COMPANY IS RELYING UPON THIS AGREEMENT IN AGREEING TO ACCEPT Submitter's SUBMISSION OF THE MATERIAL AND WOULD NOT ACCEPT Submitter's MATERIAL WITHOUT IT.

If the terms of this document are acceptable, please sign and return one copy of this document to the Company prior to submission of the Material that Submitter desires to have evaluated.

Company: Submitter:

By: _____   By: _____

Form I.14.2 Form for Rejection of All Submissions of Unsolicited Ideas

[Company Letterhead]

[Date]

[Address of Recipient]

Dear _____:

This acknowledges our receipt of your recent correspondence containing an unsolicited idea or material.

We make it our policy not to accept or consider any unsolicited ideas or materials of any kind.

We do not agree that any unsolicited idea or material you submitted will be treated as proprietary or confidential, regardless of the manner in which it was submitted by you or any conditions you placed on such submission. Nor do we agree that your submission of any unsolicited idea or material will result in any compensation to you.

As such, please refrain from sending us any further unsolicited ideas or materials. If you have previously received notice of our policy but continue to submit unsolicited ideas or materials, or should you submit additional unsolicited ideas or materials, they will be deemed our property, free and clear of any claims by you or others, and we will be able to use them for any purpose, including advertising and promotion, without compensation, payment, or any other obligation to you.

Very truly yours,

[Signature]

_____

The Business Side of Advertising

CHAPTER XV

The Relationship Between the Advertising Agency and Its Client

In the absence of a written agreement, industry practice can be referred to in establishing the rights and obligations between an advertising agency and an advertiser. With all the changes over the last decades, however, there are few industry norms remaining. Without a written agreement, the advertising agency is largely at the mercy of the advertiser when the advertiser elects to terminate the relationship. And it is safe to say that virtually every relationship will eventually be terminated. Conversely, unless matters regarding ownership of materials, assignments of contracts, and commissions are covered by a written contract, an advertising agency may have undue leverage against an advertiser upon termination.

Put bluntly, it's unprofessional not to have a written agreement. (See Forms II.15.1, II.15.2, and II.15.3.)

1. Compensation

Without doubt, the most sensitive debates surrounding an agency/client agreement concern the manner in which the agency will be compensated for its services.

For many years, the matter of compensation could not have been simpler. Until the 1980s, most advertising agencies were compensated on a commission basis, receiving 15% on all monies spent on media and 17.65% on monies spent on production. As the 1980s came to a close, however, the commission structure began to undergo profound changes. A 2000 survey conducted by the Association of National Advertisers, Inc., the leading trade association for marketers and advertisers, reported that only 21% of the advertisers surveyed were paying their agencies commission on media, down from 34% in 1997. Of those advertisers reporting in the 2000 survey, the report concludes that "…it is clear that the traditional 15% commission rate is no longer the standard." The survey found that labor-based compensation is the method of choice for the majority of U.S. advertisers, with 68% of respondents paying their agencies on a labor-based fee formula (up from 53% in 1997).

Advertisers have increasingly sought more innovative and balanced ways to compensate an agency. In some instances, advertisers have looked upon agencies as common suppliers providing a commodity that should be priced on a flat-fee basis. Today, some relationships between agencies and advertisers are based upon nothing more than an agreed-upon fee for a finite project. Such relationships are generally short-term, with transactions concluded quickly. If the agency underestimates the time required to deliver the product, it loses in the proposition. Similarly, the advertiser has no way of knowing if it paid a fair price for the job.

More often, advertisers and agencies desire long-term relationships and advertisers look upon their agencies more as partners than suppliers. Advertisers require their agency to be knowledgeable about their industry and understand their strategic marketing objectives. Agencies are expected to create targeted advertising with those strategic objectives in mind. To do so, an agency has to invest many hours in research and service on an account, all of which costs considerable funds in manpower and overhead.

Over the past decade, flat-fee- or hour-fee-based compensations have been the most common alternatives to the traditional commission structure. Other alternatives have also been proposed by advertisers, including:

a. Declining Commission

The most potent argument against a flat 15% commission arrangement is that it overly compensates an agency if the media buy is particularly large. Presumably, a 30-second commercial for a $50,000,000 media schedule costs no more to produce than a 30-second commercial for a $500,000 buy—or so the argument goes. As such, some advertisers pay a declining rate of commission as their media buy increases: e.g., 15% on the first $2 million, 12% on the next $3 million, and 9% on anything in excess of $5 million.

b. Guaranteed Profit

Less commonly, some advertisers guarantee their agency a minimum profit margin on their account. The difficulty is not in establishing the profit rate, but rather in establishing what cost factors go into the agency's overhead in determining the base factor upon which the profit calculation will be made. For example, how much of the agency's backroom costs will be factored in? Will research costs and time of personnel be allowed? What about outside costs that are not chargeable to any particular account; e.g., legal and accounting, or staff-utilization time? Every agency seems to have a different way of handling internal accounting, and a guaranteed profit arrangement can only work if the advertiser completely understands the agency's accounting system. In addition, such arrangements can be sensitive if the advertiser insists on knowing individual salaries of agency personnel, particularly the principals of the agency. In such instances, the confidentiality is maintained by allowing only the advertiser's auditors to have sensitive information or by accepting a certified statement from the agency's CPA.

c. Incentive Compensation

Incentive compensation, while increasingly popular, is difficult to apply, largely because it is all too often based upon factors that are not fully within the agency's control, e.g., increases in sales. In other instances, the criteria are too subjective and left to the whim of lower-level personnel of an advertiser. As a result, many incentive arrangements only serve to alienate the agency. If incentive compensation is to work, the thresholds must be attainable and the measures mutually agreed upon. For an incentive arrangement to be successful, experts say, the criteria should be a combination of subjective and objective standards that both the advertiser and agency agree are fair and reasonable. The determination of whether an agency has satisfied any subjective criteria should only be made by the advertiser's highest-level executives. Finally, the incentive compensation should be only a small part of the overall compensation plan. If too high a percentage of the overall compensation is incentive-based, it may be impossible for the agency to operate profitably. Industry experts say that no more than 10% of an agency's compensation should be based upon an incentive formula.

d. Guaranteed Minimum Compensation

When an agency calculates what it believes it will cost to service an account and adds a profit margin to that figure, that amount becomes the guaranteed compensation. Such a system can work if the agency can accurately calculate the manpower and administration an account will require. Unlike flat project fees, guaranteed compensation arrangements usually allow for periodic review and adjustment depending upon the shifting requirements of an account. (See Form II.19.4, paragraph 3.)

2. Advertiser Acknowledgments and Authorizations

It is not unusual to see limits placed on how much advertising agencies can spend without the advertiser's authorization. This protects both parties from potential misunderstandings. The problem, however, is often more practical than contractual.

In the advertising industry, time is of the essence and it is often impossible for an advertising agency to get written approval for expenses it incurs for its client. While contracts typically include some limit under which written approval is not required, an advertiser should recognize that practicalities make even such provisions impossible to enforce. A smart alternative is to require that an advertising agency confirm in a call report that an expense has been authorized. Of course, there should be one person designated at both the advertising agency and the advertiser who may seek or grant such authorization, and certain expenses should always require written approval of the advertiser, e.g., advertising agency and media buys, production estimates, and talent costs.

3. Dealing with Accounts Payable and Receivable

a. Invoice and Payment Schedules

The agency/client agreement should clearly define agreed-upon payment schedules. It is also important that neither party vary from the schedule unless it is stated clearly that the variation is not a modification of the standard procedure. Thus, if an advertising agency decides to give an advertiser relief from the agency's standard invoicing/payment schedule, the advertising agency should inform the advertiser that the waiver is not a permanent change in policy. Similarly, if an advertiser wishes to vary from the contractual terms, it should amend the agreement, or at least receive written acknowledgment from the advertising agency accepting the modified schedule. This can be as simple as a short letter countersigned by the advertising agency. Otherwise, technically, the advertiser may find itself in breach of the contract, able to rely only on oral testimony, a situation that benefits neither party.

b. Consequences of Arrears

An agency/client agreement should provide that an advertising agency can cancel media buys or refuse to perform additional work if it has not been paid on time. Without such a clearly defined right, a delinquent account might only worsen and create greater liabilities for the advertising agency. On the other hand, if an advertising agency cancels a media buy because of payment delinquency or disputes, and fails to notify the advertiser until after closing dates for the publications or stations involved, an advertiser can find itself flat out of luck.

c. Canceling Media

Canceling media without the authorization of the advertiser is a risky policy. First, the agency should only do so if the advertiser is clearly in breach of its obligations to the advertising agency in regard to the media purchase. The agency does not have the right to cancel media simply because it has a dispute with the advertiser over non-media-related compensation, e.g., production costs. The potential damage to the advertiser if media is canceled is too great to confuse the issue with unrelated disputes. Second, the advertising agency should be certain to give the advertiser adequate notice of the potential cancellation so that the advertiser has an opportunity to remedy the late payment.

If it directs its advertising agency to cancel media during the term of its agreement with the advertising agency, the advertiser should be aware of short-rate adjustments. Long-range media buys allow for savings off rates otherwise charged by media for spot or single insertions. Most contracts with media provide that if a long-term buy provides for a discount and the buy is canceled after the media run has begun, the media will recalculate the costs without the discount and bill the difference, known as the "short-rate adjustment." Therefore, before canceling any long-term media buy in progress, make sure the short-rate adjustment doesn't eat up most of the savings anticipated by the cancellation.

d. Recovering Collection Costs

A clause permitting recovery of collection costs is often overlooked, but shouldn't be. Parties rarely object to them. Recovery of attorneys' fees may be desired in the event of a breach of the agreement by one of the parties that results in litigation between the advertiser and its advertising agency. For example, the advertising agency's failure to acquire the scope of rights mandated in the agency/client agreement could be an expensive mistake, forcing the advertiser to incur additional expenses for outside creative, and leading to costly litigation.

4. Exclusivity

Increasingly, advertisers retain advertising agencies on a non-exclusive basis, thereby reserving the right to use any number of other agencies for their advertising work. This can be problematic depending upon the nature of the compensation formula for the agency. Understanding the different compensation systems typically used today is necessary in order to appreciate the problems that a non-exclusive arrangement can create.

a. Compensation Considerations

1. In a fee-based compensation deal, an agency is paid a fee generally based upon either an hourly charge or a set monthly fee. On occasion, the two approaches are combined and hourly charges are applied against a monthly fee with periodic reconciliations to adjust for any underage or overage. In some instances, a minimum monthly fee is guaranteed regardless of the hours of work performed.

2. Under a pure commission deal, an agency is paid a set commission rate, e.g., 15%, charged against dollars spent on media and production. In some instances, a monthly fee is agreed upon, and the commissions earned in any given month are applied against that month's fee with periodic reconciliations to adjust for any underages or overages. Sometimes a minimum monthly fee is guaranteed regardless of the commissions earned.

If the agreement between an agency and an advertiser is non-exclusive, the advertiser is free at any time to use another agency for a project. Thus, in a fee-based deal, the original agency loses the work. Similarly, in a pure commission-based deal, the original agency loses the commissions if it does not place the media. Therefore, unless a minimum monthly fee is guaranteed under the agreement between the original agency and the advertiser, a non-exclusive agreement provides no security for the agency and leaves the agency at risk of not recouping any investment it made in ramping up to service a client: e.g., hire personnel, pay for outside services, increase space, etc. On the other hand, a non-exclusive agreement provides the advertiser with the most discretion on when and by whom its advertising will be produced. Certainly, it makes no sense for an advertiser to grant exclusivity to an agency that does not have the expertise to handle certain aspects of the advertiser's marketing requirements, e.g., sales promotion or ethnic marketing. In such circumstances, any exclusivity should be narrowly defined.

Why It Matters

Suppose an advertiser has more than one agency under a non-exclusive contract, with each contract providing for payment by commissions only. In such a situation, there is nothing to prevent the advertiser from using the material prepared by one agency and allowing it to be placed by another agency. As a result, one agency has provided services to the advertiser for which it will not be compensated by commissions. Therefore, the exclusivity of the relationship is an important contract consideration. Note, however, that the problem is not as important in purely fee-based agreements, as the advertising agency will presumably be paid for all work performed, including during a notice period prior to termination.

b. Competitive Considerations

How restricted should an advertising agency be in its ability to work for companies considered competitive or antithetical to an existing advertiser client? Because such a restriction, by definition, limits the freedom of an advertising agency to offer its services in a competitive marketplace, it is viewed by agencies with great concern. On the other hand, because an agency's creative, media, and account-planning services are so vital to an advertiser's success in the market, advertisers understandably want total loyalty from, and the sole focus of, their agencies. Therein lies the conflict between competitive freedom and broad exclusivity.

In the following hypothetical negotiation, we can draw six important lessons about competitive accounts and exclusivity:

The Creative Advertising Agency has won the highly coveted Crunchy Cookie account. Compensation has been agreed to and a discussion regarding other contract provisions is under way. The topic of the moment is exclusivity. Crunchy Cookie is owned by Consolidated Products, a huge conglomerate. Consolidated wants to know what accounts Creative handles. Creative wants to know what companies Consolidated doesn't care to have it handle. Creative is naturally expected to agree not to handle any other cookie account. Creative would not argue otherwise. So far, so good.

Consolidated, however, sells a variety of products; some fall into the snack category—others do not. Is it reasonable to restrict Creative from handling anyone else's snack products? Is it fair to expect Creative to refrain from working for a client that sells, for example, salty snacks like nuts and chips? And what about a restriction that covers a competitor, regardless of the cookie-specific assignment? What if Amalgamated Industries, which has a cookie subsidiary, approaches Creative to do business? Is it fair to restrict Creative from providing any services to Amalgamated Industries, regardless of the category? Amalgamated also sells tobacco products. Should Creative be prevented from taking on Amalgamated tobacco products because Amalgamated also sells cookies? Certainly, if Crunchy Cookie is paying Creative tens of millions of dollars for fully commissioned media and advertising for print, broadcast, Internet, outdoor, POS, etc., then Consolidated may be in a position to demand very broad exclusivity. On the other hand, Creative does not want to put all its cookies in one basket and can't afford to be dependent on one client. An agency can survive only if it is free to take on a variety of accounts. Lesson One: Exclusivity must, in all fairness, have its limits.

Creative and Consolidated agree it is fair to define the exclusivity category to include all snack foods. To work on Consolidated's Crunchy Cookies and Amalgamated's salt snacks might mean Creative's key creative personnel feel conflicted between the most effective executions for the two clients, both of whom are addressing a similar consumer. Creative could make an argument that consumers do not make a conscious choice between cookies and nuts when choosing snacks. The goal is to motivate the consumer to choose to buy Crunchy Cookies rather than another cookie, not to motivate them to buy, or for that matter eat, Crunchy Cookies rather than salted peanuts when hunger strikes. Then again, one might start to wonder, wouldn't "Eat Cookies, Not Nuts" make an effective campaign?

The same issue can arise in any general category. Should a car company restrict its agency from taking on a bicycle account (transportation)? Should a credit card company prohibit its agency from representing a secondary mortgage lender (financial services)? Would it be fair to prevent an agency that handles personal organizers with email account, e.g., Palm Pilot or Blackberry, from taking on a company that sells cellular telephones (communications)? Whether two products or services compete with one another can be decidedly blurry and it is often unclear where the line should be drawn. Lesson Two: Pinning down products and services or their categories, for purposes of defining exclusivity, requires negotiation on a case-by-case basis.

The issue becomes thornier when exclusivity is extended to an entire company, not just particular products or services. Corporate conglomerates dominate the marketplace today. It is not uncommon to see giant companies consolidating entire vertical markets in food, communications, entertainment, and the like. Others dominate in horizontal markets of disparate products or services that range from electronics to entertainment to clothing to sporting goods. Still others are in markets with goods and services that defy any logical synergy, e.g., Seagram's former configuration of motion pictures and distilled spirits. Whatever the case may be, competition for market share in every product/service category is ferocious. How much "room" is there in the negotiation? Lesson Three: It's up to the advertiser and agency to clearly define the limits of who the agency may represent to be certain that conflicts do not develop. To the extent the agency does not openly communicate with its existing clients in that respect, it assumes the risk associated with such an approach.

Consolidations and mergers, however, are not unique to advertisers. Consolidation has also occurred in the agency business. Sizable holding companies control advertising agencies that actually compete with one another domestically and throughout the world. Exclusivity across the subsidiaries of such holding companies is yet another issue. Suppose Creative is a subsidiary of Agency Holding Unlimited (AHU). AHU has seven subsidiary advertising agencies, all of which are operated independently from one another. Is it fair for Consolidated Products to demand that no other AHU subsidiary will handle a cookie account in exchange for Creative winning Crunchy Cookies? Or, should Consolidated accept the argument AHU makes that its subsidiaries, including Creative, are totally independent companies that do not exchange information on accounts, share creative concepts or talent, or even consider what another sister agency is doing? The answer is not a simple one. Lesson Four: The marketplace has many examples where distant competitive arrangements among subsidiaries of the holding companies, e.g., Omnicom, WPP, and Interpublic, succeed without impeding the creative product or effective account management sought by advertisers from their agencies.

The last aspect of exclusivity that Creative and Consolidated grapple with is whether exclusivity will extend beyond the term of their contract. Creative's position is that an exclusivity clause that extends for months beyond termination prevents it from working on a competitor's account for too long a period of time. Consolidated makes numerous arguments to justify the extension. For example, Consolidated is concerned that Creative is privy to confidential information and account planning that, if known when handling a competitive account, could prove very detrimental. In addition, Consolidated does not want Creative to resign its account simply because a more lucrative competitor is up for grabs in the marketplace. Creative might also argue that it would be unfair to restrict the agency if it's the advertiser who fires the agency as opposed to the agency resigning the advertiser. Finally, a contract may be terminated for reasons that have nothing to do with account service or the agency's performance. In such circumstances, the agency should not be penalized with extended exclusivity. Lesson Five: Extended exclusivity is not unreasonable in certain circumstances, but it should not be considered *de rigeur* in every contract.

In this context, it also important to remember that a well-drafted confidentiality provision can protect an advertiser well beyond the term of the contract (assuming such a clause is part of the contract). Indeed, it would be entirely unreasonable for an agency to refuse to protect confidential information provided it is clear between the advertiser and agency what information is considered confidential. Lesson Six: A well-drafted confidentiality clause can offer as much protection to an advertiser as an extended exclusivity provision.

> *Summary of Lessons Learned:*
>
> ◆ Exclusivity must, in all fairness, have its limits.
>
> ◆ Pinning down products and services or their categories, for purposes of defining exclusivity, requires negotiation on a case-by-case basis.
>
> ◆ It's up to the advertiser and agency to communicate with one another to be certain that conflicts do not develop.
>
> ◆ The marketplace has many examples where distant competitive arrangements among wholly owned agencies succeed without impeding the creative product or effective account management sought by advertisers from their agencies.
>
> ◆ Extended exclusivity is not unreasonable in certain circumstances, but it should not be considered *de rigeur* in every contract.
>
> ◆ A well-drafted confidentiality clause can offer as much protection to an advertiser as an extended exclusivity provision.

5. Termination

Every advertising agency would like to think that its clients will remain on the agency's roster forever; assuming, of course, that the client is profitable for the agency. Likewise, every advertiser would like to stay with the same agency forever; assuming, of course, that the agency continues to come up with creative, profit-making advertising. The reality, however, is that advertising agency relationships with advertisers are almost always more short-lived than either party envisioned at the beginning of the relationship. At the start, everyone's excited about a new client, new creative input, and a new beginning. But then the need for measurements of performance begins. Sales comparisons. Profit projections. A critical eye starts to oversee the process. The ever-fickle consumer gets in the way. A new brand manager comes to town. Suddenly, the account is up for review, and while the "incumbent" will probably be invited to pitch yet again, its likelihood of winning is pretty low. So from the outset, the astute advertising executive must plan for the end of the affair.

Typical advertising agency agreements with advertisers address termination in a number of ways. To understand the wisdom behind these variations, it helps to look at the nature of agency/client relationships: how they prosper and why they fail.

a. In the Beginning: The Pitch

Most new accounts for an advertising agency are won through competitions with other agencies. Typically, a request for proposal (RFP) is sent to agencies inviting them to participate in a pitch. Often, particularly for larger advertising accounts, consultants are retained to help the advertiser in the search and to cull a few finalists from the field of contenders that will make formal presentations to the advertiser. While not always the case, these presentations may also include speculative creative. Without doubt, the finalists devote a great deal of time, effort, and expense to preparing their presentations.

If speculative creative is involved, it is not uncommon for the advertiser to pay a nominal fee to the finalists. While the fee rarely reimburses the advertising agency for the full costs of its creative, particularly if it loses the pitch, the fee provides a basis upon which ownership in the speculative creative can be determined. Usually when such a fee is paid, a written agreement between the agency and the advertiser provides that the advertiser owns the creative, regardless of whether the agency wins the account or not. Absent a written agreement, ownership of the creative remains with the agency.

b. The Win

To establish a commitment, it is not uncommon for the advertiser and agency to agree to a set minimum term of their relationship, e.g., one year. The logic is that this allows the agency to staff the account and learn about the advertiser's business without the fear of quick termination that could leave it with contingent employee liabilities and an unrecouped investment on the time, effort, and expense it devoted to gearing up to service its new account.

At the same time, the advertiser is assured that its new agency will not be looking for greener pastures too soon. Of course, an agreement may provide for early termination if based upon "cause," e.g., embezzlement of money or failure to pay, but such terminations are rare. Indeed, it is not unusual at all to see contracts between advertisers and agencies that are completely silent on termination for cause.

Once the minimum term of agreement has expired, most agreements remain in effect until terminated by either party on an agreed-upon number of days.

c. Fast Forward to Calling It Quits

Quite often, the relationship between an advertiser and its agency spoils for reasons beyond either party's control. The economy may shift. Innovative competition may enter the market. Patents may expire. Honest differences of opinion on the best creative direction may arise.

Other times, creative or other differences lead to disenchantment. The creative team may miss the mark despite clear instructions from the advertiser. The advertiser may fail to spend enough to back the market despite protestations from the agency. Priorities and management of the advertiser or agency may change. The advertiser may simply tire of the creative or the agency may see a better prospect in the market. And the list goes on.

As with marriage, honesty up front, coupled with a good "prenuptial agreement" is the best form of insurance against a painful ending. Unlike a marriage, though, the relationship between an advertiser and an agency cannot allow for one of the parties to simply walk out on the other.

A smooth transition benefits both parties, and the termination clause in the agency/client prenuptial will help guard against a hotly contested ending.

d. Postponing the Inevitable

For decades, the industry relied on a 90-day notice-of-termination period. In the past 20 years, however, the so-called "90-day clause" has become an endangered species. Indeed, it may nearly be extinct. The original thinking behind the clause was to allow the advertiser enough time to find a new agency in the event termination was made by the incumbent agency. Likewise, the clause would give the incumbent agency time to terminate employees and control expenses if it were fired by the advertiser. All in all, 90 days was the compromise period and it seemed to work well for years. Then, like everything else, it changed.

Not only did advertisers begin to reject the idea of the minimum one year term, they also began shrinking the termination notice period to 60 days, and even to 45 days. The reduction had to do with the fact that compensation to agencies also changed from principal reliance on commissions from media and markup on production to principal reliance on monthly fees, usually based upon hours devoted to the client. Thus, the longer the termination notice period, the more the advertiser was obligated to pay its agency, even if it was dissatisfied with its work. The alternative for the advertiser was to hire a new agency and, for the period of the notice, effectively pay two agencies simultaneously; clearly this was not an attractive approach.

Today, an advertiser typically wants a short notice period and no minimum term. After all, its products and services are on the line and it should be free to utilize whatever agency is best in the marketplace to maximize sales. On the other hand, the advertising agency usually wants at least 60 days with a minimum term of one year. After all, it cannot be expected to devote key creative talent and account management to an account that has no assurance of longevity.

e. Getting Along in the Transition Period

Getting along during the transition period (period after notice of termination is made), depends upon a number of issues. First, will the agency truly be able to service the advertiser during the notice period, or will it be pressured to cut personnel in anticipation of the loss? If the agency is on a fee basis, rather than commission, what does the fee cover during the termination period? If the agency is paid on commission from media, should the commission be paid on media placed during, but running after, the interim period? How are liabilities transferred? What about long-term commitments made by the agency on behalf of the advertiser? Unfortunately, there are no easy answers; each situation stands on its own.

At the end of the day, however, one thing is abundantly clear. Those terminations that result in acrimony are largely the result of a failure to communicate the respective expectations of the agency and the advertiser at the inception of the relationship. The agency/client agreement is where that communication begins and where both parties will return when the relationship ends. Yet, all too often, agencies don't have contracts with clients, or the contracts are nothing more than correspondence that doesn't address vital points. Both sides need to approach the agency/client contract mindful of the old adage about contracts—their measure of worth is taken when the contract is breached or terminated. So, however unpleasant the conversation may be, time spent early in the relationship outlining what happens when "it's over" will be time well spent.

f. Handling Existing Contractual Commitments.

Be certain that the advertising agency's contracts with outside suppliers can be freely assigned to the advertiser or its new advertising agency and that the advertiser affirmatively agrees to assume contractual responsibilities. Otherwise, it may become difficult to sever a relationship.

Why It Matters

If the advertising agency is a signatory to the Screen Actors Guild ("SAG") or American Federation of Television and Radio Artists ("AFTRA") Commercial Codes, the advertising agency guarantees the proper payments to actors performing in commercials produced by the agency on behalf of its advertiser client. If the actors' contracts are not assumed by the advertiser, the advertising agency continues to be liable for proper payment to the actors. Insofar as the unions are concerned, it is no excuse that the advertising agency is no longer the advertising agency of record for the advertiser. An advertising agency should be certain to obtain assumption-of-obligations agreements from the advertiser or its new advertising agency and must file these agreements with the appropriate talent unions. (Unfortunately most signatories neglect to routinely file the agreements with the unions).

---

g. Transfer of Ownership and Property

It is appropriate that the ownership and title to materials created by an advertising agency be transferred to its advertiser client upon termination of their relationship, provided the advertiser has paid the agency all charges associated with owning the materials. In pure commission-based agreements, the transfer may be conditioned upon the continued payment of commissions for some period of time, since commissions are the manner in which an advertising agency recoups its expenses and makes its profit. If an agreement between an advertising agency and an advertiser is terminated after materials have been produced but before they are published or broadcast, the advertising agency may be looking at a considerable loss unless it recoups a fair amount from future commissions. On the other hand, if the relationship is fee-based, i.e., the advertising agency receives a set monthly fee or an hourly rate, the transfer of ownership should not be conditioned upon commissions for future use.

It is important that the agreement also specify that only those rights the advertising agency acquired in the first place can be transferred. More often than not, rights to materials secured from third-party suppliers, e.g., music producers and photographers, are limited by license agreements. The agency/client agreement should clearly state that transfers are subject to the rights of third-party suppliers. In that connection, the advertising agency should be required to specify any limitations in rights at the time of transfer. Preferably, any such limitations should be told to the advertiser at the time the license agreements are first entered into.

h. Canceling Media and Short-rate Liability

If an advertiser terminates its agreement with its advertising agency and thereby cancels media buys, there may be short rate adjustments (see 3.c. above).

6. Indemnification

One subject that produces considerable tension between agencies and advertisers is the indemnity clause—the provision in a contract that governs who will be financially responsible when a mistake is made. With the ever-increasing instances and costs associated with litigation over advertising campaigns, this is no small issue and can cost the agency or advertiser hundreds of thousands and sometimes millions of dollars.

a. Standard Indemnifications

First, we can dispose of the easy areas, where there is rarely disagreement. Most agencies are more than willing to indemnify an advertiser for those perils covered by a standard advertising-agency insurance policy. Such risks include infringement of copyright, privacy, and publicity, as well as slander, libel, plagiarism, idea misappropriation, and other similar risks. Depending upon the policy, it may also include coverage for trademark infringement and unfair competition suits by competitors alleging false comparative advertising.

Likewise, advertisers are almost uniformly willing to indemnify their agencies with respect to any materials the advertiser supplies to the agency upon which the agency relies in crafting advertising claims. Examples include research, product specs, performance data, laboratory tests, and the like.

Finally, each party will generally agree to indemnify the other with respect to its own mistakes, such as for the destruction or loss of property entrusted to it; for acts taken beyond the scope of its respective authority, e.g., media commitments not authorized by the advertiser; and for its breach of specific obligations provided in the contract, such as timely payments, talent payments, etc.

b. Indemnification Gaps

The remaining areas contain a host of perils, both known and unknown, and often create a contentious gap between the parties. Into the gap falls the risk of a lawsuit brought by a governmental agency, a class-action lawsuit, or a private action brought by consumers or consumer groups alleging false or misleading advertising. Another area of contention involves disputes related to the failure to fulfill an offer made in an advertisement. These risks generally cannot be covered by insurance (although some say that for an outrageous premium one can buy a policy to cover almost anything). Who should bear the potentially substantial costs should these types of actions arise?

1. Practical Considerations: Often, the key to resolving the debate boils down to the relative size of the agency and advertiser. The fact remains that neither party should have confidence in an indemnity that is greater than the assets of the indemnitor. In other words, if either the advertiser or the agency is thinly capitalized or underinsured, the indemnity won't be worth the paper it's printed on. More often than not, the reality is that the agency is the smaller of the companies, and it is naive, at best, for an advertiser to think an indemnity from the agency beyond its insurance coverage has any value in the event an uninsured claim arises. In these instances, it is far better for the advertiser to be realistic, not dwell on an indemnity clause that has no real meaning, and not rely on what may be a false sense of security.

2. Minimizing Risk: There are some agencies, however, whose balance sheets are the envy of their clients. In those instances, the analysis is far more difficult. Who should bear the risk? What standards should apply to the sharing of risk? What impact does a broadly worded indemnity have on the creativity of any advertising agency? Apart from indemnities, what can an agency and advertiser do to minimize risk against uninsured claims?

First and foremost, every clause in an agency/client agreement, whether it is the indemnity clause or any other, should be put to the following test by the advertiser: Does it place an undue burden on the agency's ability to create an effective and successful advertising campaign? Often, the creative process is at its best when the legal "envelope" has been pushed. Stifling that creativity with undue fears of financial liability may be counterproductive. Instead, it is far more productive to insist that the agency have established review procedures in place.

Likewise, the agency should insist that the advertiser's legal counsel or in-house legal department review all advertising. This simple safeguard is an invaluable measure to minimize risk.

Without question, the plethora of regulations and legal limitations placed on advertising today is hardly supportive of a freewheeling creative process. But it is also clear that despite the constraints, incredibly creative advertising is produced every day without risk to anyone's bottom line. In this writer's view, those who ignore the importance of a thorough legal review are misguided. An appropriate review and approval process is worth far more than any indemnity, regardless of the assets of the agency or advertiser.

    3.   Responsibility: At the end of the day, who should be responsible for the uninsured perils that fall outside the indemnity?

The advertiser must take responsibility for its own advertising. While it can try to shift blame elsewhere, it is rarely the case that an advertiser is completely unaware that a campaign has problems. As wordsmiths and experts in the advertising business, the agency is also responsible. It cannot hide behind the advertiser's approval of a campaign.

Why It Matters

In the '70's and early '80's, an advertiser could expect an agency to assume substantial legal risk when the agency was paid 15% on a $100-million media budget, a 17.65% markup on production costs, and received a 90-day cancellation-notice period. Today that scenario is largely a fairy tale.

Speaking of fairy tales, imagine this: Neither the agency nor the advertiser indemnifies the other for uninsured claims. Instead, the marketplace determines liability. If the facts indicate that the agency is at fault, then the legal system apportions liability accordingly. If the advertiser errs, the liability remains with the advertiser. Other times, liability is shared. Could this be more expensive than an all-inclusive, definitive indemnity, free of any gaps? Sure. Would it allow for easier contract negotiations, so that brand managers, account managers, and creative departments could get on with it? Probably.

Years ago, *Rolling Stone* magazine introduced its "Perception/Reality" campaign. In many ways, the fight over indemnities is also a battle between perception and reality. The perception is that broad indemnities should be fought for tooth and nail. The reality is that, unless backed by insurance or very substantial liquid assets, even the broadest indemnity is generally not worth the heated debate it often engendered.

---

c. Violations of Law

It is against public policy for one party to indemnify another against criminal or quasi-criminal charges. Thus, a stockbroker cannot indemnify a company in a tender offer from criminal violations of the federal securities laws. Similarly, it is clear that an indemnity between an advertising agency and an advertiser cannot cover criminal or quasi-criminal charges, fines, or expenses. On the other hand, charges involving violations of civil laws can be covered by an indemnity. Thus, an action by the Federal Trade Commission (FTC) investigating alleged deceptive advertising could be covered, depending upon the fault of the respective parties. It is not clear, however, if any fines that might be levied by the FTC are the proper subject of an indemnity. If the FTC were to fine both the advertiser and its advertising agency, such fines should probably be absorbed by each company and not covered by an indemnity. Presumably, if the FTC fines both parties, there is shared culpability.

In any event, any indemnity should be carefully worded and considered, since the exposure to the party granting the indemnity can be extreme, particularly if the problem is not covered by insurance, e.g., an action by the FTC.

7. Product Liability

The liability of advertisers for injuries sustained by consumers because of defects in the products they sell is nothing new. Millions of dollars are awarded every year to plaintiffs injured by faulty products. If an advertising agency knowingly participates in the production of advertising that could cause consumers to use a product in a dangerous fashion, the advertising agency may be held liable along with the advertiser for injuries sustained by consumers who can show they relied upon the representations in the advertising.

15.a In the 1980s, the idea of naming the agency as a culpable party became an accepted practice, since the agency was responsible for showing behavior that, if duplicated, was unsafe.

Why It Matters

Late in the 1970s, plaintiffs' attorneys began naming advertising agencies in actions regarding injuries sustained by consumers as a result of using products in ways that advertising depicted them being used.

1.   The earliest cases involved the Jeep CJ5, an all-around utility vehicle, manufactured by American Motors (Chrysler had not yet acquired the company) and advertised in commercials produced by Compton Advertising. The CJ5 is no longer sold. Compton Advertising no longer exists. The commercials showed consumers driving the vehicle on a beach and in other off-road conditions, such as jumping sand dunes, crossing streams, and taking sharp turns. A problem with the CJ5, however, was its high center of gravity, which gave it a propensity to overturn. In fact, the driver's manual cautioned owners on driving in the very manner depicted in the commercials! Compton was named as a codefendant in a number of the product-liability lawsuits regarding injuries sustained by CJ5 drivers and passengers. While none of the cases that went to trial found Compton liable, naming the advertising agency as a culpable party became an accepted practice in cases where the agency was responsible for showing behavior that, if duplicated, was unsafe. (See picture 1.5a.)

2.   On November 15, 1987, 28 people were killed and 54 were injured in a Continental Airlines plane crash. Continental found itself the subject of lawsuits based, in part, upon the content of an advertising campaign touting its safety record. The commercial in question showed Continental's mechanics inspecting its competitors' aircraft, and claimed that even these competitors used Continental's mechanics to maintain their aircraft. The plaintiffs and the estates of those who died alleged that but for the claims of safety in the commercial, they would not have flown Continental and would not have been victims of the crash. In one case, the jury found that the advertising campaign was false because it conveyed the impression to the public that Continental employees performed maintenance and training work for other airlines. (According to the evidence, Continental simply rented simulator time to other airlines and occasionally changed their tires at remote locations.) In that case, a Denver jury awarded the plaintiff $800,000, although it declined to find that the plaintiff had, in fact, relied upon the advertising in her decision to fly Continental. In another action, a court held that if the plaintiffs could prove that they relied upon the false claims in the

commercial to decide on which airline to fly, the case could go to a jury. The cases against Continental were settled.

3. Mercedes-Benz reportedly found itself threatened with a class-action lawsuit in California due to advertising that depicted one of its cars being driven at high speeds on the autobahn. The plaintiffs' attorney claimed that the behavior, while legal in Germany, gave the impression that the cars could be safely driven at such speeds on American roads, where the legal speed limit is 65 miles per hour. He claimed to represent a class of consumers injured in high-speed accidents involving Mercedes-Benz automobiles.

4. Even the federal government has gotten into the act. Nissan's advertising agency, Chiat\Day, produced a commercial advertising Nissan's 300ZX. The commercial depicted a fantasy in which the driver of the 300ZX was being chased first by motorcycles, then by a racecar, and finally by a jet fighter plane. When the driver shifted into "turbo," the car sped past the jet. The commercial reportedly cost more than $1 million to produce. On the night before the commercial was scheduled to air during the Superbowl, the U.S. Department of Transportation tried to convince Nissan, and the television network airing the game, not to air the commercial because it depicted the car being driven at unsafe speeds—as if consumers would really believe that a 300ZX could outrun a fighter plane! Nissan and the network went ahead and aired the commercial, but the point was made. Depicting a product being used, even in a fantasy, in a potentially unsafe manner can give rise to government action. (See picture 15.b.)

15.b The US Department of Transportation challenged a Nissan 300ZX commercial feeling that a fantasy in which the driver of the 300ZX is being chased first by motorcycles, then by a race car, and finally by a jet fighter plane implied it was a safe to drive at excessive speeds.

5. Athletic-footwear manufacturer Reebok found itself the subject of an inquiry by the Federal Trade Commission due to a commercial depicting two adults bungee jumping off a bridge. One jumper wore Reebok Pumps, and the other wore Nikes. After they jumped, the jumper wearing the Reebok Pumps was shown safely dangling from the end of his bungee cord. Only the Nikes were left at the end of the other bungee cord, giving the impression that the jumper had slipped out of his Nikes and fallen, to his peril. It was all quite humorous, but the FTC failed to see that. The Commission was concerned that children might try to imitate the behavior shown in the commercial, believing it was perfectly safe to bungee jump, so long as you wore Reebok Pumps.

The lesson to be drawn from these cases is clear. Both an advertiser and its advertising agency should take care not to depict products used in a way that, if duplicated by consumers, could cause injuries. Perhaps that is why some car commercials today that show high-speed driving include disclaimers that the car is being driven on a "closed road," or that consumers should not duplicate the behavior shown. It is very debatable, however, whether such disclaimers are really effective. If the driving behavior being shown should not be duplicated by consumers, why show it at all?

8. Syndicated Advertising

In the late 1970s and early 1980s, the concept of "syndicating" commercials gained in popularity. While syndication had been done in the past, it had not been a prevalent practice. A commercial is syndicated when it is produced and licensed for use by a number of advertisers in different markets. The commercials are customized to mention the advertiser for its market. For example, a generic commercial for checking accounts could be used by any number of banks by simply adding the bank's logo at the end of the commercial. It is also a popular way to produce commercials for radio stations by tagging an otherwise generic commercial with the call letters of any number of radio stations in different markets. Syndication of commercials is a viable way to recoup production costs and make profits, but it is not without risk.

First, if dealing with companies that are in the business of syndicating commercials, be certain to fully check them out before licensing commercials from them or giving them commercials to license to others. Their financial stability should be fully investigated, and their paperwork and title to the commercials offered for syndication should be reviewed by legal counsel.

Second, be certain that the actors performing in the commercials have agreed to syndication and determine what limits, if any, have been placed on the use of their performances. This is particularly important if the commercials were produced by a Screen Actors Guild (SAG) or American Federation of Television and Radio Artists (AFTRA) signatory. If the commercial was produced in accordance with SAG or AFTRA codes, there are limits to how long the commercial may be used without the continued consent of the actors.

Finally, make sure any deal has frequent royalty accountings to avoid any loss of revenues due from the syndicator should the syndicator suffer financial problems.

9. Sales Tax

Sales tax in the advertising industry is a thorny and complex issue, differing from state to state. For example, in some states, masters of commercials must be stored in states other than the state in which the advertising agency has its offices to avoid sales tax liability on the entire cost of commercial production. In general, and unless indicated otherwise, the analysis in this section assumes the transactions in question are intrastate, i.e., both the buyer and seller have offices the same state. For the most part, interstate transactions, i.e., where the buyer and seller have offices in entirely different states, are exempt from sales tax.

A word about use taxes is also in order. Most states have legislation that provides for a use tax as an alternative to a sales tax in situations where the sales tax on a transaction has been avoided altogether. Here's how it works: A New Jersey advertising agency purchases supplies via mail from New York. Since the materials are being shipped out of state, the New York seller is not obligated to collect the New York sales tax. Because the sale did not occur in New Jersey, no sales tax is due there either. To address this type of transaction, states have passed use-tax legislation where, using the example, the New Jersey advertising agency would owe New Jersey a use tax, usually keyed to the same rate as the state's sales tax. While New York State loses out on the tax, it also imposes a similar use tax on in-state purchases of out-of-state products. In reality, however, use taxes are rarely paid by purchasers, and the states have not historically pursued their collection with any vigor. Therefore, while this section provides guidance on how sales tax can be legitimately avoided in many instances, there technically may be corresponding use-tax consequences.

It is impossible for this book to review the sales tax laws of each state as they apply to advertising. Local legal counsel must be consulted in this regard. Some generalities, however, do apply and may assist local counsel in evaluating a particular problem. The reader is also warned that this area is very complicated.

a. General Principles

Understanding sales tax first requires an understanding of three basic principles in its application:

1. Sales tax is imposed on the receipts from the sale of "tangible personal property," and on certain charges for services performed on such property.

2. "Tangible personal property" is defined as property having a material existence and perceptible by the human touch, e.g., color separations, mechanicals, and illustrations.

3. The point at which ownership of the property is transferred to the purchaser triggers the tax at whatever rate is imposed by the state.

b. Exceptions

With those principles in mind, the following two exceptions usually apply:

1. Property purchased for resale is not taxable. For example, if an advertising agency purchases artwork that will then be resold to its client, the purchase by the agency should not incur a sales tax. The subsequent resale to the client may, however, be a taxable event. In such instances, the advertising agency is acting as a reseller or "vendor" and may be obligated to collect sales tax when it sells property.

2. The purchase of machinery and equipment used or consumed in the production of tangible personal property that will later be sold should not trigger a tax. Examples include typography and artwork purchased to produce an advertisement that will be placed in a magazine. The key is if the material created, e.g., magazine or newspaper, will be "sold" to the consumer. If the material produced is not to be resold, e.g., collateral or "free" publications, to avoid a tax, the agency may be required to appear as "vendor," rather than an agent acting on behalf of a disclosed principal, in its contract with the supplier.

c. Advertising Agencies

Rendering of advertising services is generally exempt from sales tax. Exempt advertising services are usually defined as consultation and development of advertising campaigns and placement of advertisements with media. Purchases of materials by an agency for use in performing advertising services, however, are subject to tax; e.g., purchases of pens and paper to create a storyboard.

If sales tax is to be avoided, it is important that the status of the agency as an agent for a disclosed principal be clearly set forth in the agency/client agreement. In addition, the name of the client should be clearly disclosed to any supplier. Listing the client's account number or indicating that the purchase is "for the account of" may be insufficient. If the relationship is not disclosed, the advertising agency may be deemed the principal and become liable for sales taxes that could have been avoided. Each transaction will be evaluated individually at the failure to state the status of the agency, will not necessarily defeat a defense against the imposition of a sales tax. Nonetheless, attention to proper wording will greatly reduce any risks of tax liability. Equally, it is important that regulatory authorities not find the agency a "reseller" of the property. Status as a reseller will occur if the agency inflates its purchase price for the property when passing the costs on to the client. While commission is permitted, inflating the price upon which the commission is applied will make the transfer a taxable event should it be discovered in an audit.

With regard to the production of television commercials, if the original negative or video master is delivered to the agency's client, it may trigger a tax event. As such, many masters are stored at facilities under control of the advertising agency but outside the state where the agency has offices.

A summary of the probable sales tax implications of advertising industry transactions appears as Form II.15.5 following this chapter.

Because sales taxes are so complex, some contracts between advertising agencies and advertisers contain special clauses that typically read along the following lines:

> *Client shall promptly pay any applicable sales, use, excise, or similar taxes which may be due, assessed, or measured by Agency's performance of any of its contractual obligations and duties, other than taxes measured by any net income derived by Agency. If any taxing authority imposes any such taxes directly upon Agency, Client hereby (i) consents to the payment of such tax by Agency, (ii) acknowledges that such payment will be deemed to have been made on its behalf, and (iii) agrees to promptly reimburse Agency, provided, if Client so requests, Agency supply sufficient documentation showing that such tax payments were made on Client's behalf under the Agreement. Subject to the requirements listed above, Client will indemnify and defend Agency against any and all costs, expenses, losses, or damages (including, without limitation, attorneys' fees, taxes, interest, penalties, and fines), incurred by Agency resulting from any failure of Client to pay any tax when due after receipt by Client of written notice from Agency requesting that such tax be paid.*

WARNING

Tax laws can differ widely from state to state and are subject to local administrative rulings. As such, any regulatory inquiry regarding tax liabilities should be reviewed by local legal counsel and accountants before responding. This warning can not be overly stressed. Always consult local counsel or a qualified accountant before making any conclusions regarding the handling of sales taxes on advertising services.

WARNING

NEVER ENTER INTO ANY WRITTEN AGREEMENTS BETWEEN ADVERTISING AGENCY AND AN ADVERTISER WITHOUT FIRST CONSULTING LEGAL COUNSEL.

Chapter Fifteen Forms

Form II.15.1 Annotated Contract Between an Advertising Agency and Advertiser—Long Form (Major Global, Multimillion-Dollar Assignments)

NOTE: This form should only be used in situations where both the advertiser and the advertising agency are substantial companies and are engaged in media spending above $25 million. Below that amount, this form is "overkill" and one of the other forms is recommended.

AGREEMENT ("Agreement") entered into as of [insert month day, year] (the "Effective Date") by and between [insert name of advertising agency], a [insert state of incorporation] corporation with offices located at [insert address] ("Agency" or "Party," as appropriate) and [insert name of advertiser], a [insert state of incorporation] corporation with offices located at [insert address] ("Advertiser" or "Party," as appropriate, and, together with the Agency, the "Parties" where the context so requires).[i]

1. SERVICES

1.1 Services

Agency shall perform the services ("Agency Services") set forth in [Exhibit A] for each of the Advertiser's lines of business ("Advertiser Business Lines") set forth in [Exhibit B].[ii]

1.2 Responsibility for Mistakes

Agency will proofread all materials, including those approved in writing by Advertiser, which Agency produces for Advertiser hereunder. Agency shall be responsible for any additional costs incurred by Advertiser as a result of errors by Agency or a Third-party Supplier (as defined in [Section 3.1]) in production or proofreading, or in connection with product information.[iii]

1.3 Care of Property

Agency shall take all reasonable precautions to safeguard any and all of Advertiser's property in Agency's custody or control, and shall be responsible for loss, damage, destruction, or unauthorized use by others of Advertiser's property.

1.4 Non-Disparagement

Agency shall not act, directly or indirectly, in any way likely to damage or disparage the goodwill or reputation of Advertiser or its products or services, and will not damage or disparage the goodwill or reputation of Advertiser in any materials Agency produces or in any services Agency renders for Advertiser pursuant to this Agreement.[iv]

2. EXCLUSIVITY

2.1 Non-Exclusive Engagement

Advertiser shall not be obligated to advertise or promote any product or service exclusively through Agency.[v]

2.2 Agency Exclusivity Obligation

During the Term (as defined in [Section 7.1]) of this Agreement, unless Agency obtains prior written approval from an Advertiser Contact Person, Agency shall not accept any assignments for advertising or promoting products or services which are directly or indirectly competitive or incompatible[vi] with the Advertiser Business Lines set forth in [Exhibit B][vii] ("Competitive Representation").

2.3 List of Agency Clients

A list of Agency's clients as of the Effective Date of this Agreement is attached as [Exhibit C]. Agency agrees to update such list to Advertiser on a quarterly basis.[viii]

2.4 Termination by Agency

If this Agreement is terminated by Agency, Agency agrees not to accept any Competitive Representation without the prior written approval of Advertiser, for a period of six (6) months after the effective date of such termination.[ix]

3. DEALINGS WITH THIRD-PARTY SUPPLIERS[x]

3.1 Use and Selection

Agency shall enter into agreements, as agent for Advertiser, to make purchases of materials or services from third parties ("Third-party Suppliers") necessary for the preparation and production of Advertiser's marketing and advertising concepts and programs only in the event that Agency does not have the personnel and/or facilities to perform any such services, and only as authorized by Advertiser pursuant to [Section 3.2]. All Third-party Supplier costs shall be clearly identified on Agency estimate sheets. Agency shall use due care in selecting Third-party Suppliers. Unless Agency informs Advertiser otherwise in writing, all materials and the product of all services produced or rendered by Third-party Suppliers shall be free for exclusive use by Advertiser in perpetuity.[xi]

3.2 Authorization

Agency shall not enter into any agreement with any Third-party Supplier requiring payment or reimbursement by Advertiser without the prior written approval of Advertiser's [insert title as necessary], or such other designees as Advertiser may appoint on written notice to Agency (each, a "Contact Person").[xii] Advertiser and Agency understand and agree that, in exigent circumstances, it may not be possible for Agency to obtain advance written authorization from Advertiser. In such circumstances, an Advertiser Contact Person may give verbal authorization, and such verbal authorization shall be binding, provided that such verbal authorization is confirmed by the Advertiser Contact Person in writing within two (2) business days following such verbal authorization.[xiii]

3.3 Copies to Advertiser

Agency shall provide the Advertiser Contact Person with copies of all overscale talent agreements, music licenses, and other major contracts requiring payment or reimbursement by Advertiser of an amount equal to or greater than $[insert dollar amount], prior to the execution of such agreements.[xiv]

3.4 Losses Due to Third-party Suppliers

Agency shall take all reasonable precautions to guard against any loss to Advertiser resulting from the failure of Third-party Suppliers to properly perform their obligations, including securing adequate insurance to cover any and all losses to Advertiser as a result of any failure by a Third-party Supplier.[xv]

3.5 Use of Agency Affiliates

If Agency has any related subsidiaries or affiliates ("Agency Affiliate") which Agency intends to use to perform Agency Services, Agency shall notify Advertiser in writing of the name of the entity and its relationship to Agency prior to the performance of any such services. Agency agrees that any fees and costs incurred by an Agency Affiliate will be competitively priced and billed to Advertiser at net cost.[xvi]

3.6 Broadcast Talent

In the event Agency requires performers to be used in broadcast advertising ("Talent"), such Talent may be engaged directly by Agency or through an outside service ("Talent Payment Service"), but in no event shall such Talent be considered Advertiser's employee. Agency, or Talent Payment Service, as applicable, shall be responsible for the payment of all applicable withholding taxes and filings, workers' compensation claims and premiums, and the rates, use, reuse fees, and other obligations as may arise out of the employment of such Talent; including, but not limited to, payments to Pension and Health Trust funds, and other obligations to the Screen Actors Guild, the American Federation of Television and Radio Artists, or any other applicable union (collectively, "Union Obligations").[xvii] Agency or Talent Payment Service, as applicable, shall be solely liable for payments to, and on behalf of, Talent that may become due because of Advertiser's use of the Talent's services. Agency must include estimates of Talent payments and Union Obligations in production estimates prior to production.

3.7 Non-Broadcast Talent

Talent hired as models for print or other media uses of photography (e.g., point of sale or packaging) or other use not covered by a collective bargaining agreement shall be hired as independent contractors and in no event shall they be considered Advertiser's employees.

3.8 Media Research Expenses

Agency shall not bill Advertiser for obtaining any services or reports from standard research sources, including, without limitation, Competitive Media Reporting, Nielsen, Arbitron, MRI, Simmons, Broadcast Advertisers Reports, and LNA.[xviii]

4. CHANGE ORDERS

Advertiser reserves the right to alter, modify, reject, cancel, or discontinue any agreement, commitment, or other obligation entered into by Agency and authorized by Advertiser in accordance with this Agreement, and to alter any marketing, advertising, or other plans, schedules, or work in progress ("Change Orders"). In the event Advertiser exercises such right, Agency shall immediately take all necessary, appropriate, and lawful actions to carry out such instructions and mitigate against the incurring of any avoidable cost, liability, or obligation.[xix] Advertiser agrees to assume liability for any additional costs resulting from its Change Orders.

5. PURCHASE OF MEDIA[xx]

5.1 Types of Media

Agency shall purchase, where applicable and authorized by Advertiser, national and local television, radio, consumer and trade magazine, newspaper, and out-of-home advertising time and space for Advertiser from vendors ("Media Vendors" or "Third-party Suppliers"), based on buy specifications:

5.1.1 provided by Advertiser to Agency; or

5.1.2 developed by Agency and approved by Advertiser in writing.

5.1.3 Agency shall use due care in selecting Media Vendors.

5.2 Verification of Media Invoices

Agency will verify the accuracy of all media invoices for time, rate, and space ordered by Agency by procuring tearsheets of print advertising and similar customary proofs of performance from radio and television stations.

5.3 Retention of Media Documentation

Agency will retain media invoices for three (3) years, and tear sheets and similar customary proofs of performance from radio and television stations for one (1) year.[xxi]

5.4 Media Charges[xxii]

Advertiser shall pay or reimburse Agency the net cost of all space, time, materials, and services purchased or performed for Advertiser at the rates, free of any commission, charged by or negotiated with the Media Vendors. Once Advertiser has paid Agency for the media purchased, Agency shall be solely responsible for payment to the appropriate Media Vendor and shall specify such sole liability in its contracts with the Media Vendor. Advertiser shall reimburse Agency only for media purchases that are approved by Advertiser.

5.5 Alterations in Media Schedule(s)

Agency shall make commercially reasonable efforts to preserve Advertiser's rights to cancel media purchases. Advertiser shall have the right to cancel media purchases if such cancellation is permitted under the relevant agreement between Agency and the Media Vendor. In the event that the relevant agreement does not permit cancellation, Advertiser may request Agency to engage in good-faith negotiations with the Media Vendor to cancel the agreement. Any costs or fees resulting from such early cancellations shall be paid by Advertiser, subject to the prior written approval of such costs by a Advertiser Media Purchase Contact Person. Advertiser may request that Agency modify media buys or other services. In the event that the costs or fees associated with such modifications exceed [insert amount], such modifications must be approved in writing by an Advertiser Media Purchase Contact Person. Agency shall use its best efforts to comply immediately with such requests so as to minimize the expense to Advertiser. Agency, before fulfilling such request, shall report to Advertiser the cost of any adjustment, including any projected short-rate adjustment.

6. COMPENSATION AND EXPENSE REIMBURSEMENT[xxiii]

6.1 Agency Fee

Advertiser shall pay Agency a fee ("Agency Fee") for Agency Services as set forth in [Exhibit D].

6.2 Production Costs and Expenses[xxiv]

Advertiser shall pay or reimburse Agency for production costs and expenses that are approved by Advertiser ("Production Expenses"). Production Expenses shall be billed to Advertiser at Agency's cost (without markup or profit, and net of discount or commission, including prepayment). Any cash discount, rebate, or special offer shall inure to the benefit of Advertiser. Sales taxes or other taxes levied by outside suppliers on purchases made by Agency for Advertiser shall be billed by Agency to Advertiser on a strict pass-through (actual amount) basis.

6.3 Other Expenses

All expenses other than Production Expenses, including, without limitation, travel expenses, must be approved in writing by a Advertiser Contact Person. All travel expenses incurred by Agency shall comply with Advertiser's Travel Guidelines, as amended by Advertiser from time to time, as set forth in [Exhibit E].[xxv] Advertiser will not reimburse Agency for any travel expenses incurred in violation of the Advertiser's Travel Guidelines. In no event will Advertiser reimburse Agency for travel of Agency personnel working on Advertiser's account for trips between Advertiser's principal offices and Agency's principal offices.[xxvi]

6.4 Total Compensation

Agency shall be entitled to no compensation or reimbursement for Agency Services other than as provided in [Sections 6.1, 6.2, and 6.3] of this Agreement.

6.5 Annual Review of Agency Fee

Prior to the conclusion of each year of the Term, Agency and Advertiser will meet to discuss and resolve the Agency Fee for the succeeding year. If the Agency Fee is not agreed upon prior to the beginning of the next calendar year, Advertiser shall continue to pay a monthly fee in the amount of 1/12th of the prior year's Base Fee (as defined in [Exhibit D]) until the negotiated Agency Fee is finalized with retroactive adjustment or until this Agreement is terminated, whichever occurs first.

7. TERM AND TERMINATION

7.1 Term

This Agreement begins on the Effective Date and shall continue in effect until termination by either Party in accordance with the provisions of this Agreement (the "Term").

7.2 Termination by Advertiser

Advertiser may terminate this Agreement immediately by giving Agency written notice of termination if:

7.2.1 Agency or any of its personnel commits any act which, in Advertiser's reasonable judgment, might bring Advertiser embarrassment in the marketplace;[xxvii]

7.2.2 Agency fails to pay within three (3) business days after notice from Advertiser any invoice incurred by Agency for Advertiser's account, including any applicable late charges;

7.2.3 Agency breaches the confidentiality or exclusivity provisions of this Agreement;

7.2.4 Agency files a petition in bankruptcy or such a petition is filed against it; or

7.2.5 Except as provided in Sections 7.2.1 through 7.2.4 hereof, Agency breaches this Agreement and fails to cure the breach within thirty (30) days of receiving notice from Advertiser.

7.3 Termination by Either Party

Either Party may terminate this Agreement, with or without cause, by giving the other Party at least ninety (90) days' prior written notice (the "Termination Period").[xxviii]

7.4 Agency Solvency

In the event Advertiser has concerns regarding Agency's financial stability or solvency, Advertiser shall bring such concerns to Agency's attention and Agency shall immediately attempt to resolve such concerns. If Agency is unable to resolve Advertiser's concerns to Advertiser's satisfaction within thirty (30) days, Advertiser shall have the right to terminate this Agreement immediately by giving Agency written notice of termination.[xxix]

7.5 Agency's General Obligations Upon Termination

Agency shall transfer, assign, and make available to Advertiser or its representative all property and material in the possession or control of Agency or any Third-party Supplier which, pursuant to the terms of this Agreement, is the property of Advertiser, including all information regarding Advertiser's marketing, advertising, and promotion concepts and plans, and all orders, contracts, and other arrangements for unused space, time, services, and materials.[xxx] Upon transfer, Advertiser shall assume all future obligations and liabilities incurred by Agency and authorized by Advertiser in accordance with this Agreement in connection with the transferred materials. If any contracts made and authorized by Advertiser in accordance with this Agreement cannot be transferred, Agency shall complete the performance of such contracts, which will be paid for by Advertiser in the manner described in this Agreement.

7.6 Agency's Media Obligations Upon Termination

Upon termination of this Agreement, Agency shall assign to the entity/agency designated by Advertiser all media buy commitments entered into by Agency on behalf of Advertiser, provided that Advertiser has authorized such commitments in accordance with this Agreement. In the event such authorized media buy commitments are non-assignable, Advertiser shall have the right to make the payments due under such media commitments directly to the Media Vendor.

7.7 Advertiser's Obligations Upon Termination

Advertiser shall be liable to pay only for Agency Services actually rendered prior to the effective date of termination, which shall in no event be greater than the pro-rata portion of the Agency Fee as set forth in [Exhibit D]. Upon termination, if Agency has received payment of any portion of the Agency Fee, Agency shall refund to Advertiser the pro-rata portion of the Agency Fee in excess of the amount owing up to the date of termination. Agency shall not be entitled to any compensation, reimbursement, or commission following the effective date of termination, unless specifically provided in this Agreement.

7.8 Termination Period

Except as otherwise herein provided, during the Termination Period, the rights, duties, and responsibilities of Advertiser and Agency under this Agreement shall continue in full force.

8. BILLING PROCEDURES

8.1 Invoice Dates

All Agency invoices shall be rendered monthly on the [insert day] of the month. Advertiser shall pay Agency's properly submitted invoices within [insert number] days of receipt.

8.2 Purchases from Third-party Suppliers

On all Agency invoices that include costs for purchases from Third-party Suppliers, Agency shall:

8.2.1 attach appropriate documentation substantiating all such Third-party Supplier costs, including a copy of the Third-party Supplier's invoice; and

8.2.2 itemize such Third-party Supplier costs by Advertiser Business Line.

8.2.3 Discounts. All Third-party Supplier costs will be billed and paid in such a manner as to assure that Advertiser will achieve maximum available discounts.[xxxi] Agency will give Advertiser the benefit of any discounts, whether based upon volume or otherwise, provided to Agency by Third-party Suppliers.

8.3 Media Invoices

All invoices for the purchase of media shall be payable by Advertiser thirty (30) days from receipt thereof, but not earlier than fifteen (15) days prior to the media cancellation date listed on the invoice.

8.4 Prompt-Payment Discounts from Media Vendors

In the event that a Media Vendor offers a prompt-payment discount, Agency shall advise Advertiser of the available discount and submit an invoice to Advertiser in sufficient time to obtain such prompt-payment discount. Agency shall bill Advertiser sufficiently in advance to allow payment by Advertiser prior to the due date to the Media Vendor. Unless otherwise agreed to in writing by Advertiser, upon payment by Advertiser to Agency, Agency shall immediately pay the amount due to the Media Vendor. Agency will not hold the funds or use them for any other purpose.

8.5 Media Billing Errors

If scheduled advertising does not run, is run incorrectly, or if there exists any other problem or media billing error, Agency shall immediately advise Advertiser, and credit or appropriately adjust Advertiser's account on the next monthly billing invoice following the discovery of said media billing problem or error.

8.6 Graduated Rates for Media

If Advertiser instructs Agency to purchase media space or time in a medium having a schedule of graduated rates and

8.6.1 less space or time than contracted for is used, Advertiser shall reimburse Agency for any amount actually due such Media Vendor as a result of the deficiency, at the rate applicable to the quantity of space or time used; or

8.6.2 more space or time than contracted for is used so that a credit is due, Agency shall, on the next submitted monthly invoice, credit Advertiser for any excess amount Advertiser may have paid over the amount actually due at the rate earned.

9. AGENCY STAFFING AND HOURS TRACKING[xxxii]

9.1 Staffing Level

For each calendar year during the Term of this Agreement, Agency shall provide the Agency staff ("Agency Staff") set forth in [Exhibit F].[xxxiii] Should Agency fail to provide at least the level of Agency Staff set forth in [Exhibit F], Advertiser shall have the right, in addition to any other right set forth in this Agreement, to renegotiate the Agency Fee in light of the Agency's staffing deficiency.

9.2 Configuration and Competence

Agency acknowledges and agrees that the configuration and competence of Agency Staff is of critical importance to Advertiser. Any shifts in Agency Staff must be at Advertiser's request or upon the prior written consent of an Advertiser Contact Person, such consent not to be unreasonably withheld. Agency will consult with Advertiser in connection with the replacement of any departed employee.

9.3 Hours Tracking Requirements

Agency shall perform the following minimum time-reporting requirements:

9.3.1 Agency Staff shall identify hours worked on servicing Advertiser on a weekly basis ("Recorded Time"). Recorded Time shall be approved on a monthly basis by someone in Agency's senior management.

9.3.2 Agency shall generate formal internal policy guidelines to ensure the accuracy and completeness of the time-recording process.

9.3.3 Time spent by Agency Staff on "Administrative," "New Business Development," "Executive Management," and similar matters that are not directly related to servicing Advertiser, shall not be included in the Recorded Time, directly or indirectly.

10. AGENCY PERFORMANCE AUDIT

Advertiser shall have the right to audit Agency's performance in any way it deems appropriate to measure the adequacy of Agency's performance under this Agreement, and Agency agrees to cooperate with such audit ("Agency Performance Evaluation"). The Agency Performance Evaluation may include, where applicable, Agency's:

10.1 performance of its duties and obligations under this Agreement;

10.2 creative;

10.3 media strategies;

10.4 consumer response; and

10.5 [add additional factors, as applicable].

11. AGENCY REPORTS

11.1 Agency Financial Reports

Agency shall promptly provide Advertiser with a complete copy of each audited financial report of Agency issued during or otherwise published or memorialized during the Term of this Agreement in the normal course of Agency's business.[xxxiv]

11.2 Status Reports

At the conclusion of each quarter during each calendar year during the Term, Agency shall provide Advertiser with a written status report setting forth the following information:

11.2.1 the Agency's completed, ongoing, and proposed projects;

11.2.2 Agency Staff Recorded Time, listed by Advertiser Business Lines; and

11.2.3 [add additional items, as appropriate].

11.3 Agency Ownership and Control

Agency shall be under a continuing obligation to advise Advertiser promptly of any actual or contemplated material changes in Agency's ownership or control, or any material negative change or threatened change to Agency's financial position.

11.4 Quarterly Reports[xxxv]

Upon request by Advertiser, and promptly upon termination of this Agreement, Agency shall provide Advertiser with a written status report setting forth, for the specific time period(s) designated by Advertiser, all significant information concerning:

11.4.1 the Agency's completed, ongoing, and proposed projects;

11.4.2 Agency Staff Recorded Time;

11.4.3 reimbursable expenses;

11.4.4 any other cost, liability, or obligation Agency deems to be the responsibility of Advertiser; and

11.4.5 [add additional items, as necessary].

12. AGENCY RECORD RETENTION

12.1 Retention of Records

During the Term of this Agreement and for three (3) years thereafter, Agency shall retain all records relating to Agency Services ("Agency Records").

12.2 Audit of Records

Upon not less than five (5) business days' notice, Agency Records (other than payroll records) shall be open to inspection, copying, and audit by Advertiser or an Advertiser representative, during Agency's normal business hours at Agency's place of business.[xxxvi] Advertiser shall have the right to examine, either directly or through its authorized representatives or agents, during business hours and for a reasonable period of time, all books, records, accounts, correspondence, instructions, specifications, plans, drawings, receipts, manuals, and memoranda pertinent to this Agreement. Advertiser's right of inspection shall not apply to Agency's trade secrets or other proprietary information properly designated or asserted as such.

12.3 Overcharges

If any records audit reveals that Agency has overcharged Advertiser, Agency shall immediately refund such overcharge ("Overcharge") to Advertiser. If the Overcharge is greater than five percent (5%) of the billed charges, then Advertiser's external audit expenses shall be reimbursed to Advertiser by Agency. If Agency has not retained or cannot produce Agency Records which Advertiser requests, and as a result thereof Advertiser is required to pay a fine, penalty, or other monetary amount ("Penalty Payment"), Agency shall reimburse Advertiser the Penalty Payment and any other costs incurred by Advertiser as a result of Agency's failure to retain Agency Records for the required time period.

12.4 Third-party Supplier Records

Where commercially feasible, all contracts with Third-party Suppliers shall contain the record retention and audit requirements contained in [Sections 12.1] and [12.2] above, permitting the Advertiser to obtain and access such records to the same extent permitted by the Advertiser herein with regard to the Agency's records.

13. CONFIDENTIALITY

13.1 Confidential Information

"Confidential Business Information" means any information, whether disclosed in oral, written, visual, electronic, or other form, which Advertiser discloses or Agency observes in connection with Agency's performance of Agency Services. Confidential Business Information includes, but is not limited to:

13.1.1 business plans, strategies, forecasts, and analyses;

13.1.2 financial, employee, and vendor information;

13.1.3 software (including all documentation and code), hardware, and system designs, architectures, and protocols;

13.1.4 product and service specifications;

13.1.5 purchasing, logistics, sales, marketing, and other business processes;

13.1.6 the terms of this Agreement; and

13.1.7 [add additional items, as appropriate].

"Confidential Personal Information" means all information about Advertiser's individual customers provided by Advertiser to Agency, including but not limited to names, addresses, telephone numbers, account numbers, customer lists, and demographic, financial, and transaction information.[xxxvii] Confidential Business Information and Confidential Personal Information are collectively referred to as "Confidential Information," all of which shall be deemed confidential and not disclosed by Agency or any persons or companies with whom Agency deals, except as specifically provided herein.

13.2 Treatment of Confidential Business Information

Agency shall use Confidential Business Information only as necessary to perform the Services and its other obligations under this Agreement, and shall restrict disclosure of Confidential Business Information to its employees and Third-party Suppliers who have a need to know such information to perform the Agency Services and who have first agreed to be bound by the terms of this paragraph. Within a reasonable time after receiving Advertiser's written request, Agency shall destroy in such a manner that it cannot be retrieved, or return (as instructed by Advertiser), any materials in its possession containing Confidential Business Information.

13.3 Treatment of Confidential Personal Information

Agency shall use Confidential Personal Information only as necessary to perform the Agency Services and its other obligations under this Agreement. Agency shall not duplicate or incorporate the Confidential Personal Information into its own records or databases. Agency shall restrict disclosure of Confidential Personal Information to its employees who have a need to know such information to perform the Agency Services and who have first agreed to be bound by the terms of this paragraph. Agency shall not disclose the Confidential Personal Information to any third party, including an affiliate of Agency, permitted subcontractor, or Third-party Supplier, without prior written consent of Advertiser and the written agreement of such party to be bound by the terms of this paragraph.

13.4 Procedures to Ensure Confidentiality

Agency shall establish and maintain written policies and procedures designed to ensure the confidentiality of the Confidential Information. Copies of such policies and procedures shall be provided to Advertiser upon its request. Such policies shall include the following minimum provisions:

13.4.1 Within ten (10) days following termination of this Agreement or ten (10) days following the completion of a project for which the Confidential Information has been provided, whichever first occurs, Agency shall, upon request and at Advertiser's discretion:

13.4.1.1 return the Confidential Information to Advertiser; or

13.4.1.2 certify in writing to Advertiser that such Confidential Information has been destroyed in such a manner that it cannot be retrieved.

13.4.2 Agency shall notify Advertiser promptly upon the discovery of the loss, unauthorized disclosure, or unauthorized use of the Confidential Information.

13.4.3 Agency shall permit Advertiser to audit Agency's compliance with the confidentiality provisions of this Agreement at any time.

13.5 Exceptions to Confidential Treatment of Confidential Information

Confidential Information shall not include:

13.5.1 Confidential Business Information that is or becomes publicly available without breach of this Agreement by Agency;

13.5.2 information that is independently developed by Agency without use of any Confidential Business Information; or

13.5.3 information that is received by Agency from a third party that does not have an obligation of confidentiality to Advertiser.

13.6 Disclosure of Confidential Information

Agency may disclose Confidential Information to the extent that, in the reasonable opinion of Agency's legal counsel, it is legally required to disclose. Agency shall notify Advertiser within a reasonable time prior to disclosure and allow Advertiser a reasonable opportunity to seek appropriate protective measures.

14. COMPLIANCE WITH LAWS

14.1 Agency shall comply, at Agency's own expense, with all applicable federal, state, and local laws, rules, and regulations governing the preparation and publication of Advertiser marketing and advertising materials, and with all applicable provisions of the workers' compensation laws, unemployment compensation laws, the federal Social Security Act, the federal Fair Labor Standard Act, and all other federal, state, and local laws and regulations which may be applicable to Agency as employer (collectively, "Applicable Laws").

14.2 Agency shall obtain all necessary releases, licenses, permits, and other authorization to use names, voices, likenesses, photographs, copyrighted materials, artwork, or any other property or rights belonging to third parties for use in advertising for Advertiser, and shall hold Advertiser harmless from all claims, demands, expenses (including reasonable attorneys' fees), liabilities, suits, and proceedings (including any brought in or before any court, administrative body, arbitration panel, or other tribunal) against or involving Advertiser on account of or arising out of any such use. Agency will keep Advertiser fully informed in writing of any limitations imposed upon Advertiser's use of any names, voices, likenesses, photographs, copyrighted materials, artwork, or any other property or rights belonging to third parties that is the subject of any release or other contract.[xxxviii]

15. DEFENSE

15.1 Agency's Defense Obligation

To the fullest extent permitted by law, Agency shall, at its own expense, defend, indemnify, and hold harmless Advertiser and its affiliates, together with their respective directors, officers, employees, independent contractors, agents, and licensees (each an "Advertiser Indemnitee") from and against any and all allegations (even though such allegations may be false, fraudulent, or groundless) asserted in any third-party claim, investigation, demand, suit, cause of action, or proceeding arising out of any of the following (collectively, the "Claims Against Advertiser"), whether actual or alleged:

15.1.1 Any breach of this Agreement by Agency, including, but not limited to, failure to perform any obligation under this Agreement or any act beyond its authority provided in this Agreement.

15.1.2 Any failure by Agency or any Third-party Supplier to comply with any Applicable Law.

15.1.3 Any bodily injury or loss of property claimed to result from any act or omission of Agency or any Third-party Supplier.

15.1.4 Any contention that any Advertising Properties (as defined in ([Section 17.1]) other than those furnished to Agency solely by Advertiser, constitute:

15.1.4.1 libel, slander, and/or defamation;

15.1.4.2 infringement of any trademark, copyright, or other intellectual property right of a third party;

15.1.4.3 piracy, plagiarism, misappropriation of another's idea, confidential information, trade secrets, or unfair competition;

15.1.4.4 invasion of rights of privacy or publicity.

15.1.5 Any claim, suit, or proceeding arising out of obligations under a Union Agreement relating to the production or use of any Advertising Properties (as defined in ([Section 18.1]); or

15.1.6 Any loss, unauthorized disclosure, or unauthorized use of Confidential Personal Information by Agency or any Third-party Supplier.

15.2 Advertiser's Defense Obligation

To the fullest extent permitted by law, Advertiser shall, at its own expense, defend, indemnify, and hold harmless Agency and its directors, officers, employees, agents, licensees, and affiliates (each an "Agency Indemnitee") from and against any and all allegations (even though such allegations may be false, fraudulent, or groundless) asserted in any third-party claim, investigation, demand, suit, or cause of action arising out of any of the following (collectively, the "Claims Against Agency"), whether actual or alleged:

15.2.1 Any contention that any of the Advertising Properties (as defined in ([Section 17.1]) furnished to Agency solely by Advertiser constitute:

15.2.1.1 libel, slander, and/or defamation;

15.2.1.2 infringement of any trademark, copyright, or other intellectual property right of a third party;

15.2.1.3 piracy, plagiarism, misappropriation of another's idea, confidential information, trade secrets, or unfair competition; or

15.2.1.4 invasion of rights of privacy or publicity.

15.2.2 Any death or injury to any person, damage to property, or any other damage or loss, resulting or claimed to result in whole or in part from any defect in a product or service sold by Advertiser, unless Agency suggested or assisted in the creation of the depiction or description of the Advertiser product or service, and the death or injury resulted therefrom; or

15.2.3 Any claim or lawsuit alleging misrepresentation of the effectiveness, nature, quality, or content of Advertiser's products or services, provided the claim or lawsuit relates to advertising claims specifically approved in writing by Advertiser.

15.3 As used herein the general terms "Claim" or "Claims" or "Indemnifying Party" or "Indemnified Party" shall refer, respectively, to either claims against, or indemnity obligations and rights of, the Advertiser or the Agency, as the context requires.

15.4 Counsel

Each Party shall use counsel reasonably satisfactory to the other in satisfaction of its Defense Obligation hereunder, and shall proceed with diligence, timeliness, and good faith in such defense. Without limiting the obligations set forth in this [Section 15] and [Section 16], either Party shall have the opportunity to participate in its defense and to engage counsel of its own choice at its expense.

15.5 Consent

Neither Party may consent to the entry of any judgment or enter into any settlement of any Claims without the Indemnified Party's prior written consent.

16. INDEMNIFICATION

16.1 Agency's Indemnification Obligation

To the fullest extent permitted by law, Agency shall indemnify and hold harmless each of the Advertiser Indemnitees from and against any and all liabilities, losses, fines, penalties, costs, expenses, and reasonable attorneys' fees that arise out of the Claims Against Advertiser. An Advertiser Indemnitee need not seek recovery from a third party in order to make a claim under this [Section 16].

16.2 Advertiser's Indemnification Obligation

To the fullest extent permitted by law, Advertiser shall indemnify and hold harmless each of the Agency Indemnitees from and against any and all liabilities, losses, fines, penalties, costs, expenses, and reasonable attorneys' fees that arise out of the Claims Against Agency. An Agency Indemnitee need not seek recovery from a third party in order to make a claim under this [Section 16].

17. INSURANCE.[xxxix]

17.1 Workers' Compensation Insurance

During the Term of this Agreement, Agency shall obtain and maintain Workers' Compensation Insurance with statutory benefits, and Employer's Liability Insurance in Agency's name (both containing a waiver of subrogation in favor of Advertiser, executed by the insurance company), with limits of not less than $100,000 per accident for each employee, and $500,000 aggregate from a company having a rating of A or better in the current Best's Insurance Report, published by A.M. Best Company, Inc.

17.2 Commercial General Liability Insurance

During the Term of this Agreement, Agency shall obtain and maintain Commercial General Liability Insurance naming Advertiser as an additional insured, containing a waiver of subrogation in favor of Advertiser and having a severability of interest endorsement and including, but not limited to, coverage for personal and advertising injury and contractual liability, with limits of not less than $5,000,000 combined single limits for bodily injury and property damage per occurrence, from a company having a rating of A or better in the current Best's Insurance Report, published by A.M. Best Company, Inc.

17.3 Motor Vehicle Liability Insurance

During the Term of this Agreement, Agency shall obtain and maintain Motor Vehicle Liability Insurance, naming Advertiser as an additional insured, containing a waiver of subrogation in favor of Advertiser, in Agency's name, covering all vehicles, and including coverage for hired and non-owned automobiles, used in connection with Agency's operations under this Agreement, with limits of not less than $1,000,000 combined single limits for bodily injury and property damage per occurrence, from a company having a rating of A or better in the current Best's Insurance Report, published by A.M. Best Company, Inc.

17.4 Advertising Agency Liability Insurance

During the Term of this Agreement, Agency shall obtain and maintain Advertising Agency Liability Insurance naming Advertiser as an additional insured, specifically endorsed to insure the contractual liability assumed by Agency under this Agreement, with limits of liability of not less than $10,000,000 per occurrence, from a company having a rating of A or better in the current Best's Insurance Report, published by A.M. Best Company, Inc.

17.5 Errors and Omissions Insurance

During the Term of this Agreement, Agency shall obtain and maintain Errors and Omissions Liability Insurance specifically endorsed to insure the contractual liability assumed by Agency under this Agreement, with limits of liability of not less than $10,000,000 per occurrence, from a company having a rating of A or better in the current Best's Insurance Report, published by A.M. Best Company, Inc.

17.6 Additional Policy Requirements

Each policy obtained by Agency shall expressly provide that it shall not be subject to material change or cancellation without at least thirty (30) days' prior written notice to Advertiser. Agency shall furnish Advertiser with copies of the policies required to be obtained by Agency, or with certificates, upon Advertiser's request.

17.7 Non-Effect of Insurance on Indemnity Obligation

Failure to secure and maintain proper insurance coverage as required by this [Section 17] will not relieve Agency of its responsibility to indemnify Advertiser, and shall, of itself, constitute a material breach of this Agreement.

18. COPYRIGHT, ETC.

18.1 Ownership

Except with respect to third-party rights of which Agency has informed Advertiser in writing, all tangible or intangible property developed or prepared for Advertiser during the Term of this Agreement, including, but not limited to, plans, sketches, layouts, copy, promotions, commercials, films, photographs, illustrations, transcriptions, software, and literary and artistic materials; finished or unfinished, whether created by Agency, Advertiser, or a Third-party Supplier, or any combination thereof; and all drafts and versions thereof, whether used or unused ("Advertising Properties"), shall be and remain the exclusive property of Advertiser.[xl] Agency acknowledges and agrees that Advertiser, its employees, subsidiaries, successors, agents, and assigns, and any others acting with its permission or under its authority, and without any limitations as to time or territory, shall have the right to copyright, use, publish, reproduce, alter, and prepare derivative works of the Advertising Properties, for art, advertising, trade, or any other lawful purpose whatsoever, in or through any media or combination of media, now existing or yet to be invented, without any obligation or liability to Agency. Neither Agency nor any of its Third-party Suppliers shall permit any party (other than Advertiser) to use any Advertising Properties. Agency shall place Advertiser's copyright notice on each Advertising Property in such locations and styles as Advertiser may direct. Upon Advertiser's request, Agency will prepare and file applications for copyright registration at Advertiser's expense and in Advertiser's name.

18.2 Work Made-For-Hire

Agency acknowledges and agrees that all the copyrightable aspects of Advertising Properties are deemed "works made-for-hire" as that term is defined in Section 101 of the United States Copyright Act, 17 U.S.C. Section 101 (or any successor section thereto), that Advertiser is deemed the author or creator of the Advertising Properties, and that Advertiser is the exclusive owner of all right, title, and interest, including the copyrights and any and all other intellectual property rights, in and to the Advertising Properties. If, for any reason, any of the Advertising Properties are not found to have been created as works made-for-hire, Agency hereby assigns all its right, title, and interest in and to the Advertising Properties to Advertiser. Agency shall execute any instruments that, in the sole judgment and discretion of Advertiser, may be deemed necessary to further carry out such assignment or to protect Advertiser's rights in the Advertising Properties ("Assignment Documents"). In the event Agency fails to execute any Assignment Documents when requested by Advertiser, Advertiser is hereby irrevocably granted a power of attorney to execute Assignment Documents on Agency's behalf.

18.3 Original Work

Agency represents and warrants that all Advertising Properties will be original; or that it will have obtained all rights necessary for the unrestricted use of Advertising Properties by Advertiser (as well as for any concept or theme contained in any Advertising Property), in any manner and over any period of time, including, without limitation, rights related to patent, copyright, and trademark, right of publicity and privacy and trade secret, excepting such limitations or restrictions as Agency shall fully disclose in writing to Advertiser before the work is created. Agency agrees to secure for Advertiser all third-party consents, releases, and contracts necessary to evidence Advertiser's rights in any Advertising Properties provided by Agency under this Agreement.

18.4 Work By Third-party Suppliers

If Agency retains a Third-party Supplier to produce any Advertising Properties, Agency shall ensure that such Third-party Supplier agrees in writing to be bound by the provisions of this [Section 18]. In the event any Third-party Supplier has imposed any limits or restrictions on the transfer or use of any materials other than as provided in this [Section 18], Agency must inform Advertiser of such limitations when Agency obtains authorization to retain such Third-party Supplier.[xli]

19. TRADEMARKS

19.1 Generally

Agency will not use any trademark, service mark, name, slogan, logo, or phrase in Advertising Properties, whether Agency develops it or not, unless it has been previously approved by Advertiser's trademark counsel; and, if ultimately used in Advertising Properties, then Agency agrees that such are and shall remain Advertiser's sole property. Agency shall not obtain, or attempt to obtain, during the Term of this Agreement or at any time thereafter, any right, title, or interest in or to any trademarks owned by Advertiser or any other intellectual property used or owned by Advertiser.

19.2 Searches

Agency shall be responsible for undertaking, or retaining the services of a reputable service firm to undertake, a search of the files of the United States Patent and Trademark Office, state trademark registrations, and common-law trademark usage (to the extent reasonably available) to ensure that any new name, logo, slogan, or quotation developed by Agency for Advertiser can be protected by the filing of a United States trademark registration application. Third-party Supplier charges that are directly related to such searches shall be reimbursable as "Other Expenses" pursuant to [Section 6.3] of this Agreement, but only if approved by Advertiser pursuant to [Section 3.2] of this Agreement.

19.3 Registration

Agency hereby assigns to Advertiser the entire right, title, and interest in and to any trademark developed by Agency for Advertiser, together with all of the goodwill associated therewith. Advertiser may, in its sole determination and at its cost, apply for registration of such trademark by the United States Patent and Trademark Office or elsewhere.

19.4 Protection

Agency shall cooperate fully with Advertiser in regard to obtaining trademark protection for Advertiser and defending any such rights obtained. On all materials prepared for Advertiser by Agency, Agency shall place the appropriate trademark registration notice or notice of trademark claim, e.g., ® or ™, indicating Advertiser's trademark rights.

20. FORCE MAJEURE

Neither Advertiser nor Agency shall be liable to the other for any failure, inability, or delay in performing hereunder if caused by any occurrence beyond the reasonable control of the Party so failing, including, without limitation, an Act of God, war, strike, or fire; but due diligence shall be used in curing such cause and in resuming performance. In such event, Agency expressly acknowledges that Advertiser shall be able to seek one or more alternative service provider(s). In addition, the

Agency Fee described in [Exhibit D] shall be equitably reduced to reflect the services that were not provided by Agency. In the event performance is not resumed within thirty (30) days, the non-failing Party may terminate this Agreement immediately upon written notice.

21. INDEPENDENT CONTRACTOR/LIMITED AGENCY

21.1 Performance of Work

In connection with the production and placement of advertising materials hereunder, Agency is acting as special agent for a principal, and except as otherwise authorized in accordance with this Agreement, any other work performed by Agency or Advertiser under this Agreement shall be in that Party's capacity as an independent contractor and not as agent or representative of the other Party. It is expressly understood that this undertaking does not constitute a joint venture.

21.2 Agency Employees and Third-party Suppliers

All persons employed by Agency and all Third-party Suppliers used in the performance of services hereunder shall be under the sole and exclusive direction and control of Agency, and shall not be considered the employees of Advertiser for any purpose whatsoever. Agency and all Third-party Suppliers shall remain at all times independent contractors and shall be responsible for and shall promptly pay all federal, state, and municipal taxes chargeable or assessed with respect to their employees, including, but not limited to, social security, unemployment, federal and state withholding, and all other taxes.

22. DISPUTE RESOLUTION[xlii]

22.1 Negotiation

In the event of any controversy, claim, question, disagreement, or dispute (collectively the "Dispute") arising out of or relating to this Agreement or the relationship between the Parties, the Parties shall first use their best efforts to resolve the Dispute through negotiation. During negotiation, the Parties shall, without delay, continue to perform their respective obligations under this Agreement that are not related to the Dispute. To invoke the dispute-resolution procedures set forth in this [Section 22], the invoking Party shall give to the other Party written notice of its decision to negotiate. The notice shall include a detailed description of the issues subject to the Dispute and a proposed resolution thereof. Within five (5) business days after the written notice has been received by the other Party, both Parties shall designate representatives to settle the Dispute. The designated representatives shall be [insert appropriate level of officer, e.g., vice president] of their respective corporations, or other individuals holding comparable executive positions, with decision-making authority to settle the Dispute without further ratification by the Parties. The designated representatives shall consult and negotiate with each other in good faith and attempt to reach a just and equitable resolution satisfactory to both Parties within fifteen (15) business days after the deadline for designation of the representatives. If those designated representatives do not timely resolve the Dispute through negotiation, the Dispute may be submitted to resolution through arbitration as provided in [Section 22.2].

22.2 Arbitration

If the Parties do not resolve the Dispute after negotiations, the Parties agree to submit the Dispute to binding arbitration in [insert city and state] in accordance with the American Arbitration Association ("AAA") Commercial Arbitration Rules effective at the time of submission.[xliii] All Disputes shall be resolved by a single arbitrator. If the Parties are unable to reach agreement on the selection of the arbitrator within 15 days from the date of the arbitration demand, the AAA shall choose the arbitrator. The costs of any arbitration shall be shared equally by the Parties and neither shall recover from the other its attorneys' fees.[xliv]

22.3 Governing Law

The resolution of any Dispute under this Agreement shall be governed and interpreted in accordance with the laws of the State of [insert name of State], without regard to its conflicts of law rules or choice of law principles.

22.4 Enforcement

The agreement to arbitrate shall be specifically enforceable in any court having competent jurisdiction over either Party hereto. In the event either Party seeks relief in any court to enforce an arbitration ruling, that Party shall be entitled to its reasonable attorneys' fees and costs incurred with such enforcement. Arbitration may proceed in the absence of either Party if notice of the proceedings has been given to such Party.

22.5 Discovery

In the discretion of the arbitrator, each Party shall have the same discovery rights as afforded under the Federal Rules of Civil Procedure during arbitration.

22.6 Limitation of Liability

Except as otherwise provided in this Agreement, in no event shall either Party seek or be liable for punitive, exemplary, enhanced, or trebled damages arising from any Dispute relating to or in connection with this Agreement or the relationship between the Parties, whether such damages are claimed for breach of contract, negligence, or any other tort claim.

22.7 Confidentiality

All proceedings pursuant to this [Section 21] shall be confidential. Any admission or statement made pursuant to this [Section 21] shall not be admissible or used in any arbitration or judicial proceeding, except to enforce or vacate any arbitration award pursuant to this [Section 21].

22.8 The Federal Arbitration Act

This Agreement involves interstate commerce and is subject to the Federal Arbitration Act ("FAA"), 9 U.S.C. §§ L-16. The FAA preempts any inconsistent state or local law, rule, or regulation concerning arbitration.

23. GENERAL

23.1 Assignment

Agency shall not assign any part or all of this Agreement, or subcontract or delegate any of Agency's rights or obligations under this Agreement, without Advertiser's prior written consent. Any attempt to assign, subcontract, or delegate in violation of this paragraph is void in each instance. Advertiser may assign this Agreement to its affiliates.

23.2 Diverse Suppliers (Minority- or Women-Owned Business Enterprises)[xlv]

Advertiser has a policy that requires Agency, whenever practicable, to use diverse suppliers, including contractors and subcontractors, if such suppliers are both qualified and competitive. A diverse supplier is a for-profit enterprise located in the United States or its trust territories, which is controlled, operated, and 51 percent owned by a minority member or a woman. Minority members are individuals who are African American, Hispanic American, Native American, Asian-Pacific American, and Asian-Indian American.

23.3 Local Work Rules

Agency shall ensure that all of its personnel and any Third-party Suppliers comply with Advertiser's rules and policies while on Advertiser's premises.

23.4 Advertiser's Code of Conduct[xlvi]

Agency acknowledges that Agency has been furnished a copy of Advertiser's Code of Business Conduct (the "Code of Conduct"), and that Advertiser associates are required to follow the Code of Conduct. Agency shall support the Code of Conduct and shall not take any action which may cause an Advertiser associate to violate the Code of Conduct. Agency shall report to Advertiser any violation or attempted violation of the Code of Conduct.

23.5 Notices

23.5.1 Notices under this Agreement are sufficient if given by nationally recognized overnight courier service, certified mail (return receipt requested), facsimile with electronic confirmation, or personal delivery to the other Party at the address below:

If to Advertiser:

[name of advertiser]
[address of advertiser]
[name and/or title of person to receive delivery]
[phone number]
[fax number]
[e-mail address]
with copies to:
[insert additional recipients, if any]

If to Agency:

[name of advertiser]

[address of advertiser]
[name and/or title of person to receive delivery]
[phone number]
[fax number]
[e-mail address]
with copies to:
[insert additional recipients, if any]

23.5.2 Notice is effective:

23.5.2.1 when delivered personally;

23.5.2.2 three (3) business days after it is sent by certified mail;

23.5.2.3 on the business day after it is sent by a nationally recognized courier service for next-day delivery; or

23.5.2.4 on the business day after it is sent by facsimile with electronic confirmation to the sender.

23.5.3 A Party may change its notice address by giving notice in accordance with this paragraph. If this paragraph states no notice address for a Party, notice will be effective if given to the Party at the address specified in this Agreement's introductory paragraph or the last known address.

23.6 Waiver

Either Party's failure in any one or more instances to insist upon strict performance of any of the terms and conditions of this Agreement or to exercise any right herein conferred shall not be construed as a waiver or relinquishment of that right or of that Party's right to assert or rely upon the terms and conditions of this Agreement. Any express waiver of a term of this Agreement shall not be binding and effective unless made in writing and properly executed by the waiving Party.

23.7 Severability

If any provision of this Agreement is determined to be unenforceable, the Parties intend that this Agreement be enforced as if the unenforceable provisions were not present, and that any partially valid and enforceable provisions be enforced to the extent that they are enforceable.

23.8 Survival

The following provisions shall survive termination of this Agreement: [Section 2] (Exclusivity); [Section 12] (Record Retention); [Section 13] (Confidentiality); [Section 15] (Defense); and [Section 16] (Indemnification). In addition, any provision which, by its nature, must survive the completion, termination, cancellation, or expiration of this Agreement shall survive the completion, termination, cancellation, or expiration of this Agreement.

23.9 Injunctive Relief

23.9.1 Agency acknowledges that any material breach of this Agreement by Agency would cause Advertiser irreparable harm for which Advertiser has no adequate remedies at law. Accordingly, Advertiser is entitled to specific performance of this Agreement or injunctive relief for any such breach. Agency waives all claims for damages by reason of the wrongful issuance of an injunction and acknowledges that its only remedy in that case is the dissolution of that injunction.

23.9.2 Agency acknowledges and agrees that it shall not be entitled to any injunctive relief against Advertiser, to enjoin Advertiser's use of advertising materials produced by Agency on behalf of Advertiser, on account of Advertiser's breach of this Agreement. Agency agrees that its sole remedy shall be an action to recover monetary damages as a result of Advertiser's breach.[xlvii]

23.10 Entire Agreement

This Agreement together with all associated exhibits and schedules, which are incorporated by reference, constitutes the complete and final agreement of the Parties pertaining to the Agency Services and supersedes the Parties' prior agreements, understandings, and discussions relating to the Agency Services. No modification of this Agreement is binding unless it is in writing and signed by Advertiser and Agency.

23.11 Headings

The headings to the various Sections and paragraphs of this Agreement are solely for the convenience of the Parties, are not part of the Agreement, and shall not be used for the interpretation of the validity of the Agreement or any provision hereof.

23.12 Cumulative Rights

The rights and remedies of the Parties under this Agreement are cumulative, and either Party may enforce any of its rights or remedies under this Agreement or other rights and remedies available to it at law or in equity.

23.13 Authority

Each Party hereto warrants that it has the full authority and power to enter into and perform this Agreement and to make all representations, warranties, and grants as set forth herein. Agency further represents that it is not subject to any restrictive obligations imposed by former clients or any other person that would impair its ability to exercise its best efforts for or on behalf of Advertiser in connection with services to be performed pursuant to this Agreement.

23.14 No Third-party Beneficiaries

This Agreement is made solely and specifically among and for the benefit of the Parties hereto and their respective successors and assigns, and no other person will have any rights, interest, or claims hereunder or be entitled to any benefits under or on account of this Agreement as a third-party beneficiary or otherwise.

23.15 Counterparts

This Agreement may be executed simultaneously in two or more counterparts which, when taken together, shall be deemed an original and constitute one and the same document. The signature of any Party to the counterpart shall be deemed a signature to the Agreement, and may be appended to any other counterpart. Facsimile transmission of executed signature pages shall be sufficient to bind the executing Party.

IN WITNESS WHEREOF, the Parties hereto have caused this Agreement to be executed by their respective officers thereto duly authorized, as of the date first written below.

[Advertiser]   [Advertising Agency]

By: _____   By: _____

[Name]   [Name]

Date: _____   Date: _____

Endnotes:

i   The term "agency" in the reference to "advertising agency" is an anachronism. Historically, advertising agencies began as agents of the media (e.g., newspaper agents selling ad space and writing copy), not the advertisers. In agency-advertiser agreements, the issue is typically handled by making the agency a limited agent which must obtain prior written approval before incurring any obligation to a third party (see [Section 3.2]). Such an approach gives the advertiser more control over the agency's actions than an "agent for all purposes" designation would. At the same time, the limited agency designation makes clear that any rights obtained by the agency on behalf of the advertiser belong to the advertiser. For example, if an advertiser requires an agency to license the rights to certain music on the agency's own behalf rather than in the agency's role as an agent, and the client subsequently terminates the agency, the music rights might belong to the agency and not the advertiser. Moreover, if the agency is not designated as a limited agent, sales tax issues may arise.

ii   From a practical point of view, the description of services is relatively immaterial. As the scope of an agency's assignment often changes, it may be impractical to include a detailed "scope of work" list in the agency agreement. Each change to the agency's assignment would require a change to the agreement. An alternative way to manage the connection between the Agency Fee and the agency's services is to monitor both the level of agency staff time spent on the advertiser's work and the amount of advertiser work that is done. That approach is taken in [Section 9] of this form agreement. Disputes between agencies and advertisers in this area are rare; litigation is virtually nonexistent.

iii   It is not uncommon for agencies to seek to absolve themselves from any liability for proofing errors once the advertiser has approved the final copy and layout in a proof version of the advertisement. Advertisers should resist this approach.

iv   While it is impossible to guarantee that the agency will not stumble and commit some act or produce some materials that are problematic for an advertiser, this clause at least gives an advertiser the opportunity to cite the agency for its error and to take it into consideration in the compensation.

v   Advertisers may find that an agency wants exclusivity from the advertiser for a particular product or service. Before granting such exclusivity, the advertiser must consider if the agency can adequately handle the advertisers needs in, e.g., ethnic marketing, foreign marketing, yellow page advertising, or special services such as package design, sales promotions, event management, or the like. Because it is often impossible to anticipate marketing directions or sectors to a certainty, the non-exclusive clause suggested in this form is more advantageous to the advertiser. If the agency is on a fee rather than commission basis, the lack of exclusivity should not pose a major problem.

vi   From an advertiser's perspective, it is important to have the agency agree not to represent directly or indirectly competitive or incompatible products/services. For example, an automobile manufacturer might not allow its agency to represent a motorcycle manufacturer, even though cars and motorcycles are only indirectly competitive with one another. In addition, a retailer might not want its agency to do work for an entity that opposes the sale of imported products because such an entity's interests would be incompatible with those of the retailer. Although the phrase may be imprecise, it is intended to bring the agency to the table on exclusivity issues. The term "incompatible" is commonly used in industry contracts, but it is not usually a defined term. If an advertiser prefers or is required by an agency to include a definition, the following language can be added: "For purposes of this [Section 2.2], an 'incompatible' product or service is one which is contrary or adverse to the interests of the Advertiser or which expressly or impliedly derides Advertiser's business or the Advertiser Business Lines set forth in [Exhibit B]."

vii   The list of "Business Lines" applies throughout the agreement to cover: (i) the scope of the agency's assignment and (ii) the products and services under the agency's non-compete. Generally, assignments follow product categories matching an advertiser's Business Units (e.g., apparel, tools and so on). However, it is not unusual for an advertiser and the agency to discuss whether there are any exceptions which might not allow this concept throughout all of these areas.

viii   This request may be problematic if the agency is a subsidiary of a holding company that owns many agencies. In such instances, the list of clients is generally limited to those which are direct clients of the same subsidiary hired by the advertiser.

ix   The purpose of this provision is to provide a disincentive for the agency to terminate its agreement with the advertiser so that the advertising agency can represent one of the advertiser's competitors. Also, it seeks to prevent leakage of confidential information, such as the current year's advertising budget.

x   Agencies often use third party suppliers, e.g., printers, engravers, photographers, models, and commercial directors, when they create advertising materials.

This section does not apply to media purchases.

xi   In many instances, materials and services used by agencies in the production of advertising for an advertiser are secured with restrictions on their use. For example, photographers typically allow use of photographs only for a limited period of time in a limited geographic area. The extent of exclusivity required also has a bearing on cost. The hiring of talent engaged in television commercials is usually governed by the collective bargaining agreements of the principal performing unions wherein use of a performance is limited in time. Therefore, an advertiser must be realistic in demanding unbridled us of materials produced by agencies.

xii   An advertiser may want to consider adding a minimum dollar threshold for the written approval requirement. By doing so, the advertiser will not impede the efficient operations of the agency for purchases that are below the threshold.

xiii   This language places the burden on the Advertiser Contact Person to confirm the verbal approval in writing. Alternatively, an advertiser may choose to require the agency to provide advertiser with a written confirmation summarizing the verbal consent. However, if the written confirmation memoranda submitted by the agency are not regularly reviewed by advertiser personnel, such an approach would provide an advertiser with little practical protection. The decision regarding the approach to take depends upon the nature of the advertiser's relationship with the agency. If an advertiser chooses the agency confirmation option, the following alternate confirmation language can be used:

In such circumstances, an Advertiser Contact Person may give verbal authorization, and such verbal authorization shall be binding, provided that the Agency submits a written report confirming such verbal authorization to Advertiser within two (2) business days following such verbal authorization, and provided further that Advertiser does not dispute the Agency's written report within [insert number] days of receipt. Unless authorized under this [Section 3.2], Agency shall not enter into any agreement with any Third party Supplier requiring payment or reimbursement by Advertiser.

xiv   An advertiser should discuss the specific types of agreements and the dollar thresholds it desires.

xv   Many Third party Suppliers are likely to be small businesses (e.g., photographers, models, print shops) which cannot reasonably be expected to have sufficient insurance to cover the advertiser. The agency's insurance may provide the protection required by the advertiser, but is not likely to cover "any and all losses."

xvi   An agency may push back on this "billed at net cost" requirement, and may instead ask an advertiser for prior written approval of any Agency Affiliate Fees. "Billed at net cost" means that there is no agency profit or commission component.

xvii   Most major advertising agencies and many advertisers are signatories to the Commercial Codes of SAG and AFTRA and must abide by those Codes in the hiring of actors. Where neither the agency nor the advertiser are signatories to such Codes, however, commercials can be produced "outside" the Codes. Before embarking on such a direction, however, the advertiser and agency are well advised to seek legal advice from counsel experienced in the Codes.

xviii   At times, the agency may be requested to provide special reports from one of the cited companies. In such events, it is not uncommon, nor unfair, for the agency to seek reimbursement for any special charges from such companies.

xix   Given that Change Orders can sometimes result in the loss of volume and other discounts, it is important to require the agency to take steps to mitigate against such losses.

xx   If the agency is not buying media, this Section should be deleted, together with applicable provision in Section 3. Depending on circumstances, a section might be added requiring the Agency to collaborate with Advertiser's media buying service.

xxi   So called "proofs of performance" are rare today.

xxii   If the compensation relationship between the advertiser and agency is based upon media commissions rather than fees, the rate of commission might be as high as 15% or more of the gross media charges billed to the agency for the advertiser's media placements. Such commission percentage, however, is the subject of considerable negotiation and the rate is often substantially lower.

xxiii   This form provides for a fee based relationship rather than a commission, incentive, or guaranteed profit relationship. While commission relationships were once the norm, fee based compensation plans are now more prevalent. While incentive compensation is also quite common, incentive programs vary so widely that they are not conducive to a form approach. Before an advertiser considers incentive compensation, however, the incentive plan must be carefully reviewed to assure that it is reasonable and within the control of the agency to achieve. It is damaging to the advertiser/agency relationship to offer an incentive compensation plan that has no realistic chance of being realized by the agency.

xxiv   Were this form a commission arrangement, production costs would generally be marked up by 17.65% or a negotiated rate.

xxv   If the advertiser does not have any travel guidelines, then the following clause can be substituted: "All travel expenses incurred by Agency shall be authorized in writing by Advertiser."

xxvi   It is not uncommon for an advertiser to require its agency to absorb travel between the offices of the two companies for work routinely performed under an agreement. Agencies will generally resist such a clause. In negotiations, it is not uncommon to see this clause remain but have a limit on the number of trips the agency has to absorb on an annual basis without reimbursement.

xxvii   Agencies are linked to an advertiser's brand(s) and to its image. Improper behavior by agency personnel may harm the advertiser's image; thus, the advertiser should have the ability to terminate immediately in such a situation.

xxviii   While 90 days is preferred by advertising agencies, it can no longer be described as the norm. It is common to see shorter termination notice periods, e.g., 60 or 45 days. Shortening the period, however, is not necessarily to the advantage of an advertiser. It is important that an appropriate transition period exist. Historically, 90 days has been found to be quite appropriate, although 60 days does not generally pose a significant problem. It is also quite common for an agency to ask that the right of termination without cause on 90 days' notice not be permitted until one year has passed. The logic for such a request is that an agency may need to gear up to service an advertiser, including the hiring of personnel and the leasing of space and/or equipment. Unless the agency knows that the agreement has at least a one year term, it may not be able to recoup the investment it was required to make in order to "gear up," not to speak of recouping its "pitch" expenses.

xxix   If an agency has filed for bankruptcy, under current bankruptcy laws (3/2001), this clause may not be enforceable.

xxx   In some instances, agencies will ask that this provision be modified to indicate that advertising properties will be transferred provided that advertiser has paid the agency. In commission-based arrangements, it is reasonable to condition transfer of the materials upon payment in order to protect the agency. In a fee-based compensation agreement like this form agreement, however, conditioning transfers upon payment is not required to protect the agency.

xxxi   Agencies receive discounts from some suppliers (e.g., printers, media) for prompt payment or volume purchases. For that reason, invoices rendered by the agency for a particular month may well be based on estimated costs for future purchases of materials or media. Discounts, if obtained, should be passed on to the advertiser by the agency. If, however, the advertiser is late in paying invoices and the agency's cash is being used to pay suppliers, the advertiser should not expect to receive the benefit of any discount.

xxxii   This provision is important because the advertiser is paying the agency a retainer fee. The agency should be required to maintain staff time records that will enable the advertiser to determine whether the retainer fee amount is justified and to determine what fee may be appropriate upon renegotiation. In the agency review and evaluation process, the advertiser should compare the level of agency staffing that the agency promises to provide (contained in Exhibit F) to the level of staffing that the agency actually provides during the term of the agreement (to be tracked by the agency under [Section 9.3]). This provision allows the advertiser to claim that the agency is in breach of the agreement if the agency does not provide the staffing level that it originally promised.

xxxiii   Exhibit F, to be provided by the agency, should contain information regarding the name/function of each agency employee on the advertiser's account and the number of hours that person will spend on advertiser's account in the calendar year.

xxxiv   Smaller agencies may not have audited financial reports to provide. An advertisers may have to settle for unaudited financial reports from such agencies if it wishes to do business with them.

xxxv   As noted, one way to manage the connection between the Base Fee and the agency's services is to monitor the level of agency staff time spent on Advertiser projects. This provision is intended to require that the agency provide the advertiser with quarterly staffing/services reports to allow the advertiser to determine whether its Base for the year was appropriate. This provision is also intended to help control the agency's scope of work issue by reducing the likelihood of unexpected third and fourth quarter agency requests for additional fees because a particular project is alleged to be outside of the scope of services included in the Base Fee.

xxxvi   This audit provision is regularly included in agency agreements, but advertisers typically do not take advantage of it until difficulties arise or until the advertiser agency relationship is ending. Routine audits, from the beginning of the relationship, may prevent problems later with media and other suppliers which have failed to collect from the agency.

xxxvii   The treatment of Confidential Personal Information may be governed by state or federal law, e.g., the Gramm-Leach-Bliley Act ("GLBA"). GLBA allows a financial institution to share personally identifiable information about consumers with nonaffiliated parties only if (1) the nonaffiliated parties are contractually obligated to keep the information confidential, and (2) the practice is disclosed in the financial institution's privacy policy. If an advertiser issues its own credit card through a national bank, the advertiser is a financial institution for purposes of GLBA. Because of GLBA, an advertiser may have limited rights to negotiate on the portions of this Agreement dealing with Confidential Personal Information.

xxxviii   Advertisers must understand that many releases have limitations imposed upon the use of the materials or names or likeness of individuals that are the subject of the release. It is therefore important that the agency keep the advertiser fully informed of any such limitations.

xxxix   This provision should be reviewed by the advertiser's risk manager with particular attention to the limits on insurance policies suggested in this section.

xl   Agencies consider ideas or concepts to be their "stock in trade," and want the right to submit them to other clients if rejected by the first. Ideas cannot be protected by copyright but if they are unique, they may have some value to other advertisers. It can become contentious whether the agency should have the right to use ideas rejected by the advertiser for other agency clients. In a commission compensation arrangement, an agency may object to the transfer of property rights to rejected ideas and may want to restrict the transfer only to materials used by the advertiser. Such a position is not unreasonable in a pure commission deal. If an agency is on a fee basis, however, an advertiser may justifiably take the position that everything submitted to the advertiser was paid for, and therefore should be owned by the advertiser.

xli   Advertiser must keep in mind that many third party suppliers such as music houses, do not transfer complete ownership to an advertiser. In such instances, the agency is obligated to inform the advertiser of any limitations imposed by the third party on Advertiser's use of materials or services supplied.

xlii   The methodology for dispute resolution in agency/advertiser agreements is subject to considerable debate. The clause included provides for binding arbitration. Such inclusion, however, should not be construed as the author's endorsement of such an approach in all instances. Where resolution of disputes is preferred in courts, the provisions of this Section can be replaced with the following:

This Agreement and the rights of the Parties hereunder shall be governed by and interpreted in accordance with the laws of the State of [insert name of State], without regard to its conflict of laws rules or choice of law principles. Exclusive jurisdiction and venue for any claims made by either Party against the other shall be within the state and federal courts located in the State of [insert name of State].

xliii   The AAA is only one of the many dispute resolution bodies that can be considered. Another such body is JAMS.

xliv   The parties may want to consider the award of the costs of arbitration or attorneys fees to the prevailing party or at the discretion of the arbitrator. In addition, if arbitration is not the methodology for dispute resolution adopted by the parties, recovery of court costs and attorney's fees should be considered.

xlv   Not all agencies are required, or should be required, to comply with such a provision. It is included in this form for appropriate inclusion at the discretion of the advertiser and as the advertiser's legal counsel may advise.

xlvi   This assumes such a policy exists. If not, this paragraph should be eliminated.

xlvii   This provision may give rise to objection by an agency. It is based upon the approach taken by motion picture companies with regard to injunctive rights of actors or other creative personnel where an injunction interfering with the distribution of a completed motion picture is too onerous on the motion picture company to be allowed. The same logic holds with respect to an advertiser's use of advertising materials produced by an agency.

EXHIBIT A: AGENCY SERVICES

Agency agrees to perform the services listed below and to conform to the highest professional standards in carrying out its responsibilities and in all dealings with Advertiser and anyone associated with Advertiser:[xlviii]

A.1 Generally:

A.1.1 Familiarize itself in every respect with Advertiser's business, markets, and Business Lines, as well as the business, products, and services of Advertiser' competitors;

A.1.2 Study and analyze market and marketing potential for the Advertiser's Business Lines;

A.1.3 Keep current with all Advertiser's product and service information for the Advertiser's Business Lines, including all new or additional product and service information provided by Advertiser;

A.1.4 Upon request by Advertiser, advise Advertiser on the formulation of marketing plans, including advertising campaigns;

A.1.5 Upon request by Advertiser, create, prepare, and submit for Advertiser's approval advertising ideas and programs and campaigns for traditional and electronic media, and plans for the development and execution thereof;

A.1.6 Prepare and submit to Advertiser written and itemized estimated costs associated with the execution of marketing and advertising concepts and programs, including the cost of materials and all reasonably foreseeable expenses relating thereto;

A.1.7 Execute advertisements in finished form in accordance with Advertiser's instructions upon prior written approval;

A.1.8 Use commercially reasonable best efforts to provide all services at the most advantageous rates, terms, and conditions available;

A.1.9 Audit and pay all proper bills incurred for Advertiser's account; and

A.1.10 In accordance with Advertiser's instructions, forward advertising material with proper instructions to the media for fulfillment of the order.

A.2 Media Planning

Agency will be responsible for media planning (including initial development and plan revisions) for Advertiser, including the following:

A.2.1 As requested by Advertiser, provide plans setting forth media recommendations for each Advertiser's Business Line;

A.2.2 Prepare advance-planning calendars for each of Advertiser's Business Lines in a manner and at such frequency as reasonably requested by Advertiser;

A.2.3 Create and present formal media-plan presentations at such frequency as may be directed by Advertiser;

A.2.4 Recommend available media and/or placement opportunities that Advertiser could utilize to promote the Advertiser's Business Lines and provide points of view on such media opportunities, including obtaining and reporting on subscriber/viewer demographic profiles, at such frequency as may be directed by Advertiser;

A.2.5 Provide management of budgets and implement plan revisions as directed by Advertiser;

A.2.6 Provide competitive analyses including, without limitation, the tracking of placements of competitive advertisements;

A.2.7 Coordinate with Advertiser and its creative agencies, if any, and as necessary, to arrange for the timely delivery of materials to Media Vendors for scheduled placements; and

A.2.8 Obtain written approval from Advertiser under the terms of this Agreement for the media plan and the media buying strategy for each of Advertiser's Business Lines.

A.3 Negotiating and Buying Services

A.3.1 For national and local television and radio advertising, Agency will:

A.3.1.1 Project ratings of specific media exposures, such as specific televisions programs;

A.3.1.2 Negotiate with Media Vendors to buy national and local television and radio time, and make commercially reasonable efforts to buy media at the best and most advantageous available rates and times. Agency will purchase media as needed to meet scheduled on-air dates, according to the agreed-upon media plan;

A.3.1.3 Construct and order buy schedules based on Advertiser' budget;

A.3.1.4 Forward buy schedule summaries to Advertiser;

A.3.1.5 Consult with Advertiser as to placement opportunities, strategic and tactical goals, budgets, and other related issues, and purchase media accordingly per Advertiser's agreements and instructions; and

A.3.1.6 Provide Advertiser with post-buy reports specifying the delivery of the media purchased, as directed by Advertiser.

A.3.2 For print advertising, including consumer and trade magazines and newspapers, Agency will:

A.3.2.1 Project audience delivery and monitor circulation levels;

A.3.2.2 Negotiate with Media Vendors to buy print space, and make commercially reasonable best efforts to buy such media at the best and most advantageous available rates and times. Agency will order media as needed to meet scheduled insertion dates;

A.3.2.3 Construct and order insertion schedules based on Advertiser's budget;

A.3.2.4 Forward insertion schedule summaries to Advertiser;

A.3.2.5 Consult with Advertiser as to placement opportunities, strategic and tactical goals, budgets, and other related issues, and purchase media accordingly per Advertiser's instructions; and

A.3.2.6 Provide Advertiser with post-buy reports, specifying the delivery of the media purchased.

A.3.3 For out-of-home advertising, Agency will:

A.3.3.1 Project out-of-home ratings or "showings";

A.3.3.2 Negotiate with Media Vendors to buy out-of-home media postings, and make commercially reasonable best efforts to buy such media postings at the best and most advantageous rates and locations available;

A.3.3.3 Construct and order posting schedules;

A.3.3.4 Forward posting schedule summaries to Advertiser; and

A.3.3.5 Consult with Advertiser regarding budgets and related issues, and make media purchases accordingly per Advertiser's instructions.

A.3.4 Buy Maintenance Services. Agency will, on behalf of Advertiser, perform maintenance on all media buy orders for all media buys hereunder:

A.3.4.1 Check media contracts for accuracy, check invoices and station affidavits of performance, and ensure that the advertising placed has been published, displayed, or aired as ordered;

A.3.4.2 Pay invoices in a timely manner, provided Advertiser has made timely payments therefore under the terms of this Agreement;

A.3.4.3 Resolve billing discrepancies and negotiate rebates or "make-goods" when applicable; and

A.3.4.4 Secure, obtain, and pass over to Advertiser all available discounts.

Endnotes:

xlviii The Agency and Advertiser need to discuss any other specific desired deliverables and include them in this list.

EXHIBIT B: ADVERTISER BUSINESS LINES

[customize list based on the agency assignment]

EXHIBIT C: LIST OF AGENCY'S CLIENTS

[to be added by the agency]

EXHIBIT D: AGENCY COMPENSATION[xlix]

D.1 Option A—Fee-Based Arrangement

D.1.1 General

The Agency Fee will be: a base fee (the "Base Fee") calculated and paid in twelve (12) equal monthly installments starting in [January][l] of each calendar year.

D.1.2 Base Fee

The Base Fee for the 20_____ calendar year shall be $[_____].

D.2 Option B—Commission-Based Arrangement[li]

D.2.1 Media Service—On all media purchased by Agency on Advertiser's behalf pursuant to Advertiser's authorization, Agency shall bill Advertiser at the published card rates, or negotiated rates, as may be applicable. If no agency commission is granted or allowed on such purchases, Advertiser agrees that Agency shall invoice Advertiser a gross amount which, after deduction of Agency's cost, will yield Agency [insert percentage] percent ([insert number]%) of such gross amount as Agency commission.[lii]

D.2.2 Production—On broadcast production, artwork, engravings, type compositions, and any and all art and mechanical expenses incurred by Agency pursuant to Advertiser's authorization, Agency shall invoice Advertiser a gross amount which, after deduction of Agency's cost, will yield Agency [insert percentage] percent ([insert number]%) of such gross amount as Agency commission.[liii]

D.2.3 If Agency undertakes, at Advertiser's request, special assignments such as market counseling or sales meeting presentations, the charges made by Agency will be agreed upon in advance whenever possible. If no agreement is made, Agency shall charge Advertiser at Agency's standard rates for the work performed by Agency. In addition, for materials or services purchased from outside sources under Advertiser's authorization, Agency shall invoice Advertiser a gross amount which, after deduction of Agency's cost, will yield Agency [insert percentage] percent ([insert number]%) of such gross amount as Agency commission.[liv]

D.2.4 With respect to the engagement of talent, Agency shall bill Advertiser the authorized engagement rate, plus any taxes, insurance, pension, and health fund contributions, talent payment-service fees, etc. applicable thereto, plus a gross amount which, after deduction of Agency's cost, will yield Agency [insert percentage] percent ([insert number]%) of such gross amount as agency commission.[lv] Advertiser recognizes that Agency is a signatory to collective bargaining agreements with Screen Actors Guild and American Federation of Television and Radio Artists, and that the hiring of talent by Agency on Advertiser's behalf will be subject to the terms of such agreements.

Endnotes:

xlix   This Exhibit provides for one of two compensation formats—fee based (Option A) and commission based (Option B). While there are other compensation programs that include incentives and guaranteed profits, they are generally too unique to the facts of a particular relationship to lend themselves to any form approach. It should also be noted that it is not uncommon to see a compensation program that is a combination of both fee and commission. Therefore, this exhibit should only be used as a guide, recognizing that compensation systems can vary considerably.

l   The month may have to be changed depending upon when the agreement begins.

li A note on calculating commissions: There are two general types of commission paid to advertising agencies—commissions on media purchases and commissions on production related expenses. In the case of media commissions, most media allow an agency to deduct a percentage (usually 15%) from an invoice. For example, if a media invoice is for $100, the advertiser pays the agency the full amount, also known as the "gross". The agency, however, is obligated to the media a "net" of $85. The agency retains $15 (15%) as its commission. In the case of production expenses, deductions from invoices are not generally permitted. In such instances, it is not uncommon to see a commission of 17.65%. While such a percentage may seem odd at first glance, there is logic to it. Using the media example of $100, and agency expects to earn a commission of $15 on an $85 liability. If a production job is invoiced at $85 and billed at net to an advertiser, i.e., at the same price the agency has to pay to the third party, the agency would still expect a commission of $15. To earn the same $15 commission on a production job for which the agency had to pay the same $85, however, the net amount has to be "marked up" by 17.65% to yield the same $15 commission. Thus, it is not unusual to hear the reference, "15% on gross or 17.65% on net". Both calculations will yield the same commission. Another way to deal with the equation is to calculate "yield" rather than a net or gross commission rate. Thus, the same commission would be paid, regardless of what is billed if the commission is calculated so that it yields an agreed upon commission on whatever the agency actually pays to the third party. This form takes the yield approach. It should be noted, however, that commission rates are highly negotiable and the norm is not necessarily 15% or 17.65%.

lii The commission rate for media purchases is subject to considerable variation. Generally no higher than 15%, it is most often lower. This is particularly true if an advertiser is spending a considerable amount for media. The labor costs for a media buy do not necessarily increase as the amount spent on media increases. Thus, it does not necessarily flow that media commissions should be a flat rate regardless of how much is spent. In addition, many advertisers use media buying companies, rather than their advertising agencies, to purchase media., at commission rates that are usually quite competitive.

liii Production commissions do not vary as much as media commissions and tend to be higher, presumably because there is more labor involved in production work in relation to the dollars spent.

liv This commission rate is equivalent to the rate for production commissions. It should be noted that advertisers generally do not pay agencies the full commission in connection with the engagement of over-scale talent.

lv While subject to negotiation, it is not uncommon to see no commission paid on talent.

EXHIBIT E: ADVERTISER'S TRAVEL GUIDELINES[lvi]

[To be supplied by Advertiser]

Endnotes:

lvi   The policy included on this Exhibit is one example of such policies and is not necessarily one that will work in all circumstances. Any policy adopted should reflect one that is consistent with the advertiser's own policies.

EXHIBIT F: AGENCY STAFF

Agency staffing for the 20_____ calendar year is attached, including the following information on Agency Staff for Advertiser:

[Agency to provide chart]

Form II.15.2 Contract Between an Advertising Agency and Advertiser—Long Form (Typical Relationships)

AGREEMENT effective [insert date] by and between [insert name of advertising agency] ("Agency"), with offices located at [insert address], and [insert name of client] ("Client"), with offices located at [insert address].

1. Appointment of Agency and Scope of Appointment

   a. Client hereby appoints Agency as its [exclusive][lvii] advertising agency during the "Term" (as hereinafter defined) of this Agreement. During the Term, Agency will be [the sole company][lviii] charged with the responsibility of preparing and placing advertising with respect to Client's product(s) and/or service(s) specified in Schedule 1, attached hereto and collectively referred to herein as the "Scheduled Appointment."

   b. During the Term, Client may wish to assign additional projects, products, or services to Agency beyond the Scheduled Appointment. Agency agrees to accept such assignment upon written agreement by Client regarding compensation to be paid to Agency with respect to such additional assignment.

   c. In the performance of its services hereunder, Agency is authorized to act as Client's agent in purchasing materials and services required to produce advertising on Client's behalf.

2. Scope of Services[lix]

   Agency will perform services for Client in connection with the planning, preparing, and placing of advertising for Client as provided in Schedule 2, attached hereto.

3. Exclusivity[lx]

   Subject to the provisions of Schedule 3, attached hereto, during the Term of this Agreement, Agency will not accept any assignment with respect to products or services competitive to those assigned by Client to Agency.

4. Compensation

   Agency's compensation in consideration of its rendition of services to Client will be as provided in Schedule 4, attached hereto.

5. Billing and Payment Procedures

   Agency will invoice Client, and Client will pay Agency, in accordance with the provisions of Schedule 5, attached hereto.

6. Commitments to Third Parties

   a. Agency shall make no commitment for or on behalf of Client or for which Client shall have any liability or responsibility unless Client shall have first given its approval. If the cost of a given expenditure in connection with the foregoing exceeds the approved amount by more than 10%[lxi], Agency must obtain prior written approval from Client. If Agency is unable, due to extraordinary circumstances, to obtain such approval in writing, Agency may obtain Client's oral approval, provided Agency confirms such oral approval in writing as soon as practicable, but no later than two (2) business days from the time oral approval is obtained.

   b. Client may, during the progress of any work hereunder, by written or oral order to Agency, require additions, modifications, suspension, or termination of such assigned work. Upon receipt of such instructions from Client, Agency shall take no action which may increase the expense to Client hereunder beyond those expenses inherent in the assignment which had been agreed to prior to the receipt of instructions to modify, suspend, or terminate, and provided further that Client will hold Agency harmless with respect to any costs incurred by Agency as a result thereof.

c.   In purchasing any materials or services for Client's account, Agency will exercise due care in selecting suppliers, and make every effort to obtain the lowest price for the desired quality of materials or services. Wherever possible, Agency will obtain competitive bids. In no event will Agency purchase any materials or services from any supplier which is a subsidiary or affiliated company, or which is known to Agency to be owned or controlled by any of Agency's directors or officers, without making full disclosure to Client of any such relationship.

d.   If at any time Agency obtains discounts or rebates from any supplier, whether based on volume of work given to such supplier by Agency or otherwise, then and in such event, Agency will remit to Client, within a reasonable time after Agency's receipt of such discount or rebate, such proportion thereof as the volume of work given by Agency to such supplier on Client's behalf bears to the total volume of work given by Agency to such supplier from all of Agency's clients during the pertinent period to which the discount or rebate is applicable. For all media purchased by Agency on Client's behalf, Client agrees that Agency will be held solely liable for payments only to the extent proceeds have cleared from Client to Agency for advertising disseminated in accordance with this Agreement. For sums owing, but not cleared, to Agency, Client agrees to be held solely liable.[lxii] Agency will use its best efforts to provide in all contracts with media that Agency will be held solely liable for payments if Client has provided proceeds to Agency sufficient to cover such payments.

7.   Audit of Books

Agency shall maintain complete documentation and records relating to the media and production transactions, including, but not limited to, transactions for point-of-purchase and research billed to Client. Such documents include purchase orders, bids, vendor invoices, canceled checks, written policies and procedures, vendor contracts, and any other appropriate documentation to satisfy Client that expenditures were within industry standards and the Client-approved budget. All documents and records shall be maintained in accordance with generally accepted accounting principles consistently applied, and in such manner as may be readily audited. The documentation and records shall be available at all reasonable times for audit by Client's internal audit function or by any independent audit firm engaged by Client, both during the Term hereof and for two (2) years following the expiration or termination date of the Agreement, or until all disputes, if any, between Agency and Client have been finally resolved, whichever is later. With respect to the latter obligation, only those records in dispute need be retained.

8.   Safeguarding of Property

Agency will take all reasonable precautions to safeguard any of Client's property entrusted to Agency's custody or control, but in the absence of negligence on Agency's part or willful disregard by Agency for Client's property rights, Agency will not be responsible for any loss, damage, destruction, or unauthorized use by others of any such property. Agency will not be responsible for obtaining the return of engravings from publications after their use in publications.

9. Indemnities

    a. Client Indemnity. Client shall be responsible for the accuracy and completeness of information concerning its organization, and the description of Client's products and services which Client furnishes to Agency in connection with the performance of this Agreement. If Client supplies any other elements to Agency for use in advertising, or advises Agency that Client has the right to use the property of a third party in advertising, Client shall be responsible for such elements. (Such information or elements supplied by Client shall be referred to herein as "Organizational Information.") Client shall indemnify, defend, and hold harmless Agency, its employees, officers, directors, and shareholders from and against any and all injury, loss, damage, liability, claim, demand, costs, and expenses (including reasonable attorneys' fees and costs) which are incurred by Agency based upon or arising out of any claim, allegation, demand, suit, or proceeding made or brought against Agency with respect to any advertising or other products or services which Agency prepared or performed for Client and which were approved by Client, to the extent that such claim, allegation, demand, suit, or proceeding relates, in whole or substantial part, to the accuracy or completeness of such Organizational Information; provided, however, that Client shall not be required to indemnify Agency for any injury, loss, damage, liability, claim, demand, or expense arising out of or in any way caused by the negligence or willful misconduct of Agency.

    b. Agency Indemnity. Subject to Client's responsibility with respect to Organizational Information set forth above, Agency assumes full responsibility for, and shall indemnify, defend, and hold harmless Client, its affiliates, its and their agents, employees, officers, directors, and stockholders from and against, any and all injury, loss, damage, liability, claims, demands, costs, and expenses (including reasonable attorneys' fees and costs) which may be incurred by Client based upon or arising out of any claim, allegation, demand, suit, or proceeding made or brought against Client arising out of the production, distribution, or dissemination of materials produced hereunder, including, without limitation: (i) libel, slander, defamation, infringement or misuse of any proprietary rights, piracy, plagiarism, unfair competition, idea misappropriation, or invasion of rights of privacy or publicity; or (ii) damage to or destruction of personal property or injury to or death of any person, attributable to or arising out of Agency's performance or nonperformance hereunder.

    c. Notification of Claims. A party entitled to be indemnified pursuant to this paragraph 9, subsection (a) or (b) above (the "Indemnified Party") shall provide prompt written notice to the party liable for such indemnification (the "Indemnifying Party") of any claim or demand which the Indemnified Party has determined has given or could give rise to a right of indemnification under this Agreement. The Indemnifying Party shall promptly undertake to discharge its obligations hereunder. Additionally, the Indemnifying Party shall employ counsel reasonably acceptable to the Indemnified Party to defend any such claim or demand asserted against the Indemnified Party. The Indemnified Party shall have the right to participate in the defense of any such claim or demand, at its own expense. The Indemnified Party shall cooperate with the Indemnifying Party in any such defense. The Indemnified Party may settle or compromise such claim or demand. The Indemnified Party shall make available to the Indemnifying Party or its agents all records and other materials in the

Indemnified Party's possession reasonably required by it for its use in contesting any third-party claim or demand.

10. Ownership[lxiii]

    a. All campaigns, trademarks, service marks, slogans, artwork, written materials, drawings, photographs, graphic materials, film, music, transcriptions, or other materials that are subject to copyright, trademark, patent, or similar protection (collectively the "Work Product"), developed or prepared by Agency or its employees, agents, contractors, or subcontractors under this Agreement, are the property of the Client, provided: (i) such Work Product is accepted by the Client within twelve months of being proposed by Agency (and such acceptance is reflected in written form from Client to Agency received within such twelve-month period); and (ii) Client pays all fees and costs associated with creating, and, where applicable, producing such Work Product. Subject only to the two aforesaid Conditions (the "Conditions"), all title and interest to Work Product shall vest in Client as "works made-for-hire" within the meaning of the United States Copyright Act. To the extent that the title to any such Work Product may not, by operation of law or otherwise, vest in Client as a work made-for-hire, or any such Work Product may not be considered a work made-for-hire, all right, title, and interest therein is hereby irrevocably assigned by Agency to Client. In order to assure that its employees, agents, contractors, and subcontractors do not possess proprietary rights in the Work Product that are inconsistent with Client's possession of such rights, Agency will, as necessary, obtain the assignment and conveyance to Client, or to Agency for the benefit of Client, of any proprietary rights that such persons or entities may have or may have in the future to such Work Product.

    b. Without limiting the general rights of the Client as provided in paragraph 10(a), it is understood that Agency may, on occasion, license materials from third parties for inclusion in Work Product. In such circumstances, ownership of such licensed materials remains with the licensor at the conclusion of the term of the license. In such instances, Client agrees that it remains bound by the terms of such licenses and that it does not obtain proprietary rights in such materials beyond the terms and conditions contained in the pertinent license. Agency will keep Client informed of any such limitations.

    c. Work Product that does not meet the two Conditions in paragraph 10(a) remains Agency's property unless the failure to meet the first condition is due to the failure of Agency to submit the Work Product to the Client with a specific request that the Client either accept or reject the Work Product in question, in which case the acceptance of the Client shall be deemed to have been given, and the first condition deemed satisfied. Notwithstanding the foregoing, upon the request of Client made prior to the earlier of (1) eighteen months after Work Product is proposed by Agency and (2) the termination of this Agreement, Agency will grant Client an option to acquire at a future date all or a portion of the rights to Work Product that was not accepted by Client pursuant to paragraph 10(a) (the "Option"). The Option shall be subject to terms and conditions (including, without limitation, terms relating to consideration for and duration of the Option) negotiated in good faith by Agency and Client. Absent agreement on terms, no rights will be transferred to Client.

11. Term of Agreement

    a.   The term of this Agreement will commence on [insert date], and will continue in full force and effect until terminated by either party upon written notice of such intention given ninety (90) days in advance, provided that in no event may this Agreement be terminated effective prior to the expiration of twelve (12) months from the commencement of the Term.[lxiv] The ninety-day period of notice is referred to herein as the "Notice Period."

    b.   The rights, duties, and responsibilities of Agency will continue in full force during the Notice Period, including the ordering and billing of advertising in print media whose published closing dates fall within such Notice Period and the ordering and billing of advertising in broadcast media where the air dates fall within such Notice Period.

12. Rights Upon Termination

    a.   Upon termination of this Agreement, Agency will transfer, assign, and make available to Client, or Client's representative, all Work Product in Agency possession or control belonging to Client pursuant to paragraph 10 hereof; subject, however, to any rights of third parties of which Agency has informed Client.

    b.   Agency also agrees to give all reasonable cooperation toward transferring to Advertiser or Advertiser's designee, with approval of third parties in interest, all contracts and other arrangements with advertising media or others for advertising space, facilities, and talent, and other materials yet to be used, and all rights and claims thereto and therein, upon the Advertiser duly releasing the Agency from the obligation thereof.

    c.   Client recognizes that talent contracts with members of certain labor unions or guilds generally cannot be assigned except to signatories to the collective bargaining agreements governing the services rendered by such talent.

    d.   Upon termination of this Agreement, any projects or arrangements which remain incomplete and cannot be assigned to Client or Client's designee (as determined by Client, and in Client's sole judgment) shall be completed by Agency consistent with the terms and conditions of this Agreement. Except as provided in the previous sentence, upon termination of this Agreement, Agency shall immediately deliver to Client or Client's designee all Work Product (as herein defined) belonging to Client. Notwithstanding the foregoing, it is understood by the parties that Agency may keep archival copies of Work Product for historical purposes and internal use.

    e.   In addition to the foregoing, upon termination of this Agreement, Agency shall cooperate with Client and any successor agency designated by Client, and shall facilitate the assignment of all contracts relating to Client's advertising to the successor agency or such other party designated by Client. Client shall assume from Agency all outstanding non-cancellable contractual obligations to third parties incurred by Agency in connection with the services of Agency rendered pursuant to this Agreement, including, but not limited to, obligations to purchase materials and services for Client's account and obligations for uncompleted work approved by Client.

13. Governing Law, Jurisdiction, and Venue

This Agreement and the rights of the parties hereunder shall be governed by and interpreted in accordance with the internal laws of the State of [insert name of state], without regard to its conflict of laws, rules, or choice of law principles. Exclusive jurisdiction and venue for any claims made by either party against the other shall be within the state and federal courts located in the State of [insert name of state].

14. Entire Agreement

This Agreement constitutes the entire agreement between Agency and Client relating to the subject matter hereof, and supersedes any prior agreement or understandings between them. This Agreement may not be modified or amended unless such modification or amendment is agreed to by both Agency and Client in writing.

15. Notices

    a.   Notices under this Agreement are sufficient if given by nationally recognized overnight courier service, certified mail (return receipt requested), facsimile with electronic confirmation, or personal delivery to the other party at the address below:

If to Client:
[name of advertiser]
[address of advertiser]
[name and/or title of person to receive delivery]
[phone number]
[fax number]
[e-mail address]

If to Agency:
[name of agency]
[address of agency]
[name and/or title of person to receive delivery]
[phone number]
[fax number]
[e-mail address]

    b.   Notice is effective: (i) when delivered personally; (ii) three (3) business days after being sent by certified mail; (iii) on the business day after being sent by a nationally recognized courier service for next-day delivery; or (iv) on the business day after being sent by facsimile with electronic confirmation to the sender. A party may change its notice address by giving notice in accordance with this paragraph.

16. Additional Documents

Each party agrees to execute and deliver such additional documents and instruments and to perform such additional acts as may be necessary or appropriate to effectuate, carry out, and perform all of the terms, provisions, and conditions of this Agreement and the transactions contemplated hereby.

17. No Third-Party Beneficiaries

This Agreement is made solely and specifically among and for the benefit of the parties hereto and their respective successors and assigns, and no other person will have any rights, interest, or claims hereunder or be entitled to any benefits under or on account of this Agreement as a third-party beneficiary or otherwise.

18. Waiver

The failure of any party to seek redress for violation of, or to insist upon the strict performance of, any agreement, covenant, or condition of this Agreement shall not constitute a waiver with respect thereto or with respect to any subsequent act.

19. Successors and Assigns

This Agreement shall be binding upon and inure to the benefit of the parties and their permitted successors and assigns.

20. Paragraph Headings and Captions

Paragraph headings and captions contained in this Agreement are inserted only as a matter of convenience, and in no way define, limit, or extend the scope or intent of this Agreement or any provision thereof.

21. Severability

Wherever possible, each provision of this Agreement shall be interpreted in such a manner as to be effective and valid under applicable law, but if any provision of this Agreement shall be prohibited by or determined to be invalid under any such law, such provision shall be limited to the minimum extent necessary to render the same valid or shall be excised from this Agreement, as the circumstances require, and this Agreement shall be construed as if said provision had been incorporated herein as so limited or as if said provision had not been included herein, as the case may be, and enforced to the maximum extent permitted by law.

22. Counterparts

This Agreement may be executed in two or more counterparts, each of which shall be deemed an original, but all of which shall constitute one and the same instrument.

23. Force Majeure

Neither Client nor Agency shall be liable to the other for any failure, inability, or delay in performing hereunder if caused by any cause beyond the reasonable control of the party so failing, including, without limitation, an Act of God, war, strike, or fire; but due diligence shall be used in curing such cause and in resuming performance.

24. Assignment

Except as may be necessary in the rendition of Agency's services as provided herein, neither Agency nor Client may assign any part or all of this Agreement, or subcontract or delegate any of their respective rights or obligations under this Agreement, without the other party's prior written consent. Any attempt to assign, subcontract, or delegate in violation of this paragraph is void in each instance.

25. Public Announcement

Neither Agency nor Client may issue, without the consent of the other party, any press release, or make any public announcement with respect to this Agreement or the transactions contemplated hereby, except as may be required by law (and, if so required, such party shall give the other party a reasonable opportunity to comment thereon, if possible).

26. Compliance with Laws

Both parties will comply with the provisions of all federal, state, and local laws, ordinances, and regulations applicable to the performance of their obligations under this Agreement.

27. Independent Contractors; No Partnership or Joint Venture

Except only as otherwise specifically provided herein and necessary in connection with Agency's services provided hereunder, the parties are independent contractors, and nothing herein contained shall be construed as creating any relationship of employer/employee, partnership, agency, joint venture, or otherwise between the parties hereto, nor shall this Agreement be construed as conferring on any party any express or implied right, power, or authority to enter into any agreement or commitment, express or implied, or to incur any obligation or liability, on behalf of any other party. In addition, this Agreement shall not be construed as creating any relationship between one party and the other party's employees. Accordingly, neither party nor its employees shall be entitled, as a result of this Agreement, to any of the benefits under any employee benefit plan that the other party presently has in effect or may put into effect; nor will either party or its employees be considered employees of the other party for any purpose.

IN WITNESS WHEREOF, Agency and Client have executed this Agreement on the day and date as first appears.

[AGENCY] _____   [CLIENT] _____

By: _____   By: _____

Name:_____   Name: _____

Title:_____   Title: _____

Endnotes:

lvii   Depending upon the nature of the relationship, an agency may be appointed as an advertiser's exclusive advertising agency in general or connection with a particular assignment. While such exclusivity is not common, it is appropriate in some instances.

lviii   See footnote 2.

lix   It is important that the advertising agency and advertiser understand the scope of the services to be provided. If appropriate attention is not paid to this issue, advertisers may find themselves quite disappointed at what the advertising agency is willing or capable of doing within the compensation structure.

lx   Advertisers are often sensitive to advertising agencies dealing with product or service categories that the advertiser deems competitive or antithetical to its products or services. While advertising agencies should certainly agree not to handle any directly competitive products or services, restrictions can become more complicated if defined too broadly.

lxi   While there is no required percentage allowance, 10% is typical. It is not unusual, however, that there be no tolerance without the advertiser's written approval.

lxii   This is a somewhat controversial provision. "Sequential Liability" is not an established legal principle. It is a concept adopted by the American Association of Advertising Agencies in the 1990's. A significant portion of the media industry has rejected the concept, taking the position that the advertising agency and advertiser are jointly and severally liable (a concept that is similarly rejected by the advertising industry).

lxiii   Ownership of creative is a major issue, particularly creative that is either rejected or not used by the advertiser. Some advertisers, particularly when they are paying the agency on a fee basis as opposed to a media commission basis, take the position that everything presented to the advertiser, whether accepted or used, is owned by the advertiser. Advertising agencies, on the other hand, contend that their stock in trade is ideas and their execution. If rejected or not used by an advertiser, the creative should therefore be owned by the advertising agency. This form attempts to reach a compromise. Whether such a compromise is appropriate in a particular deal will depend upon the needs of the respective parties.

lxiv   There is some question whether a ninety day cancellation period or a one year minimum term is standard. Depending upon the nature and complexity of the assignment, however, such terms may be appropriate. Caution must be exercised by both parties with regard to the cancellation period to be certain that work in process can be completed in the time frame provided. In that regard, ninety days is generally regarded as an appropriate period, although it is not unusual to see sixty or even forty five day periods. The one year minimum is appropriate where there is a considerable lead time before advertising will be produced or where an advertising agency must make a significant investment in materials, equipment, and personnel to properly service the advertiser. A minimum term of one year may be necessary to insure a proper ramp up and return on investment for the advertising agency.

Schedule 1: Scope of Assignment

[insert description]

Schedule 2: Scope of Services[lxv]

A. Study Client's products or services;

B. Analyze Client's present and potential markets;

C. Create, prepare, and submit to Client for approval, advertising ideas and programs;

D. Employ, on Client's behalf, Agency's knowledge of available media and means that can be profitably used to advertise Client's products or services;

E. Prepare and submit to Client for approval, estimates of costs of recommended advertising programs;

F. Write, design, illustrate, or otherwise prepare Client's advertisements, including commercials to be broadcast, or other appropriate forms of Client's message;

G. Order the space, time, or other means to be used for Client's advertising, endeavoring to secure the most advantageous rates available;

H. Properly incorporate the message in mechanical or other form and forward it with proper instructions for the fulfillment of the order;

I. Check and verify insertions, displays, broadcasts, or other means used, to such degree as is usually performed by advertising agencies; and

J. Audit invoices for space, time, material preparation, and services.

Endnotes:

lxv   This is a relatively comprehensive list of potential advertising agency services and should be reviewed and edited according to the nature of the relationship and assignment.

Schedule 3: Exclusivity and Exceptions Thereto

[insert details]

Schedule 4: Compensation[lxvi]

A. Client will pay a [monthly][lxvii] fee of $_____ in consideration of the advertising services performed by Agency. Such fee will be deemed a nonrefundable advance against commissions to be received by Agency as follows:

    (1) On all media purchased by Agency, Agency will bill Client at the published card rates, or negotiated rates, as may be applicable. If no Agency commission, or less than [insert amount] percentl[xviii] ([insert amount]%) Agency commission (the "Commission Rate"), is granted or allowed on any such purchases, Client agrees that Agency may invoice Client an amount which, after deduction of Agency's cost, will yield Agency the aforesaid Commission Rate on such amount as Agency commission. During the Notice Period following notice of termination, Agency will be entitled to commissions on all orders of advertising in print media whose published closing dates fall within the Notice Period and of broadcast media where the air dates fall within the Notice Period, regardless of who may place such orders.

    (2) With respect to the engagement of talent, Agency will bill Client the authorized engagement rate, plus any taxes, insurance, pension and health fund contributions, etc. applicable thereto, plus an amount which, after deduction of Agency's cost, will yield Agency the Commission Rate on such amount as Agency commission. Client recognizes that Agency is a signatory to collective bargaining agreements with Screen Actors Guild and American Federation of Television and Radio Artists, and that the hiring of talent by Agency on Client's behalf will be subject to the terms of such agreements.[lxix]

    (3) On broadcast production, artwork, engravings, type compositions, and any and all art and mechanical expenses incurred by Agency pursuant to Client's authorization, Agency will invoice Client an amount which, after deduction of Agency's cost, will yield Agency [insert Commission Rate or other percentage] on such amount as Agency commission.

    (4) Advances against commissions will be reconciled against commissions actually received on a [monthly, quarter-annual, or other] basis. Agency will issue the appropriate credit or debit invoices.

B. Client agrees to reimburse Agency for such cash outlays as Agency may incur, such as forwarding and mailing, telephoning, telegraphing, and travel, in connection with services rendered in relation to Client's account.

C. The Agency shall be compensated during the Notice Period as provided in Schedule 4. Compensation shall include, but not be limited to, retainer and all other commissions due the Agency. Agency shall be entitled to receive the then-monthly fee whether advertising is created and/or placed by Agency or another entity. Within sixty (60) days following the Termination Date, Client and Agency shall reconcile any disparity between amounts paid pursuant to any estimate, and actual media and production billings incurred by Agency prior to the Termination Date, with a refund by Agency to Client or an additional payment from Client to Agency, as appropriate. Advances against commissions shall similarly be reconciled by such date.

D. Prior to the conclusion of each calendar year during the Term, Agency and Client will meet to discuss and resolve Agency's compensation for the next subsequent year. If Agency's compensation is not agreed upon prior to the beginning of the next calendar year, Client shall continue to pay Agency as otherwise provided in this Schedule 4 until the parties negotiate such compensation or until this Agreement is terminated, whichever occurs first.

Endnotes:

lxvii   While monthly is common, the period of payment can be longer, e.g., quarterly.

lxviii 15% is a common commission paid, although the rate is under constant challenge and can no longer be described as the "norm". It is not uncommon to see commissions as low at 10%. Advertisers that are paying on commission must be realistic and be certain that their commission rate affords the advertising agency an appropriate profit margin to insure that the quality of the work is not adversely effected by a losing relationship.

lxix   Not all advertising agencies are signatory to union agreements dealing with the employment of actors in commercials. Where an advertising agency is not a signatory, this paragraph should be eliminated.

Schedule 5: Billing and Payment Procedures

A. Estimates

Agency will furnish Client with written cost estimates, specifying in reasonable detail all anticipated costs arising in connection with all services provided under this Agreement, when the cost to Client of such service is estimated to exceed $[insert amount].

B. Bids for Jobs

Except as authorized in writing in advance by Client, Agency will obtain at least three (3) bids for all production jobs which require outside suppliers in the performance of service hereunder and which are estimated to cost in excess of $[insert amount] for each individual project. Client will advise Agency as to the form and scope of bids and qualifications required for the respective suppliers.

C. Itemized Invoices

All bills and invoices submitted to Client for payment shall be itemized in reasonable detail, supportable by appropriate documentation and proof of performance, and allocated to Client's accounts as may be specified by Client from time and in accordance with Client's accounting practices. When applicable, manufacturer's and retailer's excise, state, or municipal sales and use taxes shall be billed to Client as separate items on invoices; provided, however, Client shall in no event be liable for the payment of any taxes based on Agency's net income or gross receipts, or any property taxes. Agency agrees to furnish, on request of Client, statements evidencing that such taxes as are properly billed to Client have been paid. Under no circumstances will penalties and/or interest resulting from the late payment or non-payment of any tax by Agency become an obligation of Client, unless Client was responsible for incurring such penalty or interest. Client shall have the right to require Agency to contest with the imposing jurisdiction, at Client's expense and within Client's control, any taxes which Client may deem to be improperly levied.

D. Advance Invoicing

Agency will invoice Client for all media and third-party costs sufficiently in advance of the due date to permit payment by Client to Agency in order to take advantage of all available cash discounts or rebates.

E. Proof

On all outside purchases other than for media, Agency will attach to the invoice proof of billed charges from suppliers.

F. Timing

All invoices will be rendered on or about the first day of each month and will be payable the tenth day of the month.

Form II 15.3 Contract Between an Advertising Agency and Advertiser—Short Form

AGREEMENT between [name and address of advertising agency] ("Agency"), and [name and address of client] ("Client").

1. Appointment

    Client appoints Agency as Client's [exclusive][lxx] advertising agency in connection with the products and/or services of Client described in Schedule 1, attached hereto, for a term ("Term") as hereinafter provided.

2. Scope of Advertising Services

    Agency will provide Client with the advertising services provided in Schedule 2, attached hereto. Should Client request Agency to perform additional services beyond what is provided in Schedule 2, Agency and Client will negotiate in good faith with respect to the terms, conditions, and compensation for such additional services.[lxxi] Any agreement for additional services will be set forth in writing and considered an addendum to this Agreement.

3. Ownership[lxxii]

    All campaigns, trademarks, service marks, slogans, artwork, written materials, drawings, photographs, graphic materials, film, music, transcriptions, or other materials that are subject to copyright, trademark, patent, or similar protection (collectively, the "Work Product") produced by Agency are the property of the Client provided: (1) such Work Product is accepted in writing by the Client within twelve (12) months of being proposed by Agency; and (2) Client pays all fees and costs associated with creating and, where applicable, producing such Work Product. Work Product that does not meet the two foregoing conditions shall remain Agency's property.

    Notwithstanding the foregoing, it is understood that Agency may, on occasion, license materials from third parties for inclusion in Work Product. In such circumstances, ownership of such licensed materials remains with the licensor at the conclusion of the term of the license. In such instances, Client agrees that it remains bound by the terms of such licenses. Agency will keep Client informed of any such limitations.

4. Term

    The term of this Agreement shall commence on the date provided in Schedule 1 ("Commencement Date") and shall continue until terminated by either party upon ninety (90) days' prior written notice ("Notice Period"), provided that this Agreement may not be terminated effective prior to the expiration of twelve (12) months from the Commencement Date.[lxxiii] Notice shall be deemed given on the day of mailing or, in case of notice by telegram, on the day it is deposited with the telegraph company for transmission. During the Notice Period, Agency's rights, duties, and responsibilities shall continue.

    Upon termination, Agency will transfer and/or assign to Client: (1) all Work Product in Agency's possession or control belonging to Client, subject, however, to any rights of third parties; and (2) all contracts with third parties, including advertising media or others, upon being duly released by Client and any such third party from any further obligations. Client recognizes that Agency is a signatory to certain union agreements covering talent used in broadcast materials, which generally cannot be assigned except to signatories to such collective bargaining agreements governing the services rendered by such talent.[lxxiv]

5. Compensation and Billing Procedure

Agency will be compensated and Client will be billed as provided in Schedule 3, attached hereto.

6. Confidentiality and Safeguard of Property

Client and Agency respectively agree to keep in confidence, and not to disclose or use for its own respective benefit or for the benefit of any third party (except as may be required for the performance of services under this Agreement or as may be required by law), any information, documents, or materials that are reasonably considered confidential regarding each other's products, business, customers, clients, suppliers, or methods of operation; provided, however, that such obligation of confidentiality will not extend to anything in the public domain or that was in the possession of either party prior to disclosure. Agency and Client will take reasonable precautions to safeguard property of the other entrusted to it, but in the absence of negligence or willful disregard, neither Agency nor Client will be responsible for any loss or damage.

7. Indemnities

Agency agrees to indemnify and hold Client harmless with respect to any claims or actions by third parties against Client based upon material prepared by Agency, involving any claim for libel, slander, piracy, plagiarism, invasion of privacy, or infringement of copyright, except where any such claim or action arises out of material supplied by Client to Agency.[lxxv]

Client agrees to indemnify and hold Agency harmless with respect to any claims or actions by third parties against Agency based upon materials furnished by Client or where material created by Agency is substantially changed by Client. Information or data obtained by Agency from Client to substantiate claims made in advertising shall be deemed to be "materials furnished by Client." Client further agrees to indemnify and hold Agency harmless with respect to any death or personal injury claims or actions arising from the use of Client's products or services.

8. Commitments to Third Parties

All purchases of media, production costs, and engagement of talent will be subject to Client's prior approval. Client reserves the right to cancel any such authorization, whereupon Agency will take all appropriate steps to effect such cancellation, provided that Client will hold Agency harmless with respect to any costs incurred by Agency as a result.

If at any time Agency obtains a discount or rebate from any supplier in connection with Agency's rendition of services to Client, Agency will credit Client or remit to Client such discount or rebate.

For all media purchased by Agency on Client's behalf, Client agrees that Agency shall be held solely liable for payments only to the extent proceeds have cleared from Client to Agency for such media purchase; otherwise, Client agrees to be solely liable to media ("Sequential Liability"). Agency will use its best efforts to obtain agreement by media to Sequential Liability.[lxxvi]

9. Amendments

Any amendments to this Agreement must be in writing and signed by Agency and Client.

10. Notices

Any notice shall be deemed given on the day of mailing or, if notice is by telegram, e-mail, or fax, on the next day following the day notice is deposited with the telegraph company for transmission, or e-mailed or faxed.

11. Governing Law

This Agreement shall be interpreted in accordance with the laws of the State of [insert] without regard to its principles of conflicts of laws. Jurisdiction and venue shall be solely within the State of [insert].

IN WITNESS WHEREOF, Agency and Client have executed this Agreement.

[AGENCY]   [CLIENT]

By: _____   By: _____

Name:_____   Name:_____

Title:_____   Title:_____

Endnotes:

lxx   Depending upon the nature of the relationship, an agency may be appointed as an advertiser's exclusive advertising agency in general or connection with a particular assignment. While such exclusivity is not common, it is appropriate in some instances.

lxxi   It is important that the advertising agency and advertiser understand the scope of the services to be provided. If appropriate attention is not paid to this issue, advertisers may find themselves quite disappointed at what the advertising agency is willing or capable of doing within the compensation structure.

lxxii   Ownership of creative is a major issue, particularly creative that is either rejected or not used by the advertiser. Some advertisers, particularly when they are paying the agency on a fee basis as opposed to a media commission basis, take the position that everything presented to the advertiser, whether accepted or used, is owned by the advertiser. Advertising agencies, on the other hand, contend that their stock in trade is ideas and their execution. If rejected or not used by an advertiser, the creative should therefore be owned by the advertising agency. This form attempts to reach a compromise. Whether such a compromise is appropriate in a particular deal will depend upon the needs of the respective parties.

lxxiii There is some question whether a ninety day cancellation period or a one year minimum term is standard. Depending upon the nature and complexity of the assignment, however, such terms may be appropriate. Caution must be exercised by both parties with regard to the cancellation period to be certain that work in process can be completed in the time frame provided. In that regard, ninety days is generally regarded as an appropriate period, although it is not unusual to see sixty or even forty five day periods. The one year minimum is appropriate where there is a considerable lead time before advertising will be produced or where an advertising agency must make a significant investment in materials, equipment, and personnel to properly service the advertiser. A minimum term of one year may be necessary to insure a proper ramp up and return on investment for the advertising agency.

lxxiv   Not all advertising agencies are signatory to union agreements dealing with the employment of actors in commercials. Where an advertising agency is not a signatory, this paragraph should be eliminated.

lxxv   The indemnity in this form generally follows the insurance coverage available to advertising agencies. Some advertisers demand a broader indemnity. While such a demand may seem prudent, one must remember that most advertising agencies are small businesses that can afford only just so much insurance. Significant claims beyond their insurance coverage will more likely than not bankrupt the advertising agency. Therefore, an advertiser must be realistic in its indemnity demands.

lxxvi   This is a somewhat controversial provision. "Sequential Liability" is not an established legal principle. It is a concept adopted by the American Association of Advertising Agencies in the 1990's. A significant portion of the media industry has rejected the concept, taking the position that the advertising agency and advertiser are jointly and severally liable (a concept that is similarly rejected by the advertising industry).

Schedule 1: Products/Services Assigned to Agency

Schedule 2: Commencement Date and Scope of Services

I. Commencement Date: [supply]

II. Scope of Services:[lxxvii]

    A. Study Client's products or services;

    B. Analyze Client's present and potential markets;

    C. Create, prepare, and submit to Client for approval, advertising ideas and programs;

    D. Employ on Client's behalf, Agency's knowledge of available media and means that can be profitably used to advertise Client's products or services;

    E. Prepare and submit to Client for approval, estimates of costs of recommended advertising programs;

    F. Write, design, illustrate, or otherwise prepare Client's advertisements, including commercials to be broadcast, or other appropriate forms of Client's message;

    G. Order the space, time, or other means to be used for Client's advertising, endeavoring to secure the most advantageous rates available;

    H. Properly incorporate the message in mechanical or other form and forward it with proper instructions for the fulfillment of the order;

    I. Check and verify insertions, displays, broadcasts, or other means used, to such degree as is usually performed by advertising agencies; and

    J. Audit invoices for space, time, material preparation, and services.

Endnotes:

lxxvii This is a relatively comprehensive list of potential advertising agency services and should be reviewed and edited according to the nature of the relationship and assignment.

Schedule 3: Compensation and Billing Procedures

I.   Compensation[lxxviii]

    A.   Client will pay a [monthly][lxxix] fee of $_____ in consideration of the advertising services performed by Agency. Such fee shall be deemed a nonrefundable advance against commissions to be received by Agency as follows:

        (1) On all media purchased by Agency, Agency shall bill Client at the published card rates, or negotiated rates, as may be applicable. If no agency commission, or less than [insert amount] percent[lxxx] ([insert amount]%) agency commission (the "Commission Rate"), is granted or allowed on any such purchases, Client agrees that Agency may invoice Client an amount which, after deduction of Agency's cost, will yield Agency the aforesaid Commission Rate of such amount as Agency commission. During the Notice Period following notice of termination, Agency will be entitled to commissions on all orders of advertising in print media whose published closing dates fall within the Notice Period and of broadcast media where the air dates fall within the Notice Period, regardless of who may place such orders.

        (2) With respect to the engagement of talent, Agency shall bill Client the authorized engagement rate, plus any taxes, insurance, pension and health fund contributions, etc. applicable thereto, plus an amount which, after deduction of Agency's cost, will yield Agency the Commission Rate on such amount as Agency commission.

        (3) On broadcast production, artwork, engravings, type compositions, and any and all art and mechanical expenses incurred by Agency pursuant to Client's authorization, Agency shall invoice Client an amount which, after deduction of Agency's cost, will yield Agency the Commission Rate on such amount as Agency commission.

        (4) Advances against commissions will be reconciled against commissions actually received on a (monthly, quarter-annual, or other) basis. Agency will issue the appropriate credit or debit invoices.

    B.   Client agrees to reimburse Agency for such cash outlays as Agency may incur, such as forwarding and mailing, telephoning, telegraphing, and travel, in connection with services rendered in relation to Client's account.

II.   Billing and Payment Procedures

    A.   Agency will invoice Client for all media and third-party costs sufficiently in advance of the due date to permit payment by Client to Agency in order to take advantage of all available cash discounts or rebates.

    B.   The cost of production materials and services shall be billed by Agency upon completion of the production job, or upon receipt of supplier invoice prior thereto.

    C.   On all outside purchases other than for media, Agency will attach to the invoice proof of billed charges from suppliers.

    D.   All invoices shall be rendered on or about the first day of each month and will be payable the tenth day of the month.

    E.   Invoices shall be submitted in an itemized format. Interest will be charged on overdue invoices at a rate of [insert amount] percent ([insert amount]%) per annum, or the maximum permitted by law, whichever is less.

Endnotes:

lxxviii This form assumes a compensation method whereby the advertising agency receives a minimum monthly fee against which commissions are applied. This is a relatively common manner in which to compensate an advertising agency. There are, however, many variations of this theme, e.g., fee only, hourly rates, incentive, or commission only and just about any combination thereof.

lxxix While monthly is common, the period of payment can be longer, e.g., quarterly.

lxxx 15% is a common commission paid, although the rate is under constant challenge and can no longer be described as the "norm". It is not uncommon to see commissions as low at 10%. Advertisers that are paying on commission must be realistic and be certain that their commission rate affords the advertising agency an appropriate profit margin to insure that the quality of the work is not adversely effected by a losing relationship.

Form II.15.4 Screen Actors Guild (SAG) Television Commercials Transfer of Rights— Assumption Agreement

TRANSFEROR: TRANSFEREE:

(Company Name)   (Company Name)

(Address)   (Address)

(City, State, Zip)   (City, State, Zip)

This Agreement is effective _____.

Transferee hereby agrees with Transferor that all television commercials covered by this Agreement (listed below*) are subject to the Screen Actors Guild Commercials Contract under which the commercials were produced.

Transferee hereby agrees expressly for the benefit of Screen Actors Guild and its members affected thereby to make all payments of holding fees and use fees as provided in said Contract, and all social security, withholding, unemployment insurance, and disability insurance payments, and all appropriate contributions to the Screen Actors Guild-Producers Pension and Health Plans required under the provisions of said Contract with respect to any and all such payments, and to comply with the provisions of said Contract, including specifically the arbitration provisions and procedures contained therein, with respect to the use of such television commercials and required records and reports. It is expressly understood and agreed that the rights of Transferee to telecast such television commercials shall be subject to and conditioned upon the prompt payment to the performers involved of all compensation as provided in said Contract, and the Guild, on behalf of the performers involved, shall be entitled to injunctive relief in the event such payments are not made.

In the event of a subsequent transfer, assignment, sale, or other disposition by Transferee of any commercials covered by this Agreement, Transferee agrees to give written notice, by mail, to the Guild of each such subsequent transfer, etc. within 30 days after the consummation thereof, and such notice shall specify the name and address of the transferee, assignee, or purchaser. Transferee shall also deliver to the Guild a copy of the subsequent agreement with the subsequent transferee, assignee, or purchaser, which agreement shall be in substantially the same form as this Agreement.

*COMMERCIALS COVERED BY THIS AGREEMENT:

[Attach a list all commercials, including Title, I.D. number, product, and session date.]

[Company Name of Transferor]   [Company Name of Transferee]

By: _____   By:_____

Name_____   Name: _____

Title: _____   Title: _____

Date: _____   Date: _____

FINANCIAL INFORMATION:
(Needed only if Transferee is not signatory to SAG Commercials Contract)

Transferee's Bank: _____

Name: _____

Branch:_____

Phone: _____

Staff Referral: _____

Acct. Number: _____

APPROVED FOR SCREEN ACTORS GUILD

By: _____

Name: _____

Title: _____

Date: _____

Form II.15.5 Probable Sales Tax Scenarios

The column labeled "Agent/Principal" assumes the agency/client agreement specifies that the advertising agency is an agent for the advertiser and is authorized to purchase materials on the advertiser's behalf. The "Vendor" column refers to instances where the agency can be viewed as a seller, rather than as an agent.

Sales Tax Summary—Intrastate Transactions (unless otherwise noted)

Type of Relationship	Agent/Principal	Vendor
A. Print Media Advertisements		
1. Artwork, illustrations, layouts, drawings, mechanicals, photographs, composition, typography, etc.—produced in-house	Exempt	Exempt
2. Purchases from outside suppliers of artwork, illustrations, layouts, drawings, mechanicals, photographs, composition, typography, etc.	Exempt	Exempt
3.a. Photostats purchased from outside suppliers	Taxable	Taxable
3.b. Photostats fabricated within the agency	Taxable	Taxable
4. Reproduction Rights—Photographs	Exempt	Exempt
5. Model Fees	Exempt	Exempt
6. Retouching Charges	Exempt	Exempt
7. Preliminary Artwork (e.g., sketches or layouts) prepared in the agency for discussion and planning purposes	Exempt	Exempt
B. TV Commercials		
1. Cost of original negative, shipped out-of-state	Exempt	Exempt
2. Cost of duplicate negative, if retained in state	Taxable	Taxable
C. Agency Compensation		
1. Commissions/fees re: media advertising (space or time)	Exempt	Exempt
2. Commissions/fees on outside purchases re: media advertising	Exempt	Exempt
3. Commissions/fees on outside purchases other than media advertising	Exempt	Taxable
D. Production of Tangible Personal Property (non-media related)		
1. Purchases of finished product or materials (such as paper or ink) that will constitute an ingredient of the final product	Taxable	Exempt
2. Preliminary and intermediate services inside agency (fabricating, processing, etc.)	Taxable	Exempt

CHAPTER XVI
Website Development and Maintenance Agreements

As websites become ever more sophisticated and businesses rely more on outside firms specializing in website development, both site owners and developers have learned by trial, and all too often by error, one invaluable lesson: to begin work without a signed Website development agreement can be the prelude to a nightmare.

A site owner could find itself forced to accept unreasonably harsh terms and could pay far in excess of the agreed-upon price rather then risk the developer walking away from an incomplete project in which the site owner has made a substantial investment of time and money. On the other hand, a developer could find itself forced to add functionality and modify features without any additional compensation beyond the initial quoted price.

A website development and maintenance agreement, signed before production begins, can help prevent many potentially serious problems and misunderstandings. This chapter discusses some of the most important issues to consider and items to include in the agreement. A sample agreement that can be used as a starting point for negotiations also appears at the end of this chapter and is referred to in the various comments.

1. Development Issues

a. Site Owner's Wish List

Few, if any, business owners venturing into cyberspace have the training or experience in software design or multimedia conceptualization necessary to prepare the detailed website specifications that serve as the blueprint for the creation of a website. What they can do, however, is provide a generalized list of the business requirements and functions that they wish the website to fulfill. For example, they may want the site to provide current information about their company, advertise products, and permit customers to purchase products online. They may even have some general ideas of the content and/or layout of the website. These general business requirements should all be itemized and attached to the agreement and used by the developer as the basis for developing technical specifications for the website.

b. Website Specifications

Using the general business requirements provided by the site owner, the developer should prepare and complete detailed technical specifications for the website's features and functions before any actual Web page production begins. The development of sufficiently detailed specifications benefits both parties. It enables the developer to clearly understand the site owner's requirements and to prepare a fixed-price bid. It provides the site owner with a clear picture of the Web pages to be delivered and the price to be charged.

These specifications should include representations or prototypes of the various Web pages that will make up the website as well as scripts and flow charts indicating the interactivity between the Web pages. Once completed and approved, a copy of the final specifications should be attached to the agreement.

Seeing the website start to take shape, a site owner might be tempted to authorize production of individual Web pages prior to a final sign-off on specifications for the entire site. This is rarely a wise decision. A site owner who succumbs to this temptation might incur unnecessary and avoidable production costs if creative or practical reasons make it necessary to substantially revise or eliminate individual Web pages, or if the final specifications produced are so poor that the site owner opts to exercise a right of termination.

Specifications, once approved, serve two important purposes:

1. Specifications provide the objective criteria against which to measure the website actually delivered. From the site owner's perspective, acceptance (which typically triggers the final payment obligation) is not required if the product delivered does not conform to the specifications. The specifications also provide sufficient information regarding the scope and detail of the project to make the developer more amenable to a fixed-price rather than an uncapped hourly arrangement. From the developer's perspective, the specification process helps minimize ambiguities and misunderstandings. Objective specifications also protect the developer from falling victim to clients with poorly defined or continually changing expectations. A developer that has based its fee on a particular set of objective specifications is much better positioned to ask for additional fees from a site owner that requests additional functionality or material modifications once the production phase begins.

2. Specifications establish an objective performance standard that serves as the basis for a meaningful performance warranty (see section below entitled "Website Performance Warranties"). Site owners should always require a performance warranty because many "bugs" or deviations from the specifications will not be discovered until the website goes live and is heavily trafficked by website visitors.

2. Billing and Payment Issues

a. Fixed Price vs. Hourly Billing

Developers and site owners generally engage in a tug-of-war regarding a mutually satisfactory pricing mechanism to cover website development costs. The developer is aware that software development can be quite labor-intensive, and generally prefers an hourly billing structure to guarantee coverage of all development costs. Site owners generally should resist straight hourly rate billing, especially in situations involving complex software development. Such an arrangement provides no incentive for the developer to control costs.

The compromise that appears to produce the most satisfactory results is for the parties to develop specifications sufficiently detailed that the developer is comfortable committing to a fixed price. A fixed-price arrangement provides the added benefit of inducing the developer to staff the project as efficiently as possible to protect and maximize profit margin.

Where the website is particularly complex, the process of reviewing and finalizing these technical blueprints can involve a substantial number of hours. The site owner may be required to pay a separate hourly fee for the development of these specifications.

b. Payments Tied to Milestones (See Form II.16.1, paragraph 4.a.)

The website development project should be broken down into discrete phases to be completed by specified milestone dates, with fixed payments to be made upon the satisfactory completion of each phase.

A large down payment should be avoided because it diminishes the site owner's leverage, making it more difficult to insist on prompt and satisfactory performance. The first payment typically is one-third of the total fixed price of the project, and is delivered upon contract execution.

The second payment typically is also one-third of the total fixed price, and is made upon delivery of a completed prototype of the website to the site owner for beta testing. The final one-third payment is generally withheld until all Web pages have been delivered, tested, and accepted by the site owner. Some site owners include a provision in their agreement that allows them to retain a portion of this last payment (e.g., one-tenth of the total fixed fee) until expiration of the warranty period as leverage to induce the developer to promptly correct defects discovered once the website is "live" (up and running).

c. Ongoing Maintenance Charges (See Form II.16.1, paragraphs 4.b, 4.c, 4.d, and 5.a.)

Once operational, websites require ongoing maintenance. Web pages need to be continually updated and revised. New pages frequently need to be added to the website. Existing hyperlinks must be checked and maintained.

If the developer will also be providing the computer server on which the website will be maintained, additional installation and maintenance services are involved. Site owners often mandate performance standards for the computer server, such as minimum bandwidth requirements for the connection between the computer server and the Internet. Many limit the time periods during which the server may be disconnected for regular maintenance procedures to the off-peak traffic periods after midnight. Many site owners arrange for their developer to monitor the website's visitors for marketing purposes. In these situations, demographic, behavioral, preference, and other identifying information must be collected and forwarded to the site owner. Arrangements must be made to retrieve and respond in a timely manner to inquiries from website visitors.

Developers typically charge separately for each of these services. For any of these activities that will be conducted directly by the site owner rather than the developer, the agreement should state the amount of basic training that the developer will provide free of charge, the rates for additional training, and the availability of the developer for telephone support.

3. Ownership and Rights

a. Rights to Source Code for Custom Software (See Form II.16.1, paragraph 6.c.)

If any software designed by the developer is to be used in connection with the website, a number of issues regarding ownership and use should be resolved before signing any agreement.

If the developer is to create new software for the site, it might agree to grant ownership of the new software to the site owner. If the developer refuses to do so, or in cases where the developer is incorporating his or her own proprietary software into the website, arrangements must be made so that the site owner will have access to the source code version of such software. Software cannot be debugged, updated, or otherwise modified without the source code.

Some developers agree to make the source code available to the site owner under a licensing arrangement for use solely in connection with the developer's website. Any separate source-code license fees or special restrictions on the right of the site owner to provide another developer with access to the source code (e.g., in cases where that developer is a potential competitor of the original developer) should be delineated in the agreement before proceeding with any particular developer.

Developers sometimes refuse to make the source code available, either because it contains valuable trade secrets or to force the site owner to become a captive client for maintenance and future modifications. Without a license to the source code, the site owner will be unable to maintain or modify the software in the event that the developer goes out of business, files for bankruptcy, fails to maintain the software to satisfactory levels, or simply raises maintenance fees to unacceptable levels. Each of these risks should be carefully considered before proceeding with any particular developer.

A typical compromise to the source-code access dilemma is to require the developer to deposit a copy of the source code with an independent escrow agent. The parties sign an agreement allowing the escrow agent to release the source code to the website owner under certain agreed-upon conditions.

The escrow arrangement is not a perfect solution, as developers rarely agree to permit release of the source code on the basis of increased maintenance prices or unsatisfactory maintenance levels. Moreover, it requires the site owner to have the escrow agent periodically verify that the version on deposit is the most recent release and that the source code can in fact be compiled into usable object code.

b. Ownership of Content (See Form II.16.1, paragraphs 10.a.(1) and 10.a.(3).)

Although ownership of software created by the developer might not be critical to the site owner, it is crucial that the site owner own the copyright to any original content created by the developer that appears on the website. Without such ownership, the owner would not have the legal right to copy, update, or modify the materials, or to authorize others (e.g., a substitute developer) to do so, without first obtaining the consent of the developer that created the content.

The site owner will not obtain copyright ownership to content merely by paying for its creation. The developer, as the actual creator of the content, automatically owns the copyright to the content unless there is a written agreement providing otherwise.

1.   Obtaining Ownership from Developer

A site owner typically will obtain copyright ownership to content by including a provision in the website development agreement designating the content created by the developer as a "work-made-for-hire."

A prudent site owner will also include a backup copyright-assignment provision in the agreement, although it is ultimately preferable to obtain copyright ownership through a work-made-for-hire provision. Such a provision serves two purposes:

(a) It provides some protection to the site owner in the event that the courts determine that a multimedia work created by an independent contractor cannot be classified as a work-made-for-hire—a position advocated by the U.S. Copyright Office in the early 1980s.

(b) It provides the site owner with the only method of obtaining copyright ownership to creative materials produced by the developer prior to executing a written agreement.

The agreement should also obligate the developer to provide any documents requested by the site owner to confirm that the content and/or software created by the developer was intended to be a work-made-for-hire or to effectuate, record, or confirm the copyright assignment. Also, it should obligate the developer to help prepare all U.S. and foreign copyright, trademark, and/or patent applications covering the website content. Lastly, the agreement should require the developer to make itself available for consultation and testimony should a third party commence a copyright-infringement action challenging the site owner's right to exploit the material delivered by the developer.

2.   Obtaining Ownership from Developer's Employees and Freelancers (See Form II.16.1, paragraph 10.a.(2).)

Site owners are usually surprised to discover that the work-made-for-hire and copyright-assignment provisions included in the website development agreement do not guarantee that the developer has the right to transfer ownership to the site owner.

The developer will own the copyright to Web-page material created by its employees only if the material was created within the scope of their employment. Likewise, the developer will own the copyright to material created by freelancers only if they have signed written work-made-for-hire and/or assignment agreements. If the developer has not taken all the proper steps to secure ownership rights from its employees and freelancers, then its conveyance of ownership rights to the site owner will be incomplete.

Therefore, the site owner can guarantee that it receives all requisite rights only by requiring the developer to obtain signed agreements from its employees and freelancers. These documents should be attached to the website development agreement.

c. Obtaining Third-party Consents, Waivers, and Releases (See Form II.16.1, paragraphs 6.d and 12.g.)

The website development agreement should require the developer to warrant to the site owner that the software and content to be provided by the developer will be original and will not infringe the copyright, trademark, trade secret, or other proprietary rights of any third party. A developer might be unwilling to make such a broad representation with respect to patent rights of third parties, because pending patent applications are not available for public inspection. It is reasonable, however, to require the developer to warrant that its software and content does not violate any United States patents issued as of the date the website is delivered.

To the extent that the developer is providing any content for the website, the agreement also should require the developer to warrant that it will obtain any necessary copyright clearance to use any preexisting text, photos, video and film clips, music, and software owned by third parties. The parties should resolve in the agreement whether the cost of obtaining such clearances and/or licenses is included within, or is in addition to, any price quoted by the developer.

To the extent that the developer is providing photographs, video and film clips, or audio recordings that include the name, image, or likeness of people or individuals, the agreement should also require the developer to warrant that it will obtain any necessary right-of-privacy or -publicity consents and releases. The violation of someone's right of publicity can be quite costly, and in the traditional media context has resulted in verdicts as high as $400,000. Again, the parties should resolve in the agreement whether the cost of obtaining such consents is included within, or is in addition to, any price quoted by the developer.

4. Indemnification and Insurance (See Form II.16.1, paragraphs 14 and 20.)

The developer should agree to indemnify the site owner for any costs and losses arising from claims by third parties based upon breaches of the software and content warranties, and to defend the site owner from such claims. The developer should also warrant that if the site owner is prevented from using any of the Web pages because of a legal claim made by a third party relating to software or content supplied by the developer, the developer will pay to procure the right for the site owner to continue to use the offending Web page, or will modify the Web page at no cost to the site owner.

Be aware, however, that many developers are small, undercapitalized start-up businesses without the resources to stand behind an agreement to indemnify the site owner or to obtain the necessary legal advice in this particularly difficult area. If the site owner decides to proceed with such a developer, the site owner's legal advisor should review all documents relating to third-party rights. The final one-third payment should be conditioned upon delivery and satisfactory review of all third-party consents, waivers, and releases.

Site owners also should consider requiring the developer to obtain an errors-and-omissions insurance policy (or at least maintain such a policy directly) to cover potential claims arising from alleged copyright violations (patent violations typically are excluded from coverage), invasions of privacy, violations of rights of publicity, and defamations.

5. Website Performance Warranties (See Form II.16.1, paragraphs 12.a and 12.c.)

Developers should be required to warrant that the site will function substantially in accordance with the written website specifications for a specified period of time, and that it will make any necessary corrections reported during such period free of charge. Typically, this period will extend for 30 to 90 days following acceptance of the initial work or launch of the website, although extended warranty periods are generally available for an additional fee.

A developer should never agree that its product will perform exactly in accordance with the specifications because of the complexities inherent in software development. It should also never represent that the software is "free of defects in material and workmanship" or "error free," because software, especially custom-designed software, inevitably contains some bugs.

The agreement should also require the developer to represent that the software will contain no "Self-Help Code" designed to permit the developer to disable the software in the event of a dispute or "Unauthorized Code" designed to permit the developer to gain unauthorized access to or to erase or otherwise alter the software. The agreement should also require the developer to indemnify the site owner for any costs and losses arising from its breach of these warranties.

6. Confidential Information (See Form II.16.1, paragraph 16.)

Confidentiality obligations should apply to both the site owner and the developer. The developer could have access to confidential information regarding the site owner's marketing strategies, product information, employee passwords, business affairs, and future plans for the website. A developer could also have access to potentially salable confidential information about visitors to the website.

The site owner will have access to confidential information of the developer if it is granted a license to the developer's source code.

Both parties should agree to keep confidential, and not to use, the proprietary information of the other party for the benefit of itself or anyone else, and to return all copies of confidential information immediately upon request.

7. Limitation of Developer's Financial Liability (See Form II.16.1, paragraph 15.)

Developers face the daunting reality that defective software can cause the site owner to suffer serious financial losses resulting from the loss of data and the consequent loss of business. The developer easily could be forced out of business if it is required to reimburse the site owner for these types of consequential and incidental damages. For this reason, the developer should insist on excluding liability for consequential and incidental damages arising out of its agreement with the site owner.

Developers may seek further protection from this tremendous exposure by inducing the site owner to agree to limit the developer's financial exposure to a specified amount, usually the total price payable under the contract. Site owners will often agree to this limitation provided that the developer agrees to carve out an exception that will require it to remain fully liable for damages suffered by the site owner that result from the developer's violation of any third-party software or content rights.

8. The Right to Terminate the Agreement (See Form II.16.1, paragraph 17.)

The right to terminate the agreement is important to both parties.

As previously discussed, the site owner should include a right to terminate in the event that it is not satisfied with the specifications produced by the developer. This will enable the site owner to minimize its financial losses if it is dissatisfied with the developer's design capabilities, and begin to search for a replacement developer at the earliest possible date. A fair agreement will require the site owner to compensate the developer for its design efforts at the full hourly rate applicable to this phase of the project.

The site owner also should retain the right to terminate if the developer fails to meet the timetable for deliveries by more than a specified grace period. The developer should not be penalized for delays caused by the site owner, such as time lost due to changes in the specifications and delays in providing materials to the developer for digitization.

The agreement should include the right to terminate in the event that the site owner fails to make a required payment after a specified grace period. Site owners should limit the developer's remedies in the event of a dispute to money damages only, and require the developer to waive its right to seek a court order to shut down the website in the event of a dispute.

The agreement should also make clear that termination by either party will not terminate either the parties' obligations of confidentiality and indemnification, or provisions limiting the liability of either party.

WARNING

The foregoing material is an introduction to some of the most important legal issues to consider and items to include in a website development and maintenance agreement. The following sample Agreement can be used as a starting point for negotiations between a site owner and developer. But remember, the sample agreement might not be appropriate for your specific transaction; no two transactions are alike. Always consult a legal advisor with experience in this area before signing any agreement, and NEVER sign an agreement unless you understand the implications of each and every one of its provisions.

Chapter Sixteen Forms

Form II.16.1 Website Development and Maintenance Agreement

AGREEMENT, made and entered into as of [date] (the "Effective Date"), by and between [Name of site owner], a [state of incorporation] corporation with principal offices at [address of principal executive offices] (hereinafter "Site Owner"), and [Name of developer], a [state of incorporation] corporation with principal offices at [address of principal executive offices] (hereinafter "Developer").

WHEREAS, Site Owner is in the business of [describe site owner's line of business] ("Site Owner's Business"); and

WHEREAS, Site Owner wishes to advertise on, and market Site Owner's Business through, the international network of computers and computer networks known as the "Internet"; and

WHEREAS, Developer is in the business of providing, directly and through agents, certain software and computer consulting services pertaining to the Internet; and

WHEREAS, Site Owner desires to retain the services of Developer to (i) locate, obtain, and maintain certain computer hardware and locate, obtain, install, and maintain certain computer software required to provide Site Owner with a site on the World Wide Web protocol of the Internet (the "website"); (ii) obtain an Internet Protocol address and corresponding "domain name" and take such further acts as are necessary to establish the address of the website; (iii) adapt, translate, reformat, and otherwise modify certain text, images, music, audio, video, and other information ("Content") provided by Site Owner into digitized formats that can be loaded onto the system and accessed by others through the World Wide Web; and (iv) install the modified Content onto such system and maintain and update the website;

NOW, THEREFORE, in consideration of the mutual covenants and promises contained herein, as well as other valuable consideration, the receipt and sufficiency of which is hereby acknowledged, the parties hereto agree as follows:

1. Term of Agreement

   This Agreement shall commence as of the Effective Date and shall continue until the earlier of (a) one (1) year following the Acceptance Date (as defined in paragraph 9.b. hereof) or (b) prior termination in accordance with the terms of this Agreement, the aforementioned period of time to constitute the term of the Agreement (the "Term").

2. Basic Services

   Developer shall provide the following services to Site Owner in accordance with the delivery schedule set forth in Exhibit A to this Agreement (the "Delivery Schedule"):

   a. Website Design and Development. Developer shall develop for Site Owner a series of pages to be included at the website ("Web Pages") in accordance with the following procedures:

   (1) Content Development. Developer shall develop and submit to Site Owner specific and detailed representations of the Web Pages that will achieve the business requirements described in the applicable Exhibit A to this Agreement ("Business Requirements") in accordance with the timetable set forth therein. Such representations shall include scripts, paper-based models of screen displays, and flow charts indicating Web Page layout, content, progression, and interac-

tivity. Once Site Owner approves the representations, or modified versions of the representations, a copy of each of the representations or modified representation, as the case may be, shall be countersigned by a representative of each party and shall be consecutively numbered and annexed as a schedule hereto, whereupon such representations shall become the specifications for the Web Pages to be developed ("Specifications").

(2) Content Production. Developer shall produce and submit to Site Owner, in accordance with the timetable set forth in the applicable Exhibit A to this Agreement, digitized versions of each element of the Web Pages as described in the Specifications.

(3) Programming. Once Site Owner approves the digitized version, or modified digitized versions, as the case may be, of each element of the Web Pages, Developer shall assemble, in accordance with the timetable set forth in Exhibit A to this Agreement, the digitized Content approved by Site Owner into a completed master of the Web Pages that conforms in all material respects to the Specifications ("Master").

b. Web Page Loading and Hosting. Developer shall obtain access to and the rights to use a server ("Server") and all necessary telecommunications hardware and software necessary to connect such Server directly to the Internet (all of which may be the property of Developer or some third party) and mount the Web Pages on the Server. The Server and the systems operator ("Systems Operator") shall meet the minimum standards (including bandwidth) set forth in Exhibit B to this Agreement. Promptly after the Acceptance Date, Developer shall install the Web Pages onto the Server and shall have responsibility for maintaining the Web Pages on the Server during the Term of this Agreement.

c. Internet Address and Domain Name. Within five (5) days following the execution of this Agreement, Developer shall contact a registration service to obtain, at the request of Site Owner, on Site Owner's behalf and in Site Owner's name, an Internet Protocol address, and shall undertake all other acts necessary (including, but not limited to, payment of any registration fee) to establish the address of the website.

d. Domain Name Clearance. Developer agrees to undertake clearance for the Domain Name. Site Owner shall be responsible for trademark clearance and protection.

e. Training. If so requested by Site Owner, Developer shall provide Site Owner with [specify number] days of training in the use and features of the website. Such training shall take place in Developer's offices at a time reasonably convenient to both parties.

3. Maintenance Services

Developer shall provide the following maintenance services during the term of this Agreement:

a. Web Page Updates.

(1) Update Services. On not more than two (2) occasions during each calendar month during the term of this Agreement, Site Owner shall have the right to require Developer to change each of the advertising banners, licensee banners, pictures, and video clips appearing on its Web Pages ("Updates"), and Developer will incorporate the Updates into the Web Pages within four (4) business days following delivery by Site Owner of all data required to produce the Updates.

(2) Update Software. Upon request of Site Owner from time to time, Developer shall make available at cost any software tools necessary for Site Owner to update the Web Pages directly ("Update Software"), provided that Site Owner shall be responsible for all third-party license and/or usage fees.

    b.   Training.

    (1) Use of Coding. If so requested by Site Owner, Developer shall provide Site Owner with training in the use of coding. Such training shall take place at Developer's offices at a time reasonably convenient to both parties.

    (2) Use of Update Software. If so requested by Site Owner, Developer shall provide Site Owner with training in the use of the Update Software. Such training shall take place at Developer's offices at a time reasonably convenient to both parties.

    c.   Website Information. All technical information pertaining to the usage of the website, including but not limited to "page views," "click-throughs," and data storage space shall be transmitted to Site Owner on at least a weekly basis free of charge.

    d.   User Information. All user information available from people accessing the website, sending e-mail to the website, joining clubs or participating in chat rooms or message boards at the website, or purchasing items from the website; including, without limitation, names, ages, addresses, e-mail addresses, telephone numbers, credit card information, products requested, and any other demographic, psychographic, or other information directly or indirectly obtained from such users (collectively, "User Information") shall be recorded and transmitted to Site Owner accurately and completely, periodically as requested by Site Owner at a cost of $[price] per report, provided that all such information for the period shall be contained within a single report.

    e.   Web Server Maintenance. All occasional or periodic servicing of the Server hardware and software shall be provided promptly as necessary.

4.   Fees

    a.   Fee for Website Design and Development Services. The fee for the Website Design and Development services provided hereunder is set forth on the Specifications annexed hereto and shall be paid by Site Owner to Developer in four installments as follows: (1) 33 ⅓% upon execution by both parties hereto of this Agreement; (2) 33 ⅓% upon delivery to Site Owner of a prototype of the website for beta testing; (3) 23 ⅓% on the date following the latter of the Acceptance Date (as defined in paragraph 9.b. hereof) and the date on which the website becomes accessible by the general public (the "Live Date"), provided that Developer has theretofore delivered to Site Owner the items referenced in paragraph 6.a., 6.b., 6.c., and 6.d. hereof; and (4) 10% on the thirtieth calendar day following the Live Date, provided that Developer has theretofore corrected any reported deviations from the applicable Specifications and delivered to Site Owner any corrected Web Page Disks required under paragraph 9.b. of this Agreement.

    Developer shall also be permitted to charge Site Owner, at the applicable hourly rate set forth in Exhibit C to this Agreement, for time incurred by Developer modifying any digitized version of a Web Page if the modification requested by Site Owner causes the digitized version of such Web Page to materially deviate from the applicable Specification. In no event shall Developer be permitted to pass along to Site Owner any overtime or other charges incurred by Developer to meet the timetable set forth in the applicable Exhibit A to this Agreement unless (i) the need for such overtime arises as a result of Site Owner's acceleration of the delivery schedule set forth in the applicable Exhibit A to this Agreement or Site Owner's failure to provide Content required for the creation of the Web Pages by the deadline set forth in the applicable Exhibit A to this Agreement, and (ii) Site Owner provides Developer with prior written authorization to implement an overtime schedule. Any overtime charges passed along to Site Owner shall not exceed 1.5 times the applicable hourly rates set forth in Exhibit C to this Agreement.

b. Fees for Web Page Mounting and Hosting. The fee for Web Page Mounting and Hosting services provided hereunder shall be paid commencing on the Acceptance Date (as defined in paragraph 9.b. hereof) and continuing each month thereafter for the remainder of the Term of this Agreement. Such fee shall be at a rate of $[price] per month for (i) the first [number] megabytes of software and data storage space utilized in connection with the website and (ii) the first [number] megabytes of software and data transmitted to website Users. Additional storage and transmission space shall be available at a rate of $[price] per megabyte.

c. Fees for Maintenance Services (Other than Training). The fee for the Maintenance Services provided hereunder shall be $[price] per month during the Term of this Agreement.

d. Fees for Training. The aggregate cost of each of the eight-hour training sessions under paragraphs 2.d., 3.b.(1), and 3.b.(2) shall be $[price] per day (inclusive of all hardware, software, and location costs) for the first two days of each type of training described in such paragraphs, which fee shall be payable in full one calendar week prior to each scheduled training session. Additional training shall be available at the rates set forth in Exhibit C to this Agreement.

5. Additional Services Available

a. Web Page Linking. Developer shall check and maintain existing hyperlinks to each of Site Owner's Web Pages and actively search the Internet for new places to post hyperlinks to Site Owner's Web Pages at the hourly rate set forth on Exhibit C to this Agreement.

b. Modified Web Pages and New Web Pages. Site Owner may, from time to time during the Term of this Agreement, submit to Developer written proposals for modifications to, or the creation of new, Web Pages ("Modified Web Pages" and "New Web Pages," respectively) and any required timetable for their delivery. Developer will submit to Site Owner a written response to the written proposals within five (5) business days following receipt thereof, setting forth a fixed-price proposal for implementing same. If Site Owner agrees to the response, or to a modified version of such response, a copy of the response or modified response, as the case may be, shall be countersigned by a representative of each party, consecutively numbered and annexed as an additional Exhibit A to this Agreement, and shall become the Business Requirements for the Modified Web Pages or New Web Pages, as the case may be. The subsequent development of Specifications and production of Modified Web Pages or New Web Pages, as the case may be, shall thereupon proceed in accordance with the terms, conditions, and procedures set forth in paragraph 2(a) of this Agreement. The Modified Web Pages or New Web Pages, as the case may be, shall be subject in all respects to the provisions of this Agreement as if such Modified Web Pages or New Web Pages were the initial Web Pages.

6. Developer Deliverables

a. Web Page Disks. As further described in paragraph 9.a. hereof, Developer shall deliver to Site Owner by the delivery date set forth in the applicable Exhibit A to this Agreement, two (2) copies of digitized, machine-readable object code version of the Web Pages, stored on media appropriate for direct loading onto the Server (the "Web Page Disks"). Web Page Disks shall be subject in all respects to the provisions of this Agreement as if the information contained thereon were the initial Web Pages. Site Owner shall be permitted to make copies (or hire third parties to make copies) of the Web Page Disks as necessary.

b. License to use Server Software. Developer shall deliver to Site Owner by the delivery date set forth in the applicable Exhibit A to this Agreement, a license(s) for the object code version of all software to be installed on the Server in connection with the Web Pages. Such license(s) shall be in substantially the form annexed as Exhibit D to this Agreement.

c. Source Code for Server Software and Related License. Developer shall deliver to Site Owner by the delivery date set forth in the applicable Exhibit A to this Agreement, a copy of both the source code and license(s) for that source code of all software to be installed on the Server in connection with the Web Pages. Such license(s) shall be in substantially the form annexed as Exhibit E to this Agreement.

d. Third-party Consents, Waivers, and Releases. Developer shall deliver to Site Owner by the delivery date set forth in the applicable Exhibit A to this Agreement, all consents, waivers, and releases of third parties necessary to use all material incorporated into the Web Pages that was not supplied by Site Owner, including but not limited to, such waivers for all of the persons and other entities connected with the production of the Web Pages, and all of the persons whose names, voices, performances, photographs, likenesses, works, services, and materials will be used in the Web Pages.

7. Content Provided by Site Owner

All photographs, videos, trademarks, images, or other works owned or controlled by Site Owner that are specified by Site Owner for inclusion in the Web Pages shall be provided by Site Owner in clear and camera-ready form necessary for digital translation. Developer shall make no changes to the text or appearance of any Content without the prior written approval of Site Owner, except that Developer shall reformat the Content into digital format. In the event that Site Owner fails to provide any Content required for the creation of the Web Pages in accordance with the timetable set forth in the applicable Exhibit A to this Agreement, then Developer's obligations that are dependent on such Content shall be extended on a day-for-day basis to reflect such delay.

8. Website Portability

All agreements with Systems Operators shall expressly provide that Developer shall have the right to move the website to other Servers or Systems Operators upon thirty (30) days' prior written notice.

9. Delivery, Acceptance, and Installation of Web Pages

a. Delivery. As required under paragraph 6.a. hereof, Developer shall deliver to Site Owner by the delivery date set forth in the applicable Exhibit A to this Agreement, two (2) copies of the Web Page Disks. Developer acknowledges that its failure to deliver the Web Page Disks to Site Owner or to provide additional Web Page Disks incorporating all error correction and debugging deemed necessary by Site Owner by the applicable delivery date will result in expense and damage to Site Owner. If any delivery date is missed by more than ten (10) calendar days (as adjusted to reflect any extension required under paragraph 7 of this Agreement), Site Owner may, at its option, notify Developer in writing that it considers the delay a default of Developer under this Agreement which shall entitle Site Owner to terminate this Agreement. Should Site

Owner elect to excuse the delay, it shall do so by written notice, which notice shall include new delivery date(s).

b. Testing and Acceptance.

(1) Promptly upon receipt of the Web Page Disks, Site Owner shall immediately proceed to inspect, test, and evaluate them to determine whether the Web Page Disks conform to the applicable Specifications in all material respects, in the reasonable opinion of Site Owner.

(2) If Site Owner determines that the Web Page Disks do not conform in all material respects to the applicable Specifications, Site Owner shall give Developer written notice describing such nonconformity. Developer shall have seven (7) business days from the receipt of such notice to correct the deficiencies. Upon delivery of two (2) copies of the corrected Web Page Disks (which shall be at no additional cost to Site Owner), Site Owner shall then immediately proceed to re-inspect, re-test, and re-evaluate the Web Page Disks. If Site Owner determines that the Web Page Disks still do not conform in all material respects to the applicable Specifications, Site Owner shall have the option to (i) repeat the procedure set forth above; or (ii) invoice and recover from Developer the amount of Site Owner's reasonable out-of-pocket costs to correct, modify, and/or complete the Web Page Disks in accordance with the Specifications, and terminate this Agreement. The date on which acceptance occurs pursuant to this Agreement shall be the "Acceptance Date."

c. Installation. Developer shall have sole responsibility for installing the Web Pages onto the Server promptly after the Acceptance Date. Developer will notify Site Owner in writing when the Web Pages have been loaded onto the Server and are accessible from a remote computer linked to the World Wide Web.

10. Ownership and Rights

a. Ownership by Site Owner of Web Pages.

(1) With the sole exception of any software created by Developer hereunder and any preexisting third-party software used in connection with the satisfaction of Developer's obligations hereunder, which is identified in Exhibit F to this Agreement ("Software"); all materials, products, and related modifications thereto developed or prepared by Developer (including any of its subcontractors) in connection with the Web Pages, including, without limitation, all text, images, music, audio, video, and other information, and all code relating thereto ("Web Page Elements"), are the exclusive property of Site Owner, and all right, title, and interest thereto shall vest in Site Owner and be deemed to be a "work-made-for-hire" and made in the course of services rendered hereunder. To the extent that title to any such works may not, by operation of law, vest in Site Owner or such works may not be considered works-made-for-hire, all right, title, and interest therein are hereby irrevocably assigned to Site Owner.

(2) In the event that Developer subcontracts production or programming for the Web Pages or any of the Web Page Elements, Developer will deliver to Site Owner (i) a written agreement from each "freelancer" and subcontractor utilized by the Developer for the production or programming of the Web Page Elements, in the form annexed as Exhibit G to this Agreement, and (ii) a written agreement from each "freelancer" utilized by any subcontractor for the production or programming of the Web Page Elements in the form annexed as Exhibit H to this Agreement.

(3) All Web Page Elements shall belong exclusively to Site Owner, with Site Owner having the right to obtain and hold in its own name all copyright, patent, and trademark registrations and

such other protections as may be appropriate to the subject matter and any applications, extensions, continuations, and renewals thereof and all merchandising rights therein. Developer agrees to give Site Owner and any person designated by Site Owner, any reasonable assistance required to perfect the rights defined in this section.

b. Limited License of Content to Developer. Nothing herein shall be construed to grant any right or license to Developer in or to any Content or Web Page Elements provided to Developer hereunder by Site Owner, other than the right to use such material solely on behalf of Site Owner in accordance with the terms hereof. All of the foregoing materials, including, without limitation, any and all copyrights, trademarks, and tradenames, are and shall remain the property of Site Owner.

11. Proprietary and Legal Notices; Development Credit

a. Copyright Notice. The following copyright notice will be programmed into all Web Pages delivered hereunder so that it will appear at the beginning of all visual displays of such Web Pages: "© [year] [Site Owner]" Said notice will be affixed on all tangible versions of the Web Page Disks delivered hereunder and on any associated documentation.

b. Legal Page. The website shall include a legal page in the form annexed as Exhibit I to this Agreement (the "Legal Page"). The Legal Page shall be referenced at the bottom of the "home page" and linked to such reference via a hyperlink.

c. Development Credit. During the term of this Agreement, Site Owner shall acknowledge the contributions of Developer to the website by inserting the text "Designed by [Developer]" or reasonably equivalent text at the website. The format and placement of such development credit shall be at the sole discretion of Site Owner. It shall be the sole responsibility of Developer to provide Site Owner with sufficient information to create and update any hyperlink to Developer's home page. Such development credit shall not give Developer any trademark, copyright, or other proprietary interest or rights in the website. Nothing herein shall be construed to require Site Owner to promote Developer's website.

12. Developer Warranties and Covenants

Developer hereby warrants and covenants to Site Owner as follows:

a. Warranty of Performance. The Web Pages will operate in conformity with the performance capabilities and requirements described in Exhibit A and the applicable Specifications. If any material nonconformities are discovered, Developer shall promptly remedy them and provide revised Web Page Disks promptly to Site Owner at no additional expense to Site Owner.

b. Warranty of Title. Except for material provided by Site Owner for use in connection with the website, the materials used by Developer and its subcontractors in connection with the website shall not infringe upon any existing United States patent right or copyright, trade secret, or other proprietary right of any third party. No creative materials shall be used by Developer or its subcontractors in connection with the website shall be licensed from any third party without Site Owner's prior written approval of the form and substance of such license agreement.

c. Warranty Against Disablement. No portion of the Web Pages delivered hereunder will contain any protection feature designed to prevent their use. This includes, without limitation, any computer virus, worm, software lock, drop-dead device, Trojan horse, trap door, time bomb, or any other codes or instructions that may be used to access, modify, delete, damage, or disable the website once uploaded to the World Wide Web, or any computer server on which such Web Pages are stored or any computer system that has accessed such Web Pages through the World Wide Web. Developer will not impair the operation of any such Web Pages in any other way.

d. Warranty of Expertise. All of the services to be performed by Developer hereunder or by a subcontractor on the Developer's behalf will be rendered using sound, professional practices, and in a competent and professional manner by knowledgeable, trained, and qualified personnel. Developer acknowledges that Site Owner is relying upon the skill and expertise of Developer in Developer's performance of this Agreement.

e. Corporate Authority. Developer has the full right, power, legal capacity, and authority to enter into this Agreement and to carry out the terms hereof.

f. No Conflicts. There are and will be no liens, claims, encumbrances, legal proceedings, restrictions, agreements, or understandings that might conflict or interfere or be inconsistent with, limit, or otherwise affect any of the provisions of this Agreement or any rights of site owner to any of the Web pages or any elements thereof.

g. Third-party Rights. Except with respect to any persons or entities connected with materials supplied by Site Owner, Developer will obtain releases, in a form approved by Site Owner, from all persons and other entities whose names, voices, performances, photographs, likenesses, works, services, and materials are used in the Web Pages (the "Releases"), permitting the unrestricted use of their names, voices, photographs, likenesses, performances (including, but not limited to, any music and sound synchronized therewith), and biographical data in the program in connection with the advertising, promotion, and exploitation of the Web Pages throughout the world in perpetuity. The use by Site Owner of any materials contained on the Web Pages (excluding any materials provided by Site Owner), including, without limitation, materials used in connection with the production, marketing, and distribution of the Web Pages, will not violate the rights of any third party and will not give rise to any claim of such violation, including, without limitation, claims of libel; slander; defamation; copyright infringement; infringement of moral rights; trademark infringement; false designation of origin; disparagement; violation of privacy, publicity, identity, or other proprietary rights; violation of any existing United States patent rights, trade secret, or shop rights; piracy; or plagiarism.

h. No Obligations. Except with respect to any persons or entities connected with materials supplied by Site Owner, all obligations with respect to the production, distribution, and exploitation of the Web Pages, including, but not limited to, all salaries, royalties, deferments, license fees, service charges, music costs, laboratory charges, and the like, will be fully paid by Developer, and Site Owner shall have no obligations for salaries, royalties, residuals, deferments, music fees, license fees, service charges, laboratory charges, or similar payments.

13. Site Owner Warranties and Covenants

Site Owner hereby warrants and covenants to Developer as follows:

a. Warranty of Title. The use by Developer or its subcontractors of the materials supplied by Site Owner hereunder, in the manner contemplated by this Agreement, shall not infringe upon any existing United States patent right, copyright, trade secret, or other proprietary right of any third party.

b.   Corporate Authority. Site Owner has the full right, power, legal capacity, and authority to enter into this Agreement and to carry out the terms hereof.

c.   No Conflicts. There are and will be no liens, encumbrances, legal proceedings, restrictions, agreements, or understandings that might conflict or interfere or be inconsistent with, limit, or otherwise affect any of the provisions of this Agreement or the enjoyment by Developer of any of the rights granted to Developer by Site Owner hereunder.

d.   Third-party Rights. The use by the Developer or its subcontractors of the materials supplied by Site Owner hereunder, in the manner contemplated by this Agreement, will not violate the rights of any third party and will not give rise to any claim of such violation, including, without limitation, claims of libel; slander; defamation; copyright infringement; infringement of moral rights; trademark infringement; false designation of origin; disparagement; violation of privacy, publicity, identity, or other proprietary rights; violation of United States patent rights, trade secret, or shop rights; piracy; or plagiarism.

e.   Content Restrictions. No information and data disseminated by Site Owner via the website shall be in violation of law.

14. Indemnification

a.   Indemnification of Site Owner by Developer against Certain Liability. Developer hereby agrees to indemnify, defend, and hold harmless Site Owner and its officers, directors, employees, and agents (collectively, the "Indemnitees") from and against all demands, claims, actions or causes of action, assessments, losses, damages, liabilities, costs, and expenses, including, without limitation, interest, penalties, and attorneys' fees and expenses (collectively, the "Losses"), which shall be based upon a claim that (1) Site Owner's use of any of the materials or services supplied by Developer or any of its subcontractors pursuant to this Agreement (including any advertising or promotional use of such materials) infringes any patent, copyright, trademark, trade secret, rights of publicity or privacy, or any other proprietary right of any third party or is libelous or slanderous, (2) if true, would constitute a breach of any of Developer's representations, warranties, or agreements hereunder; or (3) arises out of the negligence or willful misconduct of Developer or any of its subcontractors.

b.   Repair or Replacement of Infringing Web Pages. If a court of competent jurisdiction imposes an injunction prohibiting Site Owner from continued use of the Web Pages or portions thereof as a result of material provided by Developer or any of its subcontractors, Developer shall, at Developer's expense and the election of Site Owner:

(1)   procure for Site Owner the right to continue to use the material pursuant to this Agreement; or

(2)   replace or modify the Web Pages to make them non-infringing, provided that the modifications or substitutions will not materially and adversely affect the performance of such Web Pages or lessen their utility to Site Owner (as determined by Site Owner).

c.   Indemnification of Site Owner Against Personal Injury and Property Damage. Developer shall indemnify the Indemnitees against any and all liability for personal injuries and physical property damage arising out of the performance of this Agreement by Developer or its employees, agents, subcontractors, or representatives.

d.   Indemnification of Developer by Site Owner against Liability for Infringement. Site Owner hereby agrees to indemnify, defend, and hold harmless Developer and its officers, directors, employees, and agents (collectively, the "Developer Indemnitees") from and against all Losses which shall be based upon a claim that (1) Developer's use of any of the materials or services supplied by Site Owner and used by Developer pursuant to this Agreement infringes any existing United States patent, copyright, trademark, trade secret, rights of publicity or privacy, or any other proprietary right of any third party or is libelous or slanderous, (2) if true, would constitute a breach of any of Site Owner's representations, warranties, or agreements hereunder; or (3) arises out of the negligence or willful misconduct of Site Owner.

e. Indemnification Procedure. Promptly after the receipt of any notice of claim or commencement of any action or proceeding against it within the scope of this paragraph 14, the indemnified party shall give notice to the indemnifying party if it wishes to assert a claim for indemnification. The indemnifying party shall then be entitled to participate in such action and, to the extent that it shall wish, to assume the defense thereof with counsel satisfactory to indemnified party; and, after notice from the indemnifying party to the indemnified party of its election so to assume the defense thereof, at its sole expense, the indemnifying party shall not be liable to the indemnified party for any fees of other counsel. If the indemnifying party assumes the defense of such an action, the indemnifying party without the indemnified party's consent (which shall not be unreasonably withheld) may effect no compromise or settlement unless:

(1) there is no finding or admission of any violation of law or any violation of the rights of any person, and no effect on any other claims that may be made against the indemnified party; and

(2) the sole relief provided is monetary damages that are paid in full by the indemnifying party. If notice is given to the indemnifying party of the commencement of any action and it does not, within ten (10) days after such notice is given, give notice to the indemnified party of its election to assume the defense thereof, the indemnifying party shall be bound by any determination made in such action or any compromise or settlement thereof effected by the indemnified party. Notwithstanding the foregoing, if the indemnified party determines in good faith that there is a reasonable probability that an action may materially and adversely affect it or its affiliates other than as a result of monetary damages, the indemnified party may, by notice to the indemnifying party, assume the exclusive right to defend, compromise, or settle such action, but the indemnifying party shall not be bound by any determination of an action so defended or any compromise or settlement thereof effected without its consent (which shall not be unreasonably withheld).

15. LIMITATION OF LIABILITY

DEVELOPER SHALL NOT BE LIABLE FOR ANY SPECIAL OR CONSEQUENTIAL DAMAGES, OR LOST PROFITS OF SITE OWNER, EVEN IF DEVELOPER HAS BEEN ADVISED OF THE POSSIBILITY OF SAME. DEVELOPER'S TOTAL LIABILITY FOR DAMAGES, COSTS, AND EXPENSES UNDER THIS AGREEMENT, EXCEPT FOR DAMAGES, COSTS, AND EXPENSES ARISING FROM ITS INDEMNIFICATION OBLIGATIONS UNDER PARAGRAPH 14 OF THIS AGREEMENT, SHALL NOT EXCEED THE TOTAL AMOUNT OF THE FEES PAID TO THE DEVELOPER BY SITE OWNER HEREUNDER.

16. Confidentiality

a. Confidentiality Obligations. Each party acknowledges that it shall receive Confidential Information (as hereinafter defined) of the other party relating to its technical, marketing, product, and/or business affairs. During the Term of this Agreement and for a period of five (5) years thereafter, all Confidential Information of the other party shall be held in strict confidence and shall not be disclosed or used without the express written consent of the other party, except as may be required by law. Each party shall use reasonable measures and make reasonable efforts to provide protection for the other party's Confidential Information, including measures at least as strict as such party uses to protect its own Confidential Information.

b.   Confidentiality of this Transaction. Developer shall not make any announcement or other disclosure to any third party of the transaction contemplated by this Agreement or any of the details of any plans for Site Owner's website until such plans have actually been implemented at Site Owner's website, or unless Developer has Site Owner's prior written consent. The form, substance, and timing of any announcement referring directly or indirectly to Site Owner's website shall be subject to Site Owner's prior approval.

c.   User Information. Without limiting the definition of Confidential Information, Developer acknowledges and agrees that the User Information shall be deemed to be Confidential Information owned exclusively by Site Owner, and that Developer shall not use the User Information for any purpose other than that of fulfilling its obligations under this Agreement. Neither Developer, nor any third party on behalf of Developer, shall have the right, directly or indirectly, to use, exploit, disclose, transmit, sell, assign, lease, or otherwise convey or make available for access by third parties, any User Information.

d.   Confidential Information Defined. Confidential information shall mean any information relating to, or disclosed in the course of, the performance of this Agreement, except for any information that (i) is or becomes generally available to the public without breach of this Agreement; (ii) is in the possession of a party prior to its disclosure by the other party; or (iii) becomes available from a third party not in breach of any obligation of confidentiality to which such third party is subject.

e.   Website Security. Developer shall provide Site Owner with, and advise Site Owner of, various security tools and procedures that can restrict access to areas of the website. Developer, however, cannot guaranty the ultimate effectiveness of any such measures, and the selection of appropriate security tools and procedures shall be Site Owner's ultimate responsibility.

17. Termination of Agreement

a.   Termination by Site Owner. Site Owner shall be entitled to terminate this Agreement: (i) if Developer fails to meet the timetable for deliveries set forth on the applicable Exhibit A by more than ten (10) calendar days (as adjusted to reflect any extension required under paragraph 7 of this Agreement) without the consent of Site Owner; (ii) upon the expiration of ten (10) calendar days following written notice to Developer of Site Owner's dissatisfaction with the performance of the Server or Systems Operator, provided that Developer has not remedied the cause of such dissatisfaction or moved the website to another Server or Systems Operator prior to the expiration of such ten-day period; (iii) upon the expiration of ten (10) calendar days following written notice to Developer of a default in the performance of any of its other obligations under this Agreement, provided that Developer has not remedied the default prior to the expiration of such ten-day period; or (iv) if a voluntary petition is filed by Developer or an involuntary petition is filed against Developer under the Bankruptcy Code that is not dismissed within thirty (30) days after filing, or upon the appointment of a receiver for all or any portion of Developer's business or operations, or any assignment of all or substantially all of the assets of Developer for the benefit of creditors, or if Developer discontinues or otherwise transfers its business or operations.

b. Termination by Developer. Developer shall be entitled to terminate this Agreement: (i) if Site Owner fails to make any payment when due hereunder, provided, however, that Developer is not then in default of its obligations under this Agreement, and provided, further, that Developer has given Site Owner ten (10) calendar days' prior written notice of its intent to terminate if such default is not remedied and Site Owner has not remedied the default prior to the expiration of such ten-day period; or (ii) if a voluntary petition is filed by Site Owner or an involuntary petition is filed against Site Owner under the Bankruptcy Code that is not dismissed within thirty (30) days after filing, or upon the appointment of a receiver for all or any portion of Site Owner's business or operations, or any assignment of all or substantially all of the assets of Site Owner for the benefit of creditors.

c. Consequences of Termination. In the event of termination of this Agreement: (i) the provisions of paragraphs 10, 12 through 17, 19, and 21 shall survive and continue in full force and effect; (ii) all rights and licenses granted to Site Owner by Developer pursuant to this Agreement shall continue and survive royalty-free and fully paid-up provided that Site Owner has paid to Developer all fees owed to Developer through the date of termination; (iii) each party shall return all copies of Confidential Information and all other property belonging to the other party and received from the other party; and (iv) each party may pursue claims it has against the other for any breach of the terms of this Agreement.

d. Waiver of Equitable Relief. Developer acknowledges that Site Owner's uninterrupted use of the Web Pages and website are the essence of this Agreement and that the damages to Site Owner in the event of an interruption cannot be reasonably or adequately compensated in an action at law and that such interruption would cause Site Owner irreparable harm and damage. Therefore, in the event of termination of this Agreement for any reason, Developer waives any rights to equitable relief by way of temporary, preliminary, or permanent injunction or such other equitable relief as any court of competent jurisdiction may have authority to order. Developer agrees that its sole remedy against Site Owner in the event of Site Owner's default or breach of this Agreement or upon the termination of this Agreement for any reason whatsoever shall be money damages.

18. Grant of Rights and License to Developer/Approvals

Subject to the terms and provisions hereof, Site Owner hereby grants to Developer the following non-exclusive, non-assignable license (the "License") during the Term hereof:

a. Operation. To operate the website on behalf of Site Owner and to process inquiries from website visitors. At all times herein, Developer will operate the website in a first-class manner to the reasonable satisfaction of Site Owner.

b. User Information. To record all User Information submitted by website visitors and to forward such information to Site Owner.

c. Trademarks. To use the trademarks (the "Trademark(s)") and the tradenames (the "Tradename(s)") listed in Exhibit J hereto to depict Site Owner's business on website. (The Trademarks, Tradenames, User Information, and the descriptions and depictions of Site Owner and Site Owner's business are hereinafter collectively referred to as the "Trade Properties.")

d.   Approvals. Without limiting the foregoing, all uses of the Trade Properties by Developer, whether exhibited on the website or in the promotion thereof, shall be subject to the approval of Site Owner. Developer will submit all such materials to Site Owner prior to use, and Site Owner shall either approve or disapprove such materials within a reasonable period of time. Developer will not take any action that would impair the rights of Site Owner in the Trade Properties or that would adversely affect their reputation or validity.

19. Employment of Each Other's Personnel

During the Term of this Agreement and for a period of one (1) year thereafter, neither party shall solicit or hire any individual who was employed by the other or their suppliers during the Term of this Agreement.

20. Insurance

Developer shall obtain all necessary and adequate insurance with respect to the production and use of the website, including, without limitation, liability insurance, workers' compensation, and errors and omission insurance in amounts and with carriers approved by Site Owner; each with limits of at least one million dollars ($1,000,000.00) on account of any one occurrence, and at least one million dollars ($1,000,000.00) for multiple occurrences of property damage. Site Owner will be named as co-insured on all such insurance policies, and copies of such policies and certificates of insurance (or binders) shall be delivered to Site Owner contemporaneously with the execution of this Agreement.

21. General Provisions

a.   Entire Agreement. This Agreement, together with all Exhibits, Specifications, and other attachments, which are incorporated herein by reference, is the sole and entire agreement between the parties relating to the subject matter hereof. This Agreement supersedes all prior understandings, agreements, and documentation relating to such subject matter. No provisions in either party's purchase orders, or in any other business forms employed by either party, will supersede the terms and conditions of this Agreement, and no supplement, modification, or amendment of this Agreement shall be binding unless executed in writing by both parties in this Agreement. In the event of a conflict between the provisions of the main body of the Agreement and any attached Exhibits, Specifications, or other materials, this Agreement shall take precedence.

b.   Modifications to Agreement. Modifications and amendments to this Agreement, including any Exhibits or Specifications attached hereto, shall be enforceable only if they are in writing and are signed by authorized representatives of both parties.

c.   No Assignment. Developer may not assign its rights or obligations under this Agreement, either in whole or in part, without the prior written consent of Site Owner. Any attempt to do so shall be void and of no effect. Notwithstanding the foregoing, Developer shall be permitted to subcontract its obligations hereunder. Site Owner shall be permitted to assign its rights and subcontract its obligations hereunder.

d.   Waiver. No term or provision of this Agreement shall be deemed waived and no breach excused unless such waiver or consent is in writing and signed by the party claimed to have waived or consented. A waiver by either of the parties of any of the covenants, conditions, or agreements to be performed by the other hereunder shall not be construed to be a waiver of any succeeding breach thereof.

e. No Duty to Investigate. Neither party shall have an affirmative duty to investigate any fact relevant to any representation or warranty made by the other party to this Agreement.

f. Force Majeure. Neither party shall be liable for delay or failure in the performance of its obligations hereunder if such delay or failure arises from the occurrence of events beyond the reasonable control of such party, which events could not have been prevented by the exercise of due care and could not have been foreseen at the time of entering into this Agreement, such as fire, explosion, flood, storm, labor strikes, acts of God, war, embargo, riot, or the intervention of any governmental authority; provided that the party suffering the delay or failure immediately notifies the other party of the reason for the delay or failure and acts diligently to remedy the cause of such delay or failure. Notwithstanding the foregoing, any delay or failure exceeding thirty (30) days shall be grounds for termination by the non-defaulting party.

g. No Partnership. Nothing contained herein will be construed as creating any partnership, joint venture, or other form of joint enterprise between the parties.

h. Independent Contractor. The parties acknowledge that Developer will perform its obligations hereunder as an independent contractor. The manner and method of performing such obligations will be under Developer's sole control and discretion. Site Owner's sole interest is in the result of such services. It is also expressly understood that Developer's employees and agents, if any, are not Site Owner's employees or agents, and have no authority to bind Site Owner by contract or otherwise. In the event Site Owner is found liable for Social Security, withholding, insurance, or other taxes due on account of Developer's employees or agents, Site Owner shall have the right to recover an equivalent amount from Developer.

i. Notices. Any notice required or permitted under this Agreement shall be in writing and shall be delivered personally against receipt; or by registered or certified mail, return receipt requested, postage prepaid; or sent by Federal Express or other recognized overnight courier service; and addressed to the party to be notified at its address set forth below or to such other address of which the parties may have given notice in accordance with this paragraph 21.i. All notices and other communications required or permitted under this Agreement shall be deemed given when delivered personally, or one day after being deposited with Federal Express or other recognized overnight courier service, or five days after being deposited in the United States mail, postage prepaid and addressed as follows, or to such other address as each party may designate in writing:

If to Site Owner:
  [Site Owner]
  [address]
  Attn:
  Telecopy:

If to Developer:
  [Developer]
  [address]
  Attn:
  Telecopy:

j.   Attorney Fees. If any action at law or in equity is necessary to enforce the terms of this Agreement, the prevailing party shall be entitled to reasonable attorney fees, costs, and expenses, in addition to any other relief to which it may be entitled.

k.   Applicable Law. This Agreement will be governed by United States copyright and intellectual property laws and the laws of the State of [state] without regard to any conflict of law principles. Both parties consent and submit in advance to the jurisdiction of any supreme court of the State of [state] and any United States District Court located therein.

l.   Severability. If any provision of this Agreement is held invalid, void, or unenforceable under any applicable statute or rule of law, it shall to that extent be deemed omitted, and the balance of this Agreement shall be enforceable in accordance with its terms.

m.   Headings Not Controlling. The headings in this Agreement are for reference purposes only and shall not be construed as a part of this Agreement.

Each party represents and warrants that on this date they are duly authorized to bind their respective principals by their signatures below.

[SITE OWNER]

By:

Name:_____

Title:_____

[DEVELOPER]

By:

Name:_____

Title:_____

CHAPTER XVII
Insurance

Schedule of Exhibits

1. Advertiser and Advertising Agency Insurance

In today's marketplace, it is poor business practice for an advertising agency or advertiser not to carry advertising liability insurance, even for the smallest of companies. The cost of insurance is not excessive compared to the potential liability costs. A variety of policies are available. One company, Media/Professional Insurance (http://www.mediaprof.com) ("Media Pro") developed a contract in conjunction with the American Association of Advertising Agencies (AAAA). Media Pro should always be included in the bidding process.

Specialized advertiser and advertising agency insurance policies afford coverage for a number of perils encountered in the advertising business. Coverage, however, is generally limited to libel, slander, defamation, copyright infringement, invasions of privacy and publicity, misappropriation, and infringement of title. Such policies are not broad errors-and-omissions policies, although new policies are being developed that expand coverage. The typical policy available today does not insure against certain problems, and advertisers and advertising agencies are increasingly looking to one another to cover such risks.

Trademark infringement is not covered under most of the basic policies available today. At least one version of the AAAA/Media Pro contract includes trademark coverage and riders, and is available from the other carriers.

Trademark liability can be very high, particularly if a labeled product on store shelves needs to be recalled. The costs associated with recalls or re-labeling can bankrupt a small- or medium-sized agency.

Comparative advertising lawsuits are another costly area. Literally millions of dollars in damages have been awarded, and at least one advertiser went bankrupt as a result of a deceptive comparative advertising campaign.

Some insurance policies available today will cover comparative advertising, but only by a special rider. Since comparative advertising can expose an advertiser and its advertising agency to considerable risk, both should carefully consider the inclusion of a comparative advertising rider. If an advertising agency chooses to forego the rider because of the expense, then the advertising agency should try to obtain an indemnification from its client for any liability concerning comparative advertising.

Be sure to review what coverage is available. Make a conscious choice whether or not to adopt the various riders that are offered. Then, determine if the indemnities between the advertising agency and the advertiser included in the agency/client agreement go beyond the insurance coverage. In those areas where there is no coverage, adopt special procedures to minimize risks, e.g., legal review and approval of questionable campaigns.

2. Production and Related Insurance

It is common for production companies to carry insurance on damage to film or tape. No production should go forward without it. Nor should any production involving out-of-doors production proceed without weather insurance.

Too often, production companies overlook specialized insurance for risky productions, or insurance covering production cost if a celebrity talent fails to perform or becomes disabled by injury or health problems during production. Insurance is available for such contingencies and, while often quite expensive, should be considered where appropriate. Other insurance to consider covers equipment, props, sets, wardrobes, and damage to third-party property. Workers' compensation should be in place, covering production crews and actors. If stunts are involved, special liability insurance is a must. Finally, an overall umbrella policy provides an additional, usually inexpensive, protection.

CHAPTER XVIII
Vendor Relationships

3. War and Terrorism Coverage

Losses incurred as a result of a declared war are generally not covered by insurance. Nor is it likely that any insurance carrier will write a special rider to cover such risks and losses. The key in such instances is whether the loss is a direct result of the war. If not, then coverage may apply.

It is not clear what acts of terrorism are excluded from coverage on standard policies. Insurance companies have not clearly defined "terrorism." Importantly, the Terrorism Risk Insurance Act requires that policies cover acts of terrorism by or on behalf of foreign individuals or entities occurring in the United States. Some carriers extend the coverage to foreign countries as well.

In addition, policies generally cover losses (except lost earnings and profits) as a result of interruptions, postponements, or cancellations of productions caused by civil authorities (in the United States and Canada). Thus, if civil authorities revoke a production permit or prohibit access to facilities under a production company's control, coverage may apply.

Note that cancellations due to *fears* of war, terrorism, or interruption by civil authorities are not covered.

The crux of the problem is defining when a country is at "war," is the victim of "terrorism," or when production interference is caused by a civil authority. While each of these instances may be easily defined in a vacuum, experience from the events of September 11, 2001, show how difficult it is to distinguish each in an actual claim.

4. Deductibles

The amount of the deductible is important for more than the obvious exposure it leaves with the insured. In many of the policies offered, the deductible also applies to the legal expenses incurred by the insurance company. Thus, if a policy has a $25,000 deductible, the insured will be liable for the first $25,000 of the legal fees incurred. The insured must, therefore, realize that a high deductible may make claims rather expensive to defend. One is well advised to take as low a deductible as can be afforded. In the advertising industry, many claims are settled for less than $50,000. If the deductible is too high, the advertiser or advertising agency is effectively uninsured for most claims.

5. Choice of Legal Counsel

Some policies offered today allow the insured to choose the counsel who will defend them. This is particularly advantageous, as the insured will be able to deal with a law firm with whom it has an existing relationship or one whose credentials are appropriate to the particular case.

1. Centralizing Controls

Relationships with outside vendors should be coordinated by a single person who is trained or experienced in negotiations. At some advertising agencies and advertisers, such people carry the title "Business Affairs Manager," "Art Buyer," or the like. While they are often part of the creative department, they are not part of the creative process. Their function is to negotiate the best possible deal for the advertising agency and the advertiser and, in many ways, to shield the creative teams from the business side of advertising.

If negotiations with vendors are left to a variety of people, there will be inconsistencies that will invariably create liabilities and embarrassment. This is particularly true where creative directors or art directors negotiate with outside creative suppliers. Creative directors and art directors are not generally trained in negotiations. Indeed, some experts believe it is the last responsibility with which a creative director or art director should be charged.

Photographers and freelance creatives typically use professional representatives to negotiate their deals. These representatives are not just experienced negotiators; they are also very astute in copyright law, union codes, and contract law. More often than not, they also have the advantage of knowing more of what happens in the marketplace than any single advertising agency or advertiser executive. Putting an amateur up against these professionals is corporate suicide. (See Forms II.18.1 and II.18.2.)

Why It Matters

The pitfalls encountered by not heeding this advice are best exemplified by the plethora of cases dealing with lost transparencies. Here's the scenario:

The art director calls his or her friendly stock photo house and asks for pictures of sunsets. "No problem, they're on their way," is the reply. True to their word, the stock photo house delivers 50 original transparencies to the advertising agency. The agency's receptionist dutifully signs the form presented by the person delivering the transparencies, without bothering to read it.

The transparencies are delivered to the art director, who immediately starts reviewing them and then puts them in a desk drawer. This process is repeated a few times, and some of the transparencies are "borrowed" by the creative director to look at as well. Finally, the creative team decides on the transparency it likes best and happily informs the friendly stock photo house. "Great, please return the transparencies you're not using," is the reply.

Unfortunately, only 25 of the 50 transparencies can be found. No one tells this to agency management. The 25 transparencies are returned to the stock photo house, and the campaign goes forward. A month or so later, the advertising agency receives an invoice from the stock photo house for $37,500: $1,500 each for the "lost transparencies," per the agreement signed by the receptionist. In all likelihood, the case will be settled for many thousands of dollars, none of which is recoupable from the advertising agency's client.

In some cases, settlements have been in excess of $30,000 and arbitration awards even higher. Stock photo houses use forms that generally specify that each lost transparency is worth $1,500 or more. While there are some arguments against such fees, the weight of judicial authority holds that the figure is legitimate and the contracts are enforceable.

There is no excuse for such a scenario, yet it happens every day because procedures are not centralized. Indeed, in most instances, it seems there are no procedures in place at all!

Strategies:

- Centralize the function of dealing with outside suppliers.

- Instruct receptionists that they are to examine a form before they sign it and ask management to review it if there are any questions.

- Keep all stock photography in a single, secure location.

- Whenever possible, instruct stock photo houses to send duplicate transparencies, not originals.

2. Purchase Orders

It is crucial that the entire understanding between an advertising agency or advertiser and an outside supplier be clearly set forth in writing and signed by the supplier. (See Form II.18.3.)

Use of a printed purchase-order form detailing conditions for the purchase of outside creative materials is key to a successful strategy in dealing with outside suppliers. Purchase orders are typically used with photographers, stock photo houses, and freelance writers, but they can be used for virtually any outside purchase. Properly drafted, the purchase order can be used as a universal form, and the purchaser will generally be adequately protected even where a purchase-order form is "mistakenly" used in certain transactions requiring specialized forms. While some suppliers may hotly contest provisions printed in a purchase-order form, special provisions can be negotiated on a case-by-case basis, with modifications written on the front of the printed form.

It is also important to remember that forms should never be viewed as "etched in stone." They are simply the basis upon which to negotiate. Be sure that qualified individuals are dealing with the outside suppliers. Such individuals should be familiar with all the conditions on the forms and should consult with upper management or legal counsel if they have any questions. In addition, any variance from the standard terms and conditions of the form should be carefully set forth on the front of the form, not in a separate document or other correspondence. Finally, a form received from a supplier should never be signed without carefully reviewing it and discussing objectionable conditions with the supplier. If it contains anything objectionable, it should be discussed with the supplier.

Strategies:

- Adopt a standard purchase-order form.
- Use the purchase order as a negotiating tool.
- Only allow qualified people to deal with the purchase order.
- Type all deviations from the standard terms and conditions onto the front of the purchase order.
- Never sign a supplier's purchase order without carefully reviewing it and discussing objectionable conditions with the supplier.

3. Obtaining Releases from People Used in Advertising

Names, photographs, caricatures, or likenesses of living persons cannot be used in advertising without their written consent. This includes the names and likenesses of advertising agency or advertiser employees and anyone else recognizable in an advertisement. It also includes all forms of advertising: print, collateral, broadcast, direct mail, and online. Therefore, signed releases must always be obtained.

Releases for materials acquired or licensed from outside suppliers can be problematic. Insist upon receiving copies of releases signed by any models who appear in stock photographs.

As with any agreement, care must be taken that key terms are clearly set forth in the release. For example, how long may the photograph or name be used? What is the geographic territory of use? Are there any approval rights? The use of a General Release form will insure that these necessary points, and all others, are covered. (See Form II.18.4.)

If the advertising in question utilizes a testimonial, be sure the Testimonial Release form includes a representation that the testimonial is true. (See Form II.18.6.)

A professional models' modeling agency may supply its own form of release for a print photo shoot. Be very wary of their forms. While their forms can be used, specialized advertising agency forms are more appropriate. All too often, model agency's forms are incomplete and do not fully address the legal issues or protect the interests of the advertiser. (See Form II.18.5.)

When hiring actors, standard union contracts are fine for scale performers; i.e., performers who are to be paid union minimums for common acting services. If an advertising agency or advertiser is not a union signatory or if it is hiring celebrity talent at above scale rates, more detailed contracts are needed.

In special circumstances, you may also need to use a Property Release, particularly if you are entering someone else's property or using a unique prop. (See Form II.18.7.)

Strategies:

- Always get a signed General Release when using a person's name, photograph, or image, even if he or she is an employee of the advertising agency or advertiser.

- If you are acquiring the right to use the name or photograph in perpetuity, be sure to pay the individual a reasonable amount of consideration, preferably not less than $100.

- If you are using releases supplied by modeling agencies, be sure they cover all negotiated points: e.g., term, territory, options, and compensation.

Why It Matters

1. In a print campaign for an herbal beauty product, a photograph of a woman walking toward a pond holding the hand of her daughter. The woman and her daughter had their backs to the camera, and they were both naked. The woman argued, and the court agreed, that she had the right to try to prove to a jury that she was recognizable, based upon her husband's testimony that he recognized her from the two dimples above her buttocks, her long slender neck, slim waist, bony elbows, indented back, and short, free-flowing hair. The case was later settled.

2. A national bank used a group shot of employees for a print campaign. No releases were obtained, although it was claimed that the employees orally consented. The employees later brought a class-action lawsuit against the bank for the unauthorized use of their photographs in the ad. The ad was pulled, and the case was settled.

3. A model who penciled onto a release "magazine use only" was held to have a cause of action against an advertiser who used the photo on a billboard.

4. A model posed for a photograph reading an educational book in bed. The photo was subsequently used in an ad juxtaposed with the photo of an old man reading a sex book in an adjacent bed. The judge found that the ad suggested that the model was a willing call girl and upheld the model's claim of defamation.

4. Obtaining Signatures from Suppliers

Obtaining supplier signatures on agreements is a particularly problematic area in the advertising industry. Many, if not most, advertising agencies today fail to secure supplier signatures on their forms. It is cumbersome and considered contrary to traditional behavior in the industry. That it is contrary to traditional behavior in the industry is irrefutable. The advertising industry is, by far, one of the sloppiest industries in this regard. It is nothing short of amazing that an industry that spends more than $135 billion a year has done so with as few problems as it has. Nonetheless, it is clear that the failure to obtain a written agreement with an outside supplier can create substantial problems. For example, without a signature consenting to terms of ownership, the U.S. Supreme Court has held that no transfer of ownership occurs and the creator of the work retains the copyright. Note that any agreement to indemnify must be signed for the indemnity to be enforceable.

Why It Matters

It is common for agency/client agreements to specify that the advertiser owns everything the advertising agency secures or creates for the advertiser, unless the advertising agency informs the advertiser otherwise. The advertising agency should not put itself into the position of breaching this clause by failing to obtain a supplier's signature on a form.

Similarly, if an advertising agency orally obtains all rights to outside creative work, but fails to get the supplier to sign a contract or form providing for the transfer, no transfer has occurred—regardless of what the oral understanding was between the advertising agency and the outside supplier. While resolution of a dispute in court might be different if the advertising agency was actively involved in the creative process, e.g., provided the layout for a photograph, the weight of authority holds that without a signature, the supplier has only granted a license, and no transfer of ownership has occurred.

5. Negotiating Options with Vendors

An agreement negotiated for outside materials or services, e.g., photography or talent, may give a false sense of security because, while it will usually cover the terms of initial use desired by the advertiser, no consideration is given to extending the campaign beyond what was originally planned. Negotiating options for the use of outside materials or services beyond the initial terms of agreement helps to avoid this problem. For example, a deal to use a photograph for a period of one year in consumer publications in the United States may satisfy the immediate needs of the advertiser. If, however, a decision is made to extend the campaign for an additional one-year period, or into other geographic territories, the advertiser is at a great negotiating disadvantage, having lost most of its leverage. If options for expanded use are negotiated at the inception of a deal, the economics will be far more favorable to the advertiser. Such options should cost nothing until they are exercised.

It is important to remember that options are generally keyed to a date by which the advertising agency or advertiser must notify the supplier that it wishes to exercise the option. Such dates have been held to be strictly binding by courts, and a missed date may force costly renegotiations with a supplier. Under such circumstances, the advertising agency and advertiser have lost all leverage with the supplier and may be at its mercy, a decidedly uncomfortable place to be. It can become a nightmare if the supplier demands an excessive amount of money or simply doesn't want to deal with the advertising agency or advertiser at all. Usually, failure of an advertising agency to properly exercise the option date is a breach of its agreement with the advertiser. Understandably, the advertiser may hold the advertising agency responsible for any additional costs necessary to re-secure the rights.

6. Alternatives to Transfers of Ownership

It is not uncommon for suppliers to refuse to transfer ownership outright, preferring to retain ownership in the underlying copyright and only license use of the materials to an advertiser. In fact, most sophisticated suppliers will insist on such an arrangement or require an excessive fee to transfer full ownership. While complete transfers can be structured legally, alternatives to ownership transfer are often necessary. Such alternatives include assignments and licenses. Where no agreement exists, a fallback position may be to argue that the materials were jointly created and that the advertiser or its advertising agency is co-owner, together with the supplier of the materials.

a. Assignments

It is the idea of transferring material as a "work-made-for-hire" that upsets most outside suppliers. In certain circumstances, material created by independent contractors can be acquired as a work-made-for-hire, vesting ownership of the work in the purchaser. Such arrangements are rare in the advertising industry. For some reason, outside suppliers look upon work-made-for-hire agreements as poison and won't even discuss the possibility in a negotiation. In situations where an advertiser or advertising agency still desires to obtain practical ownership, an assignment should be considered.

An assignment transfers complete ownership from the supplier to the agency. The supplier, however, can demand return of ownership after 35 years. In advertising, most material has a useful life of far less than 35 years. An assignment is, therefore, a legitimate alternative.

Like a work-made-for-hire agreement, assignments must be in writing and signed by the supplier in order to be effective.

b. Licenses

If a work-made-for-hire or assignment agreement is unavailable, the transfer can take the form of a license to use or exploit the materials for a specified period of time and for specified uses. Most works obtained from outside suppliers in the advertising industry are obtained via licenses. While a license can be oral, it is poor business practice to rely on anything less than a written license agreement. This is particularly true with respect to options. The key to drafting a license agreement is to be certain that the terms are very clearly set forth. In most instances, a license agreement is longer and more detailed than an assignment and tougher to negotiate since each point (e.g., area of use, term of use, media, payments, exclusivity, etc.) is open to discussion. Therefore, only the most experienced business-affairs manager should negotiate license agreements.

c. Joint Works

When all else fails and nothing is in writing, the advertiser or its advertising agency can try to argue that the materials are a joint work, owned by both the advertiser and the outside supplier. Nothing needs to be in writing to create a joint work, although a written understanding is preferred.

Whether material is a joint work depends upon the facts of each case. To claim joint ownership, a party must show that it contributed a substantial portion of the creative content of the material, i.e., was effectively the coauthor of the material. Another way to understand the concept: if neither party's contribution can stand on its own as an independent work, the finished material is probably a joint work of authorship.

In a joint authorship, each author is free to use the work or to license it to others without permission of the coauthor, unless there is an agreement to the contrary. This is the essential weakness to a joint work—neither party has control over the other's use of the material. Thus, joint-work status should only be a last resort and optimally subject to a written understanding outlining limits on usage by the respective authors.

Chapter Eighteen Forms

Form II.18.1 Agreement with Photographers—Work-Made-For-Hire/Buy-Out

[Advertising Agency/Advertiser Letterhead]

[Date]

[Photographer's Address]

Dear [Photographer's Name]:

This letter, when signed by the parties, will constitute a valid and binding agreement between [Agency/Advertiser] (hereinafter referred to as "Purchaser") and [Photographer] (hereinafter referred to as "Supplier") with respect to photography services provided by Supplier:

1. Grant of Rights. In the event that the material which is the subject of this Agreement is copyrightable subject matter, Supplier and Purchaser hereby agree that for the purposes of the agreement the photographs (hereinafter referred to as "Photographs") shall be a work-made-for-hire and the property of Purchaser. Purchaser shall have the right to secure copyright protection for the Photographs. In the event that the Photographs are not copyrightable subject matter, or for any reason cannot legally be a work-made-for-hire then, and in such event, Supplier hereby assigns all right, title, and interest to said Photographs to Purchaser and agrees to execute all documents required to evidence such assignment. Without limiting the foregoing, Supplier gives and grants to Purchaser the right to exclusive use of all Photographs prepared by Supplier pursuant to this Agreement, in all media and types of advertising and promotion of Purchaser. Purchaser shall have the unlimited right to exploit the Photographs as it sees fit, including the right to alter or rearrange the Photographs, throughout the United States and its territories and possessions. Purchaser's rights shall be exclusive, and Supplier will not use, license, or permit the use of the Photographs for any other purpose except as part of Supplier's portfolio.

2. Consideration. Purchaser agrees to pay Supplier and Supplier agrees to accept, in consideration of all services rendered by Supplier and the use of the results thereof and all rights granted by Supplier to Purchaser, the following compensation:

[insert compensation arrangement]

3. Supplier's Warranty. Unless otherwise provided in this Agreement, Supplier hereby represents and warrants: (a) that no third party has any rights in, to, or arising out of the Photographs supplied hereunder; (b) that Supplier has full right and power to enter into this Agreement; (c) that all models and any other living persons, or the representatives of any deceased persons whose names or likenesses are used in the Photographs, and the owners of any unique or unusual inanimate objects which are used in the Photographs, have executed releases allowing unlimited use by Purchaser

(Supplier shall supply Purchaser with copies of said releases with the Photographs hereunder); and (d) that the Photographs comply with Purchaser's specifications and are free from any material defects in design or workmanship; and (e) that the material supplied hereunder complies with and/or has been produced in accordance with all applicable state and federal laws and regulations.

4. Indemnity. Supplier agrees to hold Purchaser and its respective assigns and licensees harmless from and against any loss, damage, or expense, including court costs and reasonable attorneys' fees, that Purchaser and its assigns and licensees may suffer as a result of a breach or alleged breach of the foregoing warranties or as a result of claims or actions of any kind or nature resulting from the use in any manner of the Photographs. Purchaser agrees to similarly hold Supplier and its assigns and licensees harmless with respect to any material supplied by Purchaser.

5. Purchaser's Rejection and Approval Rights. Purchaser reserves the right to reject and not pay for Photographs not delivered in accordance with the specifications of this Agreement, including timely delivery, which is of the essence. Complaints, notice of defects in workmanship or design of the Photographs, or notice of rejection of any of the Photographs will be forwarded to Supplier promptly after Purchaser has reviewed the Photographs.

6. Supplier's Approval Rights. Supplier agrees that no advertisement or other material need be submitted to him or her for any further approval, and that Purchaser will be without liability to Supplier for any distortion or illusionary effect resulting from use of the Photographs.

7. Entire Agreement; Amendments. The terms and conditions set forth herein constitute the entire agreement between the parties and shall supersede all prior agreements. No waiver, modification, or addition to this Agreement shall be valid unless in writing and signed by the parties thereto.

8. Cancellation. This agreement may be canceled by Purchaser at any time prior to its acceptance of the Photographs, upon written notice to Supplier. In such event, Purchaser will pay Supplier, in lieu of the compensation specified in this Agreement, the direct non-cancelable costs theretofore incurred and any direct non-cancelable theretofore committed costs incurred by Supplier in the performance of its obligations hereunder prior to such cancellation; provided, however, that the total amount of such costs shall not exceed the price specified on the face of this Agreement.

9. Confidentiality. Supplier covenants and agrees that he or she will not disseminate, reveal, or otherwise make available to others, or use for his or her own purposes, any information of a proprietary or confidential nature concerning Purchaser learned by Supplier in the course of fulfilling this Agreement, including, but not limited to, advertising materials, ideas, plans, techniques, and products.

10. Use of Photographs. Purchaser shall not be required to utilize Supplier's services or the Photographs, it being understood that Purchaser's only obligation shall be to make the payments required pursuant to the provisions of this Agreement.

11. Assignment. The fulfillment of this Agreement, or any sums payable hereunder, may not be assigned by Supplier without the prior written consent of Purchaser.

12. Governing Law. The provisions hereof shall be interpreted in accordance with the laws of the State of _____.

[Agency/Advertiser]

By: _____

[Name]

ACCEPTED AND AGREED TO:

[Photographer]

By: _____

[Name]

Form II.18.2 Agreement with Photographers—License

[Advertising Agency/Advertiser Letterhead]

[Date]

[Photographer's Address]

Dear [Photographer's Name]:

This letter, when signed by the parties, will constitute a valid and binding agreement between [Agency/Advertiser] (hereinafter referred to as "Purchaser") and [Photographer] (hereinafter referred to as "Supplier") with respect to photography services provided by Supplier:

1. Grant of Rights. Supplier gives and grants to Purchaser for a period of _____(___) years (hereinafter referred to as the "Term") an exclusive license to use all photographs (hereinafter referred to as "Photographs"), prepared by Supplier pursuant to this Agreement, in all media and types of advertising and promotion of Purchaser. Purchaser shall have the unlimited right to exploit the Photographs as it sees fit in its advertising and promotion, including the right to alter or rearrange the Photographs, throughout the United States, its territories and possessions.

2. Consideration. Purchaser agrees to pay Supplier and Supplier agrees to accept, in consideration of all services rendered by Supplier and the use of the results thereof and all rights granted by Supplier to Purchaser, the following compensation:

[insert compensation arrangement]

3. Supplier's Warranty. Unless otherwise provided in this Agreement, Supplier hereby represents and warrants: (a) that no third party has any rights in, to, or arising out of the Photographs supplied hereunder; (b) that Supplier has full right and power to enter into this Agreement; (c) that all models and any other living persons, or the representatives of any deceased persons whose names or likenesses are used in the Photographs, and the owners of any unique or unusual inanimate objects which are used in the Photographs, have executed releases allowing unlimited use by Purchaser (Supplier shall supply Purchaser with copies of said releases with the Photographs hereunder); and (d) that the Photographs comply with Purchaser's specifications and are free from any material defects in design or workmanship; and (e) that the material supplied hereunder complies with and/or has been produced in accordance with all applicable state and federal laws and regulations.

4. Indemnity. Supplier agrees to hold Purchaser and its respective assigns and licensees harmless from and against any loss, damage, or expense, including court costs and reasonable attorneys' fees, that Purchaser and its assigns and licensees may suffer as a result of a breach or alleged breach of the foregoing warranties or as a result of claims or actions of any kind or nature resulting from the use in any manner of the Photographs. Purchaser agrees to similarly hold Supplier and its assigns and licensees harmless with respect to any material supplied by Purchaser.

5. Purchaser's Rejection and Approval Rights. Purchaser reserves the right to reject and not pay for Photographs not delivered in accordance with the specifications of this Agreement, including timely delivery, which is of the essence. Complaints, notice of defects in workmanship or design of the

Photographs, or notice of rejection of any of the Photographs will be forwarded to Supplier promptly after Purchaser has reviewed the Photographs.

6. Supplier's Approved Rights. Supplier agrees that no advertisement or other material need be submitted to him or her for any further approval, and that Purchaser should be without liability to Supplier for any distortion or illusionary effect resulting from use of the Photographs.

7. Entire Agreement; Amendments. The terms and conditions set forth herein constitute the entire agreement between the parties and shall supersede all prior agreements. No waiver, modification, or addition to this Agreement shall be valid unless in writing and signed by the parties thereto.

8. Cancellation. This agreement may be canceled by Purchaser at any time prior to its acceptance of the Photographs, upon written notice to Supplier. In such event, Purchaser will pay Supplier, in lieu of the compensation specified in this Agreement, the direct non-cancelable costs theretofore incurred and any direct non-cancelable theretofore committed costs incurred by Supplier in the performance of its obligations hereunder prior to such cancellation; provided, however, that the total amount of such costs shall not exceed the price specified on the face of this Agreement.

9. Confidentiality. Supplier covenants and agrees that he or she will not disseminate, reveal, or otherwise make available to others, or use for his or her own purposes, any information of a proprietary or confidential nature concerning Purchaser learned by Supplier in the course of fulfilling this Agreement, including, but not limited to, advertising materials, ideas, plans, techniques, and products.

10. Exclusivity and Endorsements. Supplier warrants, represents, and agrees that he or she has not authorized (which authorization is still in effect), and that throughout the Term hereof will not authorize or permit, the use of the Photographs for any other person, corporation, or business entity.

11. Use of Photographs. Purchaser shall not be required to utilize Supplier's services or the Photographs, it being understood that Purchaser's only obligation shall be to make the payments required pursuant to the provisions of this Agreement.

12. Assignment. The fulfillment of this Agreement, or any sums payable hereunder, may not be assigned by Supplier without the prior written consent of Purchaser.

13. Governing Law. The provisions hereof shall be interpreted in accordance with the laws of the State of _____.

[Agency/Advertiser]

By: _____

[Name]

ACCEPTED AND AGREED TO:

[Photographer]

By: _____

[Name]

Form II.18.3 Purchase-Order Form

[On the face of the order form, in bold type]:

DIRECTIONS FOR GENERAL PURCHASE-ORDER FORM PROVISIONS

THIS ORDER IS SUBJECT TO ALL THE TERMS AND CONDITIONS STATED ON THE FACE AND THE BACK OF THIS ORDER. IF ANY TERMS CONTAINED IN SUPPLIER'S ACCEPTANCE OF THIS ORDER OR IN SUPPLIER'S INVOICES ARE AT VARIANCE WITH THE TERMS OF THIS ORDER, THE TERMS OF THIS ORDER SHALL GOVERN. NO ORAL AGREEMENT OR OTHER UNDERSTANDING SHALL IN ANY WAY MODIFY OR CHANGE THE TERMS OF THIS ORDER UNLESS AGREED TO IN WRITING AND SIGNED BY AGENCY.

[At an appropriate place on the face of the order form]:

This order is entered into by (insert Agency's name) as agent for _____ . (Fill in blank with Agency's Client's name.)

[As a separate provision, on the face of the order form, in bold type]:

SUPPLIER MUST COUNTERSIGN A COPY OF THIS PURCHASE ORDER. UNLESS AGENCY HAS RECEIVED A COUNTERSIGNED COPY, SUPPLIER WILL NOT RECEIVE PAYMENT.

[As a separate provision, just above the space reserved for specifics
of any particular deal, in bold type, preferably red]:

UNLESS OTHERWISE NOTED IN THE FOLLOWING SPACE, ALL TERMS AND CONDITIONS ON THE BACK OF THIS ORDER ARE FULLY ACCEPTED BY SUPPLIER.

[On the reverse side of the order form]:

1. PARTIES. Agency is acting as agent for the Client named on the front of this purchase order ("PO"). The Agency will be liable for the stated payments to the Supplier only in the event that the Agency has been paid by the Client for the materials furnished hereunder. Supplier, acting as an independent contractor, warrants and represents that it has full power to accept and perform all terms and conditions of this PO.

2. DELIVERY OF RELEASES. Supplier shall not be entitled to payment for the material furnished hereunder unless all releases required herein have been delivered to Agency in a timely manner.

3. COPYRIGHT OWNERSHIP/USE. In the event that the material which is the subject of this PO is copyrightable subject matter, Supplier and Agency hereby agree that for the purposes of this PO the material shall be a work-made-for-hire and the property of Agency as agent for Client. In the event that any material which is the subject of this PO is not copyrightable subject matter, or for any reason cannot legally be a work-made-for-hire, then, and in such event, Supplier hereby assigns all right, title, and interest to said material to Agency as agent for Client and agrees to execute such documents as may be necessary to evidence such assignment(s). Any terms of ownership or use other than as provided in this paragraph must be specifically stated in writing on the front of this PO; otherwise any limitations on ownership or use shall be deemed void. Without limiting the foregoing, if Agency's right to use any material is in any way

limited in time, Supplier agrees that, during the period of use, Agency's rights shall be exclusive and Supplier will not use, license, or permit the use of the material for any other purpose, except only as may otherwise specifically be set forth on the front of this PO.

4. SCOPE OF RIGHTS. Without limiting the provisions of paragraph 3 hereof and unless otherwise provided on the front of this PO, the rights of Agency herein include, but are not limited to: (a) the right to use the material in such manner as Agency shall determine; (b) the right to alter or rearrange such material; (c) the right to secure copyright therein; and (d) the right to sell or otherwise exploit such material.

5. SUPPLIER'S WARRANTY. Unless otherwise provided on the front of this PO, Supplier hereby represents and warrants: (a) that no third party has any rights in, to, or arising out of, the material supplied hereunder; (b) that Supplier has full and exclusive right and power to enter into this Agreement; (c) that all models and any other living persons, or the representatives of any deceased persons whose names or likenesses are used in the material, and the owners of any unique or unusual inanimate objects which are used in the material, have executed releases allowing unlimited use by Agency; (d) that the material supplied hereunder complies with Agency's specifications and is free from any material defects in design or workmanship; and (e) that the material supplied hereunder complies with and/or has been produced in accordance with all applicable state and federal laws and regulations.

6. INDEMNITY. Supplier agrees to hold Agency, Client, and their respective assigns and licensees harmless from and against any loss, damage, or expense, including court costs and reasonable attorneys' fees, that Agency, Client, and their assigns and licensees may suffer as a result of any breach or alleged breach of the foregoing warranties or as a result of claims or actions of any kind or nature resulting from the use in any manner of the material furnished by Supplier hereunder. Agency similarly agrees to hold harmless Supplier and its assigns and licensees with respect to any materials supplied by Agency.

7. REJECTION AND APPROVAL RIGHTS. Agency reserves the right to reject and not pay for material not delivered in accordance with the specifications of this PO, including timely delivery, which is of the essence. Notice of defects in workmanship or design of the material, or notice of rejection of material, will be forwarded to Supplier promptly after Agency and/or Client have reviewed the material. If approval rights of Agency are to be limited in any way, it is the responsibility of Supplier to obtain Agency's written consent to such limitations, either on the front of this PO, or in a separate, written agreement signed by Agency.

8. ENTIRE AGREEMENT; AMENDMENTS. The terms and conditions set forth herein constitute the entire agreement between the parties. The price specified in this PO is firm except for the addition of sales and use taxes applicable to the services and materials provided. Agency will not recognize any claim for an increased price, unless approved by Agency in writing prior to the commencement of or during the course of completing the work. No charge will be allowed for packing, crating, transportation, or storage without the Agency's prior written consent. None of the directions provided Supplier by Agency's representatives during Supplier's fulfillment of this PO shall be considered a change of project specifications or shall justify a change in the agreed cost unless specifically agreed to in writing by the Agency.

9. CANCELLATION. This PO may be canceled by Agency at any time prior to its acceptance of the material covered by this PO, upon written notice to Supplier. In such event, Agency will pay Supplier, in lieu of the price specified on the front of this PO, the direct non-cancelable

costs theretofore incurred by Supplier and any direct non-cancelable costs committed in the performance of its obligations hereunder prior to such cancellation; provided, however, that the total amount of such costs shall not exceed the price specified on the face of this PO. Agency will not be responsible for any cancellation fees or penalties to Supplier unless so provided on the front of this PO or in a separate written agreement signed by the Agency and Supplier.

10. CONFIDENTIALITY. Supplier covenants and agrees that it will not disseminate, reveal, or otherwise make available to others, or use for its own purposes, any information of a proprietary or confidential nature concerning Agency or Client, learned by Supplier in the course of fulfilling this PO, regarding, but not limited to, trade secrets and confidential information, advertising materials, ideas, plans, techniques, and products.

11. ASSIGNMENT. The fulfillment of this PO, or any sums payable hereunder, may not be assigned by Supplier without the prior written consent of Agency.

12. AUDIT. Agency shall have the right to audit those financial records of Supplier which pertain to the material specified on the front of this PO, during ordinary business hours on not less than two (2) days' prior notice.

13. EXPENSES. In the event that pursuant to this PO, Supplier is entitled to reimbursement of expenses, said expenses must be substantiated, except for local taxi fares and gratuities, by (a) subcontractor invoices and/or vouchers, together with evidence of payment, and (b) a final and complete detailed itemization of each expenditure for which reimbursement is requested. All props or other material for which reimbursement is sought must be delivered to Agency prior to payment therefor. All expense discounts must be passed on to Agency. All expenses, except those of an incidental nature, must be in accord with prior estimates approved in writing by Agency.

14. GOVERNING LAW. The provisions hereof shall be interpreted in accordance with the laws of the State of [insert state in which agency is located].

Form II.18.4 General Release

In consideration of the payment to me of the sum of $\$$_____and other valuable consideration, receipt whereof is hereby acknowledged, I hereby agree as follows:

1. I hereby give and grant for a period of_____(_) years (hereinafter referred to as the "Term") to _____ ("Client") and _____ ("Agency/Advertiser"), and their respective licensees, successors, and assigns (herein collectively called the "licensed parties"), the right to use, publish, and copyright my name, voice, picture, portrait, and likeness in all media and types of advertising and promotion of _____, a product or service of Client.

2. I agree that all photographs of me used and taken by the licensed parties are owned by them and that they may copyright material containing same. If I should receive any print, negative, or other copy thereof, I shall not authorize its use by anyone else.

3. I agree that no advertisement or other material need be submitted to me for any further approval and the licensed parties shall be without liability to me for any distortion or illusionary effect resulting from the publication of my picture, portrait, or likeness.

4. I warrant and represent that this license does not in any way conflict with any existing commitment on my part. I have not heretofore authorized (which authority is still in effect), nor will I authorize or permit for the Term hereunder, the use of my name, picture, portrait, likeness, or testimonial statement in connection with the advertising or promotion of any product or service competitive to or incompatible with _____.

5. Nothing herein will constitute any obligation on the licensed parties to make any use of any of the rights set forth herein.

Signature _____

Print Name_____

Print Date_____

If releasor is not yet 21 years old, complete the following form:

I, the undersigned, hereby warrant that I am the _____ (insert the word "parent" or "guardian," as appropriate) of _____, a minor, and have full authority to authorize the above Release, which I have read and approved. I hereby release and agree to indemnify the licensed parties and their respective successors and assigns, from and against any and all liability arising out of the exercise of the rights granted by the above Release.

Signature of Parent or Guardian   _____

Address _____

Date: _____

Form II.18.5 Professional Model Release

In consideration of the following payments and other valuable consideration, receipt whereof is hereby acknowledged as provided herein, I hereby agree as follows:

1. I hereby give and grant to _____ ("Client") and _____ ("Agency/Advertiser"), and their respective licensees, successors, and assigns (herein collectively called the "licensed parties"), the right to use, publish, and copyright my picture, portrait, and likeness in advertising and promotion of _____, a product or service of Client, as follows:

    Term of Use ("Term"):

    Scope of Use:

    Territory:

    Compensation:

    Special Provisions:

2. I agree that all photographs of me used and taken by the licensed parties are owned by them and that they may copyright material containing same. If I should receive any print, negative, or other copy thereof, I shall not authorize its use by anyone else.

3. I agree that no advertisement or other material need be submitted to me for approval, and the licensed parties shall be without liability to me for any distortion or illusionary effect resulting from the publication of my picture, portrait, or likeness.

4. I warrant and represent that this license does not in any way conflict with any existing commitment on my part. I have not heretofore authorized (which authority is still in effect), nor will I authorize or permit for the Term hereunder, the use of my name, picture, portrait, likeness, or testimonial statement in connection with the advertising or promotion of any product or service competitive to or incompatible with _____.

5. Nothing herein will constitute any obligation on the licensed parties to make any use of the rights set forth herein.

Signature _____

Print Name _____

Print Date _____

If releasor is not yet 21 years old, complete the following form:

I, the undersigned, hereby warrant that I am the _____ (insert the word "parent" or "guardian," as appropriate) of _____, a minor, and have full authority to authorize the above Release, which I have read and approved. I hereby release and agree to indemnify the licensed parties and their respective successors and assigns, from and against any and all liability arising out of the exercise of the rights granted by the above Release.

Signature of Parent or Guardian _____

Address_____

Date: _____

Form II.18.6 Testimonial Release

In consideration of the payment to me of the sum of $_____ and other valuable consideration, receipt whereof is hereby acknowledged, I hereby agree as follows:

1. I give and grant for a period of _____(__) years (hereinafter referred to as the "Term" to _____ ("Client") and _____ ("Agency/Advertiser"), and their respective licensees, successors, and assigns (herein collectively called the "licensed parties"), the right to use, publish, and copyright my name, voice, picture, portrait, and likeness in all media and types of advertising and promotion of _____, a product or service of Client.

2. I agree that all photographs of me used and taken by the licensed parties are owned by them and that they may copyright material containing same. If I should receive any print, negative, or other copy thereof, I shall not authorize its use by anyone else.

3. I agree that no advertisement or other material need be submitted to me for any further approval, and the licensed parties shall be without liability to me for any distortion or illusionary effect resulting from the publication of my picture, portrait, or likeness.

4. I warrant and represent that this license does not in any way conflict with any existing commitment on my part. I have not heretofore authorized (which authority is still in effect), nor will I authorize or permit for the Term hereunder, the use of my name, picture, portrait, likeness, or testimonial statement in connection with the advertising or promotion of any product or service competitive to or incompatible with

5. I further agree that the licensed parties will have the right to attribute the attached statement (or statements in different words which have substantially the same meaning) to me, which is an expression of my personal experience and belief.

6. I agree that to the extent I shall require a product or service in its category, I shall continue to use Client's product or service during the term hereof.

7. Nothing herein will constitute any obligation on the licensed parties to make any use of any of the rights set forth herein.

Signature _____

Print Name _____

Print Date _____

Sworn to before me this _____ day of _____ in the year of _____

Notary Public _____

If releasor is not yet 21 years old, complete the following form:

I, the undersigned, hereby warrant that I am the _____ (insert the word "parent" or "guardian," as appropriate) of _____ , a minor, and have full authority to authorize the above Release, which I have read and approved. I hereby release and agree to indemnify the licensed parties and their respective successors and assigns, from and against any and all liability arising out of the exercise of the rights granted by the above Release.

Signature of Parent or Guardian _____

Address_____

Date: _____

Form II.18.7 Property Release

For valuable consideration, receipt whereof is hereby acknowledged, I hereby agree as follows:

1. I give and grant for a period of _____ years (hereinafter referred to as the "Term") to _____ ("Licensee") and its licensees, successors, and assigns (herein collectively called the "licensed parties"), the right to use, photograph, and publish the following property (the "Property") owned by the undersigned in all media and types of advertising and promotion of Licensee:

[Insert description of Property]

2. I agree that all photographs of the Property used and taken by the licensed parties are owned by them and that they may copyright material containing same. If I should receive any print, negative, or other copy thereof, I shall not authorize its use by anyone else.

3. The Property is owned by me and does not infringe upon or violate the copyrights or any other rights whatsoever of any person or entity. I have the full and exclusive right and authority to enter into this Agreement and to make the grant herein contained.

4. This license does not in any way conflict with any existing commitment on my part.

5. Nothing herein will constitute any obligation on the licensed parties to make any use of any of the rights set forth herein.

6. Unless otherwise agreed to in writing, the Licensee will not be responsible for any physical damage that may occur to the Property as a result of its use of the Property.

Signature _____

Print Name _____

Print Date _____

CHAPTER XIX
Dealing with Production Companies

If releasor is not yet 21 years old, complete the following form:

I, the undersigned, hereby warrant that I am the _____ (insert the word "parent" or "guardian," as appropriate) of _____, a minor, and have full authority to authorize the above Release, which I have read and approved. I hereby release and agree to indemnify the licensed parties and their respective successors and assigns, from and against any and all liability arising out of the exercise of the rights granted by the above Release.

Signature of Parent or Guardian _____

Address _____

Date: _____

1. Production Contracts

For the most part, commercial producers have adopted the standard contract for commercial production proposed by the Association of Independent Commercial Producers (AICP). While it is generally an acceptable form, there are some provisions that are less than advantageous to the advertising agency and advertiser. As a result, an advertiser or advertising agency is well advised to use its own form and negotiate the differences between that and the AICP form, when appropriate, for the particular job. A few key points deserve discussion. (See Form II.19.1.)

a. Cancellation

Of particular concern is the cancellation provision contained in the AICP form. If the production is canceled well in advance of the scheduled first day of production, the advertising agency should be required to pay the production house nothing more than its out-of-pocket expenses. If the production is canceled fewer than 30 days prior to production, problems regarding expense reimbursement and lost profits understandably arise, depending upon how short the notice actually is. The AICP form is anything but generous to the advertiser and its advertising agency in this regard. Instead, it provides for considerable payments to the production house despite adequate notice of cancellation. In addition, careful attention should be paid to the director's fee. Quite often, this fee must be paid regardless of when cancellation occurs. Since a director's fee can be substantial, this exposure should be addressed and fairly apportioned in the event of cancellation. Of course, if a top-line director is hired, it will be difficult to negotiate the cancellation fee.

b. Overages

The proper contract also covers contingencies in the event the production goes over budget, which is not uncommon. Overages can sometimes add more than 50% to a budget and, if not carefully controlled and addressed in the contract, can easily get out of hand, particularly if the director is given too much latitude to make creative changes. Always make it clear that someone from the advertising agency or advertiser has the final say as to costs. Also, any deviation from the script must be approved, even if the particular changes do not result in additional costs, as they may lead to other changes that will break the budget.

c. Audits

Auditing a production is always a problem. It is expensive and time-consuming. If a production is properly monitored during a shoot by the advertiser or advertising agency producer, auditing should generally be avoidable. Thus, the first thing to review if an audit becomes necessary is internal controls so that the mistake is not repeated. The sample form at the end of this chapter provides that if an audit is conducted and it is found that the production house is at fault, the production house will pay for the costs of the audit. Suffice it to say, this is a hotly contested provision, but one that is fair when the fault clearly lies with the production house.

d. Indemnities

Warranties and indemnities have also been strengthened in the sample form, placing additional responsibility on the production house for its contributions to the production and the conduct of its personnel during the production.

e. Ownership of Materials

The sample form also broadly defines ownership of the materials used in the course of production as the property of the advertising agency on behalf of its advertiser client. This prevents a production house from refusing to turn over a master recording or film as leverage in a negotiation with the advertising agency for additional edits, productions, or the like.

f. Paying Suppliers

Finally, delinquent payments by the production house to its suppliers used in the production can create considerable problems for the advertising agency and advertiser. The sample form allows the advertising agency to pay such suppliers directly and deduct the amount paid from future payments to the production house. This is the reason the contract must hold back at least 20% of the budget until final delivery of the commercial.

2. Fixed-Fee vs. Cost-Plus Contracts

In a fixed-fee contract, a single cost is set for the entire production. Unless an overage is approved by the advertising agency or advertiser, the completed commercial, ready for broadcast, should be delivered at no more than the fixed fee provided in the contract. Obviously, this is the preferable way to produce a commercial, since costs can be precisely budgeted. In some instances, however, exact costs cannot be determined and a cost-plus contract is the only alternative.

In a cost-plus contract, certain fees are fixed; e.g., the day rate for production personnel, the director's basic fee and day rate, and third-party rights fees, e.g., music. Otherwise, the production house is paid a fee equal to all the expenses of production, including agreed-upon overages, together with a percentage on top of it. Such percentages vary widely and can range from 10% to as much as 50%. If at all possible, cost-plus contracts should be avoided.

3. Dealing with Overages

Controlling overages is really quite simple—one person present at the shoot has the authority for overages. This individual works for the advertiser or its advertising agency and is experienced in commercial production. It sounds simple enough, but all too often overages are approved by a number of people and not confirmed in writing. The personnel at the shoot get caught up in the production, losing sight of cost controls. Someone has to be in charge at the shoot and strong enough to say "no" more often than "yes."

Chapter Nineteen Forms

Form II.19.1 Television Commercial Production Contract

[On the front side of the form]

Client: _____

Production Company: _____

Product: _____

Production Contact: _____

Agency Producer: _____

Director: _____

Agency Business Mgr.: _____

Editorial Subcontractor: _____

Special Subcontractor: _____

This agreement is entered into between _____(hereinafter referred to as the "Agency") as agent for Client, and Production Company (hereinafter referred to as the "Contractor"), for Contractor to produce a filmed and/or videotaped commercial(s) (hereinafter referred to as the "Film" and/or "Tape") in accordance with the scripts and/or storyboards in a manner satisfactory to the Agency under the following terms and conditions:

Commercial Number(s), Title(s), and Length(s):

Description of Job:

      ☐　Actual Costs, plus fixed fee:
      [or]
      ☐　Firm Bid:

Production Schedule

No. Studio Shoot Days: _____

No. Location Shoot Days: _____

Pre-Production Wk/of: _____

Shoot Date: _____

Answer Print or VTR/Master Date: _____

Production Requirements:

The following materials and elements will be furnished by Agency (Agcy.), Contractor (Ctr.), or Subcontractor (Subct.), as indicated:

	Acny.	Ctr.	Subct.
Casting	☐	☐	☐
Principal Talent Payments	☐	☐	☐
Extra Payments	☐	☐	☐
Client Products	☐	☐	☐
Color Corrected Packages	☐	☐	☐
Sets & Props	☐	☐	☐
Stock Footage	☐	☐	☐
Stylist	☐	☐	☐
Wardrobe	☐	☐	☐
Make-up	☐	☐	☐
Hairstyle	☐	☐	☐
Home Economist	☐	☐	☐
Dailies Screening	☐	☐	☐
Location	☐	☐	☐
Animation	☐	☐	☐
SFX	☐	☐	☐
Titles & Art	☐	☐	☐
Original Music	☐	☐	☐
Stock Music	☐	☐	☐
Special Insurance (Rider Attached)	☐	☐	☐
Other	☐	☐	☐

Specify:

Photography

Film:

Color	☐
B&W	☐
35mm	☐
16mm	☐

Videotape:

Color	☐
B&W	☐
1"	☐
2"	☐
3/4"	☐

Camera reports, AD reports, and script notes are to be supplied to the agency producer upon completion of photography.

Schedule of Costs:

Cost of photography/videotaping and delivery of acceptable production elements, including any special subcontracting elements. Completion of film/videotape: For approved interlock(s), (rough cut) picture(s), sound elements, videotape master, and cassettes: $ _____

Production Subtotal: $_____

Editorial Subtotal: $_____

Total Contract Price (Total Editorial and Production): $_____

Payment Schedule

_____ % upon execution of this Agreement, net _____ days;

_____ % upon execution of this Agreement, net _____ days;

_____ % upon execution of this Agreement, net _____ days.

Disposition of Elements

Production Elements—original picture negatives and dailies to:

Original videotape master(s), magnetic sound tracks, and ½" audiotape, shipped by common carrier, prepaid, and issued to Client's storage facilities at:

General

In full consideration for Contractor's satisfactory performance of all terms and conditions of this Agreement as well as all the rights granted herein, Contractor shall receive the total contract costs as listed above. Payment of said sums shall be conditioned upon delivery, approval, and acceptance of the materials listed in Section VI above as well as delivery of a proper memorandum from all Subcontractors of the commercial(s) who would have the right to exercise a lien on materials produced hereunder, advising that they have received full payment for their work on the commercial(s).

When fully executed by the parties, this Agreement, with the terms and conditions set forth on the reverse side and any rider(s) attached hereto, shall constitute the entire understanding between the parties with respect to the subject matter of this Agreement.

[Contractor]   [Agency]

                                               (acting on behalf of above-named Client)

By: _____   By: _____

Date: _____   Date: _____

[On the reverse side of the form]

Standard Terms and Conditions for Production of Television Commercials

1. Materials and Services To Be Supplied

   Except as otherwise specifically provided herein, you will supply all services and materials required for production of the commercial(s) named herein, including, but not limited to, the following: production, technical and directorial personnel, photography, sound recordings, studio facilities, locations, casting, wardrobe, animation, talent, screening facilities, and all editorial services necessary to complete and deliver to Agency the commercial elements contracted for herein and/or the completed commercial(s); without any obligation on the part of Agency, except for payment of the agreed-upon contract price stated on the face hereof, upon due performance by you.

2. Ownership

   In the event that the work and material which is the subject of this contract is copyrightable subject matter, you and Agency hereby agree that, for the purpose of this contract, the work and material shall be a work-made-for-hire and the property of Agency as agent for the within-named client. In the event that the work and material which is the subject of this contract is not copyrightable subject matter, or for any reason is determined not to be a work-made-for-hire, then you hereby grant all right, title, and interest to said work and material to Agency as agent for the within-named Client, and you will promptly execute and deliver such documents as may be requested by Agency in order to accomplish the transfer of all such right, title, and interest.

3. Agent

   In the making, execution, and performance of this contract, Agency is acting solely as agent for the within-named Client.

4. Independent Contractor

   In the making, execution, and performance of this contract, you are an independent contractor and you warrant that the commercial(s) produced under this contract shall be produced in compliance with all federal, state, and local laws. All contracts made by you in furtherance of rendering performance under this contract are entered into by you as principal and not as agent for Agency or the within-named Client.

5. Quality

   It is of the essence to this contract that any commercial(s) produced under this contract in all respects will be of first and Class A aesthetic and artistic quality and technically equal to current SMPTE and ASA standards, all subject to Agency approval and acceptance. All pertinent photography and opticals will be within the television safety margin of the motion picture or videotape frame size so as to be visible to the television viewer.

6. Agency Supervision and Approval and Price Adjustment

   The duly designated Agency production representative will be permitted to be present at any time and at all places during any stage of production of the commercial(s). Such production representative will be authorized to approve any and all elements of the production or changes in the production which are subject to or require approval by Agency. You agree to secure Agency approval prior to making any changes in, or variations from, the scripts or storyboards during the course of production. Agency will be notified in advance as to the time and place of all stages of production. At Agency's request, you will submit for its inspection and approval materials completed or in process at each completed stage of the production and will make any reasonable changes, variations, or substitutions in the work as requested. If such requests for changes, variations, or substitutions will result in additional costs for the production, and are not due to your fault or failure, Agency will pay the additional costs, if you present an estimate thereof, in writing, which estimate is first approved by the Agency's duly designated representative. Without prior written approval, Agency will not be liable for any additional costs.

7. Warranty

You warrant that you have full right and power to enter into this Agreement.

You further warrant that you will obtain and furnish to Agency, prior to the delivery of the completed commercial(s), legal and effective written consents, waivers, releases, copyright assignments, patents and licenses, authorizations, and other agreements, in form and substance requested by Agency or approved by Agency, covering all persons, work, and materials used by you in connection with the commercial(s) (except persons, matter, and materials supplied to you by Agency), you will also insure the right of the within-named Client to free, unlimited, and unrestricted broadcast exhibition and use in any way or place worldwide of said commercial(s) or any part thereof, without limitation, including, but not limited to, the right to substitute, "double," and "dub" voices, acts, poses, and sound effects by or with others in any language for any cast members either alone or in connection with other matter, in any media and by any means now known or hereafter devised, for any and all purposes including trade, publicity, and advertising without limitation as to time, products use, or otherwise, by Agency, its clients, sponsors, exhibitors, broadcasters, and others authorized by Agency or the within-named Client, except with respect to limitations imposed by applicable union agreements.

You warrant that the commercial(s) when delivered to Agency will be free and clear of any and all claims, liens, mortgages, and any other encumbrances of any kind or character (except with respect to the scripts and materials furnished by Agency and with respect to limitations imposed by applicable union agreements) and that the commercial(s) will not infringe upon the personal rights, including civil rights or privacy, of any person or group, nor violate any federal, state or local law, ordinance, or regulation.

8. Indemnification

You will indemnify and hold Agency, the within-named Client, nominees, successors, licensees, and assigns and all broadcasters, exhibitors, and other users of the commercial(s) and any elements thereof, as authorized by Agency and/or the within-named client, harmless from and against any and all damages, expenses, claims, suits, judgments, penalties, and costs including reasonable counsel fees and all costs of any kind, which may be obtained against, imposed upon, accrued against, or be suffered by Agency or any of the foregoing by reason of your breach of any of the warranties or covenants herein contained, and from any injury to persons and loss or damage to property arising out of or resulting from your negligent acts, failure to act, or willful misconduct or from any use by Agency of the commercials furnished by you hereunder. Agency will similarly indemnify you with respect to the scripts and material furnished by Agency.

9. Union Agreement

You agree to comply with all rules, regulations, and requirements of any applicable collective bargaining agreement with any union representing performers, technicians, and other personnel employed by you or in any way participating in the production of the commercial(s). Under no circumstances, however, will your compliance be deemed an agreement by either Agency or its within-named Client to become a signatory to any such collective bargaining agreement. You will indemnify and hold Agency and the within-named Client and other authorized users harmless from and against any and all damages, expenses, claims, suits, judgments, penalties, and costs, including reasonable counsel fees and all losses of any kind, arising out of your actual or alleged breach of such agreements.

10. Screen Actors Guild (SAG) and American Federation of Television and Radio Artists (AFTRA)

As an integral part of this Agreement you hereby agree that all players employed by you hereunder will be paid the minimum wage and be given all rights set forth in the current SAG or AFTRA contract, whichever is applicable, in every respect, as if you were directly a party and signatory of said contract. It is further expressly agreed for the benefit of SAG or AFTRA, whichever has jurisdiction, and the players affected thereby that the respective Guild or Federation is hereby given the full right and power on its own behalf and on behalf of said players to enforce all rights and conditions contained in the aforementioned contract against you as if this Agreement were entered into directly with SAG or AFTRA by you.

Within three (3) days after the performance of any talent, you will furnish Agency's designated representative with the following for each person employed by you in each commercial: original SAG or AFTRA employment contracts completely filled out and signed by you and the talent, appropriately completed and signed Federal and State Withholding Report forms, Production Time Reports, and Commercial Audition Report Forms. All contracts used by you must be approved by Agency as to form. Without limiting the foregoing, it is agreed that Agency's standard employment contract for television commercials, including time card and withholding certificate, when used for the employment of all performers in each commercial produced hereunder, is deemed approved. For any players hired by you and paid according to the wage scales of a collective bargaining agreement other than SAG or AFTRA, or players paid by you at negotiated rates not part of any collective bargaining agreement, you agree to furnish to Agency executed releases substantially in the forms requested by Agency and a list of all such talent in each commercial, the role each person played, and the amount paid by you to each person.

You further agree to be liable for any penalty payments resulting from late or improper payments or session fees, except when payment of session fees is the obligation of Agency and you have delivered the appropriate contracts, reports, and forms within the time limit specified above. You further agree to be liable for any penalty payments resulting from the hiring of persons "not covered" or "not in good standing" under the SAG and AFTRA contracts or for whom you failed to comply with the appropriate "preference" or "Union Security" requirements.

11. Contract Cancellation

Agency will have the right to cancel this Agreement by written notice to you at any time prior to Agency's acceptance of the completed product. In the event of such cancellation, you will repay to Agency all payments theretofore made to you under this Agreement and will deliver to Agency all completed and uncompleted films, tapes, and materials produced hereunder; and Agency will be liable to pay you, in lieu of the agreed price hereunder, a sum which will reimburse you for the reasonable direct costs and expenses which you have incurred in the normal, efficient routine of production to the date of cancellation, including any authorized third party's charges incurred by you on Agency's behalf, plus a negotiated sum not to exceed 30% of such direct costs and expenses to cover overhead, profit, directors, and creative fees. For purposes of calculating 30% of direct costs and expenses, it is expressly understood that such direct costs and expenses will not include amounts for overhead, profit, directors, and creative fees. In no case will Agency pay you more than the agreed price hereunder.

12. Insurance

You agree that you have, or will obtain from an insurance carrier acceptable to Agency, and you will, at your own expense, maintain, insurance covering all picture and sound track elements created during this commercial production. Such insurance will be in an amount sufficient to cover the replacement cost of such elements against all hazards or risks customarily insured against in the motion-picture production industry and on terms and conditions approved by Agency. It is also understood that you carry, at your own expense, the following insurance: Comprehensive General Liability Endorsement, Contractual Liability, Business Auto Liability, Workers' Compensation, Employers Liability, and Professional Liability; all with limits on the Insurers' Coverage in no event less than $1,000,000 with respect to injury or death to any one person, not less than $5,000,000 with respect to injuries to or death of any number of persons in any one occurrence, and not less than $1,000,000 in respect of damage to or loss of use of property in any one occurrence, or in the alternative a $5,000,000 Combined Single-Limit Liability to cover any injury or damage to persons, including, but not limited to, all performers, whether principals or extras engaged by you, or to any property arising out of or in any way connected with the production of the herein-named commercial(s). Agency and its Client shall be named as additional insureds to protect their interests on such insurance policies. All such policies shall further waive any right of contribution from insurance held or owned by Agency or its Client. A certificate of insurance evidencing such coverage shall be provided to Agency upon request, and must provide that such insurance may not be materially altered or canceled on less than fifteen (15) days' prior written notice to Agency.

13. Regulatory

You are cognizant of the requirements of the Federal Trade Commission and other regulatory organizations relating to demonstration techniques employed in television commercials. You agree, warrant, and represent that in the production of the commercial(s) you will not use any mock-ups or substitute materials or employ trick photography without written disclosure thereof to Agency and without first having obtained Agency's specific written approval. You will not engage in any deceptive practice in the production of the commercial(s) and will indemnify and hold harmless Agency and the within-named Client with respect to any and all costs, including counsel fees, which may arise from a violation of your obligations hereunder.

14. Return of Properties and Insurance

It is agreed that you will return all properties, products, and materials supplied to you by Agency upon the completion of production and that you will not have any right, title, and interest therein. You agree to have all properties, products, and materials covered by insurance against all loss, damage, hazard, and risk, in an amount sufficient to cover the replacement thereof.

15. Auditing

You agree that Agency, at its request, will have the right to audit the costs you have charged Agency. You therefore agree to provide all cost information, invoices, and other relevant information related to such productions, upon reasonable notice by Agency, at your place of business during normal business hours. In the event such audit reveals that you have spent or permitted the spending of more than ten percent (10%) of the original budget without proper authorization from the Agency, you will absorb the unauthorized expense and the Agency's out-of-pocket costs of conducting the audit.

16. Delinquent Supplier Payments

Agency reserves the right in cases of delinquent payments by you to suppliers performing work on or furnishing material for this production to: (a) pay such suppliers directly, irrespective of any setoff or counterclaims you may have against the supplier(s), an amount equal to the money owed such supplier(s) for work the supplier has furnished or is furnishing for this production (and such payment will be deemed payment to you and will reduce the contract price herein by the amount of any such payment), and, at Agency's election, have such supplier(s) deliver such commercials and all materials relating thereto directly to Agency (and you hereby expressly authorize such delivery), or (b) terminate this Agreement without further obligation to you, and you will immediately deliver to Agency all then-existing components of the commercial(s) and all materials related thereto.

17. Nondisclosure

You agree that all work to be performed by you herein will be treated by you in the strictest confidence and will not be disclosed to anyone other than persons authorized by Agency to receive such information. You further agree, at Agency's request, to require those you employ for this production to sign appropriate agreements not to discuss or disclose information about the product or the production.

18. Bankruptcy

If at any time prior to the complete performance hereof by you, there will be filed by or against you a petition in bankruptcy, insolvency, or reorganization, or for the appointment of a receiver or trustee of all or part of your property, or should you make an assignment for the benefit of creditors, no further payments will be due to you from Agency hereunder. In the event of any of the foregoing, at Agency's option and upon written notice to you, this Agreement will forthwith terminate, and you will immediately deliver to Agency all elements or parts of any commercial(s) fully or partially completed by you and any and all materials contained in such commercial(s), and Agency will have no further obligation to you.

19. Waiver

The failure of any party to this Agreement to exercise any rights granted herein upon the occurrence of any of the contingencies set forth in this Agreement will not constitute a waiver of any such rights upon the recurrence of any such contingency.

20. Applicable Law

    This Agreement and all matters or issues collateral thereto will be governed by the laws of the State of _____ applicable to contracts made and performed entirely therein.

21. Assignment of Contract

    This Agreement may not be assigned by either party without the written consent of the other; except that the within-named Client at any time will have the right to designate itself or any advertising agency or firm in the place and stead of Agency, and upon such designation, the contract will be read and construed as if the Client's name or the name of the advertising agency or firm so designated by the Client were substituted for "Agency" wheresoever the same shall appear in this Agreement.

22. Equal Employment Opportunity Company

    In connection with your performance hereunder, you agree not to discriminate against any employee or applicant for employment because of race, religion, color, sex, or national origin.

23. Publicity

    You agree not to use the name of Agency, the within-named Client, or the product(s) or service(s) advertised in the commercial(s) in any advertising or publicity or for any promotional purposes without Agency's prior written consent.

24. Arbitration

    All disputes between the parties concerning any matter relating to this Agreement shall be subject to arbitration under the Commercial Rules of the American Arbitration Association. Arbitration shall be the exclusive forum available to the parties, and all hearings shall take place in the City of _____ , State of _____ . [N.B.: Arbitration clause is optional; delete if not desired.]

CHAPTER XX
Dealing with Media

It is not uncommon in the advertising industry for millions of dollars to be spent without a single signed contract. Although contrary to basic legal principles, this works more often than not. Nonetheless, contracts with media should be considered, particularly with the ever-increasing friction between media and advertising agencies. (See Form II.20.1.)

Never sign a contract submitted by media without consulting legal counsel, regardless of the circumstances. Staff should be instructed accordingly.

1. Advertising Agency Media Order Liability and Sequential Liability

In the early part of the century, advertising agencies worked for the media, not the advertisers. As a result, advertising agencies were compensated with commissions from the media. In that sense, the relationship of the advertising agency to media was as a principal, not as an agent, for the advertiser. From this relationship the tradition arose that the advertising agency, not the advertiser, was responsible for payments to the media. This concept was adopted by the American Association of Advertising Agencies (AAAA) and became the rule for decades. In a 1988 release, the AAAA expressed the policy as follows:

> The AAAA believes that the principle of sole liability is relied upon through the industry and that its continued use is in the best interest of the industry as a whole and advertising agencies in particular. Therefore, we recommend that members using the new contract form require a sole liability statement as part of any agreement reflected in the contract. If no sole liability clause is included in materials received from the station from which it is buying time, we recommend that such a statement be typed or printed by the agency on the front page of the contract in a manner intended to make clear that the principle of sole liability governs the contract. Such a statement might read: "Station agrees to hold agency solely liable for payments to be made under this contract."

The 1988 language came about after several years of negotiation with the broadcast industry on new contract language for media forms that had not been changed since 1970. While agreement was reached on new language relating to a variety of issues, the AAAA and the broadcast industry were unable to agree on language regarding liability for media charges. The media insisted on joint and several liability, i.e., the right to go after either the agency or the advertiser, and were not willing to concede to any change. So as not to lose the opportunity to issue updated media forms incorporating the agreed-upon changes, the AAAA and the broadcast industry agreed that no mention of any type of liability would appear in the published agreed-upon conditions. Thus, the spot television forms issued in 1986 and the spot radio forms issued in 1988 included the language noted above, although its inclusion was not agreed upon by the broadcasting industry any more than their concept of joint and several liability was agreed upon by the AAAA.

Unfortunately, in the late 1980s and early 1990s, increasing media costs were coupled with economic recessions. Some advertising agencies went bankrupt, leaving media unpaid. In other instances, advertising agencies, particularly smaller ones, found themselves holding the bag for bankrupt advertisers, paying media and never recovering the expenses. This was largely due to the fact that media had the leverage of refusing advertising for other clients of the advertising agency if one client's account remained unpaid. (As a result, advertising agencies began inserting variations of the AAAA's policy on media's joint- and several-liability orders.) Many disclaimed any liability whatsoever, stating that their purchases were on behalf of a disclosed principal and that the advertiser was solely liable. Most media rejected such provisions. Other advertising agencies adopted policies stating that they were liable only if they were paid by the advertiser, a standard that became known as sequential liability.

In 1991, the AAAA responded to industry concerns and adopted the sequential liability theory. Under sequential liability, an advertising agency is responsible to media only if the advertising agency has been paid by the advertiser. If it has not been paid, then media must look to the advertiser for payment and the advertising agency is not responsible. The precise wording now recommended by the AAAA reads as follows (Newspaper Contract, January 2003): "Unless otherwise set forth by the Agency on the face of this form, the Publisher agrees to hold the Agency solely liable for payment to the extent proceeds have cleared from the Advertiser to the Agency for advertising published in accordance with the contract. For sums owing but not cleared to the Agency, the Publisher agrees to hold the Advertiser named on the face of this form solely liable."

Sequential liability, however, has yet to be willingly accepted by media. Given the time over which it has been a part of agency forms, however, the argument exists that it has become trade practice. That argument, however, is suspect given the relatively consistent objection from media. Therefore, unless an advertising agency has written agreements with media that sequential liability will apply, it is difficult to predict if courts will uphold the concept as a matter of trade practice. In short, the status of liability will depend upon the paperwork and the historical relationship between the parties. Hopefully, if more media become amenable to the sequential liability theory, it may be deemed accepted trade practice at some point in the future.

One reason that it will take years for the policy change to become an industry practice is that it is uncommon for an advertising agency to sign a media confirmation form or for media to sign the advertising agency's insertion order. As a result, courts are faced with the proverbial battle of the forms and it will take years to resolve the issues. Suffice it to say that inserting language in an advertising agency form is a far cry from resolving the issue.

Because of the controversy, some agencies are now requesting that their clients pay media directly and that the advertiser then remit the commission to the agency. This will work only if media agree, and qualify the advertiser as an "in-house agency" so that the advertiser gets the agency discount to pass on to its advertising agency as the agency's commission.

Why It Matters

1. A New York case decided on September 17, 1991, illustrates the problem. Press reports proclaimed that the decision dealt a severe blow to the AAAA theory of sequential liability. Unfortunately, the press reported neither the facts nor the import of the decision accurately.

    The facts were simple. Gerry Gilbert Advertising was the advertising agency for Tower Financial Corporation. The advertising agency placed insertion orders with the *Wall Street Journal* that included the disclaimer, "client is responsible for billing costs." For some reason, not discussed in the decision, Tower Financial did not pay the advertising agency and media charges went in arrears. Dow Jones, owner of the *Wall Street Journal*, sued the advertising agency for unpaid insertions.

    The court chose not to rely upon the disclaimer. Instead, it found that the course of conduct between the advertising agency and the *Wall Street Journal* negated the disclaimer and supported a finding that the advertising agency, not the advertiser, was primarily liable for the media costs. In coming to this conclusion, the court relied on the following:

    a. All invoices were sent to the advertising agency, and payments to the *Journal* were made by advertising agency checks;

b. Despite receiving dunning notices from the *Wall Street Journal*, the advertising agency never denied liability. The first denial and reliance on the disclaimer came after Dow Jones brought suit; and

c. The advertising agency sued Tower Financial for the amount due. If the advertising agency's position that it was not liable was correct, it made no logical sense for the advertising agency to sue its advertiser client. By suing the advertiser client, the advertising agency admitted that it had independent liability.

The court found that this course of dealing between the advertising agency and the *Wall Street Journal* negated the disclaimer. The court did not discuss, much less hold, that disclaimers were not sufficient to relieve an advertising agency of liability if it was never paid by an advertiser.

Of particular import is the court's devotion of two full paragraphs of its short decision to advise the parties that its findings were limited solely to the facts before the court. The court clearly stated that its decision was not intended to be a pronouncement on the relative rights of the media or advertising industries as to the question of media liability.

Thus, very little can be concluded on the basis of the Gerry Gilbert case. It cannot be cited as significant in the discussion of liability to media when an advertising agency has not been paid. Indeed, the court never discussed the theories, let alone the application, of sequential liability or the use and affect of disclaimers.

2. In a case that held against the prevailing view of advertising agency liability, a New York court ruled against the New York Times Company in its suit against an advertising agency for media bills unpaid by a bankrupt advertiser represented by the advertising agency. The court relied on basic principles of agent/principal law and dismissed the case, finding that the advertising agency was merely an agent for a disclosed principal and could not be held independently liable. The court record does not indicate that the New York Times Company sought to introduce evidence of industry practice or AAAA policies.

3. In a California case, advertising agency Scott, Lancaster, Mills & Atha, Inc. found itself a defendant in an action by ten independent television-station owners for media time ordered by the advertising agency on behalf of its then-bankrupt advertiser client, National Service Corporation. Relying largely on the older AAAA policy, the court found the advertising agency liable for the media costs, even though it had never been paid by its advertiser client.

4. In an unreported case in California, a trial court held that in the absence of a signed agreement, there was not a "meeting of the minds" as between joint and several liability (argued by the media) and sequential liability (argued by a media buying company that had not been paid by a bankrupt client for media time or space that had run). In the absence of an agreement, the court ruled that basic principles of agent/principal law applied. Under such rules, an agent for a disclosed principal is not independently liable for the obligations of the principal. As a result, the court dismissed the media's claim. While this case is unreported, its legal logic is sound.

Included as Appendix 5 is a position paper issued by the AAAA in July 1991, together with responsive comments by media ass333ociations regarding sequential liability and its evolution and acceptance in the industry. It sets forth in detail how the theory came to be and why media continue to object to it.

2. Media Refusal to Run Advertising

Generally, media are under no obligation to accept advertising from an advertiser or its advertising agency. The media have a constitutional right to refuse advertising on virtually whatever basis they choose, as long as the choice is unilateral and not part of a conspiracy. It may, for example, refuse a category of advertising, e.g., contraceptives; or a particular advertiser for internal corporate purposes, e.g., advertising for an advertiser that has criticized the editorial content of a publication. Only in the rare instance when the medium is the only available method to advertise in a particular market can it be argued that advertising must be accepted. For example, in some towns that have only one newspaper, the newspaper has been ordered to accept advertising for X-rated movies shown at theaters in the community.

Media may not, however, agree with one competitor to exclude another competitor from its pages or its airwaves. To do so risks violations of the antitrust laws.

Chapter Twenty Forms

Form II.20.1 Checklist for Print and Broadcast Media Contracts

A. Print Media

☐ 1. Reproduction material should be reviewed by print media against a proof and the insertion order to make sure it agrees in every respect.

☐ 2. Two copies of tearsheets containing the advertisement(s) should be sent to the agency with the invoice. The agency should reserve the right not to pay bills unless proof of publication is received.

☐ 3. Unless print media is a member of the Audit Bureau of Circulations, the agency should be entitled, upon request, to a statement of circulation verified by a certified public accountant or other auditing organization.

B. Broadcast Media

☐ 1. Broadcast media invoices should contain the advertiser's name, the product or service advertised, the date, time, and length of commercial announcement, media costs, and, where applicable, the assigned ISCI code for each commercial announcement.

☐ 2. The broadcast media should warrant that all information shown on its invoice is true and correct and was taken from the commercial record produced and maintained at the media.

☐ 3. Broadcast media have the right to cancel any broadcast or portion thereof covered by this Agreement in order to broadcast any program which, in its absolute discretion, is of public significance. In any such case, the media should notify the agency in advance, if reasonably possible, but where such notice cannot reasonably be given, the media should notify the agency within one (1) business day after such broadcast was canceled. If the agency and the media cannot agree upon a satisfactory substitute day and time, the broadcast time so preempted should be deemed canceled without affecting the rates, discounts, or rights provided under the contract except that the agency will not have to pay the charges for the canceled broadcast.

☐ 4. Broadcast media should be required to advise the agency by telephone, and subsequently by written confirmation, if the agency-furnished program or commercial material and scheduling instructions do not arrive three (3) business days in advance of broadcast date.

C. Print and Broadcast Media

In addition to the above, the following media-specific points should be addressed.

☐ 1. Advertising should be inserted or aired only in accordance with the schedule and instructions given.

☐ 2. If the media is unable to insert/broadcast on dates ordered, or if reproduction/broadcast material is damaged, the agency should be notified immediately.

☐ 3. Copy changes or alterations to the materials supplied by the agency should not be made unless approved by the agency prior to insertion.

☐ 4. Advance copy/proofs should be submitted to the agency for approval before insertion/broadcast if revisions or additions are made by the media.

☐ 5. All materials should be held by the media for future use or returned or disposed of as direct-

CHAPTER XXI
Dealing with Actors, Agents, and Talent Brokers

ed by the agency.

☐ 6. Advertising authorized by an order should be billed at a specified rate provided in the order.

☐ 7. Rebates should be given if the total amount of space/time used during a contract period entitles the advertiser to a better rate than that paid.

☐ 8. The media should represent that the agreement contains the minimum rate at which an equal or less amount of space/time, for the same class of advertising, to be published/broadcast in a like position, under the same conditions, within the same period of time, can be secured at the time the agreement was entered into.

☐ 9. If additional space/time is used within the period covered by the agreement, where the media have a schedule of graduated rates, any lower rate should be given, if earned, according to the media's rate card (if any).

☐ 10. The agency should be free to cancel an order prior to the cancellation or closing date stated in the media's rate card.

☐ 11. If, due to public emergency or necessity, *force majeure*, restrictions imposed by law, acts of God, labor disputes, or for any other cause, including mechanical or electronic breakdowns, beyond the media's control, there is an interruption or omission of any advertisement/commercial announcement or program contracted to be published/broadcast hereunder, the media should suggest a substitute publication or time period for the publication/broadcast.

☐ 12. If a substitute time period, or make-good, is not acceptable to the agency, the media should allow the agency a pro-rata reduction of the space, time, and/or program charges.

☐ 13. All obligations should be subject to applicable federal, state, and local laws and regulations.

☐ 14. The contract should not be assignable or transferable by the media without first obtaining the consent of the agency in writing.

☐ 15. All parties should covenant and agree that they will not disseminate, reveal, or otherwise make available to others, or use for their own purposes, any information of a proprietary or confidential nature concerning the agency or the agency's named client learned in the course of fulfilling the order, regarding, but not limited to, trade secrets and confidential information, advertising materials, ideas, plans, techniques, and products.

☐ 16. If at all possible, in placing the order, the agency should be acting solely as the authorized agent for its client, and assume no liability for the payment of any charges in connection with the order except to the extent it has received payment from its client for the purchase.

1. Making Offers

Contracts with celebrities do not have to be in writing to be enforceable. An oral agreement to hire talent is binding, and unless offers are carefully worded, an advertising agency or advertiser may be assuming liabilities before its management fully approves a transaction. All offers made by an advertising agency should provide that they are made subject to the advertiser's approval (preferably in writing). All offers made by advertisers should state that they are effective only upon approval of an appropriate executive of the company. Finally, either avoid making a firm offer altogether, or never extend a firm offer unless the appropriate executives have signed off on it.

Why It Matters

Talent agents are very expert in the process of offering and counteroffering, and without strict internal controls on those who handle the process, considerable losses may be incurred. Furthermore, if the advertising agency has been the sloppy player in the process, its client is probably justified in demanding that the advertising agency absorb all of the damages. Since celebrity-talent deals can range in the hundreds of thousands, and sometimes millions, of dollars, mistakes can be very costly.

2. Negotiating Celebrity Talent Contracts

Negotiating with celebrity talent should not be left to amateurs. Experienced talent agents generally know more about the going price for talent in commercials or print campaigns than most advertising executives. They are also expert in the many "tricks" that can be used to increase a talent's compensation, such as requiring future negotiations for rights not adequately obtained in the first negotiation. For example, if an advertising agency or advertiser does not carefully consider the impact of placing limitations on the number of commercials that can be produced, the number of days the talent can be required to perform, or the markets in which the advertising can be used, costly renegotiations may become necessary.

Why It Matters

The SAG and AFTRA union codes covering the production of television commercials contain very detailed definitions of what constitutes a "new" commercial, for purposes of calculating the number of commercials produced by a signatory producer. For example, except in very specific instances, if any new creative material is added to a commercial, the finished work is a new commercial under the codes. Thus, if an advertising agency or advertiser decides to add additional footage or to substitute footage, regardless of whether this entails additional services from the talent, the revised commercial is probably a new commercial under the union codes. If the contract (or agreement) places a limit on the number of commercials that can be produced, these code limitations definitions (or specifications) can result in the advertiser or its agency quickly reaching or exceeding the agreed-upon contractual limit.

If the number of days the talent can be required to perform is limited, how are travel days to be counted? How about days where weather necessitates a cancellation? In addition, the union codes provide that cancellation upon short notice may constitute a booking. Do such days count toward the agreed-upon limit?

Be aware that some stations broadcast and some publications are distributed beyond their immediate markets. For example, cable station TBS in Atlanta is seen nationwide. If an advertising agency or advertiser buys media time on TBS, and thereby broadcasts into a market not permitted under an agreement with talent, the additional costs in subsequently acquiring the right from talent to so broadcast can be considerable.

3. Key Contractual Elements in a Celebrity Contract

If an advertiser or advertising agency does not have an experienced negotiator to deal with celebrities, it should retain experienced legal counsel to handle the negotiations. If, despite these warnings, an advertising executive insists on experiencing the "Hollywood scene," be sure he or she covers the following points during the negotiations and uses the Celebrity Talent Negotiations Checklist provided at the end of this section. Doing so will make it easier to pick up the pieces and to correct the mistakes that invariably will be made.

a. Exclusivity

One of the most important contract provisions, the exclusivity clause restricts the scope of services a celebrity can perform for other advertisers. Its negotiation is very tricky. First, it is highly unusual for an advertiser to demand complete exclusivity, prohibiting the celebrity from performing services for any other advertiser. Unless the advertiser is prepared to pay a considerable sum of money—often in the seven-figure range—it should shy away from such far-reaching restrictions. On the other hand, the advertiser may be selling itself short if it only prohibits the talent from performing services for products or services directly competitive with the advertiser. Diversified, multi-division, or subsidiary advertisers may want a celebrity restricted from providing services to advertisers competitive with divisions or subsidiaries other than the one for which the celebrity is providing services. There could be cases where the parent company wants to prohibit a celebrity touting Pepsi-Cola from working for McDonald's as well, because McDonald's serves Coca-Cola. The geographic territory covered by the exclusivity is another issue. Do not assume that the territories only need to be those where the advertiser is permitted to run advertising featuring the celebrity. For example, even if the advertiser is running media only in the United States, it may want to consider expanding the exclusivity coverage to include Canada and Mexico as well, if concerned about possible spillover from advertising emanating from either bordering country.

b. Morals

When included in contracts, morals clauses and their coverage are often the most difficult to agree upon. Celebrity agents and their celebrity clients generally find them insulting if they go beyond convictions of felonies or lesser crimes involving indecent or immoral acts. On the other hand, advertisers are increasingly insisting they be included in contracts, given the seemingly unending surprises reported in the press today. Advertisers understandably want their celebrity endorsers to behave appropriately in public, given the risk to the goodwill of name brands as well as the millions of dollars spent on celebrity compensation, production costs, and media buys. Unfortunately, some advertisers fail to realize that "Hollywood celebrity" often brings with it a lifestyle and behavior that no morals clause will prevent or influence. The reality is that any advertiser hiring a celebrity endorser must realize that there is always risk involved. When in doubt—and the astute executive is well advised to always be in doubt—research the background of the celebrity using publicly available databases, e.g., LexisNexis, or hire an investigator.

Morals clauses vary greatly from contract to contract and are generally stronger in contracts where the celebrity is paid a considerable sum. For example, one well-known celebrity endorser who was paid millions of dollars a year agreed to the following morals clause:

> *Notwithstanding anything herein to the contrary, you hereby acknowledge that your proper conduct and reputation are of the utmost importance to [the Advertiser] and that such conduct and behavior must at all times be consistent with the dignity and high standards of [the Advertiser] and must not derogate or otherwise disparage [the Advertiser]. Therefore, you must at all times conduct yourself with due regard for public morals and decency. You warrant that you have not and will not commit any illegal or publicly obscene or indecent act or through your own malfeasance or wrongful omission become involved in any situation which has a materially adverse effect on your reputation or on the reputation of [the Advertiser], its trade name, or its affiliates. If you breach this provision, and the effect of such breach is, in the sole judgment of [the Advertiser], of sufficient magnitude to require, for commercial reasons, the discontinuance of the use of the materials produced hereunder utilizing your services, then [the Advertiser], in its sole discretion, shall have the right to terminate this Agreement forthwith. In such event, there shall be no further compensation payable to you hereunder except with respect to any sums which may be due you for services then already rendered or for authorized expenses incurred by you prior to the date of termination. The decision on all matters arising under this paragraph shall be in [the Advertiser's] sole discretion, provided that its decision to terminate hereunder must be exercised, if at all, not later than sixty (60) days after the facts giving rise to such right under this paragraph are brought to [the Advertiser's] attention.*

Just as likely, however, a contract will provide a far more narrow morals clause, such as the following:

> *If you are convicted of any felony or misdemeanor involving moral turpitude, [the Advertiser] shall have the right to immediately terminate this Agreement. [The Advertiser's] decision on all matters arising under this paragraph will be conclusive, provided that [the Advertiser's] decision to terminate hereunder must be exercised, if at all, not later than thirty (30) days after the facts giving rise to such right under this paragraph are brought to [the Advertiser's] attention.*

Such a clause (from an actual contract) may be seen as too narrow in today's tabloid-press world—both as to the requirement of a conviction and the time within which the advertiser must make its decision to terminate—unless, perhaps the compensation is only in the very low six figures. In contracts with guarantees above $250,000 but under $1,000,000, a reasonable compromise between the two clauses cited above would be as follows:

> *If you have committed or commit any act or become involved in any situation or occurrence that brings you into public disrepute, contempt, scandal, or ridicule, [the Advertiser] shall have the right to immediately terminate this Agreement. [The Advertiser's] decision on all matters arising under this paragraph will be conclusive, provided that [the Advertiser's] decision to terminate hereunder must be exercised, if at all, not later than sixty (60) days after the facts giving rise to such right under this paragraph are brought to [the Advertiser's] attention.*

Why It Matters

1. Anthony Kiedis, the lead singer of the rock group Red Hot Chili Peppers, was featured in a radio commercial for condoms. The commercial was sponsored by the Centers for Disease Control and Prevention, an agency of the U.S. Department of Health and Human Services. In the commercial,

Mr. Kiedis stated that he was naked and wearing a condom. After the commercial was aired, it was discovered that Mr. Kiedis had been convicted on charges of sexual battery and indecent exposure a number of years earlier. The Secretary for Health and Human Services was outraged, and the commercial was withdrawn. If research into Mr. Kiedis' background, readily available on any number of public databases, had been conducted prior to the time he was hired, the problem could have been avoided.

2.   Other well-known celebrity endorsements have gone sour due to the totally unforeseen behavior of the celebrities. Marilyn Chambers was the "Ivory Snow Girl" until it was discovered she had starred in the X-rated movie *Behind the Green Door*. As a newly crowned Miss America, Vanessa Williams was headed down the endorsement runway until nude photos of her appeared in a magazine. Baseball star Steve Garvey's endorsement career nearly ended when he acknowledged allegations from two women that he fathered their children out of wedlock. The list goes on and on: Michael Jackson, Madonna, Pete Rose, Mike Tyson, O.J. Simpson, etc. Celebrity endorsements can be very successful, but know the risks before playing the Hollywood game.

c. Length of Use and Run-Offs

Quite often, an advertiser or agency neglects to factor in production schedules or short run-off periods following termination. If production isn't completed until months after the celebrity is signed, a one-year deal suddenly looks rather short. Similarly, it is not as easy as it sounds to stop the distribution of advertising materials at the end of the contract term. Usually, the advertiser must start the process of removal many weeks before the expiration date. As such, a short run-off period is advisable at the end of the contract during which no new advertising can be produced, but continued use of previously produced advertising is permitted. Such run-off periods typically run from one to three months, depending upon the level of compensation paid during the basic term of the contract. Quite often, advertisers will pay additional compensation to secure longer run-off periods; dropping the exclusivity condition during run-off periods can minimize such additional compensation.

d. Area of Use

Permitted area of use can become a problem for the careless negotiator. Remember that as far as the celebrity is concerned, the area of use is wherever the media is actually distributed, not where it emanates from or where it is principally distributed. Therefore, if an advertiser or agency specified U.S. print only, it must be very careful that the ads do not find their way into international editions of magazines. Similarly, a territorial restriction covering only the southeastern United States would be violated if an advertiser or its agency bought time on Atlanta's TBS Superstation. Thus, before an area of use is defined, be certain that the media plan is consistent with the restriction.

e. Compensation and Agent's Commission

Be wary of paying all the compensation up front, even in cases where the celebrity's services are completed in the early period of the contract. Try to stretch out some of the payments; it helps remind the celebrity that he or she is still under contract. Similarly, try to avoid paying the agent's commission. It generally should be paid by the celebrity.

f. Media

Unless the permitted media is stated very broadly, e.g., "in any and all media whatsoever and without restriction," be very careful in the wording used. For example: "point-of-sale" does not mean "packaging"; "outdoor billboards" do not include "transit advertising"; "cable" does not necessarily mean "pay-per-view"; "consumer print advertising" may not include "direct mail," etc.

g. Public Relations Support

Always try to include the right to use public relations to support a campaign. Otherwise, a celebrity may object to press releases or an advertisement in Advertising Age announcing the campaign.

h. Scheduling

Celebrities can be fickle, and too often take their scheduling commitments for advertising less seriously than those for a television series or motion picture. Once a schedule has been committed to, the celebrity should not be able to cancel except for reasons beyond his or her control. The contract should provide that if a celebrity cancels without an adequate excuse, he or she will have to pay for the losses incurred in canceling a production day. Such clauses are hotly contested but are completely reasonable. Similarly, if the behavior is particularly egregious, e.g., the celebrity simply didn't feel like showing up that day, an advertiser or agency should be permitted to terminate the contract entirely.

i. Options

Always anticipate additional uses, production days, commercials, print ads, media, territories, periods of use, and the like. If possible, include expansions in these areas in the contract as an option that can be exercised by the advertiser at a set price. While additional compensation will be due to the celebrity if an option is exercised, it is safe to say that the amount of the compensation will be less than an amount negotiated after the fact, when the celebrity will have the upper hand.

j. Union Codes

Most television commercials in which celebrities perform are produced under the jurisdiction of a union agreement with either the Screen Actors Guild or the American Federation of Television and Radio Artists. These agreements have a variety of restrictions and limitations. They also require additional payments to the unions' pension and health funds. Be certain that any celebrity contract complies with the union codes.

k. Travel Expenses

Increasingly, celebrities are asking for travel expenses for themselves and a companion. Since such travel is usually first class (air travel must be first class under the union codes), the addition of a companion is expensive. Try to avoid it. In either event, also avoid open-ended expense reimbursement, e.g., "we will reimburse you for your hotel and meals while present at a production hereunder." Such clauses give the celebrity too much latitude, and room-service bills may exceed the airfare incurred getting the celebrity to the hotel. It is better to book the hotel for the celebrity and provide them a per diem for expenses, e.g., $250. In that way, expense-account abuses are kept to a minimum.

k. Agency Status

A celebrity contract with an advertising agency on behalf of one of the agency's clients should always specify that the advertiser can assign the agreement to another agency should the advertiser ever decide to terminate its relationship with the agency while a celebrity contract is still in force.

The above are only a few of the more critical elements in a celebrity contract. There can be many others, depending upon the fame of the celebrity, the sensitivity of the advertiser, and the compensation paid. A full checklist appears in the Forms section at the end of this chapter.

4. Celebrity Events and Sponsorships

Another area where advertisers become involved with celebrities is event sponsorship and promotion. Such sponsorships are quite common in sports, but advertisers are increasingly sponsoring such diverse entertainment properties as concert tours, museum exhibitions, and other public events. Many of the above concerns apply equally to celebrity contracts for event sponsorship and should be part of the consideration before embarking in this direction.

At the end of this chapter is a checklist for use when developing event-sponsorship deals.

5. Dealing with Celebrity Talent Brokers

Given the complexity of negotiating with celebrity talent, some individuals hold themselves out as celebrity brokers. Brokers will locate talent and negotiate contracts with the talent's agent on behalf of the advertising agency and advertiser. They are generally paid a fee based upon a percentage, usually 10%, of the compensation paid to the celebrity. They are paid only if the deal goes through. Some brokers will also agree to a flat fee for their services.

If an advertising agency or advertiser is not sure whom they want to use as celebrity talent, and simply wants to get ideas on cost and availability, a celebrity broker is a good source to gather such information. If the deal goes forward, the broker will negotiate the deal and be paid his or her commission. When dealing with such brokers, care should be taken in a number of areas.

First, be certain the compensation arrangement, if based upon a percentage of what is paid to the talent, is clearly defined. Generally, it should be based upon only the amount paid during the first year of the relationship, and not options. It should cover only base compensation, not expenses or other perks, e.g., first-class transportation, per diems, free product, etc.

Second, remember that in a commission deal, the more money paid to the talent, the more money the broker makes. While most brokers will swear that they are not influenced by this fact, keep it in mind and be certain that strict controls are in place on the amount offered. Quite often, an advertising agency or advertiser may want legal counsel experienced in negotiating celebrity deals to review any offer before it is made to the talent. The legal fees will be money well spent. In fact, it may be worthwhile to check with such counsel before retaining a broker in the first place. It is possible that he or she will know what the advertiser or advertising agency needs and will handle the matter at a lower cost than a broker, particularly in high-priced deals.

Third, be certain that the broker is retained for one deal at a time and not for future services. Always reserve the right to use someone else or to take over the negotiations.

Finally, any contract drafted by the broker should be reviewed and approved by a qualified attorney.

If an advertiser or advertising agency knows which celebrity it wants for a campaign or has limited its desired choices to a few, it is questionable whether a broker is needed. More likely than not, experienced legal counsel can complete negotiations more economically.

Chapter Twenty-One Forms

Form II.21.1 Offer Letter to Celebrity Talent

[Advertising Agency Letterhead]

[Date]

[Artist's Name]

[Artist's Address]

Subject: Deal Memo for [Artist's Name]

Dear [Artist's Agent]:

This will confirm our understanding of the agreement between you and us concerning our retaining the services of _____ (hereinafter "Artist') to perform the services specified below, to us ("Agency") on behalf of our Client, _____ hereinafter "Client"), to advertise the following products or services ("Product" or "Service"):

Subject to the conditions indicated below, we have an agreement to:

1. INITIAL TERM:

The term hereof commences on _____ and ends on _____ .

2. EXCLUSIVITY:

During the term hereof, Artist will not perform services or authorize or permit the use of [his/her] name or likeness in connection with any product or service competitive to or incompatible with Client's Product or Service.

It is understood that any work already done by Artist and any agreements entered into by Artist prior to the date of this offer, which are listed in Exhibit A, shall not be considered a conflict of interest.

3. SERVICES:

- Up to _____ ( ) ____-hour print photography sessions, exclusive of travel, to shoot photo stills for print advertisements. Print production dates need not be consecutive.
- Up to _____ ( ) ____-hour personal appearances.
- Up to _____ ( ) consecutive ____ -hour production days (exclusive of travel) to film or tape _____ ( ) television commercial(s).
- Up to _____ ( ) ____-hour production days to record up to ( ) radio commercials.
- Other: _____

Artist will participate in wardrobe fittings and rehearsals as required for each engagement.

The dates and times for Artist's services will be determined by Agency, subject to Artist's prior professional commitments.

In the event that distant travel is required, Client agrees to provide Artist with first-class accommodations including airfare, hotel, and ground transportation.

4. USAGE/RIGHTS:

Client shall have the right to use the Artist's image and performance in [print advertising, including but not limited to outdoor boards, kiosks, product packaging, and magazine, transit, in-store, newspaper, Internet, and direct-mail advertising]. [Delete inapplicable media.]

Client shall have the right to use the Artist's image and performance in up to ____ television commercial(s) and edited versions thereof on television, cable, [in-store, noncommercial Internet on Client's websites, and industrial]. [Delete inapplicable uses.]

5. AREA OF USE:

Worldwide

6. PUBLICITY:

Client shall have the right to publicize its association with Artist.

7. COMPENSATION:

Artist's compensation hereunder will be $_____, payable as follows: _____.

If Artist's services consist only of participation in radio or television commercials, Artist will receive the applicable minimum union scale multiplied by ____.

All commissions to Artist's agent will be paid by Artist unless otherwise set forth below.

Guarantee: In no event will Artist's compensation hereunder be less than _____ ("Guarantee"). The schedule for payment of such Guarantee will be as follows: _____. All compensation due to Artist hereunder will be applied against such Guarantee.

8. TERM OPTION(S):

Client will have two consecutive options to extend the term for one (1) year each. Artist's compensation and all other terms hereof will continue in full force and effect during any period with respect to which Client has exercised its option.

Client shall have the right to use all materials produced hereunder during such option periods. Artist's Guarantee with respect to each Option Period will be $_____, payable as follows: _____.

Notification of exercise must be given in writing no later than 30 days prior to expiration of the then-existing Term.

9. PENSION & HEALTH:

Agency will make the appropriate Pension & Health (P&H) contribution to AFTRA and SAG Pension and Health Plans for the television and radio commercials. For the purposes of calculating P&H, ____% of the Guarantee will be allocated to broadcast services.

10. BEHAVIOR

    If Artist gets involved in any personal situation which reflects unfavorably upon him or which could jeopardize his value to Client, Client will have the right to terminate all obligations to Artist.

11. APPEARANCE:

    During the Initial Term of the agreement and any option periods (if exercised), Artist shall be prohibited from altering [his/her] appearance in any way that would deviate from [his/her] original appearance when entering into this Agreement.

If the above meets with your and Artist's approval, please sign in the space provided below and we shall prepare a formal agreement including these terms and others customary in contracts of this kind. It is hereby acknowledged that until the execution of a more formal agreement, this deal memo shall serve as a binding agreement between the parties. If possible, please secure Artist's signature hereto.

If this deal memo is not signed by Artist and only signed by a representative from Artist's talent agency, the talent agency hereby agrees, represents, and warrants that such agency has received a power of attorney from Artist or is otherwise legally authorized to commit Artist to the obligations set forth herein and that the talent agency will be responsible to Client for any damages resulting from Artist's failure to comply with the terms hereof.

[Advertising Agency]

By _____

ACCEPTED AND AGREED

_____

[Artist]

[Talent Agency]

By: _____

EXHIBIT A

Complete List of Existing Commercial Relationships

Advertiser: _____

Category: _____

Territory: _____

Usage: _____

Exclusivity: _____

Term: _____

Options: _____

Advertiser: _____

Category: _____

Territory: _____

Usage: _____

Exclusivity: _____

Term: _____

Options: _____

Form II.21.2 Checklist for Celebrity Talent Negotiations

Celebrity Talent Negotiations

☐ 1.   Term

   ☐ a.   Length of Initial Term
   ☐ b.   Option(s) to Renew (specify number and length)
   ☐ c.   Use Beyond Expiration Date (allows time to get new pool of commercials and other advertising ready)

☐ 2.   Services

   ☐ a.   Television/Cable (specify number)
   ☐ b.   Radio (specify number)
   ☐ c.   Other Media
   ☐ d.   Print and Collateral
   ☐ e.   Packaging
   ☐ f.   Merchandising and Promotion
   ☐ g.   Sales & Dealer Meetings (specify number)
   ☐ h.   Personal Appearances (specify how many and for how long on each one)
   ☐ i.   Photographic Sessions (specify number—may be simultaneous with TV or radio recording)
   ☐ j.   Utilization of Film Clips in Print and Collateral
   ☐ k.   Right of First Refusal in Other Commercial Areas

☐ 3.   Availability

   ☐ a.   Notice Period
   ☐ b.   Prior Commitments
   ☐ c.   Location

☐ 4.   Ownership of Materials and Characters Performed by Celebrity

☐ 5.   Area of Use

   ☐ a.   Test (determine type; option to roll out on market by market)
   ☐ b.   Regional
   ☐ c.   National (U.S. territories, possessions, commonwealths)
   ☐ d.   Canada
   ☐ e.   Worldwide

☐ 6.   Compensation

   ☐ a.   Scale
   ☐ b.   Overscale (obtain right to apply over scale against rehearsals, holding fees, personal appearances, print use, etc.)
   ☐ c.   Payment should cover competitive protection or exclusivity as required by union code
   ☐ d.   Guarantees (if required to pay minimum guarantees, is there a right to carry excess into next period?)
   ☐ e.   Allocation of guarantees, if any, for Pension and Health Fund contribution purposes

☐ 7.   Competitive Restrictions

    ☐ a. Talent exclusivity in advertising

    ☐ b. Competitive product or line of products

    ☐ c. Extend to incompatible or antithetical products, e.g., cigarettes vs. smoking suppressors, or a denture cleaner vs. toothpaste

☐ 8.   Use of Name and Likeness

    ☐ a. Scope of Use

    ☐   (1) Specify if rights limited to TV or extended to radio, print, point-of-sale, packaging

    ☐   (2) Necessity of special photographic sessions

    ☐   (3) No approval of copy by Celebrity

    ☐ b. Endorsements (N.B.: If Celebrity is endorsing the advertiser's product or service, the Celebrity must satisfy FTC requirements and provide an affidavit of use of the product or service.)

☐ 9.   Death, Breach, Illness, Disability, and Disfigurement

    ☐ a. If a guarantee is paid in advance, Advertiser should have the right to recoup a pro-rata portion of guaranteed payment less applicable fees for services provided prior to termination.

    ☐ b. Reserve the right to use material already produced during remainder of term after Celebrity's death, disability, etc., if advertiser desires

☐ 10.   Morals

    ☐ a. Right to terminate upon certain occurrences

    ☐ b. Right to recoup at least portion of guarantee

☐ 11.   Force Majeure

    ☐ Agreement should specify that in event of strikes, boycotts, war, etc., Advertiser's right to use advertising materials is extended by period equivalent to any period Advertiser is prevented from using the materials by such events.

☐ 12.   Indemnity

    ☐ Agreement should provide for full indemnification from Celebrity for his or her breach and regarding any materials s/he supplies.

☐ 13.   Services Unique

    ☐ Celebrity should acknowledge his services are unique and of a special nature so as to permit Advertiser injunctive relief should Celebrity breach the contract.

☐ 14.   Union Membership

    ☐ If the advertising agency or the advertiser is a signatory to the Commercial Codes of the Screen Actors Guild or the American Federation of Television and Radio Artists, the celebrity should be a member of the unions or agree that he will become a member, if so required.

☐ 15.   Pay or Play

    ☐ An Advertiser is under no obligation to actually broadcast the commercials or print or use other materials produced. Advertiser's sole obligation should be to pay guarantees (if any) and fees that become due through actual services provided or use made by the Advertiser.

☐   16.   Warranties

☐   Celebrity should confirm that he or she has the right to enter into the agreement and has no prior involvement with competitive product(s).

☐   17.   Incorporated Celebrities

☐   Celebrity agrees to read and acknowledge agreement and agrees to be bound by all terms applicable to him or her. If the Celebrity is incorporated, i.e., his or her services are loaned out by a corporation, special provisions should be added to ensure that the Celebrity's corporation will comply with applicable tax laws and union rules.

☐   18.   Minors

☐   If the Celebrity is under 18 years of age, a parent or guardian must sign the agreement. Consider having the contract affirmed by a court to prevent the minor from disaffirming the agreement.

☐   19.   Notices

☐   All notices sent should be delivered by hand, certified mail, or telegram.

☐   20.   Fan Mail

☐   Any fan mail received by the Celebrity regarding his or her performance in materials produced for the Advertiser should be the Advertiser's property unless marked "Personal."

☐   21.   Governing Law

☐   Specify which state law will govern the agreement, usually the state of either the Advertiser or the advertising agency.

☐   22.   Interviews

☐   Celebrity should agree not to grant interviews or release any materials concerning Advertiser's agreement with him or her without the Advertiser's prior written consent.

☐   23.   Entire Understanding

☐   It should be stated that the written agreement is the entire understanding between the Advertiser and the Celebrity.

☐   24.   Insurance

☐   If the Celebrity's health is an issue or the production and media budgets are high, the Advertiser may want to obtain insurance, in which event a provision should be inserted under which the Celebrity agrees to submit to a physical examination.

Form II.21.3 Tournament and Event Sponsorships Checklist

☐ 1.   Official Name of Tournament/Event

☐ 2.   Tournament/Event Logo and Banners

  ☐ a. Design
  ☐ b. Placement
  ☐   (1) Print and Broadcast Advertising and Promotion
  ☐   (2) On-Line
  ☐   (3) Tickets
  ☐   (4) Programs
  ☐   (5) Announcements
  ☐   (6) Scoreboards/Venue Displays (N.B. Television Camera Placement)
  ☐   (7) Stationery
  ☐   (8) Collateral, e.g., Clothing, Brochures, POS, Premiums, etc.
  ☐   (9) Public Relations and Interviews

☐ 3.   Description(s), Date(s) and Location(s)

  ☐ a. Actual Tournament/Event
  ☐ b. Promotional Events
  ☐ c. Ancillary Events

☐ 4.   Sponsorship Rights

  ☐ a. Credentials for Sponsor Personnel and Guests
  ☐ b. Tickets
  ☐   (1) General
  ☐   (2) Special
  ☐   (3) Complimentary vs. Purchase
  ☐   (4) Parking
  ☐ c. Sponsor Product Sales at Venue
  ☐   (1) Pouring Rights
  ☐   (2) Concessions
  ☐   (3) Kiosks
  ☐ d. Sponsor Advertising at Venue
  ☐ e. Hospitality Sites
  ☐ f. Pre/Post Tournament/Event Parties, Receptions, Promotions, Events, etc.
  ☐ g. Sponsor Tie-ins with Consumer Promotions Tied to Tournament/Event
  ☐ h. Storage facilities for Sponsor Materials at Venue
  ☐ i. Infrastructure Needs of Sponsor
  ☐   (1) Electricity
  ☐   (2) Water
  ☐   (3) Communications/Media
  ☐   (4) Parking

☐   j.   Preferred Rates on Hotels, Restaurants, Airlines, Car Rentals, etc.

☐   k.   Player/Performer Appearances

☐   l.   Celebrity Spokesperson(s)/Master of Ceremonies and Sponsor's Tie-in

☐   m.   Restrictions, if any, on Sponsor Exploitation of Sponsorship Rights

☐   n.   Video Logo/Watermark on Broadcast Materials

☐   o.   Materials for Vendors/Suppliers

☐   p.   Materials for Consumers

☐   5.   Sponsorship Exclusivity

☐   a.   Competitive Companies/Sponsors

☐   b.   Affiliated Companies/Sponsors

☐   c.   Sponsorship "Levels"

☐   d.   Ambush Marketing

☐   (1)   Venue and Surrounding Area

☐   (2)   Media

☐   (3)   "Team" or Other Allied Sponsorships

☐   e.   Policing of Infringers

☐   6.   Duties of Tournament/Event Owner in Conjunction With Sponsorship

☐   a.   Stage Tournament/Event

☐   b.   Broadcast Tournament/Event

☐   c.   Promote Tournament/Event

☐   (1)   Advertising

☐   (2)   Promotion

☐   (3)   Public relations

☐   d.   Production of Sponsorship Materials

☐   e.   Contracts, Permits, and Licenses

☐   f.   Liability Insurance

☐   g.   Cancellation Insurance

☐   7.   Duties of Sponsor in Conjunction with Sponsorship

☐   a.   Media Advertising Buys

☐   b.   Production of Sponsorship Materials

☐   c.   Tournament/Event Purse Contribution

☐   (1) Cash

☐   (2) Product

☐   d.   Sponsorship Fee

☐   (1)   Amount

☐   (2)   Payment Schedule

☐   e.   Charitable Donation

☐ 8.   Approval Rights

    ☐ a. Scope
    ☐ b. Timing

☐ 9.   Term

    ☐ a. Initial Sponsorship
    ☐ b. Renewals

☐ 10.   Termination Rights

    ☐ a. Tournament/Event Cancellation
    ☐ b. Loss of Media Coverage
    ☐ c. Breach and Cure Period

☐ 11.   Indemnities

☐ 12.   Representations and Warranties

    ☐ a. Legal Authority to Enter Agreement
    ☐ b. Ownership and Use of Logo(s)

☐ 13.   Independent Parties

☐ 14.   Remedies

    ☐ a. Injunctive Relief
    ☐ b. Liquidated Damages
    ☐ c. Litigation Costs and Attorneys' fees

☐ 15.   Notices

☐ 16.   Assignment Rights and Binding Effect Upon Successors and Assigns

☐ 17.   Governing Laws and Jurisdiction

☐ 18.   Waiver

☐ 19.   Entire Agreement

☐ 20.   Severability of Unenforceable Provisions

☐ 21.   Survival of Representations

☐ 22.   Cooperation of Parties

☐ 23.   Confidentiality

☐ 24.   Paragraph Headings

☐ 25.   Force Majeure

☐ 26.   Contact Person(s)/Liaisons

CHAPTER XXII
Talent Unions

A number of unions cover the production of television and radio commercials. The Screen Actors Guild (SAG) covers actors who perform in television commercials produced on film or videotape. The American Federation of Television and Radio Artists (AFTRA) covers actors in radio commercials and television commercials produced on videotape. The American Federation of Musicians (AF of M) covers musicians. Other unions cover crews, camera operators, directors, and others who perform services in the production of commercials.

The SAG and AFTRA codes distinguish "principal performers" from extras. The distinction is important. An extra can be "bought out," i.e., paid a flat fee for services. On the other hand, principal performers must be paid minimums for as long as the commercial is used.

A principal performer is defined in the codes as:

+ someone whose face is identifiable; and

+ who appears in the foreground performance; and

+ who demonstrates or illustrates a product or service or otherwise reacts to the on- or off-camera narration of a commercial message.

All three elements must be present. If any element is lacking, the performer is an extra and can be bought out.

1. Signing Union Agreements

An advertiser or advertising agency cannot be forced to become signatories to the unions, although it is particularly difficult to avoid if professional actors are hired. Usually, advertisers can more easily avoid becoming signatories, provided they produce commercials through advertising agencies that have signed on with the unions. Similarly, performers cannot be forced to join the unions, although most professional performers are members.

By becoming a signatory, the advertiser or advertising agency guarantees to pay certain minimum compensation to performers and to comply with additional work-environment conditions. Only limited editing of commercials is allowed without incurring additional fees to the performers. Furthermore, commercials may be used only for limited periods of time before renegotiation is required with performers in the commercials.

Why It Matters

Producing union commercials can become expensive. Talent costs alone can run into many thousands of dollars if a commercial is aired extensively. It is, therefore, advisable to avoid signatory status for as long as possible.

Because of the expense, some advertising agencies are unable to represent advertisers that insist on saving costs by producing non-union commercials. In other instances, some signatory agencies produce commercials outside the United States to avoid the unions. In the worst case, some agencies simply cheat and hope not to get caught.

In major markets it is impossible for a large advertising agency not to be a signatory to the SAG and AFTRA commercial codes. Nonetheless, before becoming a signatory, or when renewal occurs, legal counsel should be consulted.

Why It Matters

Many smaller and regional advertisers object to the high cost of union talent. If an advertising agency is a signatory, it must pay all talent the full union rates, regardless of whether the talent is a member of the union. A signatory cannot buy out talent (except extras). As a result, signatory status can close an advertising agency out of competing for some accounts.

2. Payroll Services

A payroll service handles the bookkeeping and payroll records that are required under the various union collective-bargaining agreements for actors appearing in television and radio commercials. In some states, they also handle print-model compensation. Most advertising agencies and advertisers use them today, rather than handling the talent payroll in-house. The payroll service is paid on the basis of a percentage, usually from about 4% to 9%, of the total payroll.

If an advertising agency or advertiser uses a payroll service to pay talent who perform in commercials, care should be taken that payments to the payroll service are indeed used to pay talent. In recent years, a payroll service went out of business, leaving behind double liability for payments to talent; the payroll service had spent the money paid to it before it paid the talent. Since a union signatory guarantees talent payments, it is not a defense for the advertiser that a payroll service was paid. (See Form II.22.1.)

Chapter Twenty-Two Forms

Form II.22.1 Payroll Service Agreement

AGREEMENT entered into as of this _____ day of _____, 20____, by and between [insert name of payroll service company] a [insert state of incorporation of payroll service company] corporation located at [insert address of payroll service company] ("Payroll Company") and [insert name of payroll service company client] a [insert state of incorporation of payroll service company] corporation located at [insert address of payroll service company client] ("Client").

Whereas Client is an advertising agency engaged in, among other things, the creation and production of television and radio commercials, industrial films, and other promotional materials, films, and announcements (collectively "Commercials" as hereinafter defined);

Whereas Client requires the services of actors, actresses, musicians, singers, stunt drivers, and other performers in the creation, production, and use of such Commercials; and

Whereas Client desires to engage Payroll Company to, among other things, be appointed as its agent for the purpose of serving as the employer of record in connection with the hiring and payment of the Talent retained by Client for the production of Commercials, including the payment, accounting, and certain other services in connection with the retention of the Talent used by Client.

Now therefore, in consideration of the mutual promises and other good and valuable consideration as set forth herein, the receipt and sufficiency of which is hereby acknowledged, the parties hereto hereby agree as follows:

1. Definitions

    As used herein, all capitalized terms shall have respective meanings set forth herein and the following terms shall have the respective meanings indicated below unless the context otherwise requires.

    a. "Business Day" means any day other than a Saturday, Sunday, national holiday, or any other day on which the banks are closed in Chicago, Illinois.
    b. "Talent" means the actors, actresses, models, singers, musicians, and any other performers employed to appear in any Commercial.
    c. "Payroll Company System" means the hardware, software, and related procedures, and personnel, repair, and maintenance services established and maintained by Payroll Company for the purpose of making payments to, auditing, and controlling the employment of Talent.
    d. "Union" or "Unions" shall mean all or any one of the American Federation of Musicians ("AFofM"), the American Federation of Television and Radio Artists ("AFTRA"), and/or the Screen Actors Guild ("SAG").
    e. "Union Contracts" shall mean the collective bargaining agreements between the American Federation of Musicians ("AFofM"), the American Federation of Television and Radio Artists ("AFTRA"), and the Screen Actors Guild ("SAG"), on the one hand, and the ANA-AAAA Joint Policy Committee on Broadcast Talent Union Relations, as representative of the advertising industry, on the other hand, insofar as such collective bargaining agreements pertain to the employment of Talent by Payroll Company in Commercials produced by Client during the term of this Agreement.

f. "Commercials" shall mean videoed or filmed messages, recorded in any medium, where the production of such materials falls within the jurisdiction and coverage of the Union Contracts.

2. Term of Agreemen

The term of this Agreement ("Term") shall begin on the date hereof and shall continue for one calendar year through [date]. Thereafter, the term of this Agreement shall automatically be renewed for successive one (1)-year periods unless either party hereto notifies the other party in writing, not less than ninety (90) nor more than one hundred and twenty (120) days prior to the end of the initial term or the then-current renewal term, of its intention not to renew this Agreement.

3. Exclusive Appointment of Payroll Company.

During the Term hereof, Client hereby grants to Payroll Company and Payroll Company hereby accepts from Client the exclusive right to act as employer of record with respect to all Talent retained by Client who appear in Commercials produced (i) by Client or (ii) by any third-party production companies employed by Client to produce Commercials on Client's behalf. At all times Payroll Company shall be acting as Client's agent during the Term hereof, Client shall not knowingly use, authorize, or permit the use of the equipment or services of an employment-processing company or any system other than the Payroll Company System in connection with the employment of Talent in Commercials.

4. Talent Payroll Services

Employer of Record for Individual Talent. Except as otherwise provided herein, Client hereby appoints Payroll Company to act and assume all responsibilities as employer of record, and Payroll Company agrees to act and assume all responsibilities as employer of record in connection with all contracts entered into by Client with any Talent for the production of Commercials.

5. Paying Agent for Talent Utilizing Loan-Out Corporation

Where Talent has elected to provide his or her services through a loan-out corporation, Payroll Company shall act as the paying agent of Client for such loan-out corporation. Payroll Company, as Client's paying agent, shall make all payments to and in respect of such loan-out corporations according to Client's instructions pursuant to the terms of this Agreement.

6. Supervisio

Payroll Company services hereunder shall be subject to Client's direction, approval, and notification, which shall be provided within a reasonable time so as to permit Payroll Company to perform its obligations hereunder. Client shall be fully responsible for and shall supervise all of the activities of Talent at the production of the Commercials, notwithstanding the status of Payroll Company as designated employer.

7. Residual Reporting

Client shall timely provide to Payroll Company the information necessary to make all use-, reuse-, and holding-fee payments (collectively, "Residual Payments") to Talent, to the extent payable during the term of this Agreement in accordance with the Union Contracts. Such information is to be provided on Talent Advice Forms provided by Payroll Company or on forms supplied by Client in a format acceptable to Payroll Company.

8. Union Compliance

    Client agrees that it shall fully adhere to and comply with, and is a signatory of, the Union Contracts and shall remain a signatory thereto so long as this Agreement is in force. Client and Payroll Company shall abide and comply with the applicable provisions of the Union Contracts and the applicable rules and regulations of respective Unions. Payroll Company recognizes that Client may be represented by the ANA-AAAA Joint Policy Committee on Broadcast Talent Union Relations and will defer to Client's interpretation in the event of a conflict, provided, however, that Client shall be solely responsible for compliance with the Union Contracts in connection with such interpretations. At all times and with respect to all commercials produced by Client for which Payroll Company renders services hereunder, Client shall be deemed the "Producer," as such term is defined in the Union Contracts. Nothing herein shall constitute agreement by Payroll Company to become a signatory to the Union Contracts nor, except as specifically provided herein, to be bound by such Union Contracts.

9. Non-Union Signatory Status

    Notwithstanding anything herein to the contrary, in the event that Client is not a signatory to any of the Union Contracts or fails to remain a signatory to any of the Union Contracts, Client hereby agrees that all Commercials produced by it for which Payroll Company renders any services hereunder are subject to the Union Contracts ("Covered Commercials"). In that connection and solely with respect to the Covered Commercials, Client hereby, expressly for the benefit of the Unions and their members effected thereby, is to make all payments of session fees, holding fees, and use fees as provided in the Union Contracts and all Social Security, withholding, unemployment insurance, and disability insurance payments, and to otherwise comply with the Union Codes as if Client were or continued to be a signatory thereto.

10. Pension and Welfare

    Payroll Company will make, in a timely manner, all payments and prepare and file all reports in respect to union pension and welfare contributions due on the compensation payable to Talent pursuant to the Union Contracts. Payroll Company will invoice Client, and Client will reimburse Payroll Company, for such pension and welfare contributions.

11. Late-Payment Penalties

    As Client's sole remedy for any late-payment penalties that occur as a result of the failure of Payroll Company to make timely payments to Talent hereunder, Payroll Company shall be responsible for any late-payment penalties to Talent; provided, however, that Payroll Company only may be liable for such penalties where the Client has provided Payroll Company with complete production reports, Talent Advice Forms, and/or required tax forms at least three full Business Days prior to any payment due date, as specified in Union Codes. If such information is not timely provided before three Business Days as provided for herein, Payroll Company shall not be liable for any penalty, but shall nevertheless exercise every reasonable effort to complete payments on time, including that these payments shall be marked "Special Handling." In the event any late-payment penalties are assessed by any Union when Client failed to provide the necessary information before the three Business Day–period provided for above, Client shall be responsible for the timely payment of all such late-payment penalties.

12. Payment and Report Schedule

    a.   Payments. So long as Client is not in default hereunder, Payroll Company shall make all payments due to Talent, including all session, residual, and related payments to Talent due and payable during the term of this Agreement, and issue checks to each Talent including details for services being paid, making all proper deductions, and will forward such checks as required by the applicable Union Contracts. All payments shall be in accordance with such Union Contracts, and in the event that an error results in an under-scale payment, Client agrees to reimburse Payroll Company for the amount necessary to correct such error.

    b.   Payroll Deductions and Reporting. With respect to all Talent for which Payroll Company is the designated employer, Payroll Company will discharge the obligations imposed by federal, state, and local law with respect to the filing of all required returns and reports, the withholding and remittance, in a timely manner, of all sums to be withheld from Talent's compensation, and the employer's obligations with respect to Social Security, income taxes, unemployment compensation, workmans' compensation, and disability benefits. Payroll Company will be responsible for the processing of all unemployment compensation claims for all Talent employed or supplied hereunder.

13. Required Tax Forms

Client shall provide Payroll Company, on a timely basis, with all required tax forms, including but not limited to federal and state W-4s. Any liability or penalty resulting from Client's failure to provide, or to timely provide, this information shall be the responsibility of Client.

14. Forms and Accuracy

Payroll Company's responsibilities in connection with payroll deductions, reporting, tax forms, and similar obligations as set forth above, shall be completed solely on the basis of Production Reports, Talent Advice Forms, and required tax forms received from Client. Payroll Company will assume all liability for the accuracy of all its arithmetic computations based on the information as supplied by Client; provided, however, that Client shall be solely responsible for all interpretations of the applicable Union Contracts.

15. Errors

    a.   Payroll Company will assist Client in attempting to recover any excess payments to Talent made through error, induced by fraud, or otherwise not actually due. If and when Payroll Company does recover any such payment to which Client is entitled, Payroll Company will credit Client's account with such recovery.

    b.   Client will reimburse Payroll Company for payments made to correct miscalculations by Payroll Company which result in underpayment to Talent, provided that Client's total cost will not exceed the amount that would have otherwise been due on an accurate calculation.

16. Payments to Payroll Company

    a.   Client, in its capacity as Producer under the Union Contracts, shall pay to Payroll Company and shall be directly liable to Payroll Company for the full amount of all payments advanced hereunder by Payroll Company on behalf of Client, including the gross wages and other payments advanced by Payroll Company on behalf of Client to Talent, plus the Union Pension and

Welfare Fund contributions, and any penalty payments provided for herein and for any taxes paid as required by law.

b. Client shall pay to Payroll Company any and all costs or expenses incurred by Payroll Company in connection with the payment of Talent through loan-out corporations.

c. In consideration of Payroll Company's continuing services to be performed in connection herewith, Client shall pay Payroll Company in accordance with the base fees provided for in its annual rate card in effect at the time. The Payroll Company Rate Card in effect upon the commencement of the term of this Agreement is attached to this Agreement as Exhibit A.

d. Payroll Company shall make its special-guarantee payment-tracking system available to Client, and Client shall pay to Payroll Company the charges for this service in accordance with the provisions contained in Exhibit B attached to this Agreement.

e. Any services, fees, or charges other than those specified herein must be agreed to in writing.

17. Billing and Payment

a. Invoice. Payroll Company will render daily invoices to Client with respect to the engagement of Talent or a payment due with respect to Talent. Client shall review the Payroll Company invoices promptly upon receipt, and Client shall notify Payroll Company within three (3) Business Days of any respect in which a Payroll Company invoice is inconsistent with Client's instructions or records. Where Client has notified Payroll Company of a discrepancy in an invoice as provided in this paragraph, Payroll Company and Client shall cooperate with one another to resolve the discrepancy promptly in order that the appropriate payment for Talent be made timely in accordance with the Union Contracts and without incurring a late-payment penalty.

b. Payment. (i) Client shall pay to Payroll Company all invoices rendered by Payroll Company not later than ten (10) days from invoice date. If payment is delinquent, Payroll Company shall provide written notice of such delinquency to Client. In the event of such a delinquency (with or without such written notice), Client shall pay to Payroll Company a 2.00% monthly service charge of the total invoice amount in each month during which a delinquency exists, but in no event shall such charge be greater than the maximum amount allowable by law. (ii) Client acknowledges and agrees that Payroll Company is retained hereunder as its agent, and that it is directly, fully and solely responsible for the payment to Payroll Company of all invoices authorized and issued to Client. Payment to Payroll Company shall be in accordance with the terms of paragraph 11(b)(i) hereof and shall not, in any event be predicated or conditioned upon the receipt by Client of any payments due Client from any third party. Client's obligation to pay Payroll Company shall be absolute and unconditional and shall not be subject to setoff, counterclaim or abatement for any reason whatsoever.

c. Client agrees to pay to Payroll Company any costs incurred by Payroll Company in connection with collection of any amount owed to Payroll Company or enforcement of any of its rights including, without limitation, any claims Payroll Company may have hereunder or with respect to any outside attorneys fees and disbursements incurred in connection with any collection efforts or enforcement of its rights hereunder.

d. Payroll Company shall have the right to apply or offset any funds of Client in the possession of Payroll Company against any amounts due and owing from Client, or against any claims against Client. Further, if said delinquency is not cured by Client within five (5) Business Days after mailing written notice of such default to Client, Payroll Company then has the option of placing Client on a C.O.D. basis and withholding all services hereunder; or, in the alternative, Payroll Company reserves the right to immediately cancel this Agreement and provide notice of such fact to the relevant unions and Talent guilds. Notwithstanding other provisions in this Agreement, Payroll Company will not be responsible for any payments when a delinquency exists due to Client.

18. Taxes

Client shall pay (or reimburse Payroll Company for) all sales, use, or excise taxes, if any, due upon the use of the services rendered by Payroll Company pursuant to this Agreement. Payroll Company may pay such taxes and invoice Client for such payments. If Client wishes to contest any such taxes, it may do so after reimbursing Payroll Company for the taxes as provided, and Client shall indemnify and hold Payroll Company harmless from any costs or expenses entailed in such contest, including penalties and attorneys' fees. Client shall have no liability for franchise tax or taxes measured by the income or profit of Payroll Company.

19. Audit

Client shall have the right, at its own expense, to audit the written records of Payroll Company regarding Talent employed by Payroll Company at the request and direction of Client, to assure its compliance with the terms of this Agreement. Payroll Company shall make its written records directly pertaining to the activities, data, and information concerning Talent in connection with this Agreement available for inspection by Client or its designated agent, at Payroll Company's office, at reasonable times, during business hours, upon reasonable written notice from Client.

20. Confidentiality

The terms, conditions, and provisions of this Agreement are confidential and shall not be disclosed by either party, other than to each party's employees and representatives that need to be aware of its provisions, without the consent of the other party. The parties recognized by the parties that certain information supplied by Client is confidential, involving the business of Client that it may not wish to have made known publicly. Accordingly, Payroll Company further agrees that it will not furnish any confidential information concerning matters covered hereby except to Client, an advertiser for whom Client is acting, the unions involved, and Talent or corporations controlling Talent's services with respect to such Talent's own individual payments; in the event of being required to do so by law by any court order or as it may be requested to do so by an authorized government officer, including, without limitation, any agent of the Internal Revenue Service or any federal, state, or local law-enforcement officer. Payroll Company will cooperate with Client in any effort to prevent its employees from being required to furnish any such information to persons other than those described in the preceding sentence, including participating in any reasonable legal process as may be reasonably requested and paid for by Client.

21. Financial Information

Client shall furnish Payroll Company with its income statement, balance sheet, and statement of changes in financial position (and such other financial information as Payroll Company may reasonably request) at least once per calendar quarter within 90 days after the end of the preceding quarter. Such statements may be unaudited but certified as true and correct by Client's chief financial officer with the exception of the statements to be delivered at the end of Client's fiscal year, which shall be audited by an independent public accounting firm. All such statements shall be in accordance with generally accepted accounting principles, consistently applied.

22. Client's Solvency

In the event that Payroll Company has concerns, based on credible information that Payroll Company has obtained regarding Client's longevity, financial stability, or solvency, Payroll Company shall bring such concerns to Client's attention and Client shall immediately attempt to resolve such concerns. If Client is unable to resolve Payroll Company concerns to Payroll Company's reasonable satisfaction within five (5) days of being notified of such concerns by Payroll Company, then Payroll Company shall have the right in its sole discretion to terminate this Agreement effective immediately by giving Client written notice of termination.

23. Representations and Warranties

a. Each party represents and warrants to the other that:
(i) It is duly organized and in good standing under the laws of the State indicated as its state of organization in the first paragraph of this Agreement and has adequate power to enter into and perform this Agreement;
(ii) This Agreement has been duly authorized, executed, and delivered on behalf of such party and constitutes the legal, valid, and binding agreement of such party, enforceable in accordance with its terms; and
(iii) The entering into and performance of this Agreement will not violate any judgment, order, law, regulation, or agreement applicable to such party or any provision of such party's charter or bylaws, or result in any breach of, constitute a default under, or result in the creation of any lien, charge, security interest, or other encumbrance upon any assets of such party pursuant to any instrument to which such party is a party or by which it or its assets may be bound.

b. Client represents and warrants to Payroll Company that:
(i) Client has the right and authority to employ Talent and produce Commercials;
(ii) Client shall comply with each of its obligations as set forth herein with respect to Payroll Company and all Talent retained by Payroll Company on behalf of Client; and
(iii) Client shall fully comply with all applicable federal, state, or local laws and regulations and any other legal or contractual obligations, including but not limited to the Screen Actors Guild Commercial Contract, to the extent Client is a signatory thereto or otherwise bound thereby, concerning the hiring, performance, employment, working conditions, and termination of employment with respect to Talent, including but not limited to those laws and regulations regarding workplace safety and equal opportunity, notwithstanding the status of Payroll Company as designated employer.
(iv) Without limiting the foregoing, Client shall fully comply in all respects with all Federal and applicable state laws and regulations and the Union Contracts as regards the terms and conditions under which minors may be lawfully employed. If Client requests any minor to be employed by Payroll Company, Client will furnish to Payroll Company all requisite work permits.
(v) Client shall be responsible for any unauthorized use of Commercials, including violations of Talent's rights of privacy or publicity, unless such unauthorized use is a result of Payroll Company's negligence or other breach of this Agreement, in which event Payroll Company will

take full responsibility and indemnify Client with respect to any such claims.

c. Payroll Company represents and warrants to Client that:

(i) Payroll Company has the right and authority to be designated as employer of the Talent; and

(ii) Payroll Company shall comply with all applicable Union Contracts, and federal, state, and local laws and regulations regarding the payment of Talent retained by Payroll Company on behalf of and as agent for Client.

d. The representations and warranties contained in this paragraph shall be deemed "material" for all purposes related to this Agreement.

24. Event of Default

a. The occurrence of any of the following events, continued for 10 days (3 days in the event (i) is applicable and 2 days in the event either party voluntarily files any petition action under any bankruptcy or insolvency law) or any other time period specifically set forth herein after receipt by the defaulting party of written notice thereof and the defaulting party's failure to cure the same, shall, at the non-defaulting party's option, constitute an Event of Default hereunder:

(i) the nonpayment by either party of any sums required to be paid or remitted to the other party hereunder;

(ii) the default by either party under any material term, covenant, or condition of this Agreement, or the breach by either party of any material representation or warranty contained herein;

(iii) any affirmative act of insolvency by either party, whether voluntary or involuntary, or the filing by either party, or any third person against either party, of any petition or action under any bankruptcy, reorganization, insolvency, or moratorium law or any other law or laws for the relief of, or relating to, debtors; provided, however, that no such act shall constitute an Event of Default unless and until such party shall be unable to meet its obligations to the other party under the terms of this Agreement; and provided that the parties agree that this Agreement constitutes a financial accommodation by Payroll Company to Client as such term is utilized in 11 U.S.C. § 365; or

(iv) the exposure of a substantial part of either party's property to any levy, seizure, assignment, or sale for or by a creditor or governmental agency.

b. Upon an Event of Default by Payroll Company, Payroll Company shall, without demand, forthwith pay to Client all amounts due and owing pursuant hereto, and Client may

(i) require Payroll Company to be removed as designated employer of record; and

(ii) terminate this Agreement.

c. Upon an Event of Default by Client, Client shall, without demand, (a) forthwith pay to Payroll Company all amounts due and owing pursuant hereto, and Client authorizes Payroll Company to offset any amounts owed to Payroll Company hereunder with respect to any particular Talent against any amounts held by Payroll Company and its successors, assigns, officers, directors, employees, and agents (collectively, for purposes of this section, "Payroll Company Indemnitees"), and (b) hold Payroll Company Indemnitees harmless with respect to any such particular Talent. Payroll Company may:

(i) terminate Client's rights hereunder; and

(ii) terminate this Agreement.

d. No remedy referred to in this paragraph 24 is intended to be exclusive, but each shall be cumulative and in addition to any other remedy herein or otherwise available by law or in equity.

25. Indemnification

    a. Client shall indemnify and hold Payroll Company Indemnitees against, and hold Payroll Company Indemitees harmless from and any and all claims, actions, liabilities, costs, expenses, and damages, including but not limited to attorneys' fees and costs, with respect to any claims imposed on, incurred by, or asserted against Payroll Company Indemnitees occurring as a result of, or in connection with (i) erroneous information provided by Client, (ii) any breach by Client of any clause, condition, representation, warranty, or provision of this Agreement, (iii) Client's designation of Payroll Company as employer with respect to the retention of Talent, except to the extent that any such claim shall relate to Payroll Company's default hereunder or negligence or willful misconduct with respect thereto, (iv) any breach or violation by Client of any applicable law, (v) any act or failure to act by Payroll Company at the request of Client whether on account of any ambiguity or interpretation of any Union Contract or other agreement or otherwise, or any claim resulting from such deference to Client's interpretation of any Union Contract as provided herein, and (vi) any other claim or cause resulting from any act or failure to act by Client in accordance with this Agreement.

    b. Payroll Company shall indemnify and hold Client and its successors, assigns, officers, directors, employers, and agents (collectively, for purposes of this paragraph "Client Indemnitees") harmless from and against any and all claims, actions, liabilities, costs, expenses, and damages, including but not limited to outside attorneys' fees and costs, with respect to any claim imposed on, incurred by, or asserted against Client Indemnitees occurring as a result of or in connection with (i) erroneous information provided by Payroll Company, (ii) any breach or violation by Payroll Company of any clause, condition, representation, warranty, or provision of this Agreement, (iii) any breach by Payroll Company of any applicable law, or (iv) any other claim or cause resulting from any act or failure to act by Payroll Company in accordance with this Agreement, except to the extent that any claim shall relate to Client's default hereunder or negligence or willful misconduct with respect thereto.

26. Governing Law

This Agreement shall be governed by the laws of the State of _____ without reference to its conflict of law rules. The courts of such State shall have exclusive jurisdiction over all controversies arising out of or in connection with this Agreement. The parties hereby consent to venue and personal jurisdiction in the courts of such State, waive any objections to jurisdiction or venue of such courts, and agree that process may be served upon them in any such action by registered mail at the address stated in the notice section of this Agreement or personally within or without said State. The prevailing party in any action hereunder shall be entitled to recover its reasonable outside attorneys' fees and disbursements.

27. Assignment.

This Agreement may not be assigned by either party without the written consent of the other; provided, however, that Payroll Company may subcontract or delegate any of its obligations or rights hereunder without Client's consent, provided that Payroll Company shall remain fully obligated hereunder. Any attempt by either party to assign this contract without the required consent shall be deemed void. No third party shall be considered an intended beneficiary of this Agreement or entitled to any benefit hereunder.

28. Waiver of Jury Trial

THE PARTIES HERETO WAIVE ALL RIGHT TO OR ENTITLEMENT TO TRIAL BY JURY IN CONNECTION WITH ANY DISPUTE THAT ARISES OUT OF OR RELATES IN ANY WAY TO THIS AGREEMENT.

29. Entire Agreement

This Agreement and attached Exhibits incorporate the entire agreement between the parties with respect to its subject matter and supersede all prior representations, negotiations, agreements, and understandings. This Agreement cannot be modified or amended except in writing signed by the parties.

30. Waiver

The failure of a party to enforce or to insist upon strict compliance with a provision of this Agreement shall not constitute a waiver of such provision or preclude its enforcement in the future. Any waivers granted hereunder are effective only if recorded in writing signed by the parties.

31. Limitation of Liability

In the event of any breach of this Agreement by Payroll Company which may be caused by the malfunction of its system or software or its failure to provide required service, the limit of any claim of loss by Client shall be no greater than the proven financial loss sustained by virtue of such breach. In no event shall Payroll Company be liable for incidental, consequential, or punitive damages for any breach of this Agreement. Neither occasional short-term interruptions of service which are not unreasonable under comparable industry standards, nor interruptions of service resulting from events or circumstances beyond the control of Payroll Company hereunder render Payroll Company in default under this Agreement. Notwithstanding the foregoing and without limitation thereto, Payroll Company shall in no event be liable to Client for any consequential damages or loss of profits suffered by Client as a result of a breach of this Agreement by Payroll Company.

32. Notices

    a. Notices under this Agreement are sufficient if given by nationally recognized overnight courier service, certified mail (return receipt requested), facsimile with electronic confirmation, or personal delivery to the other party at the address below:

        If to Client: [address]
        With a copy to:
        If to Payroll Company: [address]
        With a copy to:

    b. Notice is effective: (i) when delivered personally, (ii) three (3) business days after sent by certified mail, (iii) on the business day after being sent by a nationally recognized courier service for next-day delivery, or (iv) on the business day after being sent by facsimile with electronic confirmation to the sender. A party may change its notice address by giving notice in accordance with this Section.

33. Severability

   If any provision of this Agreement is determined to be unenforceable, the parties intend that this Agreement be enforced as if the unenforceable provisions were not present and that any partially valid and enforceable provisions be enforced to the extent that they are enforceable.

34. Captions

   The paragraph headings in this Agreement are for ease of reference only, and shall not affect the construction or interpretation of this Agreement.

35. Counterparts

   This Agreement may be executed in two or more identical counterparts, each of which shall be deemed to be an original and all of which taken together shall be deemed to constitute the Agreement when a duly authorized representative of each party has signed a counterpart. The parties may sign and deliver this Agreement by facsimile transmission. Each party agrees that the delivery of this signed Agreement by facsimile shall have the same force and effect as delivery of original signatures.

IN WITNESS WHEREOF the parties have caused this Agreement to be executed by their duly authorized officers as of the date first written below.

[Payroll Company]_____   [Client]

By: _____   By:_____

(Signature)   (Signature)

Date:_____   Date: _____

Exhibit A

Payroll Company Rate Card as of [insert current date]

Employers of Record

When Payroll Company is designated as Employer of Record, Client will reimburse Payroll Company for gross compensation and all applicable union payments advanced by Payroll Company with respect to the employment of Talent. Additionally, Client will reimburse Payroll Company the following percentages for employer payroll taxes, insurance, and handling fees based on gross compensation paid by Payroll Company to Talent on Client's behalf:

[insert rates]

Other Talent

When Payroll Company is not designated as Employer of Record (i.e. Talent is employed by Client, advertiser, or corporation), Client will reimburse Payroll Company for gross Talent compensation and all applicable union payments advanced by Payroll Company with respect to the employment of Talent. Additionally, Client will reimburse Payroll Company the following percentages of gross compensation paid by Payroll Company to Talent on Client's behalf:

[insert rates]

Exhibit B

Special Guarantee

A special guarantee is defined as one which provides for the services of Talent at a rate of pay significantly higher than scale (often times referred to by the industry as a celebrity performer) and for a specified period of time, which normally is one year. Payroll Company shall make its special-performer guarantee payment-tracking system available to Clients who engage Talent under guarantee contracts. Payroll Company rates for this special-guarantee contract service are as follows:

Non-Incorporated Talent

Payroll Company tax factor and handling fee charge is applied as outlined in Exhibit A. There is no handling fee charge for amounts in excess of the Social Security maximum. This rate is for the term of the guaranteed amount and is not affected by the number of payments required, but must be applied on a calendar year basis because of employer payroll taxes.

Incorporated Talent

A flat handling fee of $_____ to process each special performer guarantee of $15,000 and over. This rate is for the term of the guaranteed amount and is not affected by the number of payments required. Each guarantee is also subject to a charge for workers' compensation insurance up to an annual maximum of $_____ ($_____ wage limit).

BANK REFERENCES
ADVERTISER AND ADVERTISING AGENCY

Bank name and address: _____

_____

Name of bank representative: _____

Bank account number: _____

Bank phone number: _____

Signatory Status:	Yes	No
SAG	☐	☐
AFTRA TV	☐	☐
AFTRA RADIO	☐	☐
AF of M	☐	☐

CHAPTER XXIII
Considerations in Mergers and Acquisitions of Advertising Agencies

The scope of this chapter is limited to mergers and acquisitions in the advertising agency business. Advertisers are too diverse for a single chapter to address matters they should consider with regard to mergers, shareholders, and partners. This discussion, however, may nonetheless provide insight that smaller advertisers can apply to their businesses as well. The author would also like to acknowledge the assistance of Richard B. Rodman, Esq., his partner, in the preparation of this chapter.

Historically, mergers and acquisitions in the advertising agency business have had mixed results. At times, an advertising agency merges out of weakness, not strength. Unless an advertising agency thoroughly reviews and understands the factors at stake before a change in ownership occurs, a merger will likely fail. Quite often, an advertising agency can save itself a lot of time and effort if it asks and answers many key questions before committing the time and expense to draft formal agreements. The checklist at the end of this chapter may assist in that regard. (See Form II.23.1.)

Too often, advertising agencies spend innumerable hours and incur considerable expense courting one another only to find that the merger won't work. Worse yet, some become so committed to buying or selling that they move forward despite complications and lose sight of the consequences of a bad deal until it's too late.

Before contemplating a merger or acquisition, the principals of an agency should consider the questions presented here. Doing so will reveal important issues and afford both sides to a transaction the opportunity to resolve differences early on, thereby increasing the likelihood that the transaction will be successfully completed and business objectives will be met.

1. What Important Steps Should both the Seller and Buyer Take Prior to Exchanging Information and During Negotiations?

a. Letter of Intent

A letter of intent sets forth the basic terms of a deal. While a letter of intent is not a legally binding agreement, it is important to set forth the basic assumptions of the buyer and the seller before undertaking the long and complicated process of due diligence. Most often, the buyer prepares the letter of intent.

b. Confidentiality Agreement

A confidentiality agreement sets forth the mutual obligations of the buyer and seller to keep any information they receive from one another confidential and to return all copies of any materials exchanged immediately upon the termination of negotiations should either the seller or buyer elect not to proceed with the transaction.

c. Due Diligence List

At the very outset of negotiations and prior to undertaking a due diligence investigation, the buyer should furnish a due diligence list to the seller setting forth the scope of the due diligence review.

d. Communication Plan

A clear understanding of when and how the buyer may contact the seller's accounts to inquire about account changes or discuss the transaction with the seller's employees must be established.

2. How will the Deal be Structured?

How the deal will be structured depends on whether the transaction is a merger or an acquisition. Most often in the advertising agency business, a deal is structured as an acquisition, with a seller and a buyer.

In general, there are two ways to structure an acquisition. Either the buyer purchases the stock of the seller or the buyer purchases the assets of the seller. Each alternative has significant financial ramifications.

a. Stock Purchase Considerations

Generally, a stock purchase is advantageous to a seller primarily for tax reasons. The consideration paid for the stock gives rise to capital gains taxes for the seller. Selling stock is also a very simple way to transfer control of the agency without obtaining the consents from third parties that are often required in the sale of assets.

A stock purchase may be disadvantageous to a buyer for tax reasons. For example, the buyer cannot allocate any part of the purchase price to depreciable assets. In addition, in a stock acquisition, the buyer assumes the history and obligations, known and unknown, of the seller, including taxes, disclosed and undisclosed liabilities, and so forth.

b. Asset Purchase Considerations

The advantage in an asset purchase lies with the buyer. First, the buyer can choose what assets it will purchase and avoid those it does not want. Second, the buyer can allocate the purchase price to depreciable assets for tax purposes. Most importantly, however, the buyer can determine the liabilities it is assuming with some degree of certainty, which is not always the case in a stock sale. That is, the buyer will only be assuming certain, disclosed liabilities in an asset sale. This fact becomes important to a buyer in pricing an agency.

An asset acquisition provides little advantage to a seller unless the seller is an "S" corporation. If the seller is a "C" corporation, there will be double tax at both the corporate and shareholder level. If the seller is a "C" corporation and a buyer must purchase stock to avoid the double taxation, the buyer should either discount the purchase price (to compensate for lost tax benefit) or consider allocating part of the purchase-price payments to non-compete agreements, signing bonuses, consulting agreements, and the like. Doing so will allow the buyer deductible expenses.

c. Can the Transaction be Structured as a Tax-Free Reorganization or Merger?

A tax-free reorganization is possible if at least 50% of the purchase price is to be paid by issuance of buyer's stock. In such instances, tax on the value of the stock is deferred until the stock is sold. Any cash received from the sale is taxed upon receipt at capital gains rates. The vehicle most commonly used is known as a "statutory merger" of the target company into a subsidiary of the buyer. Such structures are complicated but may offer the tax benefits necessary to make the transaction advantageous to both the seller and the buyer.

3. Does the Transaction Constitute a Purchase of a "Minority-Owned Enterprise"?

Various programs have been established in both the public and private sectors for the purpose of fostering business with qualified minority-owned companies. A company will be deemed minority owned where at least 51% of the company's voting stock is controlled by minority owners. In order to maintain a company's status as minority owned, equity acquisitions often are structured so as to ensure that the purchaser acquires no more than 49% of the voting stock. The balance of the voting equity may be purchased at a subsequent date by using call options on the part of the buyer and put options on the part of the seller. Also, advertising agreements with certain advertisers, such as governmental agencies, may require that the agency be a qualified minority-owned company. Such restrictions do not necessarily make an acquisition any less attractive, because the deal can be structured so that the seller retains its status while the buyer's investment is protected.

4. What is the Purchase Price?

In determining the purchase price of an advertising agency, the seller and buyer should consider a variety of ways the purchase price can be "allocated" to differing factors.

a. How will the Purchase Price be Determined?

1. AGI: A percentage of annual gross income ("AGI") may determine the purchase price. While a percentage of AGI is not the most common way to value an agency, it is appropriate in instances where the financial condition of the agency is best reflected in the AGI figure. For example, if an agency is marginally profitable but has accounts the buyer would particularly like to secure, the seller may only view the transaction as attractive based on a percentage of the AGI.

2. EBITDA: Much more often, however, the purchase price is leveraged and based upon a formula that looks to past and future financial performance. In such instances, the most common approach is to use a multiple of the average after-tax net or pre-tax income or average earnings before interest, taxes, depreciation, and amortization ("EBITDA") for a period of time, going backward and forward, to be paid over a period of years. The multiples can and often do vary. When dealing with an EBITDA formula, the multiple generally ranges from 4 to 6.5 of average EBITDA over a period of years (usually three). The multiple can also be based upon a sliding scale depending upon the target company's profit margin, cumulative revenue growth, a mixture of both, etc. In addition, the seller and buyer can protect themselves from drastic changes in the selling price by providing for a minimum purchase price ("cuff") and a maximum purchase price ("collar").

Generally, a seller can anticipate receiving anywhere from 25% to 50% of the estimated purchase price at the time of the closing of the sale. The balance generally is contingent upon future performance. The seller should make sure that the agreement provides that the down payment represents the minimum purchase price to be paid and cannot be recovered by the buyer if future performance is disappointing.

The seller's shareholders are usually entitled to retain the seller's net worth as of the date of closing, over a designated threshold amount that is left in the company to meet working capital needs. For example, if the seller has $500,000 in cash in the bank but only needs half of that amount as working capital, then the seller's shareholders would be entitled to $250,000. The amount necessary for operating capital is often the subject of intense negotiations. Generally, the buyer likes to see three months or more of working capital. The seller, on the other hand, generally wants a smaller sum. In the end, the amount necessary is largely dependent upon the seller's cash flow.

A word of caution in determining the purchase price: While the valuation methods and multiples cited above are commonly used, they are not necessarily valid denominators in all transactions. Often, the type of buyer that wants to acquire an agency in a particular market determines the value of an agency. In many instances, sellers must face the reality that their agencies are not going to be acquired by the publicly owned, international holding companies that have both cash and stock to use in structuring a deal. At times, the seller must face the harsh reality that the purchase price will be significantly less than a high percentage of AGI or high multiple of EBITDA and may more often depend upon the financial resources of a small group of potential buyers. The measures of value discussed above, however, are good starting points, even in difficult markets.

5. What Amount of the Purchase Price Should be Allocated to Employment Agreements?

If the seller is a closely held company, employment agreements and incentive compensation for new and increased business can be negotiated simultaneously with the purchase. From a tax point of view, it is often in the buyer's interest to seek a lower purchase-price payment by increasing compensation since the compensation can be expensed immediately. This is especially so if the buyer is not a publicly owned company and not overly concerned with its bottom-line earnings numbers. From the seller's perspective, such an allocation may be attractive if the offset offers lucrative compensation and sufficient perquisites and/or incentives for the seller, provided the seller understands that he or she will be turning capital gains (purchase-price payments) into ordinary income payments. A seller should also note that if the purchase price of the agency is contingent upon future performance, and more particularly, based upon EBITDA or pre-tax or after-tax net income, increased compensation to the principals may have a material adverse effect upon future purchase-price payments.

6. How will the Purchase Price be Paid?

A buyer will want to pay as little as possible up front. If a substantial up-front payment is required, it is generally no more than one-quarter to one-half of the projected purchase price.

If the purchase price is a contingent amount payable over time, and if a substantial down payment has been made at the closing, the buyer may want a "clawback" provision if business is lost. Under a clawback provision, the buyer is entitled to reimbursement of monies paid to the seller if the purchase-price payments already made exceed the formula purchase price that is based upon future performance.

If the purchase price is contingent upon subsequent performance, interim payments can be made, but the buyer must ensure that such payments are on the low side in the event of a downturn of business. Alternatively, the buyer can provide for a clawback if performance criteria are not met. Obviously, sellers have a distinct dislike of clawbacks, while buyers often see clawbacks as insurance against unanticipated downturns.

The purchase price (in both stock and asset deals) can be paid so as to maximize tax benefits to the buyer, e.g., incentive compensation pursuant to employment agreements, signing and annual bonuses, payments for covenants not to compete, and consulting agreements with retiring principals of the seller. However, where the buyer is a publicly owned company, it generally does not want purchase-price payments to adversely affect earnings flow, and in many cases it would rather have payments treated as purchase-price payments rather than deductible compensation. Similarly, sellers may resist increased compensation payments where contingent purchase-price payments are based upon net income. In the end, it's all a matter of balancing the tax and economic needs and requirements of the buyer, the seller, and the seller's shareholders.

7. Can the Buyer Help Decrease the Seller's Expenses and Overhead, Thereby Increasing the Potential Payout?

When buying an advertising agency, it is common to eliminate employee and overhead redundancies and thereby decrease the seller's expenses. Consequently, a purchase price that is dependent upon future profits may be improved by the decreased overhead offered by sellers. Such benefits most often relate to accounting services, human resources, and research services. They may also include a host of other services that the buyer may be able to offer the seller. If these benefits reduce overhead, they are generally attractive. A seller must be cautious, however, with respect to what it will be charged by the buyer for such services. Quite often, in order to minimize the auditing and calculation of such charges, a buyer will charge the seller a set percentage of the seller's AGI. In such instances, depending upon the percentage, such charges can have a very significant impact on the profits and thereby reduce the buy-out price. It may be better for the seller to negotiate an "a la carte" price for each of the services it may, in its discretion, request. In that way, the seller can retain control of how it will seek savings. Alternatively, all or part of the administrative charge can be excluded from the payout calculation. For example, if a seller was charged 6% of AGI for services, the buyer and seller could agree that only 2% of the charges will be deducted from AGI for purposes of making the payout calculation.

8. How will Potential Client Conflicts be Handled?

Where the purchase price is based on future revenues, the loss of accounts as a result of client conflicts can prove costly. In such situations, the buyer and seller need to consider whether the payout formula should be adjusted in cases where a conflict results in a loss of a seller's client. If an adjustment is warranted, the revenues that would have been earned on the account are considered in calculating the future payouts.

9. What does the Seller's Past and Future Financial Performance Indicate?

In evaluating the seller's business, look at financial statements for at least the previous three years. If the seller is a closely held corporation, evaluate the financials to determine if items were expensed that might not otherwise be appropriate under the accounting practices of the buyer. If so, recast the financials so that comparisons are based on generally accepted accounting principles. The buyer should also determine how long the accounts have been with the seller, particularly if the accounts are products or services of a multiproduct service company. Such accounts offer growth opportunities that the seller may not have the resources to pursue.

10. How Deep is the Seller's Management?

From a buyer's perspective, it is important to determine if there is a management succession plan. In addition, the buyer needs to determine whether any key agency employees are closely tied to clients. If relationships are close, and non-shareholders control accounts, the buyer may want to include employment agreements with non-shareholders. At the very least, the buyer should attempt to get nonsolicitation covenants from such employees effective during and after any termination of employment. The operative question is: Who is essential to the future operation of the company? Quite often, it is not the owners of the seller, but key account managers. Buyers are well advised to probe deeply on this issue.

11. Are there any Pending or Threatened Lawsuits?

The last thing a buyer needs is to find out too late that the seller is a plaintiff or defendant in a lawsuit that will warrant the attention and resources of the seller's and buyer's personnel. The buyer should also ask whether there are any threatened lawsuits so that it can avoid unpleasant surprises after the acquisition is completed. Similarly, the seller should disclose if there are any active settlement agreements or other legal obligations owed to others as a result of past lawsuits. Finally, the buyer should determine if the seller is the subject of any governmental or regulatory orders or consent decrees.

12. Are there any Pending or Threatened Audits?

The risk of an IRS or other regulatory audit is serious, particularly in the case of closely held companies. The buyer should satisfy itself that the seller's accounting practices and accounting firm have properly handled accounting and tax issues. Audits can also arise from the IRS seeking to determine if an agency has properly paid its employees. It is a known and often risky practice in the advertising agency business to treat certain individuals as independent contractors rather than employees, even though they are devoting all or most of their time to agency business. The IRS may take the position that such individuals are, in fact, agency employees and that the agency should have paid the appropriate withholding tax. The agency may be responsible for making IRS withholding payments, plus interest and penalties. A buyer is well advised to ascertain whether a seller has made a practice of using independent contractors and whether its independent contractors are, in fact, employees. A sales-tax audit can also result in unanticipated and substantial liability. Care should be taken to ensure that the seller has been making all required sales tax payments.

13. How Profitable are the Accounts?

The buyer needs to ascertain if some accounts are carrying others or if some are so-called "loss leaders." The reality is that most "loss leaders" only lead to endless losses and do not attract new business, despite what a seller might lead a buyer to believe. On the other hand, if an agency's revenues are dominated by one or two significant accounts, it is easy to lose sight of the fact that smaller accounts can also be profitable. Determining profitability is a function of examining each account rather than the agency as a whole.

14. Will the Future Operation be Autonomous or Merged under Singular Management?

From a seller's perspective, particularly if the purchase price is contingent on future performance, it is important that a significant degree of autonomy is maintained. Since the seller's future payout is based upon performance, it stands to reason that the seller's management should be permitted to continue to operate the business in the ordinary course until the earn-out period has expired, unless, of course, the seller's performance suffers to a point where the business proposition for both sides becomes unprofitable. In such instances, the buyer must have the right to step in and either take control of or have a strong voice in the daily operations of the business.

15. What Lease or Other Contractual Obligations Must be Assumed?

The terms of all real estate leases must be examined closely. Is the landlord's consent necessary to an assignment? The answer is usually "yes." Is the landlord's consent necessary if there is a stock sale rather than an asset sale? In many leases, a change of control (i.e., more than a 50% change in stock ownership) is treated as an assignment and requires the landlord's consent. Does the landlord have the right to terminate the lease? In addition to real estate leases, a seller may have lease obligations on equipment and even onerous employment agreements with employees providing for incentive compensation based on how well the agency does. Are there any bank loan agreements? How are they to be handled? Do agreements with advertisers provide that the agency cannot handle competitive brands, and how does this affect the deal with a potential buyer? These sample questions are posed to highlight the importance of an appropriate due diligence review on the part of the buyer prior to the completion of any sale.

16. What is the Fate of Branch Offices?

It is not unusual to see transactions where a seller's branch offices are involved. Branch offices are often established to service a client located in a particular market and are not free-standing offices in any real sense. If offices are going to be closed as a result of an acquisition or merger, both the seller and buyer must carefully review any liabilities that may arise as a result. It is a mistake to assume that the only issue to consider is whether a particular account can be properly serviced if a branch office is closed. While that is certainly an important question, the costly mistake is failing to consider any hidden liabilities associated with the closing.

17. What Representations and Warranties do the Buyer and Seller Want? What Will They Give?

Some of the most difficult provisions in an agreement are the representations and warranties the buyer wants from the seller. From the buyer's perspective, representations and warranties constitute a recitation of the assumptions upon which the buyer is basing its decision to purchase. Thus, a violation of the representations and warranties constitutes a breach of the agreement by the seller that gives rise to various remedies to protect the buyer, including, if material enough, rescission of the entire deal. From the seller's perspective, certain of the representations and warranties may include factors that are beyond the seller's control or knowledge. This conflict can lead to contentious negotiations

Listed below are some of the areas typically covered by representations and warranties. It is not unusual to see many more subjects covered, depending on the buyer's concerns.

- Has the seller confirmed its financial condition and assured the buyer there are no material adverse changes?
- Has the seller confirmed that there are no pending account terminations or budget reductions?
- If an asset deal, has the seller confirmed that there will be no pre-billing or prepayments for services that are to be rendered subsequent to the closing?
- Does the seller own the assets free and clear of any liens or encumbrances?
- Has the seller disclosed all material agreements to which it is a party and all material liabilities relating to the business?
- Has the seller disclosed any litigation or claims against seller?
- What is the collectibility of accounts receivable? Will seller's principal(s) guarantee them?

- Are there any agreements or transactions between the seller and related parties that may undermine the deal?

- Has the seller maintained the kind of insurance policies that are customary in the advertising agency business?

18. Are there Material Issues Concerning Employees?

One of the unique aspects of an acquisition or merger in the advertising agency business is that the buyer is actually acquiring very little in the way of hard assets. In truth, the buyer is acquiring an intangible asset, that is, the goodwill the employees built. As a result, issues relating to the seller's employees are critical. Questions that should be addressed include:

- How many employees of the seller will become employees of the buyer?

- What are the reasons for excluding particular employees from the merger and what obligations does the seller have towards those employees?

- Who is responsible for accrued vacation and severance for terminated employees of the seller?

- Has there been an honest evaluation of key account and creative employees (other than the owners of the seller)? Are employment agreements and restrictive covenants going to be necessary to make the deal work?

- How are deserving key executives who are not stockholders of the seller going to be compensated on the sale of business? One method is redirecting part of the purchase price to an incentive compensation arrangement. Another, but more complicated method, is a restructuring of the seller's stock ownership prior to the acquisition.

19. How is the Employment of the Seller's Owners to be Handled?

At the end of the day, those who own the agency being acquired are generally the most important employees of that agency. Employment agreements with owners who are active in the operations of the agency being acquired are therefore a critical element of a deal.

All too often, the terms and conditions of their employment agreements are left to the end of the negotiation process. It is far better to address the issues early in the negotiations than to risk derailment of a deal after weeks or months of negotiation and due diligence. Questions to address include:

- What will be their specific duties and to whom will they report?

- Will there be a guaranteed term of employment?

- What will be the base salary? This can become a contentious issue in transactions where the purchase price is dependent on a multiple of future profits. In such instances, the owners will want to minimize their salaries and receive the multiple on profits. On the other hand, the buyer is justified in wanting to pay the owners a legitimate, deductible, salary. Finding a balance is key.

- Will there be any incentive compensation? If so, will it relate to old accounts? New accounts? Profitability?

- What fringe benefits and perquisites will they receive?

- Will the buyer have a right to renegotiate or terminate employment agreements if the gross or net income of the business acquired falls below certain threshold amounts?

- What will be the scope of restrictive covenants prohibiting the seller's owners from inducing employees to leave, from soliciting or servicing accounts, or from engaging in competitive activities for a designated period of time after termination of employment?

- If an owner of the seller is retiring and will not remain an employee of the buyer, has the buyer considered a consulting arrangement from both a business point of view (continuity) and as a means of paying a portion of the purchase price on a tax-deductible basis?

- Will any of the seller's principals or key executives receive stock or options to purchase the stock of the buyer, and, if so, what are the terms?

Chapter Twenty-Three Forms

Form II.23.1 Checklist for Advertising Agency Mergers and Acquisitions

☐ 1.   What are the potential client conflicts?

☐ 2.   How long have accounts been with seller?

    ☐ a.   Are accounts multiproduct?
    ☐ b.   What are the growth opportunities?

☐ 3.   How deep is seller's management?

    ☐ a.   Is there succession management?
    ☐ b.   Are there close ties between any officer and clients?
    ☐ c.   Are there employment agreements?
    ☐ d.   Who is essential to the future operation of the company?

☐ 4.   Review accounting and legal procedures.

☐ 5.   Any pending lawsuits?

☐ 6.   How profitable are the accounts?

    ☐ a.   Are some accounts carrying others?
    ☐ b.   How dominant are the largest accounts?

☐ 7.   Will the future operation be autonomous or merged under singular management?

☐ 8.   What lease or building obligations must be assumed?

☐ 9.   What is the fate of branch offices?

☐ 10.   How will the deal be structured?

    ☐ a.   If a stock purchase, is it:
    ☐   (1)   Advantageous to seller for tax reasons, but
    ☐   (2)   Disadvantageous to buyer
      ☐   (a) for tax reasons; and/or
      ☐   (b) because it cannot allocate purchase price to depreciable assets; and/or
      ☐   (c) because it assumes history and obligations of seller; e.g., taxes, disclosed and undisclosed liabilities, etc.
    ☐ b.   If an asset purchase, is it:
    ☐   (1)   Advantageous to buyer because
      ☐   (a) it can purchase certain assets;
      ☐   (b) it can allocate purchase price for tax purposes; and/or
      ☐   (c) it can select which liabilities are to be assumed; but
    ☐   (2)   May be disadvantageous to seller unless "S" corporation, double tax.
    ☐   (3)   Do assets purchased include accounts (goodwill), work in process (inventory), furniture and equipment, accounts receivable?

☐   (4)   Alternatively, assets purchased may not include accounts receivable but, if so, payables not to be assumed; this would impact on purchase price to be paid.

☐   c.   Should it be structured as an exchange of stock, particularly if buyer is a listed company? If so, no immediate capital gains tax, but sellers' assets are still concentrated.

☐   11.   What is the purchase price?

    ☐   a.   How will it be determined?

    ☐   (1) A percentage of annual gross income, or

    ☐   (2) A multiple of average after-tax; net income for a period of time going forward to be paid over that period of time, or

    ☐   (3) Book value plus incentive compensation to principals under employment agreements based on performance of acquired business, or

    ☐   (4) Nominal purchase price; seller retains its assets other than accounts and work in process; incentive compensation based on future performance of business.

    ☐   b.   How will it be paid?

    ☐   (1) Buyer will want to pay as little as possible up front; or if required to make substantial up-front payment, it is generally no more than one-third of projected purchase price.

    ☐   (2) If purchase price is fixed amount payable over time and if a large part of business is represented by a few large accounts, the buyer may want forfeiture provisions if business is lost.

    ☐   (3) The purchase price (in both stock and asset deal) can be paid so as to maximize tax benefits to buyer, e.g., incentive compensation pursuant to employment agreements, signing and annual bonuses, and covenants not to compete and consulting agreements with retiring principals of the seller.

☐   12.   What are the representations as to the existing business?

    ☐   a.   Has the seller confirmed its financial condition and assured the buyer of no material adverse changes?

    ☐   b.   Has the seller confirmed that there are no pending account terminations or budget reductions?

    ☐   c.   If asset deal, has the seller confirmed that there will be no pre-billing or prepayments for serv☐ ices to be rendered subsequent to the sale?

    ☐   d.   Has the seller disclosed all material agreements to which seller is a party and all material liabilities relating to the business?

    ☐   e.   Has the seller disclosed any litigation or claims against seller?

    ☐   f.   What is the collectibility of accounts receivable?

☐   13.   Are material issues concerning employees resolved?

    ☐   a.   How many employees of seller will become employees of buyer?

    ☐   b.   Who is responsible for accrued vacation time and severance pay (or packages) for terminated employees of buyer?

    ☐   c.   Has there been an honest evaluation of key account and creative employees (other than the owners of the seller) who may require employment agreements and restrictive covenants to make the deal work?

☐   14.   How is the employment of the seller's owners to be handled?

    ☐   a.   What will be their specific duties and to whom will they report?

☐   b.   Will there be a guaranteed term of employment?

☐   c.   What will be the base salary?

☐   d.   Will there be any incentive compensation? If so, will it relate to old accounts, new accounts, profitability?

☐   e.   What fringe benefits and perquisites will they receive?

☐   f.   Will the buyer have a right to renegotiate or terminate employment agreements if gross or net income of the business acquired falls below certain threshold amounts?

☐   g.   What will be the scope and duration of restrictive covenants prohibiting principals from inducing employees to leave and from soliciting or servicing accounts after termination of employment?

☐   h.   If a principal owner of seller is retiring and will not become an employee of buyer, has the buyer considered a consulting arrangement both from a business point of view (continuity) and as a means of paying a portion of purchase price on a tax-deductible basis?

☐   i.   Will any of the seller's principals receive stock or options to purchase stock of buyer, and, if so, what will the terms be?

☐   15.   Practical considerations for negotiation:

☐   a.   Letter of confidentiality

☐   (1) Secrecy re: client information

☐   (2) Will buyer agree not to solicit seller's accounts for specific period if deal is not consummated?

☐   b.   When may buyer contact seller's accounts to inquire whether an account is considering any changes in its relationship with the seller?

Appendix

APPENDIX I

Copyright Application Forms TX, VA and PA

Author's Nationality or Domicile: Give the country of which the author is a citizen or the country in which the author is domiciled. Nationality or domicile **must** be given in all cases.

Nature of Authorship: After the words "Nature of Authorship," give a brief general statement of the nature of this particular author's contribution to the work. Examples: "Entire text"; "Coauthor of entire text"; "Computer program"; "Editorial revisions"; "Compilation and English translation"; "New text."

SPACE 3: Creation and Publication

General Instructions: Do not confuse "creation" with "publication." Every application for copyright registration must state "the year in which creation of the work was completed." Give the date and nation of first publication only if the work has been published.

Creation: Under the statute, a work is "created" when it is fixed in a copy or phonorecord for the first time. Where a work has been prepared over a period of time, the part of the work existing in fixed form on a particular date constitutes the created work on that date. The date you give here should be the year in which the author completed the particular version for which registration is now being sought, even if other versions exist or if further changes or additions are planned.

Publication: The statute defines "publication" as "the distribution of copies or phonorecords of a work to the public by sale or other transfer of ownership, or by rental, lease, or lending." A work is also "published" if there has been an "offering to distribute copies or phonorecords to a group of persons for purposes of further distribution, public performance, or public display." Give the full date (month, day, year) when, and the country where, publication first occurred. If first publication took place simultaneously in the United States and other countries, it is sufficient to state "U.S.A."

SPACE 4: Claimant(s)

Name(s) and Address(es) of Copyright Claimant(s): Give the name(s) and address(es) of the copyright claimant(s) in this work even if the claimant is the same as the author. Copyright in a work belongs initially to the author of the work (including, in the case of a work made for hire, the employer or other person for whom the work was prepared). The copyright claimant is either the author of the work or a person or organization to whom the copyright initially belonging to the author has been transferred.

Transfer: The statute provides that, if the copyright claimant is not the author, the application for registration must contain "a brief statement of how the claimant obtained ownership of the copyright." If any copyright claimant named in space 4 is not an author named in space 2, give a brief statement explaining how the claimant(s) obtained ownership of the copyright. Examples: "By written contract"; "Transfer of all rights by author"; "Assignment"; "By will." Do not attach transfer documents or other attachments or riders.

SPACE 5: Previous Registration

General Instructions: The questions in space 5 are intended to show whether an earlier registration has been made for this work and, if so, whether there is any basis for a new registration. As a general rule, only one basic copyright registration can be made for the same version of a particular work.

Same Version: If this version is substantially the same as the work covered by a previous registration, a second registration is not generally possible unless: (1) the work has been registered in unpublished form and a second registration is now being sought to cover this first published edition; or (2) someone other than the author is identified as copyright claimant in the earlier registration, and the author is now seeking registration in his or her own name. If either of these two exceptions applies, check the appropriate box and give the earlier registration number and date. Otherwise, do not submit Form TX. Instead, write the Copyright Office for information about supplementary registration or recordation of transfers of copyright ownership.

Changed Version: If the work has been changed and you are now seeking registration to cover the additions or revisions, check the last box in space 5, give the earlier registration number and date, and complete both parts of space 6 in accordance with the instructions below.

Previous Registration Number and Date: If more than one previous registration has been made for the work, give the number and date of the latest registration.

SPACE 6: Derivative Work or Compilation

General Instructions: Complete space 6 if this work is a "changed version," "compilation," or "derivative work" and if it incorporates one or more earlier works that have already been published or registered for copyright or that have fallen into the public domain. A "compilation" is defined as "a work formed by the collection and assembling of preexisting materials or of data that are selected, coordinated, or arranged in such a way that the resulting work as a whole constitutes an original work of authorship." A "derivative work" is "a work based on one or more preexisting works." Examples of derivative works include translations, fictionalizations, abridgments, condensations, or "any other form in which a work may be recast, transformed, or adapted." Derivative works also include works "consisting of editorial revisions, annotations, or other modifications" if these changes, as a whole, represent an original work of authorship.

Preexisting Material (space 6a): For derivative works, complete this space **and** space 6b. In space 6a identify the preexisting work that has been recast, transformed, or adapted. The preexisting work may be material that has been previously published, previously registered, or that is in the public domain. An example of preexisting material might be: "Russian version of Goncharov's 'Oblomov.'"

Material Added to This Work (space 6b): Give a brief, general statement of the new material covered by the copyright claim for which registration is sought. **Derivative work** examples include: "Foreword, editing, critical annotations"; "Translation"; "Chapters 11-17." If the work is a **compilation**, describe both the compilation itself and the material that has been compiled. Example: "Compilation of certain 1917 Speeches by Woodrow Wilson." A work may be both a derivative work and compilation, in which case a sample statement might be: "Compilation and additional new material."

SPACE 7, 8, 9: Fee, Correspondence, Certification, Return Address

Deposit Account: If you maintain a Deposit Account in the Copyright Office, identify it in space 7a. Otherwise leave the space blank and send the fee of $30 with your application and deposit.

Correspondence (space 7b): This space should contain the name, address, area code, telephone number, fax number, and email address (if available) of the person to be consulted if correspondence about this application becomes necessary.

Certification (space 8): The application cannot be accepted unless it bears the date and the **handwritten signature** of the author or other copyright claimant, or of the owner of exclusive right(s), or of the duly authorized agent of author, claimant, or owner of exclusive right(s).

Address for Return of Certificate (space 9): The address box must be completed legibly since the certificate will be returned in a window envelope.

Author's Nationality or Domicile: Give the country of which the author is a citizen or the country in which the author is domiciled. Nationality or domicile **must** be given in all cases.

Nature of Authorship: After the words "Nature of Authorship," give a brief general statement of the nature of this particular author's contribution to the work. Examples: "Entire text"; "Coauthor of entire text"; "Computer program"; "Editorial revisions"; "Compilation and English translation"; "New text."

SPACE 3: Creation and Publication

General Instructions: Do not confuse "creation" with "publication." Every application for copyright registration must state "the year in which creation of the work was completed." Give the date and nation of first publication only if the work has been published.

Creation: Under the statute, a work is "created" when it is fixed in a copy or phonorecord for the first time. Where a work has been prepared over a period of time, the part of the work existing in fixed form on a particular date constitutes the created work on that date. The date you give here should be the year in which the author completed the particular version for which registration is now being sought, even if other versions exist or if further changes or additions are planned.

Publication: The statute defines "publication" as "the distribution of copies or phonorecords of a work to the public by sale or other transfer of ownership, or by rental, lease, or lending." A work is also "published" if there has been an "offering to distribute copies or phonorecords to a group of persons for purposes of further distribution, public performance, or public display." Give the full date (month, day, year) when, and the country where, publication first occurred. If first publication took place simultaneously in the United States and other countries, it is sufficient to state "U.S.A."

SPACE 4: Claimant(s)

Name(s) and Address(es) of Copyright Claimant(s): Give the name(s) and address(es) of the copyright claimant(s) in this work even if the claimant is the same as the author. Copyright in a work belongs initially to the author of the work (including, in the case of a work made for hire, the employer or other person for whom the work was prepared). The copyright claimant is either the author of the work or a person or organization to whom the copyright initially belonging to the author has been transferred.

Transfer: The statute provides that, if the copyright claimant is not the author, the application for registration must contain "a brief statement of how the claimant obtained ownership of the copyright." If any copyright claimant named in space 4 is not an author named in space 2, give a brief statement explaining how the claimant(s) obtained ownership of the copyright. Examples: "By written contract"; "Transfer of all rights by author"; "Assignment"; "By will." Do not attach transfer documents or other attachments or riders.

SPACE 5: Previous Registration

General Instructions: The questions in space 5 are intended to show whether an earlier registration has been made for this work and, if so, whether there is any basis for a new registration. As a general rule, only one basic copyright registration can be made for the same version of a particular work.

Same Version: If this version is substantially the same as the work covered by a previous registration, a second registration is not generally possible unless: (1) the work has been registered in unpublished form and a second registration is now being sought to cover this first published edition; or (2) someone other than the author is identified as copyright claimant in the earlier registration, and the author is now seeking registration in his or her own name. If either of these two exceptions applies, check the appropriate box and give the earlier registration number and date. Otherwise, do not submit Form TX. Instead, write the Copyright Office for information about supplementary registration or recordation of transfers of copyright ownership.

Changed Version: If the work has been changed and you are now seeking registration to cover the additions or revisions, check the last box in space 5, give the earlier registration number and date, and complete both parts of space 6 in accordance with the instructions below.

Previous Registration Number and Date: If more than one previous registration has been made for the work, give the number and date of the latest registration.

SPACE 6: Derivative Work or Compilation

General Instructions: Complete space 6 if this work is a "changed version," "compilation," or "derivative work" and if it incorporates one or more earlier works that have already been published or registered for copyright or that have fallen into the public domain. A "compilation" is defined as "a work formed by the collection and assembling of preexisting materials or of data that are selected, coordinated, or arranged in such a way that the resulting work as a whole constitutes an original work of authorship." A "derivative work" is "a work based on one or more preexisting works." Examples of derivative works include translations, fictionalizations, abridgments, condensations, or "any other form in which a work may be recast, transformed, or adapted." Derivative works also include works "consisting of editorial revisions, annotations, or other modifications" if these changes, as a whole, represent an original work of authorship.

Preexisting Material (space 6a): For derivative works, complete this space **and** space 6b. In space 6a identify the preexisting work that has been recast, transformed, or adapted. The preexisting work may be material that has been previously published, previously registered, or that is in the public domain. An example of preexisting material might be: "Russian version of Goncharov's 'Oblomov.'"

Material Added to This Work (space 6b): Give a brief, general statement of the new material covered by the copyright claim for which registration is sought. **Derivative work** examples include: "Foreword, editing, critical annotations"; "Translation"; "Chapters 11-17." If the work is a **compilation**, describe both the compilation itself and the material that has been compiled. Example: "Compilation of certain 1917 Speeches by Woodrow Wilson." A work may be both a derivative work and compilation, in which case a sample statement might be: "Compilation and additional new material."

SPACE 7,8,9: Fee, Correspondence, Certification, Return Address

Deposit Account: If you maintain a Deposit Account in the Copyright Office, identify it in space 7a. Otherwise leave the space blank and send the fee of $30 with your application and deposit.

Correspondence (space 7b): This space should contain the name, address, area code, telephone number, fax number, and email address (if available) of the person to be consulted if correspondence about this application becomes necessary.

Certification (space 8): The application cannot be accepted unless it bears the date and the **handwritten signature** of the author or other copyright claimant, or of the owner of exclusive right(s), or of the duly authorized agent of author, claimant, or owner of exclusive right(s).

Address for Return of Certificate (space 9): The address box must be completed legibly since the certificate will be returned in a window envelope.

Author's Nationality or Domicile: Give the country of which the author is a citizen or the country in which the author is domiciled. Nationality or domicile **must** be given in all cases.

Nature of Authorship: After the words "Nature of Authorship," give a brief general statement of the nature of this particular author's contribution to the work. Examples: "Entire text"; "Coauthor of entire text"; "Computer program"; "Editorial revisions"; "Compilation and English translation"; "New text."

SPACE 3: Creation and Publication

General Instructions: Do not confuse "creation" with "publication." Every application for copyright registration must state "the year in which creation of the work was completed." Give the date and nation of first publication only if the work has been published.

Creation: Under the statute, a work is "created" when it is fixed in a copy or phonorecord for the first time. Where a work has been prepared over a period of time, the part of the work existing in fixed form on a particular date constitutes the created work on that date. The date you give here should be the year in which the author completed the particular version for which registration is now being sought, even if other versions exist or if further changes or additions are planned.

Publication: The statute defines "publication" as "the distribution of copies or phonorecords of a work to the public by sale or other transfer of ownership, or by rental, lease, or lending." A work is also "published" if there has been an "offering to distribute copies or phonorecords to a group of persons for purposes of further distribution, public performance, or public display." Give the full date (month, day, year) when, and the country where, publication first occurred. If first publication took place simultaneously in the United States and other countries, it is sufficient to state "U.S.A."

SPACE 4: Claimant(s)

Name(s) and Address(es) of Copyright Claimant(s): Give the name(s) and address(es) of the copyright claimant(s) in this work even if the claimant is the same as the author. Copyright in a work belongs initially to the author of the work (including, in the case of a work made for hire, the employer or other person for whom the work was prepared). The copyright claimant is either the author of the work or a person or organization to whom the copyright initially belonging to the author has been transferred.

Transfer: The statute provides that, if the copyright claimant is not the author, the application for registration must contain "a brief statement of how the claimant obtained ownership of the copyright." If any copyright claimant named in space 4 is not an author named in space 2, give a brief statement explaining how the claimant(s) obtained ownership of the copyright. Examples: "By written contract"; "Transfer of all rights by author"; "Assignment"; "By will." Do not attach transfer documents or other attachments or riders.

SPACE 5: Previous Registration

General Instructions: The questions in space 5 are intended to show whether an earlier registration has been made for this work and, if so, whether there is any basis for a new registration. As a general rule, only one basic copyright registration can be made for the same version of a particular work.

Same Version: If this version is substantially the same as the work covered by a previous registration, a second registration is not generally possible unless: (1) the work has been registered in unpublished form and a second registration is now being sought to cover this first published edition; or (2) someone other than the author is identified as copyright claimant in the earlier registration, and the author is now seeking registration in his or her own name. If either of these two exceptions applies, check the appropriate box and give the earlier registration number and date. Otherwise, do not submit Form TX. Instead, write the Copyright Office for information about supplementary registration or recordation of transfers of copyright ownership.

Changed Version: If the work has been changed and you are now seeking registration to cover the additions or revisions, check the last box in space 5, give the earlier registration number and date, and complete both parts of space 6 in accordance with the instructions below.

Previous Registration Number and Date: If more than one previous registration has been made for the work, give the number and date of the latest registration.

SPACE 6: Derivative Work or Compilation

General Instructions: Complete space 6 if this work is a "changed version," "compilation," or "derivative work" and if it incorporates one or more earlier works that have already been published or registered for copyright or that have fallen into the public domain. A "compilation" is defined as "a work formed by the collection and assembling of preexisting materials or of data that are selected, coordinated, or arranged in such a way that the resulting work as a whole constitutes an original work of authorship." A "derivative work" is "a work based on one or more preexisting works." Examples of derivative works include translations, fictionalizations, abridgments, condensations, or "any other form in which a work may be recast, transformed, or adapted." Derivative works also include works "consisting of editorial revisions, annotations, or other modifications" if these changes, as a whole, represent an original work of authorship.

Preexisting Material (space 6a): For derivative works, complete this space **and** space 6b. In space 6a identify the preexisting work that has been recast, transformed, or adapted. The preexisting work may be material that has been previously published, previously registered, or that is in the public domain. An example of preexisting material might be: "Russian version of Goncharov's 'Oblomov.'"

Material Added to This Work (space 6b): Give a brief, general statement of the new material covered by the copyright claim for which registration is sought. **Derivative work** examples include: "Foreword, editing, critical annotations"; "Translation"; "Chapters 11-17." If the work is a **compilation**, describe both the compilation itself and the material that has been compiled. Example: "Compilation of certain 1917 Speeches by Woodrow Wilson." A work may be both a derivative work and compilation, in which case a sample statement might be: "Compilation and additional new material."

SPACE 7,8,9: Fee, Correspondence, Certification, Return Address

Deposit Account: If you maintain a Deposit Account in the Copyright Office, identify it in space 7a. Otherwise leave the space blank and send the fee of $30 with your application and deposit.

Correspondence (space 7b): This space should contain the name, address, area code, telephone number, fax number, and email address (if available) of the person to be consulted if correspondence about this application becomes necessary.

Certification (space 8): The application cannot be accepted unless it bears the date and the **handwritten signature** of the author or other copyright claimant, or of the owner of exclusive right(s), or of the duly authorized agent of author, claimant, or owner of exclusive right(s).

Address for Return of Certificate (space 9): The address box must be completed legibly since the certificate will be returned in a window envelope.

Author's Nationality or Domicile: Give the country of which the author is a citizen or the country in which the author is domiciled. Nationality or domicile **must** be given in all cases.

Nature of Authorship: After the words "Nature of Authorship," give a brief general statement of the nature of this particular author's contribution to the work. Examples: "Entire text"; "Coauthor of entire text"; "Computer program"; "Editorial revisions"; "Compilation and English translation"; "New text."

SPACE 3: Creation and Publication

General Instructions: Do not confuse "creation" with "publication." Every application for copyright registration must state "the year in which creation of the work was completed." Give the date and nation of first publication only if the work has been published.

Creation: Under the statute, a work is "created" when it is fixed in a copy or phonorecord for the first time. Where a work has been prepared over a period of time, the part of the work existing in fixed form on a particular date constitutes the created work on that date. The date you give here should be the year in which the author completed the particular version for which registration is now being sought, even if other versions exist or if further changes or additions are planned.

Publication: The statute defines "publication" as "the distribution of copies or phonorecords of a work to the public by sale or other transfer of ownership, or by rental, lease, or lending." A work is also "published" if there has been an "offering to distribute copies or phonorecords to a group of persons for purposes of further distribution, public performance, or public display." Give the full date (month, day, year) when, and the country where, publication first occurred. If first publication took place simultaneously in the United States and other countries, it is sufficient to state "U.S.A."

SPACE 4: Claimant(s)

Name(s) and Address(es) of Copyright Claimant(s): Give the name(s) and address(es) of the copyright claimant(s) in this work even if the claimant is the same as the author. Copyright in a work belongs initially to the author of the work (including, in the case of a work made for hire, the employer or other person for whom the work was prepared). The copyright claimant is either the author of the work or a person or organization to whom the copyright initially belonging to the author has been transferred.

Transfer: The statute provides that, if the copyright claimant is not the author, the application for registration must contain "a brief statement of how the claimant obtained ownership of the copyright." If any copyright claimant named in space 4 is not an author named in space 2, give a brief statement explaining how the claimant(s) obtained ownership of the copyright. Examples: "By written contract"; "Transfer of all rights by author"; "Assignment"; "By will." Do not attach transfer documents or other attachments or riders.

SPACE 5: Previous Registration

General Instructions: The questions in space 5 are intended to show whether an earlier registration has been made for this work and, if so, whether there is any basis for a new registration. As a general rule, only one basic copyright registration can be made for the same version of a particular work.

Same Version: If this version is substantially the same as the work covered by a previous registration, a second registration is not generally possible unless: (1) the work has been registered in unpublished form and a second registration is now being sought to cover this first published edition; or (2) someone other than the author is identified as copyright claimant in the earlier registration, and the author is now seeking registration in his or her own name. If either of these two exceptions applies, check the appropriate box and give the earlier registration number and date. Otherwise, do not submit Form TX. Instead, write the Copyright Office for information about supplementary registration or recordation of transfers of copyright ownership.

Changed Version: If the work has been changed and you are now seeking registration to cover the additions or revisions, check the last box in space 5, give the earlier registration number and date, and complete both parts of space 6 in accordance with the instructions below.

Previous Registration Number and Date: If more than one previous registration has been made for the work, give the number and date of the latest registration.

SPACE 6: Derivative Work or Compilation

General Instructions: Complete space 6 if this work is a "changed version," "compilation," or "derivative work" and if it incorporates one or more earlier works that have already been published or registered for copyright or that have fallen into the public domain. A "compilation" is defined as "a work formed by the collection and assembling of preexisting materials or of data that are selected, coordinated, or arranged in such a way that the resulting work as a whole constitutes an original work of authorship." A "derivative work" is "a work based on one or more preexisting works." Examples of derivative works include translations, fictionalizations, abridgments, condensations, or "any other form in which a work may be recast, transformed, or adapted." Derivative works also include works "consisting of editorial revisions, annotations, or other modifications" if these changes, as a whole, represent an original work of authorship.

Preexisting Material (space 6a): For derivative works, complete this space **and** space 6b. In space 6a identify the preexisting work that has been recast, transformed, or adapted. The preexisting work may be material that has been previously published, previously registered, or that is in the public domain. An example of preexisting material might be: "Russian version of Goncharov's 'Oblomov.'"

Material Added to This Work (space 6b): Give a brief, general statement of the new material covered by the copyright claim for which registration is sought. **Derivative work** examples include: "Foreword, editing, critical annotations"; "Translation"; "Chapters 11-17." If the work is a **compilation**, describe both the compilation itself and the material that has been compiled. Example: "Compilation of certain 1917 Speeches by Woodrow Wilson." A work may be both a derivative work and compilation, in which case a sample statement might be: "Compilation and additional new material."

SPACE 7,8,9: Fee, Correspondence, Certification, Return Address

Deposit Account: If you maintain a Deposit Account in the Copyright Office, identify it in space 7a. Otherwise leave the space blank and send the fee of $30 with your application and deposit.

Correspondence (space 7b): This space should contain the name, address, area code, telephone number, fax number, and email address (if available) of the person to be consulted if correspondence about this application becomes necessary.

Certification (space 8): The application cannot be accepted unless it bears the date and the **handwritten signature** of the author or other copyright claimant, or of the owner of exclusive right(s), or of the duly authorized agent of author, claimant, or owner of exclusive right(s).

Address for Return of Certificate (space 9): The address box must be completed legibly since the certificate will be returned in a window envelope.

Author's Nationality or Domicile: Give the country of which the author is a citizen or the country in which the author is domiciled. Nationality or domicile **must** be given in all cases.

Nature of Authorship: After the words "Nature of Authorship," give a brief general statement of the nature of this particular author's contribution to the work. Examples: "Entire text"; "Coauthor of entire text"; "Computer program"; "Editorial revisions"; "Compilation and English translation"; "New text."

SPACE 3: Creation and Publication

General Instructions: Do not confuse "creation" with "publication." Every application for copyright registration must state "the year in which creation of the work was completed." Give the date and nation of first publication only if the work has been published.

Creation: Under the statute, a work is "created" when it is fixed in a copy or phonorecord for the first time. Where a work has been prepared over a period of time, the part of the work existing in fixed form on a particular date constitutes the created work on that date. The date you give here should be the year in which the author completed the particular version for which registration is now being sought, even if other versions exist or if further changes or additions are planned.

Publication: The statute defines "publication" as "the distribution of copies or phonorecords of a work to the public by sale or other transfer of ownership, or by rental, lease, or lending." A work is also "published" if there has been an "offering to distribute copies or phonorecords to a group of persons for purposes of further distribution, public performance, or public display." Give the full date (month, day, year) when, and the country where, publication first occurred. If first publication took place simultaneously in the United States and other countries, it is sufficient to state "U.S.A."

SPACE 4: Claimant(s)

Name(s) and Address(es) of Copyright Claimant(s): Give the name(s) and address(es) of the copyright claimant(s) in this work even if the claimant is the same as the author. Copyright in a work belongs initially to the author of the work (including, in the case of a work made for hire, the employer or other person for whom the work was prepared). The copyright claimant is either the author of the work or a person or organization to whom the copyright initially belonging to the author has been transferred.

Transfer: The statute provides that, if the copyright claimant is not the author, the application for registration must contain "a brief statement of how the claimant obtained ownership of the copyright." If any copyright claimant named in space 4 is not an author named in space 2, give a brief statement explaining how the claimant(s) obtained ownership of the copyright. Examples: "By written contract"; "Transfer of all rights by author"; "Assignment"; "By will." Do not attach transfer documents or other attachments or riders.

SPACE 5: Previous Registration

General Instructions: The questions in space 5 are intended to show whether an earlier registration has been made for this work and, if so, whether there is any basis for a new registration. As a general rule, only one basic copyright registration can be made for the same version of a particular work.

Same Version: If this version is substantially the same as the work covered by a previous registration, a second registration is not generally possible unless: (1) the work has been registered in unpublished form and a second registration is now being sought to cover this first published edition; or (2) someone other than the author is identified as copyright claimant in the earlier registration, and the author is now seeking registration in his or her own name. If either of these two exceptions applies, check the appropriate box and give the earlier registration number and date. Otherwise, do not submit Form TX. Instead, write the Copyright Office for information about supplementary registration or recordation of transfers of copyright ownership.

Changed Version: If the work has been changed and you are now seeking registration to cover the additions or revisions, check the last box in space 5, give the earlier registration number and date, and complete both parts of space 6 in accordance with the instructions below.

Previous Registration Number and Date: If more than one previous registration has been made for the work, give the number and date of the latest registration.

SPACE 6: Derivative Work or Compilation

General Instructions: Complete space 6 if this work is a "changed version," "compilation," or "derivative work" and if it incorporates one or more earlier works that have already been published or registered for copyright or that have fallen into the public domain. A "compilation" is defined as "a work formed by the collection and assembling of preexisting materials or of data that are selected, coordinated, or arranged in such a way that the resulting work as a whole constitutes an original work of authorship." A "derivative work" is "a work based on one or more preexisting works." Examples of derivative works include translations, fictionalizations, abridgments, condensations, or "any other form in which a work may be recast, transformed, or adapted." Derivative works also include works "consisting of editorial revisions, annotations, or other modifications" if these changes, as a whole, represent an original work of authorship.

Preexisting Material (space 6a): For derivative works, complete this space **and** space 6b. In space 6a identify the preexisting work that has been recast, transformed, or adapted. The preexisting work may be material that has been previously published, previously registered, or that is in the public domain. An example of preexisting material might be: "Russian version of Goncharov's 'Oblomov.'"

Material Added to This Work (space 6b): Give a brief, general statement of the new material covered by the copyright claim for which registration is sought. **Derivative work** examples include: "Foreword, editing, critical annotations"; "Translation"; "Chapters 11-17." If the work is a **compilation**, describe both the compilation itself and the material that has been compiled. Example: "Compilation of certain 1917 Speeches by Woodrow Wilson." A work may be both a derivative work and compilation, in which case a sample statement might be: "Compilation and additional new material."

SPACE 7, 8, 9: Fee, Correspondence, Certification, Return Address

Deposit Account: If you maintain a Deposit Account in the Copyright Office, identify it in space 7a. Otherwise leave the space blank and send the fee of $30 with your application and deposit.

Correspondence (space 7b): This space should contain the name, address, area code, telephone number, fax number, and email address (if available) of the person to be consulted if correspondence about this application becomes necessary.

Certification (space 8): The application cannot be accepted unless it bears the date and the **handwritten signature** of the author or other copyright claimant, or of the owner of exclusive right(s), or of the duly authorized agent of author, claimant, or owner of exclusive right(s).

Address for Return of Certificate (space 9): The address box must be completed legibly since the certificate will be returned in a window envelope.

Author's Nationality or Domicile: Give the country of which the author is a citizen or the country in which the author is domiciled. Nationality or domicile **must** be given in all cases.

Nature of Authorship: After the words "Nature of Authorship," give a brief general statement of the nature of this particular author's contribution to the work. Examples: "Entire text"; "Coauthor of entire text"; "Computer program"; "Editorial revisions"; "Compilation and English translation"; "New text."

SPACE 3: Creation and Publication

General Instructions: Do not confuse "creation" with "publication." Every application for copyright registration must state "the year in which creation of the work was completed." Give the date and nation of first publication only if the work has been published.

Creation: Under the statute, a work is "created" when it is fixed in a copy or phonorecord for the first time. Where a work has been prepared over a period of time, the part of the work existing in fixed form on a particular date constitutes the created work on that date. The date you give here should be the year in which the author completed the particular version for which registration is now being sought, even if other versions exist or if further changes or additions are planned.

Publication: The statute defines "publication" as "the distribution of copies or phonorecords of a work to the public by sale or other transfer of ownership, or by rental, lease, or lending." A work is also "published" if there has been an "offering to distribute copies or phonorecords to a group of persons for purposes of further distribution, public performance, or public display." Give the full date (month, day, year) when, and the country where, publication first occurred. If first publication took place simultaneously in the United States and other countries, it is sufficient to state "U.S.A."

SPACE 4: Claimant(s)

Name(s) and Address(es) of Copyright Claimant(s): Give the name(s) and address(es) of the copyright claimant(s) in this work even if the claimant is the same as the author. Copyright in a work belongs initially to the author of the work (including, in the case of a work made for hire, the employer or other person for whom the work was prepared). The copyright claimant is either the author of the work or a person or organization to whom the copyright initially belonging to the author has been transferred.

Transfer: The statute provides that, if the copyright claimant is not the author, the application for registration must contain "a brief statement of how the claimant obtained ownership of the copyright." If any copyright claimant named in space 4 is not an author named in space 2, give a brief statement explaining how the claimant(s) obtained ownership of the copyright. Examples: "By written contract"; "Transfer of all rights by author"; "Assignment"; "By will." Do not attach transfer documents or other attachments or riders.

SPACE 5: Previous Registration

General Instructions: The questions in space 5 are intended to show whether an earlier registration has been made for this work and, if so, whether there is any basis for a new registration. As a general rule, only one basic copyright registration can be made for the same version of a particular work.

Same Version: If this version is substantially the same as the work covered by a previous registration, a second registration is not generally possible unless: (1) the work has been registered in unpublished form and a second registration is now being sought to cover this first published edition; or (2) someone other than the author is identified as copyright claimant in the earlier registration, and the author is now seeking registration in his or her own name. If either of these two exceptions applies, check the appropriate box and give the earlier registration number and date. Otherwise, do not submit Form TX. Instead, write the Copyright Office for information about supplementary registration or recordation of transfers of copyright ownership.

Changed Version: If the work has been changed and you are now seeking registration to cover the additions or revisions, check the last box in space 5, give the earlier registration number and date, and complete both parts of space 6 in accordance with the instructions below.

Previous Registration Number and Date: If more than one previous registration has been made for the work, give the number and date of the latest registration.

SPACE 6: Derivative Work or Compilation

General Instructions: Complete space 6 if this work is a "changed version," "compilation," or "derivative work" and if it incorporates one or more earlier works that have already been published or registered for copyright or that have fallen into the public domain. A "compilation" is defined as "a work formed by the collection and assembling of preexisting materials or of data that are selected, coordinated, or arranged in such a way that the resulting work as a whole constitutes an original work of authorship." A "derivative work" is "a work based on one or more preexisting works." Examples of derivative works include translations, fictionalizations, abridgments, condensations, or "any other form in which a work may be recast, transformed, or adapted." Derivative works also include works "consisting of editorial revisions, annotations, or other modifications" if these changes, as a whole, represent an original work of authorship.

Preexisting Material (space 6a): For derivative works, complete this space **and** space 6b. In space 6a identify the preexisting work that has been recast, transformed, or adapted. The preexisting work may be material that has been previously published, previously registered, or that is in the public domain. An example of preexisting material might be: "Russian version of Goncharov's 'Oblomov.'"

Material Added to This Work (space 6b): Give a brief, general statement of the new material covered by the copyright claim for which registration is sought. **Derivative work** examples include: "Foreword, editing, critical annotations"; "Translation"; "Chapters 11-17." If the work is a **compilation**, describe both the compilation itself and the material that has been compiled. Example: "Compilation of certain 1917 Speeches by Woodrow Wilson." A work may be both a derivative work and compilation, in which case a sample statement might be: "Compilation and additional new material."

SPACE 7,8,9: Fee, Correspondence, Certification, Return Address

Deposit Account: If you maintain a Deposit Account in the Copyright Office, identify it in space 7a. Otherwise leave the space blank and send the fee of $30 with your application and deposit.

Correspondence (space 7b): This space should contain the name, address, area code, telephone number, fax number, and email address (if available) of the person to be consulted if correspondence about this application becomes necessary.

Certification (space 8): The application cannot be accepted unless it bears the date and the **handwritten signature** of the author or other copyright claimant, or of the owner of exclusive right(s), or of the duly authorized agent of author, claimant, or owner of exclusive right(s).

Address for Return of Certificate (space 9): The address box must be completed legibly since the certificate will be returned in a window envelope.

Author's Nationality or Domicile: Give the country of which the author is a citizen or the country in which the author is domiciled. Nationality or domicile **must** be given in all cases.

Nature of Authorship: After the words "Nature of Authorship," give a brief general statement of the nature of this particular author's contribution to the work. Examples: "Entire text"; "Coauthor of entire text"; "Computer program"; "Editorial revisions"; "Compilation and English translation"; "New text."

SPACE 3: Creation and Publication

General Instructions: Do not confuse "creation" with "publication." Every application for copyright registration must state "the year in which creation of the work was completed." Give the date and nation of first publication only if the work has been published.

Creation: Under the statute, a work is "created" when it is fixed in a copy or phonorecord for the first time. Where a work has been prepared over a period of time, the part of the work existing in fixed form on a particular date constitutes the created work on that date. The date you give here should be the year in which the author completed the particular version for which registration is now being sought, even if other versions exist or if further changes or additions are planned.

Publication: The statute defines "publication" as "the distribution of copies or phonorecords of a work to the public by sale or other transfer of ownership, or by rental, lease, or lending." A work is also "published" if there has been an "offering to distribute copies or phonorecords to a group of persons for purposes of further distribution, public performance, or public display." Give the full date (month, day, year) when, and the country where, publication first occurred. If first publication took place simultaneously in the United States and other countries, it is sufficient to state "U.S.A."

SPACE 4: Claimant(s)

Name(s) and Address(es) of Copyright Claimant(s): Give the name(s) and address(es) of the copyright claimant(s) in this work even if the claimant is the same as the author. Copyright in a work belongs initially to the author of the work (including, in the case of a work made for hire, the employer or other person for whom the work was prepared). The copyright claimant is either the author of the work or a person or organization to whom the copyright initially belonging to the author has been transferred.

Transfer: The statute provides that, if the copyright claimant is not the author, the application for registration must contain "a brief statement of how the claimant obtained ownership of the copyright." If any copyright claimant named in space 4 is not an author named in space 2, give a brief statement explaining how the claimant(s) obtained ownership of the copyright. Examples: "By written contract"; "Transfer of all rights by author"; "Assignment"; "By will." Do not attach transfer documents or other attachments or riders.

SPACE 5: Previous Registration

General Instructions: The questions in space 5 are intended to show whether an earlier registration has been made for this work and, if so, whether there is any basis for a new registration. As a general rule, only one basic copyright registration can be made for the same version of a particular work.

Same Version: If this version is substantially the same as the work covered by a previous registration, a second registration is not generally possible unless: (1) the work has been registered in unpublished form and a second registration is now being sought to cover this first published edition; or (2) someone other than the author is identified as copyright claimant in the earlier registration, and the author is now seeking registration in his or her own name. If either of these two exceptions applies, check the appropriate box and give the earlier registration number and date. Otherwise, do not submit Form TX. Instead, write the Copyright Office for information about supplementary registration or recordation of transfers of copyright ownership.

Changed Version: If the work has been changed and you are now seeking registration to cover the additions or revisions, check the last box in space 5, give the earlier registration number and date, and complete both parts of space 6 in accordance with the instructions below.

Previous Registration Number and Date: If more than one previous registration has been made for the work, give the number and date of the latest registration.

SPACE 6: Derivative Work or Compilation

General Instructions: Complete space 6 if this work is a "changed version," "compilation," or "derivative work" and if it incorporates one or more earlier works that have already been published or registered for copyright or that have fallen into the public domain. A "compilation" is defined as "a work formed by the collection and assembling of preexisting materials or of data that are selected, coordinated, or arranged in such a way that the resulting work as a whole constitutes an original work of authorship." A "derivative work" is "a work based on one or more preexisting works." Examples of derivative works include translations, fictionalizations, abridgments, condensations, or "any other form in which a work may be recast, transformed, or adapted." Derivative works also include works "consisting of editorial revisions, annotations, or other modifications" if these changes, as a whole, represent an original work of authorship.

Preexisting Material (space 6a): For derivative works, complete this space **and** space 6b. In space 6a identify the preexisting work that has been recast, transformed, or adapted. The preexisting work may be material that has been previously published, previously registered, or that is in the public domain. An example of preexisting material might be: "Russian version of Goncharov's 'Oblomov.'"

Material Added to This Work (space 6b): Give a brief, general statement of the new material covered by the copyright claim for which registration is sought. **Derivative work** examples include: "Foreword, editing, critical annotations"; "Translation"; "Chapters 11-17." If the work is a **compilation**, describe both the compilation itself and the material that has been compiled. Example: "Compilation of certain 1917 Speeches by Woodrow Wilson." A work may be both a derivative work and compilation, in which case a sample statement might be: "Compilation and additional new material."

SPACE 7, 8, 9: Fee, Correspondence, Certification, Return Address

Deposit Account: If you maintain a Deposit Account in the Copyright Office, identify it in space 7a. Otherwise leave the space blank and send the fee of $30 with your application and deposit.

Correspondence (space 7b): This space should contain the name, address, area code, telephone number, fax number, and email address (if available) of the person to be consulted if correspondence about this application becomes necessary.

Certification (space 8): The application cannot be accepted unless it bears the date and the **handwritten signature** of the author or other copyright claimant, or of the owner of exclusive right(s), or of the duly authorized agent of author, claimant, or owner of exclusive right(s).

Address for Return of Certificate (space 9): The address box must be completed legibly since the certificate will be returned in a window envelope.

Author's Nationality or Domicile: Give the country of which the author is a citizen or the country in which the author is domiciled. Nationality or domicile **must** be given in all cases.

Nature of Authorship: After the words "Nature of Authorship," give a brief general statement of the nature of this particular author's contribution to the work. Examples: "Entire text"; "Coauthor of entire text"; "Computer program"; "Editorial revisions"; "Compilation and English translation"; "New text."

 SPACE 3: Creation and Publication

General Instructions: Do not confuse "creation" with "publication." Every application for copyright registration must state "the year in which creation of the work was completed." Give the date and nation of first publication only if the work has been published.

Creation: Under the statute, a work is "created" when it is fixed in a copy or phonorecord for the first time. Where a work has been prepared over a period of time, the part of the work existing in fixed form on a particular date constitutes the created work on that date. The date you give here should be the year in which the author completed the particular version for which registration is now being sought, even if other versions exist or if further changes or additions are planned.

Publication: The statute defines "publication" as "the distribution of copies or phonorecords of a work to the public by sale or other transfer of ownership, or by rental, lease, or lending." A work is also "published" if there has been an "offering to distribute copies or phonorecords to a group of persons for purposes of further distribution, public performance, or public display." Give the full date (month, day, year) when, and the country where, publication first occurred. If first publication took place simultaneously in the United States and other countries, it is sufficient to state "U.S.A."

 SPACE 4: Claimant(s)

Name(s) and Address(es) of Copyright Claimant(s): Give the name(s) and address(es) of the copyright claimant(s) in this work even if the claimant is the same as the author. Copyright in a work belongs initially to the author of the work (including, in the case of a work made for hire, the employer or other person for whom the work was prepared). The copyright claimant is either the author of the work or a person or organization to whom the copyright initially belonging to the author has been transferred.

Transfer: The statute provides that, if the copyright claimant is not the author, the application for registration must contain "a brief statement of how the claimant obtained ownership of the copyright." If any copyright claimant named in space 4 is not an author named in space 2, give a brief statement explaining how the claimant(s) obtained ownership of the copyright. Examples: "By written contract"; "Transfer of all rights by author"; "Assignment"; "By will." Do not attach transfer documents or other attachments or riders.

 SPACE 5: Previous Registration

General Instructions: The questions in space 5 are intended to show whether an earlier registration has been made for this work and, if so, whether there is any basis for a new registration. As a general rule, only one basic copyright registration can be made for the same version of a particular work.

Same Version: If this version is substantially the same as the work covered by a previous registration, a second registration is not generally possible unless: (1) the work has been registered in unpublished form and a second registration is now being sought to cover this first published edition; or (2) someone other than the

author is identified as copyright claimant in the earlier registration, and the author is now seeking registration in his or her own name. If either of these two exceptions applies, check the appropriate box and give the earlier registration number and date. Otherwise, do not submit Form TX. Instead, write the Copyright Office for information about supplementary registration or recordation of transfers of copyright ownership.

Changed Version: If the work has been changed and you are now seeking registration to cover the additions or revisions, check the last box in space 5, give the earlier registration number and date, and complete both parts of space 6 in accordance with the instructions below.

Previous Registration Number and Date: If more than one previous registration has been made for the work, give the number and date of the latest registration.

 SPACE 6: Derivative Work or Compilation

General Instructions: Complete space 6 if this work is a "changed version," "compilation," or "derivative work" and if it incorporates one or more earlier works that have already been published or registered for copyright or that have fallen into the public domain. A "compilation" is defined as "a work formed by the collection and assembling of preexisting materials or of data that are selected, coordinated, or arranged in such a way that the resulting work as a whole constitutes an original work of authorship." A "derivative work" is "a work based on one or more preexisting works." Examples of derivative works include translations, fictionalizations, abridgments, condensations, or "any other form in which a work may be recast, transformed, or adapted." Derivative works also include works "consisting of editorial revisions, annotations, or other modifications" if these changes, as a whole, represent an original work of authorship.

Preexisting Material (space 6a): For derivative works, complete this space **and** space 6b. In space 6a identify the preexisting work that has been recast, transformed, or adapted. The preexisting work may be material that has been previously published, previously registered, or that is in the public domain. An example of preexisting material might be: "Russian version of Goncharov's 'Oblomov.'"

Material Added to This Work (space 6b): Give a brief, general statement of the new material covered by the copyright claim for which registration is sought. **Derivative work** examples include: "Foreword, editing, critical annotations"; "Translation"; "Chapters 11-17." If the work is a **compilation**, describe both the compilation itself and the material that has been compiled. Example: "Compilation of certain 1917 Speeches by Woodrow Wilson." A work may be both a derivative work and compilation, in which case a sample statement might be: "Compilation and additional new material."

 SPACE 7,8,9: Fee, Correspondence, Certification, Return Address

Deposit Account: If you maintain a Deposit Account in the Copyright Office, identify it in space 7a. Otherwise leave the space blank and send the fee of $30 with your application and deposit.

Correspondence (space 7b): This space should contain the name, address, area code, telephone number, fax number, and email address (if available) of the person to be consulted if correspondence about this application becomes necessary.

Certification (space 8): The application cannot be accepted unless it bears the date and the **handwritten signature** of the author or other copyright claimant, or of the owner of exclusive right(s), or of the duly authorized agent of author, claimant, or owner of exclusive right(s).

Address for Return of Certificate (space 9): The address box must be completed legibly since the certificate will be returned in a window envelope.

Author's Nationality or Domicile: Give the country of which the author is a citizen or the country in which the author is domiciled. Nationality or domicile **must** be given in all cases.

Nature of Authorship: After the words "Nature of Authorship," give a brief general statement of the nature of this particular author's contribution to the work. Examples: "Entire text"; "Coauthor of entire text"; "Computer program"; "Editorial revisions"; "Compilation and English translation"; "New text."

SPACE 3: Creation and Publication

General Instructions: Do not confuse "creation" with "publication." Every application for copyright registration must state "the year in which creation of the work was completed." Give the date and nation of first publication only if the work has been published.

Creation: Under the statute, a work is "created" when it is fixed in a copy or phonorecord for the first time. Where a work has been prepared over a period of time, the part of the work existing in fixed form on a particular date constitutes the created work on that date. The date you give here should be the year in which the author completed the particular version for which registration is now being sought, even if other versions exist or if further changes or additions are planned.

Publication: The statute defines "publication" as "the distribution of copies or phonorecords of a work to the public by sale or other transfer of ownership, or by rental, lease, or lending." A work is also "published" if there has been an "offering to distribute copies or phonorecords to a group of persons for purposes of further distribution, public performance, or public display." Give the full date (month, day, year) when, and the country where, publication first occurred. If first publication took place simultaneously in the United States and other countries, it is sufficient to state "U.S.A."

SPACE 4: Claimant(s)

Name(s) and Address(es) of Copyright Claimant(s): Give the name(s) and address(es) of the copyright claimant(s) in this work even if the claimant is the same as the author. Copyright in a work belongs initially to the author of the work (including, in the case of a work made for hire, the employer or other person for whom the work was prepared). The copyright claimant is either the author of the work or a person or organization to whom the copyright initially belonging to the author has been transferred.

Transfer: The statute provides that, if the copyright claimant is not the author, the application for registration must contain "a brief statement of how the claimant obtained ownership of the copyright." If any copyright claimant named in space 4 is not an author named in space 2, give a brief statement explaining how the claimant(s) obtained ownership of the copyright. Examples: "By written contract"; "Transfer of all rights by author"; "Assignment"; "By will." Do not attach transfer documents or other attachments or riders.

SPACE 5: Previous Registration

General Instructions: The questions in space 5 are intended to show whether an earlier registration has been made for this work and, if so, whether there is any basis for a new registration. As a general rule, only one basic copyright registration can be made for the same version of a particular work.

Same Version: If this version is substantially the same as the work covered by a previous registration, a second registration is not generally possible unless: (1) the work has been registered in unpublished form and a second registration is now being sought to cover this first published edition; or (2) someone other than the author is identified as copyright claimant in the earlier registration, and the author is now seeking registration in his or her own name. If either of these two exceptions applies, check the appropriate box and give the earlier registration number and date. Otherwise, do not submit Form TX. Instead, write the Copyright Office for information about supplementary registration or recordation of transfers of copyright ownership.

Changed Version: If the work has been changed and you are now seeking registration to cover the additions or revisions, check the last box in space 5, give the earlier registration number and date, and complete both parts of space 6 in accordance with the instructions below.

Previous Registration Number and Date: If more than one previous registration has been made for the work, give the number and date of the latest registration.

SPACE 6: Derivative Work or Compilation

General Instructions: Complete space 6 if this work is a "changed version," "compilation," or "derivative work" and if it incorporates one or more earlier works that have already been published or registered for copyright or that have fallen into the public domain. A "compilation" is defined as "a work formed by the collection and assembling of preexisting materials or of data that are selected, coordinated, or arranged in such a way that the resulting work as a whole constitutes an original work of authorship." A "derivative work" is "a work based on one or more preexisting works." Examples of derivative works include translations, fictionalizations, abridgments, condensations, or "any other form in which a work may be recast, transformed, or adapted." Derivative works also include works "consisting of editorial revisions, annotations, or other modifications" if these changes, as a whole, represent an original work of authorship.

Preexisting Material (space 6a): For derivative works, complete this space **and** space 6b. In space 6a identify the preexisting work that has been recast, transformed, or adapted. The preexisting work may be material that has been previously published, previously registered, or that is in the public domain. An example of preexisting material might be: "Russian version of Goncharov's 'Oblomov.'"

Material Added to This Work (space 6b): Give a brief, general statement of the new material covered by the copyright claim for which registration is sought. **Derivative work** examples include: "Foreword, editing, critical annotations"; "Translation"; "Chapters 11-17." If the work is a **compilation**, describe both the compilation itself and the material that has been compiled. Example: "Compilation of certain 1917 Speeches by Woodrow Wilson." A work may be both a derivative work and compilation, in which case a sample statement might be: "Compilation and additional new material."

SPACE 7, 8, 9: Fee, Correspondence, Certification, Return Address

Deposit Account: If you maintain a Deposit Account in the Copyright Office, identify it in space 7a. Otherwise leave the space blank and send the fee of $30 with your application and deposit.

Correspondence (space 7b): This space should contain the name, address, area code, telephone number, fax number, and email address (if available) of the person to be consulted if correspondence about this application becomes necessary.

Certification (space 8): The application cannot be accepted unless it bears the date and the **handwritten signature** of the author or other copyright claimant, or of the owner of exclusive right(s), or of the duly authorized agent of author, claimant, or owner of exclusive right(s).

Address for Return of Certificate (space 9): The address box must be completed legibly since the certificate will be returned in a window envelope.

Author's Nationality or Domicile: Give the country of which the author is a citizen or the country in which the author is domiciled. Nationality or domicile **must** be given in all cases.

Nature of Authorship: After the words "Nature of Authorship," give a brief general statement of the nature of this particular author's contribution to the work. Examples: "Entire text"; "Coauthor of entire text"; "Computer program"; "Editorial revisions"; "Compilation and English translation"; "New text."

SPACE 3: Creation and Publication

General Instructions: Do not confuse "creation" with "publication." Every application for copyright registration must state "the year in which creation of the work was completed." Give the date and nation of first publication only if the work has been published.

Creation: Under the statute, a work is "created" when it is fixed in a copy or phonorecord for the first time. Where a work has been prepared over a period of time, the part of the work existing in fixed form on a particular date constitutes the created work on that date. The date you give here should be the year in which the author completed the particular version for which registration is now being sought, even if other versions exist or if further changes or additions are planned.

Publication: The statute defines "publication" as "the distribution of copies or phonorecords of a work to the public by sale or other transfer of ownership, or by rental, lease, or lending." A work is also "published" if there has been an "offering to distribute copies or phonorecords to a group of persons for purposes of further distribution, public performance, or public display." Give the full date (month, day, year) when, and the country where, publication first occurred. If first publication took place simultaneously in the United States and other countries, it is sufficient to state "U.S.A."

SPACE 4: Claimant(s)

Name(s) and Address(es) of Copyright Claimant(s): Give the name(s) and address(es) of the copyright claimant(s) in this work even if the claimant is the same as the author. Copyright in a work belongs initially to the author of the work (including, in the case of a work made for hire, the employer or other person for whom the work was prepared). The copyright claimant is either the author of the work or a person or organization to whom the copyright initially belonging to the author has been transferred.

Transfer: The statute provides that, if the copyright claimant is not the author, the application for registration must contain "a brief statement of how the claimant obtained ownership of the copyright." If any copyright claimant named in space 4 is not an author named in space 2, give a brief statement explaining how the claimant(s) obtained ownership of the copyright. Examples: "By written contract"; "Transfer of all rights by author"; "Assignment"; "By will." Do not attach transfer documents or other attachments or riders.

SPACE 5: Previous Registration

General Instructions: The questions in space 5 are intended to show whether an earlier registration has been made for this work and, if so, whether there is any basis for a new registration. As a general rule, only one basic copyright registration can be made for the same version of a particular work.

Same Version: If this version is substantially the same as the work covered by a previous registration, a second registration is not generally possible unless: (1) the work has been registered in unpublished form and a second registration is now being sought to cover this first published edition; or (2) someone other than the author is identified as copyright claimant in the earlier registration, and the author is now seeking registration in his or her own name. If either of these two exceptions applies, check the appropriate box and give the earlier registration number and date. Otherwise, do not submit Form TX. Instead, write the Copyright Office for information about supplementary registration or recordation of transfers of copyright ownership.

Changed Version: If the work has been changed and you are now seeking registration to cover the additions or revisions, check the last box in space 5, give the earlier registration number and date, and complete both parts of space 6 in accordance with the instructions below.

Previous Registration Number and Date: If more than one previous registration has been made for the work, give the number and date of the latest registration.

SPACE 6: Derivative Work or Compilation

General Instructions: Complete space 6 if this work is a "changed version," "compilation," or "derivative work" and if it incorporates one or more earlier works that have already been published or registered for copyright or that have fallen into the public domain. A "compilation" is defined as "a work formed by the collection and assembling of preexisting materials or of data that are selected, coordinated, or arranged in such a way that the resulting work as a whole constitutes an original work of authorship." A "derivative work" is "a work based on one or more preexisting works." Examples of derivative works include translations, fictionalizations, abridgments, condensations, or "any other form in which a work may be recast, transformed, or adapted." Derivative works also include works "consisting of editorial revisions, annotations, or other modifications" if these changes, as a whole, represent an original work of authorship.

Preexisting Material (space 6a): For derivative works, complete this space **and** space 6b. In space 6a identify the preexisting work that has been recast, transformed, or adapted. The preexisting work may be material that has been previously published, previously registered, or that is in the public domain. An example of preexisting material might be: "Russian version of Goncharov's 'Oblomov.'"

Material Added to This Work (space 6b): Give a brief, general statement of the new material covered by the copyright claim for which registration is sought. **Derivative work** examples include: "Foreword, editing, critical annotations"; "Translation"; "Chapters 11-17." If the work is a **compilation**, describe both the compilation itself and the material that has been compiled. Example: "Compilation of certain 1917 Speeches by Woodrow Wilson." A work may be both a derivative work and compilation, in which case a sample statement might be: "Compilation and additional new material."

SPACE 7,8,9: Fee, Correspondence, Certification, Return Address

Deposit Account: If you maintain a Deposit Account in the Copyright Office, identify it in space 7a. Otherwise leave the space blank and send the fee of $30 with your application and deposit.

Correspondence (space 7b): This space should contain the name, address, area code, telephone number, fax number, and email address (if available) of the person to be consulted if correspondence about this application becomes necessary.

Certification (space 8): The application cannot be accepted unless it bears the date and the **handwritten signature** of the author or other copyright claimant, or of the owner of exclusive right(s), or of the duly authorized agent of author, claimant, or owner of exclusive right(s).

Address for Return of Certificate (space 9): The address box must be completed legibly since the certificate will be returned in a window envelope.

Author's Nationality or Domicile: Give the country of which the author is a citizen or the country in which the author is domiciled. Nationality or domicile **must** be given in all cases.

Nature of Authorship: After the words "Nature of Authorship," give a brief general statement of the nature of this particular author's contribution to the work. Examples: "Entire text"; "Coauthor of entire text"; "Computer program"; "Editorial revisions"; "Compilation and English translation"; "New text."

SPACE 3: Creation and Publication

General Instructions: Do not confuse "creation" with "publication." Every application for copyright registration must state "the year in which creation of the work was completed." Give the date and nation of first publication only if the work has been published.

Creation: Under the statute, a work is "created" when it is fixed in a copy or phonorecord for the first time. Where a work has been prepared over a period of time, the part of the work existing in fixed form on a particular date constitutes the created work on that date. The date you give here should be the year in which the author completed the particular version for which registration is now being sought, even if other versions exist or if further changes or additions are planned.

Publication: The statute defines "publication" as "the distribution of copies or phonorecords of a work to the public by sale or other transfer of ownership, or by rental, lease, or lending." A work is also "published" if there has been an "offering to distribute copies or phonorecords to a group of persons for purposes of further distribution, public performance, or public display." Give the full date (month, day, year) when, and the country where, publication first occurred. If first publication took place simultaneously in the United States and other countries, it is sufficient to state "U.S.A."

SPACE 4: Claimant(s)

Name(s) and Address(es) of Copyright Claimant(s): Give the name(s) and address(es) of the copyright claimant(s) in this work even if the claimant is the same as the author. Copyright in a work belongs initially to the author of the work (including, in the case of a work made for hire, the employer or other person for whom the work was prepared). The copyright claimant is either the author of the work or a person or organization to whom the copyright initially belonging to the author has been transferred.

Transfer: The statute provides that, if the copyright claimant is not the author, the application for registration must contain "a brief statement of how the claimant obtained ownership of the copyright." If any copyright claimant named in space 4 is not an author named in space 2, give a brief statement explaining how the claimant(s) obtained ownership of the copyright. Examples: "By written contract"; "Transfer of all rights by author"; "Assignment"; "By will." Do not attach transfer documents or other attachments or riders.

SPACE 5: Previous Registration

General Instructions: The questions in space 5 are intended to show whether an earlier registration has been made for this work and, if so, whether there is any basis for a new registration. As a general rule, only one basic copyright registration can be made for the same version of a particular work.

Same Version: If this version is substantially the same as the work covered by a previous registration, a second registration is not generally possible unless: (1) the work has been registered in unpublished form and a second registration is now being sought to cover this first published edition; or (2) someone other than the

author is identified as copyright claimant in the earlier registration, and the author is now seeking registration in his or her own name. If either of these two exceptions applies, check the appropriate box and give the earlier registration number and date. Otherwise, do not submit Form TX. Instead, write the Copyright Office for information about supplementary registration or recordation of transfers of copyright ownership.

Changed Version: If the work has been changed and you are now seeking registration to cover the additions or revisions, check the last box in space 5, give the earlier registration number and date, and complete both parts of space 6 in accordance with the instructions below.

Previous Registration Number and Date: If more than one previous registration has been made for the work, give the number and date of the latest registration.

SPACE 6: Derivative Work or Compilation

General Instructions: Complete space 6 if this work is a "changed version," "compilation," or "derivative work" and if it incorporates one or more earlier works that have already been published or registered for copyright or that have fallen into the public domain. A "compilation" is defined as "a work formed by the collection and assembling of preexisting materials or of data that are selected, coordinated, or arranged in such a way that the resulting work as a whole constitutes an original work of authorship." A "derivative work" is "a work based on one or more preexisting works." Examples of derivative works include translations, fictionalizations, abridgments, condensations, or "any other form in which a work may be recast, transformed, or adapted." Derivative works also include works "consisting of editorial revisions, annotations, or other modifications" if these changes, as a whole, represent an original work of authorship.

Preexisting Material (space 6a): For derivative works, complete this space **and** space 6b. In space 6a identify the preexisting work that has been recast, transformed, or adapted. The preexisting work may be material that has been previously published, previously registered, or that is in the public domain. An example of preexisting material might be: "Russian version of Goncharov's 'Oblomov.'"

Material Added to This Work (space 6b): Give a brief, general statement of the new material covered by the copyright claim for which registration is sought. **Derivative work** examples include: "Foreword, editing, critical annotations"; "Translation"; "Chapters 11-17." If the work is a **compilation**, describe both the compilation itself and the material that has been compiled. Example: "Compilation of certain 1917 Speeches by Woodrow Wilson." A work may be both a derivative work and compilation, in which case a sample statement might be: "Compilation and additional new material."

SPACE 7, 8, 9: Fee, Correspondence, Certification, Return Address

Deposit Account: If you maintain a Deposit Account in the Copyright Office, identify it in space 7a. Otherwise leave the space blank and send the fee of $30 with your application and deposit.

Correspondence (space 7b): This space should contain the name, address, area code, telephone number, fax number, and email address (if available) of the person to be consulted if correspondence about this application becomes necessary.

Certification (space 8): The application cannot be accepted unless it bears the date and the **handwritten signature** of the author or other copyright claimant, or of the owner of exclusive right(s), or of the duly authorized agent of author, claimant, or owner of exclusive right(s).

Address for Return of Certificate (space 9): The address box must be completed legibly since the certificate will be returned in a window envelope.

Author's Nationality or Domicile: Give the country of which the author is a citizen or the country in which the author is domiciled. Nationality or domicile **must** be given in all cases.

Nature of Authorship: After the words "Nature of Authorship," give a brief general statement of the nature of this particular author's contribution to the work. Examples: "Entire text"; "Coauthor of entire text"; "Computer program"; "Editorial revisions"; "Compilation and English translation"; "New text."

SPACE 3: Creation and Publication

General Instructions: Do not confuse "creation" with "publication." Every application for copyright registration must state "the year in which creation of the work was completed." Give the date and nation of first publication only if the work has been published.

Creation: Under the statute, a work is "created" when it is fixed in a copy or phonorecord for the first time. Where a work has been prepared over a period of time, the part of the work existing in fixed form on a particular date constitutes the created work on that date. The date you give here should be the year in which the author completed the particular version for which registration is now being sought, even if other versions exist or if further changes or additions are planned.

Publication: The statute defines "publication" as "the distribution of copies or phonorecords of a work to the public by sale or other transfer of ownership, or by rental, lease, or lending." A work is also "published" if there has been an "offering to distribute copies or phonorecords to a group of persons for purposes of further distribution, public performance, or public display." Give the full date (month, day, year) when, and the country where, publication first occurred. If first publication took place simultaneously in the United States and other countries, it is sufficient to state "U.S.A."

SPACE 4: Claimant(s)

Name(s) and Address(es) of Copyright Claimant(s): Give the name(s) and address(es) of the copyright claimant(s) in this work even if the claimant is the same as the author. Copyright in a work belongs initially to the author of the work (including, in the case of a work made for hire, the employer or other person for whom the work was prepared). The copyright claimant is either the author of the work or a person or organization to whom the copyright initially belonging to the author has been transferred.

Transfer: The statute provides that, if the copyright claimant is not the author, the application for registration must contain "a brief statement of how the claimant obtained ownership of the copyright." If any copyright claimant named in space 4 is not an author named in space 2, give a brief statement explaining how the claimant(s) obtained ownership of the copyright. Examples: "By written contract"; "Transfer of all rights by author"; "Assignment"; "By will." Do not attach transfer documents or other attachments or riders.

SPACE 5: Previous Registration

General Instructions: The questions in space 5 are intended to show whether an earlier registration has been made for this work and, if so, whether there is any basis for a new registration. As a general rule, only one basic copyright registration can be made for the same version of a particular work.

Same Version: If this version is substantially the same as the work covered by a previous registration, a second registration is not generally possible unless: (1) the work has been registered in unpublished form and a second registration is now being sought to cover this first published edition; or (2) someone other than the author is identified as copyright claimant in the earlier registration, and the author is now seeking registration in his or her own name. If either of these two exceptions applies, check the appropriate box and give the earlier registration number and date. Otherwise, do not submit Form TX. Instead, write the Copyright Office for information about supplementary registration or recordation of transfers of copyright ownership.

Changed Version: If the work has been changed and you are now seeking registration to cover the additions or revisions, check the last box in space 5, give the earlier registration number and date, and complete both parts of space 6 in accordance with the instructions below.

Previous Registration Number and Date: If more than one previous registration has been made for the work, give the number and date of the latest registration.

SPACE 6: Derivative Work or Compilation

General Instructions: Complete space 6 if this work is a "changed version," "compilation," or "derivative work" and if it incorporates one or more earlier works that have already been published or registered for copyright or that have fallen into the public domain. A "compilation" is defined as "a work formed by the collection and assembling of preexisting materials or of data that are selected, coordinated, or arranged in such a way that the resulting work as a whole constitutes an original work of authorship." A "derivative work" is "a work based on one or more preexisting works." Examples of derivative works include translations, fictionalizations, abridgments, condensations, or "any other form in which a work may be recast, transformed, or adapted." Derivative works also include works "consisting of editorial revisions, annotations, or other modifications" if these changes, as a whole, represent an original work of authorship.

Preexisting Material (space 6a): For derivative works, complete this space **and** space 6b. In space 6a identify the preexisting work that has been recast, transformed, or adapted. The preexisting work may be material that has been previously published, previously registered, or that is in the public domain. An example of preexisting material might be: "Russian version of Goncharov's 'Oblomov.'"

Material Added to This Work (space 6b): Give a brief, general statement of the new material covered by the copyright claim for which registration is sought. **Derivative work** examples include: "Foreword, editing, critical annotations"; "Translation"; "Chapters 11-17." If the work is a **compilation**, describe both the compilation itself and the material that has been compiled. Example: "Compilation of certain 1917 Speeches by Woodrow Wilson." A work may be both a derivative work and compilation, in which case a sample statement might be: "Compilation and additional new material."

SPACE 7,8,9: Fee, Correspondence, Certification, Return Address

Deposit Account: If you maintain a Deposit Account in the Copyright Office, identify it in space 7a. Otherwise leave the space blank and send the fee of $30 with your application and deposit.

Correspondence (space 7b): This space should contain the name, address, area code, telephone number, fax number, and email address (if available) of the person to be consulted if correspondence about this application becomes necessary.

Certification (space 8): The application cannot be accepted unless it bears the date and the **handwritten signature** of the author or other copyright claimant, or of the owner of exclusive right(s), or of the duly authorized agent of author, claimant, or owner of exclusive right(s).

Address for Return of Certificate (space 9): The address box must be completed legibly since the certificate will be returned in a window envelope.

APPENDIX II

FTC Policy Statement Regarding Advertising Substantiation

Introduction

On March 11, 1983, the Commission published a notice requesting comments on its advertising substantiation program.[1] To facilitate analysis of the program, the notice posed a number of questions concerning the program's procedures, standards, benefits, and costs, and solicited suggestions for making the program more effective. Based on the public comments and the staff's review, the Commission has drawn certain conclusions about how the program is being implemented and how it might be refined to serve better the objective of maintaining a marketplace free of unfair and deceptive acts or practices. This statement articulates the Commission's policy with respect to advertising substantiation.

The Reasonable Basis Requirement

First, we reaffirm our commitment to the underlying legal requirement of advertising substantiation-that advertisers and ad agencies have a reasonable basis for advertising claims before they are disseminated.

The Commission intends to continue vigorous enforcement of this existing legal requirement that advertisers substantiate express and implied claims, however conveyed, that make objective assertions about the item or service advertised. Objective claims for products or services represent explicitly or by implication that the advertiser has a reasonable basis supporting these claims. These representations of substantiation are material to consumers. That is, consumers would be less likely to rely on claims for products and services if they knew the advertiser did not have a reasonable basis for believing them to be true.[2] Therefore, a firm's failure to possess and rely upon a reasonable basis for objective claims constitutes an unfair and deceptive act or practice in violation of Section 5 of the Federal Trade Commission Act.

Standards for Prior Substantiation

Many ads contain express or implied statements regarding the amount of support the advertiser has for the product claim. When the substantiation claim is express (e.g.., "tests prove", "doctors recommend", and "studies show"), the Commission expects the firm to have at least the advertised level of substantiation. Of course, an ad may imply more substantiation than it expressly claims or may imply to consumers that the firm has a certain type of support; in such cases, the advertiser must possess the amount and type of substantiation the ad actually communicates to consumers.

Absent an express or implied reference to a certain level of support, and absent other evidence indicating what consumer expectations would be, the Commission assumes that consumers expect a "reasonable basis" for claims. The Commission's determination of what constitutes a reasonable basis depends, as it does in an unfairness analysis, on a number of factors relevant to the benefits and costs of substantiating a particular claim. These factors include: the type of claim, the product, the consequences of a false claim, the benefits of a truthful claim, the cost of developing substantiation for the claim, and the amount of substantiation experts in the field believe is reasonable. Extrinsic evidence, such as expert testimony or consumer surveys, is useful to determine what level of substantiation consumers expect to support a particular product claim and the adequacy of evidence an advertiser possesses.

One issue the Commission examined was substantiation for implied claims. Although firms are unlikely to possess substantiation for implied claims they do not believe the ad makes, they should generally be aware of reasonable interpretations and will be expected to have prior substantiation for such claims. The Commission will take care to assure that it only challenges reasonable interpretations of advertising claims.[3]

Procedures for Obtaining Substantiation

In the past, the Commission has sought substantiation from firms in two different ways: through industry-wide "rounds" that involved publicized inquiries with identical or substantially similar demands to a number of firms within a targeted industry or to firms in different industries making the same type of claim; and on a case-by-case basis, by sending specific requests to individual companies under investigation. The Commission's review indicates that "rounds" have been costly to both the recipient and to the agency and have produced little or no law enforcement benefit over a case-by-case approach.

The Commission's traditional investigatory procedures allow the staff to investigate a number of firms within an industry at the same time, to develop necessary expertise within the area of investigation, and to announce our activities publicly in circumstances where public notice or comment is desirable. The Commission intends to continue undertaking such law enforcement efforts when appropriate. However, since substantiation is principally a law enforcement tool and the Commission's concern in such investigations is with the substantiation in the advertiser's possession, there is little, if any, information that the public could contribute in such investigations. Therefore, the Commission anticipates that substantiation investigations will rarely be made public before they are completed.

Accordingly, the Commission has determined that in the future it will rely on nonpublic requests for substantiation directed to individual companies via an informal access letter or, if necessary, a formal civil investigative demand. The Commission believes that tailored, firm-specific requests, whether directed to one firm or to several firms within the same industry, are a more efficient law enforcement technique. The Commission cannot presently foresee circumstances under which the past approach of industry-wide rounds would be appropriate in the ad substantiation area.

Relevance of Post-Claim Evidence in Substantiation Cases

The reasonable basis doctrine requires that firms have substantiation before disseminating a claim. The Commission has on occasion exercised its discretion, however, to consider supporting materials developed after disseminations The Commission has not previously identified in one document the circumstances in which it may, in its discretion, consider post-claim evidence in substantiation cases.[4] Such guidance can serve to clarify the program's actual operation as well as focus consideration of postclaim evidence on cases in which it is appropriate.

The Commission emphasizes that as a matter of law, firms lacking a reasonable basis before an ad is disseminated violate Section 5 of the FTC Act and are subject to prosecution. The goal of the advertising substantiation requirement is to assure that advertising is truthful, however, and the truth or falsity of a claim is always relevant to the Commission's deliberations. Therefore, it is important that the agency retain the discretion and flexibility to consider additional substantiating evidence, not as a substitute for an advertiser's prior substantiation, but rather in the following circumstances:

1. When deciding, before issuance of a complaint, whether there is a public interest in proceeding against a firm;

2. When assessing the adequacy of the substantiation an advertiser possessed before a claim was made; and

3. When deciding the need for or appropriate scope of an order to enter against a firm that lacked a reasonable basis prior to disseminating an advertisement.

First, using post-claim evidence to evaluate the truth of a claim, or otherwise using such evidence in deciding whether there is a public interest in continuing an investigation or issuing a complaint, is appropriate policy. This does not mean that the Commission will postpone action while firms create post-claim substantiation to prove the truthfulness of claims, nor does it mean that subsequent evidence of truthfulness absolves a firm of liability for failing to possess prior substantiation for a claim. The Commission focuses instead on whether existing evidence that claims are true should lead us in the exercise of our prosecutorial discretion to decline to initiate a law enforcement proceeding. If available post-claim evidence proves that the claim is true, issuing a complaint against a firm that may have violated the prior substantiation requirement is often inappropriate, particularly in light of competing demands on the Commission's resources.

Second, post-claim evidence may indicate that apparent deficiencies in the pre-claim substantiation materials have no practical significance. In evaluating the adequacy of prior substantiation, the Commission will consider only post-claim substantiation that sheds light on pre-existing substantiation. Thus, advertisers will not be allowed to create entirely new substantiation simply because their prior substantiation was inadequate.

Finally, the Commission may use post-claim evidence in determining the need for or appropriate scope of an order to be entered against a firm that lacked a reasonable basis. Thus, when additional evidence offered for the first time at trial suggests that the claim is true, the Commission may frame a narrower order than if there had been no post-claim evidence.

The Commission remains committed to the prior substantiation requirement and further believes that these discretionary factors will provide necessary flexibility. The Commission will consider post-claim evidence only in the circumstances listed above. But, whether it will do so in any particular case remains within its discretion.

Self Regulation Groups and Government Agencies

The Commission traditionally has enjoyed a close working relationship with self regulation groups and government agencies whose regulatory policies have some bearing on our law enforcement initiatives. The Commission will not necessarily defer, however, to a finding by a self-regulation group. An imprimatur from a self-regulation group will not automatically shield a firm from Commission prosecution, and an unfavorable determination will not mean the Commission will automatically take issue, or find liability if it does. Rather the Commission will make its judgment independently, evaluating each case on its merits. We intend to continue our useful relationships with self-regulation groups and to rely on the expertise and findings of other government agencies in our proceedings to the greatest extent possible.

By direction of the Commission.

---

[*] The distinction between pre-claim and post-claim evidence is only relevant when the charge is lack of substantiation. For other chases, such as falsity, when evidence was developed is irrelevant to its admissibility at trial.

[1] 48 FR 10471, March 11, 1983.

[2] Nor presumably would an advertiser have made such claims unless the advertiser thought they would be material to consumers.

[3] Individual Commissioners have expressed differing views as to how claims should be interpreted so that advertisers are not held to outlandish or tenuous interpretations. Notwithstanding these variations in approach, the focus of all Commissioners on reasonable interpretations of claims is intended to ensure that advertisers are not required to substantiate claims that were not made.

[4] The Commission's evidentiary rule, 16 C.F.R. 3.40, has sometimes been interpreted as precluding introduction of post-claim substantiation. In fact, it does not. Section 3.40 only provides a sanction against the introduction of evidence that should have been produced in response to a subpoena, but was not.

APPENDIX III

National Advertising Division, Children's Advertising Review Unit & National Advertising Review Board Procedures

NAD/NARB/CARU Procedures

Effective May 1, 2002

1.1 Definitions

A. The term "national advertising" shall include any paid commercial message, in any medium (including labeling), if it has the purpose of inducing a sale or other commercial transaction or persuading the audience of the value or usefulness of a company, product or service; if it is disseminated nationally or to a substantial portion of the United States, or is test market advertising prepared for national campaigns; and if the content is controlled by the advertiser.

B. The term "advertiser" shall mean any person or other legal entity that engages in "national advertising."

C. The term "advertising agency" shall mean any organization engaged in the creation and/or placement of "national advertising."

D. The term "public or non-industry member" shall mean any person who has a reputation for achievements in the public interest.

2.1 NAD/CARU

A. Function and Policies

The National Advertising Division of the Council of Better Business Bureaus (hereinafter NAD), and the Children's Advertising Review Unit (CARU), shall be responsible for receiving or initiating, evaluating, investigating, analyzing (in conjunction with outside experts, if warranted, and upon notice to the parties), and holding negotiations with an advertiser, and resolving complaints or questions from any source involving the truth or accuracy of national advertising, or consistency with CARU's Self-Regulatory Guidelines for Children's Advertising.

B. Advertising Monitoring

NAD and CARU are charged with independent responsibility for monitoring and reviewing national advertising for truthfulness, accuracy and, in the case of CARU, consistency with CARU's Self-Regulatory Guidelines for Children's Advertising.

C. Case Reports

The Council of Better Business Bureaus shall publish at least ten times each year the Case Reports, which will include the final case decisions of NAD, CARU and NARB, and summaries of any other matters concluded since the previous issue. Each final NAD, CARU and NARB case decision shall identify the advertiser, challenger, advertising agency, product or service, and subject matter reviewed. It shall also include a summary of each party's position, NAD, CARU or the NARB's decision and its rationale, and a concise Advertiser's Statement, if any. (See Section 2.9).CARU shall publish in the Case Reports a summary of CARU's actions, other than formal cases, during the preceding month. Included in this Activity Report, shall be the following:

(i)   Inquiries—summaries of informal inquiries under CARU's Expedited Procedures (see Section 2.12 below);

(ii) Pre-Screening/Submissions—summaries of story-boards or videotapes of proposed advertising submitted to CARU for prescreening; and

(iii) Commentaries—information, either news or policy, which CARU believes is appropriate to disseminate to its readership.

D. Confidentiality of NAD/CARU Proceedings

It is the policy of the National Advertising Division of the Council of Better Business Bureaus not to endorse any company, product, or service, and a decision of "Advertising Substantiated" (see Section 2.8) should not be construed as such. Correspondingly, an advertiser's voluntary modification of advertising, in cooperation with NAD/ CARU's self-regulatory efforts, is not to be construed as an admission of any impropriety. To ensure the integrity and cooperative nature of the review process, parties to NAD/CARU proceedings must agree: 1) to keep the proceedings confidential throughout the review process (See Section 2.2 (B) (vii)); and 2) not to subpoena any witnesses or documents from NAD/CARU/NARB regarding the review proceeding in any future court or other proceeding (except for the purpose of authentication of a final, published case decision by a staff member) and to pay attorneys fees and costs if such a subpoena is attempted and successfully resisted; and, 3) after a decision has been published, not to mischaracterize any NAD/CARU/NARB case decision or use and/or disseminate any NAD/CARU/NARB case decision for any advertising and/or promotional purposes. NAD/CARU may issue a public statement, for clarification purposes, if any party violates any of the provisions of this Section.

E. Referrals to Law Enforcement Agencies

When NAD/CARU commences a review pursuant Section 2.2 of these Procedures, and the advertiser elects not to participate in the self-regulatory process, NAD/CARU shall prepare a review of the facts with relevant exhibits and, after consultation with the NARB Chair, shall forward them to the appropriate federal or state law enforcement agency. Reports of such referrals shall be included in the Case Reports.

2.2 Filing a Complaint

A. Any person or legal entity, including NAD/CARU as part of their monitoring responsibility pursuant to Section 2.1 (B) of these Procedures, may submit to NAD/CARU any complaint regarding national advertising, regardless of whether it is addressed to consumers, to professionals or to business entities. All complaints (except those submitted by consumers), including any supporting documentation, must be submitted in duplicate hard copy and in an electronic format (including evidentiary exhibits when possible.) To help ensure a timely review, challengers should strive to limit the length of their submissions to 8 double-spaced typewritten pages (excluding evidentiary exhibits) and limit the number of issues raised in a challenge to those that are the most significant. A challenger may further expedite the review of the contested advertising by waiving its right to reply (see Section 2.6 B) or by requesting an "Expedited Review" pursuant to Section 2.11 of these Proceedings.

    (i) Filing Fee- All competitive challenges shall be filed together with a check, made payable to the Council of Better Business Bureaus, Inc., in the amount of $1,500 (for CBBB members) or $2,500 (for non-members), as a filing fee to help defray some of the administrative costs associated with the advertising review process. The President of the National Advertising Review Council (NARC) shall have the discretion to waive the fee for any challenger who can demonstrate economic hardship.

B. Upon receipt of any complaint, NAD/CARU shall promptly acknowledge receipt of the complaint and, in addition, shall take the following actions:

    (i) If, at the commencement or during the course of an advertising review proceeding, NAD/CARU concludes that the advertising complained of is: (a) not national in character; (b) the subject of pending litigation or an order by a court; (c) the subject of a federal government agency consent decree or order; (d) permanently withdrawn from use prior to the date of the complaint and NAD/CARU receives the advertiser's assurance, in writing, that the representation(s) at issue will not be used by the advertiser in any future advertising for the product or service; (e) of such technical character that NAD/CARU could not conduct a meaningful analysis of the issues; or (f) without sufficient merit to warrant the expenditure of NAD/CARU's resources, NAD/CARU shall advise the challenger that the complaint is not, or is no longer, appropriate for formal investigation in this forum. Upon making such a determination, NAD/CARU shall advise the challenger that a case will not be opened, or in the event that an advertising review proceeding has already been commenced, shall administratively close the case file and report this action in the next issue of the Case Reports. When it can, NAD/CARU shall provide the challenger with the name and address of any agency or group with jurisdiction over the complaint.

    (ii) If the complaint relates to matters other than the truth or accuracy of the advertising, or consistency with CARU's Self-Regulatory Guidelines for Children's Advertising, NAD/CARU shall so advise the challenger, as provided above, and where a significant national advertising issue is raised, shall forward a copy of the complaint to the NARC President who, in consultation with the NARB Chair, shall consider whether the complaint is appropriate for a consultive panel.

    (iii) If, in its discretion, NAD determines that a complaint is too broad or includes too many issues or claims to make resolution within the time constraints proscribed by these Procedures feasible, NAD may request that the challenger limit the issues or claims to be considered in the review proceeding, or, in the alternative, advise the challenger that the matter will require an extended schedule for review.

(iv) If a complaint challenges advertising for more than one product (or product line) NAD may return the complaint to the challenger and request that separate complaints be submitted for each of the advertised products.

(v) If the complaint relates to the truth or accuracy of a national advertisement, or consistency with CARU's Self-Regulatory Guidelines for Children's Advertising, NAD/CARU shall promptly forward the complaint by facsimile, overnight, or electronic mail to the advertiser for its response.

(vi) Complaints regarding, specific language in an advertisement, or on product packaging or labels, when that language is mandated or expressly approved by federal law or regulation; political and issue advertising, and questions of taste and morality (unless raising questions under CARU's Self-Regulatory Guidelines for Children's Advertising), are not within NAD/CARU's mandate. If the complaint, in part, relates to matters other than the truth and accuracy of the advertising, or consistency with CARU's Self-Regulatory Guidelines for Children's Advertising, NAD/ CARU shall so advise the challenger.

(vii) NAD/CARU reserves the right to refuse to open or to continue to handle a case where a party to an NAD/ CARU proceeding publicizes, or otherwise announces, to third parties not directly related to the case the fact that specific advertising will be, is being, or has been, referred to NAD/CARU for resolution. The purpose of this right of refusal is to maintain a professional, unbiased atmosphere in which NAD/CARU can affect a timely and lasting resolution to a case in the spirit of furthering voluntary self-regulation of advertising and the voluntary cooperation of the parties involved.

C. Complaints originating with NAD shall be considered only after the General Counsel of the NARB has reviewed the proposed complaint and has determined that there is a sufficient basis to proceed. This provision shall not apply to complaints originating from CARU's monitoring efforts.

D. In all cases, the identity of the challenger must be disclosed to NAD/CARU who shall advise the advertiser of the identity of the challenger. 2.3 Parties to NAD/CARU/NARB Proceedings The parties to the proceeding are

(i) NAD/CARU acting in the public interest,

(ii) the advertiser acting in its own interest, and

(iii) the challenger(s), whose respective rights and obligations in an NAD/CARU/NARB proceeding are defined in sections 2.2, 2.4, 2.5, 2.6, 2.7, 2.8, 2.9, 2.10, 2.11, 2.12, 3.1, 3.2, 3.3, 3.5, and 4.1 of these Procedures.

2.4 Information in NAD/CARU Proceedings

A. All information submitted to NAD/CARU by the challenger and the advertiser, pursuant to Sections 2.4 through 2.11 of these Procedures, shall be submitted in duplicate hard copy and in an electronic format (including evidentiary exhibits when possible). Upon receipt of a filing by any party, NAD/CARU shall forward a copy to the other party by messenger, facsimile, electronic or overnight mail. All transmittals by NAD/CARU during the course of an advertising review proceeding shall be paid for by the challenger, unless the challenger is a consumer or otherwise demonstrates economic hardship, in which case all transmittals shall be paid for by NAD/CARU.

B. Time periods for all submissions to NAD, CARU and NARB shall commence on and include the first day of business following the date of delivery of the triggering document and shall not include Saturdays, Sundays or Federal holidays.

C. NAD/CARU shall not consider any data submitted by a challenger that has not been made available to the advertiser, and any materials submitted by a challenger on condition that they not be shown to the advertiser shall promptly be returned. In the case of studies, tests, polls and other forms of research, the data provided should be sufficiently complete to permit expert evaluation of such study, poll, test or other research. NAD/CARU shall be the sole judge of whether the data are sufficiently complete to permit expert evaluation. If a party initially submits incomplete records of data that is then in its possession, and later seeks to supplement the record, NAD/CARU may decline to accept the additional data if it determines that the party's failure to submit complete information in the first instance was without reasonable justification.

D. An advertiser may submit trade secrets and/or proprietary information or data (excluding any consumer perception communications data regarding the advertising in question) to NAD/CARU with the request that such data not be made available to the challenger, provided it shall:

   (i) clearly identify those portions of the submission that it is requesting be kept confidential in the copy submitted for NAD/CARU's review; and

   (ii) redact any confidential portions from the duplicate copy submitted to NAD/CARU for NAD/CARU to forward to the challenger;

   (iii) provide a written statement setting forth the basis for the request for confidentiality;

   (iv) affirm that the information for which confidentiality is claimed is not publicly available and consists of trade secrets and/or proprietary information or data; and

   (v) attach as an exhibit to NAD/CARU's and the complainant's copy of the submission a comprehensive summary of the proprietary information and data (including as much non-confidential information as possible about the methodology employed and the results obtained) and the principal arguments submitted by the advertiser in its rebuttal of the challenge. Failure of the advertiser to provide this information will be considered significant grounds for appeal of a decision by a challenger. (See Section 3.1)

E. Prior to the transfer of data to the advertiser or challenger, NAD/CARU shall obtain assurances that the recipients agree that the materials are provided exclusively for the purpose of furthering NAD/CARU's inquiry; circulation should be restricted to persons directly involved in the inquiry, and recipients are required to honor a request at the completion of the inquiry that all copies be returned.

2.5 The Advertiser's Substantive Written Response

The advertiser may, within 15 business days after receipt of the complaint, submit to NAD/CARU, in duplicate hard copy and an electronic format (including exhibits when possible), a written response that provides substantiation for any advertising claims or representations challenged, any objections it may have to the proceedings on jurisdictional grounds, as defined in Sections 2.2(B)(i)-(v), together with copies of all advertising, in any medium, that is related to the campaign that includes the challenged advertising. To help ensure a timely review, advertisers should strive to limit the length of their submissions to 8 double-spaced typewritten pages (excluding evidentiary exhibits). Advertiser responses addressed to the issue of NAD/CARU jurisdiction, should be submitted as soon as possible after receipt of the complaint, but in any event, must be submitted no later than 15 business days after the advertiser receives the initial complaint. (See also Section 2.10 Failure to Respond.)

2.6 The Challenger's Reply

A. If the advertiser submits a written response, NAD/CARU shall promptly forward the copy of that response prepared by the advertiser for the challenger, that shall have any material designated as confidential redacted, and shall include, as an exhibit, a comprehensive summary of the redacted information in the manner set forth in Section 2.4 above. Within ten business days of receipt of the advertiser's response, the challenger shall submit in duplicate hard copy and an electronic format (including exhibits when possible) its reply, if any, to NAD/CARU. To help ensure a timely review, challengers should strive to limit the length of their reply to 8 double-spaced typewritten pages (excluding evidentiary exhibits). This reply should include a short Executive Summary summarizing the key points in the challenger's position on the case and cite to the supporting evidence in the record. If the challenger does not submit a reply, NAD/CARU shall proceed to decide the challenge upon the expiration of the complainant's time to reply, subject to a request by NAD/CARU for additional comments or data under Section 2.8(A).

B. Expediting Review by Waiving the Reply – After the challenger has reviewed the Advertiser's first substantive written response; the challenger may notify NAD in writing that it elects to waive its right to add to the record thereby expediting the proceeding. In the event that a challenger waives its right to reply, additional information from either party may be submitted only upon request from NAD and shall be treated in the same manner as requests for additional comments or data under Section 2.8(A) of these procedures and any meetings with the parties will be held at the discretion of the NAD.

2.7 Advertiser's Final Response

If the challenger submits a reply, NAD/CARU shall promptly forward a copy of that reply to the advertiser. Within ten business days after receipt of the complainant's reply, the advertiser shall submit a response, if any, in duplicate hard copy and an electronic format (including exhibits when possible). To help ensure a timely review, advertisers should strive to limit the length of their response to 8 double-spaced typewritten pages (excluding evidentiary exhibits). This response should include a short Executive Summary summarizing the key points in the advertiser's position on the case and cite to the supporting evidence in the record.

2.8 Additional Information and Meetings with the Parties

A. In the event that NAD/CARU deems it necessary and request further comments or data from an advertiser or challenger, the written response must be submitted within six business days of the request. NAD/CARU will immediately forward the additional response to the advertiser or challenger, who will be afforded six business days to submit its own response to the submission. Unless NAD/CARU requests further comments or data under this paragraph, no additional submissions will be accepted as part of the case record, and any unsolicited submissions received by NAD/CARU will be returned.

B. NAD/CARU, in its discretion, may, in addition to accepting written responses, participate in a meeting, either in person or via teleconference, with either or both parties. In the event that

NAD/CARU participates in a meeting in which only one party participates, NAD/CARU shall notify the other party that a teleconference or meeting has been scheduled to take place and after the meeting shall summarize the substance of the information exchanged for the other party (or have such a summary provided by the attending party). Where feasible, upon request, an advertiser shall be afforded the opportunity to schedule its meeting with NAD/CARU after the date of challenger's meeting.

C. The period of time available for all communications, including meetings and written submissions, shall not exceed the time limits set forth in Sections 2.4 through 2.8 above except upon agreement of NAD/CARU and the parties. 2.9 Decision A. The Final Case Decision Within 15 business days of its receipt of the last document authorized by Rules 2.5 to 2.8, above, NAD/CARU will formulate its decision on the truth and accuracy of the claims at issue, or consistency with CARU's Self-Regulatory Guidelines for Children's Advertising; prepare the "final case decision;" provide a copy to the advertiser and invite the advertiser to add an Advertiser's Statement within five business days of receipt. B. Advertiser's Statement In the event that NAD/CARU decides some or all of the advertising claims at issue are not substantiated, the advertiser shall, within five business days of receipt of the decision, submit an Advertiser's Statement stating whether the advertiser agrees to modify or discontinue the advertising or chooses to take the issues to appeal, as specified in Section 3.1. The Advertiser's Statement should be concise and may not exceed one double spaced page in length. Whether an advertiser intends to comply or appeal, an advertiser may include in this statement an explanation of why it disagrees with NAD/CARU. However, this is not the venue to reargue the merits of the case, bring in new facts, or restate or summarize NAD/CARU's conclusions. NAD/CARU reserves the right, upon consultation with the advertiser, to edit for length or inappropriate material. In the event that the advertiser fails to submit an Advertiser's Statement as required by this Section, NAD/CARU may refer the matter to an appropriate government agency for review and possible law enforcement action. C. Publication of the Decision Upon receipt of the final version of the Advertiser's Statement, NAD/CARU shall provide copies of the "final case decision" to the advertiser and the challenger, by facsimile, electronic or overnight mail or messenger, and make the decision available to the public through press announcements and publication of the decision in the next Case Reports.

D. Case Report Headings

NAD/CARU's decisions in the Case Reports shall be published under the headings:

- Advertising Substantiated
- Advertising Referred to NARB
- Advertising Modified or Discontinued
- Administrative Closing
- Advertising Referred to Government Agency
- No Substantiation Received
- Compliance

E. Summary

The first issue of the Case Reports each calendar year shall include a summary, prepared by NAD/CARU, which includes the number, source and disposition of all complaints received and cases published by NAD/CARU during the prior year.

2.10 Failure to Respond

A. If an advertiser fails to file a substantive written response within the period provided in Section 2.5 above, NAD/ CARU shall release to the press and the public a "notice" summarizing the advertising claims challenged in the complaint, and noting the advertiser's failure to substantively respond.

B. If the advertiser fails to file a substantive written response within an additional 15 business days, NAD/CARU, may refer the file to the appropriate government agency and release information regarding the referral to the press, the public, and the media in which the advertising at issue has appeared, and shall report the referral in the next issue of the Case Reports.

C. If a challenger fails to file a reply within the time provided by Rule 2.6, or an advertiser fails to file a response within the time provided in Rule 2.7, the untimely document shall not be considered by NAD/CARU, or by any panel of the NARB.

2.11 NAD Expedited Proceeding

A challenger may, with the consent of the advertiser, request that the NAD engage in an expedited review of the contested advertising. This request must be made in the challenger's initial challenge letter to NAD, which shall not exceed four double-spaced typewritten pages. Based on the complexity of the challenge, NAD shall determine whether the matter is appropriate for an expedited review. If a challenger's request for an expedited proceeding is accepted, the challenger automatically waives its right to reply to the Advertiser's substantive written response. The advertiser will have 15 business days in which to respond to NAD's inquiry. NAD will forward the advertiser's response to the challenger. Thereafter, NAD may, in its discretion, request additional information from either party. NAD will issue a summary decision within 15 business days after the close of the evidentiary record. If NAD determines that the advertising should be modified or discontinued, the advertiser may then request a full review (with any additional submissions permitted by these Procedures) and a detailed decision. In such a case, the advertiser will be required to discontinue the challenged advertising until the final decision is issued. In an expedited proceeding, the parties' rights to appeal (as described in Sections 3.1(A) and 3.1(B) of these Procedures) attach only in the event that the advertiser requests a full review and after a detailed decision is issued on the merits.

2.12 CARU Expedited Procedure

Notwithstanding 2.2 through 2.11 above, if the advertiser responds within five business days of receipt of an inquiry regarding non-compliance with CARU's Guidelines and the advertising is substantiated, or if within an additional five business days the advertising is modified to comply with CARU's Guidelines, no formal case will be opened, and the results will be published in the CARU Activity Report.

3.1 Appeal

A. When an advertiser does not agree to comply with NAD/CARU's decision on one or more issues involved in a case, the advertiser shall be entitled to panel review by the NARB. To appeal an NAD/CARU decision, an advertiser shall make a request for a referral to the NARB and specify any and all issues for its appeal in the Advertiser's Statement it prepares in response to NAD/CARU's decision pursuant to Section 2.8(A). All advertiser requests for an appeal to NARB shall be submitted together with a check made payable to the Council of Better Business

Bureaus, Inc. in the amount of $500 (for CBBB Members) or $1000 (for non-members). In such cases, NAD/CARU shall publish its decision and the Advertiser's Statement in the next Case Reports, under the heading "Advertising Referred to NARB".

B. Within ten business days after the date of receipt of a copy of NAD/CARU's final case decision, the challenger may request review by the NARB by filing a letter, not to exceed 20 double spaced pages plus any relevant attachments from the NAD/CARU case record, explaining its reasons for seeking review. The letter should be addressed to the Chair, NARB, Attention: Executive Director, 70 West 36th Street, 13th Floor, New York, NY 10018. All Challenger request for permission to appeal shall be filed together with a check made payable to the Council of Better Business Bureaus, Inc. in the amount of $500. The challenger shall send a copy of this letter to the advertiser and to NAD/CARU. Within ten business days after receipt of the copy of the request for review, the advertiser may and NAD/CARU shall submit a response to the NARB Chair, not to exceed 20 double spaced pages plus any relevant attachments from the NAD/CARU case record. A copy of the advertiser's and NAD/CARU's responses shall be sent by the advertiser and NAD/CARU, respectively, to the other parties, except that portions of the case record that were submitted to NAD/CARU on a confidential basis shall not be sent to the challenger unless the advertiser consents. No other submissions shall be made to the NARB Chair. These letters, together with the relevant sections of the case record provided by the parties, will be reviewed by the NARB Chair, who within ten business days after the time for the last submission under this rule has expired shall (1) determine if there is no substantial likelihood that a panel would reach a decision different from NAD/ CARU's decision; or (2) proceed to appoint a review panel as outlined in Section 3.2. The NARB Chair shall return the record to NAD/CARU after (s)he makes his or her determination. With the exception of the time period within which a challenger must file a request for NARB review of an NAD/CARU decision, the NARB Chair reserves the right to extend the time intervals provided in this Section for good cause, notifying all interested parties of such extension.

C. When an advertiser appeals to the NARB pursuant to Section 3.1(A), or if the NARB Chair grants a complainant's request for NARB review pursuant to Section 3.1(B), the appellant shall pay a filing fee by check made payable to the Council of Better Business Bureaus, Inc. in the amount of $500 (for a CBBB member) or $1000 (for a non-member). NAD/CARU shall prepare the relevant portions of the case record and forward them to the NARB within five business days. The NARB shall thereafter make copies of and mail the case record to the parties, except that portions of the case record that were submitted to NAD/CARU on a confidential basis shall not be sent to the challenger unless the advertiser consents. The appellant shall pay for all NARB copying and transmittal costs incurred as a result of an appeal or request for appeal, pursuant to Sections 3.1 through 3.6 of these Procedures. Where the advertiser and the challenger both appeal, these costs shall be divided equally between them. In any event, NARB shall pay these costs for any party that can demonstrate economic hardship. The party appealing shall, within ten business days of receipt of the case record prepared by NAD/CARU, submit to the NARB Chair, addressed as indicated in Section 3.1(B), a letter not to exceed 30 double spaced pages explaining its position. The appellant shall send a copy of the letter to the other parties, who shall each have ten business days of receipt of which to submit a response, not to exceed 30 double spaced pages, to the NARB Chair, with copies to the other parties. No other submissions shall be made. D. In the event that the advertiser shall exercise its right to an appeal under Section 3.1(A), the challenger shall have the right to appeal any additional issues considered by the NAD/CARU that have not been appealed by the advertiser. In the event that a challenger's request to appeal is granted by the NARB Chair under Section 3.1(B), the advertiser may appeal any additional issues considered by the NAD/CARU that have not been appealed by the challenger, notwithstanding that its time to file an appeal as of right has expired. The challenger or advertiser may exercise the right to appeal under this paragraph by submitting a letter to the NARB at the address listed in Section 3.1(B), requesting the appeal and specifying the additional issues it wishes to appeal. In the case of the challenger, the letter shall be due within five business days of receipt of the final case decision with the advertiser's statement indicating the advertiser's election to appeal; in the case of the advertiser, the letter is due within five business days of the date of receipt of the NARB Chair's determination granting the challenger's request to appeal. Copies of these letters shall be sent by the issuing party to all of the other parties. The advertiser shall be deemed thereafter to be the appellant for purposes of the order of submissions.

3.2 Appointment of Review Panel

The Chair, upon receipt of an appeal by an advertiser, or upon granting a request to appeal by a challenger, shall appoint a panel of qualified NARB members and designate the panel member who will serve as panel Chair.

3.3 Eligibility of Panelists

An "advertiser" NARB member will be considered as not qualified to sit on a particular panel if his/her employing company manufactures or sells a product or service which directly competes with a product or service sold by the advertiser involved in the proceeding. An "agency" NARB member will be considered as not qualified if his/her employing advertising agency represents a client which sells a product or service which directly competes with the product or service involved in the proceeding. A NARB member, including a non-industry member, shall disqualify himself/herself if for any reason arising out of past or present employment or affiliation (s)he believes that (s)he cannot reach a completely unbiased decision. In addition, the Executive Director shall inform the advertiser, challenger, and the Director of NAD/CARU of their right to object, for cause, to the inclusion of individual panel members, and to request that replacement members be appointed. Requests will be subject to approval by the NARB Chair. If the NARB Chair is unable to appoint a qualified panel, (s)he shall complete the panel by appointing one or more alternate NARB member(s).

3.4 Composition of Review Panel

Each panel shall be composed of one "public" member, one "advertising agency" member, and three "advertiser" members. Alternates may be used where required. The panel will meet at the call of its chair, who will preside over its meetings, hearings and deliberations. A majority of the panel will constitute a quorum, but the concurring vote of three members is required to decide any substantive question before the panel. Any panel member may write a separate concurring or dissenting opinion, which will be published with the majority opinion.

3.5 Procedure of Review Panel

A. As soon as the panel has been selected, the Executive Director will inform all parties as to the identity of the panel members. At the same time, (s)he will mail copies of all submissions under Section 3.1(C) to each of the panel members, and will, in like manner, send them any response or request submitted by any other party or parties. Within ten days after receiving copies of the appeal, the panel members shall confer and fix the time schedule that they will follow in resolving the matter.

B. The panel, under the direction of its chair, should proceed with informality and speed. If any party to the dispute before NAD/CARU requests an opportunity to participate in the proceedings before the panel, (s)he shall be accommodated. All parties to a matter before the panel shall be given ten days notice of any meeting at which the matter is to be presented to the panel. Such notice shall set out the date and place of the meeting, and the procedure to be followed.

C. The case record in NAD, CARU and/or NARB proceedings shall be considered closed upon the publication of the "final case decision" as described in Section 2.8. No factual evidence, arguments or issues will be considered within the case record if they are introduced after that date.

D. The decision of the panel will be based upon the portion of the record before NAD/CARU which it has forwarded to the panel, the submissions under Section 3.1 (C), and any summaries of the record facts and arguments based thereon which are presented to the panel during its meeting with the parties. A party may present representatives to summarize facts and arguments that were presented to NAD/CARU, and members of the panel may question these persons. If the advertiser has declined to share any of its substantiation with the challenger, the panel will honor its request for confidentiality, even though the challenger may have instituted the appeal. The challenger will therefore be excluded from the meeting during the time when such confidential substantiation is being discussed by the panel with NAD/CARU and the advertiser. The panel will consider no facts or arguments if they are outside the facts presented to, or inconsistent with the arguments made before, NAD/CARU. However, in the event that newly discovered, significant evidence germane to the issues to be decided by the panel becomes available, the panel may remand the case back to NAD/CARU for its further consideration and decision.

3.6 Timing and Reporting of Panel Decisions

When the panel has reached a decision, it shall notify the NARB Chair of its decision and the rationale behind it in writing and shall endeavor to do so within 15 business days. The Chair, upon receipt of a panel's decision, shall transmit such decision and rationale to NAD/CARU and then to the advertiser. The advertiser then has five business days to respond indicating its acceptance, rejection or any comments it may wish to make on the panel's decision and shall state whether or not it will comply with the panel's decision. Thereafter, the Chair shall notify other parties to the case of the panel's decision, incorporating therein the response from the advertiser, and make such report public. In the event that a panel has determined that an advertising claim has not been substantiated or is untruthful and/ or inaccurate, and the advertiser fails to indicate that the specific advertisement(s) will be either withdrawn or modified in accordance with the panel's findings within a time period appropriate to the circumstances of the case, the Chair will issue a Notice of Intent to the advertiser that the full record on the case will be referred to the appropriate government agency. If the advertiser fails to respond or does not agree in writing to comply with the decision of the panel within ten days of the issuance of the Notice of Intent, the Chair shall so inform the appropriate government agency by letter, shall offer the complete NARB file upon request to such government agency, and shall publicly release his/her letter. The Chair and/or Executive Director of the NARB shall report to the NARB at its annual meeting on, among other things, the number, source and disposition of all appeals received by the NARB.

3.7 Closing a Case

When a case has been concluded with the publication of a NAD/CARU decision or, when a panel has turned over a decision to the Chair, and when the Chair has executed the procedures in Section 3.6 of these "Procedures," the case will be closed and, absent extraordinary circumstances, no further materially similar complaints on the claim(s) in question shall be accepted by NAD/CARU or NARB, except as provided for in Section 4.1.

3.8 Confidentiality of Panel Procedures

All panels, through the Executive Director, shall maintain a record of their proceedings, but a verbatim record is not required. All deliberations, meetings, proceedings and writings of a panel other than the written statement of its conclusions and the rationales behind them shall be confidential, with the sole exception of those which the Chair of the NARB determines must be made available to an agency of the government. A published NAD/CARU decision and an NARB Panel Report, in those cases referred to a panel, are the only permanent records required to be kept as to the basis of an inquiry, the issues defined, the facts and data presented, and the conclusions reached by NAD/CARU and a NARB Panel, if one has been involved in the process.

4.1 Compliance

A. After an NAD, CARU or NARB panel decision requesting that advertising be "Modified or Discontinued" is published, together with an Advertiser's Statement indicating the advertiser's willingness to comply with NAD, CARU or the NARB panel's recommendations, NAD/CARU, either on its own or at the behest of a challenger or a third party, may request that the advertiser report back on the status of the advertising at issue, and explain the steps it has taken to bring its advertising into compliance with the decision. Any evidence that NAD relies on as a basis for its request for a report on compliance shall be forwarded to the advertiser together with the request for a status report.

B. If, after reviewing the advertiser's response to a request for a status report on compliance, pursuant to Section 4.1, or, if the advertiser fails to respond, after NAD/CARU independently reviews the current advertising, NAD/CARU determines that the advertiser, after a reasonable amount of time, has not made a bona fide attempt to bring its advertising into compliance with NAD, CARU or the NARB panel's recommendations and/or the representations with respect to compliance made in its Advertiser's Statement, NAD/CARU may refer the file to the appropriate government agency and release information regarding the referral to the press, the public, and to the media in which the advertising at issue has appeared, and shall report the referral in the next issue of the Case Reports. The amount of time considered reasonable will vary depending on the advertising medium involved.

C. If NAD/CARU determines that the advertiser has made a reasonable attempt to comply with an NAD, CARU or NARB panel decision, but remains concerned about the truthfulness and accuracy of the advertising, as modified, NAD/CARU will notify the advertiser, in writing, detailing these concerns. The advertiser will have ten business days after receipt of NAD/CARU's notice to respond, unless NAD/CARU expressly agrees to extend the advertiser's time to answer. Within 15 days of receipt of the advertiser's response, NAD/CARU will make a determination regarding the advertiser's compliance, and:

(i) if NAD/CARU concludes that the advertising is in compliance with NAD, CARU or the NARB panel's decision, NAD/CARU will notify the advertiser and close the compliance inquiry;

(ii) if NAD/CARU recommends that further modifications be made, to bring the advertisement into compliance with NAD, CARU or the NARB panel's original decision, NAD/CARU will notify the advertiser of its findings and any further recommendations for compliance.

    (a) If the advertiser accepts NAD/CARU's compliance findings, and agrees to discontinue the advertising at issue until it makes the further modifications recommended by NAD/CARU, NAD/CARU shall report this in the next issue of the Case Reports and shall continue to monitor for compliance.

    (b) If the advertiser indicates that it disagrees with NAD/CARU's compliance findings and refuses to make the further modifications recommended by NAD/CARU, the advertiser may, within five business days of receiving NAD/CARU's letter, submit a statement documenting its disagreement. Upon receipt of such statement, or in the event an advertiser fails to respond within five days, NAD/CARU:

        (1) shall, where compliance with an NARB panel decision is at issue, refer the matter to the NARB Chair for review under Section 3.6 above; and

        (2) may, where compliance with an NAD/CARU decision is at issue, refer the matter to the appropriate government agency and report this action to the press, the public, and any medium in which the advertising at issue appeared; and shall report its findings in the next issue of NAD Case Report.

GENERAL PROVISIONS

5.1 Amendment of Standards

Any proposals to amend any advertising standards which may be adopted by NARB may be acted on by a majority vote of the entire membership of the NARB at any special or regular meeting, or by written ballot distributed through the United States mails, provided that the text of the proposed amendment shall have been given to the members 30 days in advance of the voting date Once NARB voting is completed and tallied, the NARC President shall take it to the NARC Board of Directors for their approval.

5.2 Use of Consultive Panels for Matters Other Than Truth and Accuracy, or Consistency with CARU's Self-Regulatory Guidelines for Children's Advertising

From time to time, NARB may be asked to consider the content of advertising messages in controversy for reasons other than truth and accuracy, or consistency with CARU's Self-Regulatory Guidelines for Children's Advertising, or the NARC or the NARB may conclude that a question as to social issues relative to advertising should be studied. In such cases the following procedures shall be employed to deal with such issues:

5.3 Consultive Panels

The NARB Chair may consult regularly with the NARC President, the NARC Board of Directors or with the NARB to determine whether any complaints have been received, or any questions as to the social role and responsibility of advertising have been identified, which should be studied and possibly acted upon. If so, a consultive panel of five NARB members shall be appointed, in the same proportions as specified for adjudicatory panels in Section 3.4 above.. 5.4 Panel Procedures Consultive panels shall review all matters referred to them by the Chair and may consult other sources to develop data to assist in the evaluation of the broad questions under consideration. No formal inquiry should be directed at individual advertisers.

5.5 Confidentiality

All panel investigations, consultations and inquiries shall be conducted in complete confidence.

5.6 Position Paper

If a consultive panel concludes that a position paper should be prepared to summarize its findings and conclusions for presentation to the full NARB, the paper shall be written by one or more members of the panel, or by someone else under its direction. The contents of the paper should reflect the thinking of the entire panel, if possible, but any panel member may write a separate concurring or dissenting opinion, which will be published with the panel report, if it is published.

5.7 Voting on Publication

Any such report prepared by a consultive panel will be submitted to the NARB Chair, who will distribute copies to the full NARB for its consideration and possible action. The members of the NARB will be given three weeks from the date of such distribution within which to vote whether to publish the report or not. Their votes will be returned to the Executive Director of the NARB If a majority of the NARB members vote for its publication the report will be distributed to NARC for its review and will be published only if a majority of NARC vote for its publication.

5.8 Publication

If a majority of the NARB and NARC vote for publication, the paper will be published promptly with appropriate publicity.

APPENDIX IV

Enforcement Policy Statement On U.S. Origin Claims

Federal Trade Commission
December 1997

I. Introduction

The Federal Trade Commission ("FTC" or "Commission") is issuing this statement to provide guidance regarding its enforcement policy with respect to the use of "Made in USA" and other U.S. origin claims in advertising and labeling. The Commission has determined, as explained below, that unqualified U.S. origin claims should be substantiated by evidence that the product is all or virtually all made in the United States. This statement is intended to elaborate on principles set out in individual cases and advisory opinions previously issued over the course of many years by the Commission. This statement, furthermore, is the culmination of a comprehensive process in which the Commission has reviewed its standard for evaluating U.S. origin claims. Throughout this process, the Commission has solicited, and received, substantial public input on relevant issues. The Commission anticipates that from time to time, it may be in the public interest to solicit further public comment on these issues and to assess whether the views expressed in this statement continue to be appropriate and reflect consumer perception and opinion, and to determine whether there are areas on which the Commission could provide additional guidance.

The principles set forth in this enforcement policy statement apply to U.S. origin claims included in labeling, advertising, other promotional materials, and all other forms of marketing, including marketing through digital or electronic means such as the Internet or electronic mail. The statement, moreover, articulates the Commission's enforcement policy with respect to U.S. origin claims for all products advertised or sold in the United States, with the exception of those products specifically subject to the country-of-origin labeling requirements of the Textile Fiber Products Identification Act,[1] the Wool Products Labeling Act,[2] or the Fur Products Labeling Act.[3] With respect to automobiles or other passenger motor vehicles, nothing in this enforcement policy statement is intended to affect or alter a marketer's obligation to comply with the requirements of the American Automobile Labeling Act[4] or regulations issued pursuant thereto, and any representation required by that Act to appear on automobile labeling will not be considered a deceptive act or practice for purposes of this enforcement policy statement, regardless of whether the representation appears in labeling, advertising or in other promotional material. Claims about the U.S. origin of passenger motor vehicles other than those representations required by the American Automobile Labeling Act, however, will be governed by the principles set forth in this statement.

II. Background

Both the FTC and the U.S. Customs Service have responsibilities related to the use of country-of-origin claims. While the FTC regulates claims of U.S. origin under its general authority to act against deceptive acts and practices, foreign-origin markings on products (e.g., "Made in Japan") are regulated primarily by the U.S. Customs Service ("Customs" or "the Customs Service") under the Tariff Act of 1930. Specifically, Section 304 of the Tariff Act, 19 U.S.C. § 1304, administered by the Secretary of the Treasury and the Customs Service, requires that all products of foreign origin imported into the United States be marked with the name of a foreign country of origin. Where an imported product incorporates materials and/or processing from more than one country, Customs considers the country of origin to be the last country in which a "substantial transformation" took place. A substantial transformation is a manufacturing or other process that results in a new and different article of commerce, having a new name, character and use that is different from that which existed prior to the processing. Country-of-origin determinations using the substantial transformation test are made on a case-by-case basis through administrative determinations by the Customs Service.[5]

The FTC also has jurisdiction over foreign origin claims in packaging insofar as they go beyond the disclosures required by the Customs Service (e.g., claims that supplement a required foreign origin marking, so as to represent where additional processing or finishing of a product occurred). In addition, the Commission has jurisdiction over foreign-origin claims in advertising, which the U.S. Customs Service does not regulate.

Where Customs determines that a good is not of foreign origin (i.e., the good undergoes its last substantial transformation in the United States), there is generally no requirement that it be marked with any country of origin. For most goods, neither the Customs Service nor the FTC requires that goods made partially or wholly in the United States be labeled with "Made in USA" or any other indication of U.S. origin.[6] The fact that a product is not required to be marked with a foreign country of origin does not mean that it is permissible to promote that product as "Made in USA." The FTC will consider additional factors, beyond those considered by the Customs Service in determining whether a product is of foreign origin, in determining whether a product may properly be represented as "Made in USA."

This statement is intended to address only those issues related to U.S. origin claims. In developing appropriate country-of-origin labeling for their products, marketers are urged also to consult the U.S. Customs Service's marking regulations.

III. Interpreting U.S. Origin Claims: The FTC's Deception Analysis

The Commission's authority to regulate U.S. origin claims derives from Section 5 of the Federal Trade Commission Act ("FTC Act"), 15 U.S.C. § 45, which prohibits "unfair or deceptive acts or practices." The Commission has set forth its interpretations of its Section 5 authority in its Deception Policy Statement,[7] and its Policy Statement Regarding Advertising Substantiation Doctrine.[8] As set out in the Deception Policy Statement, the Commission will find an advertisement or label deceptive under Section 5, and therefore unlawful, if it contains a representation or omission of fact that is likely to mislead consumers acting reasonably under the circumstances, and that representation or omission is material. In addition, objective claims carry with them the implication that they are supported by valid evidence. It is deceptive, therefore, to make a claim unless, at the time the claim is made, the marketer possesses and relies upon a reasonable basis substantiating the claim. Thus, a "Made in USA" claim, like any other objective advertising claim, must be truthful and substantiated.

A representation may be made by either express or implied claims. "Made in USA" and "Our products are American made" would be examples of express U.S. origin claims. In identifying implied claims, the Commission focuses on the overall net impression of an advertisement, label, or other promotional material.

This requires an examination of both the representation and the overall context, including the juxtaposition of phrases and images, and the nature of the transaction. Depending on the context, U.S. symbols or geographic references, such as U.S. flags, outlines of U.S. maps, or references to U.S. locations of headquarters or factories, may, by themselves or in conjunction with other phrases or images, convey a claim of U.S. origin. For example, assume that a company advertises its product in an advertisement that features pictures of employees at work at what is identified as the company's U.S. factory, these pictures are superimposed on an image of a U.S. flag, and the advertisement bears the headline "American Quality." Although there is no express representation that the company's product is "Made in USA," the net impression of the advertisement is likely to convey to consumers a claim that the product is of U.S. origin.

Whether any particular symbol or phrase, including an American flag, conveys an implied U.S. origin claim, will depend upon the circumstances in which the symbol or phrase is used. Ordinarily, however, the Commission will not consider a marketer's use of an American brand name[9] or trademark,[10] without more, to constitute a U.S. origin claim, even though some consumers may believe, in some cases mistakenly, that a product made by a U.S.-based manufacturer is made in the United States. Similarly, the mere listing of a company's U.S. address on a package label, in a nonprominent manner, such as would be required under the Fair Packaging and Labeling Act,[11] is unlikely, without more, to constitute a "Made in USA" claim.

IV. Substantiating U.S. Origin Claims: The "All or Virtually All" Standard

Based on its review of the traditional use of the term "Made in USA," and the record as a whole, the Commission concludes that consumers are likely to understand an unqualified U.S. origin claim to mean that the advertised product is "all or virtually all" made in the United States. Therefore, when a marketer makes an unqualified claim that a product is "Made in USA," it should, at the time the representation is made, possess and rely upon a reasonable basis that the product is in fact all or virtually all made in the United States.[12], [13]

A product that is all or virtually all made in the United States will ordinarily be one in which all significant parts[14] and processing that go into the product are of U.S. origin. In other words, where a product is labeled or otherwise advertised with an unqualified "Made in USA" claim, it should contain only a de minimis, or negligible, amount of foreign content. Although there is no single "bright line" to establish when a product is or is not "all or virtually all" made in the United States, there are a number of factors that the Commission will look to in making this determination. To begin with, in order for a product to be considered "all or virtually all" made in the United States, the final assembly or processing of the product must take place in the United States. Beyond this minimum threshold, the Commission will consider other factors, including but not limited to the portion of the product's total manufacturing costs that are attributable to U.S. parts and processing; and how far removed from the finished product any foreign content is.

A. Site of Final Assembly or Processing

The consumer perception evidence available to the Commission indicates that the country in which a product is put together or completed is highly significant to consumers in evaluating where the product is "made." Thus, regardless of the extent of a product's other U.S. parts or processing, in order to be considered all or virtually all made in the United States, it is a prerequisite that the product have been last "substantially transformed" in the United States, as that term is used by the U.S. Customs Service — i.e., the product should not be required to be marked "made in [foreign country]" under 19 U.S.C. § 1304.[15] Furthermore, even where a product is last substantially transformed in the United States, if the product is thereafter assembled or processed (beyond de minimis finishing processes) outside the United States, the Commission is unlikely to consider that product to be all or virtually all made in the United States. For example, were a product to be manufactured primarily in the United States (and last substantially transformed there) but sent to Canada or Mexico for final assembly, any U.S. origin claim should be qualified to disclose the assembly that took place outside the United States.

B. Proportion of U.S. Manufacturing Costs

Assuming the product is put together or otherwise completed in the United States, the Commission will also examine the percentage of the total cost of manufacturing the product that is attributable to U.S. costs (i.e., U.S. parts and processing) and to foreign costs.[16] Where the percentage of foreign content is very low, of course, it is more likely that the Commission will consider the product all or virtually all made in the United States. Nonetheless, there is not a fixed point for all products at which they suddenly become "all or virtually all" made in the United States. Rather, the Commission will conduct this inquiry on a case-by-case basis, balancing the proportion of U.S. manufacturing costs along with the other factors discussed herein, and taking into account the nature of the product and consumers' expectations in determining whether an enforcement action is warranted. Where, for example, a product has an extremely high amount of U.S. content, any potential deception resulting from an unqualified "Made in USA" claim is likely to be very limited, and therefore the costs of bringing an enforcement action challenging such a claim are likely to substantially outweigh any benefit that might accrue to consumers and competition.

C. Remoteness of Foreign Content

Finally, in evaluating whether any foreign content is significant enough to prevent a product from being considered all or virtually all made in the United States, the Commission will look not only to the percentage of the cost of the product that the foreign content represents, but will also consider how far removed from the finished product the foreign content is. As a general rule, in determining the percentage of U.S. content in its product, a marketer should look far enough back in the manufacturing process that a reasonable marketer would expect that it had accounted for any significant foreign content. In other words, a manufacturer who buys a component from a U.S. supplier, which component is in turn made up of other parts or materials, may not simply assume that the component is 100% U.S. made, but should inquire of the supplier as to the percentage of U.S. content in the component.[17] Foreign content that is incorporated further back in the manufacturing process, however, will often be less significant to consumers than that which constitutes a direct input into the finished product. For example, in the context of a complex product, such as a computer, it is likely to be insignificant that imported steel is used in making one part of a single component (e.g., the frame of the floppy drive). This is because the steel in such a case is likely to constitute a very small portion of the total cost of the computer, and because consumers purchasing a computer are likely, if they are concerned about the origin of the product, to be concerned with the origin of the more immediate inputs (floppy drive, hard drive, CPU, keyboard, etc.) and perhaps the parts that, in turn, make up those inputs. Consumers are less likely to have in mind materials, such as the steel, that are several steps back in the manufacturing process. By contrast, in the context of a product such as a pipe or a wrench for which steel constitutes a more direct and significant input, the fact that the steel is imported is likely to be a significant factor in evaluating whether the finished product is all or virtually all made in the United States. Thus, in some circumstances, there may be inputs one or two steps back in the manufacturing process that are foreign and there may be other foreign inputs that are much further back in the manufacturing process. Those foreign inputs far removed from the finished product, if not significant, are unlikely to be as important to consumers and change the nature of what otherwise would be considered a domestic product.

In this analysis, raw materials[18] are neither automatically included nor automatically excluded in the evaluation of whether a product is all or virtually all made in the United States. Instead, whether a product whose other parts and processing are of U.S. origin would not be considered all or virtually all made in the United States because the product incorporated imported raw materials depends (as would be the case with any other input) on what percentage of the cost of the product the raw materials constitute and how far removed from the finished product the raw materials are.[19] Thus, were the gold in a gold ring, or the clay used to make a ceramic tile, imported, an unqualified "Made in USA" claim for the ring or tile would likely be inappropriate.[20] This is both because of the significant value the gold and the clay are likely to represent relative to the finished product and because the gold and the clay are only one step back from the finished articles and are integral components of those articles. By contrast, were the plastic in the plastic case of a clock radio that was otherwise all or virtually all made in the United States found to have been made from imported petroleum, the petroleum is far enough removed from, and an insignificant enough input into, the finished product that it would nonetheless likely be appropriate to label the clock radio with an unqualified U.S. origin claim.

V. Qualifying U.S. Origin Claims

A. Qualified U.S. Origin Claims Generally

Where a product is not all or virtually all made in the United States, any claim of U.S. origin should be adequately qualified to avoid consumer deception about the presence or amount of foreign content. In order to be effective, any qualifications or disclosures should be sufficiently clear, prominent, and understandable to prevent deception. Clarity of language, prominence of type size and style, proximity to the claim being qualified, and an absence of contrary claims that could undercut the effectiveness of the qualification, will maximize the likelihood that the qualifications and disclosures are appropriately clear and prominent.

Within these guidelines, the form the qualified claim takes is up to the marketer. A marketer may make any qualified claim about the U.S. content of its products as long as the claim is truthful and substantiated. Qualified claims, for example, may be general, indicating simply the existence of unspecified foreign content (e.g., "Made in USA of U.S. and imported parts") or they may be specific, indicating the amount of U.S. content (e.g., "60% U.S. content"), the parts or materials that are imported (e.g., "Made in USA from imported leather"), or the particular foreign country from which the parts come ("Made in USA from French components").[21]

B. Claims about Specific Processes or Parts

Regardless of whether a product as a whole is all or virtually all made in the United States, a marketer may make a claim that a particular manufacturing or other process was performed in the United States, or that a particular part was manufactured in the United States, provided that the claim is truthful and substantiated and that reasonable consumers would understand the claim to refer to a specific process or part and not to the general manufacture of the product. This category would include claims such as that a product is "designed" or "painted" or "written" in the United States or that a specific part, e.g., the picture tube in a television, is made in the United States (even if the other parts of the television are not). Although such claims do not expressly disclose that the products contain foreign content, the Commission believes that they are normally likely to be specific enough so as not to convey a general claim of U.S. origin. More general terms, however, such as that a product is, for example, "produced," or "manufactured" in the United States, are likely to require further qualification where they are used to describe a product that is not all or virtually all made in the United States. Such terms are unlikely to convey to consumers a message limited to a particular process performed, or part manufactured, in the United States. Rather, they are likely to be understood by consumers as synonymous with "Made in USA" and therefore as unqualified U.S. origin claims.

The Commission further concludes that, in many instances, it will be appropriate for marketers to label or advertise a product as "Assembled in the United States" without further qualification. Because "assembly" potentially describes a wide range of processes, however, from simple, "screwdriver" operations at the very end of the manufacturing process to the construction of a complex, finished item from basic materials, the use of this term may, in some circumstances, be confusing or misleading to consumers. To avoid possible deception, "Assembled in USA" claims should be limited to those instances where the product has undergone its principal assembly in the United States and that assembly is substantial. In addition, a product should be last substantially transformed in the United States to properly use an "Assembled in USA" claim. This requirement ensures against potentially contradictory claims, i.e., a product claiming to be "Assembled in USA" while simultaneously being marked as "Made in [foreign country]." In many instances, this requirement will also be a minimum guarantee that the U.S. assembly operations are substantial.

C. Comparative Claims

U.S. origin claims that contain a comparative statement (e.g., "More U.S. content than our competitor") may be made as long as the claims are truthful and substantiated. Where this is so, the Commission believes that comparative U.S. origin claims are unlikely to be deceptive even where an unqualified U.S. origin claim would be inappropriate. Comparative claims, however, should be presented in a manner that makes the basis for the comparison clear (e.g., whether the comparison is being made to another leading brand or to a previous version of the same product). Moreover, comparative claims should not be used in a manner that, directly or by implication, exaggerates the amount of U.S. content in the product, and should be based on a meaningful difference in U.S. content between the compared products. Thus, a comparative U.S. origin claim is likely to be deceptive if it is made for a product that does not have a significant amount of U.S. content or does not have significantly more U.S. content than the product to which it is being compared.

D. U.S. Customs Rules and Qualified and Comparative U.S. Origin Claims

It is possible, in some circumstances, for marketers to make certain qualified or comparative U.S. origin claims (including claims such as that the product contains a particular amount of U.S. content, certain claims about the U.S. origin of specific processes or parts, and certain comparative claims) even for products that are last substantially transformed abroad and which therefore must be marked with a foreign country of origin. In making such claims, however, marketers are advised to take care to follow the requirements set forth by the U.S. Customs Service and to ensure, for purposes of Section 5 of the FTC Act, that the claim does not deceptively suggest that the product is made with a greater amount of U.S. parts or processing than is in fact the case.

In looking at the interaction between the requirements for qualified and comparative U.S. origin claims and those for foreign origin marking, the analysis is slightly different for advertising and for labeling. This is a result of the fact that the Tariff Act requires foreign origin markings on articles or their containers, but does not govern claims in advertising or other promotional materials.

Thus, on a product label, where the Tariff Act requires that the product be marked with a foreign country of origin, Customs regulations permit indications of U.S. origin only when the foreign country of origin appears in close proximity and is at least of comparable size.[23] As a result, under Customs regulations, a product may, for example, be properly marked "Made in Switzerland, finished in U.S." or "Made in France with U.S. parts," but it may not simply be labeled "Finished in U.S." or "Made with U.S. parts" if it is deemed to be of foreign origin.

In advertising or other promotional materials, the Tariff Act does not require that foreign origin be indicated. The Commission recognizes that it may be possible to make a U.S. origin claim in advertising or promotional materials that is sufficiently specific or limited that it does not require an accompanying statement of foreign manufacture in order to avoid conveying a broader and unsubstantiated meaning to consumers. Whether a nominally specific or limited claim will in fact be interpreted by consumers in a limited matter is likely to depend on the connotations of the particular representation being made (e.g., "finished" may be perceived as having a more general meaning than "painted") and the context in which it appears. Marketers who wish to make U.S. origin claims in advertising or other promotional materials without an express disclosure of foreign manufacture for products that are required by Customs to be marked with a foreign country of origin should be aware that consumers may believe the literal U.S. origin statement is implying a broader meaning and a larger amount of U.S. content than expressly represented. Marketers are required to substantiate implied, as well express, material claims that consumers acting reasonably in the circumstances take from the representations. Therefore, the Commission encourages marketers, where a foreign-origin marking is required by Customs on the product itself, to include in any qualified or comparative U.S. origin claim a clear, conspicuous, and understandable disclosure of foreign manufacture.

Endnotes:

1.   15 U.S.C. § 70.

2.   15 U.S.C. § 68.

3.   15 U.S.C. § 69.

4.   49 U.S.C. § 32304.

5.   For goods from NAFTA countries, determinations are codified in "tariff shift" regulations. 19 C.F.R. § 102.

6.   For a limited number of goods, such as textile, wool, and fur products, there are, however, statutory requirements that the U.S. processing or manufacturing that occurred be disclosed. See, e.g., Textile Fiber Products Identification Act, 15 U.S.C. § 70(b).

7.   Letter from the Commission to the Honorable John D. Dingell, Chairman, Committee on Energy and Commerce, U.S. House of Representatives (Oct. 14, 1983); reprinted in Cliffdale Associates, Inc., 103 F.T.C. 110, appendix (1984).

8.   49 Fed. Reg. 30,999 (1984); reprinted in Thompson Medical Co., 104 F.T.C. 648, appendix (1984).

9.   This assumes that the brand name does not specifically denote U.S. origin, e.g., the brand name is not "Made in America, Inc."

10.   For example, a legal trademark consisting of, or incorporating, a stylized mark suggestive of a U.S. flag will not, by itself, be considered to constitute a U.S. origin claim.

11.   15 U.S.C. § 1451 et seq.

12.   For purposes of this Enforcement Policy Statement, "United States" refers to the several states, the District of Columbia, and the territories and possessions of the United States. In other words, an unqualified "Made in USA" claim may be made for a product that is all or virtually all manufactured in U.S. territories or possessions as well as in the 50 states.

13.   In addition, marketers should not represent, either expressly or by implication, that a whole product line is of U.S. origin (e.g., "Our products are Made in USA") when only some products in the product line are, in fact, made in the United States. Although not the focus of this Enforcement Policy Statement, this is a principle that has been addressed in Commission cases both within and outside the U.S. origin context. See, e.g., Hyde Athletic Industries, FTC Docket No. C-3695 (consent order December 4, 1996) (complaint alleged that respondent represented that all of its footwear was made in the United States, when a substantial amount of its footwear was made wholly in foreign countries); New Balance Athletic Shoes, Inc., FTC Docket No. 9268 (consent order December 2, 1996) (same); Uno Restaurant Corp., FTC Docket No. C-3730 (consent order April 4, 1997) (complaint alleged that restaurant chain represented that its whole line of thin crust pizzas were low fat, when only two of eight pizzas met acceptable limits for low fat claims); Häagen-Dazs Company,

Inc., FTC Docket No. C-3582 (consent order June 7, 1995) (complaint alleged that respondent represented that its entire line of frozen yogurt was 98% fat free when only certain flavors were 98% fat free).

14.   The word "parts" is used in its general sense throughout this enforcement policy statement to refer to all physical inputs into a product, including but not limited to subassemblies, components, parts, or materials.

15.   It is conceivable, for example, that occasionally a product imported into the United States could have a very high proportion of its manufacturing costs be U.S. costs, but is nonetheless not considered by the U.S. Customs Service to have been last substantially transformed in the United States. In such cases, the product would be required to be marked with a foreign country of origin and an unqualified U.S. origin claim could not appropriately be made for the product.

16.   In calculating manufacturing costs, manufacturers should ordinarily use as their measure the cost of goods sold or finished goods inventory cost, as those terms are used in accordance with generally accepted accounting principles. Such costs will generally include (and be limited to) the cost of manufacturing materials, direct manufacturing labor, and manufacturing overhead. Marketers should also note the admonishment below that, in determining the percentage of U.S. content, they should look far enough back in the manufacturing process that a reasonable marketer would expect that it had accounted for any significant foreign content.

17.   For example, assume that a company manufactures lawn mowers in its U.S. plant, making most of the parts (housing, blade, handle, etc.) itself from U.S. materials. The engine, which constitutes 50% of the total cost of manufacturing the lawn mower, is bought from a U.S. supplier, which, the lawn mower manufacturer knows, assembles the engine in a U.S. factory. Although most of the parts and the final assembly of the lawn mower are of U.S. origin and the engine is assembled in the United States, the lawn mower will not necessarily be considered all or virtually all made in the United States. This is because the engine itself is made up of various parts that may be imported and that may constitute a significant percentage of the total cost of manufacturing the lawn mower. Thus, before labeling its lawn mower "Made in USA," the manufacturer should look to its engine supplier for more specific information as to the engine's origin. For instance, were foreign parts to constitute 60% of the cost of producing the engine, then the lawn mower would contain a total of at least 30% foreign content, and an unqualified "Made in USA" label would be inappropriate.

18.   For purposes of this Enforcement Policy Statement, the Commission considers raw materials to be products such as minerals, plants or animals that are processed no more than necessary for ordinary transportation.

19.   In addition, because raw materials, unlike manufactured inputs, may be inherently unavailable in the United States, the Commission will also look at whether or not the raw material is indigenous to the United States, or available in commercially significant quantities. In cases where the material is not found or grown in the United States, consumers are likely to understand that a "Made in USA" claim on a product that incorporates such materials (e.g., vanilla ice cream that uses vanilla beans, which, the Commission understands, are not grown in the United States) means that all or virtually all of the product, except for those materials not available here, originated in the United States. Nonetheless, even where a raw material is nonindigenous to the United States, if that imported material constitutes the whole or essence of the finished product (e.g., the rubber in a rubber ball or the coffee beans in ground coffee), it would likely mislead consumers to label the final product with an unqualified "Made in USA" claim.

20.   Nonetheless, in these examples, other, qualified claims could be used to identify truthfully the domestic processing that took place. For example, if the gold ring was designed and fabricated in the United States, the manufacturer could say that (e.g., "designed and fabricated in U.S. with 14K imported gold"). Similarly, if the ceramic tile were manufactured in the United States from imported clay, the manufacturer could indicate that as well.

21.   These examples are intended to be illustrative, not exhaustive; they do not represent the only claims or disclosures that would be permissible under Section 5 of the FTC Act. As indicated, however, qualified claims, like any claim, should be truthful and substantiated and should not overstate the U.S. content of a product. For example, it would be inappropriate for a marketer to represent that a product was "Made in U.S. of U.S. and imported parts" if the overwhelming majority of the parts were imported and only a single, insignificant part was manufactured in the United States; a more appropriate claim would be "Made in U.S. of imported parts."

22.   On the other hand, that the last substantial transformation of the product takes place in the United States may not alone be sufficient to substantiate such a claim. For example, under the rulings of the U.S. Customs Service, a disposable razor is considered to have been last substantially transformed where its blade is made, even if it is thereafter assembled in another country. Thus, a disposable razor that is assembled in Mexico with a U.S.-made blade and other parts of various origins would be considered to have been last substantially transformed in the United States and would not have to bear a foreign country-of-origin marking. Nonetheless, because the final assembly of the razor occurs abroad, it would be inappropriate to label the razor "Made in U.S. of U.S. and imported parts." It would, however, likely be appropriate to label the razor "Assembled in Mexico with U.S.-made blade," "Blade made in United States, razor assembled in Mexico" or "Assembled in Mexico with U.S. and imported parts."

23.   19 C.F.R. § 134.46. Specifically, this provision provides that:

> In any case in which the words "United States," or "American," the letters "U.S.A.," any variation of such words or letters, or the name of any city or locality in the United States, or the name of any foreign country or locality other than the country or locality in which the article was manufactured or produced appear on an imported article or its container, and those words, letters or names may mislead or deceive the ultimate purchaser as to the actual country of origin of the article, there shall appear, legibly and permanently, in close proximity to such words, letters or name, and in at least a comparable size, the name of the country of origin preceded by "Made in," "Product of," or other words of similar meaning.

   In a Federal Register notice announcing amendments to this provision, the Customs Service indicated that, where a product has a foreign origin, any references to the United States made in the context of a statement relating to any aspect of the production or distribution of the product (e.g., "Designed in USA," "Made for XYZ Corporation, California, U.S.A.," or "Distributed by ABC, Inc., Colorado, USA") would be considered misleading to the ultimate purchaser and would require foreign country-of-origin marking in accordance with the above provision. 62 Fed. Reg. 44,211, 44,213 (1997).

APPENDIX IV
Sequential Liability

A Position Paper from the American Association of Advertising Agencies

I. AAAA Re-Emphasizes Its Position on Sequential Liability for Media Payments

Since 1991, the American Association of Advertising Agencies has maintained that advertisers and their agencies are "sequentially liable" for media payments.

Under "sequential liability," a medium could look to the agency for payment if the agency had been paid by the advertiser, but would be limited to seeking payment directly from the advertiser if the agency had not yet been paid.

The specific wording adopted by the AAAA Board of Directors and reflected in AAAA standard media contract forms is:

The agency shall be solely liable for payment of all media invoices if the agency has been paid for those invoices by the advertiser. Prior to payment to the agency, the advertiser shall be solely liable.

II. Media Trade Association Leaders Disagree with the AAAA Position

Media trade associations resist the concept of sequential liability, preferring "dual liability" (otherwise known as "joint and several liability"). This would mean that both the client and agency continue to remain liable for payments to the media, if the client had already paid the agency, or if the agency had not yet been paid for purchased media services.

Although beneficial to media, this position is in one sense illogical; you cannot hold everyone simultaneously liable for payment. Sequential liability is fair to the agency (i.e., it is liable to the media only if it has been paid) and fairer to the client (i.e., the client is no longer liable once it has paid).

III. Re-Emphasizing the AAAA Position on Sequential Liability is Particularly Relevant Today

Increasingly, the growth in marketing and advertising spending is from thinly capitalized companies, including dot-coms and other start-ups, many of which have limited probability of long-term, standalone success. Questionable viability and/or under-capitalization increases the need to focus on risk and provides media companies, agencies and others with an incentive to mitigate or eliminate their credit exposure.

Any liability theory other than sequential liability benefits the media and works against agencies' interests when future payments may not be assured. When the media rejects sequential liability, you should consider requiring payment from the client in advance and in full before commitments become non-cancelable. As an alternative, you might consider requiring the advertiser to be the contracting party, with the agency performing its services as media consultants.

IV. Recommendations to AAAA Members

Media Contracts:

All AAAA media contract forms include a sequential liability statement. This statement indicates that unless otherwise set forth in writing by the agency, the agency will be solely liable for payment to the medium to the extent proceeds have cleared from the advertiser to the agency for advertising run in accordance with the contract. For sums owing but not cleared to the agency, the advertiser named on the contract will be solely liable.

These forms carry only AAAA approval and are not endorsed by any media organization. (Available forms can be obtained from the AAAA Media Services Division.) Use of these forms by AAAA agencies is entirely voluntary.

Credit Applications:

Media credit applications usually provide for dual liability and terminology establishing liability is often included within a range of unrelated provisions and printed on the reverse side of the application. Subject to the advice you receive from your agency's attorney, the AAAA recommendation is to amend these forms by striking the dual liability phrase and incorporating the sequential liability language which is previously detailed in this paper. You should initial any changes that you make.

Client Agreements:

To properly define the agency's role, and to reduce its exposure in event of a default, it is important to include within the client agreement a clause stating that, for media and production purchases, the Agency is functioning as an agent for a disclosed principal.

V. Rejection of an Order

A medium may reject an agency's insertion order or contract (or its own credit application, if it has been amended by the agency) because it contains a "sequential liability" provision. If this occurs, there are usually three options available to the agency and advertiser:

1. The advertiser can refuse to place the order under any terms other than sequential liability.

2. The agency can continue to submit an insertion order or contract containing sequential liability language, but the advertiser should be made aware that the medium's use of different liability language could, under the worst circumstances, mean that the advertiser could be liable to pay twice.

3. The agency and the advertiser can accept the medium's proposed liability terms. If this alternative is chosen, your client should be aware of his potential "double exposure" if dual liability is imposed.

VI. The Order is Accepted and the Insertion Order/Contract is Returned, Annotated with a Different Liability Clause

In this instance there are typically three available courses of action:

1. The advertiser may elect to cancel the order.

2. The agency can send the medium a written statement that it rejects any liability language different from its proposed language.

3. Advertiser and agency may choose to ignore the medium's endorsement or annotation changing the agency's initial verbiage, and let some future court decide which liability clause is enforceable, if the need arises.

VII. The Parties

Liability involves three parties: the advertiser, the medium, and the agency. All should discuss these liability issues with their attorneys in order to understand them.

Writings on this issue have too often only focused on the agencies and the media, while the clients' stake is tremendous. Sequential liability is in the clients' and agencies' best interests and both should leverage their interests by making their preferences known to the media.

Sequential liability offers an added level of financial comfort to advertisers. The credit record of AAAA members is exemplary and we believe that AAAA members offer, in most cases, an extra level of financial stability to their clients. But many advertisers may use a variety of firms to service their particular advertising and promotion needs. If any of these firms are thinly capitalized or in questionable financial condition, the advertiser could face the risk of dual payment if that firm suffers financial reversals and a dual liability contract is in place.

VIII. A Closing Recommendation to AAAA Members

The economy is in a robust growth cycle, and as is often stated, this growth is largely from companies with great ideas and technology, but which are either thinly capitalized or financed by venture capital, which can be withdrawn.

Suppliers and partners to these companies are aware that there is potential credit exposure, and are likely to attempt to minimize their individual risk. One way that media and production companies, and other third-party suppliers, may attempt to mitigate their loss exposure is to adhere to joint liability provisions or to look to agencies as guarantors of payment.

We recommend that you discuss risk with your attorneys and your clients and that you have this discussion on an up-front basis, before making any substantial third-party commitments. When appropriate, you should consider requiring payment before media closing or cancellation dates. This is becoming more widespread in doing business with dot.coms and, depending on your particular circumstance, may be a prudent path to follow.

Adopted by AAAA Board of Directors, February 1991 · Revised April 2000

Index

Index